OLD ENGLISH PLATE

OLD ENGLISH PLATE

ECCLESIASTICAL, DECORATIVE, AND DOMESTIC: ITS MAKERS AND MARKS

WILFRED JOSEPH CRIPPS

SPRING BOOKS · LONDON

First published 1878
This edition published 1967 by
The Hamlyn Publishing Group Ltd,
Hamlyn House, The Centre, Feltham, Middlesex

2nd Impression 1968

Printed in Great Britain by Fletcher & Son Ltd, Norwich
and bound by Richard Clay (The Chaucer Press) Ltd,
Bungay, Suffolk

PREFACE TO THE SIXTH EDITION.

———◆———

SINCE the appearance of the first edition of this Handbook, Old English Plate has attracted a constantly increasing share of public attention. A knowledge of its many points of interest has become more general: and whilst specimens of ancient secular plate are more eagerly sought for than ever before by collector and connoisseur, the preservation of our old church-plate has become better assured owing to the lively interest now taken by County and Diocesan Archæological Societies in what remains of it within their respective districts.

Before these days few persons, whether amongst the clergy or laity, understood the great interest of old English church-plate, or possessed the requisite knowledge to take proper account of it; and the literature on the subject consisted of the papers of the late Mr. Octavius Morgan, upon which the chapter on Ecclesiastical Plate in this volume is founded, together with the not less valuable notes and observations of the late Sir A. W. Franks, the late Rev. J. Fuller Russell, Mr. J. T. Micklethwaite, Professor A. H. Church, and others. It was not, in fact, till the year 1880, two

years after the first publication of *Old English Plate*,
that the author, by the kind present from the Rev.
C. R. Manning of a copy of his interesting pamphlet
on the church-plate of the Deanery of Redenhall,
Norfolk, became aware that he and his earliest
coadjutor, Mr. T. M. Fallow, had any fellow-labourer
in the work of making systematic local enquiry into
the history of old church-plate.   Mr. Manning's work,
brought to the notice of the late Rev. H. Whitehead
by the present writer, suggested the paper on the plate
of the Deanery of Brampton in Cumberland, which led
up to the publication, in 1884, of a complete account
of the church-plate of the counties of Cumberland and
Westmorland forming the Diocese of Carlisle, under
the able editorship of Chancellor Ferguson.   This
admirable treatise drew general attention to the great
interest of its subject, and was the means of inducing
the late Mr. J. E. Nightingale shortly afterwards to
undertake an examination of the old ecclesiastical plate
of Dorset and Wilts.   It is not too much to say that
the volume relating to Wiltshire church-plate is the
model of what such a treatise should be.   Since then
the late Rev. A. Trollope has written very fully on the
church-plate of Leicestershire ; that of the small county
of Rutland has been catalogued by Mr. R. C. Hope ;
Mr. C. Markham has compiled a good account of the
Northants church-plate ; the Suffolk Institute of Archæology has completed one for that county, edited by the
Rev. F. Haslewood ; and Mr. E. H. Freshfield has

devoted three beautifully illustrated quarto volumes to the plate of the churches in the city of London and in the counties of London and Middlesex. Besides these complete histories, a great deal of material has been collected towards similar descriptions of the treasures in Kent, Northumberland, Durham, Norfolk, Berks, Surrey, and Oxfordshire, chiefly in the form of papers in the Transactions of the Archæological Associations of those counties. A good commencement, and in some cases more than that, has been made in Herefordshire, Devon, Cornwall, Lincolnshire, Derbyshire, Warwickshire, Worcestershire, and Gloucestershire. The Rev. E. H. Bates has described very carefully the plate of several deaneries in the county of Somerset.

Besides the above local enquiries, and following upon an excellent general notice of Scottish communion-plate by Prof. Norman Macpherson, a complete and quite monumental work on the same subject by Rev. T. Burns and Mr. A. J. S. Brook, most admirably illustrated, appeared in 1892, whilst a valuable classification of mediæval English chalices and patens by Mr. W. H. St. John Hope and Mr. T. M. Fallow has been contributed to the *Archæological Journal.* As regards secular plate, Corporation plate and insignia have been treated of in a large work by the late Mr. Llewellyn Jewitt and Mr. W. H. St. John Hope ; an account of the curious and rare plate of the Hull Trinity House has been published by Mr. T. M.

Fallow; and papers on Mazers and Spoons are to be found in recent volumes of *Archæologia*.

It is good evidence of the great interest now taken in old plate, that later writers should devote time to enlarging chapters or sections from the following pages into articles, such as those last named, in preference to spending it upon more original work. The sections relating to Salts, Ewers and Basins, and the like, are as suitable for treatment of this kind as those upon Mazers and Spoons.

It may here be mentioned that a great part of *Old English Plate* has been reproduced, almost word for word, with many of its illustrations and all its tables of date-letters, in an American work, described in the preface as "based upon" it : and to this it is by no means a satisfactory set-off, that the work of a foreign author may be similarly appropriated by the English book-maker, and with as little acknowledgment, or none at all.

If *Old English Plate* has been not indirectly the moving cause of these widely spread researches, it is to some of them that its own pages owe, from time to time, much of their fresh information. This is especially the case as regards the late Mr. J. E. Nightingale's volume on Wilts church-plate and the great work mentioned above on Scottish Communion Plate, to the authors of which the present writer is indebted for many names and dates added to former entries in Chapter VI.

It is plain that if the successive editions of *Old English Plate* aimed only at being a summary of the literature on its subject, brought up as far as possible to date, they would need all the careful emendation they have received; and the author can hardly acknowledge too freely and fully the help in this behalf of the friends, but especially the Rev. C. R. Manning and Mr. Fallow, whose names have been already mentioned in these prefatory words, and also Mr. Edwin H. Freshfield, as well as the kindness of many correspondents, amongst them Mr. T. Wainwright, of Barnstaple, the Rev. W. H. Wayne, the Rev. E. H. Bates, Mr. Robert Harvey, of Thorpe, Norwich, Mr. J. R. Boyle, of Hull, and Mr. Cecil C. Woods, of Cork, who have favoured him with notes of much interest.

To Mr. Thomas Taylor of Chipchase Castle the author is indebted for nearly all the newer information given about the goldsmiths of Newcastle-upon-Tyne, in the eighteenth century; and to the Kent Archæological Society for wood-cuts.

From the *Memorials of the Goldsmiths' Company* compiled by its learned clerk, Sir Walter S. Prideaux, and privately printed in 1896, it has proved possible to identify the marks of a number of working goldsmiths of the seventeenth century with so high a degree of probability as to amount in most cases to certainty. For the privilege of access to these *Memorials*, as well as to the original records, when necessary, the writer of these lines has to thank the Worshipful Company, which has also done him the honour of giving him its Freedom and Livery.

W. J. C.

Cirencester :
March, 1890.

PREFACE TO THE EIGHTH EDITION.

THIS new edition of *Old English Plate* requires but few words of preface. The notable Loan Exhibitions of Old Plate held in London, one in 1901 at the Burlington Fine Arts Club, and the other in the summer of 1902 in aid of the Hospital for Sick Children, Great Ormond Street, have more fully than ever testified to the interest of its subject, and their valuable Catalogues to the utility of its pages.

If any further proof of this were required, it would be found in the astonishing prices of the auction room during past seasons, whenever good specimens of ancient plate have been offered for sale. There can be no doubt that their real interest and value is understood as it never was before.

To the literature upon the subject mentioned in the preface to the sixth edition of *Old English Plate* must be added an excellent account of the Church Plate of the Diocese of Llandaff, by Mr. G. E. Halliday, F.R.I.B.A., the Diocesan Surveyor; and the author has now to acknowledge gratefully some valuable notes from Mr. H. F. Berry, M.R.I.A., on Dublin goldsmiths, some of which unfortunately reached him too late for insertion in the present edition, but which he hopes to give at some future day.

W. J. C.

CIRENCESTER :
October, 1902.

PREFACE TO THE ELEVENTH EDITION

A FEW words will suffice for the preface to this the eleventh edition of *Old English Plate*.

There have been no startling discoveries since the last, but many interesting sales have taken place at which the good pieces have more than maintained their high prices. Leaving aside those organized by the Red Cross and St. John's Society, as partaking more of the nature of charity, there have been the Ashburnham, Methuen, Swaythling, Sneyd, and Mulliner sales, to mention only a few. Looking through Christie's catalogues of these last years is sad reading, for it shows how many of the old families have been obliged to part with their valuable old plate owing to the effects of the war. The Sneyd and Mulliner sales following closely on each other could boast of sconces in their list. This was curious, for these pieces are very rare. The Victoria and Albert Museum has been fortunate in acquiring a fine Salt of 1592. A full description of this piece has appeared in *Country Life* of January 2, 1926.

One interesting event in the plate world must not be forgotten, namely the return of some of the Hanoverian plate to England. The collection was noteworthy, not for containing unique pieces of early date or exceptional interest, but rather for the great number of articles, to be reckoned by dozens, of which in other collections perhaps only one or two specimens are to be found. The retention of this plate, as well as some jewels, by the Duke of Cumberland when succeeding to the throne of Hanover on the death of King William IV., was the cause of great coolness between Queen Victoria and her uncle. He claimed it, as belonging to the Crown of Hanover, under the Salic law, and she did not recognize his right to do so. In 1866 a special train conveyed plate and jewels to Vienna, only just in time to save them from the Prussians, who entered the town of Hanover very shortly after the train had left. Thus the treasures escaped annexation with the rest of the kingdom.

Some church-plate has been restored to its proper use in Scotland, and Mr. Walter has been instrumental in getting back the cup and paten stolen from Boston in Norfolk. A small parish in Gloucestershire has been less fortunate. An Elizabethan paten with an uncommon maker's mark disappeared from the church a few years ago and so far has not been recovered. One cannot but wonder, when on this subject, what has become of the many pieces of English plate in Russia, noted in 1880 by the author, who often said that there were more Elizabethan flagons in that country than in England. All art treasures in public museums are reported by Sir Martin Conway to be safe, but what of those in private hands? One must hope that these, or most of them, when taken from their rightful owners, were also deposited in the museums.

Not much has been done in the way of cataloguing church-plate. Mr. Evans has finished Gowert and will soon have Oxfordshire ready. Mr. Carey Curtis has made an exhaustive catalogue of all Channel Island marks and church-plate. Mr. Hopper and Lieutenant Colonel Manuel Sympson had up to the time of their death worked at Norfolk and Lincolnshire, and their work is being continued by Mr. John Walter and Mr. Maurice Wright. Sussex has been described by Mr. T. E. Couchman, and Devonshire has been finished, but no further progress has been made in Ireland.

The help and advice of all these must be gratefully acknowledged. Owing to Mr. Carey Curtis, the chapter on the Channel Islands has been greatly improved. Mr. Walter and Mr Maurice Wright have sent valuable notes, Mr. M'Call and Mr Taylor of Chipchase have drawn attention to some mistakes. Mr. Dudley Westropp of the National Museum of Ireland has kindly supplied some information on Dublin date letters. This except in a few instances agreed with notes made by Mr. Cripps twenty-three years ago. Mr. Westropp has also drawn attention to some misprints in the names of the Dublin goldsmiths. Lastly, Mr. Walter Prideaux's advice and help have been readily given on many occasions.

CIRENCESTER :
January, 1926.

PUBLISHER'S NOTE TO THE 1967 EDITION

The present reissue of Wilfred Joseph Cripps's celebrated book can claim to be the 12th edition of the work to have appeared since its original publication in 1878.

The book has been out of print for 40 years and the present edition is based on the 11th impression of 1926. Apart from reversing the order of the Prefaces to previous editions and omitting 11 plates for technical reasons, the book is presented in its original form, complete and unabridged.

BOOKS AND PAPERS ON CHURCH PLATE

A FULL list of books or papers on church plate is added as far as they are known to the writer, who as an excuse for adding them would like to quote from a correspondent who wrote saying how grateful he was for having had his attention drawn to these books in the prefaces of *Old English Plate*, otherwise he would not have known of them.

List of Plate Marks on the Church Plate belonging to the Parishes of Redenhall Deanery, Norfolk, Rev. C. R. Manning, 1880.

Old Church Plate in the Diocese of Carlisle, edited by Chancellor Fergusson, 1882.

Church Plate in the Archdeaconry of Worcester, by Rev. William Lea, Archdeacon of Worcester, 1884.

Church Plate in Kent, by Canon Scott Robertson, 1886-1887.

The Church Plate of the County of Dorset, by J. S. Nightingale, F.S.A., 1889.

Inventory of the Church Plate of Leicestershire, by the Rev. A. Trollope, 1890.

Church Plate of the County of Rutland, by R. C. Hope.

The Church Plate of the County of Wilts, by J. S. Nightingale, F.S.A., 1891.

The Church Plate of Surrey, by the Rev. T. S. Cooper, 1892.

Old Scottish Plate, by the Rev. Th. Burns, etc., 1892.

Old Church Plate in the Counties of Northumberland and Durham, by Wilfred J. Cripps, 1894.

The Church Plate of the County of Northampton, by C. A. Markham, F.S.A., 1894.

The Communion Plate of the Churches in the City of London, E. Freshfield, jun., F.S.A., 1894.

The Communion Plate of the Parish Churches in the County of London, E. Freshfield, jun., F.S.A., 1895.

The Communion Plate of the Parish Churches in the County of Middlesex, E. Freshfield, jun., F.S.A., 1897.

Church Plate in the County of Suffolk, edited by the Rev. Francis Haslewood, F.S.A., 1897.

The Communion Plate of the Parish Churches of the County of Essex, Part I., by E. Freshfield, jun., F.S.A., 1899.

Llandaff Church Plate, by G. E. Halliday, F.R.I.B.A., 1901.

An Inventory of Church Plate in Somerset, edited by the Rev. H. Bates, 1897-1903.

The Church Plate of the County of Hereford, by the Hon. B. Scudamore Stanhope, Archdeacon of Hereford, and H. C. Moffatt, 1903.

The Church Plate of Pembrokeshire, by the Rev. J. T. Evans, 1905.

The Church Plate of Gloucestershire, by the Rev. J. T. Evans, 1906.

The Church Plate of the Diocese of Bangor, by E. Alfred Jones, 1906.

The Church Plate of the Isle of Man, E. Alfred Jones.

The Church Plate of Carmarthenshire, by the Rev. J. T. Evans, 1907.

The Church Plate of the City of Chester, by T. Stanley Ball, 1907.

The Church Plate of the Diocese of Cork, Cloyne, and Ross, by the Rev. C. A. Webster, B.D., M.R.S.A.I., 1909.

The Church Plate of Hampshire, by the Rev. P. R. P. Braithwaite, 1909.

The Church Plate of the Diocese of Lincoln; paper by E. Mansel Sympson, M.D., in *The Archæological Journal*, 1910.

The Church Plate of Radnorshire, by the Rev. J. T. Evans, 1910.

The Church Plate of Breconshire, by the Rev. J. T. Evans, 1912.

Sussex Church Plate, by Mr. T. E. Couchman, 1913.

The Church Plate of Cardiganshire, by the Rev. J. T. Evans, 1914.

Yorkshire Church Plate, begun by J. M. Fallow, F.S.A., completed and edited by H. B. McCall, F.S.A., 1917.

The Church Plate of the Deanery of Jersey, by S. Carey Curtis, 1917.

The Church Plate of the Deanery of Guernsey, by S. Carey Curtis, 1919.

The Church Plate of Gowerland, by the Rev. J. T. Evans, 1921.

CONTENTS.

xix

LIST OF WOODCUTS.

BIBLIOGRAPHY OF THE BOOKS AND PAMPHLETS BY THE LATE WILFRED J. CRIPPS, Esq.,C.B.

The Royal North Gloucester : being Notes from the Regimental Orders and Correspondence of the Royal North Gloucester Militia, with Introductory Chapters (Preface dated from Cirencester, Dec. 1874), 1875.

Notes on Some Specimens of Ancient Plate in the Possession of the Worshipful Company of Merchant Taylors, 1877.

On Some Ancient Church Plate at Cirencester (in *Trans. of Bristol and Gloucestershire Archæological Society,* vol. ii. pp. 92-103), 1877.

Old English Plate—Ecclesiastical, Decorative, and Domestic : its Makers and Marks, 1878.

Old French Plate : its Makers and Marks. (1st ed. 1880; 2nd ed. 1893 ; 3rd. ed. 1926.)

College and Corporation Plate : a Handbook to the Reproductions of Silver Plate in the South Kensington Museum from Celebrated English Collections, 1881.

(Ed.) *Pedigree of the Family of Harrison with Notices of Several Members of the Family* (privately printed), 1881.

Queen Anne Plate (in *Cassell's Magazine of Art,* 1882, pp. 277-82), 1882.

Notes on the Church Plate at Northleach (in *Trans. of the Bristol and Gloucestershire Archæological Society,* vol. vii. pp. 191-3), 1882-3.

English and Foreign Silver Work : with Remarks upon the Plate Duties Compulsory Hall Marking, and the Constitution of the Goldsmiths' Company (in *Journal of the Society of Arts,* May 11, 1883), 1883.

Report of the Plate at Welbech, 1882.

Old Cotswold Houses and Families (in *Wilts and Gloucestershire Standard*), 1886-9.

A "J. P.'s" View of County Government (in *Murray's Magazine,* vol. l. pp. 317-26), 1887.

Old Family Plate (in *Murray's Magazine,* vol. iii. pp. 637-45), 1888.

The Reproductions of Foreign Arts in the South Kensington Museum (in *The Art Journal,* 1888, pp. 171-5 and 235-8), 1888.

A Bronze Grave-Chalice from Hexham Priory Church (from the *Archæologia Aeliana*, vol. xcv. pp. 192-3), 1891.

On a Mediæval Chalice and Paten found in Wales (reprinted from *Archæological Journal*, vol. xlix. p. 83), 1892.

Recent Roman Finds in Cirencester [chiefly on the Ashcroft estate] (in *Trans. of Bristol and Gloucestershire Archæological Society*, vol. xvii. pp. 12-16), 1892.

Old Church Plate and How to Describe It (in *Trans. of Bristol and Gloucestershire Archæological Society*, vol. xviii. pp. 75-81), 1893.

Old Church Plate in the Counties of Northumberland and Durham (from the *Archæologia Aeliana*, vol. xvi.), 1894.

Pre-Reformation Chalices (in *The Minster*, vol. i. no. 1, Jan. 1895, pp. 84-92), 1895.

Report on the Discovery of the Roman Basilica of Corinium at Cirencester (from the *Proceedings of the Society of Antiquaries*, June 23, 1898), 1898.

Roman Altar and Other Sculptured Stones found at Cirencester in April 1899 (from the *Proceedings of the Society of Antiquaries*, May 10, 1900), 1900.

OLD ENGLISH PLATE.

CHAPTER I.

GOLD and silver, the best known of the noble metals, seem
marked out by their natural beauty, their cost, and by the
facility with which they lend themselves to the designs of the
artist and the craftsman, as the appropriate materials for all
the articles, whether of utility or ornament, that are specially
devoted to the service of magnificence and splendour. From
the earliest times devotion and luxury have habitually taken
expression in their use.

The beauty and rarity of these metals having thus early
attracted attention, it is not wonderful that the properties
which render them so available to the workman should have
long been understood and appreciated. Their malleability,
ductility, and the brilliant polish of which they are susceptible,
have been known from time immemorial, and valued by every
nation that has left any distinct mark upon the pages of history.
The Egyptians, Assyrians, Phœnicians, Greeks, and Romans,
were all well acquainted with both gold and silver, and high
authority places the vessels recently found on the supposed site
of Troy and at Mycenæ amongst genuine relics of pre-Hellenic
or, more indefinitely still, *Homeric* times.

The early historical books of the Bible show that even a
nomad tribe in their desert wanderings were able to carry
the art of the goldsmith to a high state of perfection fifteen
centuries before the commencement of the Christian era.
The malleability of gold must have been well understood by
him who "did beat gold into thin plates" (Exod. xxxix. 3),

and could "cut it into wires to work it into fine linen with cunning work." Adorning it with jewels must have been a familiar art to those who "wrought onyx stones enclosed in ouches of gold" (Exod. xxxix. 6); and what more like work of some modern artist than the candlestick wrought by the Israelitish smith of old, with its six branches of beaten work, "his shaft, and his branch, his bowls, his knops, and his flowers of the same; three bowls made after the fashion of almonds in one branch, a knop and a flower; and three bowls made like almonds in another branch, a knop and a flower; so throughout the six branches going out of the candlestick" (Exod. xxxvii.).

It is unnecessary to multiply these early Biblical evidences— gold and silver are mentioned on every page; the fining pot for silver, the furnace for gold, and the refiner's fire are used as familiar images ; suffice it to say, that from the time of Joseph's cup of silver and Solomon's drinking vessels of gold, all the more costly articles of household decoration and use have been made of those precious metals, and that from the time of the ark and the tabernacle, devotion has lavished them upon the adornment of its shrines and the fabrication of utensils dedicated to the service of religion.

Turn we to Homer and we find the same; the κρατήρ, wine bowl of silver, sometimes with brim of gold, sometimes all gilt, stands in the entrance hall on a tripod; silver wine cups are given as rewards; gold thread, gold plate, refined gold, gold vessels of every kind constantly mentioned; Greek words compounded of χρυσὸς (gold) and ἄργυρος (silver) are to be counted by hundreds.

Roman homes gleamed with silver in the days of Horace— *ridet argento domus* (Hor. Od. iv. 11. 6). Cicero speaks of a shipload of wrought and stamped silver; Pliny of suppers served on pure and antique silver (Plin. Ep. iii. 1. 9); Virgil of libations poured out of golden bowls—*pateris libamus et auro* (Georg. ii. 192).

Silver and gold have ever since been prized in the same way, and modern nations vie with the ancients and one another in the taste and art with which they apply them, and add to their beauty and value, whether by the aid of jewels or enamels, chasing, engraving, or the exquisite work that may be produced by even the hammer alone, wielded by skilful hands.

Before proceeding to consider the gold and silver plate of our own country, and the makers' and other marks from which, as we shall find, it is often possible for the expert to gather much curious information, it will be well to note what may seem to be of use to the amateur and collector of old plate, as to the precious metals themselves and their alloys, and as to the modes adopted from time to time of ascertaining the proportion of pure gold and silver contained in given portions of such alloys, or articles made of them, not forgetting some remarks upon the English standards, and the weights used by the English goldsmiths. And first as to gold.

GOLD.

This is one of the most widely distributed of all metals, being found alike in volcanic rocks and alluvial deposits, sometimes in small masses or nuggets, but more often in a granular form. It is found both in the old and new worlds ; Hungary, Brazil, the Ural Mountains, Mexico, and Peru, have all furnished large quantities, but none of them anything like the amount supplied by California, Australia, and South Africa in modern times. According to Cernuschi, its production annually up to 1850 was but equal to £6,000,000. From 1872 to 1878 it averaged about £19,000,000 ; in 1889 it amounted, according to the Director of the United States Mint, to about 179 tons of the metal, which would be worth something like £25,000,000 ; and from 1896 to 1901 the average yield was £50,500,000, with a yearly wear and tear not more than one-half. From 1871 to 1885 production and waste about balanced.*

The British Isles have contributed their share, gold having been found in Cornwall, Wales, Scotland, and in the Wicklow Mountains in Ireland ; we find the Crawford Moor district (Wanlockhead, &c., in Lanarkshire) once yielding no less than £100,000 of gold in three years' washing ; and Mr. Patrick Dudgeon of Cargen notices a mention of gold in Scotland, in a grant by King David I., A.D. 1125, to the Church of the Holy Trinity at Dunfermline, of his tenth of all the gold found in Fife and some other places.

In Wanlockhead nuggets of gold have been found, and gold in grains may even now be obtained by washing. A piece of

---

* Production in 1925, £81,000,000 at nearly 85s. per fine oz.

quartz having veins of gold in it was found there in 1872, and is described by Mr. Dudgeon. An analysis of this gold, made by Professor A. H. Church, gave him the following result, viz.:

Gold	86·60	
Silver	12·39	sp. gr. 16·50.
Iron	·35	
Other substances and loss	·66	

A sample of Sutherlandshire gold has given the same analyst a smaller proportion of pure gold, viz.:

Gold	79·22	sp. gr. 16·62,
Silver	20·78	

To these may be added analyses on the same and other high authority, from each of the other districts mentioned above, and also one of gold from Ashanti by way of comparison. The Wicklow and Wales analyses are by the late David Forbes, F.R.S.

Wicklow...Gold	92·32	Cornwall...Gold	90·12
Silver	6·17	Silver	9·05
Wales......Gold	90·16	Ashanti ...Gold	90·05
Silver	9·26	Silver	9·94

It will be observed that in the specimen from Ashanti there was found but $\frac{1}{10,000}$ part of anything but gold and its invariable companion, silver.

It remains to notice the physical properties of gold, which are the same wherever it is found,—its great density and weight, its malleability, ductility, its beautiful yellow colour, and the brilliant polish of which it is susceptible. Even in its least dense state, as cast gold, its specific gravity is 19·25, that is to say, it is 19¼ times heavier than water, whilst, by hammering or rolling, its specific gravity can be made up to 19·30 or even 19·40.

Its weight is correspondingly great: a cubic inch weighs 10·16 oz. Troy, a cube measuring six inches every way will therefore weigh no less than 182·88 lb. Troy, or about as much as a man can lift. Gold is so malleable that it can be beaten into leaves the $\frac{1}{200,000}$ part of an inch thick, and so ductile that a grain can be drawn into more than 500 feet of wire; it is these properties that are of such importance to the worker in gold.

SILVER.

This metal is also very widely distributed; the chief sources of supply in former days were Hungary, Transylvania, and Spain, but since the discovery of America an enormous quantity has come from thence, and especially from Peru and Mexico; it also exists in large quantities in sea water. It is, however, very seldom found pure, being usually in combination with other substances, often with lead, and it is by separating silver from lead that a great deal of British silver is produced at the present time. A mention of this process is noticed by Mr. Dudgeon in an Act of Parliament of James I. of Scotland, passed in 1424.

It has been estimated that up to 1830 silver was produced in threefold quantities compared with gold; the annual production for the ten years ending 1871 being about £10,000,000. In 1872 and up to 1875, valued at the same rate in relation to gold, it would be £13,700,000; and if we assume that the ratio of 1 : 15½ represents the proportion between the value of silver and that of gold, then the annual production of both metals for twenty-four years represents £33,000,000. It is said that the total amount of silver produced throughout the world in 1889 was 3,920 tons, which would, at 4s. per Troy ounce, represent a value of rather more than £25,500,000; and, further, that the production of silver in 1899 would be worth about fifty-two millions of money at its coin value in England of 5s. 6d. per ounce. Its intrinsic value would be much less than half of this sum at the market price. A specimen of native Cornish silver (Wheal Ludcott) gave the late Sir A. Church—

Silver	97·86	
Silver Chloride	·71	
Gold and antimony	·21	sp. gr. 10·26.
Iron	·15	
Loss, &c.	1·07	

Silver is not so malleable as gold, although it may be beaten into leaves no more than the $\frac{1}{100,000}$ part of an inch thick, and it may be drawn into a wire finer by far than human hair, such is its ductility.

Its specific gravity differs greatly from that of gold, being from 10·40 to 10·60 according to circumstances, and the weight of a cubic inch is 5·52 oz. Troy, or not much more than half the weight of a similar cube of gold.

ALLOYS.

We have now noted what is necessary as to pure gold and pure silver, and the importance of some of the details recorded, especially those relating to their specific gravity, will presently be seen. But both these metals when in a state of purity are too soft for the purposes of either coin or plate. It has therefore been found expedient from the earliest times to employ some other metal as an alloy to give them the required degree of hardness without materially affecting their colour.

Let it be remarked in passing that the word *alloy* is often said to be derived from the French *à la loi*, the proportion of baser metal that might be used for the purpose having been from very early days regulated by law. But the word seems more often than not used for the mixed metal itself rather than for the portion of base metal added to the pure gold or silver; and coupling this with the fact that the French express it by *alliage*, there is reason to think that the word may not impossibly be derived from *allier* rather than *à la loi*. In mint language the alloy is the base metal added to the more precious one, following the language of successive ordinances down even to the Coinage Act of 1870.* It will be found used in both senses in these pages.

However this may be, the necessity of alloying pure gold and silver is certain, and it is found that while silver or copper are the metals which can be most usefully employed in forming such an alloy with gold, copper only can be advantageously used for the alloy with silver.

The admixture of silver alone with gold renders the alloy paler and greener than pure gold, whilst copper makes it more red. Copper and silver, when both present, make it of a yellow hue. In the case of silver it is found that the other white metals render it brittle and not easily workable. The maximum hardness of an alloy of silver is obtained when the copper amounts to one-fifth of the silver, but the colour is

---

* See Prof. W. Chandler-Roberts' Cantor Lectures on *Alloys used for Coinage. Proceedings of the Society of Arts,* 1884.

scarcely impaired when the alloy consists of equal parts of the
two metals, hence a means of committing great frauds.

The proportions found by experience to produce the best
results are, for gold twenty-two parts (in technical terms called
carats) of fine or pure gold, and two parts of alloy; and for
silver 11 oz. 2 dwts. of fine silver and 18 dwts. of copper in the
Troy pound of 12 oz., or in other words 222 parts of fine silver
to 18 such parts of copper. If the quality of silver is given
in thousandth parts, as is often the case, our standard silver,
which contains in every 1000 parts 925 of fine silver, would be
reported as 925· fine, and the higher or Britannia standard,
which will be presently mentioned, as 959· fine. Standard gold,
expressed in the same way, is of millesimal fineness 916·66;
whilst 18-carat gold would be represented by 750·.* It must be
added with regard to the estimation of the fineness of gold in
carats, that originally the Troy ounce was divided into twenty-
four carats, and each carat into four grains, but the carat is
now only understood to be the $\frac{1}{24}$ part of the metal, and gold
of twenty-two carats means a mixture of twenty-two parts of
fine gold with two parts of alloy, gold of eighteen carats a
mixture of eighteen parts of pure gold with six parts of alloy,
and so on.

Some interesting facts about these alloys are to be found in
the Report for 1873 of Prof. W. Chandler-Roberts, F.R.S.,†
chemist to the Royal Mint. He states that the alloying metal
now employed for the English coinage, both gold and silver,
is copper only, and that the gold-copper alloys, of one of which
" standard " gold is formed, are practically homogeneous—that
is to say, every part of the mixture is of the same quality.
They are considered by Matthiessen to be " solidified solutions
of allotropic modifications of the metals in each other." The
result in the case of standard silver alloy is not so satisfactory.
This appears to be a " solidified *mechanical mixture* of two solutions, and the cooling of such an alloy is accompanied with a
remarkable molecular re-arrangement, in virtue of which certain
combinations of the constituents of the molten alloy become
segregated from the mass, and its homogeneous character is
destroyed." Portions taken from different parts of a trial

---

* 20 lbs. Troy of gold (standard) are coined into 934 sovereigns and one half-
sovereign (and see p. 19).

† The late Sir W. C. Roberts-Austen, K.C.B., F.R.S.

plate of such metal would not necessarily be all of quite the
same degree of fineness, though the whole plate as a mass
might be of exactly the correct standard. Levol is said by
Prof. Chandler-Roberts in this Report to have proved, as the
result of a series of experiments conducted in the Mint at
Paris, that it is only the alloy containing 71·893 per centum of
silver which is absolutely homogeneous, and that while in alloys
containing more silver than this amount, the centre of the
solidified mass is richer than the exterior, in alloys of lower
fineness than 71·893 per centum, the centre contains less silver
than the external portions. Prof. Chandler-Roberts' own experiments upon standard silver confirm Levol's statement as to the
concentration of silver towards the centre of the mass; but they
also prove that the molecular re-arrangement is comparatively
slight if the mass is slowly and uniformly solidified.

THE ENGLISH STANDARDS.

The proportions which have been mentioned above, viz., for
gold 22 parts or carats of fine gold and 2 parts of alloy, and for
silver 11 oz. 2 dwts. of fine silver and 18 dwts. of copper, are
those which form our "standard" or "sterling" alloys in
England, and with small exception this has been so in the
case of gold since the Restoration in 1660, and in the case of
silver from far earlier times. They are signified whenever the
expressions "standard gold" and "sterling silver" are used,
and they were the standards of the present gold and silver coin
of the realm.* The word "sterling" is derived, be it said with
some doubt, from the name by which the inhabitants of Eastern
Germany, who were called Easterlings in the twelfth and thirteenth centuries, were known. The purity of their money was
famous, and it is said that coiners were fetched from thence to
improve the quality of our own currency.

In connection with this it may be noted, that a statute of
1343 (17 Edw. III.), providing that good "sterling" money
should be made in England, also provides that good Flemish
money shall pass current, but voluntarily, that is to say,
its circulation was permitted, without making its acceptance
compulsory, nor the offer of it a legal tender.

In many other countries besides our own, legislation on this

---

* See p. 19.

subject has been found necessary or advisable, but as far as English plate is concerned, it is enough to detail the English standards, and even as regards these it will be convenient to reserve for the next chapter such more minute changes as are found to occur now and then in the course of the legal history of the goldsmith's craft.

For the sake of clearness the following table is appended, which will give at a glance a comparative view of the fineness of English gold and silver money, and gold and silver plate from time to time.

COMPARATIVE TABLE OF THE STANDARD FINENESS OF GOLD MONEY AND GOLD PLATE.

Gold Money.	Carats fine.	Gold Plate.	Carats fine.
41 Henry III. .	24 carats (pure gold). Varied from 23 c. 3½ gr. to 22 carats, but never lower than the latter, except from 37 Hen. VIII. to 3 Edw. VI., when it was 20 carats. 22 carats, at which it has remained ever since.	28 Edward I. .	("Touch of Paris") 19¼ carats.
18 Edw. III. to 12 Chas. II.		17 Edward IV. 18 Elizabeth . 38 George III. 17 & 18 Vict. .	18 carats. 22 carats. 22 carats and 18 carats. 3 lower standards of 15, 12, and 9 carats respectively added.
12 Charles II.			

COMPARATIVE TABLE OF THE STANDARD FINENESS OF SILVER MONEY AND SILVER PLATE.

Silver Money.	Fine.	Alloy.	Silver Plate.	Fine.	Alloy.
	oz. dwts.	oz. dwts.		oz. dwts.	oz. dwts.
28 Edward I. .	11 2	0 18	28 Edward I. .	"As good as sterling."	
	(being sterling silver.)		8 & 9 Will. III.	11 10	0 10
34 Henry VIII.	10 0	2 0		(New sterling, or "Britannia" standard.)	
36 ditto .	6 0	6 0			
37 ditto .	4 0	8 0	6 George I. .	11 2	0 18
2 Edward VI. .	6 0	6 0		Being the old sterling standard restored; this and the above new sterling have both been legal standards from 1720 to the present day.	
4 ditto .	3 0	9 0			
6 ditto .	11 1	0 19			
1 Mary . . .	11 0	1 0			
2 Elizabeth. .	11 2	0 18			
	Being sterling standard restored, at which it has remained ever since.				

It must be understood that the standard of fineness remained the same from any one date in the above table, until the next entry occurs.

Formerly, the standard gold of the English coinage was alloyed with silver as well as copper, and it was consequently of the paler yellow colour we notice in the case of old sovereigns, and Australian sovereigns up to recent years. This older mixture contained according to the standard trial plates of 1728 and 1829 respectively, the following proportions of gold and alloying metals :—

	1728	1829
Gold	916·1	915·3
Silver	50·4	37·6
Copper	33·5	46·5

Since 1829 or thereabouts, copper only has been used as an alloy, and the specific gravity has been reduced from about 17·82 to 17·57 ; whilst more recently even the traces of silver existing in the natural gold have been removed. This is effected by passing a stream of chlorine gas through the molten gold, by a process invented by Mr. F. B. Miller, which purifies it not only from the silver, but from other metals, some of them injurious to the gold if required for coining purposes. This process has been of late years extensively employed for recovering silver from gold, and for toughening the latter metal. The trial plate of 1873 shows gold 916·61 and copper 83·39. The specific gravity of our English standard or sterling silver is 10·30.

The last three Mint trial plates for silver show respectively :—

	1728	1829	1873
Silver	928·9	925·0	924·96
Copper	71·1	75·0	75·04

The remedy or permitted variation from standard has varied from time to time in the case of gold as well as silver. The earliest known remedy for the gold coin, then of 23·3½ carats fine, was ⅛th a carat, or 5·2 thousandths. This was allowed by Edward III., in 1345. The most ancient trial plate now preserved is for this standard, and is of the year 1477. It shows

Gold	993·15
Silver	5·15
Copper, &c.	1·35

This, or sometimes ⅙th of a carat or 6·9 thousandths, remained the rule till 1649, since which time till 1817 ⅙th of a carat has continually been the remedy for the 22-carat coinage gold. In this last year an effort was made to attain greater accuracy in the coinage, and the remedy was reduced from $\frac{1}{8}$th to $\frac{1}{16}$th of a carat, or 2·6 thousandths. It is now 2·0 thousandths. The silver remedy was 2 dwts. or 8·4 thousandths from 1601 to 1817, when 1 dwt. or 4·2 thousandths was substituted. At the present time it is 4·0 thousandths.

THE ASSAY.

Proceeding to consider the modes by which the fineness of the precious metals and their alloys may be tested, we must not forget the old story of Hiero's golden crown, and how it was referred to Archimedes to ascertain whether the suspicions of the king that it was alloyed with silver, were well founded. The picturesque account of his bath overflowing on his entering it, thereby suggesting to his philosophic mind a mode of solving the difficult problem, and of his flight home, forgetting even his garments in his haste, that he might set about it at once, may be true; but certain it is that, well skilled in mechanics and hydrostatics, he used the means with which he was most familiar, and detected the fraud by the aid of what we should call the specific gravity of the metal, instead of by a chemical analysis, at that time not understood.

It will be obvious that a test depending entirely upon the weight and bulk of the object to be examined, as compared with water, can only be usefully applied to a mass of some metal, or of mixed metals, of the same density throughout and free from any hollows, for the occurrence of any foreign substance of a different specific gravity, or of hollow places in the middle of a mass, would render its application useless.

It is, however, not without its value, and especially in the case of gold, owing to the very marked difference between the weight of equal bulks of gold and of silver or copper, or a mixture of the two. A short table which has been compiled from figures given by a well-known professional assayer,* will show this very clearly :—

1 cubic inch of pure gold	.... sp. gr.	19·25	=	10·16 oz. Troy.
1	,,	pure silver.........	10·47	=	5·52 oz. ,,
1	,,	copper	8·72	=	4·60 oz. ,,
1	,,	11 parts of silver and 7 of copper	=	5·16 oz. ,,
		(The usual alloy for gold.)		
1	,,	equal parts of silver and copper	=	5·06 oz. ,,
N.B.—sp. gr. 18 c. gold alloyed with copper............	=	16·61 oz. ,,
	,,	,,	copper 7, silver 11	=	16·87 oz. ,,
		(as above).		

* *The Book of Hall Marks*, by A. Lutschaunig, London, 1872.

The writer now quoted draws attention to the fact that a quantity of the last alloy mentioned in this list is almost exactly half the weight of an equal bulk of pure gold. There are two cases in which these facts can be made of use; if the quality of the metal be known, it can be ascertained whether an article made of it is solid throughout, or hollow; and again, if it be known to be solid throughout, as for instance in the case of a beaten plate of metal, its specific gravity will readily show whether it is formed of pure gold, or of gold mixed with alloy. Archimedes must have satisfied himself that Hiero's crown was solid throughout, before he could have founded a decision that it was alloyed with silver on the fact that when immersed in a vessel containing water it displaced a certain greater quantity of water than was displaced when the same weight of pure gold was put into the vessel. It will of course be a good test for articles suspected to be plated.

But as these early times do not immediately concern the present inquiry, we must pass to the mode used in what are called the Middle Ages, and even in more modern times, of testing the fineness of gold and silver by the touchstone, or *pierre de touche*. King Henry VII. by his will directs that " there be made a tomb of stone called Touche sufficiently large both for our dearest late wife the Queen and ourself." This Touchstone or Basanite is an imperfect black jasper or black flinty slate, originally brought from Mount Tmolus in Lydia, and therefore called *lapis Lydius;* it is, however, found in various parts of the world, and indeed any hard black siliceous substance, or even a piece of black pottery, will serve the purpose. The great Josiah Wedgwood made such, stamped with $^{WEDGWOOD}_{ETRURIA}$ about 1770 or 1780.

This mode of trying the fineness was called " touching," and the word obtained for a long time after the adoption of the chemical assay. The word " touch " seems to have been applied indifferently to the trial, to the quality of the metal tested, and to the mark impressed upon it. A curious mention of the word in this last sense occurs in 1536, when it is said that a report was widely spread in the north country that everybody was to bring in his plate in order that it might have the " touch of the Tower" struck on it.* This has,

---

* *State Papers, Domestic, Henry VIII.* (1536), Vol. XI., No. 768, fo. 296.

however, in all probability little really to do with our present subject, most likely referring to a matter of taxation, and to what in modern French plate affairs is called a " *recense,*" and not to assaying generally.

For the trial of gold, sets of touch-needles or bars were used, one set alloyed with copper, another with silver, and in some cases a third set alloyed with silver and copper mixed, twenty-four in each set, according to the twenty-four carats' fineness of gold. The streak or touch made on the touchstone with the piece under examination was compared with the streaks made by the needles; these streaks were also washed with *aquafortis,* which dissolving the alloying metals, left the gold pure, and by the comparison its fineness was determined.

For testing silver, sets of needles were also used. In Germany the set consisted of sixteen, after the sixteen *loth** according to which the standard of fineness was there computed, but doubtless the number varied in different countries according to the computation of the standard. In skilful hands much information could be derived from the sensations of greasiness or dryness, roughness or smoothness, imparted by the stroke; but this test has been little used for many centuries, and it could never have been a satisfactory mode of ascertaining the purity of silver, into which so much copper could be introduced without materially affecting its colour, though it is probable that the hardness of the alloy aided in the detection of fraud. The "touch," however, long continued the mode of trying gold, and indeed is even used at the present day for rough examinations.

The period at which the chemical assay by the cupel was first introduced is not exactly known, but it was certainly practised in the thirteenth century, and, as we shall see, was the mode of examination adopted by the authorities in the fourteenth century. In the latter it was practised at Montpellier in France, a city famous for its goldsmiths.

In the following chapter we shall come to definite mention of the "Assay" in 1300, which is early enough for our purpose.

The process of the *assay* in contradistinction to the *touch* is as

---

* The Cologne pound was divided into 2 marks, and each mark into 16 loth. The mark = 3608 gr. English.

follows :—for gold, to a portion of metal scraped off the article
to be examined, say about eight grains, after being accurately
weighed, is added three times its weight of silver, and a
proper proportion of lead, the latter by wrapping the gold and
silver in a piece of sheet-lead. The whole is placed in a small
shallow porous crucible made of bone ashes, called a cupel, and
exposed to a bright-red heat; the metals melt, and whilst the
silver and gold combine, the lead and alloying metals become
oxidised, and the oxides are absorbed by the cupel, leaving a
button of pure gold and silver. This button is then flattened,
rolled out into a strip, which is then coiled into a sort of screw,
called a "cornet"; this is placed in hot diluted nitric acid, by
which the silver is dissolved and the gold alone remains, the
cornet is then treated with stronger nitric acid, washed, and
lastly made red-hot : when cold it is weighed again, and the
difference between its present weight and the original weight
of the scrapings carefully determined. For silver the process is
much the same : a certain portion, usually about ten or twenty
grains, is scraped off the article, some being taken from each
separate part : this is wrapped in lead of proportionate weight,
and the whole heated in the cupel. The result is the same
as in the case of gold, except that the button remaining is of
pure silver only; the difference between the weight of this
button and the original weight of the portion operated upon,
shows the amount of alloy. The portion of metal taken off for
examination is called the " diet."

Of this process a minutely-detailed account was given in
a small book published more than two centuries ago, called
*A Touchstone for Gold and Silver Wares,** and the process is
now carried on at Goldsmiths' Hall in precisely the same
manner as then, even to the mode of folding up the papers
to contain the scrapings of the metal to be assayed. If the
article examined is found to be of the required fineness, the
marks are stamped on it·with punches; but if the metal is not
of the proper quality, the article is crushed, and so delivered
back to the maker. It is scarcely credible that every separate
part of every separate article made of gold and silver (with the

---

* The title of the edition quoted is | *Wares*, by W. B., of London, goldsmith,
A New Touchstone for Gold and Silver | 2 ed. 1679.

few exceptions that will appear later) in this country, goes through this process of examination, either in London or in one of the provincial assay-towns, but such is the fact; and the public are greatly indebted to the companies of goldsmiths, and especially to the great London guild, for the effectual protection afforded by their vigilance against the frauds which prevailed in earlier times.

There is yet another mode of testing silver, an account of which has been partly taken from Brande and Cox's *Dictionary of Science, Literature, and Art,* together with some of the notes which follow it. This mode, the assay of silver in the humid way, may be adopted where the quality of the alloy is approximately known. The process depends upon the precipitation of the silver by a standard solution of common salt, each 1000 grains of which contain a sufficient quantity of salt to precipitate ten grains of silver, so that supposing the silver and the salt to be pure, ten grains of silver dissolved in nitric acid would be entirely precipitated by 1000 grains of the standard solution. The process is as simple as that of assaying by the cupel. The metal scrapings after being weighed are put into a small bottle and dissolved in nitric acid, to this solution is then added the standard solution of salt, as long as it produces cloudiness; at the moment when no further change occurs, the number of measures of salt solution used is read off, and the fineness of the alloy determined with great accuracy by the amount of the standard solution of salt which has been required to precipitate completely the silver from its solution; thus supposing we were operating upon fine silver, we should have used 1000 such measures, but with the same weight of sterling silver, say silver coin, 925 only would have been required.

It may be that assaying by means of the spectroscope may some day supersede these older methods, but the attempts which have been made as yet in this direction have only served to prove that in the present state of science, little or no practical use can be made of this beautiful instrument for assaying purposes.

Some experiments made by Prof. Chandler-Roberts at the Mint with Professor Hughes' Induction Currents Balance seem to show that it is more probable that some day electricity may be pressed into the service of the assayer. A detailed description of this invention would be out of place here; suffice it to say, that it is capable of revealing the existence of very minute proportions of gold in silver, and of silver in gold, and thus, already useful in the examination of certain alloys of the precious metals, may eventually become of practical value in assaying them. It was thought at first that by its means when combined with what Professor Hughes called a *sonometer*, and with a telephone, the difference might be detected in the sound produced by two shillings both fresh from the Mint, one of which has been rubbed between the fingers and the other not.* This is perhaps rather more than can be said to have been really accomplished as yet, but it will doubtless be achieved at no very distant day.

Enough has now been said about processes, which after all can only be carried out by expert hands, and we may pass on to a few notes of general utility belonging to the chemical part of the subject, referring those whom the subject of practical assaying may interest to the standard works on Metallurgy, especially Dr. Percy's volume on Silver.

A word will be expected about the "frosted" silver, and what is called the "coloured" gold, that is so often seen in the windows of the goldsmiths' shops : and first, what is "coloured gold "? It is metal from the immediate surface of which the copper or other alloy has been removed, so as to leave an outer coat of pure gold. An article treated in this way has all the appearance of being made of purer gold than it is, but the coating of fine gold is one of almost inconceivable thinness, "not thicker," says Mr. Lutschaunig, "than the hundredth part of the breadth of a hair. It is the same as if the article were gilt or electro-plated, only that in the one instance the alloy is taken out of the gold on the surface, leaving the pure gold, and that in the other the gold is put on. Any gold over nine carats can be coloured by boiling in nitric acid, or other preparation acting in the same manner." "Frosted" silver is silver similarly dealt with. If silver mixed with copper, our own standard silver for example, be heated to a dull red heat in air, it becomes of a black colour from the formation of a film of oxide of copper, and if this be removed by its being dipped in hot

---

* *Nineteenth Century Review*, October, 1879.

diluted sulphuric acid, the silver becomes of the beautiful white appearance called "frosted" silver, owing to a film of pure silver being left on its immediate surface.* We find the celebrated London silversmith of the last century, Paul Lamerie, who died in 1751, directing in his will that all the plate in hand at the time of his death should be "forthwith finished and made fit for sale by being *boiled* and burnished." New coins owe their brilliancy to this mode of treatment before being struck, the darker appearance of their projecting parts after some wear is occasioned by the alloy showing through the pure surface. Articles of plate may also be deadened, matted, or frosted by being boiled in bi-sulphate of potash, which acts in the same way as the diluted sulphuric acid.

The bad quality of the silver of which base coin or any other article of base metal is made may be detected immediately by the use of a solution of common nitrate of silver. If thirty grains of this salt be dissolved in an ounce of distilled water, and a drop or two of the solution be placed upon the suspected coin or metal, a brown or black film or spongy mass of metallic silver will appear in the case of base metal, and its quantity will form a rough measure of the degree of baseness.

Some interesting directions for the care and cleaning of silver-gilt plate, are preserved with the church-plate of Stinsford, in Dorsetshire.† They are dated June, 1737, and are headed "Directions to keep the Gilt Plate clean from the Silversmith that made it," the silversmith being none other than Paul Lamerie himself. They run as follows :—" Clean it now and then with only warm water and soap, with a Spunge, and then wash it with clean water, and dry it very well with a soft Linnen Cloth, and keep it in a dry place, for the damp will spoyle it." Compare with this extract, the instructions given by the silversmith who made the plate for Carlisle Cathedral in 1679, for they are equally well worth our attention. " Be carefull," he says, " to wipe it with a clean soft linnen cloath, and if there chance be any staines or spotts that will not easily come off with a little water, the cloath being dipp'd therein, and so rubb the flagons and chalices from the topp to the Bottome, not crosswise, but the Bason and patens are to be rubb'd roundwise, not acrosse, and

---

* In Mint language this is called "blanching."
† *The Church Plate of Dorset.* Salisbury, 1889.

by noe means use either chalke, sand, or salt."* These last
words cannot be too strongly emphasised. It is sad to see how
much damage has been done to beautiful old plate by excessive
rubbing and the use of injurious cleaning materials. The simple
directions given above by Paul Lamerie and his brother silversmith are still as good a guide as those can wish for, who value
their old silver and silver-gilt plate.

GOLDSMITHS' WEIGHTS.

In former times the Tower pound, or *pois d'orfèvres*, the old
pound sterling of silver, was used by the goldsmiths, and in the
earlier inventories, such as those of the Treasury of the Exchequer
and in the Wardrobe Accounts, the weight of articles of plate
is recorded in such pounds, and in marks, shillings, and pence
for sub-divisions. This ancient pound was equal to 5,400 grains
Troy, and was divided into twenty shillings, and these last into
twelve pence or pennyweights; the mark was two-thirds of the
Tower pound.

These, however, ceased to be legal mint weights in the reign
of Henry VIII. They had long before that fallen out of common
use, but in 1526-7 (18 Hen. VIII.) the Tower pound was
abolished by royal proclamation. The Troy pound then substituted for the Tower pound is said to have been introduced
into England as early as the great French wars of the reign of
Edward III., or perhaps earlier, and its name was no doubt
derived from the French town of Troyes, where a celebrated
fair was held. It has been used ever since by the trade of goldsmiths for all gold or silver wares in England, but as its
sub-divisions are not so commonly known as the avoirdupois
weights of commercial life, it will be useful to give in addition
to a table of the Troy weights, a table by which the weight of
plate as ascertained by the ordinary domestic avoirdupois scale,
may be easily and quickly converted into the Troy reckoning
by which it would have to be valued or sold.

TROY WEIGHTS.

24 grains =   1 dwt. (pennyweight).
480 grains =   20 dwts. = 1 oz. (ounce).
5,760 grains = 240 dwts. = 12 oz. = 1 lb. (pound).

* *Old Church Plate in the Diocese of Carlisle*, by R. S. Ferguson, M.A., F.S.A.
London, 1882.

AVOIRDUPOIS WEIGHTS.

$437\frac{1}{2}$ grains = 1 oz.

7000 grains = 16 oz. = 1 lb.

The grain is the same in both cases.

COMPARATIVE TABLE OF TROY AND AVOIRDUPOIS WEIGHTS.

Avoirdupois.		Troy.				Avoirdupois.		Troy.			
¼ oz. =	—	4 dwts.	13¾ gr.			8 oz. =	7 oz.	5 dwts.	20	gr.	
½ ,, =	—	9 ,,	2¾ ,,			9 ,, =	8 ,,	4 ,,	1½	,,	
1 ,, =	— 18	,,	5½ ,,			10 ,, =	9 ,,	2 ,,	7	,,	
2 ,, =	1 oz. 16	,,	11 ,,			11 ,, =	10 ,,	0 ,,	12½	,,	
3 ,, =	2 ,, 14	,,	16¼ ,,			12 ,, =	10 ,,	18 ,,	18	,,	
4 ,, =	3 ,, 12	,,	22 ,,			13 ,, =	11 ,,	16 ,,	23½	,,	
5 ,, =	4 ,, 11	,,	3½ ,,			14 ,, =	12 ,,	15 ,,	5	,,	
6 ,, =	5 ,, 9	,,	9 ,,			15 ,, =	13 ,,	13 ,,	10½	,,	
7 ,, =	6 ,, 7	,,	14½ ,,			16 ,, =	14 ,,	11 ,,	16	,,	

192 oz. (12 lbs.) Avoirdupois = 175 oz. Troy, being 84,000 gr. each.

The weight of an article of plate was always given in ounces and pennyweights; thus 5 lb. 5 oz. 5 dwts. would be called 65 oz. 5 dwts., but it is now-a-days given in ounces and decimal parts of an ounce, in compliance with modern legislation on the subject.   It will be convenient also to remember that a pound Troy of standard gold is coined in England into $46\frac{28}{40}$ sovereigns, the weight of a sovereign being 123·27447 gr.   A pound Troy of sterling silver is coined into 66 shillings, the weight of a shilling being 87·27272 gr., and of a sixpence 43·63636 gr.   New silver coins, therefore, to the amount of 5s. 6d. will weigh an ounce Troy, and could be used at that rate as a substitute for ordinary weights on an emergency.   It fell no less than 16d. between 1891 and 1894, and about 4d. in the next eight years. In 1902 and 1903 it stood at 2s., but gradually rose until in 1907 it reached 2s. 6d.   Then there was a sudden drop to 2s., a figure which nearly represents the average yearly price of standard silver until quite recently.   In the last five years the fluctuations in the price of silver have been great.   In 1920 it reached the record price of 89½d., going down by degrees to under 30d. in 1923.   Then there was a moderate recovery to a little over 36d. in October 1924.   At present it stands over 30d.   The intrinsic value of plate made of sterling standard would be (Jan. 1926) about 2s. 6d. per ounce.

Owing to the high price of silver, melting silver coins became a profitable undertaking, and so in 1920 the Coinage Act was passed, under which the proportion of fine silver was reduced from 925 parts to 500 parts in every 1000, so that what are now called silver coins are in fact only half silver.

MINT PRICES FOR GOLD.

Lastly, dividing the number of sovereigns contained in one pound Troy of standard gold by twelve, the value of an ounce of such gold (22 carat) will be found to be £3 17s. 10½d., or 3s. 6½d. for each $\frac{1}{24}$ part (or carat) of fine gold in the ounce weight. The following table gives the value per ounce of all the other qualities of gold that it has been necessary to mention, at this Mint price. No account is taken of the material used for alloying the gold, which would in any case be of trifling value. The alloying metal in an ounce of 22 carat gold, if sterling silver alone were used for the alloy, would hardly be worth 2½d. at the present market price of silver; in other words the silver in a sovereign made of such an alloy would be worth less than a single penny.

	£	s.	d.	
24 carats (or pure gold)	4	4	11½	per oz
23 car. 3½ gr. (old gold coin. See table, p. 9)	4	4	6¼	,,
22 car. (present gold coin and first goldware standard)	3	17	10½	,,
20 car. (gold coin temp. Henry VIII. See table, p. 9). Also an Irish standard	3	10	9½	,,
19⅛ car. (touch of Paris. See table, p. 9)	3	7	11½	,,
18 car. (second goldware standard)	3	3	8½	,,
15 car. (third ditto)	2	13	1	,,
12 car. (fourth ditto)	2	2	5¾	,,
9 car. (fifth ditto)	1	11	10½	,,

CHAPTER II.

THERE are no articles in the manufacture of which such extensive frauds can be committed in so small a compass as those made of the precious metals, and there are no frauds more difficult of detection by ordinary persons. We have seen, too, that whilst a certain amount of base metal must needs be introduced into all such articles, it is only by a minute scientific examination that the proportion of base metal so introduced can be known for certain, and but few persons can possess either the skill or the means to conduct the necessary operations. The great profit to be made by fraudulent practices, the difficulty of detection, and the consequent probability of escape from it and from punishment, have at all times exposed the dishonest work-man to irresistible temptations. In very early times, those who carried on particular trades or handicrafts were accustomed to form themselves into guilds or fraternities for the purpose of protecting and regulating the trade, or mystery as it was called, which they exercised. These were at subsequent periods incor-porated by royal charters, which gave them power and authority to carry out their objects more effectually. Amongst such associations, those of the goldsmiths seem to have been early formed in many countries of Europe. In 1260 it became neces-sary for the provost of Paris to issue a code of statutes for the regulation of the goldsmiths, who already existed there as a corporate body. Not only was gold of an inferior quality sub-stituted for good gold, but articles made of laten were gilt and palmed off for gold, and pewter was silvered and sold for the genuine metal. In these statutes, gold is ordered to be of "the touch of Paris," and silver as good as "Sterlings" (*esterlins*), which was the standard of the English coin, as we

have seen.   In 1300 the mark of Paris was known even abroad,
for it is referred to in the English Wardrobe Accounts of that
year (28 Edw. I.) in these terms :—

"8 coclear' argenti signata in collo signo Parisius, scilt. de
quodam flore glegelli."

A second and more extensive code was issued by John II. of
France, in the shape of Letters of Confirmation given at St.
Ouen in Aug. 1355,* when it was ordered that every goldsmith
who was approved by the masters of the craft should have a
puncheon with a countermark of his own.   Amongst other
things they were forbidden to work in gold unless it be of the
touch of Paris, or better, and the statutes add that this standard
is better than all the gold which they work in other lands (*en
mille terres*), and that its fineness is nineteen and one-fifth carats.
They are also forbidden to work in base metal, to use false stones
or glass, or to put coloured foil beneath real stones.   Their
silver was to be *argent de roy*, 11 deniers 12 grains fine,† and
jurors (*prudhommes*) were appointed to guard the trade, with
power to punish those who worked in bad metal.   At Montpellier the goldsmiths in the fourteenth century constituted a
fraternity governed by statutes, and they had a standard of
their own, which, however, does not seem to have been a high
one, since silver might contain one-third part of alloy, or such
silver as would come white out of the fire, and gold of fourteen
carats fine might be worked.   They were expressly forbidden
to manufacture articles in gilt or silvered copper or brass, save
ornaments and utensils for churches, to mount real stones in
jewellery of base metal, or to set false stones in gold or silver.
We shall presently see how much light the history of the
goldsmiths of Montpellier throws upon that of their English
brethren.

At Nuremberg and Augsburg, cities most famous for their
metal-workers, as well as in many other places, similar guilds
of goldsmiths, regulated by statutes, existed.

---

* *Collection de pièces relatives à l'histoire de France*, par C. Leber, Paris, 1838. Vol. XIX. 348.

† *Denier* was the term used in France to denote the fineness of silver as carat is for gold.   The silver is divided into twelve deniers, and each denier into two *oboles* or twenty-four grains ; hence silver of twelve deniers was pure, and eleven deniers one obole had only one twenty-fourth part alloy.   This quality was the *Argent de Roy.*

In England a fraternity or guild of goldsmiths had existed from an early period, for in 1180, the twenty-sixth year of the reign of Henry II., it was amongst other guilds amerced for being adulterine, that is, set up without the king's licence. It was not, however, incorporated by charter for nearly a hundred and fifty years after this time, although it had special duties assigned to it, one of the duties of the wardens of the craft being to protect their trade against fraudulent workers by holding official examinations of the above-mentioned kinds, and placing marks upon articles so examined.

Some such marks must have been necessary in order to certify to the purchaser, and for other purposes, a certain standard purity of metal in articles so examined, and the official stamps by which it was certified seem to have been the origin of the marks which are found on the gold and silver plate of most countries.

Every person who is possessed of any article of gold or silver plate, has, most probably, observed a small group of marks stamped upon some part of it. Few, perhaps, have regarded them in any other light than as a proof that the article so marked is made of the metal of which it is professed to be made, and that the metal itself is of a certain purity. And this is, in fact, the ultimate intention of these marks; but besides this the archæologist can often deduce from them other important and interesting information,—as to the year in which any article bearing them was made; the place at which it was made, or at all events, assayed: the maker's name, and other particulars. As regards England, an historical notice of the Goldsmiths' Company of London and its charters, and the legislation which from time to time has regulated the trade of the goldsmith, will elucidate in its course the meaning of all the marks to be found on English plate.

Some notes of the provincial guilds and assay offices, including those of Scotland and Ireland, and of their respective marks, will be reserved for separate chapters.

Except for the early trace of a guild in 1180, which has already been noticed, we have to wait until the commencement of the thirteenth century before we come to any definite regulation of the mystery of the goldsmiths of London, and even then their formal incorporation had not yet taken place.

However, by this time they were a numerous and powerful craft, for in an affray which occurred in 1267 between the goldsmiths and the tailors, those trades met and fought to the number of 500 men on each side, of whom some were killed, the dead being, it is said, thrown into the Thames, and others wounded, before the bailiffs of the city could part them and apprehend the ringleaders, some of whom were hanged.* But, truth to say, their turbulence was not their only failing, for the frauds that seemed so common in France had their place also in England, and by the year 1238 were of such extent as to call for a mandate from the king, to be found in the Close Rolls of that year.† This, which is entitled "*De auro fabricando in civitate Londoniarum*," commands the mayor and aldermen to choose six of the more discreet goldsmiths of the city, who were to superintend the craft, seeing that no craftsmen worked any gold of which a mark was not worth a hundred shillings at least, nor any silver of less intrinsic value than the king's money—"*quod non valeat in se quantum valeat moneta Regis.*" They were also to prevent any one working in secret, or anywhere but in the public street, to see that gold bore no colour but its own, except in the case of gold thread, and that no one put gold upon laton or copper. There are also provisions as to the use of precious and counterfeit stones. Fifty years later, the first actual statute on the subject, passed in 1300, recognizes these discreet goldsmiths by the name of wardens, and for the first time establishes their powers on a firm basis, ordaining as follows, viz. (28 Edward I., Stat. 3, cap. 20) :—"That no goldsmith should make any vessel, jewel, or other thing of gold or silver unless it be of good and true alloy, *i.e.*, gold of the standard of the touch of Paris (*tuche de Parys*) and silver of the sterling alloy, or better (*argent del alloy de le esterling ou de meilleur*), and that none work worse silver than money. And that no vessel of silver depart out of the hands of the workers until it be assayed by the wardens of the craft, and marked with the leopard's head (*e q'ele soit signée de und teste de leopart*). That the wardens (*gardiens*) should go from shop to shop (*de shope en*

---

* *Chronicles of the Mayor and Sheriffs of London*, edited by H. T. Riley, London, 1863. Such affrays are also men-   tioned in Herbert's *History of the London Livery Companies.*
† Close Roll, 22 Henry III., m. 6.

shope) among the goldsmiths and assay (*assaient*) the gold, and
if they should find any other it should be forfeit to the King.
That no false stones should be set in gold, and that all the good
towns of England where any goldsmith be dwelling shall be
ordered according to this Estatute as they of London be, and
that one shall come from every good town for all the residue
that be dwelling in the same unto London for to be ascertained
of their Touch. And if any goldsmith be attainted that he
hath done otherwise, he shall be punished by imprisonment and
by ransom at the King's pleasure."

Here, then, we have mention, not only of wardens of the
craft, but of an assay and of a distinct mark for standard
metal. Mr. Octavius Morgan notes that the phraseology of
this statute more than suggests that such a mark was now
ordered for the first time, it being termed "*une* teste." This
is indeed an important step in the history of which we are
tracing the course. It is the earliest mention, too, of an assay.

Now that the duty of the wardens is laid down, we have
naturally not long to wait for the regular incorporation of a
Goldsmiths' guild in London, and in 1327 it was so incorporated
by letters-patent from Edward III., under the name of " The
Wardens and Commonalty of the Mystery of Goldsmiths of the
City of London."

This charter, which is in old French, and is dated 30 May,
1 Edw. III., is given at length, both in French and English,
in Herbert's *History of the London Livery Companies*. It first
recites and then grants as follows :—that the goldsmiths of our
City of London had by their petition exhibited to the King and
Council in Parliament, holden at Westminster, shown that
theretofore no private merchants or strangers were wont to bring
into this land any money coined, but plate of silver to exchange
for our coin ; that it had been ordained that all of the trade of
goldsmiths were to sit in their shops in the High-street of
Cheap, and that no silver or gold plate ought to be sold in the
city of London, except in the King's Exchange or in Cheap,
among the goldsmiths, and that publicly, to the end that
persons in the trade might inform themselves whether the
seller came lawfully by it ; but that of late both private
merchants and strangers bring from foreign lands counterfeit
sterling whereof the pound is not worth sixteen sols of the

right sterling, and of this money none can know the right value but by melting it down ; and that many of the trade of goldsmiths do keep shops in obscure streets, and do buy vessels of gold and silver secretly without inquiring whether such vessels were stolen or come lawfully by, and immediately melting it down, make it into plate, and sell it to merchants trading beyond sea, and so make false work of gold, silver, and jewels, in which they set glass of divers colours, counterfeiting right stones, and put more alloy in their silver than they ought, which they sell to such as have no skill in such things ; and that the cutlers cover tin with silver so subtilely and with such sleight that the same cannot be discovered nor separated, and so sell the tin for fine silver, to the great damage and deceipt of us and our people ; we, with the assent of our Lords spiritual and temporal, and the commons of our realme, will and grant for us and our heirs that henceforth no one shall bring into this land any sort of money, but only plate of fine silver, and that no plate of gold or silver be sold to sell again, or to be carried out of the kingdom, but shall be sold openly for private use ; that none of the trade shall keep any shop, except in Cheap, that it may be seen that their work be good ; that those of the trade may by virtue of these presents elect honest and sufficient men, best skilled in the trade, to inquire of the matters aforesaid, and that they who are so chosen reform what defects they shall find, and inflict punishment on the offenders, and that by the help of the mayor and sheriffs, if need be ; that in all trading cities in England where goldsmiths reside, the same ordinance be observed as in London, and that one or two of every such city or town for the rest of the trade shall come to London to be ascertained of their touch of gold, and there to have a stamp of a puncheon of a leopard's head marked upon their work as it was anciently ordained.

For some years they were governed by the provisions of this charter, but in 1363 further legislation became necessary, and by an Act of that year (37 Edw. III. cap. 7) it was ordained that no goldsmith, as well in London as elsewhere within the realm, should work any gold or silver but of the alloy of good sterling (*alloy de bon esterlyng*) ; that every master goldsmith should have a mark by himself which should be known by them who should be assigned to survey their work and allay; that the goldsmiths should not set their mark till their work was assayed; and that after the assay made, the surveyor should set the king's mark upon it, and then the goldsmith his mark for which he should answer; that no goldsmith should charge for silver vessel but 1s. 6d. for the pound of two marks as at Paris; that no silversmith should meddle with gilding; and that no gilder should work in silver. This brings us another stage, and introduces us to a maker's mark for the first time in England. We have a standard mark since 1300, and now a maker's mark dating from 1363.

It is pretty clear that in the fourteenth century, owing to the frauds committed, a great move was made throughout Europe with respect to goldsmiths, France and perhaps Montpellier taking the lead.

Turn we therefore, by the way, to Montpellier, of whose history the *Publications de la Société Archéologique de Montpellier* give many interesting particulars, and we find that by 1355 a dispute which had arisen between the consuls of the town and the goldsmiths, in consequence of the great abuses introduced into the trade of the latter, led to the following regulations of that year :—

That all vessels and works of silver made by the *argentiers* of Montpellier must be of the standard of eleven deniers and one obole, or twelve grains, at the least.* The goldsmiths were to make two patterns or trial pieces of silver, of the standard of eleven deniers fourteen grains, marked with the puncheon of Montpellier (for Philippe le Hardi had, in 1275, ordained that each city should have a particular mark for works in silver), after which the goldsmiths should work with an allowance of two grains. One of these trial pieces should be kept at the consulate, and the other by the warden of the goldsmiths. That a third trial piece shall be made of eleven deniers and one obole, also marked, which should remain with the consuls for trial with suspected works. Every master silversmith should mark with a particular mark the pieces of his work, and deliver them himself to the warden. The warden, before marking the piece with the puncheon of Montpellier, should remove a portion of

---

* See Note, p. 22.

the silver, called, in the language of Montpellier, "borihl," (a technical term for a portion of metal removed with a buril, burin or graver, for the purpose of the assay), which he should put into a box, keeping a separate box for each workman, and once or twice a year make an assay of these "borihls," and if the standard was found below the eleven deniers one obole they should denounce the worker to the consuls, who should make a second assay, and if they found the fraud confirmed, should deliver him over to justice. Moreover the wardens might break such articles as seemed to them insufficient. In the original documents nothing is said of the method of performing the operation of the assay ; but as it is expressly ordered that in assaying the trial pieces and "borihls" the same ashes (probably bone-ashes to form the crucible), *lead* and fire, should be used, it is clear that the assay was by the cupel.

Nothing had hitherto been done or said about gold; but though less worked than silver there were equal abuses ; and in 1401 the consuls and wardens of the mystery, assisted by several argentiers, made a regulation in presence of the consuls of the city, by which the standard of gold, which originally was only fourteen carats, and had by a subsequent decree been raised to eighteen carats, was now reduced to sixteen carats ; and there is here a question of the trial of gold by the "touch," showing that it was then in use.

In the fifteenth century abuses and frauds in the trade had greatly multiplied. Public clamour was raised against the principal silversmiths for working below the standard of 1355. A process was instituted against them in 1427. The consuls seized several of their works, had them assayed, found them fraudulent, and made the makers appear before the tribunal. In their defence they pleaded that the ordinances of 1355 were obsolete with regard to small "orfèvreries." They were condemned to pay a fine of ten marks of silver each, and on appeal the sentence was confirmed. They claimed exemption from marking girdles and small works. An inquest was held, and the following ordinances resulted, which were solemnly renewed in 1436 with still stricter conditions, and they show with what care the fabrication of works of gold and silver was regulated. To ensure the legal standard they ordained, besides the ordinary precaution of the box, the "borihls," the trial pieces, and the name of the silversmith, that the name of the warden of the mystery, inscribed on the register of the city and on the private book of the silversmiths, should be followed by *one of the letters of the alphabet,* which should be reproduced beneath the shield of arms (*ecusson*) of the town on each work, in order that it might be known under what warden it was made. These proceedings of the goldsmiths of Montpellier are highly interesting, since they not only give us an account of the frauds and the alteration of the standard, together with the particulars of the assay, which in its system with the box and trial pieces bears a very strong analogy to our trial of the Pyx,* but also give us the date, origin and establishment of three very important marks, viz., the mark of the country or city, the mark of the maker, and the annual letter, two of which we had already adopted in this country, whilst the use of the third, the annual letter, was soon to be established.

If we may turn aside for a moment to see how the goldsmiths put their powers into actual use, we gather that their original charter must have served its purpose to some extent. Proceedings taken against one Peter Randolfe, a Latoner, are enough to show that it was at all events not a dead letter in 1376, for upon interrogation for exposing two circlets for

---

* The important duty of testing the purity of the coinage from time to time has been entrusted for ages to the Goldsmiths' Company. The ceremony of doing this has been conducted with the same formalities from time immemorial, and is called "The trial of the Pyx." Such a trial is known to have taken place in 9 & 10 Edw. I., and it has been held at short but irregular intervals ever since; it is now an annual event. A specimen coin, taken formerly from each "journey" or day's work, but in modern days from each melting of metal, whether gold or silver, is placed in a chest kept at the Mint, called the Pyx. At the proper time a jury of the Goldsmiths' Company is summoned, who after being sworn and solemnly charged, proceed to an assay of the coins found in the Pyx, and to compare their quality with the standard trial plates in the custody of the Warden of the Standards. Their verdict is the deliverance of the authorities of the Mint, who are virtually placed upon their trial. Since the Coinage Act of 1870, the proceedings have been somewhat shorn of their circumstance, owing to the jury being summoned to Goldsmiths' Hall, and there charged by the Queen's Remembrancer, instead of by the Lord Chancellor himself at Westminster, where the assay was formerly conducted, in an apartment specially prepared for the purpose. The mode of procedure thenceforward to be adopted on these occasions is completely set forth in the above Coinage Act (33 Vict. c. 10), and in the Queen's Order in Council of 29 June, 1871.

mazers of mixed silver, we find him promising not to interfere
with the goldsmiths' trade again.*

The names of many of the great London goldsmiths of this
generation are known.   Thomas Hessey was the king's goldsmith in 1366, and Nicholas Twyford held the same office
shortly afterwards; the latter is mentioned in accounts of 1379.
The names of John de Chichester and Thomas Reynham,
John Hiltoft and also his executors, all occur in the Wardrobe
Accounts as enjoying royal patronage between this time and
the end of the century.   The great goldsmith, Sir Drew
Barentyn, who died in 1415, was a man of more than civic note.

Here, however, the charter of Edward III. was found
insufficient for want of proper persons being named in it;
therefore Richard II. in 1392-3 re-incorporated them by
another charter dated 6 Feb. 16 Ric. II., confirming the first
and giving them power to choose wardens and other officers.

Edward IV. in 1462 not only confirmed the charter of
Richard II., but constituted the Goldsmiths' Company a body
corporate and politic, with perpetual succession, power to use
a common seal, hold lands, etc., and by this charter, dated
30 May, 2 Edw. IV., invested them with a privilege of searching,
inspecting, trying, and regulating all gold and silver wares, in
the City of London, and the suburbs thereof, and in all fairs
and markets, and all cities, towns and boroughs, and all other
places whatsoever throughout our kingdom of England, with
power to punish offenders for working adulterated gold or
silver.   These powers were continually exercised, and from the
records of the company it appears that periodical progresses
through the country were made by the assay-wardens for that
purpose.   Several kings at various times have given them new
charters, enlarging and confirming the older ones.   The latest
are *Inspeximus* Charters of James I. (2 Jac. I.) and Charles II.
(18 Car. II.), which recite and confirm all those previously
granted.   The latter of these is recited in the Act of 12 Geo. II.
c. 26, and empowered the wardens to commit offenders to
prison and to set fines upon them.   The guild thus incorporated
is now one of the greatest and wealthiest of the City Companies,

---

* Riley's *Memorials of London and* | *XV. centuries.* London, 1868, p. 398.
London Life in the XIII., XIV., and |

and one to which the archæologist and antiquary are indebted for the ready information and assistance it has given to those who have from time to time sought permission to consult its records, which, commencing about 1331, are carried down to the present day. They consist of the wardens' accounts, which begin in that year, and amount to many large volumes, the ordinances, and other books relating to their estates, all of which contain curious and interesting particulars. The members of the fraternity were originally all goldsmiths, as mentioned in their first charter, and the Company is governed by a Prime Warden, three other wardens, and twenty-one assistants, with a livery of 150 members, exclusive of honorary members and members by special grant. The wardens are now annually elected on May 29th ; previously, however, to the Restoration, in compliance with their ordinances, St. Dunstan's Day, being that of their patron saint, was their proper day of election. On the day of election, when the new Prime Warden enters upon the duties of his office, the new punches for the mark having been prepared, are delivered by him to the officers of the Assay Office. Formerly the old punches were all preserved, but not many years ago the accumulation being very great and found inconvenient, it was considered that such a mass of old iron was useless, and they were destroyed. It is much to be regretted that impressions were not taken of them on a copper-plate previous to their destruction, though it is hardly probable that there were any earlier than the time of the fire of London in 1666.

The ordinances or statutes of the Company are contained in a fine MS. on vellum, with illuminated initial letters. It is therein stated that "thys boke was made and ordeynyd by Hugh Bryce, Altherman, Henry Coote, Mylys Adys, and Willyam Palmer, wardens, the xx day of September in the yere of our lorde god MCCCCLXXVIIJ and in the XVIIJ yere of the Reigne of King Edward the fourth. Humfrey Hayford then Mayre of the Cyte of london, John Stokker and Henry Colett, Śheryffys of the same Cyte." The index of the same volume is further described as follows : " Thys Kalendar was made and ordeynyd for this boke by Henry Coote, Stephyn Kelke, John Ernest, and Alen Newman, wardens, the last day of August in the yere of oure lorde god MCCCCLXXXIIJ and in the ffurst yere of the

Reygne of King Richard the thiyd. Sir Edmond Shaa, Knyght, then Mayre of the Cyte of london, Williā Whyte and John Mathew, Sheryffys of the same Cyte."

It contains first the oaths for the wardens and officers; and secondly the ordinances for the government of the Company, which chiefly consist of regulations for the masters of the craft and the taking, keeping and conduct of apprentices; but also "for the working of gold and silver to the standard, and how it shall be delivered." The following may be quoted as examples :—

"Also it is ordeyned that no goldsmith of England, nor nowhere else within the realme, work no manner of vessel nor any other thing of gold nor silver, but if it be of the verry alloy according to the standard of England, called sterling money or better."

"That no manner of vessel or any other thing be borne out from the hands of the workers, nor sold till it be assayed by the wardens of the craft or their deputy, the assayer ordained therefore, and that it be marked with the lyperde's head crowned according to the acts of diverse parliaments, and the mark of the maker thereof."

No worker was to be a freeman of the Company until he had been apprenticed seven years; and the ordinances were to be read publicly on St. Dunstan's Day. At the end of the book are some additional ordinances of the year 1507, being the twenty-second of Henry VII., by which it was provided that no goldsmith should put up to sale any vessel or other work of gold or silver *until he had set his mark upon it;* that he should take it to the assay house of the Hall of the Goldsmiths to be assayed by the assayer, who should *set his mark upon it,* and should deliver it to the warden, who should set on it *the leopard's head crowned.*

Again, in another MS. book on vellum which has the arms of the Goldsmiths' Company emblazoned on the first page, and contains ordinances dated July 5th, 1513, being the fifth year of Henry VIII., we find that it is ordained that before any work of gold or silver is put to sale the maker shall set on it his own mark, that it shall be assayed by the assayer, who shall set on it his mark, and that the wardens shall mark it with the leopard's head crowned.

Here then in both these sets of ordinances we have three distinct marks mentioned: the maker's, the assayer's, and the leopard's head or king's mark. What this assayer's mark was we are not expressly told, but it must almost necessarily be the annual letter, now therefore to be added to the leopard's head of 1300 and the maker's mark of 1363. We shall give reasons when dealing specially with this mark for attributing its inauguration to the year 1478.

The course of State legislation had proceeded *pari passu* with the ordinances of the Goldsmiths' Company, and before passing the ill-omened gulf in the history of English plate which occurs between 1513 and the commencement of the reign of Queen Elizabeth, we must bring it down to the earlier of these dates. And first comes a statute which, but for the fact that it is not found amongst "the statutes" properly so called, and seems therefore to have been only provisional and not confirmed on the assembling of parliament, would appear to have crippled the new-found powers of the goldsmiths' guild, and to have rendered them inoperative outside the city of London. Indeed, it was only assented that this ordinance should commence at the feast of St. John, and should last till the next parliament, to try in the meantime if it were profitable or not.

It is found in 1379 on the Rolls of Parliament of the second year of Richard II., No. 30, and would have ordained not only that each smith should put his mark on his work, but that it should be marked with the mark of the city or borough wherein it was assayed, and that the assay should belong to the mayors, etc., of the cities and boroughs, with the aid of the master of the mint. For the reasons mentioned, this statute was probably not acted upon very generally; though, as we shall presently see, in the case of York, a recognised touch is mentioned in civic records of 1410.

The next Act, in 1381 (5 Richard II., cap. 2), forbade the export of gold and silver in any shape, *or et argent si bien monoie vessell plate* et joialx.* These provisions are reinforced in 1402

---

* The word "plate" here stands for bar or sheet gold and silver, rather than for articles made of them, which were called "vasa" and "jocalia," or, in English, "vessel," until about the middle of the fifteenth century. In the wills and inventories of the latter half of that century, the word begins to occur in its modern sense; to give a single example, one Thomas Brygg, in 1494, bequeaths

by another Act forbidding any person to carry gold or silver in money, vessell or plate out of the realm, without the king's licence.

In 1404 (5 Henry IV., cap. 13), in order to prevent frauds, it was enacted that no artificer, nor other man, whatsoever he be, shall gild nor silver any locks, rings, beads, candlesticks, harness for girdles, chalices, hilts, pomels of swords, powder-boxes, nor covers for cups (*pur hanapes*) made of copper or latten, on pain to forfeit to the king c shillings at every time that he shall be found guilty; but that chalices excepted, artificers may work ornaments for the Church of copper and latten, and the same gild and silver, so that at the foot or some other part, the copper and the latten shall be plain, to the intent that a man may see whereof the thing is made for to eschew the deceit aforesaid.

In 1414 (2 Henry V., Stat. 2, cap. 4) it was enacted for that the goldsmiths of England, of their covin and ordinances, will not sell the wares of their mystery gilt, but at the double price of the weight of silver of the same, which seemeth to the king very outrageous and too excessive a price; the king for the ease of his people hath ordained that all goldsmiths of England shall gild no silver wares worse than of the alloy of the English sterling; and that they take for a pound of Troy gilt but 46 shillings and 8 pence at the most; and of greater weight and less according to the quantity and weight of the same; and that which shall be by them gilt from henceforth shall be of a reasonable price and not excessive, and if any goldsmith do

---

"omnia mea vasa argentea voc' le plate," using the ordinary Latin word and the less familiar term then just coming into use in juxtaposition.

In the following statutes of the fourteenth century, "plate" appears to mean merely the wrought or flattened metal, which is a more strictly accurate use of the word, derived as it is from a common origin with the Greek πλατύς, our own *flat*, and the Spanish *plata*, than its later and secondary application as a general term to vessels formed of such metal :—

9 Edw. III. Stat. 2. Statute of Money :

c. 1. "Argent en plate ne vessel dor ne dargent."

" Monoie plate ou vessel dor ne dargent."

27 Edw. III. Stat. 2. The Statute of the Staple :

" Plate of silver and billets of gold."

A "plate of ale" is the expression used at Trinity College, Cambridge, for one of the silver tankards purchased by fellow-commoners for their own use, and left by them as a parting present to the college (Wordsworth's *Social Life at the English Universities in the 18th Century*); and the same term is applied at Queen's College, in the sister university, to the caudle-cups with ring-handles which are now used for beer.

contrary to this statute, he shall forfeit to the king the value of the thing so sold.

In 1420 (8 Henry V., c. 3) it was forbidden to gild any sheaths or any metal but silver, and the ornaments of Holy Church; or to silver any metal but knights' spurs, and all the apparel that pertaineth to a baron and above that estate.

A more important statute now follows, viz., that of 1423 (2 Henry VI., cap. 14), by which it was ordained that no goldsmith or jeweller within the City of London should sell any article of silver unless it was as fine as sterling, nor set it to sell before it be touched with the touch of the leopard's head if it may reasonably bear the same touch, and also with the mark or sign of the workman of the same, upon pain of forfeiture of the double as afore is said; and that the mark or sign of every goldsmith be known to the wardens of the same craft; and that the keeper of the touch if he shall touch any harness with the leopard's head, except it be as fine as sterling, shall for everything so proved not as good in alloy as the said sterling, forfeit the double value to the king and the party. By this statute also it is ordained that the city of York, Newcastle upon Tine, Lincoln, Norwich, Bristol, Salisbury, and Coventry, shall have divers touches, and further that no goldsmith anywhere shall work silver of worse alloy than the sterling, and shall set his mark upon it before he set it to sale, upon the same penalties as if in London. This is the first mention of provincial assay towns, of which more will be said in a succeeding chapter.

Next, in 1477 (17 Edward IV., cap. 1), by reason of the provisions of the Act of 2 Henry VI., cap. 14, having been daily broken by the goldsmiths and other workers of silver, as well in London as elsewhere, it was directed *inter alia* that no goldsmith or worker of gold or silver should work or put to sale any gold under the fineness of eighteen carats, nor silver unless it be as fine as sterling, except such thing as requireth solder; also that no goldsmith work or set to sale harness of silver plate, or jewel of silver, from the feast of Easter, within the city of London or within two leagues (*leukez*) of London, before it be touched with the leopard's head crowned, such as may bear the said touch, and also with a mark or sign of the worker of the same so wrought, upon pain of forfeiture of the double value of such silver wrought and sold to the contrary; that the

mark or sign of every goldsmith be committed to the wardens
of the same mystery; and if it be found that the keeper of the
touch of the leopard's head crowned, do mark or touch any
harness with the leopard's head, if it be not as fine in alloy as
sterling, he shall forfeit double the value of the silver; and that
the craft of goldsmiths of London shall be answerable for the
non-sufficiency of the warden. The statute was enacted for
seven years, and was afterwards re-enacted for twenty years in
1489, and again for twenty years in 1552 by 7 Edward VI.,
cap. 6.

In 1488-9 (4 Henry VII., Parl. 3, cap. 2) it was found that
whereas in previous times finers and parters of gold and silver
had used to fine and part all the gold and silver needful for the
mints of London, Calais, Canterbury, York, and Durham, and
the fellowship of goldsmiths, under the rules and orders of those
mints, but now they dwelt abroad in every part of the realm,
and out of the rules aforesaid, and carried on their trade so that
men can get no fine silver; and it was enacted that the finers
and parters should not alloy fine gold nor silver, nor sell anything
else, nor to any persons except the officers of mints and the
goldsmiths; that silver be made so fine that it bear 12 pennyweight of alloy in the pound weight, and yet be as good as
sterling, and that all finers set their marks upon it.

We have now brought down both the ordinances of the goldsmiths and those of the statute book to the time of Henry VIII.,
and it will presently be seen what a disastrous period in the
history of the art has been reached. We have come to the
time when the accumulated treasures of the Church were swept
away, and the wealth of lay corporations extorted for the
service of the crown and state. Monastic and cathedral plate
disappears on the Reformation in the reign of Henry VIII., the
possessions of the parish churches follow at the end of that of
Edward VI., whilst the "benevolences" of Queen Mary ransack
the treasure-rooms of the great secular guilds and companies.

A number of goldsmiths' names occur in the Church inventories of Edward VI., and it may be as well to give a few
of them for the chance of their initials being here and there
recognised on vessels made by them for the reformed use, some
of which, as we shall see, still remain. One Christopher Terry
is noted about 1515; and between 1530 and 1553 may be found

working at their craft in London Thomas Calton, Robert
Danbe, John Palterton, Raufe Lathom, John Waberley, Thomas
Metcalfe, John Danyell, Robert Reyns, Fabyan Wythers, and
Robert Wygge—Wigg and Dickson are mentioned in the
inventory of St. George's Chapel, Windsor—and to these must
be added the name of a lady, one Margery Herkins, who carried
on business in Lombard Street. In various accounts rendered
by London churchwardens, temp. Edward VI. occur:—Jasper
ffysher, Geo. Dalton, William Kelwaye, John Wickes, John
Clarke, R. Maynarde, Mr. Hartop, W. Dyckeson, Thos. Muschamp, Thos. Dewey, Robert Trappes, Richard Lounde, John
Mabbe, Wm. Southwood and Robert Danbe. Of these, Jasper
ffysher was Prime Warden, and Rob. Wygge and John Clarke
were Wardens of the Goldsmiths' Company in 1566.

In the early years of Queen Elizabeth the names that most
frequently occur are those of Robert Tayleboys, found from
1559 to 1572, Thomas Muschampe, who made a communion
cup for Chelmsford, which is unfortunately not now in existence,
and Thomas Turpyn. Mr. Anthony, of the Queen's Arms in
Cheapside, was one of the Queen's goldsmiths at the beginning
of her reign, and it was under the auspices of this respectable
tradesman that the first lottery of which there is any record
was brought out in 1569; a little later one Hughe Kayle held a
similar appointment amongst the Queen's servants.*

The pedigrees and coats of arms of no fewer than thirteen
goldsmiths were entered at the visitation of London by the
heralds in 1568, those of the above-mentioned Dericke Anthony,
Thomas Metcalfe, and Thomas Muschampe among the number.
In this record Affabel Partridge, Esq., is styled "Principal
Goldsmith" to Queen Elizabeth. The others were George
Dalton, Henry Gilbert, John Mabbe, Francis Heton, Chris-
topher Wace, Francis Jackson, Henry Gaynsford, and Thomas
Gardiner. Four of these were members of the Court of
Assistants of the Goldsmiths' Company in 1566, Metcalfe,
Muschampe, Mabbe, and Gardiner. There were sixty-eight
goldsmiths living in Chepe in 1569, besides some twenty in
Lombard Street. These were the chief resorts of the craft.
It is curiously seldom that the name of the maker can be traced
by the sign of his shop forming part of his registered mark,

---

* The Countess of Shrewsbury, "Bess of Hardwicke," was buying quantities of
plate in 1591 and 1592 of one Prescotte, Goldsmith.

but it may be interesting to record some of them, as the following :—

Goldsmiths in Chepe, 1569.

John Lannyson	Acorn.	John Mabbe	Cuppe.
Christopher Wace	Green Dragon.	W. Calton	Wheelbarrow.
Manasses Stockton	Keye.	Beereblocke	Legge.
Wm. Marten	White Lyon.	John Mabbe, sr.	Bottell.
Wm. ffynstwayte	Myter.	Thos. Metcalf	Bell.
Hy. Gilberd	Rose.	Thos. Conell	Talbott.
Edmund Cornwall	Squirrell.	Geo. Waren	Crowne.
Hy. Sutton	Ploughe.	Thos. Gardener	Red Crosse.
Nichs. Sutton	Harrowe.	Fras. Heaton	Tonne.
Richd. Howe	Griffon.	Robt. Wright	Wyndmylle.
Thos. Bampton	Falcon.	Geo. Gatchet	King's Head.
Ant. Bate	St. John's Head.	Hy. Gaynesford	Crane.
Thos. Clerke	Angell.	Gabl. Newman	Pyke.
Diricke Antonie	Queen's Arms.	Richd. Hanberrie	Maydenhead.
Wm. Dyxson	Flour de luce.	Robt. Wygge	Greyhound.
Fras. Jackson	Black Spread Eagle.	Stephen Durrant	Blewe Bore.
Thos. Harrison	Swan.	Richd. Hanberrie	Connie.
John Harryson	Broad Arrow.	Edward Gilberd	Ship.
John Goodrich	Unicorn.	Richd. Martin	Harp.
Robt. Brandon	Gylte Lion.	Robt. Aske	Lamb.
Robt. Durrant	Half Moon.	Richd. Rogers	Gilt Eagle.
Robt. Medley	White Horse.	John Ealeston	White Hind.
Antonie Bate	Black Boye.	Richd. Rogers	Goat.
Thos. Hartoppe	White Cocke.	Christopher Ffulke	Three Legges.
Nichs. Bartlemewe	Woolsacke.	John Keale	Belhouse.
Affabell Partrige	Black Bull.	John Foxe	Gilt Fox.
Aldern. Langley	Adam and Eve.	Geo. Martin	Locke.
Robt. Sharpe	Basket.	Thos. Maye	White Beare

In St. Matthew's Alley.

George Longedale.	Affabell Partridge.
Thos. Denham.	Geo. Warrenson.
John Pinfold.	Wm. Burneye.

North Side of Chepe.

Wm. Holborne.	Andrew Palmer.
Wm. Foxe.	Robt. Signell.
Jas. Storke.	

In Lumbard Street.

Thos. Benson.	Thos. Pope.
Richd. Sharpe.	John Wetherhyil.
Wm. Jones, jr.	Thos. Muschampe.
Robt. Tayleboyes.	Umphrey Stevens.
Hughe Keale.	Richd. Robyns.
James Alleyn.	John Bull.
Wm. Jones, sr.	Robt. Hawkyns.
John Kettelwood.	Thos. Sympson.
W. Alsoppe.	Wm. ffeake.
Edward Creake.	Robt. ffrye.

CHAP. II.]　ELIZABETHAN GOLDSMITHS.　39

It will be inferred that with the accession of Queen Elizabeth, brighter days succeeded to a quarter of century of plunder and destruction. The debased standards of the last twenty or thirty years were raised once more to their former purity, and none knew better than the Queen herself the importance of this step, in which she took much personal interest. But it was not at first a very popular measure, and the promulgation by royal proclamation was necessary of a "summarie of certaine reasons which moved the Queen's majestie to procede in reformations of her base and coarse monies, and to reduce them to their values in sorte as they may be turned to fine monies," before the public, who saw only the loss that the reform would occasion them on the coin then in their possession, realised the great benefit it would be to the nation. This was dated from Hampton Court on 29 September, 1560, and on 19 February, 1560–61, the base money was called in also by proclamation. The Queen went herself in state to the Mint, and striking some coins with her own royal hand, gave them to those standing about her, ordering that a medal should be struck to commemorate the event. The Minutes of the Goldsmiths' Company record that the diet tried on 18th June, 1561, was "the first dyett of the newe Standard."

Stringent measures, too, were adopted to prevent fraud and to preserve the purity of the re-established standard. Twenty-eight goldsmiths were fined in the course of 1566, a not exceptional year in this respect ; and amongst them are some of the leading members of the craft. Legislation also was resorted to, and in 1575-6, on February 8 (18 Eliz. cap. 15), it was enacted with this view, that after the 20th of April then next ensuing, no goldsmith should work, sell, or exchange any plate or ware of gold less in fineness than twenty-two "carrects" (carats), and that he use no sother amell or other stuffing more than is necessary for finishing the same, nor make, sell, or exchange, any wares of silver less in fineness than 11 ounces 2 pennyweight, nor take above twelvepence for the ounce of gold or pound of silver "beyond the fashion" (more than the buyer shall or may be allowed for the same at the Queen's exchange or mint) ; nor put to sale any ware before he hath set his own mark on so much thereof as may conveniently bear the same ; and if after the above day any gold or silver wares shall be touched for good by the wardens or masters of the mystery, and there shall afterwards be found fraud or deceit therein, the wardens shall pay forfeit the value of the thing so marked.

The Goldsmiths' Company, resuming its good work, seems to have exercised its powers even harshly. There are constant entries in the Minute-Books of plate broken and penalties exacted for silver work, usually buckles or clasps, but often larger pieces, found on assay to be worse than standard, and goldsmiths of good name and standing are found amongst the defaulters, and were dealt with as stringently as the rest. Great dissatisfaction was given in 1583 by one Thomas Kelynge, then the assayer at Goldsmiths' Hall, who from over zeal, or baser motives as it was alleged, made himself very unpopular with the craft. Amongst the records of the mint are preserved some papers detailing "the grefes of us poor goldsmiths against our assay master," one Richard Mathewe and a fellow-craftsman named Henry Colley charging Kelynge with breaking their plate unjustly, and stating that when they had refashioned a part of the broken plate differently, and sent it in again under another maker's mark, it passed. Colley describes cutting out part of a condemned platter and making it into a taster which passed, and he further complained that out of a nest of bowls or of a tankard of no more than thirty ounces, Kelynge took as much as a quarter of an ounce, or at least half a quarter, for himself.* There were however faults on both sides, and the strict supervision of the Goldsmiths' Company was still both exercised and needed, as the following entry found among their records testifies:—"4th May, 1597—Edward Cole, Attorney-General, filed an information against John Moore and Robert Thomas; that whereas it had been heretofore of long time provided by divers laws and statutes for the avoiding deceit and fraud in the making of plate, that every goldsmith should before the sale of any plate by him made, bring the same first to the Goldsmiths' Hall for trial by assay, to be touched or marked and allowed by the wardens of the said company of Goldsmiths; the which wardens did by their indenture in their search, find out the aforesaid deceitful workmanship and counterfeit also of plate and puncheons; yet the said John

---

* Public Record Office—*Exchequer, Q. R. (Mint. Miscell.), temp. Eliz.*

Moore and R. Thomas being lately made free of the Gold-smiths' Company, did about three months past make divers parcels of counterfeit plate debased and worse than her Majesty's standard 12^d and more in the oz.; and to give appearance to the said counterfeit plate being good and lawful, did thereto put and counterfeit the marks of her Majesty's Lion, the leopard's head limited by statute and the alphabetical mark approved by ordinance amongst themselves, which are the private marks of the Goldsmiths' Hall, and be and remain in the custody of the said wardens and puncheons to be worked and imprinted thereon, and the said John Moore did afterwards sell the same for good and sufficient plate to the defrauding of her Majesty's subjects, &c."

It remains to be said that they were convicted and sentenced to stand in the pillory at Westminster, with their ears nailed thereto, and with papers above their heads stating their offence to be "for making false plate and counterfeiting her Majesty's touch." They were then put in the pillory at Cheapside, had one ear cut off, and were taken through Foster Lane to Fleet Prison, and had to pay a fine of ten marks. Here we have the first actual mention by name of the *Lion* and an *alphabetical letter*, though both had been long in use, the former for about half a century, and the latter for more than double that time.

There is nothing now to note for a long time except that in 1624 (21 Jac. I. c. 28) certain portions of the earlier enactments of 28 Edw. I., 37 Edw. III., and 2 Henry VI. were repealed, and that a few years later the goldsmiths' hall marks were fully recog-nised as a guarantee of the quality of silver bearing them; for when Charles I. resorted to forced loans for the means of carrying on the war, warrants dated from Oxford in 1643, demanded of the individuals to whom they were addressed so much money " or the value thereof in plate, toucht plate at five shillings, and untoucht plate at foure shillings foure pence per ounce."*

Mention is made in the records of 1635 of pewter marked like silver, and a petition by the Goldsmiths' Company to the Lords of the Council, pointing out the undesirability of the practice; and other similar entries occur later.

In these and such like transactions, as well as in other greater

---

* *Coll. Top. et Gen.*, vol. vii., p. 102.

affairs, the goldsmiths bore an important part, and that their business was right profitable is attested by the wealthy and notable men that are found amongst them at this time. Who has not heard of George Heriot, goldsmith to James VI. of Scotland, and of the noble hospital founded by him in Edinburgh ? A goldsmith by descent, for his father was an eminent Scotch goldsmith and money dealer, like other people he removed to London with his royal master on his accession to the English throne, and there constantly increased in eminence and wealth till his death in 1623-4.* The Vyners too, and the Jenners both owed their prosperity to the great business which they carried on as goldsmiths in the middle years of this century. The transactions of Sir Thos. Vyner with the Mercers' Company as their goldsmith extend from 1620 to 1643. He died in 1665.

The name of Vyner must be invoked to justify digression for a little while to a subject of considerable archæological, indeed national, importance. More than fifty years ago Mr. Robert Cole, F.S.A., read before the Society of Antiquaries a paper† upon some interesting documents that had then lately come into his possession relating to the Regalia made for the coronation of King Charles II. They were two in number, one of them being the order dated 20th June, 1662, for the payment from the Royal Treasury to Sir Robert Vyner, his Majesty's goldsmith, nephew of Sir Thomas, of the sums of £21,978 9s. 11d., and £10,000, "for two Crowns, two Sceptres, and a Globe of Gold, set with diamonds, rubyes, saphires, emeralds, and pearls, St. Edward's Staff, the Armilla, Ampull, and other the Regalia, all of gold." The second document was the receipt of Sir Robert Vyner for part of this money, and it bears the signature of Sir Robert Vyner himself, dated July 1, 1662. It is quite clear from a contemporary MS. record that because " all the royal ornaments and regalia theretofore preserved from age to age in the treasury of the Church of Westminster had been taken away, sold and destroyed," the Committee appointed to order the ceremony met several times, not only to direct the remaking, but even " to settle the form and fashion of each particular, all which did then retain the old names and

---

* One Wm. Sankey made and altered much royal plate in 1647.—*Exch. Miscel.*
† *Archæologia*, vol. xxix., p. 262.

fashion although they had been newly made and prepared."
A third and later document, dated Feb. 23, 1684-5, procured
by Mr. Cole in the same way and at the same time as the other
two, was afterwards communicated to the Society. It contained not only a list but the weights of the articles comprised
in the Regalia, and seemed to have been prepared as a sort
of estimate of some of the probable expenses of the approaching
coronation of James II., which took place in April, including
the providing of articles such as on the former occasion were
delivered to the great officers of state for fees. It is of considerable interest, and as the Transactions of the Society of Antiquaries are at the disposal of comparatively few persons, no
apology is needed for reprinting it here as follows.*

"A List of yᵉ Regalias provided for his late Maᵗʸ'ˢ Coronation, and are now in
yᵉ Custody of Sʳ Gilbert Talbot, Knt., Master and Treasʳ of his Maᵗʸ'ˢ Jewells and
Plate, vizᵗ. :—

	oz.	dwt.	gr.	li.	s.	d.
Imprim. Sᵗ Edward's Crowne . . . . . poiz 82	5	16				
For yᵉ addition of Gold and Workemanship				350	00	00
For yᵉ Loane of yᵉ Jewells returned				500	00	00
Itᵐ One Crowne of State† . . . . . poiz 72	01	00				
For yᵉ Gold, Jewells, and Workemanship				7,870	00	00
Itᵐ One Scepter with a Dove . . . . . poiz 34	03	20				
For yᵉ Gold, Jewells, and Workemanship				440	00	00
Itᵐ One other Scepter with a Cross. . . . poiz 32	11	10				
For yᵉ Gold, Jewells, and Workemanship				1,025	00	00
Itᵐ One Sᵗ Edward's Staffe . . . . . poiz 45	08	08				
For yᵉ Gold and Workemanship				225	06	02
Itᵐ One Gloobe with a Crosse . . . . poiz 49	07	12				
For Gold, Jewells, and Workemanshᵖp				1,150	00	00
Itᵐ One Pair of Spurrs . . . . . . poiz 12	18	00				
For Gold and Workemanship				63	07	06
Itᵐ Two Armillas . . . . poiz 6	12	22				
For Gold and Workemanship				44	18	06
Itᵐ One Ampulla or Eglet . . . . . poiz 21	08	00				
For Gold and Workemanship				102	05	00
Itᵐ The Anointing Spoon . . . . . poiz 3	05	00				
For Silver and Workemanship				2	00	00
Itᵐ One Chalice and Paten . . . . . poiz 61	12	12				
For Gold and Workemanship				277	06	03

£12,050 03 05
G. TALBOT."

* *Proceedings of the Society of Antiquaries*, 1852, vol. ii., No. 31, p. 222.
† The framework of this crown was
taken by Messrs. Rundell and Bridge,
in part payment for a new crown made
by them in 1838, and is now in the possession of Lord Amherst of Hackney.

"A List of Regalias provided for his late Ma^tes Coronation, wch were delivered for Fees, &c., by Order, and are out of ye Custody of Sr Gilbert Talbot, Kn^t, Master and Treas^r of his Maj'^s Jewells and Plate, and are now to be provided, &c. :—

		oz. dwt. gr.	£. s. d.
Imprim^s One Ld High Constable's Staffe . . .	poiz	15 00 00	
For Silver and Workemanship			08 15 00
It^m One Earle Marshall's Staffe	poiz	9 00 00	
For Silver, Gilding, and Workemanship			07 15 00
It^m Six Canopy Staves	poiz	180 02 12	
For Silver and Workemanship			76 11 01
It^m One Crown for Garter King at Arms . . .	poiz	24 10 0	
For Gold and Workemanship			116 17 6
It^m One Chaine and Jewell	poiz	5 13 3	
For Gold and Workemanship			43 06 07
It^m One Banner and Rod . . . . ,	poiz	3 13 3	
For Golde and Workemanship			37 14 03
It^m One Collar of SS	poiz	19 10 0	
For Silver, Guilding, and Workemanship			24 18 09
It^m Two Coronets	poiz	30 12 12	
For Silver, Gilding, and Workemanship			22 19 04
It^m Two Collars of SS	poiz	34 07 12	
For Silver and Workemanship			33 11 10
It^m Six Collars SS	poiz	89 15 00	
For Silver and Workemanship			82 08 09
It^m Two Ingots	poiz	19 00 00	
For Gold and Workemanship			75 05 00
It^m One Cup	poiz	19 07 00	
For Gold and Workemanship			80 05 03
It^m Coronation Meddalls—Twelve . . .	poiz	3 10 16	
For Gold and Workemanship			25 c6 08
It^m Jewells, 75 for Kn^ts of the Bath, of wch seven are in custody	poiz	35 10 12	
For Gold and Workemanship			433 04 4
			£1,067 19 4

G. TALBOT."

Interesting as this curious history of the Regalia is in itself, and as showing that none of the old Regalia, not even the Anointing Spoon,* as it would seem, survived the Commonwealth, it is also of no little importance to note the mode in which these and other documents came into Mr. Cole's hands. The instructive particulars of his acquisition of them shall be told in his own words. He says :

"It will be in the recollection of the Society that some two

---

* When exhibited by gracious permission of Her late Majesty Queen Victoria, at the rooms of the Society of Antiquaries | in 1850, the Coronation Spoon was considered by some to be the original one, and of high antiquity, but this can hardly be so.

or three years ago the then Lords of the Treasury directed the selection and mutilation of many tons weight of Exchequer Records (as they were not improperly called), and which, after being mutilated, were sold as waste paper. It is not necessary for me to make any observations on the propriety or impropriety of this order for the destruction of original documents, nor on the manner in which that order was executed : the report of the committee appointed by the House of Lords to inquire into the subject is before the public, and to that, and the evidence taken on the occasion, I would refer the Society. The contractor with the Government for the purchase of the mutilated records re-sold the mass in various parcels, and a portion of about two tons weight came into my hands, from which I selected many very curious and interesting documents, one of them the subject of my present communication."

In view of any similar wholesale destruction of ancient public records in future, the necessity cannot be too strongly urged of examining them far more carefully and by more expert hands than hitherto, before they are altogether condemned ; and it may help to save some of them to show, by fragments that have accidentally escaped, what valuable historical information may easily be overlooked and destroyed.

Returning to the Vyners and the Jenners, it must not be forgotten that from this time until 1700 or even later the London goldsmiths frequently combined the business of banking with their trade, many of the gentry in those troublous times being glad to adopt the practice of keeping "running cash balances" with their goldsmiths for safety's sake instead of keeping gold in their own houses. This, indeed, is the origin of modern London banking, and in some cases existing firms actually represent ancestors who came in for their business in this way, and gradually dropped their earlier calling for the new one.

Not that the goldsmiths' craft was thought by any means a despicable one; they are found resenting association with men of "meaner trades," even as dwellers in the same street, and in the time of Charles I., the influence of the king himself was on occasion exercised for the removal of such people from Cheapside, which was then almost exclusively inhabited by the goldsmiths.

The interesting history of Messrs. Childs' banking house,
tells of the apprenticing in early life of the great Sir Francis
Child, Lord Mayor in 1699, to his grandfather, William Wheeler
the elder, a goldsmith at Temple Bar ; of his marriage with his
cousin Elizabeth Wheeler, the only daughter and heiress of his
uncle, William Wheeler the younger, and of his succession in
1681 to the business, which has ever since been carried on at
the sign of the Marigold in the same name.

This brings us a step further towards modern banking, for
a list of goldsmiths is given, and it includes Charles Duncomb
of the Grasshopper, Francis Kenton of the King's Arms,
Thomas Fowle of the Black Lion, J. Heriot of the Naked Boy,
and John Mawson & Co. of the Golden Hind, all in Fleet
Street, and John Coggs of the King's Head in the Strand,
who prior even to 1700 kept accounts with Childs' instead of
carrying on a joint goldsmith's and banking business for the
benefit of their customers, or even taking care of their own
money.   The same account gives the names of William
Rawson and John Marryott in 1666, Thomas Williams of the
Crown in 1677, William Pinckney of the Golden Dragon, Inner
Temple Gate in 1663, Joseph Horneby, John Portman, Robert
Welsted, and Thomas Rowe, all goldsmiths of more or less
note in the time of Charles II., besides the better known one
of Edward Backwell, who died in 1679, ruined by his dealings
with that sovereign.   In a bill drawn upon Atwills, by Francis
Tyssen and accepted by Mr. William Atwill and Company,
23 March, 1703, that well-known banking firm are only called
"Goldsmiths of London."

But in the midst of more interesting historical remarks, the
working goldsmith and his regulations must not be forgotten ;
and so far as these are concerned, we find that things remained
where we left them early in the century, till in 1675, for the
prevention and redress of great abuses, the Goldsmiths' Company put forth a notice dated from their Hall on Feb. 23,
to the following effect :—That whereas divers small wares were
frequently worked and put to sale worse than standard, and
also divers pieces of silver plate sold, not being assayed at
Goldsmiths' Hall, and not marked with the leopard's head
crowned, and whereas to prevent such frauds the wardens had
formerly required all plate workers and small workers to cause

their respective marks to be brought to the said Hall, and
struck there in a table kept in the Assay Office, notice was by
this order given to all goldsmiths in and about the cities of
London and Westminster to repair to the hall, and there strike
their marks in a table appointed for that purpose, and likewise
enter their names and their dwellings in a book, and that
workers and shopkeepers should forbear to sell any gold or
silver wares not being agreeable to standard, gold of 22 carats,
and silver of 11 oz. 2 dwts. fine, nor before the workman's
mark be struck thereon, and the same assayed at Goldsmiths'
Hall, and there approved for standard by striking thereon the
lyon and *Leopard's head crowned*, or one of them, if the works
would conveniently bear the same, and the order concludes
with a caution as to the penalty for infringing it.   Advantage
of this order seems to have been sometimes taken in later days
for the marking of small wares, such as teaspoons, with the
lion passant only.

Passing mention must be made of "the Plate Lotteries" of
Charles II. before going on to a later reign.   These seem to
have been a contrivance for rewarding the fidelity of those who
had served the Crown during the interregnum, and for raising
money at the same time for present needs.   The mode of dis-
tributing gifts of plate from the Crown as prizes by means of
lotteries, probably recommended itself by the opportunity it
offered of farming out to advantage the right of setting up and
bringing out the lotteries, in various parts of England, and of
selling the tickets.   Mr. Hone, speaking of this ingenious mode
of increasing the revenue, gives from Malcolm's *Manners* a public
advertisement of the year 1669, as follows*:—"This is to give
notice that any persons who are desirous to farm any of the
counties within the kingdom of England or the dominion of
Wales, in order to the setting up of a plate lottery, or any other
lottery whatsoever, may repair to the lottery office at Mr.
Philip's house in Mermaid Court, over against the mews, where
they may contract with the trustees commissioned by His
Majesty's letters patent for the management of the said lotteries
on the behalf of the truly loyal, indigent officers."

We now come to legislation of a different character.   The

---

* Hone's *Every Day Book*, ii. 1413.

order of 1675 had had its effect, and it became necessary rather to protect the coin of the realm from being melted down for plate, than to insist on the fineness of the plate itself.

Large quantities of plate had been sacrificed for King and Parliament, or confiscated by one or the other in this disturbed century, and now that quiet times had come again, the rich turned their attention to replenishing their tables and cupboards with the necessary plate, and even tavern-keepers supplied themselves with silver drinking-vessels. We find the grand jury of Middlesex presenting in 1695 that the frequent and common use of silver basons, monteaths, silver tankards, bowls, cups and tumblers of silver in public-houses and taverns have occasioned many burglaries and murders, and praying the Bench to make application to His Majesty's Council or Parliament or both to find out means to prevent such common use of silver in such places. All classes seem to have resorted to the supply of metal that was nearest at hand—the silver coin of the realm.

In consequence, therefore, of this practice of melting down the coin, legislation for its protection became necessary, and in 1696 (8 & 9 Will. III. c. 8) with this object the standard for plate was raised above that of the silver coinage, so as to make the silver of the coinage less easily available for plate making. It was enacted that on and after March 25, 1697, no worker of plate should make any article of silver less in fineness than 11 oz. 10 dwts. of fine silver in every pound Troy, nor put to sale, exchange or sell any article made after that day but of that standard, nor until it had been marked with the marks now appointed to distinguish plate of this new standard. These marks were to be as follows :—The worker's mark to be expressed by the *two first letters of his surname*, the marks of the mystery or craft of the goldsmiths, which instead of the leopard's head and lion were to be the figure of a *lion's head erased* and the figure of a woman, commonly called *Britannia*, and a distinct and variable mark to be used by the warden of the same mystery, to denote the year in which such plate was made. The plate made at this period is often called of " Britannia standard " to distinguish it.

But here another difficulty arose, for this Act mentioning no provincial offices practically deprived them of the privilege of stamping any plate at all, as they were not empowered to use the marks appointed for the new, and now the only legal, standard. The result of this was that from 1697 until the establishment of certain provincial offices, as we shall see, in 1701, no plate was properly stamped anywhere but in London, and what little plate was made in the provinces was stamped irregularly.*

Leaving, however, the provincial offices for the present, some further provisions of the Act of 1697 must not be forgotten, for it not only protected the coin by raising the standard, but adopted means for increasing the supply of it. This was effected by providing for the ready purchase by the mint of any wrought plate bearing the stamps of the Goldsmiths' Company at 5s. 4d. per ounce, and such an offer, no doubt, brought about a further destruction of some of the ancient plate that had escaped previous storms.

From this time forward, owing to the re-registration of makers' marks, which now became necessary, considerably more is known about plateworkers' names than is the case in earlier days. Some of them were artists of great merit, and the names and abodes of all those of much note have been entered against their marks in an appendix at the end of this volume. The best patronised of them will be known by the number of recorded examples of work stamped with their respective marks.

In the course of the next twenty years the object of the last-mentioned statute was accomplished, though somewhat slowly, and at length the necessity for its continuance no longer existed. Added to this it seems to have been found that articles made of the higher quality of silver were not so durable nor so serviceable as those of the old standard.

Even as late as 1718, silver coin was very uncomfortably scarce,† and this scarcity was one of the principal matters to which the Parliament of that year directed its attention. Lord Stanhope, in his official statement as head of the Treasury, ascribed it to three causes—first, the increasing luxury in relation to plate; secondly, the export of plate or other bullion to the East Indies; and thirdly, to the clandestine trade carried on of exporting silver and importing gold to and from Holland,

---

* See p. 127.   † Lord Mahon's *History of England*, vol. i., p. 443.

Germany, and other countries. In 1717 the East India Company had exported three million ounces of silver, which far
exceeded the imports, so that large quantities of silver specie
must have been melted up to supply the export of the silversmiths. Lord Stanhope also hinted at "the malice of some
persons, who by hoarding up silver thought to distress the
Government." However this may be, the "old sterling"
standard was restored with its old marks from June 1, 1720
(6 Geo. I., c. 11), and took its place beside the new or Britannia
standard, which, with its own special marks, was left a lawful
standard for such as preferred it.

Provisions against dishonesty were again found to be necessary, and in 1739, in consequence of great frauds which are
detailed in the Act of that year (12 Geo. II., cap. 26), particularly in the use of excessive quantities of solder, the standards
were again fixed at 22 carats for gold, and 11 oz. 2 dwts. for
silver, though the higher standard was not abolished, and the
marks to be used were resettled, the maker's initials to be those
of his Christian name and surname, instead of the first two
letters of his surname as was ordered in 1697, likewise the
character or alphabet of the initial letters used was to be in
each case changed also. The marks to be used by the country
assay offices were also dealt with, but, as will be seen in a
subsequent chapter, not so clearly as could have been wished.*
As before, the general re-registration of marks has stored
the books of the Goldsmiths' Company with a quantity of
information as to the names of the goldsmiths of the day.

Except for the lower standards of gold, we have now been
carried through all the marks to be found on plate stamped
in London, save one only—the mark of the sovereign's head.
This was introduced in 1784 (24 Geo. III., c. 53) by an Act
granting a duty from December 1 in that year of 8s. per oz. on
gold plate, and of sixpence per oz. on silver. It directed the
wardens or assay master to mark the pieces with a new mark, viz.
the king's head over and above the several marks already used.

Some further details as to duties payable, articles exempted,
and dealers' licences will be found under the head of the duty
mark in the next chapter.

---

* See Chap. V., p. 140.

Last of all we come to some quite recent improvements in the system of marking gold, and to the authorisation of the above-mentioned lower gold standards, a step brought about by the use of that precious metal amongst larger classes of society. These provisions are the last on our list relating to marks, and are perhaps the least interesting of all from an antiquary's point of view, however valuable they may be to the purchaser in the every-day dealings of trade. The lower standards, or rather all those below 18 carats, have never been much used nor appreciated by the public, and it will not be necessary to refer to them at any length. The Act, however, is an important one (38 Geo. III., c. 69), which in 1798 authorised the much-used standard of 18 carats fine for gold, and provided for its being marked with a crown and the figures 18 instead of the lion passant; for it had the good effect of giving gold a different distinguishing mark from silver for the first time, a distinction which should have been made long before. It must always be remembered that until 38 Geo. III. there was no special distinguishing mark for gold, and then only for 18-carat gold, and further that it was not until 1844 that 22-carat gold was marked otherwise than as silver would have been. By 7 & 8 Vict. c. 22, s. 15, this last improvement was made, and 22-carat gold has from that time been marked with a crown and 22, instead of the lion passant, to the great advantage of the public.

The still lower standards for gold were legalised in 1854 (17 & 18 Vict. c. 96), by a provision enabling the Sovereign in Council to allow any gold standard of not less than one-third of fine gold. In pursuance of this, three reduced standards were ordered to be marked as follows, viz. :—15-carat, with the figures 15 and ·625 ; 12-carat, with 12 and ·5 ; and 9-carat, with 9 and ·375—the second figure in each case being the proportion of fine gold expressed in decimals.

The Act called "the Goldsmiths' Act " of 1844, which has been already mentioned as regulating the marking of 22-carat gold (7 & 8 Vict. c. 22), also regulates the trade as regards forgeries of dies or marks, the selling of plate worse than standard, and other such frauds. But as this is rather a matter of present day interest than connected with the history of the craft or their marks, a fuller consideration of it is reserved for a separate chapter devoted to frauds and offences.

The result of this somewhat long historical and legal notice
is that we shall find, on plate made in London, the following
marks, or some of them, in accordance with the various
statutes and ordinances that have been recounted.   Stated
for clearness in their chronological order, they are as follows :—

1. The Leopard's head, from 1300.
2. The Maker's mark, from 1363.
3. The Annual letter, from 1478.
4. The Lion passant, from 1545.
5. The Lion's head erased, and figure of Britannia, from 1697.*
6. The Sovereign's head, from 1784.

The following table gives a summary of what has here been
said of the London marks; and each of them is treated of more
fully in the next chapter.

-----

* From 1697—1720 used for silver instead of the leopard's head crowned and
lion passant, which were discontinued
during that interval.   Since 1720, used,
when required, for plate made of the
higher standard silver.

TABLE OF THE MARKS FOUND UPON PLATE MADE IN LONDON FROM THE EARLIEST TIMES.

QUALITY.	STANDARD.	DATE.	DUTY.	MAKER.
Silver, old sterling (none from 1697—1720).	Leopard's head crowned (without crown from some time in 1821-2). Lion passant (added about 1545).	Annual letter, from 1478 on all descriptions of plate alike.	Sovereign's head (from Dec. 1, 1784—1890) on all except exempted articles.	Initials or device, or both, till 1697; from that time initials, with or without addition of device; on all descriptions of plate alike.
Silver, new sterling (from 1697).	Lion's head erased. Figure of Britannia.			
			NOTE. The duty was taken off plate in 1890.	NOTES. For new sterling silver, from 1697—1739 the first two letters of the surname were used.
Gold, 22-c. (until 1844).	Leopard's head crowned (without crown from some time in 1821-2). Lion passant (added about 1545).			From 1739 initials of Christian and surname have been used on all descriptions of plate alike.
Ditto, 22-c. (since 1844).	Ditto. Crown and 22.			
Ditto, 18-c. (since 1798).	Ditto. Crown and 18.			
Ditto, 15-c. (since 1854).	Ditto. 15 and ·625.			
Ditto, 12-c. (since 1854).	Ditto. 12 and ·5.			
Ditto, 9-c. (since 1854).	Ditto. 9 and ·375.			

CHAPTER III.

THE LEOPARD'S HEAD.

THOUGH, in all probability, workers in the precious metals had
been, from even earlier times, in the habit of signing their work
each with his own distinguishing symbol, the ancient mark of a
leopard's head appointed by statute in 1300 is the first which is
mentioned in any law or ordinance regulating the goldsmith's art
in England. In the translation of the original Norman-French
of this enactment, as given in the Statutes at Large, the words
used are "*the* leopard's head," as if it were some known and
recognised symbol, but in the original itself the words are
"*une* teste de leopart," and Mr. O. Morgan has suggested that
the article "*une*" implies that it was a new mark invented for the
purpose. On the other hand, the first charter of the Goldsmiths'
Company, dated 1327, refers to the mark as ordained ". of ancient
times," and this would seem a somewhat inappropriate description of a mark instituted within living memory.*

However this may be, from 1300, if not before, it was, until
the introduction of the lion passant, the king's mark for "gold
of a certain touch," and "silver of the sterling allay." And
first, some confusion and error seem to have existed with regard
to the term "*Leopard's* head," it being, in fact, a Lion's head.
It will, however, be remembered, that in Old French, the
language alike of heraldry and of our early statutes, the term
"*leopart*" means a lion passant guardant. The arms of England
from the time of Henry III. have been three such lions, and in
the Old French heraldic works they are described as three
"*leoparts*" or "*lions leopardies*." The leopard's head, therefore,
is properly the head of a lion passant guardant, which, in fact,
is a lion's front face ; and all the early examples of this mark

---

* A very early mention of it is to be found in 1329, when thirty-six spoons, plain
white, stamped with the leopard, value 59*s*. 10*d*., occur in an "Inventory of the
Crown Jewels of Edward III.," *Arch.*, vol. x., 241.

show a fine bold lion's face with mane and beard, having on the head a ducal crown. It was in all probability, therefore, taken from the arms of the sovereign, and the crown added as a further indication of its being the King's mark. It is actually called "the King's mark" in the next statute in which it is mentioned, that of 1363. It must here be remarked that although in the Act of 1300, the charter of 1327, and the Act of 1423, it is only termed "the leopard's head," in the earliest goldsmiths' ordinances it is spoken of as "the Liberds hede *crowned*," whilst in the Act of 1477 it is described in both ways: later, in the Goldsmiths' records of 1597, it appears as the leopard's head only, though it is certainly and always found bearing a crown, upon plate of that period, and as far back at all events as 1478. It may be that it was crowned from the first, and that it is a mistake arising out of the wording of the Act of 1477, to date the addition of the crown from that year. To set against this two or three spoons of the fifteenth century seem to have an uncrowned leopard's head within a beaded circle in the bowls; but as none of them have any mark on the handle, it is not safe to draw any conclusion from them. It is not at all impossible that the crown originated with the date letter in 1478.

It is a very doubtful point too whether the mark should be called, as it often is, the *London* hall-mark. It certainly was not so originally, except in the sense that in early times the Goldsmiths' Company in that city were the only authorised keepers of "the king's touch." In 1477 it was not used as a London mark only, for the Act of that year, speaking of the prevalent abuse of setting this mark on gold and silver that was not fine, recites as a grievance that the "said touch of the Leopard's head is oftentimes put on such things by the keeper of the said touch of London *and other places*." Here the "said touch of the Leopard's head" is recognised as the sign of the standard used, as well in London as elsewhere. The right reading of the Acts is that in 1423 it was intended to limit the leopard's head mark to London, other places in future to use "divers touches"; and that it was to carry this into better effect that the Act of 1477 explicitly ordained that within the city of London and for two leagues round, the leopard's head crowned should be used. When the goldsmiths of Norwich were setting

their house in order in 1565, and establishing a proper touch
for that city, they adopted as a standard one which they
describe as of the same fineness and better than the "lyberd's
hedde with the crowne." This practically means that they
adopted the national standard, as worked in London and as
guaranteed by the mark, which had become very much limited
to London since 1423, and from 1477 was expressly so. It had
no doubt gained a great reputation, as we gather from the
*Touchstone** that in the seventeenth century it was practically
necessary to send to London to have the touch of the leopard's
head applied. But this is not quite the same thing as saying
that it was the London mark, and in point of fact when the
leopard's head crowned was abolished for a time (1697-1720),
together with the lion passant, in favour of two new marks, those
two new marks were both used under the Acts which, shortly
afterwards, established the provincial assay offices ; neither of
them was reserved specially for the Goldsmiths' Company, as
would probably have been the case if its own peculiar hall mark
had been abolished, and the inference is strong that at that
time it was considered a national standard mark and not the
London hall mark at all. Further, upon the restoration of
the old sterling standard of silver in 1720, the leopard's head
crowned was resumed in ordinary course by several of the provincial offices for metal of that degree of fineness, and in one
such office, viz., Newcastle-upon-Tyne, it was so used until
recent years.

It should also be noted that even when the leopard's head
and the lion passant were disused on silver, they still remained
in force for standard gold, and it may favour the view of the
leopard's head being a standard mark rather than the distinguishing mark of the London Goldsmiths' Hall, that it was
used at this time on one metal assayed there, but not on
the other.

Like the question of the derivation of the mark, this point is,
however, rather of antiquarian interest than of practical importance, for even if it were the standard mark until the invention
of the lion passant practically released it, if we may say so,
from doing duty in that capacity, it may perhaps not unfairly

---

* See p. 14.

since that date, say from 1545, when found on London-made plate, be looked upon as answering the same purpose as the shields of arms used as their distinguishing hall-marks by assay-offices in the provinces.

When we come to consider the London date letter, we shall urge its claim to be the London mark properly so called.

In conclusion, although evidently not always confined to London, the leopard's head crowned has been used at Goldsmiths' Hall for whatever purpose from time immemorial on standard gold, and on old sterling silver whenever such silver has been worked.*

The appearance of the stamp has from time to time been altered, and always for the worse. It is found within a circular line from 1478 to 1547. From 1548 to c. 1680 it is on a stamp with its outline following that of the crown and the head. The crown is an open ducal one at first, but at certain periods, for instance about 1515, 1531, and some other years, the crown appears almost as if it had four balls instead of the more open design. This is probably the effect produced by using a worn punch rather than of any alteration in the style of the crown. The size of the lion's head was somewhat diminished in the year 1729, when he was also shorn of much of his mane and beard, the character of the crown being also altered; and in the course of the goldsmith's year 1821-2, from the fact, it is believed, of the mention of a simple "leopard's head" being found in some of the earlier documents and especially in the Act 12 Geo. II., c. 26, without being followed by the word "crowned," the form of the stamp was altogether changed; and the head, deprived of its crown, was made to present an object far more resembling the head of a cat than the fine bold face of former days, which we would fain see restored to its pristine form.

The wording of 12 Geo. II., c. 26 in this particular was no doubt somewhat a matter of chance: but however this may be, it deserves to be remarked, that in and after 1824-5, but for the omission of the crown, it would be somewhat difficult to distinguish the small Roman letters then current from those of

---

* Some small wares, especially teaspoons, in the eighteenth and nineteenth centuries, do not show the leopard's head, but only the lion passant, the latter mark being no doubt thought a sufficient guarantee in such cases.

the former small Roman alphabet of 1776-1795. Until then the letters would be sufficiently distinguished by the fact that the earlier alphabet, down to the "i" of 1784, would be unaccompanied by a king's head mark; but this distinction ceasing with that letter in 1784, there would for the rest of the cycle be nothing but a slight difference in the royal portrait to depend upon, were it not for the absence of the crown from the leopard's head. This consideration seems however to have had nothing to do with the innovation, which accidentally proves so useful.

THE WORKER'S OR MAKER'S MARKS.

The next thing to be considered in the chronological series is the maker's mark. Following closely, as we have seen, on its adoption in other countries, such a mark was first instituted in England by statute in 1363, when it was directed that every master goldsmith should have a mark of his own, known by those who should be appointed by the king to survey the works; which marks, for which the goldsmiths should answer, should be set on the works after they had been assayed. The Goldsmiths' Company made similar provisions in their earliest known ordinances, to that which now became the law of the land; and almost every subsequent statute provides, under heavy penalties, for the marking of plate with the *mark* or *sign* of the worker.

These marks were at first, in many cases, emblems or symbols; probably often selected in allusion to the name of the maker. In early times most shops had signs by which they were known, and some retain the custom even to the present day, especially on the Continent. This no doubt arose from the fact that, as few persons could read, the writing of the name would be of little use, whereas the setting up of some sign, such for instance as the golden ball, which was easily understood, gave a convenient name to the shop; it is therefore not improbable that the goldsmiths, in some cases, took for their mark the sign of their shop.

Several of the old goldsmiths' signs are well known, as, for instance, the "grasshopper" of Sir Thomas Gresham's house in Lombard Street, now occupied by Messrs. Martins, and the "marigold" which a century later distinguished the house where the Childs carried on their banker-goldsmith business in Fleet Street. The squirrel, too, which we find on plate of 1599 (see Appendix A), may remind us of the three squirrels still to be seen on the front of Messrs. Goslings' banking-house also in Fleet Street. The Golden Bottle has always been the distinguishing sign of Messrs. Hoare's bank, now in the same thoroughfare, but formerly in Cheapside. Neither are there wanting notices here and there of the signs of more obscure working goldsmiths, especially in the accounts of parish church-wardens in the reigns of Edward VI. and Queen Elizabeth. In accounts of 1551, one Calton is found working at the sign of "the Purse in Chepe," and a fellow-craftsman of the name of Wark at "the George in Lomberde Strete;" another account of 1560 mentions a "Mr. Muschamp, goldsmith of London," as of "the Ryng with the Rube," also in "Lumbarde St." A spoon of 1525 has the figure of a heart stamped thus ♡ as the maker's mark, and many early specimens have similar symbols. Some few marks of the earlier goldsmiths resemble those so well known as merchants' marks, or the mason's marks on ancient buildings; see for example what seems to have been the trade mark of Robert Harding, alderman and goldsmith, who died in 1503, having served as master of the Goldsmiths' Company in 1489. An engraving of this is given in the margin.* Another somewhat simpler, viz. is found on a small cup of 1599, in the possession of the Armourers' Company. It has, however, been previously remarked how very seldom the shop sign of a maker is reproduced in his mark. Some half-dozen pieces of plate alone in the early Elizabethan period, and those somewhat doubtfully, are all that can be attributed to their proper maker by the mark they bear. The fleur-de-lys found on plate of 1562 may possibly belong to William Dyxson living at "the Fleur de Luce in Chepe," in 1569; the leg of 1550 to William Beereblocke, of "the Legge in Chepe," also in 1569; Robert Wright, of "the Wyndmylle," in 1569, may have made a cup bearing that symbol in 1578; the covered cup found in 1548 and 1561, may be the mark of John Mabbe, of "the Cup in Chepe," in 1569; Thomas Bampton, of "the Falcon," in 1569, may have made plates

---

* *Surrey Archæological Society's Transactions*, vol. vi., part i., p. 36.

bearing that mark in 1567. John Harysson, in 1569, of "the Broad Arrow," may have made the Tokerys Bowl in 1534. Lastly William Southwood is likely to have made the Communion cup with covered cup for mark at St. Lawrence, Jewry, in 1548. Short as this list is, even fewer goldsmiths can be identified by the occurrence of their initials on articles made by them. Robert Danbe certainly made the Communion cup at St. Peter's, Cornhill, which bears the maker's mark of **RD** in linked letters, for his dealings with the parish are recorded; and R. Maynarde was probably the goldsmith using for mark the **RM** found on a Communion cup of 1553 at Great Houghton, Northants.

The Communion cups at the Temple Church were bought in 1609 of one Terry, a goldsmith of note. They bear the mark of **FT** in linked letters, which may be his mark; but a workman named Thomas Francis was making goods at this time for dealers who only kept shops, and this mark may denote his work.

In these early days initials were not so often used for workers' marks as later, but eventually they became the rule; indeed, symbols and emblems unaccompanied by any initial letters hardly ever occur later than the commencement of the seventeenth century. The examination of a great number of specimens of that century has given us not more than a dozen such marks; a water-bird in a dotted circle found on an example belonging to the Hon. Society of the Middle Temple of the year 1682, and other pieces down to 1693, being the very last, and except this and a mark of three storks found in 1685, there is nothing of the kind later than 1661, when the Communion-plate at Gloucester Cathedral is found to bear some animal or other not easily to be recognised, on a shaped shield, or a mullet with an escallop found in 1663.

The anonymous author of the *Touchstone for Gold and Silver Wares,** writing in 1679, makes the following remarks as to the supervision exercised by the Goldsmiths' Company over the makers' marks:—"In this office" (referring to the Assay-Office at Goldsmiths' Hall) "is likewise kept for publique view a table or tables artificially made of columns of parchment or velom, and several of the same sorts; in the lead columns are struck

---

* See p. 14.

or entered the workers' marks (*which are generally the first two letters of their Christian and surnames*), and right against them, in the parchment or velom columns, are writ and entered the owners' names; This is that what is meant in the before-recited statutes, by the expression of *making the workers' mark known to the surveyors or wardens of the craft;* which said wardens' duty is to see that the marks be *plain* and of a *fit size*, and *not one like another*, and to require the thus entering the said marks, and also the setting them clear and visible on all gold and silver work, not only on every work, but also on every part thereof that is wrought apart and afterwards soldered or made fast thereto in finishing the same.   Our law makers (as I conceive) did think the thus setting the marks on the work, to be the securest way to prevent fraud in this kind; for if it would not deter from the working and selling coarse silver and gold wares, yet would it be a sure way to find out the offenders and to have the injured righted.   But if the marks might be omitted, and the works should pass but into a third owner's hand, for the most part it would be impossible to discern one man's work from another, by reason that divers workers make all sorts of work in shape so near alike."

Much of the information once possessed by the Goldsmiths' Company as to workers' names or their places of abode down to the year 1697, is unfortunately lost, together with those tables, and it is only by the examination of ancient inventories and accounts that here and there a name can be put to a mark; as, for instance, when the accounts of churchwardens give the name of the goldsmith from whom Communion-plate was purchased, and it chances that their successors in office are still in possession of the article so procured.

At Headcorn in Kent is a Communion cup of 1562 bearing for maker's mark the initials **WC** with a cricket or grasshopper. This is most probably the William Cater mentioned in the books of the Goldsmiths' Company as follows :—" Friday the 12th of February, 1562.   At this Court, William Cater promised to bring in within this month a Communion cup which he made and sold into the country untouched."

" Friday the 26th of February 1562.   At this Court William Cater brought in a Communion cup according to his promise here made the 12th day of this month, which cup he sold into

Kent untouched, and the same at the assay was found good and so delivered to the said Cater again."*

The only official record now in existence of any of their marks prior to 1697, is a copper-plate, preserved in the Assay-Master's Office, carefully framed and glazed to save it from further harm, which contains a number of impressions in nine parallel columns from the punches used by the makers who were working between 1675 and 1697.

This plate bears the following inscription, viz. :—" On the above Plate are the Marks from Workmen taken at this Office Prior to the Fifteenth of April, A.D. 1697, of which not any other Entry is to be found." It was at one time thought possible that it contained the marks of workers for generations past, and its importance in that case could hardly have been overrated : but it is now clear that it owes what interest it has to being the identical table referred to in the Goldsmiths' Order of 1675 (see p. 46). Almost every maker's mark found on plate from 1675 to 1697 is registered thereon, but none of any other period. The book referred to in the same order as appointed for the entry of names, has perished with the earlier tables; and this one remaining table, interesting as it is as a relic, is therefore but a bare record of certain marks used for those few years only, without any names against them. It cannot be said to possess the value, and is not of the interest, that would attach to a portion of an unbroken series, but all the more important marks upon it will be found in the list of examples given later. From 1697 onwards, impressions of the marks from the makers' own punches have been taken regularly, and are preserved in volumes with the owners' names and addresses, apparently in their own handwriting entered against their respective marks. In that year it will be remembered, we came at last to an express enactment that the workers' mark should be *the first two letters of his surname,* and this must have caused a general change of marks throughout the trade, indeed we can trace it in certain instances; for example, we may safely assume that the mark of **P·H** under a crown and two ermine spots found on the copper plate was the earlier mark of the Peeter Harracke who entered his new one of **HA**

---

* Note communicated by Mr. H. D. Ellis.

with the same accessories in compliance with this Act in the month of October, 1698. A number of working goldsmiths at this time and onwards were foreigners. An entry in the books of the Goldsmiths' Company records at the admission of "Peter Haraske" on July 21, 1682, that he had "lately come from France for to avoid persecution." His mark, like that of one John Chartier and some others, has all the characteristics of French goldsmiths' marks of the period.

The first letters of the surname were alone used (and on gold as well as silver) as long as the use of the higher standard of silver was compulsory, that is to say from 1697 until 1720; but on the restoration of the old sterling standard in 1720, makers seem to have thought themselves at liberty to use their ordinary initials, at all events, on wares of the restored standard; and from that year till 1739, their practice was somewhat uncertain, for initials have been found in that interval which could by no possibility have been the first two letters of any surname whatever. Many makers in 1720 registered a new mark of their ordinary initials for use on "old sterling," and so had two marks, one for each standard; thus Paul Crespin signs his work of the Britannia standard with **CR**, but old sterling silver with **PC**; Isaac Callard with **CA** and **IC** respectively, and so on. One or two old established smiths brought into use again the old mark they had used on their work before 1697, without entering it afresh at Goldsmiths' Hall. This was done by Timothy Ley and Benjamin Pyne, whose marks as found on the copper-plate re-appear on work in and after 1720. This want of uniformity was effectually remedied for the future by the Act of 1739, which came into operation on May 28th, and ordered the makers to destroy their existing marks, and to substitute for them *the initials of their Christian and surnames*, directing in addition, that the new letters should, in each case, be of a different character or alphabet from those used before. This was no doubt to further secure the destruction of the old punches.

The marks of the celebrated silversmith Paul Lamerie illustrate this course of things throughout. His first registered mark in 1712 was **LA**; his second in 1733 **P·L**; his third being, in accordance with the provisions of 1739, *PL* in what may be termed script letters, registered in the month of June, in that year.

The initial letters of the Christian and surname have been used from 1739 to the present time. Watch-case makers of the seventeenth and eighteenth centuries seldom use an escutcheon ; their initials are merely stamped in without any accessories, except perhaps a crown. It only remains to note that the minute mark often found beside the maker's is a workshop mark to show which particular workman was employed upon the article bearing it.

The more important London makers' marks have now been carried down in Appendix A, part 2, of this volume, to about 1841.

THE ANNUAL LETTER; ASSAYER'S OR WARDEN'S MARK.

This is perhaps the most interesting of all the marks, for it goes far to enable us to ascertain the precise year in which any piece of plate was made. It may seem somewhat of a paradox to begin by stating that it is by no means certain when it was itself introduced. This is nevertheless strictly true. If nothing is better ascertained than that the mark must have been in use from the latter part of the fifteenth century, it will scarcely be believed that there is no positive mention of it till 1597, when at last it occurs in the Attorney-General's information, in which it is styled " The alphabetical mark approved by ordinance among the goldsmiths " ; and no one has been able to discover the ordinance by which it was appointed, nor any earlier notice of it by name, although the mark itself is plain enough upon plate of generations before that time.

Those who would claim for it the highest degree of antiquity depend upon a supposed mention in 1336 of a " sayer's " mark in addition to the maker's mark and the leopard's head crowned in a goldsmith's ordinance.

No such ordinance is to be found amongst those preserved at Goldsmiths' Hall, the very earliest of which profess themselves to be in accordance " with the Acts of diverse Parliaments," and cannot therefore be nearly so early as that year. It is, however, pretty clear how the mistake arose.

Mr. Herbert, in his history of the Goldsmiths' Company,* gives a summary of the provisions contained in their "ancient ordinances," in the course of which all three marks, including a sayer's mark, and also the "assayer's book," are mentioned, but without any dates. His paragraph proceeds as follows :—

"The entries as to the assay just given show the practice to have been very early exercised by the company, in addition to the notice of William Speron in 1336 (now five hundred years ago), we find it ordained in 1366 by general assent that none of the fraternity shall go to fairs, to trade without having all the goods of the mystery [goldsmith's work] first assayed before the wardens for the year; and in 1444, a member is fined 6s. 8d. 'for withstondyng the wardens in taking of assaie.'"

On an earlier page Mr. Herbert had given some extracts from the accounts of the company, and amongst them the following entry of the year 1336, "Argent baille, a William Speron, des am'ciam's cest assaie vi s viij d."

It is probable that by connecting without any good reason the year mentioned in one sentence with the ordinances referred to in another, a date which referred only to an early mention of the assay itself, has been sometimes attributed to an annual letter as an assayer's mark. There seems no ground for attaching William Speron's date to any part of Mr. Herbert's summary of the ordinances. That summary is an accurate one of all the successive ordinances taken together, but if the originals are examined in detail it will be seen that whilst in the earlier of the ordinances the assayer's mark was the leopard's head, in those of 1507 and of 1513 another assayer's mark is mentioned for the first time.

It will be remembered also that, in the ancient Acts of 1363 and 1423 the mark to be fixed by the surveyor, "gardien," or warden, is always described as the king's mark, or leopard's head; and although all the marks to be used are described in detail in these enactments, no mention whatever is to be found of any mark besides that leopard's head mark and the mark of the maker. The terms "assayer" and "warden" refer to one and the same officer, for the assay was then conducted by the

---

* Herbert's *History of the Livery Companies*, vol. ii., 175.

wardens, or "their deputy, the assayer ordained thereto," to quote from one of the ordinances.

A more moderate, but probably still too high, antiquity was assigned to it by Mr. Octavius Morgan, who, thinking that with certain exceptions he had been able to obtain examples of all the various alphabets used from 1438 but none earlier, came to the conclusion for the reasons we are about to quote, that that date was the period of the first adoption of the annual letter.

It has already been seen from the proceedings of the Montpellier goldsmiths that, in consequence of repeated and increased frauds, new securities were invented from time to time to provide against them, till at last, in the year 1427, it was ordained as a fresh security that, in order to insure the fineness of the articles assayed after that time, the name of the warden of the mystery inscribed on the register of the city should be followed by one of the letters of the alphabet, which letter should be reproduced beneath the arms of the town on the piece of plate in order that it might be known under what warden it was made, so that in effect he might be held answerable for having made a fraudulent assay, and suffered bad silver to be sold as good standard. The fact of the Montpellier ordinances giving the specific reason for the introduction of a new mark seems very like the origin of it, and it led Mr. Morgan to attribute the first invention and adoption of this mark to the authorities of Montpellier in 1427. When once adopted in one place, it probably soon became a custom in others as an improved security against fraud, and the date of the first alphabet of the English use of which Mr. Morgan thought any trace is to be found, commencing as it does in 1438, very well agreed with the supposition of that being the period of its first introduction into this country.

Further than this, he observed the curious coincidence that the first Act rendering the wardens responsible for abuses committed during their respective periods of office is that of 1423, which provides that "if it may be found that the keeper of the touch touch any such harness with the leopard's head except it be as fine in allay as the sterling, that then the keeper of the touch for everything so proved not as good in allay as the said sterling, shall forfeit the double value to the king and the party."

What more probable than that here, as in France, the want of some means of fixing the right offender in each case with the responsibility for his default was soon felt, and that the Goldsmiths' Company in 1438 adopted the practice that had ten years before commended itself to their brethren of Montpellier? So much for 1438.

It now seems, with some hesitation be it said, a safer conclusion that the real date of the introducing of a date-letter into their system of hall-marking by the London goldsmiths was 1478.

Mr. Morgan was certainly right in considering that the object of our annual date-letter was the same as in the case of Montpellier. The statute of Elizabeth in 1576 again asserts the liability of the wardens, ordaining that if any article shall be touched for good by the wardens, and there shall afterwards be found fraud or deceit therein, the warden shall pay forfeit the value of the thing so marked; and at last in 1679 the author of the *Touchstone*,* writing of the date-letter, says plainly, " The reason for changing thereof is (as I conceive), for that by the aforesaid recited statutes, it is provided that if any silver work that is worse than sterling be marked with the Company's marks, the wardens and corporation for the time being shall make recompence to the party grieved, so that if any such default shall happen, they can tell by the letter on the work in what year it was assayed and marked, and thereby know which of their own officers deceived them, and from them obtain over a recompence."

If it is true that the wardens were made responsible in 1423, it is much more to the purpose that in the Act of 1477 the craft was made answerable for the non-sufficiency of the warden. It then became an immensely more important thing for the company to be able to know, in the words of the *Touchstone*, "which of their own officers deceived them, and from them obtain over a recompence."

This would not perhaps in itself be conclusive, but there is the further fact that though in 1478 a date-letter was certainly used, no mention of it is found in the important Act of the

---

* See p. 14.

preceding year, which says much about both the other marks, viz., the leopard's head crowned and the maker's mark, and, as above mentioned, makes the company responsible for its warden.

It seems very unlikely that the date-letter would have escaped mention here, had such a mark been in use ; but it seems very likely indeed that the company would then and there institute one. Had it been in existence already, the only way of accounting for its not being mentioned in 1477 would be that the warden's mark not being one ordered by Parliament, but only a domestic arrangement of the Goldsmiths' Company, did not obtain recognition by the legislature in the same manner as the leopard's head and the maker's mark. This is, however, at best rather a far-fetched explanation, especially as in later days the variable mark is mentioned in Acts of Parliament. It would certainly be referred to in some of the goldsmiths' own ordinances within a certain time of its introduction, and, so far from being mentioned soon after 1438, it is not till 1507 that any notice of it occurs. In ordinances of 1507 and 1513, as we shall remember, an assayer's mark, in addition to the leopard's head and the maker's mark, is spoken of ; and as the date-letter was then not only in use, but the only mark used except the two others just mentioned, it was clearly the assayer's mark referred to. If this is so, we can carry back mention of a date-letter from 1597 to 1507, or within a very few years of 1478. The great book of Ordinances and Statutes of the Goldsmiths' Company was itself commenced in the year 1478; and everything seems to show that it was a point of fresh departure for the craft. Further than this, there is but one single piece of marked plate in existence, to which there has ever been positively attributed a date earlier than 1478. This is the Pudsey spoon, which has been supposed upon certain historical evidence to belong to the year 1445. Its marks, however, upon careful examination cannot be distinguished from those of 1525, the spoon may have at some time or other been accidentally changed for another in the absence of any inscription or other means of preserving its identity, and it is on the whole much more probable that something of this kind has happened, than that two cycles of date-letters, for which no other evidence exists, should have run their unknown course before the date at which so many

circumstances concur in indicating that a date-letter was introduced. In the following pages and tables the year 1478 is, for
all these reasons, given as the commencement of the London
series of alphabets.

It is only fair to say that some consider England to have
given the lead to France in these matters. A distinguished
writer* remarks that, to judge by dates, "the change from
makers' marks alone to guild marks preceded in England, by
more than half a century, the same change in France"; and
he cites a letter of Charles V., written in 1376, which seems to
speak of a maker's mark only, as follows:

"*Quelconques orfevres ne porront tenir ne lever forge ne ouvrer
en chambre secrete se ilz ne sont approuvez devant les maistres du
mestier et estre temoigner souffisament de tenir forge et d'avoir poinçon
a contresaign et autrement non.*"

This hardly, however, precludes the possibility of there being
other marks also in use at the same time, and the wording
seems taken from earlier statutes, in which the touch of Paris
is ordained as a standard, as, for instance, those of King John
of France in 1355, which again are themselves only letters of
confirmation of still more ancient regulations, taking us back as
far as 1260.

The parallel passage from King John's letter of confirmation
provides that he who wishes to be a goldsmith of Paris must
either be apprenticed, "*ou qu'il soit tel éprouvé par les maistres et
bonnes gens du mestier estre souffisant estre orfevre et de tenir et lever
forge et d'avoir poinçon a contreseing*"; but a later clause adds
that, "*nul orfevre ne peut ouvrer d'or a Paris qu'il ne soit a la
touche de Paris, ou meilleur la quelle touche passe tous les ors dont
l'on euvre en mille terres.*" It must have been long a celebrated
touch to be spoken of in such terms, and it is clear that in 1300
the lily was well known and recognised even here in England
as the Paris mark; † add to this that Philip le Hardi had
ordained in 1275 that each city should have a particular mark
for works of silver. In all these cases the word "touch" must
be taken to refer to the mark by which the quality of the metal
is certified as well as to that quality itself. It is so used in our

---

* *Quarterly Review*, April, 1876.
† Wardrobe accounts of that year, 28 Edward I. (see p. 22).

own early statutes, in which the phrases "touched with the touch," "bearing the touch," "touched with the leopard's head," occur as well as another set of expressions in which it is used rather to denote the standard of the metal, for instance, "gold of a certain touch."

Two "chargeours de touche London," are mentioned in the inventory of the goods of Richard de Ravenser, Archdeacon of Lincoln, who died in 1386; a quart pot of silver with the "touche of Parys," and also dishes of silver of "London makyng" occur in a will of 1443;* "spones marked with the touche of London" in a will proved in the Canterbury Prerogative Court in 1463; "peciam dez markes Franciæ" in 1481; and "spones having the toche of the goldesmyths" in another will of 1522.

The foregoing remarks, it will be observed, deal with the comparative antiquity of the leopard's head and the lily quite as much as with the English and French date-letters; indeed they apply to either pair of marks alike, and have only found a place here rather than earlier, because they followed naturally upon a comparison of the periods at which the guilds of London and Montpellier respectively adopted a warden's mark.

Some might say, as we have seen, that neither the leopard's head nor the lily is a guild mark properly so called, but rather the mark of the royal or national standard, each for its own country; and in the case of England, everything points to the date-letter as the only special mark of the London guild. It is the date-letter which is described in 1597 as the mark approved by ordinance amongst the goldsmiths themselves, whereas the two other marks then used are " Her Majesty's " and " appointed by statute " respectively.

It would be somewhat of an anomaly to find that of all places in the world, London should have been the one without a peculiar mark of its own, other than its date-letter, if it were not that in times when the Goldsmiths' Company was the only keeper of the national touch, that touch might so easily come to be regarded in practice almost as much the mark of the guild as of the standard. It is a point of no practical importance, at all events since the appointment of a special mark for each

---

* *Test. Ebor.* see note Art. *Spoons*, chap. x.

provincial assay office; but to be strictly accurate, we should have to say that London plate is distinguished by the absence of any provincial mark rather than by the presence of any special mark of its own, unless we admit the claim of its peculiar series of date-letters to that character. These it has undeniably used from 1478, in the form of a succession of alphabets, each consisting of twenty letters; J, U or V, W, X, Y and Z, being the letters omitted. From 1560-1 they have, with hardly any exception, been enclosed in regular heraldic shields of various shapes, but till then the letters are surrounded with a line more or less closely following their own outline; the ends of the punches having been originally of the shape of the letters they bore, and afterwards of a shield shape, with the letter sunk in the centre of the shield. The most notable exceptions to this rule are the letters L of 1726-7, and M of the following year, which are often, if not always, found on a square punch.* From 1678, if not earlier, more than one size of punch is found to have been used, large and small articles having been stamped with marks of different sizes, the smaller ones being often on plain square punches with the corners slightly cut off, instead of in more heraldic shields. Very small letters indeed are found towards the end of the seventeenth century in the inside of watch cases. In certain years also the letters on the punches in use differ a little in form from one another. Two forms of the letter for 1619-20 occur; and the differences to be noted at 1567-8, 1575-6, and at 1658-9 are also so marked as to require representation in the tables.

The introduction of a shield in 1560-1, in the middle of an alphabet be it noted, curiously enough coincides exactly with the restoration of the old sterling standard silver by Queen Elizabeth, which has been spoken of in the preceding chapter; and the probability that an event of such importance to the Goldsmiths' Company was marked by them in this or some other particular way suggested a careful examination of the journals of the Company, which resulted in the discovery of the following minute for 16 December, 1560 :—

"Also forasmuch as Mr. Wardens and the Assistants have found that the moneys of our sovereign Lady the Quene conteyne in fynesse (xi oz.) eleven ounces and upward therefore it is by them agreed that after the feast of the Epiphaine of our Lord God next comynge the assaymaster and wardens of this companie shall touch no plate

* No doubt the punch in these cases is of the second size.

under the fynesse of (xi oz. ii dwt.) eleven ounces two pennie weight and for a certe
knowledge to be had betwene the same plate and other before touched it is agreed that
the letter of the yeare shall be grayved round about for a difference." *

This positive proof of the reason for the shield lends additional
weight to the suggestion which is to be made when the lion
passant comes under notice, that its invention in 1545 marks
the divergence of the standard of the silver coinage from that
of silver plate which then took place. It would be very odd if
the degradation of the coinage from the sterling quality maintained throughout for plate, and its subsequent restoration to
that standard of purity, were events of two years, in each of
which is found to occur a novel feature in the system of hall
marking practised by the Goldsmiths' Company, and if one of
the alterations in the marks, but not the other, were connected
with the coincident changes of the standard. The fleur-de-lys
and pellets which accompany in some instances the letter for
1575-6 no doubt relate to the Act of that year, as in later days
the Act of 1739-40 is marked by the adoption of a new shape
of shield for the rest of the letters of the then current alphabet.

The variation noted for 1658 is merely due to the use of a
damaged punch, probably towards the end of the year; but the
annulet under the letter for 1567, and the two forms of letter
found in 1619 are happily accounted for. In 1567 it appears
from the Minute Books of the Court of the Goldsmiths'
Company that a long-standing dispute with the Assay Master
Richard Rogers came to a head. The Company required him
to give up his house in Chepe and to come and dwell in the
proper apartments for the Assay Master at the Hall, as early as
in August, 1566. From that time forward there are constant
entries of his delays and excuses until at last in Aug. 1567 he
promised to come in to the Hall or yield up his office next
quarter-day. It was then found necessary to come to close
quarters, and ten days more were given him on Nov. 3, 1567,
to make up his mind in. The next entry relating to the matter
records that on Dec. 24, he was "discharged of the office of
assayer." Thomas Keelynge was appointed to be his successor;
and on commencing work he no doubt adopted the annulet under
the date-letter for the remaining portion of the year. So too in

---

* This restoration of the sterling standard seems to have been marked at York by
the introduction of a new alphabet, if indeed it did not originate the use of a date-letter
in that city.

1619 the second form of the letters is accounted for by the death of the assayer Thomas Dymock in the month of September, and the appointment a month later of John Reynolds.

The letters have been annually changed on the day of election of the new wardens, that being St. Dunstan's Day prior to the Restoration; the new punches were accordingly handed to the assay-warden for use, on or about May 19 in each year, and were continued to the same time in the year following.   Since 1660 the new punches have been first used on the morning of May 30, the new wardens having been elected the day before.

No entry is found of the letter for the year in the goldsmiths' journals, until the occurrence of some dispute with the officers of the assay, after which the letters were mentioned.   Their earliest note is of the letter for 1629, but from that time the notices are sufficiently regular to indicate the character of all the alphabets.   For the earlier letters, it was only by the examination of a great many pieces of ancient plate, chiefly belonging to public companies, colleges, corporations, and churches, of which the histories are known, that Mr. Octavius Morgan was able to collect the information necessary to enable him to construct a table of the alphabets used.   The difficulty was increased by the obvious fact that the dates which are engraved on ancient plate cannot always be relied on for the date of the work.   Oftentimes pieces of plate which individuals or their families have had in their possession for many years, have afterwards been given or bequeathed by them to public bodies, and then the date of the gift is recorded in the inscription which will not agree with the period of the work.   Again, plate given to public bodies, having been worn out, has been remade at subsequent periods, or exchanged for more useful articles, and the original date has been engraved on the new-made piece.   As an illustration of this difficulty, one of the loving cups of the Goldsmiths' Company itself goes by the name of "Hanbury's Cup," and bears engraved on it the record of its having been the gift of Richard Hanbury in 1608. The form and workmanship of the cup are clearly of the period of Charles II., and that was confirmed by the annual letter. In searching the books of the Company, Mr. Morgan found by accident a memorandum stating that "Hanbury's cup, weight 60 oz., was sold with other plate in 1637, and re-made in 1666."

This latter date agrees precisely with the annual letter it bears. The present writer's experiences on this point are the same. He was somewhat surprised to find, when examining the plate of the Salters' Company, that though bearing the arms and dates of Sir Nicholas Crispe, Knt. and Bart., and other great salters of the reigns of Charles I. and Charles II., it all seemed made in 1716 by a well-known goldsmith named Humphrey Payne. At last a Monteith dated 1660 appeared. This was too much of an anachronism; and a reference to the old books of the Company being kindly permitted, some curious facts, which had been entirely lost sight of and forgotten, came to light. It appeared that the Company had resolved, in 1711, to sell all their plate, after carefully registering the weights of the articles, and also the dates, names, and arms of the donors which might be engraved upon them, in order to invest the proceeds in lottery tickets (it will be remembered that State lotteries were then just a new thing, having been first authorized by Parliament in 1709). It further appeared that in 1716, it was determined to replace the plate, the lottery tickets were sold, tenders by London goldsmiths were invited, and the tender of Humphrey Payne and Co., which was the lowest of three sent in, being accepted, new plate of the same weight, but not in articles of the same description, as that sold in 1711, was made by him for the Company; and it was ordered that the names, arms, and dates of the donors of the old plate should be placed upon the new. Humphrey Payne's receipt for " self and Co." is extant amongst the minutes of the year 1716.

In this way were gradually put together the alphabets published in 1853 by Mr. Octavius Morgan, who succeeded in ascertaining the forms of no less than sixty-five letters previously unknown, including specimens of every alphabet as far back as 1478. To these many more have now been added, and some of the occasional gaps later than 1629, which existed in the original tables, filled up. Some time after their publication by Mr. Morgan, these alphabets were reproduced with the addition of shields, by the late Mr. W. Chaffers, who seems to have adopted Mr. Morgan's tables and data; but some of the letters, and the shields in many cases, were incorrect, and a somewhat doubtful improvement upon the original tables thus laboriously compiled.

The cycles of twenty years seem to have proceeded regularly from 1478 to 1696, when, on the occasion of the new standard being introduced and new marks appointed for it, a fresh alphabet was commenced. The entries in the Goldsmiths' minutes are as follows:—

"A.D. 1696, May 29th.—New puncheons received; the letter for the year being **t** in a scutcheon .

"A.D. 1697, March 27th.—The puncheons for the remaining part of this year were received, being according to an Act of Parliament, a Lyon's head erased, a Britannia, and for the letter the great court **a** in an escutcheon ."

It must be borne in mind that as the new letters were not fixed till May 29, each letter served for a portion of two years, even in days before the change of style. This **t** and **a**, therefore, between them, served as the letters for the goldsmiths' year 1696-7, that is, for the year beginning May 30, 1696; the court-hand letter for 1697-8 coming into use on May 30, 1697.

Some instances of a small black letter **u** for the year 1697-8 are said to exist; and if so, no doubt it is upon certain articles made, but not marked or sold, previous to the adoption of the new standard. It would have been very hard on those who had expended time and skill upon old sterling silver in the year 1696-7, with no notice of the impending alteration in the standard, if such wares had been thereby rendered unsaleable. The Act was, however, so worded as to avoid doing this injustice, and such articles would be stamped with the old marks, including the **u** that would have denoted 1697-8 in ordinary course. The new court-hand alphabet was applicable only to plate of the new standard inaugurated with it.

New and carefully constructed tables of the alphabets, and their shields or other inclosures, are given at the end of this volume.

THE LION PASSANT.

There is no mark so well known and at the same time so little understood as the lion passant. Far from being the ancient sign of sterling silver, it is not found at all until the middle of the sixteenth century. The most careful enquiry

has failed to produce an earlier instance than one of the
year 1545, and it is not mentioned in any statute, ordinance,
or other proceeding until the indictment by the Attorney-
General in 1597, in which it is called *Her Majesty's Lion*,
whilst the other two marks are described respectively as "the
leopard's head *limited by statute*," and "the alphabetical mark
approved by ordinance amongst themselves" (*i.e.*, the Goldsmiths'
Company).

In earlier days the leopard's head was the king's mark; does
the lion passant now take its place?

Its origin, intention, and even the precise date of its introduction are all equally obscure. It is never found before 1543,
nor is it ever absent after 1545; but there is no article of plate
known to exist of the intervening year. In one or the other of
the years 1544 and 1545 it must have been introduced. Its
description in 1597 would imply that it had been appointed to
be used by some royal order, but the Registers of the Privy
Council and the records of the Goldsmiths' Company have
alike been searched in vain; there is no mention of it in the
latter, and the volume of the former for just this period is
almost the only one of a long series that is missing. We are
therefore thrown back upon a conjecture, but one which there
seems good ground for adopting.

It will be remembered that it was in 1542 that the fineness
of the silver coin of the realm was, for the first time since
the Conquest, lowered; not that the pound sterling of silver
had not been lessened in value several times in that long
period, but it had always been effected by diminishing its
weight, leaving the fineness of the silver unaltered. In 1542,
however, Henry VIII. not only diminished the weight but
reduced the standard from 11 ounces 2 dwts. fine to 10 ounces
fine, and again in 1544 from 10 ounces to 6 ounces, leaving but
6 ounces of fine silver in a troy pound, this being followed
by a further and final degradation in 1545. It will also be
remembered that the touch of the leopard's head crowned
certified only that the silver was of "the alloy of the sterling
or better." What security then would the buyer have had
after 1542 that plate bought by him was of any better silver
than the debased coinage of the day? None whatever. May
we not, therefore, hazard a conjecture that the lion passant

was adopted at about this period to show that plate bearing it was not only as good as the coin, but was of the old sterling standard ?

No later writer has attempted to penetrate the mystery since Mr. Octavius Morgan first drew attention to it, and the Quarterly Reviewer, in 1876, who may be taken to sum up modern learning on the point, does so in a wish that "some of those laborious gentlemen who are engaged in calendering the State Papers, may fall, in the course of their researches, on some Order in Council or Gracious Proclamation enjoining the addition of this royal lion—for it at least came out of the coat-armour of the sovereign—to the three marks rendered imperative by statute."

From 1545 the lion passant, or more properly lion passant guardant, has invariably been found upon silver of the old sterling, and until 1844 upon standard gold; and, whilst it must be confessed that this theory does not account for its appearance on gold plate, there is nothing improbable in the assumption that it was thought convenient, on its adoption for silver for the reason we have given, to adopt it also for gold for the sake of uniformity in the standard marks. It is an important landmark to the archæologist, for whilst its presence or absence alone tells him something, the alterations which are observed in its size and shape from time to time are often of material assistance to him in fixing the date of the articles on which it appears.

In the first few years the beast is thin and spirited in shape, and a small crown appears over the head of the lion. This is so in 1547 and 1549. From 1550 the crown disappears, and from that year till 1557, the animal is in a plain oblong shield, whilst from 1557 to 1677 the shape of the escutcheon follows the outline of the animal.

THE LION'S HEAD ERASED AND FIGURE OF BRITANNIA.

Of these two marks there is little to be said. They were appointed by the statute of 1696-7, which raised the standard for silver plate from 11 ounces 2 dwts. to 11 ounces 10 dwts. fine, in order to distinguish the plate so made from that which had previously been made of silver of the old sterling, and they

were for this purpose substituted for the leopard's head crowned
and lion passant.

The new marks were in sole use from March 27, 1697, until
June, 1720, when the old sterling standard was restored, and
its own old marks with it, not, however, to the exclusion of
the new. Since that year, therefore, both standards, each to
bear its own marks, have been legal. For some short time after
the restoration of the old standard a good deal of plate made
of the new or higher standard silver seems still to have been
stamped, but it quickly fell into disuse, and, after 1732 or
thereabouts, the lion's head erased and the Britannia are very
rarely to be met with. The higher standard is occasionally
used even at the present day, and in such cases is of course
distinguished by its proper marks.

The Britannia stamp is sometimes found of a rectangular
and at other times of an oval shape; in one instance that has
come under the writer's notice it is absent altogether, a set
of loving cups of the year 1716 in the possession of the Worshipful Company of Salters bearing no Britannia, but instead of
it a second impression of the lion's head erased placed beside
the first, and of a different size. It may be noted also that
several pieces of plate bearing irregular marks occur in the
year or two next after the restoration of the old sterling
standard in 1720. For old sterling silver some of the punches
disused since 1697 seem to have been put into commission again, and confusion was doubtless occasioned by
the two sets of marks being in daily use at the assay-office.
The writer has seen a candlestick bearing both old and new
standard marks. Even more remarkable is a salver of 1721
bearing the Britannia and an old leopard's head crowned,
but both partially obliterated, the former by having a lion
passant and the latter a lion's head erased stamped over it.
The original combination and the correction are equally
without meaning.

THE SOVEREIGN'S HEAD.

This mark is found on all plate that has been liable to the
duty imposed from Dec. 1, 1784 (24 Geo. III. c. 53); that is to
say, upon all plate liable to be assayed, the only exemptions

from the control of the assay-offices, and therefore from duty, being :—

(1.) Certain gold articles exempted by 12 Geo. II. c. 26.*

(2.) Certain silver articles exempted by 30 Geo. III. c. 31.†

(3.) Watch cases, by 38 Geo. III. c. 24. These are exempted from duty, and so from being marked with the sovereign's head, but are not amongst the exemptions from the general marking requirements of 12 Geo. II. c. 26. An Order in Council of 1887 regulating the marking of foreign watch cases imported from abroad will be found mentioned later (see Chap. VIII.).

It will be observed that, from 1738 until 1790, the silver as well as the gold exempted was so under 12 Geo. II. c. 26, which

---

* 12 Geo. II. c. 26.—

Exemptions :—

s. 2. Any jewellers' works, that is to say, any gold or silver wherein any jewels or other stones are or shall be set (other than mourning rings), any jointed night ear-rings of gold, or gold springs of lockets.

s. 6. Rings, collets for rings, or other jewels, chains, necklace beads, lockets, hollow or raised buttons, sleeve buttons, thimbles, corral sockets and bells, ferrils, pipe-lighters, cranes for bottles, very small book-clasps, any stock or garter clasps jointed, very small nutmeg-graters, rims of snuff boxes whereof tops or bottoms are made of shell or stone, sliding pencils, toothpick cases, tweezer cases, pencil cases, needle cases, any philligree work, any sorts of tippings or swages on stone or ivory cases, any mounts, screws, or stoppers to stone or glass bottles or phials, any small or slight ornaments put to amber or other eggs or urns, any wrought seals, or seals with cornelians or other stones set therein, or any gold or silver vessel, plate, or manufacture of gold or silver so richly engraved, carved, or chased, or set with jewels or other stones, as not to admit of an assay to be taken of, or a mark to be struck thereon, without damaging, prejudicing, or defacing the same, or such other things as by reason of the smallness

or thinness thereof are not capable of receiving the marks hereinbefore mentioned, or any of them, and not weighing ten pennyweights of gold or silver each.

† 30 Geo. III. c. 31.—

Exemptions :—

s. 3. Chains, necklace beads, lockets, any philligree work, shirt buckles or broaches, stamped medals, or spouts to china, stone or earthenware teapots, or any of them, of any weight whatsoever.

s. 4. Tippings, swages or mounts, or any of them, not weighing ten pennyweights of silver each, save and except only necks and collars for castors, cruets or glasses appertaining to any sort of stands or frames.

s. 5. Any wares of silver whatsoever not weighing five pennyweights of silver each, save and except only the following silver wares (that is to say), necks, collars, and tops for castors, cruets or glasses appertaining to any sort of stands or frames, buttons to be affixed to or set on any wearing apparel, solid sleeve buttons and solid studs, not having a bissilled edge soldered on, wrought seals, blank seals, bottle tickets, shoe clasps, patch boxes, salt spoons, salt shovels, salt ladles, tea spoons, tea strainers, caddy ladles, buckles (shirt buckles or broaches before mentioned excepted), and pieces to garnish cabinets, or knife cases, or tea chests, or bridles, or stands or frames.

was repealed in 1790 as to silver by 30 Geo. III. c. 31; and it must be added that by 18 & 19 Vict. c. 60, wedding-rings pay duty even though of less weight than 10 dwts.

The mark itself, when first introduced, was in intaglio instead of in relief, looking like the matrix of a seal instead of its impression; in this form it is found in conjunction with the letters i and k, standing for 1784-5 and 1785-6 respectively, specimens of both of which are in the writer's possession, and the profile is, in these cases, turned to the left. The date-letter for 1784-5 is of course sometimes with, and at other times without, the King's-head mark, the duty not having been imposed till the middle of the Goldsmiths' year.

After the end of 1785-6 it is always found in relief like the other assay-marks, and with the profile to the right. Her late Majesty Queen Victoria was, however, turned to the left again.

The head is in a rectangular stamp with corners clipped in 1784 and 1785. It occurs in a sort of trefoil stamp, about 1804 to 1808. This is the case at York, Sheffield and Edinburgh; and so no doubt at all the provincial assay-offices, as well as in London. At all other times it is in a plain oval shield.

A duty of sixpence per ounce troy was first imposed upon plate in 1720 when the old standard of silver was revived and by the same statute (6 Geo. I. c. 11), but it was taken off again in 1758 (31 Geo. II. c. 32) by an Act which substituted a dealer's licence costing 40s. per annum.*

The Act of 1784 re-imposed a duty, but this time of 8s. per ounce on gold plate, as well as 6d. per ounce on silver; which amounts were, omitting intermediate stages, increased finally in 1815 (55 Geo. III. c. 185) to 17s. per ounce for gold, and 1s. 6d. for silver, calculated on ⅞ths of the weight to allow for waste in finishing. At these rates they remained, the duty being paid through Goldsmiths' Hall at the time of assaying, and the money returned with the articles if they were cut as being below the proper standard.

---

* Dealers' licences are now regulated by 30 & 31 Vict. c. 90.

Dealers in gold exceeding 2 dwts. and under	2 oz.	}	£2 6s.			
,, silver ,, 5 ,,	,,	30 ,,	} per annum.			
,, gold 2 oz. or upwards						
,, silver 30 oz. or upwards	}	£5 15s. per annum.				
Gold and silver refiners, etc.	}					

A drawback of the whole duty was allowed upon plate made in the United Kingdom for export and exported new. The Act of 1784 directed that such plate should be specially marked with a figure of Britannia which was used like the first stamp of the king's head as an intaglio. This direction was, however, repealed by 25 Geo. III. c. 64, in consequence of the damage done to plate by stamping it after it was finished, and the mark disused after an existence of only seven months. The provisions as to the drawback itself were not altered. The plate duties were finally abolished in 1890; and the King's-head mark ceased to be used.

CHAPTER IV.

THE PROVINCIAL ASSAY TOWNS AND THEIR MARKS PRIOR TO 1701.

THE ACT OF 1423—HISTORICAL NOTES OF THE GOLDSMITHS OF NEWCASTLE AND YORK—THE RELATIONS OF THE LONDON WITH THE PROVINCIAL GOLDSMITHS FROM TIME TO TIME — EXTINCTION OF THE OLD PROVINCIAL GOLDSMITHS' COMPANIES IN 1697 — YORK — NEWCASTLE-UPON-TYNE — NORWICH — CHESTER — EXETER — HULL, GATESHEAD, LEEDS, CARLISLE, LINCOLN, TAUNTON, DORCHESTER, BARNSTAPLE, KING'S LYNN, SANDWICH, SHERBORNE — DOUBTFUL PROVINCIAL MARKS — TABLE OF OLD PROVINCIAL MARKS.

WE now come to the consideration of the marks found upon plate assayed in the provinces ; but as the Act of 1700 established, or in certain cases re-established, the provincial assay-offices on an entirely new basis and with entirely new marks to distinguish them, the history of provincial marks divides itself into two distinct portions, the earlier of which terminates at that year. There is nothing more certain than that goldsmiths' guilds existed in mediæval days in many English provincial towns and cities. There is nothing less certain than that what is known of their work as a trade matter is practically nothing. A few purely antiquarian vestiges are what they have left behind.

It is not until 1423 that provincial "touches," except the touch of York, can with any certainty be said to have existed at all, so far as any legislation about such things is concerned. In very early days all goldsmiths were required to bring their wares to London to be marked; and even in 1379 the enactment found on the Rolls of Parliament for establishing an "assay of the touch" in cities and boroughs under the superintendence of their Mayors and Governors, with the aid of the Master of the Mint, if there be one, who should put the mark of the city or borough where it was assayed upon plate, does not, as we have already seen, appear to have become law.

At best, for reasons already given, its provisions were but temporary ; and it is clear that even in parts of England distant from the metropolis there was no general custom at this time of marking plate with peculiar local marks ; indeed, there is some direct evidence to the contrary in the claims of the Wardens of the Goldsmiths in 1404 to have had the right from time immemorial to have the governance of all manner of gold and silver work as well within the city of London " *as elsewhere within the kingdom of England.*"

Let us quote, as an instance of the exercise of this jurisdiction, the case of one John of Rochester, who, in 1414, was taken by the master of the trade of goldsmiths there for counterfeiting mazer bonds in copper and brass plated over with silver or gilded, and brought up to London, having sold them within the city.*

It is not clear, from this particular instance, whether the jurisdiction of the governors of the craft in London would or would not have extended to the case, if the fraudulent wares had been sold as well as made in Rochester ; it only shows that the maker of articles, sold as these were within the city, was amenable to it wherever he resided and worked. Had they been sold in Rochester or elsewhere in the provinces, the case would probably have been dealt with in the same manner, but without bringing the culprit up to London ; the " venue," to borrow a legal phrase, would have been local. At all events, with the increase of population, the necessity of sending every article of plate to London to be stamped, became a greater hardship upon country goldsmiths, and the legislation which proposed to meet it in 1379, shows that a need of some such measure was already found to exist. Accordingly, less than half a century later, in 1423,† the divers touches of York, Newcastle-upon-Tyne, Lincoln, Norwich, Bristol, Salisbury, and Coventry, were set up " according to the ordinance of Mayors, Bailiffs, or Governors of the said towns ; " and it was enacted, " that no goldsmith nor other workers of silver nor keepers of the said touches within the said towns shall set to sell nor touch any silver in other manner than is ordained before, within the City of London," upon pain of forfeiture. The Act further provides that no goldsmith anywhere in

---

* Riley's *Memorials of London and London Life*, p. 601. † 2 Hen. VI. c. 14 (see p 35).

England should work silver of worse allay than the sterling, nor without setting his mark or sign upon it before he set it to sale, upon the same penalties as if in London ; and it empowered justices of the peace, mayors, and bailiffs to hear and enquire of such matters.

Mints had been established at York and Bristol in the preceding year, possibly also in the other places now associated with them ; and it is well ascertained that most, if not all, of these cities and towns had guilds or fraternities of goldsmiths already established in them.

As to Newcastle-upon-Tyne, it would appear* that at so remote a period as 1249, Henry III. commanded the bailiffs and good men to choose four of the most prudent and trusty men of their town for the office of moneyers there ; and other four like persons for keeping the king's mint in that town, also two fit and prudent goldsmiths to be assayers of the money to be made there. In 1536, the goldsmiths were, by an ordinary, incorporated with the plumbers, glaziers, pewterers and painters, and the united Company required to go together, on the Feast of Corpus Christi, and maintain their play of "the three kings of Coleyn." They were to have four wardens, one goldsmith, one plumber, one glazier, one pewterer or painter; and it is quaintly added that no Scotchman born should be taken apprentice or suffered to work in Newcastle. The first "goldsmith" warden was Thomas Cramer. There were four other "goldsmiths" at this time; but only thirteen names of goldsmiths occur afterwards till that of William Ramsey, the earliest whose work still remains to be seen, and it is not known whether any of the number were actually working goldsmiths. Their hall in Morden Tower was granted them in the mayoralty of Sir Peter Riddell, in 1619, and the association of the goldsmiths with the other tradesmen lasted till 1717, when owing to something which necessitated reference to the Recorder, it ceased. They did not, however, take a leading place in this brotherhood, though it will be seen that they were in full work during the second half of the seventeenth century.

There is an exceedingly early mention of Durham work in the Wardrobe accounts of 28 Edward I., in which a pastoral

---

* From *An impartial History of the Town and County of Newcastle-upon-Tyne*, published anonymously in 1801, p. 429.

staff is described as "de opere Dunolm;" and as to York, "coclearia facta in Ebor," are bequeathed in a York will of as early a date as 1366.

In the latter city the art seems to have flourished, and the names of many goldsmiths working there during the second half of the fourteenth and in the following century are known. Alan de Alnewyk, goldsmith of York, whose shop was in "Stayngate," bequeaths, in 1374, his tools to his kinsman William, when he shall attain twenty years of age, provided he attain that age "in bonâ conversatione ad discendum ad scolas et ad artem aurifabri," quaintly adding "ac sit humilis, ac bonorum morum nec arguendo uxorem meam," or in plain English, that he must keep on good terms with the testator's widow. The names of two goldsmiths, Wormod and Jonyn, almost certainly of York, occur in the will of an archdeacon of Richmond proved at York in 1400; and the wife of a third, bearing a no less singular name, Wermbolt Harlam, leaves her gold knopped ring, in 1401, to the wife of John Angowe, a craftsman of the same mystery. Besides these, the wills of two goldsmiths settled at York in the fifteenth century, both of them containing interesting trade details, are to be found amongst those proved in that city. By one of them, John Luneburgh, in 1458, leaves some of his working tools to his friends and fellow-goldsmiths, Robert Spicer and John Pudsay, and 6s. 8d. to the craft—"aurifabrorum arti,"—towards buying a new silver crown. His small stock-in-trade included, amongst other things, the following articles, viz.:—"incudem meam secundariam et j malleum vocatum j forchyngamer, sex limas vocatas files et vj gravers, incudem meam minimi valoris in opellâ meâ j planysshing stithy et j planysshing hamer." The other will, that of John Colan, dated 1490, gives us a full inventory of the working tools and appliances then considered necessary for carrying on the goldsmith's business. The contents of his "opella," from its quaint spelling and curious mixture of Latin, French, and English words, form a list too curious to curtail.

Opella. De j lez wirkyng bord cum j lez deske xx^d
  De ij stethez iij^s iiij^d
  De ij sparhawke stethez x^d
  De vi grett lez forgeyng hamers ij^s

De v lez planeshyng hamers xii^{d}

De j lez hake hamer et j lez strenyng hamer iij^{d}

De v small lez clenches iiij^{d}

De ij lez spoyn tayses x^{d}

De ij lez stampis xiiij^{d}

De iij lez swages vi^{d}

De j lez rownde stake cum j lez flatt stake et j lez nebid stake iiij^{d}

De iiij paribus de lez sherithez xvi^{d}

De j pari de lez spanne taynges cum ij paribus de lez plyorys iii^{d}

De ij paribus de lez fyre taynges cum j pari parvo lez taynges vii^{d}

De j shavyng hooke cum j lez standard cupri v^{d}

De j long lez lokker cum lez pounsones xx^{d}

De ij lez drawyng teynges cum ij lez drawyng toyllys xiiij^{d}

De ij lez paribus of skaylettes cum pertinentiis iiij^{d}

De j parvo lez stethe cum lez hoylles in it j^{d}

De ij lez yngottes cum j pari lez pounsones iiij^{d}

De j lez lokker cum lez gravers et lez shavers iiij^{d}

De j candelabro cum lez fayn j^{d}

De j lez lokker cum lez fyilles viiij^{d}

De ij aliis lez lokkers cum lez pounsones iiij^{d}

De j rownd lez stampe auricalci cum ij lez bossellys ij^{d}

De j parvo lez tryblett cum j pair lez wood spanne taynges oh.

De iiij les pattron lokkers cum veteribus lez pattrones viij^{d}

De j lez pyill cum iij paribus lez ballance ij^{s} ij^{d}

De ij paribus ballance pro auro iiij^{d}

De j lez sairse pixide cum j lez reyn spyndyll ij^{d}

De j lez gylttyng plater cum pertinentiis iiij^{d}

De j enaymelyng lez lokker vi^{d}

De j foco cum j pari follium xii^{d}

De iij tyn peyces x^{d}

De j veteri lez bord cum lez deske iij^{d}

De ij lapidibus de lez sclait j^{d}

Non legata. De j grett lez pyill weght cum j pari balance' v^{s} De j osculatorio argenti pond' xii un. et di., pris unc. iij^{s} ij^{d}

Summa xxxix^{s} vii^{d}

De iij mirrarum lez bandys cum j pede murræ pond. xii unc. pris unc. iij^{s} iiij^{d}, xl^{s}

De j mirræ lez band cum j lez lokker cum argento fracto pond. xii un. et di. xli^{s} viii^{d}

De j arcu argenti cum catapulto argenti et j nola auri v^{s}

De j cocliari argenti sine lez knope xii^{d}

De xx peirlys ii^{s}

De ij cristaules viii^{d}

De iij foliis de lez booke gold iij^{d}

De j lez heft cultelli de lez greyn cerpentyn j^{d}

De j lez maser shell xii^{d}

De j pari balance' j^{d} ; de j lez stampe iiij^{d}

De j Premario vi^{d}

De ij aliis libris veteribus ij^{d}

De j cresmatorio de lez tyn ij^{d}

De j lez sarce pixid' ij^d
De j pari precularium de le jeitt ij^d
De lez swepynges dictæ opellæ xx^s

Summa ix^{li} iii^s x^d ob.

Thomas Skelton goldsmith of York, is found selling mazers in the middle years of the fifteenth century. It is worth noticing that the names of several of these goldsmiths point to their foreign descent. Luneburgh and Harlam must have come from those cities; Colan, or Colam, was not improbably from Cologne; and the Christian name of his son Herman, who is mentioned in his will, points in the same direction. But notwithstanding these glimpses of the tradesmen of York and their families, there is no single bit of marked plate left to show that this city, nor indeed any of the others, until much later days exercised the privilege conferred upon them in 1379 or in 1423, of touching their plate with their own touches. Very interesting documentary evidence was, however, found by the late Canon Raine amongst the archives of York of the existence of a common touch there in 1410-1. In that year a dispute arose in the craft as to whether there should be three or only two "searchers," and the question is laid before the mayor, aldermen, and other good citizens on 5th March, 12 Henry IV., with the result that two searchers, Englishmen born, and no more, were to be chosen and duly sworn. The goldsmiths were to bring their touch and mark "come la statut purport," and those who had none, to make themselves new punches, "en complisement de justice come le comune ley ent demand." They were to forfeit 6s. 8d. if they sold anything of gold or silver before "le comune touch de la dite cite" and its maker's mark were properly applied to it. All this came under review again in 1561, when the "ancient ordynances of the mystery or occupation of goldsmiths of the citie of Yorke" were diligently perused and examined "by the right worshipfull Parsyvall Crafourth, mayour, the aldremen and pryvay councell" at their assembly in "the counsell chamber upon Ousebrig," 10th April, 3 Eliz., and reformed, to be thenceforth firmly observed and kept for ever. Thomas Sympson and Robert Gylmyn, the two searchers under the old ordinances, and the other good men masters of the craft, were present. The old ordinance of Henry IV. as regards the two searchers was ratified and confirmed and as regards

makers' punches. It was also ordained that all work should be
"towched with the pounce of this citie called the half leopard
head and half flowre de luyce" as the statute purporteth.
Gold was to be of the "touche of Paryse," and of silver none
of "worse alaye than sterlyng" might be worked, except that
"sowder" should be allowed for, under pain of forfeiting the
double value. A great deal followed about apprentices and
fraudulent work, to a great extent according with the provisions
of the Acts of 1404 and 1420, especially as regards work done
for Holy Church, knights' spurs, and so on. But despite all
these regulations 1582 was a stormy year at York, when the two
searchers, Martyne Dubiggyn and William Peareson got themselves committed to ward—Peareson for one day, but his fellow
at the Lord Mayor's pleasure, and to be deprived of his office.
It appears from later records that the new searcher then
(10th May, 1583) appointed in his place was Thomas Waddy, who,
with Peareson his colleague, was soon in fresh difficulties with
one George Kitchin, which were at last settled by arbitration
23 Sept., 1583. The next searchers appointed, 5 Jan., 1583-4,
were John Stocke and William ffoster ; and a year later than
this (27 Jan., 1584-5) it was ordained that from henceforth the
searchers were to be chosen on the fourth day after the Feast
of St. James, the apostle, to continue till that day year (July 29).
In 1606 some fresh orders were made about apprentices and
searching; and in these the "towch and mark belonginge to
this cittye called the halfe leopard head and half flower-de-luce"
is again mentioned. On Sept. 1, 1684, the searchers were fined
40s. a man for having omitted to call the meeting to choose
their successors, and the company was ordered to meet that day
fortnight to choose them.

From about 1500 the leading craftsmen occasionally figure in
the list of the Lord Mayors of York. Thomas Gray serves this
office in 1497, William Willson in 1513, George Gaile in 1534,
and Ralph Pullein in 1537 ; but then several generations elapse
before a goldsmith again attains the civic chair in the person of
John Thompson, Lord Mayor in 1685, to be followed in 1697
by Mark Gill. Charles Rhoades was sheriff in 1694. The mark
of each of these last three worthies occurs upon plate. The
goldsmiths in 1623 paid only 2s. a year towards the repair of the
Mote Hall called St. Anthony's Gild, whereas the " Merchants

or Mercers " paid as much as 5 shillings. At about this time, too, a glimpse of craft life, and the more interesting because relating to goldsmiths much of whose work remains to be seen at the present day, comes from the will of Christopher Harrington of York. Dying in 1614, he leaves to the company of the trade of goldsmiths a silver spoon of ten shillings price, and after a bequest of some tools to his " mann James Plummer," devises the rest to his son Robert Harrington, and a drawing-book between them, six leaves of paper apiece.* Plate by all these three will be found in our list of old York plate.

To return from this York digression, the Act of 1477 speaks of the keepers of the touch in London *and other places;* but in 1488, when the statute of that year notices " the rule and order of the mints of London, Calice, Canterbury, York and Durham," also of "the Goldsmiths' Hall of London," and recites that " finers and parters dwell abroad in every part of the realm out of the rules aforesaid," no mention is made of any of the country assay offices; and it may be presumed that they did little or no business towards the end of that century. Even later, in 1509, it is expressly stated in one of the charters of the Goldsmiths' Company in London, that search for and punishment of abuses in the trade was but seldom executed out of London.

Possibly the supervision of the Goldsmiths' Company in London was exercised at first in a spirit that did not encourage the development of the trade in the provinces; for the confirmation of their charter by Edward IV. in 1462, gave them the inspection, trial, and regulation of all gold and silver wares, not only in London, but in all other parts of the kingdom; and these powers were continually exercised, periodical progresses being made by the assay wardens throughout the country for the purpose. It is recorded in 1493, that the costs of the wardens to " Sturbitch Fair," amounted to £2; and from the accounts relating to the sixteenth century we may take the following extracts :—

" 1512. Agreed that Mr. Wardens shall ride into the country this year, to make search ' in div^{rs} feyres, cytyes, and townys,' as they had done in tymes past."

" 1517. Agreed ' that the wardens shall ryde at Seynt Jamys'

---

* Communicated by Mr. T. M. Fallow, F.S.A.

Feyre' and to such other places and towns in the west parts of England as they shall think most necessary."

But such circuits as these were clearly not every-day events; it would seem as if nothing of the kind had taken place for some years previously to 1512, and the provincial authorities did but little in the absence of any higher supervision.

Much more plate was melted than made during the half-century which followed this outburst of energy; and country goldsmiths gradually fell, equally no doubt with those of London, into the abuses which called so loudly for enquiry at the commencement of the reign of Queen Elizabeth. Up to that time, at all events, their work does not seem to have been held in very high estimation. The touches of London and Paris are constantly mentioned in the wills and inventories of the fifteenth century; that of Bruges is also occasionally referred to : but no mention will be found of any English touch except that of London; and in the inventories of church furniture made in the reign of Edward VI., in which the names of many London goldsmiths occur, there are not to be found those of any provincial craftsmen, even in the case of parishes far from the capital, and comparatively near one or other of the local centres at which that mystery would seem to have had a settlement. This is the more significant, as in the self-same documents the sale of pewter to pewterers resident in various country towns is recorded, which would warrant a presumption that broken or superfluous silver plate would have been in like manner disposed of to neighbouring goldsmiths, had there been any such to be found.

The country goldsmiths shared, however, in the general revival of the trade that now followed, and provincial marks are often found on Elizabethan church plate, which is still in abundance in every part of England. This is especially the case in the neighbourhood of Norwich, York, and Exeter; but in most other districts, even when remote and inaccessible from London, the occurrence of any marks but those of the Goldsmiths' Company is very rare. The wardens in 1567 were again directed to "ryde a searchynge this year to Sturbridge" and were allowed four pounds for their charge "according to the old custom;" this again showing that such an expedition was not undertaken every year.

The mints in the provinces did not flourish so well, for the precious metals were somewhat scarce, and much was being made into plate. Harrison, chaplain to Lord Cobham, writing in 1586, says that divers mints had been suppressed within his own recollection, "as Southwarke and Bristow, and all coinage brought up to one place, that is to say, the Tower of London."

Domestic as well as ecclesiastical plate of country manufacture is not unknown, and the goldsmiths of York and Norwich commanded a good deal of the custom of their counties. Apostles' spoons are marked at Norwich and Exeter in some quantity from 1560 to 1650, some of the plate of the Corporation of Norwich was home made between 1560 and 1570, and specimens of plate of all kinds, from that time down to the end of the seventeenth century, are referable to the goldsmiths of York.

It is difficult to reconcile this entirely with the account given of the provincial assay offices by the author of the *Touchstone*,* who writes thus of them in 1679 somewhat more contemptuously than they would otherwise seem to deserve : "but what are the particular Marks the respective chief Governors of those seven places set on the Silver works I can give no account thereof. But this I can assert, that by reason the Marks of those places are little known they bear as little Credit, and therefore the Goldsmiths in those and other remote places do frequently send up their Silver Works to receive the *London touch*."

Our practical author remarks upon the obligation of country goldsmiths to make their marks known, not only to the local chief magistrate but to the wardens of the London goldsmiths, who had the ultimate supervision of the craft in all places, including the seven towns ; and goes on to comment upon the danger provincial corporations ran of losing their charters and being disfranchised in consequence of lax exercise of their duties and privileges, especially " now since by the favour of our King's predecessors and their Parliaments Goldsmiths in those seven towns are remitted those extremities of bringing their vessels of silver to London to be stamped with the Leopard Head, but are allowed each of them a Touch by themselves to pass their works upon."

---

* See p. 14.

He refers also to the debased quality of work executed in country places, in consequence of the remissness of the magistracy in prosecuting their authority in making search, assaying and marking the goldsmiths' work, and of the infrequency with which the Wardens of the Goldsmiths of London made search in the country, and strongly recommends intending purchasers of plate to spend their money in London.

If this was all true, it is not surprising to find that in 1697 when, owing to the scarcity of silver coin, it was desirable to encourage persons having wrought plate to bring it to be coined, although it was provided that such plate as plainly appeared to have thereupon "the mark commonly used at the hall belonging to the company of Goldsmiths in London, besides the workman's mark," should be received at the mints without question, and paid for at the rate of 5s. 4d. per oz., no cognizance was taken of any other marks. All plate not bearing the above marks was to be melted and assayed before it was allowed for, unless the vendor were satisfied with a rough valuation made upon oath by the master of the mint. Lastly, whether prosperous or not up to the year 1697, the provincial offices were all then extinguished at a blow, for the further provisions of this Act,* after proceeding to establish a higher national standard of fineness for silver plate as a protection to the coinage which its earlier clauses were intended to call into existence, entrusted the marking of all new plate to the warden of the craft of the Goldsmiths only, and made no mention of any other corporations whatever.

That great inconvenience was by this measure occasioned to the goldsmiths remote from the city of London is clear from the preamble of the Act by which, only three years later, in 1700-1, this hardship was removed by the appointment of wardens and assay masters for assaying wrought plate in the cities of York, Exeter, Bristol, Chester, and Norwich, being the cities in which mints had then lately been erected for recoining the silver moneys of the kingdom. Newcastle-upon-Tyne was added to the number in 1702. The next chapter will be devoted to these modern offices and their marks ; meanwhile it will be convenient to notice in detail the ancient marks used in the places now under consideration.

The ground may be somewhat cleared by saying that nothing

_____

* 8 & 9 Will. III. c. 8.

is known at present of any of the old provincial touches except those of York, Norwich, and Newcastle-upon-Tyne. Minting certainly was carried on at Bristol ; but there are only the faintest indications that goldsmiths' work was carried on there, nor can any town marks be appropriated to Lincoln, Salisbury, or Coventry.* Casual mention of goldsmiths at Bristol is all that is found in local records. One W. Halteby, goldsmith, dwelt at the end of the bridge of Avon there in 1396, and in a will of 1414, E. Pounsot, goldsmith, is said to have then lately possessed houses in Horse Street. "Goldsmiths dwelling in the Goldesmythes Rewe, nowe y callyd the Cookyn Rewe," are mentioned amongst the benefactors of the church of All Halow Bristowe in a ledger belonging to that church, and this entry may be attributed to the first half of the fifteenth century. Early as this the row named after them had therefore lost its name, although goldsmiths are mentioned in various parish records later in the century, and dealings with them for church plate recorded. There is also extant a complaint made to Thomas Cromwell in the reign of Henry VIII. concerning some Bristol goldsmiths.† L. Farrowe, Ths. Wynsmowre and Rd. Thomas are mentioned in it. These scattered references to individual goldsmiths of Bristol, coupled with the fact that a seal-head spoon, with a punch of the arms of Bristol struck in the bowl, was noted a few years ago as being in the hands of a London dealer, are absolutely all that can be said as to Bristol. The fact, moreover, that Elizabethan church plate in and about Bristol always bears London or Exeter marks clearly shows that, if in 1423 a touch was set up in Bristol, goldsmiths' work in that town did not long call for its continuance.

If a touch was set up in Lincoln, where goldsmiths appear to have been at work in the fifteenth century,‡ there is evidence that by the time of Elizabeth it, too, had fallen into abeyance. In nearly fifty Lincolnshire parishes Elizabethan Church plate exists with the same maker's mark (an M. with an I. over it in a shield of very peculiar shape), without the mark of any town. In the city of Lincoln itself the only old local plate extant, including an Elizabethan cup, bears makers' marks alone.

On the other hand, certain towns not named in the Act of 1423 marked plate, notably so Exeter, Chester, and Hull. The

---

* A company existed here from 1684-1822, but neither town mark nor name of any goldsmith appears in the books.

† P.R.O. State Papers, Henry VIII., Vol. 7, No. 692.

‡ *The Early History of Hedon.* Boyle, p. cx.

marks of these towns, together with the touches of York, Norwich, and Newcastle-upon-Tyne, may now be considered.

YORK.

It has at length proved possible, by means of the records referred to on a preceding page, to identify the well-known old English mark of a fleur-de-lys and leopard's head crowned, both being dimidiated and conjoined in a plain circular shield, as that which was anciently used at York. The number and *locale* of the specimens on which it had been found by the writer and others had already left the matter no longer open to question, but previously the evidence had been wholly circumstantial.

Unfortunately, the mark itself being only found on much-worn plate, and being often very indistinct, the half leopard's head looks much more like a half-rose, and it long seemed hazardous to say for which it was intended. It is now clearly proved to be a half leopard's head crowned. The exact date of the introduction of the old York mark is unknown. A date-letter was very probably adopted for the first time in consequence of the enquiry into the working of the craft which took place in 1561. An alphabet of twenty-four letters must have been used, the omitted letters being I or J, and also U or V. A table containing the known instances, and carried down to 1698, is given at the end of this volume. At certain points some of the letters seem a year wrong for a short period, and this may be accounted for by searchers having been removed and a fresh letter needed on one if not two occasions ; but even after consultation with the late Mr. Fallow, who had seen more Yorkshire hall-marks than all other antiquaries put together, the author was unable to make any alteration in the tables of date-letters that would not result in creating far more difficulties and discrepancies than it would remove. The following are the articles which have served as authority for the construction of this table ; many of them, it will be observed, are actually dated, and the fashion of the others enables them to be placed, without any hesitation, in their proper cycles.

The names are added to the initials from documentary evidence kindly contributed by the late Canon Raine, through the author's friend Mr. Fallow, which has corroborated in detail the correctness of the York date-letter tables originally compiled by the author without any better help than the specimens of plate which came to his notice from time to time.

These tables, which the author compiled with great trouble

and care, have again been thoroughly revised and a few additional letters added, but only such as occur on pieces of public
plate, so that the letters in the tables cannot be called in question
as regards their authenticity.

EXAMPLES OF OLD YORK PLATE.

DATE.	MAKER'S MARK AND NAME.		ARTICLE.
1570	TS	Thos. Symson, 1548 *	Communion cup and cover.—Salkeld, Cumb.
Do.	H	Christopher Hunton, 1551, d. 1582.	Communion cup.—Thorpe Basset, Yorks.
Do.	FW	William Foster, 1569, d. 1610.	Communion cup. — Old Byland, Yorks.
Do.	RB	Robert Beckwith, 1546, d. 1585.	Communion cups.—Yorks.
Do.	RG	Robert Gylmyn, 1550	Communion cups.—Yorks.
Do.	GK	George Kitchyng, 1561, d. 1597.	Communion cup.—Rufforth, Yorks.
Do.	M	Probably Mark Wray, 1563.	Com. plate.—Yorks.
1571	. . .	Robert Gylmyn, as in 1570.	Com. cup, with crossed belts, but no foliage.—Handsworth, Yorks.
1576	RG	. . . . . .	Seal-headed spoon. — From the Staniforth Collection.
1577	. . .	G. Kitchyng, as in 1570.	Mount of stoneware jug, dated 1576.—From the Addington Collection.
1579	. . .	[None]	Small communion cup, with peculiar Elizabethan belt. — Adwick - on - Dearne, Yorks.
Do.	H	Christopher Hunton	
1583	. . .	G. Kitching as in 1570	Com. plate.—Yorks.
Do.	WR	William Rawneson †	Com. cup.—Long Preston, Yorks.
1585	Do.	Do.	Communion cup, rude Elizabethan belt.—Troutbeck, Westmoreland.
1593	Do.	Do.	Communion cup, with usual belt.—Crathorne, Yorks.
Do.	RG	. . . . . .	Spoon.—Staniforth Coll.
1600	. . .	William Rawneson as in 1583.	Communion cup, from a church near Cawood, Yorks.—Late T. W. U. Robinson, Esq.
1607	RC	Robert Casson . .	Com. plate.—Yorks.
1608	PP	Peter Pearson, 1603	Communion cup. — Brantingham, Yorks.
1609	Do.	Do.	Communion cup with cover, dated 1609.—Sutton-on-Derwent, Yorks.
Do.	FT	Francis Tempest, 1597	Communion cup.—Cottam, Yorks.
1611	. . .	Peter Pearson, as in 1608.	Cup, gift of Coniston Wrightington. —Trinity House, Hull.

* When a date follows the name, it is the year in which the goldsmith took up his
freedom.   The date of his death is given where known.
† W. Rawneson was not free of the city.   The Dean and Chapter dealt with him
in 1578 and 1579, and he probably lived in the "Liberty of St. Peter," adjoining
the Minster, exempt from the city.   Those goldsmiths who did so were permitted to
enter their marks at the City Hall, but were under no compulsion in the matter.

DATE.	MAKER'S MARK AND NAME.		ARTICLE.
1612	CH	Chris. Harrington, 1595, d. 1614.	Small communion cup.—Patterdale, Cumb.
1613	Do.	Do.	Communion cup with engraved belt. —Pickering, Yorks.
1614	Do.	Do.	Beaker cup.—From the Dasent Collection.
1615	Do.	Do.	Apostle spoon.—From the Staniforth Collection.
Do.	. . .	Francis Tempest, as in 1609.	Communion cup. — Irthington, Cumb.
Do.	. . .	Peter Pearson, as in 1608.	Communion cup, dated 1615. — Slingsby, Yorks.
Do.	CM	Chris. Mangy, 1609 .	Communion cup, dated 1615. — St. Cuthbert's, York.
1617	. . .	Francis Tempest, as in 1609.	Communion cup, Elizabethan belt, Cleator, Cumb.
Do.	. . .	Do.	Communion cup. — Hemingbro, Yorks.
Do.	. . .	Do.	Do.—Spennithorne, Yorks.
1619	SC	Sem. Casson, 1613, d. 1633.	Do.—Bilbrough, Yorks.
1620	. . .	Peter Pearson, as in 1608.	Do., dated 1619.—Bempton, Yorks.
1622	. . .	Do.	Silver rim, dated 1622, under Scrope mazer.—York Minster.
Do.	RH	Robert, son of Christr. Harrington, 1616, d. 1647.	Communion cup.—Darton, Yorks.
1623	. . .	Peter Pearson, as in 1608.	Com. cup and cover.—Holy Trin., Goodramgate, York.
1624	RW	Robert Williamson, 1623, d. 1667.	Communion cup. — Howden, Yorks.
1625	. . .	S. Casson, as in 1619 .	Do.—Naburn, York.
1626	T·H	Thos., son of Christr. Harrington, 1624, d. 1642.	Apostle spoon.—From the Staniforth Collection.
1627	. . .	. . . .	Communion cup. — Cawthorne, Yorks.
1628	. . .	Robert Harrington, as in 1622.	Do. — Thornton Watlass, Yorks. Also cup, dated 1628.—Lotherton, Yorks.
Do.	IP	James Plummer, 1616, d. 1663.	Do.—Hayton, Yorks. Also in 1623, Com. plate.—Yorks.
1630	. . .	Christr. Mangy, as in 1615.	Do., dated 1630.—Bewcastle, Cumb.
1631	. . .	S. Casson, as in 1619 . .	Do., Pickhill, Yorks.
Do.	. . .	Robert Harrington, as in 1622.	Do.—Ebberston, Yorks.
Do.	. . .	James Plummer, as in 1628.	Do.—Headingley, Yorks.
Do.	. . .	Christr. Mangy, as in 1615.	Do.—Thirsk, Yorks.
Do.	W	Thos. Waite, 1613, d. 1662.	Com. cup, given by Abp. Harsnet, in 1630.—All Saints, North St., York.
1632	. . .	Robert Williamson, as in 1624.	Communion cup.—Calverley, York.
1633	. . .	Robert Harrington, as in 1622.	Cup and paten, dated 1633 —Chapel Allerton, Yorks.

DATE.	MAKER'S MARK AND NAME.	ARTICLE.
1633 . . .	S. Casson, as in 1619 . .	Com. cup.—St. Helen's, York.
Do. . . .	. . . .	Do., dated 1632.—Kirkby Malham, Yorks.
Do. . . .	Thos. Harrington, as in 1626.	Communion cup.—St. Olave's,York.
1634 . . .	James Plummer, as in 1628.	Communion cup.— Danby Wiske, Yorks.
Do. . . .	Robert Williamson, as in 1624.	Do.—Bilton-in-Ainsty, Yorks.
Do. . . .	Thos. Waite, as in 1631 .	Do., Elizn. belt.—Burton·in-Kendal, Westmor.
1635 . . .	Thos. Harrington, as in 1626.	Do., plain pricked belt, dated 1634, —Threlkeld, Cumb.
Do. IT	John Thompson, 1633, d. 1692.	Com. cup. — Conistone Kilnsey, Yorks.
1636 . . .	Thos. Harrington, as in 1626.	Do.—Cundall, Yorks.
Do. . . .	James Plummer, as in 1628.	Do.—Northallerton, Yorks.
1637 FB	Francis Bryce, 1634, d. 1640.	Plain cup on baluster stem (bearing a forged inscription as to Norwich, dated 1578). — Formerly in the Bohn Collection.
Do. . . .	Robert Harrington, as in 1622.	Com. cup.—Lanercost, Cumb.
Do. . . .	James Plummer, as in 1628.	Do. Billingham, Durh.
1638 . . .	Do.	Cup and paten.—Flaxton, Yorks.
Do. TH	Thos. Harrington, 1624, d. 1642.	Communion cup, dated 1728. — Scammonden, Yorks.
Do. . .	Robert Harrington, as in 1622.	Cup and paten.—Levisham, Yorks.
Do. . . .	Robert Williamson, as in 1624.	Plain com. cup.—Elmley, Yorks.
1639 . . .	Robert Harrington, as in 1622.	Communion cup. — Hunmanby, Yorks.
Do. . . .	Robert Williamson, as in 1624.	Do., dated 1638.—Thorner, Yorks.
1641 . . .	Robert Harrington, as in 1622.	Tazza-shaped com. cup, date 1640. —Guisbrough, Yorks.
Do. . . .	John Thompson, as in 1635.	Cup and paten.—Melsonby, Yorks.
1642 . . .	Thos. Harrington, as in 1638.	Communion cup. — Wheldrake Yorks.
1645 . . .	Chris. Mangy, as in 1615.	Com. plate.—Yorks.
1650 . . .	James Plummer, as in 1628.	Commonwealth mace.—Richmond, Yorks.
1654 TW	Thos. Waite. - . .	Communion cup. — Stockton - on - Forest, Yorks.
1655 . . .	. . . . . .	Beaker used as com. cup.—Cumberworth, Yorks.
1657 IP	John, son of James Plummer, 1648.	Paten.—Stillingfleet, Yorks.
1660 Do.	Do.	Cup, gift of R. Hunter, who died 1659.—Thornton Dale, Yorks.
Do. MB	Marmaduke Best, 1657 .	Tankard, given 1666. — Corpn. of Hull.

DATE.	MAKER'S MARK AND NAME.		ARTICLE.
1661	🛡️	Wm. Waite, 1653, d. 1689.	Small two-handled basin on ball feet.—T. M. Fallow, Esq.
Do.	. . .	John Plummer, as in 1657	Spoon, flat stem.—From the Staniforth Collection.
1662	. . .	Do.	Cup and paten cover, dated 1663.—Aldbrough, E. Yorks.
Do.	. . .	Do.	Com. cup, undated.—Otley, Yorks.
Do.	. . .	Do.	Do., dated 1663.—Brafferton, Yorks.
Do.	. . .	. . . . . .	Do., dated 1662.—Birkin, Yorks.
Do.	. . .	Marmaduke Best, as in 1660.	Do., and cover, undated.—Healaugh, Yorks.
Do.	(RW)	Robert, son of Robert Williamson, 1653.	Do.—Alne, Yorks.
1663	. . .	Marmaduke Best, as in 1660.	Cup and paten cover. — Bolton Abbey, Yorks.
Do.	(GM)	George, son of Christopher Mangy, 1638; living 1666.	Cup and paten, dated 1663.—St. Mary, Cottingham, Yorks.
1664	. . .	Robert Williamson, as in 1662.	Com. cup and paten.—Tadcaster, Yorks.
Do.	. . .	John Plummer, as in 1657	Large paten, dated 1666.—Beverley Minster.
Do.	(TM)	Thos., son of Geo. Mangy, 1664.	Communion cup.—Catterick, Yorks.
1667	Do.	Do.	Large repoussé dish on foot, given 1668.—Corporation of Hull.
1668	. . .	Marmaduke Best, as in 1660.	Communion cup and cover.—Cartmel, Lancashire.
1669	. . .	Thos. Mangy, as in 1664	Communion cup.—Sandal, Yorks.
Do.	(PM)	Philemon Marsh, 1652, d. 1672.	Silver lining, dated 1669, of Scrope mazer.—York Minster.
Do.	. . .	Thos. Mangy, as in 1664 .	Paten, dated 1669. — Almondbury, Yorks. Also plain cup on baluster stem, dated 1670. — (Edmund James Coll.)
1670	. . .	Rt. Williamson, as in 1674.	Com. plate.—Yorks.
1671	. . .	Marmaduke Best, as in 1660.	An "article" ordered 19 April, 1672. —Corp. of York.
1672	. . .	Do.	Gold loving cup, dated 1672.—Corporation of York.
Do.	. . .	Do	Cup and paten cover, gift of Leonard Milbourne, who died in 1672.—Skelton, Cumberland.
Do.	. . .	Do.	Do., no cover, given by the same.—Ousby, Cumb.
Do.	(WM)	William Mascall, 1664 .	Candlesticks, dated 1673. — York Minster.
1673	. . .	Marmaduke Best, as in 1660.	Communion cup. — Appleton - on-Wisk, Yorks.
Do.	. . .	William Mascall, as in 1672.	Communion cup.—Penistone, Yorks.
Do.	(IT)	John Thompson, see 1635.	Paten.—St. Cuthbert's, York.
1674	(RW)	Robert Williamson, see 1662.	Cup and cover, dated 1674.—St. Mary Bishophill, senior, York.

DATE.	MAKER'S MARK AND NAME.	ARTICLE.
1674	. . . Marmaduke Best, as in 1660.	Tankard, dated 1674.—Corporation of York.
Do.	. . . John Plummer, as in 1657	Another.
Do.	(RK) Roland Kirby, 1668. . .	Tumbler cup.—The Author.
1675	. . . John Plummer, as in 1657	Communion plate, dated 1676.—Ripon Minster.
Do.	. . . John Thompson, as in 1673.	Communion cup, dated 1676.—Ormesby, Yorks.
Do.	(TM) Thos. Mangy, see 1664 .	Paten, dated 1675. — Ecclesfield, Yorks.
1676	. . . Do.	Paten, dated 1676.
1678	. . . John Plummer, as in 1657	Paten, dated 1677.—Kirby Malzeard, Yorks.
Do.	. . . Marmaduke Best, as in 1660.	Com. cup, dated 1678.—St. Michael's, Spurriergate, York.
Do.	. . . Do.	Cup, dated 1677.—Drax, Yorks.
Do.	. . . John Thompson, as in 1673.	Com. cup, dated 1679.—Leathley, Yorks.
1679	. . . John Plummer, as in 1657	Peg tankard, dated 1680; inherited by its present owners from the family of Osbaldeston, of Hunmanby, Yorks.—Lord Amherst of Hackney.
Do.	. . . Roland Kirby, as in 1674.	Cup and paten, dated 1679.—Shipton Thorpe, Yorks.
1680	. . . Marmaduke Best, as in 1660.	Do., dated 1681.—Brotton-in-Cleveland, Yorks.
1681	(GG) George Gibson, 1678 . .	Cup, dated 1682.—Sancton, Yorks.
Do.	(CR) Charles Rhoades, 1677 .	Com. cup.—Gargrave, Yorks.
Do.	(WB) Wm. Busfield, 1679 . .	Com. cup.—St. Laurence, York. Also 1680, Com. cup, dated 1681.—Bentham, Yorks.
1682	(TM) Thos. Mangy, see 1664 .	Smaller cup, dated 1684.—St. Laurence, York.
Do.	. . . Robert Williamson, see 1662.	Lid of com. cup, and paten on stem.—Guiseley, Yorks.
Do.	. . . Roland Kirby, as in 1674.	Com. cup.—All SS., Pavement, York.
Do.	. . . John Thompson, as in 1673.	Sockets to Abp. Sancroft's candlesticks.—York Minster.
1683	. . . Charles Rhoades, as in 1681.	Paten, dated 1687. — Whitkirk, Yorks.
Do.	. . . George Gibson, as in 1681	Caudle cup. The late Canon Raine.
Do.	(MG) Mark Gill, 1680 . .	Com. cup.—Carnaby, Yorks.
1684	. . . George Gibson, as in 1681	Plain flat-lidded tankard. – (Edm. James Coll.)
Do.	. . . Wm. Busfield, as in 1681.	Large paten.—St. Martin's, York.
Do.	. . . Thos. Mangy, as in 1682	Com. cup.—Todwick, Yorks.

DATE.	MAKER'S MARK AND NAME.		ARTICLE.
1685	(IO)	John Oliver, 1676 . .	Paten cover.—St. Maurice's, York.
Do.	Do.	Do.	Flagon.—Lowther, Westmor.*
Do.	. . .	Thos. Mangy, as in 1682	Paten cover.—Featherstone, Yorks.
1686	. . .	John Oliver, as in 1685 .	Caudle cup, with acanthus decoration. —From the Staniforth Collection.
1688	. . .	Do.	Alms-dish, dated 1689.—St. Michael le Belfry, York. Also Com. cup, tulip band, dated 1689.—Stockton, Durh.
1689	(CW)	Christopher Whitehill, 1676.	Cup and paten.—Oswaldkirk, Yorks.
1690	. . .	Wm. Busfield, as in 1681.	Com. cup.—Holtby, Yorks.
1691	. . .	Robert Williamson, see 1674.	Spoon.—Noted by T. M. Fallow, Esq.
1692	. . .	Wm. Busfield, as in 1681.	Paten, dated 1694.—Farnham, Yorks.
Do.	. . .	John Oliver, as in 1685 .	Com. cup and cover.—Kettlewell, Yorks.
1694	C★R	Charles Rhoades, mark imperfect, free 1677.	Plain com. cup and cover.
1695	. . .	Wm. Busfield, as in 1681.	Com. plate.—Yorks
1696	. . .	C. Rhoades, as in 1694 .	Com. cup dated 1700. — Mytton, Yorks.
1697	. . .	Wm. Busfield, as in 1681.	Paten.—Darfield, Yorks.
Do.	. . .	Do.	Com. cup.—Rilstone, Yorks.
1698	. . .	Do.	Do.—Barmby Moor, Yorks.

NEWCASTLE-UPON-TYNE.

Notwithstanding the proved existence of a guild of goldsmiths in this town from 1536 and earlier, but little remains of their work until we come to the later part of the seventeenth century, when specimens of church-plate are to be met with, and enough to show that a date-letter was not used in Newcastle at this period. The hall-mark, at that time, consisted of three castles, arranged, as in later days, two above and one below, on a shield of irregular outline, in some instances smaller at the lower part, where it had to surround only one tower, than at the top. Sometimes the castles are in a small plain shield. A good deal of church-plate, dated from 1670 to 1700, is found in Cumberland, bearing the three towers in shields of one or other of these shapes. **WR** is the most usual maker's mark on these pieces, and it is frequently accompanied by a rose on the same or a separate punch. This is the mark of one William Ramsey, who took up his freedom in 1656, and worked till towards the

---

* In 1874, before the old York mark had been identified by the author, this flagon was sent to London to have a spout added to it. Instead of hall-marking the new spout, the Goldsmiths' Company placed the following remarkable inscription on it — "Goldsmiths' Hall, 6 May, 1874. This lip weighing 2oz. 16dwt. to an old flagon of uncertain mark and assay."

end of the century. He was mayor of the town in 1690, and died in 1698. Another mark, probably attributable to Newcastle, is on church-plate at Gateshead, dated 1672. This is a single heraldic castle or tower, on a small shield, and accompanied by a lion passant on a plain oval shield, but turned to the right.* The lion passant mark is struck twice on these pieces. The same marks occur on a communion cup at Boldon, also dated 1672. The maker's mark is **ID** in both cases, and stands for John Douthwayte, who died in 1673, having taken up his freedom in 1666. In addition to other marks, a communion cup of c. 1685 at St. Nicholas', Newcastle, bears what seems to be a Roman letter on a shaped shield; but this single instance is the only trace of a date-letter that has at present been found on ancient Newcastle plate. For fifty years before 1656, the date of William Ramsey's freedom, no goldsmith's name at all appears in the Minute Book; but from then to 1697 more than a dozen are noted in the following order, viz.: John Wilkinson, free 1658, died 1664 or 5; William Robinson, admitted 1666, died 1674; John Douthwayte, free 1666, died 1673; John Norris, admitted 1674; Francis Batty, who worked from 1674, and is spoken of as dead in an entry of 13th Sept., 1707; Albany Dodgson, admitted 1679; Eli Bilton, admitted 1679, who was apprenticed to Douthwayte, became free in 1683, and died 1712; Cuthbert Ramsey; William Ramsey, junior, admitted 1691, died 1716; Abraham Hamer, admitted 1691; Robert Shrive, free in 1694, and Thomas Hewitson, free in 1697. A John Ramsey was admitted in 1698, but he died before 1708.

Some of these men will be mentioned again in the next chapter.

It remains only to say here that in the interval between the suppression of the Newcastle assay office and its re-establishment in 1702, the Morden Tower was partly rebuilt, and that amongst the subscribers to the cost of this were the above-named Francis Batty, W. Ramsey, junior, Thomas Hewitson, Eli Bilton, Robert Shrive, and John Ramsey, besides Richard Hobbs, admitted 1700; Thomas Leightley, admitted 1700; Thomas Armstrong, admitted 1700; and Roger West, admitted 1701; who belong more properly to the later period.†

---

* This curious variation may be observed on modern Newcastle plate from 1721 to 1727.

† Per Mr. J. R. Boyle.

EXAMPLES OF OLD NEWCASTLE PLATE.

DATE.	MAKER.				ARTICLE.
1664	[marks]				John Wilkinson.
					Com. cup and cover, dated 1644. Ryton-on-Tyne, Durham.
N. D.	Do.	do.	do.	do.	Do. — Com. cup.—Warkworth, Northumb.
1672	Do.	do.	do.	[ID mark]	John Dowthwayte. — Flagons, dated 1672. — Gateshead.
Do.	Do.	do.	do.	do.	Do. — Com. cup.—Boldon, Durham.
N. D.	Do.	do.	do.	do.	Do. — Do.—Ormside, Westmor.
1670	[marks]				Wm. Ramsey. — Flagon, dated 1670.—Sawley, near Ripon.
N. D.	Do.	do.	do.	do.	Do. — Com. cup and paten.—Aspatria, Cumb.
N. D.	. .	[WR mark]	[mark]	(each twice)	Do. — Paten.—St. John's, Newcastle.
1680	[marks]				Do. — Cup and paten, dated 1680.—Ennerdale, Cumb.
N. D.	Do.	do. (each twice)			Do. — Do.—Torpenhow, Cumb.
1681	Do.	do. (each twice)			Do. — Com. cup, dated 1681.—Kelloe, Durham.
Do.	Do.	[WR] (each twice)			Do. — Paten, dated 1681. — Boldon, Durham.
N. D.	Do.	do. (do.)			Do. — Paten.— Corbridge-on-Tyne, Northumb.
1684	Do.	[mark]	[WR] (maker twice)		Do. — Com. plate, dated 1684.—Rose Castle Chapel.
c. 1685	[marks]				Do. — Com. cup.—St. Nicholas', Newcastle.
Do.	Do.	do.			Do. — Do.—Brampton, Cumb.
1686	[marks]		(each twice)		Do. — Flagon and patens, dated 1686.—St. Nicholas', Newcastle.
1687	Do.	do. (do.)			Do. — Paten.—Haverton Hill, Durham
N. D.	Do.	do. (maker twice)			Do. — Alms-dish. — Warkworth, Northumb.
N. D.	. .	do. (twice)			Do. — Com. cup.—Bywell St. Peter, Northumb.
1688	Do.	do. (each twice)			Do. — Com. cup, dated 1688.—Howick, Northumb.
c. 1690	Do.	[AH mark] (each twice)			Abr. Hamer. — Porringer, Chinese fashion.—Thos. Taylor, Esq.
1698	Do.	[TH mark]			Thos. Hewitson. — Flagon, dated 1698. — All Saints', Newcastle.
c. 1698	[marks]				Robert Shrive. — Flat-lidded tankard.
1701	Do.	[BB mark] (each twice)			Eli Bilton. — Porringer, dated 1701.—Taylor's Guild, Carlisle. Also Com. cup, dated 1687.—Chollerton, Northumb.
Do.	[I*R mark] (thrice)				John Ramsey. — Tankard, given 1702.—Taylor's Guild, Carlisle.
1697—1702	[marks]		(each twice)		Probably Wm. Ramsey the younger. — Noted by T. Taylor, Esq.

NORWICH.

Plate was made, assayed, and marked in this city at an early period, but the trade has long ceased to exist there. It has now no Goldsmiths' Company, nor does any vestige remain of the hall which is mentioned by Blomefield. Its old distinguishing mark was an escutcheon with the city arms, viz., a castle in chief above a lion passant in base, and it is found on plate belonging to the Corporation of Norwich of 1560–70, also on Norfolk church-plate of about the same date, in a shaped shield; later the same arms were borne on a plain, angular, heraldic shield with pointed base. Peter Peterson, a Norwich goldsmith of eminence in the reign of Elizabeth, is one of the few provincial craftsmen whose fame as well as name has been handed down to our times; in 1574 he is found presenting the Corporation with a standing cup gilt, on being excused serving the office of sheriff, and it is probable that the "sun" often found on Norwich plate was his mark. Born about 1518, he died in July, 1603, and his will, dated May 15, 1603, was proved at Norwich on August 1 of the same year. He left an immense quantity of plate, including a pot "of Cobbold's making," and speaks of the London and also of the "Anwarp" touch, as well as of "the castle and lion touch of Norwich." Amongst this plate is "a hanncepott graven upon the covers with the sonne, the Lion and the Castle of Norwich touch of my owne making," and a great deal more is either "graven with the sonne" or "having knoppes of the sonne"; pewter vessels also "marked with the sonne" are mentioned. The sun was therefore clearly Peterson's badge or crest, and as a sun in splendour is well known amongst the Norwich makers' marks of the period, it is the more likely that it was also his mark as a goldsmith. To set against this, an inscription on the "Peterson" cup, belonging to the Corporation of Norwich, presented by him in 1574 on being excused serving as sheriff, runs as follows: **THE+MOST+HERE+ OF + IS + DVNE+BY + PETER + PETERSON**, and this bears the equally well-known maker's mark of an orb and cross, or cross-mound. At first sight this would seem to make it more probable that the cross-mound was his mark. But it is clear that this cup was not wholly of his making, and perhaps

it was only finished up by Peterson, but bears the mark of him
who began it.   As regards the cross-mound mark too, we find
a communion cup at Haddiscoe, co. Norf., with Norwich marks
for 1569, bearing it, and as well the inscription " made by John
Stone and Robert Stone."*   It occurs also on the beaker cups
till lately belonging to the Dutch Church in Norwich, which
are not much, if at all, earlier than 1595, and this would be
probably long after Peterson had ceased to work, at all events,
with his own hand.   Altogether, the question is left at present
in a little uncertainty ; but the weight of evidence seems on the
side of the sun being the mark of Peterson.   An almost conclusive fact is the sun mark upon a communion cup at St.
Margaret's, Norwich, in 1568, the church accounts recording
the payment to Peterson of 6d. per ounce " worken " for the
making of it.   Norfolk archæologists have collected the names
and some few particulars of other less known members of the
craft in their county from the reign of Edward III.   It is
known, for example, that two wealthy goldsmiths of Norwich,
John Bassingham and John Belton, occupied the same house
successively in that city, and that the mark to be found upon
it belonged to one of them, probably the latter, who
was buried in the church of St. Andrew, Norwich, prior
to 1521, for in that year his wife was buried beside
him.†   John, Son of Robert Belton, goldsmith, was
admitted freeman of Norwich, 6 Henry VII., John
Basyngham in 8 Henry VIII., and John Basyngham, the
younger, in 30 Henry VIII.; Ffelyx Puttok, alderman, and goldsmith, bought plate of the churchwardens of Saint Andrew's,
Norwich, in 2 Edward VI.; whilst Peter Peterson, apprenticed
to John Basyngham, was admitted in 1 & 2 Philip and Mary.

A little later than this there must have been a number of
goldsmiths in Norwich, the Corporation plate bearing the
symbols of several different makers, whilst others occur on the
early Elizabethan communion cups in the country round.   One
William Cobbold, a leading goldsmith, is mentioned in the
Corporation records for 1581, and a Mr. Skottow as providing
beer-cups and wine-cups in 1634.   Cobbold is perhaps the
. . . Cobolde apprenticed to one Thomas Bere, and admitted

---

* In a different shield it occurs on a curious double cup in the Dunn-Gardner Coll.,
c. 1600.

† *Norfolk and Norwich Archæological Society's Transactions*, vol. iii., 195.

freeman in 5 Edw. VI. The name of Bere occurs in the lists at intervals from 6 Henry VI. But however many early goldsmiths worked in Norwich, there is good evidence in the city records that they went pretty much as they pleased until 1565, and that the Norwich city mark, mentioned above, was in point of fact first set up in that or the following year. To the industry of Mr. R. C. Hope, F.S.A.,* we owe the interesting discovery of a petition made by the company or fellowship of the Art or Science of Goldsmiths within the City of Norwich to the Mayor, Sheriffs, and Commonalty on 2 Oct., 7 Eliz. (1565), that whereas no standard had been set up for Norwich as for other places, and abuses had consequently become common, and whereas they had no common stamp or mark, it might be ordained as follows :—that masters and servants should work honestly under penalties ; that after the ensuing Michaelmas Day the Norwich standard should be of the same fineness and goodness, and better as the standard " of the lyberds hedde with the crowne " is and hath been always hitherto adjudged ; that a common stamp or touch should be provided bearing the castle and lion, the arms of the city ; that all work should be brought to be tried before being set for sale and in an "unburnished" state, under penalties ; that the wardens should only charge a fixed fee ; that every artificer should have a several punch or mark and should set it on his work after it had been assayed and stamped by the wardens; and lastly, that the wardens should once a quarter search for defaults and have right of entry to houses and shops for that purpose. A date-letter was used, at all events from 1566, but probably from 1565, when the first known alphabet seems to commence. Of some 186 specimens of plate bearing the letter C, no less than 69 are dated 1567, whilst 33 are dated 1568, facts which strongly point to the commencement of the alphabet in the earlier year. Unfortunately, although a number of dated specimens bearing the letters for 1565, 1566, 1567, 1568, and 1569 exist, the writer has been able to find no dated specimens from that time until the year 1627, in which the letter was D ; luckily an H for 1631, I for 1632, K for 1633, L for 1634 are to be found ; N is seen on an article dated 1636, O for

---

* See *Reliquary*, vol. iv., N.S., p. 208.

1637, P for 1638, R of the same alphabet, on a specimen dated
1640, and S for 1641.   This rather points to the use of alphabetical cycles consisting of twenty letters each, as in London, but
not without some slight irregularity, and the Table at the end of
this volume has been constructed on this principle, which is no
doubt correct, down to the middle of the seventeenth century.
From about 1660 to 1685 no date-letter at all was used, but at the
very end of the century there are traces of a renewal of the use.

If the first town-mark used at Norwich was that so often
found upon Elizabethan church-plate in Norfolk, a fresh punch
was adopted in 1624, when an entry in the books of the
Corporation of Norwich dated " 1624 ultimo Julii " states that
by the authority of the Mayor, a mark, viz. the castle and lion,
was then delivered to the wardens and searchers of the trade of
goldsmiths.   It is found on plate of 1627 and other years ; the
shape of the shield containing the lion and castle being somewhat more regular than before, though still shaped out, and the
castle altered from the rudely outlined building represented on
older stamps into a tower of the conventional heraldic pattern.

Norwich seems also to have used various standard marks ; at
one time it was a double-seeded rose, surmounted with a crown.
Mr. Octavius Morgan had a spoon stamped in the bowl with
that mark just in the place where the leopard's head is found
on ancient spoons of London make, from which it may be
supposed that it was used as the standard mark.   This spoon
has the Norwich arms on an escutcheon with other marks on
the back of the stem (see table, p. 108, c. 1637).

This rose is not found on Elizabethan specimens, but it
occurs on apostles' spoons and other plate of the reign of
Charles I.; it is also found towards the end of the century.
Other specimens of plate, which seem to belong to the interval
between 1660 and 1685, bear a rose-sprig or else a seeded rose,
and a crown on two separate stamps, instead of the usual rose
crowned.   This is as far as the matter can be carried at present,
except to say that a seeded rose crowned is occasionally found
on plate of Dutch manufacture, and that it is no doubt a Dutch
as well as an English mark.   It may be put down to the town
of Dordrecht in Holland, when not found in conjunction with
the Norwich arms.   This mark is not the only connecting link
between Dutch and Norwich plate, for many pieces of known

Norwich work show obvious signs of Dutch influence. There
was a Dutch colony in Norwich with its own church. The
earliest P. Peterson in the city records is styled " Dutchman,"
and became free 10 Henry VII.; and the greater Peter
Peterson left money to " the poorest sort of the Dutch nation "
in the city.

The following list of articles will serve as authority for the
Table in Appendix B, and for what has been stated here as to
the Norwich marks. The letter A for 1565 was discovered, and
kindly brought to the author's knowledge by the late Rev. C. R.
Manning, M.A., who published most interesting lists of the
church-plate in the rural deanery of Redenhall, and in the city
of Norwich itself, with the marks that are to be found on each
piece as well as an illustrated monograph upon the mediæval
patens in Norfolk, of which there is such a remarkable number.
To his papers in the *Norfolk and Norwich Archæological Society's
Transactions*, the author is indebted for many of the above
particulars as to the old goldsmiths of Norwich. The TH above
a star on a plain shield, which is the mark of Thomas Havers,
and is found from 1675 to 1697, is almost the only mark,
except that of Peter Peterson and T. Skottowe, which can be
identified with any certainty.

EXAMPLES OF OLD NORWICH PLATE.

TABLE I. C. 1550—1650.

DATE.	MAKER'S MARK.	ARTICLE.
1565	. . . . .	Communion cup.—Diss, Norfolk.
Do.	Do.	Communion cup and paten. — St. Saviour's, Norwich.
1566	The sun, no shield .	Cup on stem.—Lord Zouche.
1567	Do.	Paten, dated 1568.—Aylsham, Norf.
Do.	Do.	Civic plate, dated 1567.—Corporation of Norwich.
Do.	Estoile of six rays .	Communion cup, undated. — Beighton, Norf.
Do.	Orb and cross, as in 1565 .	Communion cups, all dated 1567.—Buxton, Bressingham, Pulham, and Aylsham, Norf.
Do.	Do.	Communion cup, dated 1568 (formerly at Raveningham, Norf.).

DATE.	MAKER'S MARK.	ARTICLE.
1567	Maidenhead, in plain shield.	Communion cup, undated. — Newton, Booton, and Skeyton, Norf.
Do.	Do.	Do., dated 1567 —Oulton and Cawston, Norf.
Do.	Do.	Do., dated 1568.—Northwold, Norf.
Do.	Do.	Do., undated (formerly at Whissonsett, Norf.).—(Edm. James Coll.)
Do.	Trefoil slipped in plain shield.	Do., dated 1567.—Erpingham, and Beeston Regis, Norf. ; also Wenhaston, Suffolk.
Do.	Do.	Do., undated.—North Tuddenham, Norf.
Do.	Do.	Civic plate, dated 1568.—Corporation of Norwich.
Do.	Flat fish in oval shield.	Communion cup and paten, dated 1568.—Sall, Norf., and St. Martin-at-Oak, Norwich.
Do.	Do.	Communion cup, undated.—Winfarthing, Norf.
Do.	. . . . .	Communion cup.—Kempston.
Do.	Trefoil	Com. cup, dated 1567.—Stockton, Norf.
1568	Orb and cross, as in 1565 .	Standing salt, gift of Peter Reade, who died 1568.—Corporation of Norwich.
Do.	Do.	Communion cup and paten.—St. Martin's-at-Palace, Norwich.
Do.	Cross pattée	Cup and paten, dated 1570.—St. Stephen's, Norwich.
1569	Inscribed "made by John Stone and Robart Stone."	Cup and paten, undated.—Haddiscoe, Norf.
Do.	. . . . .	Mount of stoneware jug.—(Edm. James Coll.).
1570	John Tesmond, free 1566.*	Communion plate.—Norfolk.
1586	Bishop's staff . .	Do.—Norfolk.
c. 1595	. . . .	Four beaker cups. — Formerly at the Dutch Ch., Norwich.
1627	A Pegasus	Flagon, dated 1628.—St. Gregory's, Norwich.
1631	Pelican	Paten.—Blickling.
1632	. . . .	Communion cup, dated 1632. — Great Melton, Norf.
Do.	Lion rampant, in shaped shield.	Do., dated 1634.—SS. Simon and Jude, Norwich.
1633	Arthur Heaslewood, free 1625.	Com. cup, dated 1634.—Aspall, Suff.
1634	. . . . . .	Paten, dated 1635.—Booton, Norf.
Do.	. . . . . .	Paten, undated.—Cawston, Norfolk.
Do.	Lion rampant, in shaped shield, as in 1632.	Paten of Communion cup, dated 1634.—SS. Simon and Jude, Norwich.
1636	A large bird ; probably pelican vulning herself.	Button-headed spoon, dated 1636.—From the Staniforth Collection ; also paten, undated.—Holton St. Peter, Suff.
1637	T S, linked as below, in 1640.	Beaker cups, dated 1638.—Formerly at Meeting Chapel, Great Yarmouth.
c. 1637	Lion rampant, as in 1632 .	Seal-head spoon, pricked with date 1637.—O. Morgan Collection.
1638	Do.	Seal-head spoon, pricked date 1637.—Milbank Collection ; also Com. plate, undated.—South Elmham and Gislingham, Suff.

* R. C. Hope, English Goldsmiths.

DATE.	MAKER'S MARK.	ARTICLE.
1638	A large bird, as in 1636 .	Paten, undated.—Skeyton, Norf.
1640	. . . .	Com. cup, dated 1640.—Lamas, Norf.
Do.	Probably Timothy Skottowe.*	Paten, Riddlesworth, Norf.
1641	cf. 1680 . . .	Cocoa-nut cup.—Marquess of Breadalbane.
Do.	A large bird, as in 1636 .	Communion plate, Norfolk.

TABLE II. C. 1650—1700.

DATE.	MAKER'S MARK.				ARTICLE.
1661					Communion cup, dated 1661.—Southwold, Suff.
c. 1662	Do.	do.	do.		Communion plate, given c. 1662.—Bishop's Palace Chapel, Norwich.
Do.	Do.	do.	do.		Civic plate.—Norf.
c. 1675	Do.				Paten, undated.—Pakenham, Suff. Probably the mark of Thomas Havers, free 1674, d. 1732.
1675	Do.	do.		do.	Paten, dated 1675.—St. Peter's, Hungate, Norwich.
1679	Do.	do.	do.	do.	Paten, dated 1679.—St. Peter's, Mountergate, Norwich.
1680	(As on Bp.'s Palace Chapel plate of c. 1662.)				Cup and paten, dated 1680. — Melton Constable, Norfolk.
Do.		do.	do.		Communion cup, dated 1680. — East Dereham, Norfolk.
1685	As paten, 1675.—St. Peter's, Hungate.				Paten, dated 1685.—Frostenden, Suff. (town mark illegible).
1688			E H		Communion plate, Norfolk.
c. 1689	Do.	do.			Tankard, c. 1689.—Late Rev. H. P. Marsham, Rippon Hall, Norwich.
1691	Do.	do.	do.		Flagon, dated 1691.—St. Michael's-at-Plea, Norwich.
1692	Do.	do.	do.	do.	Paten, dated 1692.—St. Paul's, Norwich.
1694	Do.	do.	†	do.	Basin, dated 1694.—St. Stephen's, Norwich.
Do.	Do.	do.		do.	Com. cup., dated 1694.—Stockton, Norf. This maker's mark occurs by itself on an undated paten at Ellingham, Norf.
c. 1695	As in 1694.—St. Stephen's, Norwich.				Flat-handled spoon. — Late Albert Way, Esq.
Do.	Do.	do.		do.	Do., dated 1695.—Rev. W. Jex Blake, Thurgarton, Norf.
c. 1696	Do.	do.			Fluted porringer, c. 1696.—Late R. Fitch, Esq., Norwich.
c. 1697	Do.	do. . . .			Flat-handled spoon (maker's mark illegible). Per late Rev. C. R. Manning.
Do.	Do.	do.		do.	Communion plate.—Norfolk.

* Timothy Skottowe became free 1617, son of Richard S., mercer.
† One James Daniel, son of Joseph D., took up the freedom of Norwich, 1693.—
Per Mr. R. C. Hope, F.S.A.

CHESTER.

The goldsmiths of Chester, though not mentioned in 1423, are known to have enjoyed chartered privileges from an early date—local tradition says from the time of Edward I. This seems to some extent borne out by references to ancient charters in the records still preserved at Chester. There is a full list of the members of the guild, including its aldermen and stewards, for the year 1585, and a notice of the admission of a brother even earlier, on October 4, 1573. There is certainly reason to believe that a charter granted by Queen Elizabeth was only a confirmation of ancient rights, for there is no mention of the receipt of a charter as if for the first time, nor of the fresh formation of a company in the records of that date.

Minutes regulating the trade are found entered in the books before we come to the above entry of 1573, and they are presumably of earlier date. One of them ordains as follows :—

" It^m that noe brother shall delevere noe plate by him wrought unles his touche be marked and set upon the same beffore deleverie thereof upon paine of forfeture of everie deffalt to be levied out of his goods iij^s iiij^d."

Another quaint notice is to the following effect :—" It is agreed by the consent of the Alderman and Steward of the Gouldsmyths that who soe ever shall make the bell that shalbe made against Shrouftide ffor the Sadlers shall have ffor his paines iij^s iiij^d and yf any of the Compeney shall offend in the premisses shall pay unto the Alderman and Steward ane the reste of the Compeney being iij^s 4^d.

" And yt all the oulde bells shalbe broke and not any of the Compeney to by any to be new burnished or sould to the peneltie aforesaid iij^s iiij^d."

The arms of the company of goldsmiths in Chester are mentioned in a list of 1579; and the coat is the same as that of the London Company, but the crest is different, being a crowned male figure holding a golden cup.*

There are, however, few or no remains of the work of these ancient artificers.

---

* Harleian MSS. 2167, fo. 230.

The large silver gilt mace belonging to the Mayor and Corporation, which was given by the Earl of Derby when he was Mayor in 1668, is stamped with a goldsmith's mark and the arms of the City of Chester as they were then borne, viz., three lions pass., dim., impaled with three garbs, dim. It bears neither leopard's head, lion passant, nor annual date-letter, and the marks which are there have been nearly obliterated when the mace was re-gilt. It is almost too late in the day for the antiquary to suggest that when ancient plate is repaired or regilt, silversmiths should be careful not to deface the marks, for many are past recall. Possibly now that the interest, and therefore value, which attaches to plate of which the precise age and date can be ascertained is better understood, the danger lies in the opposite direction.

On this point the Quarterly Reviewer in 1876 took occasion to make a remark which will be borne out by the experience of every one who has studied the matter, namely, that the region over which the forger seems to have specially delighted to range is England, outside the metropolitan district. The fraudulent worker has availed himself freely of the field afforded by the doubtful provincial marks, and the buyer cannot be too much on his guard against being imposed upon by pieces of apparently ancient plate, bearing what purport to be marks of this description.

Returning to Chester it may be said that its history as an assay town practically commences with its charter from King James II., dated March 6, 1685. The first notice in the books of the Goldsmiths' Company there of the marks to be used, is of the following year, 1686, a date which barely anticipates the modern re-settlement of 1701.

The following extracts are all that relate to the subject down to 1697, when the ancient offices were extinguished :—

1686.	Feb. 1st. And it is further concluded that the Warden's Marks shall be the Coat and crest of the Citty of Chester on two punsons with a letter for the year.	
1687.	Paid for ye tuches engraving	0 12 0
	,, for ye three punsons	0 00 6
1690.	June 2nd. And the same day the letter was changed from A to B, and so to continue for one year.	
1692.	April. Paid for a puncheon and engraving ye letter c . .	1 6
1692.	Nov. Paid Mr. Bullen for copper plate and punson . . .	00 04 00
1694.	Paid Mr. Bullen for a new letter punson	01 00
1697.	Paid for the punson and carriage . , ...	05 8

This points to the adoption of a date-letter in the year 1689, and the regular change of letter each year following. The copper plate bought in 1692 may be the very same that is now preserved in the Chester Assay Office, but none of the punch marks with which it is covered seem referable to an earlier date than 1701.

The alphabet adopted in 1689 is given as of Roman capitals in the minutes ; though this is not, of course, conclusive evidence, especially as it is known that the letters for 1689 and 1690 were not of that character. In any case it must have come to a premature end with the letter I for 1697-8. This fragment of an alphabet is given after the old Norwich alphabets, in Appendix B.

The coat of the city as used at this time for the "punson" was a dagger between three garbs. It so appears on a flagon of 1690, the property of the Independent Chapel at Oswestry. The crest was a sword erect with a band across the blade. These marks disappear in 1701, having probably only been used from 1686 till that year.

A number of so-called "goldsmiths" were free of the city at the end of the seventeenth century as well as at all other periods : but few working craftsmen were among them.* The names of Alex. Pulford, R. Walley, P. Pennington, P. Edwards and P. Pemberton are all that seem known of the latter class. After these comes the Richardson family, which temp. Queen Anne seems to have made nearly all the Chester plate, though some may have been sent from Shrewsbury and other places to be marked there.

EXAMPLES OF OLD CHESTER PLATE.

DATE.	MAKER'S MARK AND NAME.					ARTICLE.
1685				P. Pember-ton.		Church Plate—Chester.
1689					P. Edwards.	Box. — E. H. T. Wynne, Esq.
Do.	Do.	Do.	Do.	Do.	Do.	Monteith, Carrington & Co.
Do.					Ralph Walley, ent. 1682.	Flat-handled spoon.—Noted by author.
1690					Do.	Flat-lid tankard. Independent Chapel, Oswestry.

* See pp. 147-150.

EXETER.

Although there are no records of an assay office at Exeter until the commencement of its modern history, an ancient guild of goldsmiths flourished in that city, and the title " In Aurifabria " given to the Chapel of All Hallows would seem to indicate that a part of the city was called after the guild. Goldsmith Street still exists. Much information concerning early workers in Exeter has been collected—together with many curious historic details—by the Rev. G. F. Chanter, M.A., in a paper from which the following statement has been compiled :

The name John Wewlingworth, a goldsmith, is recorded in the fourteenth century ; those of Thomas Colyne and Thomas White in the fifteenth. In the sixteenth century several goldsmiths were eminent citizens of Exeter and holders of municipal offices ; but neither the mark nor any work of any of them is known. The guild of which they were in all probability members was not incorporated until the year 1700, the reason assigned by Mr. Chanter for this condition being that the Goldsmiths' Company of London had, by their charters, a right of jurisdiction over all workers of gold and silver in the kingdom, and that this central authority of the Metropolitan Company formed a bar to the incorporation of local guilds. The facts recorded in his paper point clearly to a setting in order of the Devonshire goldsmiths about the year 1571, and it may be surmised that officers of the Company were sent at that season to visit the city. A list of goldsmiths practising their craft in that year in Exeter still exists, and contains nine names of masters and three of apprentices. " At the same time," says Mr. Chanter, "there were at Barnstaple, the only other town in Devon at which goldsmiths were to be found, ' John Cotton ' and ' Thomas Mathew.' " The marks of these two makers appear on many examples of plate in their own county and in Cornwall. A year or two later the Exeter town-mark makes its appearance, which was a large Roman capital letter **X** crowned. It is borne by much of the church and domestic plate of the sixteenth and seventeenth centuries in Devon and Cornwall. Examples of it are not uncommonly found even in other parts of England. Hardly any two marks are exactly alike, some of them being surrounded with a plain, others with a dotted circle; whilst in later times than Elizabethan the escutcheon follows the shape of the contained letter. Very occasionally the **X** is not crowned.

In the sixteenth century, the letter, enclosed in a plain or dotted circle, is usually accompanied by two pellets, mullets, or quatrefoils, one in each side angle of the **X**, but in the next century these are wanting. In the case of spoons it is always found in the bowls in the usual place.

It is almost invariably accompanied by a maker's mark, which is the whole, or sometimes what seems to be a part, of the surname, and, in the latter cases, somewhat unintelligible. A good many of the Elizabethan communion cups still to be seen in Exeter parish churches, nearly all of them being of the years 1572, 1573, or 1574, bear the word **IONS** with or without the crowned **X**, and this same mark is found on many village communion cups of the same date and fashion in Somerset, Devon, and Cornwall. At Trevalga it appears on a communion cup and paten with the Exeter mark undated, and at Littleham near Bideford on a cup of 1576. The latest example at present noted is of 1579. We are fortunately enabled to identify this as a mark of an Exeter craftsman of that day by an entry in the Churchwardens' accounts of St. Petrock's in that city, which records that in 1571 they paid " Iohn Ions Goldsmith for changing the chalice into a cup £1 15s. 5d." The cup itself, engraved with the date of 1572 on its paten-cover, and duly marked by its maker, is still the property of the parish, which much values so interesting a possession.

Of several other goldsmiths named in the 1571 list marked work still remains. Richard Hilliard, who appears at its head, and whose birth can hardly have been later than about 1537, is the earliest Exeter man of whose work any example is known. Communion cups bearing his mark—**R. H.** " in a circle with a concentric ring of dots "—are found at Lamerton as well as in other places. His eldest son, Nicholas, was the well-known English miniaturist.

John North was undoubtedly the maker of a chalice at Curry Mallet, Somerset, which is dated 1573 and marked **I. NORTH**; an Elizabethan chalice at St. David's, Exeter, marked **I. N**, may perhaps also be his work.

Steven More, whose mark consisted of **S** in a shield and **MORE** in an oblong, was the maker of chalices existing at Halwell and Slapton, the latter having a very conical bowl and trumpet-shaped stem. Some of his work is stamped with a "quatrefoil charged with a roundel in each foil and in the centre." Mr. Chanter is of opinion that More did not exercise his craft in Exeter itself, but in the neighbouring district.

Two stoneware jugs, formerly in the Staniforth Collection, have respectively **ESTON** and **EASTON** as their makers' marks, whilst a third, formerly in the Bernal Collection, bears the name **HORWOOD**; all these are accompanied by the usual Exeter mark. **ESTON** is found on a communion cup at St. Andrew's, Plymouth, of which the date is 1590, and **EASTON** on the cup formerly at Venn Ottery, dated 1582. A kind of rude letter **C** is usually found with the **ESTON** mark, which may be the initial letter of that maker's Christian name. To another mark, that of one **JASPER RADCLIFF**, as is the case of the **IONS** and **ESTON** marks, it is possible to assign a date, for it appears on a cup at St. Petrock's church in Exeter, engraved with 1640, a date which corresponds well with the year 1637 pounced on an apostle spoon with the same maker's mark, in the Staniforth Collection. These last each bear the maker's initials, on a separate stamp, as well as his name in full, and are good examples of the Exeter mark of the time. The mark on the apostle spoon is as follows:—

That on the cup gives the same initials in monogram instead of with the little flowers between them, the other marks being the same as those on the spoon. An earlier form of the Exeter mark will be found in the Table at the end of this chapter. The name **COTON** occurs upon church-plate of the Elizabethan period sometimes with **D** and sometimes with **I** for initial letter.

Spoons occasionally bear the initials in the bowl, instead of the crowned **X**, and have the whole name on the back of the stem; some seal-headed baluster-ended spoons among the domestic plate still in use at Cotehele, the ancient Cornish seat of the Earls of Mount Edgcumbe, bear **TM** in monogram

within a dotted circle in their bowls, and |MATHEV| on the
stems; on others the word |BENTLY| is to be found, with the
Exeter mark in the bowl. **YEDS**, the mark of John Yeds, who
sometimes spelt his name Eydes, occurs on a flat-stemmed
spoon, and 🜚 on an apostle spoon of the late Mr. Staniforth's,
both bearing the Exeter mark. **OSBORN** with the Exeter
mark is the name on an apostle spoon with a pricked date 1638,
and also on a lion-sejant spoon dated in the same way 1663.

The mark (RO) is on an undated lion-sejeant spoon and (A)
(Edward Anthony died in 1667) on a seal-head spoon,
the first the property of Earl Amherst and the other of the
author : both of these were formerly in Dr. Ashford's collection.
R O perhaps signifies Osborn, but the spoon itself looks rather
of the sixteenth than the seventeenth century.

William Norwood's mark consisted of his surname in full.
He died in 1614.

R H interlinked with **HERMAN** on an oblong and the
Exeter shield was seen on a spoon sold in London in April
1903.

William Bartlett, who died in 1646, left his mark, $\frac{B}{W}$ in a
shield, with the Exeter town-mark, on a spoon in the Bartle
Frere Collection and on a communion cup in Somersetshire.

An assayer was appointed at the same period, and the letters
which, in later examples of the town-mark, sometimes appear
in the side angles of the **X** or below it are considered by
Mr. Chanter to be the initials of the assayer's name.

A third mark, the letter **A**, is found upon some chalices of
1575, and is thought to be a date letter for that year, the rather
that dated chalices of 1576 bear the letter **B**.

It is, however, impossible to say for certain, even after the
examination of so many specimens as are described here,
whether a date-letter was ever used at Exeter. The stoneware
jugs and the communion cups of the Elizabethan period sometimes bear two letters, one of which might be for dating them,
and the other for an initial, but nothing at all like a date-letter
is found upon spoons. On nearly all the communion cups
which bear the mark **IONS**, the Roman letter **I** is to be seen

put on in such a way that it might be a date-letter or the initial letter of the maker's Christian name. But as these were not all made in the same year, and as on other Exeter examples a letter which is known to be the maker's initial is found as well as his name, it would be safe to say that this letter **I** is not a date-letter. **C** is in this way found with **ESTON** or **EASTON**, and **T** with **MATHEV**. The date of the letter is probably 1565 to 1585.* Cups marked by the name **EASTON** or **ESTON** in oblongs in conjunction with the letters **C, G, N,** or **P,** exist at Stockleigh Pomeroy (1576); Cadbury (1582) and St. Andrews, Plymouth (1590); another was formerly at Venn Ottery (1582). Spoons and a cocoanut mount are by the| same maker, the initial of whose Christian name Mr. Chanter supposes to be represented by the letter **C,** the others being probably date-letters. Further research may clear up the question, but it is almost certain that a date-letter was not regularly used in the sixteenth and not at all in the seventeenth century. With the end of the seventeenth century the history of the goldsmiths of Exeter enters upon a fresh stage, and is continued in another chapter. The specimens in the following table bear of course the Exeter mark as well as the maker's and other marks given against each.

EXAMPLES OF OLD EXETER PLATE.

DATE.	MAKER'S MARK.	ARTICLE.
N. D.	⊕	Paten.—Devon.
c. 1571	Ⅱ IONS	Communion cup and paten cover.—Trevalga, Cornwall.
1572	Do.	Do., dated 1572.—St. Petrock's, Exeter.
1574	Do.	Do., dated 1574.—St. Winnoe, Cornwall.
c. 1575	D COTON	Communion cup.—Stoke Rivers, Devon.
c. 1575	I COTON	Do,—Morwenstow, Cornwall.
1575	I IONS A	Cup and cover, dated 1575.—Lympston, Devon.
N. D.	Do.	Do., undated.—St. Kerrian's (now with St. Petrock), Exeter.
1575	IO IONS F	Paten cover, dated 1575.—Duloe, Cornwall.

* Mr. Chanter thinks he is somewhat later.

DATE.	MAKER'S MARK.	ARTICLE.
1576	T MATHEV	Communion cup, with paten cover, dated 1576.—St. Gennys, Cornwall.
Do.	IONS B	Do., dated 1576.—Tamerton Foliot, and Little-ham, Devon.
Do.	ESTON	Do., dated 1576.—Stockleigh Pomeroy, Devon.
Do.	I IONS B	Do., dated 1576.—Perran-Uthnoe, Cornwall.
c. 1580	C ESTON D	Mount of cocoanut cup, no date.—Mrs. Capel Croome.
1581	G ESTON	Mount of stoneware jug, dated 1581.—Menheniot, Cornwall.
1582	EASTON ✸	Cup and paten cover, dated 1582.—Formerly at Venn Ottery, Devon
Do.	IF C ESTON	Communion cup, dated 1582.—Cadbury, Devon.
1590	C ESTON N	Communion cup and cover, dated 1590.—St. Andrews, Plymouth.
c. 1600	R.W	Spoon noted by Author.
1637	I R RADCLIFF	Apostle spoon, pricked date 1637.—Staniforth Collection.
1638	OSBORN	Apostle spoon, pricked date 1638.—Late Sir T. Thornhill, Bart.
1640	R RADCLIFF	Communion cup, dated 1640.—St. Petrock's, Exeter.
1641	W	Seal-head spoon, dated 1641.—Cotehele House.
c. 1688	IP (twice) and lion passant.	Hind's-foot spoon.—Noted by Author.

HULL.

Hull is not known to have marked plate in early times, and it would appear that goldsmiths' work was not carried on there on a large scale in the fifteenth century, from the fact that the wardens of the adjacent church of St. Augustine at Hedon dealt with a comparatively distant goldsmith at Lincoln in the middle of that century, instead of one at Hull only seven or eight miles away. However, there is evidence, somewhat later, that a goldsmiths' company had been in existence for some time prior to 1598.

In that year the Mayor and Burgesses proceeded " as moche as in theim is " to unite several old trade companies of a very heterogeneous character " into one intire company." The companies thus consolidated are enumerated as those of the goldsmiths, smiths, pewterers, glaziers, painters, musicians, stationers, bookbinders, and basket-makers, and they were united "to the intente that the said artes, occupacions, and misteries, may better flourish within the towne of Kingston-upon-Hull." This combined company was to be called "The Company of Goldsmithes and Smithes and others their Bretheren." The Company was to have one Warden over it, and two Searchers, but nothing is said in the ordinances as to the marking of the goldsmiths' wares. The goldsmiths who took part in this "composition" (as it was called), were George Harwood, James Watson, James Carlill, Martin Moone, and Edmond Bussell.* At a still later period we again hear of the "Company of Goldsmiths and Braziers of Hull" as presenting a petition to James II.

In and near Hull there is a good deal of plate, chiefly of the seventeenth century, bearing either the letter **H** (for Hull), or the town arms of three ducal crowns one above the other, or both these marks combined, and in every case accompanied by a maker's mark. These latter are the maker's initials in shields of very marked shape, and all but two of them with some distinguishing emblem, such as a crown, star, or other like addition. It may be further noted that the town mark, whether it be the **H** or the three crowns, always varies in form with the different makers' marks, and so suggests that it was struck by the goldsmith himself, and not by the officials of any local Goldsmiths' Hall. Possibly a similar explanation may account for the varieties of the old Exeter mark, neither Exeter nor Hull possessing touches authorized by the Act of 1423.

Twelve different Hull goldsmiths' marks have been noted on some sixty pieces of plate, dated from 1587 to 1712. Towards the end of the seventeenth century, a date letter seems to have been adopted for some six years, or so, and then abandoned. A communion cup at Trinity House bears the maker's mark **KM** accompanied by a shield of the town arms, and a large capital italic *E*, very like the York letter of 1666. The letters *A*, *D*, and *F*, corresponding in character with the *E*, have also been found in conjunction with the maker's mark **EM**.

---

* *Two Thousand Years of Gild Life.* Lambert, p. 262. In this work the history of the Hull trade gilds is traced, and their ordinances printed.

About 1630 both the **H** mark and the three-crowns mark are found together on pieces of plate, and this seems to indicate the period of change from the one town mark to the other.

The following is a list of examples of Hull-marked plate.

EXAMPLES OF HULL PLATE.

TOWN MARKS.	MAKER'S MARK.	DATE.	ARTICLE.
H . .	(IC) J. Clarkson, or J. Carlile.	1587	Com. cup.—Trinity Church, Hull; also (N.D.) seal-head spoon.—Trin. Ho., Hull.
Do. . .	(PC) Peter Carlill, d. 1598.	1571	Com. cup.—Cabourne, Lincs. Do. dated 1571, Ludford, Lincs.
H and 3 crowns.	(HR) (twice) . . .	1621	Beaker cup.—Trin. Ho., Hull.
H and 3 crowns.	(RR) R. Robinson, free 1617.*	1629	Com. cup and paten.—North Frodingham, Yorks.; and silver mount of cocoanut.—Trin. Ho., Hull.
Do. . .	Do.	1630	Com. cup.—Hessle, Yorks.
Do. . .	Do.	1638	Com. cup and paten.—Burton Pidsea, Yorks.
Do. . .	Do.	1640	Com. cup and cover.—Welwick, Yorks.; also, undated, several com. cups in Yorkshire and Lincolnshire.
3 crowns in bowl, **H** on shanks.	Do. (on shanks) . . .		Two seal-head spoons.—Trin. Ho., Hull.
H (twice)	(CW) Chr. Watson* .	1638	Two com. cups and covers.—St. Mary's, Hull. Also paten, dated 1622.—Lincs.
H (on shank).	Do. on bowl and on shank.	. .	Seal-head spoons.—Trin. Ho., Hull, and T. M. Fallow, Esq.
3 crowns (twice).	(IB) (twice) Jas Birkby, free 1651.*	. .	Two-handled porringer.—Hon. and Rev. S. Lawley.
3 crowns (twice).	(EM) Edw. Mangie, free 1660.*	1666	Com. cup and cover.—Beverley Minster.
3 crowns (once).	Do.	1668	Com. cup.—Marfleet, Yorks.
. . .	(IW) James Watson .		Spoon.

* Per Mr. R. C. Hope, F.S.A.

TOWN MARKS.	MAKER'S MARK.	DATE.	ARTICLE.
3 crowns (twice).	E M (as before) . .	1674	Paten.—Barnoldby-le-Beck, Lincs.
Do. . .	Do.	1676	Com. cup.—Kirk Ella, Yorks.
Do. . .	Do.	1678	Com. cup.—Elloughton, Yorks.
Do. . .	Do.	. .	Small mace, Hull, and several pieces of plate at Trinity Ho., Hull, besides church plate in Yorks. and Lancs. not dated.
3 crowns (once).	Do. and date letter.	. .	Sugar sifter with Frodingham family arms. — Bohn collection; also mace.—Great Grimsby.
3 crowns (twice).	Do. (twice) and date letter.	. .	Com. cup.—Copgrove, Yorks.
Do. . .	Do. and date letter.	. .	Tankard.—Trin. Ho., Hull.
3 crowns (twice).	Tho. Hebden, free 1681.	1689	Peg tankard.—Hedon Corporation.
Do. .	Do.	1689	Tumbler and (not dated) caudle cup.—Trin. Ho., Hull; and paten.—Preston, near Hull.
Do. .	I GA	. .	Com. plate.—Lincs.
3 crowns (once).	KM and date letter	. .	Com. cup.—Trin. Ho. Chapel, Hull. Also com. plate.—Lincs.
	KM		Paten cover.
3 crowns (twice).	K.M. (in pointed shield).	1695	Com. cup.—Skeffling, Yorks.
Do. . .	K.M. (in shaped shield).	1697	Tobacco box.—Trin. Ho., Hull.*
3 crowns (twice).	AB †	1708	Yorkshire ch. plate.
Do. . .	Do.	1712	Lid of Com. cup.—Thorgumbald, Yorks.; and (N.D.) com. cup.—Preston, near Hull; also small tumbler cup.—Late T. M. Fallow, Esq.

* Trinity House bought this of "Mr." Mangie, but his Christian name is not entered in the accounts.

† A. B. is apparently the mark of Abraham Barachin, who was only free of the town of Hull in 1706. The Corporation is found dealing with him in February, 1712—13 (W. H. St. John Hope, *Corporation Plate*, etc., Vol. II., 530), and this is also the date on his work at Thorgumbald, which seems to imply that he made and marked plate between 1706 and 1713 at Hull, in spite of the legislation of 1697 and 1701.

GATESHEAD.

A little plate was made and marked in Gateshead at the same period as in Hull. A tankard with flat lid of the later part of the seventeenth century, and a small mug in the possession of the late Rt. Hon. Sir J. R. Mowbray, Bart., both of which can be traced to a Northumbrian family, have a goat's head couped in a circle and the initials **A·F**, also in a circular stamp, both marks twice repeated. The goat's head was a sort of *rebus* for the name of the town. It is found on a carved chair of the year 1666 in the vestry of Gateshead church; and it also occurs on a tradesman's token of a certain John Bedford, who was one of "the twenty-four of Gateshead" in 1658.*

LEEDS.

The mark of a pendant lamb, like the badge of the Order of the Golden Fleece, is possibly referable to Leeds. It occurs with a maker's mark of **TB** in a heart-shaped shield on a paten at Almondbury Church in Yorkshire, and on a tumbler cup in the author's possession, etc. It is also found with maker's mark of **ST** in linked letters on a shaped escutcheon on a pair of patens, one of which is dated 1702, at Harewood Church in the same county, and with a fleur-de-lys and maker's mark **A.M.** (probably A. Mangey) on a rat-tail spoon in the E. James coll. Another spoon † has the mark in a square shield, maker's mark **BB** in a heart-shaped shield, and an italic *B*.

		Com. cup.—Almondbury, Yorks.
		Also rat-tail spoon.—Richd. Wilson, Esq.
Do.	do.	Tumbler cup.—The Author.
Do.		Pair of patens, one dated 1702.—Harewood, Yorks.

CARLISLE.

A single maker of village church plate in the neighbourhood of Carlisle seems to have used a seeded rose as well as his initials. His name was probably Edward Dalton, and his mark is found on small and rudely made communion cups of

---

* Boyne's *Tokens of the Seventeenth Century.*   † Noted by Mr. Stanyforth.

the early Elizabethan period at Ireby, Bolton, Long Marton, and Cliburn, all in the county of Cumberland.

  Rude Communion cups.—Ireby, Bolton, &c., Cumb.

There are two other cups in Cumberland of precisely the same make and fashion in every detail, both dated 1571, but bearing no marks,—one at Uldale and the other at Lazonby. As it is practically certain that, though unmarked, they must be by the same maker as the Ireby cup and the other examples mentioned above bearing the **ED** mark, the date of the whole group may be considered not to be a matter of any doubt. The seeded rose is taken from the old city arms; and the same mark was used for stamping weights and measures at Carlisle.

LINCOLNSHIRE.

A mark usually found alone, and therefore only a maker's mark, occurs on about sixty Elizabethan communion cups in Lincs., and may pretty safely be assigned to a local craftsman, probably working at Boston or Gainsboro'.* It is on a specimen of 1569 at Osbournby and of 1570 at Auborn and Upton-cum-Kexby, besides being on undated pieces at Haxey, Boultham, Scotton, Lea near Gainsboro', Heapham, and Thimbleby.

 Communion cup, dated 1569.—Osbournby, North Cockerington, and Marsh Chapel, Linc.

    Do.   dated **1570.**—Auborn and Upton-cum-Kexby, Linc.

    Do.   undated.—Haxey, Boultham, Scotton, &c., Linc.

On the two examples of the year 1570, at Auborn and Upton-cum-Kexby respectively, a pointed star, formed of nine small indentations without any shield or escutcheon, is found, as well as the above-mentioned maker's mark, and is accompanied by a capital Roman I. *incuse.*

TAUNTON.

A mark of considerable interest is on a spoon pricked with 1673 for date. It consists of a tun or barrel placed across the stem of a large letter **T,** and no doubt stands for the town of Taunton. It is in the bowl of the spoon, which has **TD** with a fleur-de-lis under the letters on an escutcheon for

---

* "Churchwarden's Accounts of Addlethorpe and Ingoldmells," by Rev. R. Dudding. *Lincs. Notes and Queries,* 1923.

maker's mark on the back of the handle. This spoon is
in the collection of Mr. Chichester, of Hall. The same marks
are found on a beaker in the Staniforth collection; on a
paten dated 1676 at Wootton Courtenay in Somersetshire;
and on spoons of 1686 and 1691, noted by the Somersetshire
Archæological Society.

 Spoon, dated 1673.—C. Chichester, Esq., Hall, Devon.

Do.   Paten, dated 1676.—Wootton Courtenay, Som.
Do.   Communion cup, dated 1678.—Woolavington, Som.

DORCHESTER.

The following mark has lately been identified as that of
Lawrence Stratford, of Dorchester, who in 1579, 1583 and
1593, is mentioned in the Corporation and other records.

 ✠ Paten cover, dated 1574.—Maiden Newton, Dorset.

This mark is found on Elizabethan communion plate in no
less than thirty Dorsetshire parishes; and the pieces are dated
from 1573 to 1578, but most of them are of 1574. His mark is
also found on a communion cup with cover, the latter engraved
1578 at Weston Bamfylde, Som.

One John Stratforde, also goldsmith of Dorchester, is
mentioned in 1526; and a man named Radcliffe, described
as a goldsmith at Dorchester, was fined £5 by the London
Goldsmiths' Company in 1617.

BARNSTAPLE.

A spoon, bearing the following group of marks, viz:—

was made by John Peard, of Barnstaple. He was buried there
15 Nov. 1680.* It is a flat-handled spoon, having some good
chasing on the bowl, and was in the late Mr. R. Temple
Frere's well-known collection.

---

* Communicated by Mr. T. Wainwright, Sec. of the North Devon Athenæum,
Barnstaple.

Besides this John Peard, Mr. Chanter, in his researches, has come upon the names of several goldsmiths who lived at Barnstaple—Thomas Matthews (1563–1611), John Cotton (1567–1601), Peter Quick (1573–1610), besides a younger Matthews (1596–1632), son of Thomas, and a younger J. Peard (1680–1724), among the number. It seems, however, as if only specimens of the work of the three first have survived to this day. For examples of J. Cotton and T. Matthews, the reader is referred to the Exeter chapter. P. Quick's mark ▣ is found on communion plate in Devonshire.

KING'S LYNN.

About twelve examples of church-plate are now known, marked with the arms of Lynn, sometimes accompanied by a maker's mark. This town mark consists of a shield bearing three congers' heads erect, each with a cross fitché in the mouth; and it is found on a communion cup at the church of St. Peter, Southgate, Norwich, and on a paten in St. Nicholas' Chapel, King's Lynn, with the maker's mark, **H. W.** On one piece of plate the Lynn mark has been partly obliterated by the ·Norwich town mark accompanied by the **T.S** maker's mark in an unusual shield and the **S** reversed. The piece may have been repaired at some time at Norwich. The mark has also been noted on two spoons.

SANDWICH.

A very peculiar communion cup of tazza form and early sixteenth century date, at St. Mary's, Sandwich, bears with other marks a lion passant and ship's hull dimidiated and conjoined, from the town arms. Its approximate date is known by the coincidence of the cup exactly matching a tazza, also used as a chalice, at Wymeswold in Leicestershire, which is hall-marked 1512, and also a similar tazza in the possession of Sir S. Montagu, of the year 1500. Both these last mentioned pieces bear an inscription round the bowl in Tudor capitals **SOLI DEO HONOR ET GLORIA,** whilst the Sandwich cup has in the same way the words, also in Tudor capital letters, **THIS IS THE COMMVNION COVP**; but this last inscription can hardly be much earlier than 1550. Mention occurs of a goldsmith of Sandwich in 1514, named Christopher Johnson, *alias* Coper, *alias* Goldesmyth, and called "of Sandwich Goldsmith." This occurs in *Foreign and Domestic State Papers*, Henry VIII., Vol. I., No. 5548.

SHERBORNE.

A mark frequently found by the late Mr. J. E. Nightingale, in Dorsetshire, has now been identified as that of Richard Orenge, of Sherborne.   Of fourteen specimens of Dorsetshire church-plate, three were dated 1574, 1582, and 1607 respectively; and a number of examples have since been found by Rev. E. H. Bates, in the adjoining county of Somerset, dated pieces of 1572, 1573, 1574, and 1603 being amongst them.

   Dorsetshire church-plate from 1574 to 1603.
Somersetshire do. from 1572 to 1603.

It was the example of 1603 at Charlton Horethorne, Som., which led to the identification of the mark, owing to its having a second mark of **RO** struck upon it   All the pieces were found within a moderate distance of Sherborne, and as the result of further local research it was found that one Richard Orenge was churchwarden there in 1585 and 1596, and dealings with him are mentioned in the church accounts of 1594-5.   His will, proved Nov. 24, 1606, describes him as "of Sherborne, goldsmith."   The later examples of his mark after 1582 show a small stem or handle projecting from the device.   This version of the mark may represent a " range," which is the local word for a sort of sieve, whilst the older mark may represent an orange both by way of *rebus* for the maker's name.

CHANNEL ISLANDS.

Although the Channel Islands never possessed an Assay Office, yet a considerable amount of plate, both ecclesiastical and secular, is found with local marks.   These marks are but seldom found in both Guernsey and Jersey.   In some examples the vessels which were stamped with the marks were dated, but the date is that of the gift and not the year of fabrication. In other examples the London marks have been obliterated by local marks, showing that the new marks were not necessarily those of the actual manufacturer.

The majority of secular examples on which these marks are found are the christening cups, which it was the local custom for the godparents to give to the newly born child at its baptism, generally with an inscription and date recording the gift.   Most of these cups were two handled, for beer or cyder : those without handles were for wine.   There was a slight but distinct difference in the pattern of those from Guernsey to those made in Jersey. There are also tankards, candlesticks, wine tasters, snuff boxes, and other articles in every-day domestic use at the time which also bear those marks.

The earliest mark we have met with is dated 1659, and there are a few pieces of the remainder of the seventeenth century. They seemed to be most frequent in the middle of the eighteenth century, and there are few, if any, examples of the nineteenth.

It is probable that the Massacre of St. Bartholomew (1572) and the Revocation of the Edict of Nantes (1685) were responsible for the influx of silversmiths into the Channel Islands, and it will be noted that the French version of a crown and the fleur-de-lis form a favourite feature of the mark.

The actual names of the silversmiths are rarely recorded, and it is only by chance in going through old diaries and documents that it is possible to assign a name to any set of initials.

		ECCLESIASTICAL.	SECULAR.
1.	**TB**	St. Clement, Jersey, 1659.	
2.	**I·G**	Alms dish, St. Helier, Jersey, 1731. Platter, do. do. 1740. Cup, St. Martin, Jersey, 1747. Baptismal dish, St. Laurence, Jersey, 1745. Do. St. Aubin, Jersey, 1750.	Bowl, Jersey, n.d.
3.	**P·A**	Flagons, St. Helier, Jersey, 1766. Baptismal dish, St. Peter, Jersey, 1775. Flagon, Câtel, Guernsey, 1768.	
4.	**P·B**	Paten, St. Ouen, Jersey, 1743.	
5.	**AH**	Two cups, Grouville, Jersey, 1684. (le Thr^er de Grouville m'a produitte).	
6.	**72**	Ewer, Grouville, Jersey, 1781. Baptismal dish, do. 1782.	
7.	**WY**	Platter, Grouville, Jersey, 1688.	
8.	**P·A**	Two cups, St. Helier, Jersey, 1767. Two do. do. 1777.	Christening cup, Jersey, n.d.
9.	**T·D**	Platter, St. John, Jersey, 1677.	Mug, Jersey, n.d.
10.	**P·D**	. . . .	Christening cup, Jersey, n.d.
11.	**T·M**	. . . .	Christening cup, Jersey, n.d.

<table>
<tr><td></td><td></td><td align="center">ECCLESIASTICAL.</td><td align="center">SECULAR.</td></tr>
</table>

12.   . . . .   Christening cup, Jersey, n.d.

13.   . . . .   Christening cup, Jersey, 1763.

14. *a*

   b   *a, b, c*, Platter, St. Helier, Jersey, 1704.   ⎧ *a, b, c*, Wine taster, Guernsey, n.d.

   c   *a, b, c, d*, Two cups, Forest, Guernsey, 1698.   ⎨ *c*, Sugar basin, Jersey, n.d.

   d

15. *a*   (Pierre Maingy), *a, b, c*, Flagon, Forest, Guernsey, 1756.   ⎧ *a, b, c*, Christening cup, Guernsey, 1757.

   b   ⎨ *c*, Christening cup, Guernsey, n.d.

   c

16. *a*   ⎧ *a, b, c*, Two christening cups, Guernsey, n.d.
    a, Christening cup, Jersey, n.d.

   b   *a, b, c*, Platter, Câtel, Guernsey, 1735.   *a, b, c*, Candlesticks, Guernsey, n.d.
a, b, d, Do. St. Sampson, Guernsey, 1757.   *a, b, c*, Tankard, Guernsey, 1735.
a, b, d, Cup, Sark, 1765.   *a, b, c*, Tankard, Guernsey, 1738.

   d   ⎩ *a*, Snuff box, Guernsey, 1760.

17. *a*   Cup, St. Sampson, Guernsey, 1714.

   b

18.   . . . .   Christening cup, Guernsey, n.d.

19. *a*   *a*, Paten, Torteval, Guernsey, 1727.
a, Baptismal jug, St. Andrew, Guernsey, 1729.

   b   *b*, Baptismal jug, Câtel, Guernsey, 1729.

20. *a*   Cup, St. Sampson, Guernsey, 1714.

   b

	ECCLESIASTICAL.	SECULAR.
21.	(Probably John or James Perchard), Platter, Forest, Guernsey, n.d.	
22. *a*		*a, b,* Christening cup, Sark, n.d.
b		*b,* Spoons, Guernsey, about 1760.
23.		Christening cup, Jersey, n.d.
24.		Tankard, Guernsey, 1758.
		Christening cup, Guernsey, 1760.
25.		Christening cup, Guernsey, n.d.
26.		Flat christening bowl, Jersey, n.d. Spoons, Jersey, n.d.
27.		Sugar tongs, Jersey, n.d.
28.		Spoon, Jersey, n.d.
29.		Do. do. n.d.
30.		Do. do. n.d.
31.		Do. do. n.d.
32.		Do. do. n.d.
33.		Christening cup, Jersey, n.d.
34.		Christening cup, Jersey, n.d.
35.		Christening cup, Jersey, n.d.

DOUBTFUL AND OTHER PROVINCIAL MARKS.

The above are perhaps all the local marks which can at present be traced home with certainty, and it will therefore be better to follow Sir Hercules Read's advice, and to exercise

the greatest caution in assigning marks to special localities.   A
wrong attribution only confuses the matter, making ultimate
identification more difficult.   There are, however, other marks,
many of them pretty well known, that are of interest to
us to note.   Of some of them all that can be said is, that as
they are found on plate, often spoons, apparently of English
make, and of the middle of the seventeenth century, the articles
bearing them probably escaped more regular marking owing to
the social disturbances with which their makers were surrounded.
Others occur often in certain districts, and become almost identified with the localities in which they are found.

A well-known mark is a fleur-de-lis within a plain or sometimes beaded circle.   It is often found in the bowls of spoons ;
e.g., in the Staniforth and Octavius Morgan collections.   Another
is a cross in a beaded circle, pricked date 1628.

Yet another is a small and indistinct mark of a circle crossed
and re-crossed with lines, some of them running, like the spokes
of a wheel, to the centre.   This was found in the bowl of a
spoon in the collection of the late Mr. R. Temple Frere, and
of one at Cotehele : both of these have a small sitting figure
like Buddha, by way of knop, and both have as maker's mark
the letters RC with a five-pointed star between them on the
back of the stems ; a seal-headed spoon also at Cotehele bears
the same marks, and 1647 for date pricked upon it.

A fourth mark of the same kind is four small hearts arranged
with the points inwards, so as to form a sort of quatrefoil.

Other such devices and monograms in great variety occur,
sometimes the same monogram, in the bowl and on the handle
of the spoon, two or even three times repeated in the latter
position.   Amongst them is occasionally to be recognised the
registered mark of some London maker, but so seldom that in
most cases they may safely be said to be of provincial origin,
and of about the period we have mentioned.   Exceptions may
of course be found : a few are certainly of the earlier part of
the same century ; but as a general rule, these marks may be
referred to the reign of Charles I., or the Commonwealth.

The most puzzling doubtful mark that has ever come under
the author's notice is on a piece of church-plate at Bradford.
It bears a catherine wheel, and italic *h* for date-letter, and as
maker's mark the letters SS crowned on a shield repeated
twice.   It is dated 1691, and is almost certainly of Yorkshire

make, for the same set of marks are to be found on plate
at Todwick, also in Yorkshire, and of the very same year, 1691.
The maker's mark is one of those registered at Goldsmiths'
Hall, but may well belong to a provincial maker for all that;
and as the catherine wheel occurs on more than one specimen
of plate, and in more than one form, it is in all probability the
local mark of some northern town.

It is given in the following list together with a few others:

S   ⊕   [MORE]   Communion cup, Eliz. band.—Halwell, Devon.

[RF]   [R]   Paten, dated 1570.—Worc.

[JG]   [Sta]   Com. cup.—N. Wales.

[GP]   ⊛   Com. cup and cover, dated 1572.—Stanton, Glouc.

[M]   ⊕   Church-plate, dated 1574—75—76.—Somersetshire.   The second
mark is often found sideways.

[N]   In bowl and twice on handle.   Maidenhead spoon (from Edkins collection).—The Author.

[R]   In bowl.   [T]   [⬧]   [T]   On handle.   Seal-head spoon, c. 1620.—The Author.

⊛   ⚓   ⊛   Paten, c. 1680.—Hants.

[ℏ]   [SS]   [⊗]   [SS]   Church-plate, dated 1691.—Bradford and Todwick, Yorks.

[BB]   [STER LING]   [BB]   Ben Brancker, born 1675.—Church-plate, Liverpool.

[RH]   [STER LING]   [RH]   Spoon, c. 1698.—Private Coll.

[BH]   [Sta]   Church-plate, dated 1718.—Yorks.   Also porringer, dated 1717,
late Chancellor Ferguson.

[SH]   STER LING   [SH]   Rat-tailed spoon.—T. M. Fallow, Esq.

Some spoons with very similar marks to the example of 1620
above were in the late Mr. R. Temple Frere's collection. They
are of about the same date, one being pricked 1629.

The following marks occur mostly alone as follows :—

⊛   Paten, c. 1510.—Norfolk.

[RI]   (Probably Richard Hilliard,* 1548-94.)   Com. cup.—N. Devon.

[CR]   Cup and paten, dated 1569.—Lincoln.

[JL]   (Probably John Lyngley).   Com. cup, c. 1570—N. Wales.

[B]   Elizabethan com. cup at Snave, Kent, with the letter R reversed.

* Per Rev. J. F. Chanter.

Com. cups, with Eliz. bands, dated 1570–76–77.—Cricklade St. Mary and Somerford Keynes, Wilts. ; Winchcomb, Glouc. ; and others sometimes with another mark—**W.**

 Com. cup, dated 1571.—Upcerne, Dorset.

 Com. cups, dated 1573 and 1577.—Swepston and Dadlington, Leics. ; Preston Bagot, Warwicks, 1591.

 Com. cup, Exeter pattern, dated 1574.—Curry Mallet, Som.

 Com. cup, Exeter pattern, dated 1574.—Exton, Som.

 Com. cup, Exeter pattern, dated 1574.—Libstock, Som.

 Com. cup, c. 1575.—Fransham.

 Early Eliz. com. cup and cover.—Preston-on-Stour, Glouc.

 (Probably Wm. Mutton of Chester, d. 1588). Com. cup, given 1574.—Clynnog, N. Wales ; and church-plate in Chester.

 1587.—Long Itchington, Warwickshire.

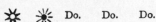 Paten-cover, dated 1575.—Nolton, S. Wales. This mark occurs on much church-plate in St. David's Diocese, dated from 1574 to 1587.

 Com. cup, c. 1575.—Moulton.

 Com. cups, c. 1600.—Yorks.

 Com. cup, c. 1600.—Hants.

  Do.   Do.   Do.

 (Probably Griffith Edwards). Com. cup, c. 1610.—Lancs.

 Com. cup, 1619.—Gosberton, Linc.

 Twice. Com. cup, c. 1620.—Hants.

 Alms box, c. 1638.—Hants.

 Alms dish.—St. Mary, South Baily, Durham City ; and on the smaller mace at Wilton, Wilts. The latter piece is inscribed Ric. Grafton fecit, 1639.

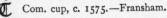 Paten, c. 1640.—Tisbury, Wilts.

 Com. cup, 1650.—Hants.

 Three times. Com. cup, c. 1650.—Hants.

 Com. cup, c. 1655.—Wraxall, Dorset.

 (Probably Thos. Vyner, see p. 42.) Gold chalice of middle of seventeenth century.—Chapel Royal, St. James's Palace.

RA as in 1660 (p. 438), only mark on cup and paten.

 Mace, c. 1668.

Much church-plate bearing these marks is found in Suffolk. Both occur together on church-plate in Norfolk and on a spoon in a private collection, c. 1668, with a rude leopard's head.

 (Probably Wm. Cossley of Gloucester, d. 1691.) Four times on flagon. —S. Nicholas, Glouc. Given 1668.

 (Probably Nath. Bullen of Chester, adm. 1669, steward 1683).—S. Mary's, Chester. Also spoon in private coll.

 Flagon, c. 1672.—Portsmouth.

 Candlesticks, c. 1675.—Som.

 Plate, c. 1675.—Bath.

 (Perhaps Rt. Harstronge). Norwich-shaped cup. Paten, dated 1676.—Cambridgeshire.

 Com. cup, seventeenth century.—Som.

 Three times. Church-plate.—Yorks.

 Com. cup and paten, dated 1677.—Bishop's Knoyle, Wilts. Also paten, undated.—Winkfield, Wilts.

 Paten, 1680.—Hants.

 Four times repeated. Com. cup, 1680.—Cheshire.

 Spoon, pricked date 1685.—Dunn-Gardner Coll. Charles II. tankard 1683.—Per Mr. L. Reid.

 Inscribed 1695.—Yorks. Church-plate.—Yorks.

 c. 1695. Church-plate.—Yorks.

 Twice. Church-plate.—Som.

 Flagon, given 1700.—Corsley, Wilts. Also paten given 1704. Kingston Deverill, Wilts.

 Four times ; c. 1700. Church-plate.—Som.

 Set of church-plate, dated 1706.—Bruton, Som.—Also paten undated.—Ansford, Som. Also cup and its salver with casing of pierced work.—Colerne, Wilts. Also paten, dated 1707.—Poulshot, Wilts.

 Cup, inscribed 1710.—Yorks.

 Four times. Beaker, 1728.—Kirkham.

 . . . . Cake basket, circa 1740. Lord Cromwell.

 Three times. Cup, renewed 1744.—Yorks.

 Three times. Warden's staff.—Ashton-under-Lyne.

Three times. Warden's staff.—Oldham.

Three times. Com. cup, c. 1760.—Lanc.

Only. Cup.—Harrington.

Sometimes the same single mark, usually a very indistinct one, occurs on a good many examples of church-plate in the same neighbourhood. The late Mr. Trollope found a sort of

indistinct rose very prevalent in Leicestershire, and also instances
of a leopard's head uncrowned without any other mark, on
village church-plate; just as Mr. Nightingale found in Dorsetshire a quantity of examples of the marks engraved on p. 124
and p. 126. Mr. Trollope also found in Leicestershire the
curious mark of a small and indistinct shield flanked by the
letters **N** and **G,** one on each side of it. In two examples of
this last the letters appear upside down and turned the wrong
way. This mark also occurs in Derbyshire and Nottingham-
shire. The leopard's head uncrowned (struck from punches of
different sizes) is also found in Lincs., Notts. and South
Yorkshire. The indistinct rose mark found by Mr. Trollope in
Leicestershire prevails widely on Elizabethan church-plate in
Warwickshire, and the cinquefoil or five-petalled flower, as at
Long Itchington, Warwickshire, 1587, is also a recognised
Warwickshire mark. It is not unfrequently found on seal-head
spoons in the Midlands. Both the two last-named marks,
occurring as they do near Coventry, may be referable to that
city or to goldsmiths there.

The **G** and fleur-de-lys (the latter mark at first *incuse,* but
later in a circular punch) may be Ipswich town marks at
different periods, the **G** indicating the older form of the name
of that town—Gippeswic. On one piece of church-plate in
East Anglia both the **G** and fleur-de-lys are found together,
accompanied by the initials **TS.** in monogram, the latter
apparently a maker's mark. Occasionally a wavy cross is
indented by the side of the **G.** This seems, like the Norwich
zigzag, to be the mark made in scraping silver for assay, and
tends to confirm the idea that the **G** is an official, and not a
private mark. Further examples of these marks, having been
found by Mr. Hopper during his researches among the church-
plate of Norfolk, corroborate this suggestion, made by Mr.
Fallow, more than twenty years ago, when he first came across
the mark somewhere in East Anglia. Besides the **G** and the
fleur-de-lys marks a sexfoil, the letter **W** under a crown, and
the mark of four hearts in a cross are common on church-plate
in parts of Suffolk. Picton, in his *History of the Municipal
Records of Liverpool,* says nothing of a goldsmiths' company
having existed in that city. Yet there seem to have been
several goldsmiths working there besides those mentioned on
page 147. On Oct. 5, 1698 : " The Council orders that a piece

of plate be made for the use of St. Peter's Church to the value
of twelve pounds, and that Mr. Robt. Shields, goldsmith, take
the direction of the minister about the fashion thereof." * This
Rt. Shields is described in the Register as "silversmith of
Water Street." His will was proved in 1710 by his widow.
Unfortunately the plate made in 1698 has disappeared, or
it may have been "remodelled" like that at other Liverpool
churches in the nineteenth century.† It is possible that Rt.
Shields' mark is the **SH** on the spoon mentioned on page 129.
Another well-known Liverpool silversmith was Ben Brancker,
who not only supplied London pieces to a Liverpool church,
but whose mark **B.B** with a bird above, probably the Liverpool
"Laver," is found on church-plate in that neighbourhood. This
list will be prolonged by the experience of most readers of this
volume.

It remains to notice in conclusion another very interesting
and perhaps unique mark, though it can hardly be called a
doubtful one. It will be remembered that no provincial offices
seem to have had any right to mark plate from 1697 to 1701,
and the inconvenience to the trade and the public occasioned
by this has already been noticed. It appears, however, that
plate made in the provinces between those years is not entirely
unknown, as a saltcellar (see engr. chap X., art. Salts), in the
form of a lighthouse, formerly amongst the family plate at
Tredegar, will show. It bears for goldsmiths' marks the three
words Britan, Rowe, and Plin°, each on a plain oblong punch
(like the word Radcliff on page 115), and it may be safely
attributed to the year 1698 or the early part of 1699. The
marks taken together indicate that it was made by one Rowe
of Plymouth, of silver of the then new Britannia standard.
The piece is not only of considerable historical interest, as will
be seen later on, but of great rarity as a specimen of provincial
silversmith's work and marking at a period when but little was
made, and none could by proper right be marked, except in
London.

The following table gives a summary, in a form convenient
for reference, of all that has been said about ancient provincial
English hall marks, and some illustrations of those which are
of the most importance to the collector of old plate :—

---

* Picton's *History of the Municipal Records of Liverpool*.
† Per Mr. Henry Peet.

TABLE OF MARKS USED BY THE PROVINCIAL ASSAY TOWNS PRIOR TO 1701.

TOWN.	TOWN MARK.	STANDARD.	DATE MARK.	MAKER'S MARK.
YORK.	Leopard's head crowned and fleur-de-lis dimidiated in circular stamp. *	None.	Annual letter.	Initials or symbol, or the two combined.
NEWCASTLE-UPON-TYNE.	Three castles in shield. Found in c. 1665-85. c. 1685. 1686-97. 1664, 1672.	A lion passant turned to the right on an oval punch is found in 1664 and 1672 with the single castle.	None.	Ditto.
NORWICH.	City arms on shield, being a castle in chief and lion passant in base. 1566. 1624. 1692.	A seeded rose crowned. Found 1630-40 and circa 1690. Sometimes a crown and a seeded rose (or else a rose-sprig), on separate punches, circa 1660-85.	Annual letter, with interruptions.	Ditto.
CHESTER.	Coat and crest of the city on two punches till 1686, viz., 3 lions pass. dimid. per pale with 3 garbs dimid., and a sword erect for crest, From 1686-1701, see p.112.	None.	Annual letter from 1689 to 1697.	Ditto.
EXETER.	Letter X crowned. 1572. 1640. c. 1620-1700.	None.	Doubtful.	Ditto.
HULL.	Before c. 1620.	None.	None.	Ditto.

* Five different punches were used for striking this mark. They are, however, so indistinct, as a rule, that an attempt to indicate them

CHAPTER V.

THE PROVINCIAL ASSAY OFFICES AND THEIR MARKS SINCE 1701.

THE ACTS OF PARLIAMENT ESTABLISHING THEM—YORK—EXETER—CHESTER—
NORWICH — NEWCASTLE-UPON-TYNE — BIRMINGHAM—SHEFFIELD—TABLE OF
MODERN PROVINCIAL MARKS.

WE come now to the re-establishment of provincial assay
offices in 1701 and 1702 under the circumstances mentioned at
an earlier page. The Acts of Parliament* which appointed
York, Exeter, Bristol, Chester, Norwich, and Newcastle-upon-
Tyne for the assaying and marking of wrought plate may be
taken together. They incorporated the goldsmiths and plateworkers of each place under the name of the " Company of
Goldsmiths," for carrying out their various provisions. No
plate was to be made less in fineness than the standard of
the kingdom, and the following marks were appointed :—The
worker's mark, to be expressed by the two first letters of his
surname, the lion's head erased, the figure of Britannia, and
the arms of the city where such plate shall be assayed, and a
distinct and variable letter in Roman character, which shall be
annually changed upon the election of new wardens to show
the year when such plate was made. Every goldsmith and
silversmith in each city was required to enter his name, mark,
and place of abode with the wardens, and not to stamp plate
with any other mark than the mark so entered. The assay-
master was to be sworn in before the mayor.

It seems almost certain that Bristol† never exercised the
power of assaying plate, and Norwich soon abandoned the
privilege. The other places named carried the provisions of
the Act into effect by establishing assay offices, none of

---

* 12 & 13 Will. III., cap. 4, York,
Exeter, Bristol, Chester, and Norwich.
1 Anne, cap. 9, Newcastle-upon-Tyne.

† There are some anomalous marks
originally found by Mr. Fallow in 1879,
on a spoon at the Temple Church,
Bristol, which might be taken for Bristol
hall-marks, but the civic archives of the
period do not record the establishment
of any Goldsmiths' Company, nor the
swearing-in of any assay master before
the mayor, as prescribed in the Act.

which, however, except that of Chester, still continue in active operation.

In 1773, after an inquiry by Parliament into the working of these offices, Birmingham and Sheffield were appointed for the same purpose; goods made in these towns having, as it appeared, until that time, been sent at great inconvenience and expense to Chester or London to be marked. The provisions of the Act appointing them are, speaking generally, much like those by which the older assay offices were regulated, except that the later provisions were more precise and complete, an advantage to be attributed, it is pertinently suggested by Mr. Ryland in his *Assay of Gold and Silver Wares*, to the opposition of the Goldsmiths' Company in London, which was a little jealous of rival offices. Out of this wholesome rivalry arose the parliamentary inquiry and report, without which the statute establishing the offices at Sheffield and Birmingham would have been far less complete and satisfactory.

A few words must be said about each of the provincial offices in turn, except Bristol, which may be considered to be disposed of; premising that the later general Acts of the last and present century, regulating the goldsmith's trade, and noticed in Chapter II., apply to all offices alike.

YORK.

This office has had a somewhat fitful existence. Re-established in 1701, it is mentioned with the rest in the Acts of 1739 and of 1784, although it was certainly not working at the time of the parliamentary inquiry of 1773. Perhaps the Company was stirred up by it a little, and started work again in 1774 with a new alphabet. At any rate, at the commencement of the last century its operations were more regular, and there is a record in existence of the work done from 1805-21.* From this it appears that duty to the amount of about £300 a year was paid through the York office for work sent to be assayed by some four or five silversmiths; the articles made by them consisting of household plate, now and then some articles of communion plate for a York church, and some wedding rings;

---

* One of the register-books of the Assay-Office was in the possession of the late Canon Raine, who kindly furnished the following notes from it.

"a coffin plate" is mentioned more than once. Later on, in 1848, it is again to be heard of, but working as before on a very small scale. A return then obtained shows it to have assayed on an average no more than 2000 ounces of silver, besides an insignificant quantity of gold in the five preceding years; and in 1856 the office had practically ceased to exist. The annual date-letter seems to have been changed more or less regularly from 1800, and perhaps earlier, nearly down to the time of the discontinuance of the office, but owing to the loss of its books and the small quantity of work done, it is hopeless to attempt any complete list of the letters used in the previous century. An alphabet of Roman capitals seems to have been commenced about 1774, and to have been continued for some ten letters, but in 1787 a new one was begun with a capital Roman A and continued with small letters till we reach a capital M for 1798. Then follow capitals in order. A letter J is found with the York arms and the incused King's Head, and seems to fit in pretty well with other pieces of known date. From the M of 1798, the Tables given in the Appendix are certainly correct.

The distinguishing mark of the York office was a shield of the arms of the city, which are five lions passant on a cross.*

The usual Britannia standard marks and perhaps Roman capitals for date-letters were used from 1701 to 1720, but a court-hand letter I appears on one Communion cup dated 1706, and on another dated 1714, both in Yorks; and the same letter is found on an undated tumbler-cup in the author's possession. All these pieces have for maker's mark **LA** for John Langwith in a shield with escalloped top. Afterwards, from the time of the restoration of the old sterling standard for silver in the year 1720 until about 1847, York, like some of the other provincial assay towns, used the leopard's head, but without any very good reason after 1739, though the practice is defensible until then according to the wording of the Act which restored the old standard.

A well-known legal authority characterises the addition of the leopard's head mark in these cases as an unnecessary incumbrance;† and from 1739 this is clearly the case. The

---

* See Table at the end of this chapter.　　† Tilsley's *Stamp Laws*.

Act of 1720 restoring the old sterling standard with its proper marks says nothing about the provincial offices, which accordingly adopted the ordinary London marks ; but in 1739 these matters were further regulated by 12 Geo. II. c. 26, and standard gold and old sterling silver were to be marked " as followeth (that is to say) with the mark of the maker or worker thereof, which shall be the first letter of his Christian and surname, and with the marks of the Company of Goldsmiths in London, viz., the leopard's head, the lion passant, and a distinct variable mark or letter to denote the year in which the plate was made ; or with the mark of the worker or maker, and with the marks appointed to be used by the assayers at York, Exeter, Bristol, Chester, Norwich, or Newcastle-on-Tyne." A reference to the Acts of Will. III. and Anne shows the marks appointed to be the arms of the cities, and a variable mark or letter, which from 1720 should properly have been used, in conjunction with the mark of the maker.

The names of the York goldsmiths which can be traced in the early part of the eighteenth century, are as follows :—

Daniel Turner, free 1700, died 1704.
Joseph Buckle, free 1715, died 1761.
John, son of Marmaduke Best, free 1694.
William, son of John Williamson, free 1694.
Clement Reed, free 1698.
John Morrett, jeweller, free 1721.

Thos. Parker, silversmith, son of Edward Parker, free 1721.
Wm. Hudson, silversmith.
John Bentley, silversmith, 1725.
John Busfield, goldsmith, son of Wm. Busfield, goldsmith, free 1727.
Jonathan Atkinson, goldsmith, 1735.

The above-named J. Buckle, J. Busfield, and W. Hudson, together with a Stephen Buckle, son of Joseph Buckle, are all who voted as goldsmiths according to poll-books of 1741. S. Buckle was apprenticed to Cookson of Newcastle in 1732, for seven years. He was not the only Newcastle apprentice from York, in fact York men entered their marks at Newcastle, and the York trade seems to have gone there for all the middle years of the century.

Goldsmiths are found voting also in 1758, amongst them Stephen Buckle again. In 1774 John Prince of Coney Street appears with others. Several names occur in 1758, 1774, and 1784; but few or any of them were working goldsmiths, though two or three were watchmakers.

EXAMPLES OF MODERN YORK PLATE.

INSCRIBED DATE.	DATE LETTER.	MAKER'S MARK.	ARTICLE.
		YORK BRITANNIA STANDARD.	
1702	(B)	BE Probably John Best, free 1694	Racing cup, inscribed "Maggot on Kiplingcotes, 1702."—Rise Park, Hull.
N. D.	(C)	LA John Langwith,* free 1699.	Yorkshire church-plate.
1705	Do.	·Bŭ· Probably Wm. Busfield, free 1679.	Com. cup and paten. — St. Michael's, Malton.
1714	(d)	Do. . .	Com. cup.—Hauxwell. Also cup inscribed 1706.—Yorks.
N. D.	Do.	Do. . . .	Tumbler cup.—W. Cripps, Esq., C. B.
N. D.	(D)	Wi Probably Wm. Williamson, free 1694.	Yorkshire church-plate.
N. D.	(F)	John Langwith .	Do.
N. D.	(G)	LA in plain pointed shield, probably another mark for J. Langwith.	Do.
N. D.	Do.	Do. . . .	Do.
N. D.	Do.	WI Wm. Williamson .	Com. cup.—Kirkby Ravensworth.
		REVIVED YORK OFFICE.	
N. D.	(D)	I·H / I·P Hampston and Prince.	Noted on a piece of Yorkshire family plate.
	(F)	Do. . . .	Flagons, dated 1780. — All Saints', North Street, York.
1780	(G)	Do.	Paten, dated 1780.—All Saints', North Street, York.
1780(twice)	(H)	Do. . . .	Paten, dated 1780.—Kirkburton, Yorks.
1784 Do.	Do.	Do. . . .	Communion cup, dated 1784.— Huntington, Yorks.
	(J)	H+P Do.	Communion cup. — Holme-on-Spalding Moor, Yorks. This piece bears the incused King's Head mark.
1787	(A)	Do. . . .	Yorkshire church-plate.
1788	Do.	Do.	Yorkshire church-plate.
1791	(d)	Do. . . , .	Flagon, dated 1791.—St. John's, Ousebridge, York.
1792	(e)	Do.	Flagon, dated 1792. — Kirk Deighton, Yorks.
N. D.	(i)	Do. . . .	Communion cup. — Askham Bryan, Yorks.
N. D.	(k)	Do.	Yorkshire church-plate.

For a continuation of York date-letters to 1856, when the Office closed, see Appendix B, Modern York date-letters. After the Revival c. 1774 the city mark is often omitted.

---

* He registered his mark also at Newcastle-on-Tyne, see p. 151. His mark occurs alone on a plain com. cup at N. Otterington, Yorks. A com. cup at Sherburn is marked IL in a sort of quatrefoil shield, probably his old sterling mark.

The firm of Prince was in 1805 Prince & Cattle, and until 1807, when it is Richard Cattle.   From 1808 Cattle & Barber till 1814; then Barber & Whitwell, with $\frac{RC}{JB}$ and $\frac{JB}{WW}$ for marks. The only other makers of the early part of the nineteenth century were W. Astley of York, and G. Booth of Selby.

EXETER.

This city availed itself forthwith of the powers conferred upon it in 1701, and its office carried on work until 1885. Eleven goldsmiths met on August 7th, 1701, and proceeded to elect William Ekins and Daniel Slade as their first wardens. Steps were taken to procure a convenient house for an assay office, resolutions for its management passed, and punches for marking plate ordered in November, one Edward Richards having been appointed assay-master in the preceding month, an office which he seems to have held till January, 1707-8.

Early in the following year such goldsmiths of Devon, Cornwall, Somerset, and Dorset, as had not yet entered their marks, were notified that the office was ready to assay plate according to the Act of Parliament.

The distinguishing mark of the office is a castle of three towers.   At first the mark used was a somewhat bold one : the two outer towers, which are lower in the shield than the central one, are bent inwards towards it, and the shield is shaped ; but after 1709, or thereabouts, the shield was reduced in size, and was made of the ordinary plain angular heraldic pattern, with the towers smaller and upright.   In the case of both the shields there is what might be taken for a small flaw running from the central tower to the bottom of the shield ; this in reality denotes the partition *per pale* of the field on which the triple castle of the city of Exeter is borne.   (See Table at end of chapter.)

The minutes of the year 1710 give the first actual mention of the alphabetical date-letter, which was for that year K; we may say, therefore, that the first alphabet used was one of Roman capitals, and commenced on Michaelmas Day, 1701, in which year the observance of the Act became obligatory.   The letters A and B are found in ornamental or shaped shields.   Later on the letter was changed on August 7th.   It will be seen from the Table given at the end of this volume that Roman letters, capital or small, were used until the commencement of an alphabet of old English capitals in 1837; we shall also notice that since 1797 the same letters have been used as at the Goldsmiths' Hall in London. This Table shows them just as they are written in the minute-book, which is the safest course to adopt, even though printed letters may not be exact facsimiles in all cases of the punches used. The letters for the present century, and perhaps a longer period, have been in square shields with the corners slightly cut off, or sometimes with the upper corners of the shield cut off and the lower end rounded, as best suited the letter enclosed.

The early makers' marks were, in compliance with the Act, the first two letters of the surname; but, most unfortunately, a leaf is now missing from the Company's record-book which contained the first twenty-three entries. The earliest of those left is the twenty-fourth, entered on Nov. 13, 1703, and is that of "Mr. Peeter Eliot of Dartmouth," whose mark was to be **EL**.

Other marks follow at the rate of one or two in each year, entered by goldsmiths residing at Launceston, Plymouth, Dunster, Truro, and other places as well as Exeter, some examples of which may be given, viz. :—

DATE.	MARKS.	NAME.	DATE.	MARKS.	NAME.
1703	EL	Peeter Eliot, of Dartmouth.	1705	Ha	Thos. Haysham, Bridgewater.
Do.		Jacob Tyth, of Launceston.	1706	SA	Thos. Sampson, Exon.
Do.	:As:	Mary Ashe, of Launceston.			
1704	Wj	Richard Wilcocks, of Plymouth.	Do.	SY	Pent. Simons, Plymouth.
Do.	HO	Mr. Richard Holin, of Truro.	1710	TR	Geo. Trowbridge, Exeter.
Do.	SW	Edward Sweet, of Dunster.			
Do.	VA	Richard Vavasor, of Tottoness.	1711	Jo:	—— Tolcher, Plymouth.
1705	Ca	Robert Catkitt, Exon.	1714	Wo	Andrew Worth.
Do.	St	James Strong, Exon.	Do.	Sy	Pent. Symonds.
Do.	Ma	John Manby, Dartmouth.			
Do.	RE	Thos. Reynolds, Exon.	1716	Lo	Abraham Lovell.
Do.	PL	Richard Plint, Truro.	1723	JE	John Elston, junior, Exon.

In 1723 may be noted an instance of the change to the
initials of the Christian and surname when John Elston,
junior, of Exeter, entered as his mark *JE* under a small
heraldic label on a shield. An example of his work remains in
the shape of a plain two-handled cup of 1725, at the Baptist
Chapel in South Street, Exeter, of the congregation of which
he was a member.

The other makers, whose names and marks are entered or
re-entered up to about 1730, are :—

John Suger, 1712.	Jane Maryen, 1722.
Adam Hutchins, 1714.	Abr. Lovell, 1722.
Peter Arno, 1716.	Samuel Wilmott, 1723.
Pent. Symonds, 1720.	Philip Elston, 1723.
Joseph Collier, 1720.	John Webber, 1724.
John Reed, 1720.	Thos. Clarke, 1725.
John Marsh, 1720.	Anty. Tripe, 1725.
Zachariah Williams, 1720.	Jas. Marshall, 1725.
Sampson Bennett, 1721.	Jas. Strong, 1726.
Samuel Blachford, 1721.	John Boutell, 1726.
Henry Muston, 1721.	John Torkington, 1727.
James Stevens, 1721.	Sam'. Blachford, 1728.
Andrew Worth, 1721.	Richard Plint, 1729.

These all used from 1720 the usual initials on old sterling
silver, or the first letters of the surname when new sterling was
worked. But singularly little of their plate has ever been found
by the author in Devon, Cornwall, or elsewhere. The names of
some Exeter goldsmiths in 1701 are recorded, but not their
marks nor whether they were all goldsmiths by trade. They
are John Audry, Wm. Briant, Nichs. Browne, Wm. Drake,
John Ekins, John Elston, Thos. Foote, Joseph Leigh, John
Mortimer, E. Richards, Danl. Slade and Edw. Spicer.*

Some rites and ceremonies took place on the initiation or
new members of the Company, for, say the minutes of Aug. 7,
1767, "at this Court appeared Mr. Thomas Kaynes and Mr.
Richard Freeman, Paid their coltage, and were duly shod."

From the parliamentary return of 1773 we find that the
Company then consisted of five members (but seventeen
plateworkers' marks were registered, being those of tradesmen
residing at Plymouth and Dartmouth, as well as Exeter itself),

---

* *English Goldsmiths*, by R. C. Hope, F.S.A.

and that the average weight of plate assayed in each of the seven preceding years was about 4479 oz.* The names of 1773 were: Edward Broadhurst, Roger Berryman Symons, Mr. Welch, Jason Holt, James Jenkins, Thos. Thorne, Benj. Symons Nathan, John Tingcombe, David Hawkins, John Brown, Thos. Strong, William Harvey, Thos. Beer, and Richard Bidlake, all of Plymouth or Plymouth Dock, William Eveleigh of Dartmouth, and Richard Jenkins and William Coffin of Exeter. According to the later return of 1848, the office was carrying on an extensive business, more, in fact, than any other provincial office except Sheffield. It had stamped, in that year, no less than 44,451 oz. of silver, besides 266 oz. of gold. In 1856 its business had somewhat increased, but almost all its work came from a single firm at Bristol.

At last in the early part of 1885, this firm finding it more convenient to have its produce assayed elsewhere, the Exeter office was closed from want of work, and it is not likely ever again to be re-opened.

Except for the city arms, the marks of Exeter are the same as those given in the Table for York; and, as at York, the Exeter office adopting the leopard's head in 1720, continued its use long after the passing of the Act of 1739. It may be again remarked here that the retention of that mark after 1739 by those offices was probably owing to a misinterpretation of the Act of that year, which no doubt intended to confine the use of the leopard's head for the future to London. It was used at Exeter on an unusually large oblong stamp, and forms a fine bold mark; indeed this may be said of all the punches employed in this city, the lion's head erased being of large size, and the Britannia on a rectangular punch as bold in its way as that adopted for the leopard's head crowned in 1720. This last was still in use in 1773, but was discontinued a good many years ago. The date of its discontinuance is not recorded in the books of the Company, and is unknown.

---

* Nearly all of it buckles, tea trays or spoons.

EXAMPLES OF MODERN EXETER PLATE.

DATE.	MAKER'S MARK.	ARTICLE.
1701	Fo	(Perhaps Thos. Foote, d. 1708.) Flat-stemmed spoon.—Rev. Canon Raine, York.
1702	El:	(Probably Elston, of Exeter.) Large paten or ciborium, with cover.—St. Martin's, Exeter.
1704	. . . .	Straining spoon.—St. Petrock's, Exeter.
1705	FR	(Perhaps Richard Freeman.) Tankard, dated 1706.—St. Goran, Corn.
Do.	WI	(Probably Zachariah Williams, before 1720.)
1706	El	(Elston, as in 1702.) Plain alms-dish or large paten.—St. Mary Arches, Exeter.
1709	FV	Communion cups, with covers.—St. Stephen's, Exeter.
Do.	El	(Elston, as in 1702.) Patens on feet, dated 1710.—St. Sidwell's, Exeter.
1710	SW	(Edw. Sweet, of Dunster.) Flat-stemmed spoon.—From the Staniforth Collection.
1712	Ri	(Probably Edw. Richards, of Exeter.) Flagons dated 1712.—St. Sidwell's, Exeter. Church plate, 1709.—Bentham, Yorks.
Do.	El	(Elston, as in 1702). Communion plate.—Padstow, Corn.
1713	Do. . .	Paten, dated 1713.—Mamhead, Devon.
1714	Do. . .	Large paten, on foot, dated 1714.—St. David's, Exeter.
1715	TR	(George Trowbridge, of Exeter.) Salver.—Redruth, Corn.
Do.	Mo	(John Mortimer, of Exeter.) Flagon.—Do.
Do.	Sy	(Pentecost Symonds, of Plymouth.) Paten.—St. Gennys, Corn.
1716	Do. . .	(Do.) Communion cup and paten.—Redruth, Corn.
1717	Do. . .	(Do.) Paten.—Tamerton Foliot, Devon.
1718	Ri	(Richards, as in 1712.) Two-handled cup and cover, dated 1717.—St. David's, Exeter.
1719	Bu	(Probably John Burdon.) Com. plate.—Exeter.
1725	SB	(Probably Saml. Blachford.) Flagon, given 1726.—Lelant, Corn.
Do.	JE	(John Elston, jun., of Exeter.) Two-handled cup, dated 1725. — Baptist Chapel, Exeter. Also 1729, paten.—Melksham, Wilts.
1726	JB	(Probably John Boutell, ent. 1726.) Paten.—Ashbrittle, Som.
1728	J E	(Elston, jun., as in 1725.) Paten, dated 1728.—Morwenstow, Corn.
Do.	P.E	(Philip Elston, ent. 1723.) Flagons, dated 1728. — St. Edmund's, Exeter.
1729	. . . .	Small communion cup for the sick.—St. Martin's, Exeter.
1730	. . . .	Straining spoon.—Exeter Cathedral.
1731	JC	(Probably Joseph Collier.) Plain chocolate pot—noted by author.
1734	SB	(Sampson Bennett, ent. 1721) Paten, dated 1736.—Constantine, Corn. NOTE.—This maker's mark appears alone on cup and paten, dated 1726.—Lelant, Corn.
Do.	ER	(Probably E. Richards.) Church-plate.—Devon.
1735	TC	(Probably Thos. Coffin.) Com. plate.—Exeter.

Date.	Maker's Mark.	Article.
1740	*JB* (crowned)	Flagon, dated 1741.—Talland, Corn.
1743	*JB*	(Probably John Boutell.) Pair of collecting basins with handles.—St. Ives, Corn.
1747	*TB*	(Probably Thos. Blake, 1724—59.) Alms-bowl, dated 1747.—Crediton, Devon.
1748	*J·S*	Small paten on foot.—St. Martin's, Exeter.

CHESTER.

The office established here in 1701 has been at work ever since, though sometimes on a small scale ; but the growth of Liverpool and Manchester has not added as much as might have been supposed to its work in recent times. The date-letters, as in the case of the other provincial offices, commence with the Roman capital A in 1701, and they have been changed regularly every year on July 9th, until 1839, since which time the change has been made the same day in August. Its business was at one time very small, dwindling from 824 oz. in 1766, to no more than 161 oz., or the weight of a single salver of moderately large size, in 1769 ; but a great increase seems then to have suddenly taken place, for, in 1770, 1771, and 1772 it stamped about 2200 oz. a year. The Company consisted of nine goldsmiths and watchmakers in 1773, though only two of them were goldsmiths by trade, Joseph Duke and Geo. Walker, and even Joseph Duke does not seem to have had a registered mark of his own. Seventeen plateworkers' names had been entered there from Manchester, Liverpool, Shrewsbury, Birmingham, Chester, and Warrington. Their names were William Hardwick of Manchester, Ralph Wakefield of Liverpool, T. Prichard of Shrewsbury, Joseph Walley of Liverpool, John Gimlet of Birmingham, Christopher Thinne of Liverpool, Geo. Walker of Chester, Geo. Smith of Warrington, William Pemberton of Chester, Richard Richardson of Chester, Ralph Walker of Liverpool, James Dixon of Chester, John Wyke and Thos. Green of Liverpool, Bolton and Fothergill (no doubt of Soho), and Gimble and Vale of Birmingham.

The fidelity and skill with which the operations of the office were conducted, secured the special commendation of the Parliamentary Committee in that year.

At the date of the next inquiry, in 1848, it again appears to have been doing but little business; 656 oz. had been the greatest total weight of silver stamped as liable to duty in any of the five preceding years, to which must be added an average of about 200 oz. of gold wares. It however received from Liverpool and from a maker at Coventry a large number of watch-cases for assay, which did not increase the duty payable through the office, though it added greatly to the business done in it. In 1885 it was stamping some 25,000 oz. annually of silver, and 10,000 oz. of gold of this description of wares.

Its distinguishing mark was at first a shield bearing the city arms of three lions passant guardant dimidiated, *per pale* with three garbs also dimidiated. This was the coat used, it will be remembered, before 1686. It was again changed in the later part of the eighteenth century for a dagger erect between three garbs ; but it is known that the Goldsmiths' Company continued the use of the old arms some years after the city had adopted the new coat. It seems somewhat uncertain in what year the new coat first found favour at the Hall ; the present assay-master is of opinion that the change was made in the year 1784 or thereabouts, and this is corroborated by the occurrence of the letter "i," which appears to be the letter for that year, accompanied sometimes by the old and at other times by the new arms. The rest of the marks correspond with those of the other provincial towns, the leopard's head having been used from 1720—1839, when it was discontinued.

Partly owing to the smallness of the business done at Chester, and partly owing to the loss of one of the books, which contained the records from 1803 to 1818, it is a matter of some doubt and difficulty to give a list of the date-letters used. Those from 1701 to 1726, and from 1818 to the present day, are recorded ; but in the interval between 1726 and 1818 the only information the books afford is that from 1726 to 1803 they were regularly changed. Happily, however, the letters for certain years are known in other ways, such as the italic *M* for 1738-9, the Roman capital u in the next alphabet for 1772-3, and a small

Roman i found without the king's head, and also with the king's head in intaglio. This last must therefore almost certainly be the letter for 1784; and it would seem to indicate that at Chester the preceding alphabet was shortened by two letters, and a new cycle commenced in 1776 with the same letter as that used in London. This uniformity of practice has not, however, been maintained. The evidence of the marks found on a number of undated specimens of plate corresponds with that afforded by the fixed points mentioned; and our Table will be practically a safe guide to the Chester date-letters. It will of course be seen that the lengths of the alphabets have necessarily had to be cut to fit, but the position of any given letter will not be affected by more than a year, and the uncertainty occasioned is therefore of little consequence. The only well-known smiths of the Queen Anne epoch are the Richardsons, whose marks constantly occur 1714-48. It is Ri in the Britannia period, and appears as two Roman capital letters RR linked back to back, on old sterling silver after 1720. The word Sterl. as a second mark occurs with the Ri mark on the mace dated 1718 at Carnarvon. It is also found about 1683 with other makers' marks.

EXAMPLES OF MODERN CHESTER PLATE.

DATE.	MAKER'S MARK AND NAME.	ARTICLE.
c. 1701	**Bu** Nathl. Bullen, adm. 1669.	
Do.	**Ta**	
Do.	**Co**	
Do.	**Gi** Perhaps Tho. Gittens, of Shrewsbury, 1695—1741.	Entries on the Chester copper plate, c. 1701. These are not here given in facsimile.
Do.	*Sa* Perhaps Thos. Sandford, of Shrewsbury, 1682—1741.	
1703	Bu N. Bullen . .	Spoon.
Do.	Pe Probably P. Pennington, see p.112.	Paten.—N. Wales.
Do.	Ro Thos. Robinson, 1682—1710.	Spoon.
1704	Ri Richard Richardson.	Large oval snuff-box, dated 1704.—Corporation of Chester.
1705	Pe as above in 1703 . .	Spoon.
Do.	. . . . .	Communion cup.—Worthenbury, Wrexham.
1709	. . . . .	Silver oar.—Corporation of Chester.
1713	Ri Richard Richardson.	Communion cup and flagon, dated 1716.—St. Peter's, Chester.
Do.	. . . . .	Spoon, dated 1715.—Corporation of Chester.

Date.	Maker's Mark and Name.	Article.
1714	. . . . . .	Paten.—St. John's Blue Coat School, Chester.
1715	. . . . . .	Communion plate.—St. Mary's, Chester.
1717	. . . . . .	Alms-dish, dated 1719.—St. John's, Chester.
1718	. . . . . .	Communion cup, dated 1720.—St. Bride's, Chester.
1719	(Ri) Richardson . .	Spoon.—C. S. Mainwering, Esq.
1721	Ri, as in 1713 . . .	Tumbler-cup, Shoemakers' Guild, Carlisle.
1722	. . . . . .	Punch-ladle, dated 1722.—Corporation of Chester.
Do.	(Ma) Thos. Maddock . .	
1723	Ri, as in 1719 . .	Punch-ladle, dated 1724.—Duke of Westminster, Eaton House.
Do.	. . . . .	Paten.—St. Michael's, Chester.
1728	. . . . . .	Cup.—T. Hughes, Esq.
Do.	(R) R. Richardson .	Cup for sick communicants, given 1728.—Kendal, Westmoreland. Others of 1732, 1734, and 1736, all by Richardson, are at Whitehaven and Workington, Cumberland, and Kirkby Lonsdale, Westmoreland.
1730	. . . . . .	Silver seal.—Corporation of Chester.
1736	RR, as above in 1728 .	Communion cup and paten, dated 1735.—Poulton-le-Fylde, Lanc.
1738	RR, as above in 1728 .	Paten, dated 1737.—Chester Cathedral.
1739	(RR)	Com. cup.—N. Wales.
1748	(R·R)	Mark noted by author.
1762	RR, as above in 1739 .	Com. plate noted by Author.
1769	Do.	Paten, given 1767.—Tattenhall, Cheshire.
Do.	. . . . .	Sugar-ladle.—W. R. M. Wynne, Esq., Peniarth.
1770	(WP) Wm. Pemberton .	Com. plate.—N. Wales.
1772	. . . . . .	Date-letter U.—Report of Parliamentary Committee.
1774	(GW) Geo. Walker .	Plain skewer.—The late E. W. Colt, Esq.
1775	(CW)	
1779	(IW) Jos. Walley . .	
1786	(TP) T. Pierpoint . .	Beaker.
1790	(I·H) Isaac Hadwine .	
1793	(RI) Rd. Jones . .	Cup, dated 1795.

NORWICH.

As to modern Norwich, nothing seems to be known except that on July 1, 1702, one Robert Harstronge was sworn in assayer of gold and silver plate to the Company of Goldsmiths in that city. This is the only evidence at all that any step was taken to put in force the powers of the Act of Will. III.; it is clear that as far as Norwich is concerned, the privileges con-

ferred by it soon fell into disuse, and for a very long time past
no plate has been assayed there. Mr. Hopper, however, has
come across several pieces among Norfolk church-plate, showing
that some assaying was done. In one case the cup has the
Britannic mark, lion's head erased, date-letter **A** and **H A** as
maker's mark; the paten has besides the Norwich castle and
lion.

Also a spoon with the following anomalous marks has been
noted—leopard's head, letter **N**, lion erased, the words **F Sil**
and the maker's mark **ID**, as in 1696, p. 109.

NEWCASTLE-UPON-TYNE.

Although this town, lately become a city, was one of those
anciently appointed to have a touch of its own, it was not
included amongst the offices re-established in 1701. Its claims
were, however, made good in 1702, upon a representation of its
ancient rights and of the ruin impending over its goldsmiths
and their families in consequence of its omission from the list. A
Company was then established in the same manner as in the case
of the other offices; and its first assay-master, Francis Batty,
senior, was elected June 24, 1702. This was the first meeting of
the new Company, and Robert Shrive and Thomas Armstrong
were elected wardens for the ensuing year. Those who attended
the meeting were Francis Batty, Eli Bilton, Robert Shrive,
Richard Hobbs, Thomas Leightly and Alexander Campbell,
admitted in 1701, all of whom have been mentioned already
except Campbell. Francis Batty was succeeded in his office in
1707 by Jonathan French, and French in his turn by Thomas
"Heweson" in 1712. Mark Grey Nicholson was sworn assay
master in 1718, and William Pryor in 1722.

The Newcastle mark is a shield with three towers or castles
upon it, being the city arms, and is found at first with an ornamental, afterwards with a heart-shaped shield, later still with a
shield having a pointed base almost the shape of an egg. The
other marks are the same as those of the other provincial offices,
the leopard's head crowned being used from 1720. Of late it
was the only provincial town retaining that mark, but the crown

upon the leopard's head served to distinguish it from the London
stamp for some time from 1822 onwards. Some quite modern
Newcastle plate shows the leopard's head uncrowned. The lion
passant is to sinister, that is to say, turns to the right, from 1721
to 1727.

The annual date-letter was probably changed on June 24th
till 1707, since when it has been changed on May 3rd—the first
alphabet, covering the years from June 1702 to 1720, did not run
in the regular order of the letters. The letter M is the first one
entered in the books. It was for 1712 and the only other letters
of this alphabet so mentioned are P, Q, D, E, for 1717, 1718,
1719, 1720. The letters were old English capitals, though they
are not given so in the minute books. From this time the
alphabets seem to run continuously onwards to the present time
except for a break between the years 1760 and 1769, which is
evident from, but otherwise unexplained by, the books of the
Company, which are fairly complete as regards the minutes ;
but the first Assay Book commences only in 1747 and ends in
1755, whilst the next does not begin till 1761. Old English
capitals were used until 1864, when a small letter (Roman)
was introduced.

The letters in the tables at the end of the volume are given
as they appear in the books of the Company, but some of the
earliest alphabets were, as we have seen above, certainly not
exactly as there shown. The Roman capital letter S for 1784
is found with and also without the Sovereign's head, which last
is in intaglio when it occurs on plate of 1784 or 1785, as it is on
London plate of the same years. More than one instance of
the incused form of duty mark coupled with the letter U of the
year 1786 is known. It is also open to doubt whether a letter
T was ever used in 1758. And there is much to indicate that
the letter S was in use for a longer period than the year 1757
only.

The chief silversmiths of the time of Queen Anne were
Francis Batty, senior, who has already been mentioned as the
first appointed assay-master in 1702 ; Eli Bilton, Thomas
Hewitson, and John Ramsey, who have also been mentioned
before. Jonathan French, who became free in 1703, was
apprenticed to Robert Shrive in 1695, and died in 1732, and one
John Younghusband became free in 1706 and died in 1718. A

younger Francis Batty takes up the freedom in Nov. 1708, and died in 1727-8, and the mark of a younger John Ramsey is found 1721-28. Eli Bilton died in 1708. The leading men of the reigns of George I. and George II. were James Kirkup, who, apprenticed to Bilton in 1705, became free in 1713 and worked to 1753; Isaac Cookson, whose name occurs from 1728-54; William Dalton, 1724-67, John Langlands, 1754-78, and William Partis of Sunderland, the mark of the last-mentioned occurring 1733-59. Other makers' marks are of very rare occurrence. All the above makers use their initials as marks for old sterling plate and the first letters of their surname on new sterling. Robert Makepeace, admitted in 1718, was before 1739 using his initials in old English characters: and afterwards plain Roman capitals as **R·M**: he died in 1755; and James Crawford, 1763-95, puts his initials **IC** under a two-handled covered cup. Isaac Cookson and John Langlands have their initials under a gem ring, the former using italics after 1739. Payments for assays occur in 1717, and some following years as made by John Langwith and Joseph Buckle, both of York. W. Beilby, from 1739-61, sent work from Durham; and Samuel Thompson of the same city from 1750-85. One Wilkinson sends some from Sunderland 1747-52, as well as Thomas Partis, 1720-33, and the William Partis mentioned above. Other outsiders sent very trifling amounts.

At Newcastle itself, too, the bulk of the trade was very much in a few hands. By far the largest business was that of Isaac Cookson, followed by his apprentice and journeyman, John Langlands. Cookson averages 7,100 oz. from 1747 to 1754. In 1778 John Langlands, senior, seems to have taken John Robertson into partnership, and in 1793 to have been replaced by his son, John Langlands, junior, who only, however, remained with John Robertson for two years, till 1795. Langlands and Robertson then separated and carried on distinct businesses, both of which were considerable ones. John Robertson worked thus till 1801, and John Langlands, junior, till 1804. The latter was succeeded by Dorothy Langlands, 1804 to 1814. John Robertson's initials are found associated with those of David Darling in the single year 1795. Langlands and Robertson averaged 11,700 oz. from 1778 to 1784, when the plate duty was imposed; and

6,500 oz. from 1784 to 1793. Lesser men than these, such as James Kirkup, Robert Makepeace, John Kirkup(1753-74,d.1784), son of James Kirkup, James Crawford, David Crawford, and later on William Stalker and John Mitchison (1775-1784) in partnership, as well as Pinkney and Scott also partners, were all in fair work, as will be seen by the subjoined list, which gives the necessary details as to their dates. The rest were but very small workers indeed, only made buckles and other such small wares.

In 1773 Newcastle shared with Chester the praise bestowed on the operations of the goldsmiths' companies in these two places, but the Company consisted of three persons only, viz., John Langlands, John Kirkup, and another. There were, however, nine makers' marks registered, their owners residing at Newcastle itself, Durham, and Sunderland ; and it then stamped about 12,000 oz. of silver per annum (of which John Langlands averaged 10,000 oz.), but no gold. These persons were Langlands, Kirkup, Samuel James, James Crawford, John Jobson, and James Hetherington, all of Newcastle ; together with Samuel Thompson of the city of Durham, and John Fearney of Sunderland. The office was doing much the same amount of business in 1848, and also in 1856, when such matters were again made the subject of parliamentary inquiry ; but it was finally closed in 1885. The last assay made of silver had been on April 22, and of gold on May 2, 1884. No gold plate was assayed here before March 1785.

EXAMPLES OF MODERN NEWCASTLE PLATE.

DATE.	MAKER'S MARK AND NAME.		ARTICLE.
1702	[Bi]	Eli Bilton, d. 1708 . .	Flat-handled rat-tailed table-spoons.—Rev. J. Arlosh, Woodside, Carlisle. Also com. cup, dated 1702.—St. Mary, South Baily, Durh. city.
Do.	[Ho]	Richard Hobbs . .	1702—1718.
Do.	[Sh]	Robert Shrive . .	
1703	. .	Eli Bilton, as in 1702	Church-plate, dated 1704.—Stanhope, Durham.
Do.	[Ra]	John Ramsey, free 1698.	Com. cup.—Kirkbampton, Cumb.
Do.	[Ba]	Francis Batty, senior .	Com. cup and cover.—Askham, Westmor.
1706?	. .	Eli Bilton, as in 1702 .	Paten, dated 1707.—Kirkandrews-on-Esk, Cumb.
1707	. .	do. . . .	Com. cup, dated 1707.—Castle Eden, Durham.
1711?	[Yo]	John Younghusband .	Flagon, dated 1711.—Askham, Westmor.
Do.	Do.	do. . . .	Tumbler-cup, given 1711—Taylors' Guild, Carlisle.
Do.	Do.	do.	Com. cup.—Ainstable, Cumb.
Do.	[Fr]	Jon. French . .	Com. Cup, dated 1712.—Esh, Durham.
Do.	[Ba]	Francis Batty, junior, adm. 1708.	Paten, dated 1712.—Ormeside, Westmor.
1712	Do.	do. . . .	Com. cup.—St. Michael's, Bongate, Appleby, Westmor.
Do.	Do.	do.	Small tumbler, used as com. cup.—Blawith, Lanc.
Do.	. .	J. Younghusband, as in 1711.	Flagon and paten, dated 1712.—Sherburn Hospital, Durham.
Do.	[LA]	John Langwith, of York, 1717—22.	Com. cup, dated 1708.—Newton Kyme, Yorks.
1713	[Ki]	James Kirkup (new sterling).	Made much plate, 1728—1748.
c. 1717	[BV]	Joseph Buckle, of York.	Occurs c. 1717.
1718	[C]	John Carnaby, adm. 1718 (new sterling).	
1719	[Ma] [Ba]	Robt. Makepeace, jun., and T. Batty, jun.	Punch-bowl, dated 1719.—T. T. Dale, Esq.
1720	[WW]	Wm. Whitfield . .	Old English capitals, from 1739.
1721	[FB]	Francis Batty, junior 1708—27—8 (old sterling).	Tankard, dated 1722.—Hexham Abbey. Also paten, dated 1722.—Wooler, Northumb.
Do.	Do.	do. . . .	Communion plate, dated 1722.—St. John's Newcastle.
Do.	[JR]	John Ramsey, jun. . .	
1722	[JC]	John Carnaby, adm. 1718 (old sterling).	Com. cup.—St. Mary's, Gateshead.
1724	Do.	do.	Paten.—St. Nicholas', Newcastle.
Do.	[WD]	Wm. Dalton . . .	1724—1739.

DATE.	MAKER'S MARK AND NAME.	ARTICLE.
1724	(JF) Jonathan French . .	Com. cup —Dufton, Westmor.
Do.	. . Francis Batty, junior as in 1721.	Com. cup.—Bowness, Cumb.
1725	(CB) (GB) Geo. Bulman . .	1725—1739.
1727	T P Thos. Partis, of Sunderland.	Flagons, dated 1727.—Ryton-on-Tyne, Durham.
1728	. . . . . .	Paten, dated 1728.—Ch. Ch., Tynemouth.
Do.	(IF) Jonathan French . .	
1729	(JM) Th. Makepeace, 1729—1738.	
1730	(IC) Isaac Cookson, 1728—1739.	Paten.—Barningham, Yorks.
Do.	(IK) James Kirkup . .	Tankard, dated 1730.—Corpn. of Carlisle.
1731	(RM) Robt. Makepeace . .	Flagon, given 1731.—Rothbury, Northumb.
1732	Do. do. . . .	Paten, dated 1734.—St. Mary's, Morpeth, Northum.
1733	(WP) William Partis, of Sunderland.	1733—1759.
1738	. . Isaac Cookson, as in 1730.	Com. cup.—Allendale Town, Northumb.
Do.	(WB) (IB) Probably W. Beilby and Co., Durham, 1739—61.	Hand candlestick.—Ravensworth Castle. Also 1728, cup dated 1730. —St. Andrew's, Newcastle.
1739	(WB) (JB) Do. do.	Occurs in and after 1739.
Do.	(GB) Geo. Bulman, 1738—1743.	Tumbler cup, late T. M. Fallow, Esq.
1740	(WP) William Partis, of Sunderland	Flagon, dated 1740.—Boldon, Durham.
Do.	(SB) Steven Buckle, of York.	Flagon.—St. Martin-cum-Gregory, York.
Do.	. . James Kirkup, as in 1730.	Flagon.—Kirkandrews-on-Esk, Cumb.
Do.	(WD) William Dalton . .	Com. cup, dated 1741.—Burgh-by-Sands, Cumb.
1743	(IC) Isaac Cookson, from 1739.	Com. cup, dated 1743.—Birtley, Northumb. Also flagons, dated 1743. — Hartburn. Also 1740, com. cup.—Halton, Lanc.—Also 1742, com. cup.—Yorks.
1744	Do. do.	Porringer.
1746	Do. do. . . .	Com. flagon, dated 1746.—Holy Trinity, Goodramgate, York.
Do.	. . Wm. Partis, as in 1740	Paten, dated 1747.—All SS., Cockermouth.
1748	. . Isaac Cookson, as in 1742	Paten.—Ripon Minster.
Do.	(WB) Probably Wm. Beilby, of Durham, d. 1765.	Com. cup.—St. Mary-le-Bow, Durham city.
1749	Do. do. . . .	Com. plate.—Yorks.
1750	Do. do. . . .	Chocolate pot, dated 1750.
1754	(IL) (JG) John Langlands and John Goodrick, d. 1757 ; 1754—1757.	Paten, dated 1755.—Elsdon, Northumb.
Do.	(R·M) Robert Makepeace . .	d. 1755.
1755	. . J. Langlands and J. Goodrick, as in 1754	

DATE.	MAKER'S MARK AND NAME.		ARTICLE.
1757	**I·K** / **JK**	John Kirkup, 1753—1774, d. 1784.	Flagon, given 1763.—Long Benton, Northumb.
Do.	*RB*	Name unknown.	
Do.	**I·L**	John Langlands, 1757—1778.	Com. flagon, given 1761.—Billingham, Durh. Com. plate dated 1762.—Blyth, Northumb. Flagon, dated 1760.—South Shields. Com. plate, given 1762.—Enderby, Leics.
1759	.	John Langlands, as in 1757.	Com. flagon.—Calverley, Yorks. Also com. cups, dated 1764.—Hexham, Northumb. Also alms-dish, given 1765.—Castle Eden, Durh.
1763	**S I**	Sam. James . . .	1763—1765.
1765	**P I**	Peter James . .	1765—1767.
1766	**I·F**	John Fearney . .	1760—c. 1773.
1768	**DC**	David Crawford .	1768—1784.
1769	I·K	John Kirkup, as in 1757.	Com. plate given by Bp. of Durham.—St. Anne's, Newcastle.
1770	. .	John Langlands, as in 1759.	Flagon, dated 1771.—Rokeby, Yorks.
1772	**I·H**	Jas. Hetherington	1772—1782.
Do.	**I·H H·E** **H&E**	Jas. Hetherington.	1772—1782. Marks used when he was for a short time partner with a man named Edwards.
Do.	. .	John Langlands, as in 1759.	Flagon, St. Giles', Durham.
Do.	**IC**	James Crawford, 1763—1795.	Flagon, dated 1773.—Holy Trin., Whitehaven. Also 1773, com. cup, given 1773.—Belford, Northumb.
1774	. .	John Langlands, as in 1759.	Flagon, dated 1776.—St. Andrew's, Newcastle.
Do.	.	do. . . .	Paten, dated 1776.—Bothal, Northumb.
Do.	. .	James Crawford, as in 1772.	Com. cup.—Laithkirk, Yorks.
Do.	*ST*	Samuel Thompson, of Durham, 1750—1785.	Spoons.
Do.	**WS IM**	Wm. Stalker and John Michison.	1774—1784.
1776	. .	J. Langlands, as in 1757.	Com. plate.—Yorks.
1777	**PB**	Peter Beatch, c. 1777.	
1783	**I·L I·R**	Langlands and Robertson, 1778—1795.*	Communion cup, dated 1784.—Ovingham, Northumb.
1784	Do.	do. . . .	Alms-dish, dated 1784 (no king's head.—St. Andrew's, Newcastle.
Do.	**L&R**	Another mark for Langlands and Robertson	
Do.	▨	do. . . .	Spoon, late T. M. Fallow, Esq.

* Also entered at Goldsmith's Hall, London, in March, 1780, "by letters of attorney."

DATE.	MAKER'S MARK AND NAME.	ARTICLE.
1784	I·M John Mitchinson, 1784 —1792.	
Do.	RP RS Pinkney and Scott, 1779 —1790.	Flagon, dated 1785 (king's head in- cuse).—St. Mary's, Gateshead.
1787	R P R S Pinkney and Scott, 1779 —1790, as in 1784.	Paten, dated 1788.—St. Andrew's, Newcastle.
Do.	P&S Another mark for Pink- ney and Scott.	
1788	. . Langlands and Robert- son, as 1783.	Com. cup, dated 1789.—Holy Island.
1790	CR Christian Reid, from 1790.	Flagon.—Greystoke, Cumb.
Do.	RP Robert Pinkney . .	1790—1825.
Do.	RS Robert Scott . .	d. 1793.
1793	TW Thos. Watson . .	1793—1845.
1795	IL in oval. J. Langlands, Junr.	1795—1804.
Do.	IR DD John Robertson and David Darling.	Com. cup and cover, dated 1795.— Chester-le-Street, Durh.
Do.	R&D Another mark for Robertson and Darling.	. . . .
1800	I·R John Robertson, 1796 —1801.	Alms-dishes, dated 1800.—St. John's, Newcastle.
Do.	DD David Darling . .	Church-plate, Hants.
Later.	DD TB Darling and Bell . .	
1801	AR Anne Robertson . .	
1810	D·L in oval. D. Langlands .	1804—1814.
1819	CR DR Reid & Co. . .	

SHEFFIELD AND BIRMINGHAM.

Lastly, we have Sheffield and Birmingham, established by an Act of 1773 as the result of the parliamentary inquiry to which we have so frequently referred. This Act* enabled them to assay silver goods only, but both offices are now empowered to stamp gold. A district of thirty miles radius round the town was originally assigned to Birmingham, and one of twenty miles to Sheffield, for the better support of the offices.

Owing to their comparatively recent establishment their work has not yet acquired any archæological interest; but their marks are—the maker's, which is to be the first letters of his Christian and surname, the lion passant, a distinct variable

---

* 13 Geo. III. cap. 52 (local).

letter to be changed annually upon the election of new wardens for each company, and the mark of the Company. This mark is a crown in the case of Sheffield, whilst an anchor distinguishes articles assayed at Birmingham. For silver of the higher standard, the Britannia stamp alone, unaccompanied by that of the lion's head erased, has been used by these offices. The Birmingham date-letters have been regular alphabets, but at Sheffield for the first half-century the letters were selected at random; since 1824, however, both have used regular alphabets, though Sheffield has here and there omitted some letters. In both cases the letter is changed in July, at Sheffield, on the first Monday in that month, on which day the annual meeting of the Company is held. These offices have both carried on an extensive and well-conducted business, earning the commendation of those whose duty it was to report upon the working of the provincial assay offices, before a Select Committee of the House of Commons, which sat in 1856. The Diet is sent up from both Sheffield and Birmingham to the Mint for trial annually as their Act directs. This is one of the improvements and safeguards owed to the more modern legislation under which they were established. The other provincial offices are only liable to the obligation of sending their diet up to the Mint, "to be tried as the pix of the coin of this kingdom is tried," if required to do so by the Lord Chancellor, and it appeared in 1856 that it had never been sent for within living memory from any of them.

EXAMPLES OF SHEFFIELD PLATE.

DATE.	MAKER'S MARK AND NAME.		ARTICLE.
1773	I W & Cº	Probably John Winter & Co., ent. 1773.*	Table candlesticks.—Col. A. Tremayne, Carclew.
Do.	Do.	. . . . .	Do.—New College, Oxford.
1775	G:A & C	Geo. Ashfield & Co., ent. 1773.*	Do.—Rev. E. F. Wayne.
1777	H·T T·L	In plain square . . Tudor and Leader, ent. 1773.*	Sauce boats, drapery over medallions.—Capt. M. Longfield.
1785	I P & Cº	John Parson & Co., ent. 1783.*	Table candlesticks.—Sir Geo. Chetwode, Bt.
1792	Do.	. . . . .	Do. do.
1793	N. S. & Co.	Natt. Smith & Co.	Pierced sugar spoon.
1794	I G & Cº	John Green & Co., ent. 1792.*	Table candlesticks, given 1795. — Corpn. of Oswestry.

* *English Goldsmiths.* R. C. Hope, F.S.A.

GENERAL REMARKS.

Two general remarks must here be made upon the subject-matter of this and the preceding chapter: one is, that it must not be supposed that there is not plenty of genuine plate, bearing old English provincial marks, to be found in modern collections; and if the writer has based his remarks chiefly on ancient specimens of church-plate, and in other cases upon specimens of which it can safely be said that they have never changed hands at all, it is only that the absolute authenticity of the data relied on may be ensured beyond all possible question.

The other remark is a caution that in the case of specimens of provincial make of which the date-letter is doubtful, no help can be obtained from the alphabets of the Goldsmiths' Company in London. The York and Norwich Tables, which will be found in Appendix B., are enough to show that in respect of their date-letters the provincial goldsmiths used different alphabets from those adopted by their metropolitan brethren. They occasionally, in the seventeenth century, sent up their wares to be touched in London, and in that case they seem to have registered the same mark at Goldsmiths' Hall as that by which they were known to the local assay-wardens. Two such instances, both of goldsmiths in the north of England, and one of a Scottish goldsmith, have come under the writer's notice.

The following tabular summary of the marks dealt with in this chapter, is constructed on the same plan as the Tables already given at the end of Chapters II. and IV.

TABLE OF MARKS USED BY THE PROVINCIAL ASSAY OFFICES SINCE 1701.

OFFICE.	QUALITY.	STANDARD.	DATE.	DUTY FROM DEC. 1, 1784, TO 1890.	MAKER.	OFFICE MARK.
YORK.	Silver, N.S.	Lion's head erased.	Annual letter.	Sovereign's head.	Initials, viz.: 1701—1720, two first letters of surname. 1739 onward, first letters of Christian and surname.	City Arms: 5 lions passant on a cross. c. 1710. c. 1780. c. 1787—1788. from circa 1790.
	Ditto, O.S., since 1720.	Leopard's head crowned.*	Britannia, § Lion passant				
	Gold, 22-c., till 1844.	Ditto.	Ditto.			
EXETER.	Silver, N.S.	Lion's head erased.	Ditto.	Ditto.	Ditto.	City Arms: a castle with 3 towers. circa 1701—1709. 1709. from circa modern.
	Ditto, O.S., since 1720.	Leopard's head crowned.†	Britannia. Lion passant			
	Gold, 22-c., till 1844.	Ditto.†	Ditto.			
CHESTER.	Silver, N.S.	Lion's head erased.	Ditto.	Ditto.	Ditto.	City Arms, 1701—1784, 3 lions passant dim., impaled with 3 garbs dim.; from 1784 sword erect between 3 garbs.
	Ditto, O.S., since 1720.	Leopard's head crowned.‡	Britannia. Lion passant.			
	Gold, 22-c., till 1844.	Ditto.‡	Ditto.			

* Discontinued about 1847.   † Discontinued about the end of the 18th century.   ‡ Discontinued in 1839.

§ Before 1714 the Britannia marks were rudely engraved and in large punches.

TABLE OF MARKS USED BY THE PROVINCIAL ASSAY OFFICES SINCE 1701—*continued.*

OFFICE.	QUALITY.	STANDARD.	DATE.	DUTY FROM DEC. 1, 1784, TO 1890.	MAKER.	OFFICE MARK.
NEWCASTLE-UPON-TYNE.	Silver, N.S.	Lion's head erased.	Annual letter.	Sovereign's head.	Initials (see preceding page).	City Arms: 3 castles.
	Ditto, O.S., since 1720, Gold, 22-c., till 1844.	Leopard's head crowned. (See p. 152.) Ditto.	Britannia. Lion passant. Ditto.			to circa 1725. circa 1725 to 1758. 1758 to 1778. from circa 1778.
BIRMINGHAM, since 1773.	Silver, O.S. Ditto, N.S. Gold. 1824—1844.	... ... As in London; but anchor instead of leopard's head.	Lion passant. Britannia.	Ditto.	Ditto.	An anchor.
SHEFFIELD, since 1773.	Silver, O.S. Ditto, N.S.	... ...	Lion passant. Britannia.	Ditto.	Ditto.	A crown.

N.B. As to Gold.—Since 1798, 18-carat gold has been allowed; to be stamped with a crown and 18 for standard marks, the other marks as given above.

Since 1844, 22-carat gold has borne a crown and 22 for standard marks, instead of the standard marks given above.

In 1854, 3 lower standards { 15-carat } to bear { 15 and ·625 } respectively; together with date, maker's and town of gold were authorised { 12-carat } the { 12 and ·5 } for standard } marks; and sovereign's head, if on as follows:— { 9-carat } figures { 9 and ·375 } marks; } articles liable to duty.

CHAPTER VI.

SCOTLAND.

SCOTCH LEGISLATION—THE EDINBURGH GOLDSMITHS—THEIR MARKS, DEACONS
AND ASSAY-MASTERS—OLD PROVINCIAL MARKS—MODERN GLASGOW—TABLE
OF EDINBURGH AND GLASGOW MARKS.

IN Scotland attention was paid at an early period to the fineness of wrought gold and silver, and steps were taken by the Legislature to prevent frauds in the working of those metals.

For in the reign of King James II., A.D. 1457,* a statute was passed by the Parliament of Scotland, enacting that "anent the reformation of gold and silver wrocht be Goldsmithes, and to eschew the deceiving done to the kingis lieges, there sall be ordained in ilk burgh, quhair Goldsmithes workis ane understandard, and a cunning man of gude conscience quhilk sall be Deakone of the craft. And quhen the warke is brocht to the goldsmithe and it be gold, what gold that beis brocht till him he sall give it foorth again in warke na war nor xx grains, and silver xi grains fine.† And the said Goldsmith sall take his warke or he give it foorth and passe to the deakone of the craft and gar him examine that it be sa fine as before written. And the said deakone sall set his marke and taken thereto togidder with the said Goldsmithes. And gif faulte be founden therein afterwards, the deakone aforesaid and Goldsmithes gudes sall be in escheit to the King, and their lives at the kingis will and the said deakone sall have to his fee of ilk ounce wrocht an penny. And quhair there is no Goldsmithes bot ane in a towne, he sall shew that warke takened with his awin marke to the head officiates of the towne quhilkis sall have a marke in like maner ordained therefore and sall be set to the said warke. And quhat Goldsmith that givis foorth his warke utherwaies then is before written his gudes sall be confiscat to the King and his

---

* Fourteenth Parliament, VI. of March, 1457. 65. Of the Deacon of Goldsmithes; and of the marking of their warke.

† That is : 20 grains or parts of fine gold in 24 ; 11 of pure silver in 12.

life at the Kingis will." We have thus early, therefore, a maker's mark established, and in addition to it, a deacon's mark in towns where goldsmiths are established or a town mark in places where but a single goldsmith resides.

In 1483 the thirteenth parliament* of the next reign, that of James III., further ordains as follows : " that for the eschewing of the great damnage and skaithes that our Sovereign Lordis lieges sustein be the goldsmithes in the minishing the fines of the silver warke that fra thine furth there be in ilk burgh of the realm quhair goldsmithes ar, ane deacon and ane searcheour of the craft. And that ilk goldsmithes warke be marked with his awin marke, the deakone's marke and the marke of the Towne of the finesse of twelve-penny fine. And quhair there is ony sik warke within the said finesse, the warke to be broken the workman to upmake the avail of the finesse aforesaid, and the said workman to be punished therefore at the King's will."

It further provides that no goldsmith be a master, nor hold open booth unless he be admitted by the officers of the craft and the whole body of it. This same year we come to the grant by the Town Council of Edinburgh, of certain privileges to the goldsmiths and members of some other trades, all being included under the name of " Hammermen," in answer to a petition in which they complained of infractions upon the "auld gude rule " of their craft.

Next follows, in 1489, another statute,† to the same effect as the earlier ones, providing " that ilk goldsmith have ane special marke, signe and taiken to be put in his said warke quihilk he makis. And they samin warkes to be of fines of the new warkes of silver of *Bruges*. And that there be ane deakon of the craft of goldsmithes quihilk sall examine the said warke and fines thereof and see that it be als gude as the said wark of *Bruges*. And thereafter the samin deakon to put his marke and signe on the said warke, and to answer thereupon his life and gudes. And as touching the warke of gold, that it be maid als fine as it is first molten in the presence of the awner, like as the touch and assaie given to him quhen it is first molten."

---

* **XXIV.** Feb. 1483. 96. Of Goldsmiths.
    † James IV. Second Parliament, **XV.** Feb. 1489. 13. Of Goldsmithes.

In 1555, an Act* to regulate "the finesse of goldsmith's warke and the marke thereof" proceeds:—"Forasmuch as there is great fraud and hurt done unto the lieges of the realm by goldsmiths that make silver and gold of no certain finesse but at their pleasure by which there is some silver warke set furth of such baseness of alloy viz., of six and seven penny fine against the public weal of the realm, it is ordained that na goldsmith make in warke nor set foorth either of his awin or uther mennis silver under the just finance of elleven pennie fine under the paine of death and confiscation of all their gudes moveable. And that everie goldsmith marke the silver warke that he makis with his awin marke and with the townis marke. . . . And als that na goldsmith make in warke or set furth of his awin or uther mennis gold under the just finesse of twentie twa carat fine under the pains aforesaid."

Then come letters-patent of King James VI., granted in 1586, and ratified by parliament in the following year, to the deacon and masters of the Goldsmiths' craft in Edinburgh, which gave further effect to these statutes by empowering that body to search for gold and silver work, and to try whether it were of the fineness required by law and to seize all that should appear deficient; this gave them a monopoly of their trade and the entire regulation of it, separating them finally from all association with the "hammermen" or common smiths. The working rules of the craft received in 1591 the ratification of the Town Council; but they contain no further mention of marks to be used. We may remark that George Heriot, a name so well known in the mystery, was "deykin" of the goldsmiths in Edinburgh that same year. This most distinguished of all the Scotch goldsmiths was born in 1563, and was eldest son of another George Heriot, who belonged to the Company of Goldsmiths in Edinburgh. The younger Heriot has already been mentioned; but it may be interesting to note in this chapter that his father, who died in 1610, was also a man of eminence, having been a commissioner in the convention of estates and parliament of Scotland, and a convener of the trades of Edinburgh at five different elections of the council.† Lastly,

---

* Mary, Sixth Parliament, XX. June, 1555.

† Hone's *Every Day Book*, ii., 747.

the Charter of Incorporation of the Goldsmiths of Edinburgh, granted by James VII., in 1687, confirms their previous privileges and extends their powers over the whole kingdom of Scotland.

It seems clear that at this time but little plate, and henceforward none at all, was assayed, except in Edinburgh, until the establishment of the office at Glasgow in the present century. In earlier times several towns used marks in compliance with the early Acts of Parliament, but few instances of plate bearing them are now to be found: such as there are will be noted presently.

The earliest marks, therefore, were the maker's and deacon's punches only, to which the mark of the town is added in 1483; though we must not forget, as a piece of antiquarian information, the mention of a town mark as early as the Act of 1457.

The introduction of a variable date-letter seems nearly coincident with the granting of the charter of James VII., the first mention of it being in Sept., 1681, when a small black letter а was adopted as the letter for the ensuing year. It has been changed regularly ever since on the first hall-day in October.

In the Goldsmiths' books, there is a wonderfully consecutive record of the date-letters used from that time forward, but no note of the shape of the shields surrounding them, except for impressions from the actual punches used in the earliest cycle, which are struck upon the pages containing the minutes.

A new and carefully corrected Table was prepared expressly for this volume, by the late Mr. James H. Sanderson, well known as one of the best authorities on the subject of Scotch plate, and time has only proved its accuracy. The extensive MS. collections made by this painstaking antiquary with a view to a complete history of Scottish plate and its marks, which unfortunately proved too great a work for a lifetime, passed at his death into the possession of the present writer. Such a history has since been accomplished for Scottish Communion-plate and its marks by Rev. T. Burns,* and Mr. A. J. S. Brook,

---

* *Old Scottish Communion Plate*, by Rev. T. Burns, Edinburgh, 1892, from which many dates and names are added to entries given in the earlier editions of this chapter, and as far as possible in square brackets in order to show their origin.

in a work which was mentioned as forthcoming in the preface to the fourth edition of *Old English Plate*. The authors of this monumental volume have really exhausted their subject, but have hardly done as much justice to the labours of their predecessor as they would if they had been aware of the extent of ground covered by Mr. Sanderson, and of the mass of information as to Scottish plate and plate marks collected by him, much of it very laboriously, in the course of journeys made on foot in every part of Scotland. Almost all the marks noticed by Mr. Brook had been found, and the difficulties connected with many of them discussed, in almost the same detail by Mr. Sanderson; whilst much of Mr. Sanderson's work that the present writer had hesitated to use, until he had the opportunity of verifying it, has been so entirely corroborated by Mr. Brook's researches, as to place the accuracy of either inquirer beyond question.

We have now enumerated four of the marks to be found on plate assayed in Edinburgh,—the maker's, the deacon's, the castle, and the date-letter. Two others have to be mentioned, one an alteration, and the other an addition. In 1759, the deacon's mark was abolished, the standard mark of a thistle being substituted for it; and in 1784, as in England, the Sovereign's head was ordained as a duty mark.

Returning to the course of legislation there is nothing to notice, and the old laws seem to have remained in force, until the date of the general enactment* which now, to quote from its title, fixes the standard qualities of gold and silver plate in Scotland, and provides for the marking and assaying thereof. Its provisions much resemble those of the Acts establishing the more modern of the English provincial assay offices, except as regards the standard and the city mark. It prohibits the sale not only of plate manufactured in Scotland, but of any plate without the marks of one of the Scotch assay offices, so that no plate made in London or elsewhere out of Scotland can be sold in Scotland, unless it be re-assayed and stamped at the Edinburgh or Glasgow offices. Of the Glasgow office, established in 1819, presently.

---

* 6 & 7 Will. IV c. 69.

The Act recapitulates the marks to be used, and they are as follows:—

For *gold* of 22 carats, the five stamps of which mention has been made—the maker's initials, the town, the standard, the duty and date marks.

For *gold* of 18 carats, the same, with the additional stamp of the figures 18.

For *silver* of the old standard, the same stamps as for gold of 22 carats.

For *silver* of the new standard, the same stamps with the additional mark of Britannia.

It may be remarked that the higher standard silver has been but little used in Scotland.

To sum up in chronological form, the Edinburgh marks are:—

1. Maker's mark, from 1457.

2. Standard mark, being deacon's initials from 1457 to 1681; and assay-master's from 1681 to 1759, when the thistle was substituted for it.

3. The town mark of a castle, from 1483.

4. The date-letter from 1681-2.

5. The duty mark of the Sovereign's head, from 1784, as in England.

As so much of our means of dating old Scotch plate depends upon the Deacon's mark, the first thing to do is to give a list of the Deacons of the craft from early times down to the year 1681, when the Deacon's initials ceased to be used as the standard mark; and after doing so, it will be as well to give a tabular view of some typical examples of Edinburgh marks from 1617 to 1778, in order that the character of Scotch hall marking may be seen at a glance, with short notices of the makers, deacons, and assay-masters of that period. In certain very exceptional cases the deacon's mark appears instead of the usual Assay-Master's mark, later than 1681. When any mark except that of the proper Assay-Master appears, it is always that of the goldsmith who was Deacon at the time, who seems therefore to have been prepared to act as Assay-Master in any emergency. Cases occur in 1717 when P. Turnbull was

Deacon and stamps plate as Assay-Master, and also in 1740 to 1744 when Dougal Ged and Edward Lothian were Deacons successively and in their years acted as Assay-Masters.

LIST OF EDINBURGH DEACONS.*

1525.	ADAM LIES [LEIS].	1588.	ADAME CRAIGE.
1526.	THOMAS RYND.	1589.	GEORGE HERIOT, S^R.
1529.	MICHAELL GILBERT.	1590.	Do.
1530.	JAMES COLLIE [COKKIE].	1591.	WILLIAM COLIE [COKIE].
1531.	ALLANE MOSSMAN.	1592.	Do.
1532.	JOHN LYLE [KYLE].	1593.	Do.
1534.	GEORGE HERIOT.	1594.	Do.
1535.	THOMAS RYND.	1595.	CLAUDERONE BEYEARD.
1544.	JOHN LYLE [KYLE].	1596.	[DAVID HERIOT].
1547.	ARCHIBALD MAYSONN.	1597.	DANIELL CRAUFUIRD, J^R.
1548.	JOHN GILBERT.	1598.	GEORGE HERIOT, J
1550.	JOHN LYLE [KYLE].	1599.	DAVID HERIOT.
1551.	MICHAELL RYND.	1600.	Do.
1552.	THOMAS EWING.	1601.	GEORGE FOULLIS.
1553.	Do.	1602.	Do.
1554.	Do.	1603.	GEORGE HERIOT.
1556.	THOMAS RYND.	1604.	ROBERT COLIE.
1558.	MICHAELL GILBERT.	1605.	GEORGE FOULLIS.
1561.	THOMAS EWING.	1606.	Do.
1562.	GEORGE RIND.	1607.	GEORGE HERIOT.
1563.	JAMES COLLIE [COK].	1608.	ROBERT DENNISTOUN.
1564.	Do.	1609.	Do.
1565-6-7.	GEORGE HERIOT.	1610.	GEORGE FOULLIS.
1568.	JAMES MOSMAN.	1611.	DAVID PALMER.
1572.	ADAM CRAIG.	1612.	Do.
1573.	Do.	1613.	JAMES DENNISTOUN.
1574.	DAVID DENNISTON.	1614.	Do.
1575.	GEORGE HERIOT.	1615.	GEORGE CRAWFURD.
1577.	WILLIAM COLIE [COKIE].	1616.	Do.
1578.	Do.	1617.	JOHN LINDSAY.
1579.	EDWARD HAIRT.	1618.	Do.
1580.	Do.	1619.	JAS. DENNISTOUN.
1581.	DAVID DENNEISTOUN.	1620.	Do.
1582.	EDWARD HAIRT.	1621.	GEORGE CRAWFURD.
1583.	[THOMAS ANNAND.	1622.	Do.
1584.	GEORGE HERIOT.	1623.	GILBERT KIRKWOODE.
1585.	JOHN MOSMAN].†	1624.	Do.
1586.	ION MOSMAN.	1625.	ALEX. REID.
1587.	ADAME CRAIGE.	1626.	Do.

* The small discrepancies between this list and the list as it appears in *Old Scottish Communion Plate*, are given in square brackets.

† These three names appear in the city records as goldsmiths, members of the town council : so they were probably the Deacons, but there are no minutes of the Goldsmiths for these years.—W. J. C.

1627.	ADAM LAMB.
1628.	Do.
1629.	ALEX. REID.
1630.	Do.
1631.	JAS. DENNISTOUN.
1632.	Do.
1633.	GEORGE CRAWFURD.
1634.	Do.
1635.	ADAM LAMB.
1636.	Do.
1637.	JOHN SCOTT.
1638.	Do.
1639.	ADAM LAMB.
1640.	THOS. CLEGHORN.
1641.	Do.
1642.	JAS. DENNISTOUN.
1643.	Do.
1644.	ADAM LAMB.
1645.	Do.
1646.	JOHN SCOTT.
1647.	Do.
1648.	GEORGE CLEGHORN.
1649.	Do.
1650.	JAS. FAIRBAIRN.
1651.	Do.
1652.	Do.
1653.	ANDREW BURNETT [BURRELL].
1654.	Do.
1655.	GEORGE CLEGHORN.

1656.	GEORGE CLEGHORN.
1657.	JAS. FAIRBAIRN.
1658.	Do.
1659.	ANDREW BURNETT [BURRELL].
1660.	Do.
1661.	PATRICK BORTHWICK.
1662.	Do.
1663.	EDWARD CLEGHORN.
1664.	Do.
1665.	JAS. SYMONTONE.
1666.	Do.
1667.	ALEX. SCOTT.
1668.	Do.
1669.	ALEX. REID.
1670.	Do.
1671.	EDWARD CLEGHORN.
1672.	Do.
1673.	THOS. CLEGHORN.
1674.	EDWARD CLEGHORN [ALEX. REID].
1675.	W. LAW.
1676.	Do.
1677.	ALEX. REID.
1678.	Do.
1679.	EDWARD CLEGHORN.
1680.	Do.
1681.	THOS. YOURSTON.
1682.	Do.

There seems to be some small doubt as to who was Deacon in certain years; but the above list, which the author owes greatly to the care of Dr. Norman Macpherson, is nearly correct, compared as it is throughout with that of Mr. Brook in *Old Scottish Communion Plate.* The Deacons were appointed in the month of September in each year. All the Deacon's marks that have been noted by the author will be found engraved in one or other of the two following lists of marks.

To illustrate the use of the Deacon's mark in dating old Scotch plate, it is the proper place to turn here to our tabular view of marks on old plate. The sets of marks are numbered to correspond with the biographical notes which belong to and follow them. The maker's mark is as a rule found on the left of the Edinburgh mark, and the deacon's or assay-master's on the right of it.

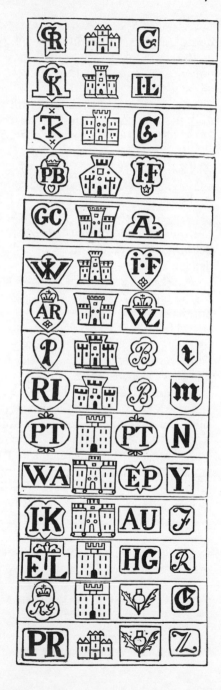

1.—1617. Edinburgh City mace.

2.—1618. Fyvie com. cup.

3.—1633. Trinity College bread-plate.

4.—1642. Tolbooth Church com. cups, Edinburgh.

5.—1646. Newbattle com. cup.

6.—1657. Dunbar com. cups.

7.—1677. Pittenweem com. cup.

8.—1686. Dunblane com. cups.

9.—1692. Culross com. cups, dated 1693.

10.—1717. Legerwood com. cups, dated 1717.

11.—1728. William Aytoun.

12.—1735. James Kerr.

13.—1746. Edward Lothian.

14.—1760. Robt. Gordon.

15.—1778. Patrick Robertson.

1. *George Robertson* was master of the Cuinziehous (coining-house), and made the Mace belonging to the city of Edinburgh in the year 1617. Between that date and 1629 we have his punch six times, as the maker of church-plate. [He was admitted 1616.]

The deacon GC in monogram was George Crawford. We find his punch on church-plate nine times between 1617 and 1638. He was Deacon in 1615-6 and 1621-2 as well as later in 1633-4. His mark occurs again at No. 3 in this list. [He was admitted 1606.]

2. *Gilbert Kirkwoode* was deacon of the Goldsmiths' Craft in the years 1623-4. He made the Fyvie parish communion-plate (Aberdeenshire) in the year 1618, and that of the parishes of Marnock and Beith in 1623-4; we have his punch many times between those dates; at Marnock and Beith as both maker and deacon. [He was admitted 1609.]

The deacon's mark I·L occurs a number of times, circa 1618; his name was Johnne Lyndsay, deacon 1617-18. [He was admitted 1605.]

3. Maker's mark is found on several examples in 1633, including the plate in the Tron Church, Edinburgh, at Forgue Church, and at Marnock, all dated pieces of 1633. [His name Thos. Kirkwoode, adm. 1632.]

The deacon's mark is the same as in the first example; being the mark as deacon of George Crawford. It occurs on many pieces of 1633, mostly with that of Thos. Kirkwoode as maker.

4. *From the Tolbooth* parish communion-plate (Edinburgh). The maker PB crowned, for Peter Borthwick. [Admitted 1642.] We have his punch four times between the years 1642 and 1662, in this last year at Fogo both as maker's and deacon's mark, being struck twice on the same piece. In 1645 he appears as maker at Haddington with Adam Lamb for deacon.

The deacon's punch is that of James Fairbairn,* admitted master in 1641. It occurs on so many pieces of church-plate

---

* Mr. Brook attributes this Deacon's mark to one John Frazer, adm. 1624, who acted, he thinks, at some period as a Deacon though never mentioned as such. But the mark occurs on a cup at Dalmellington dated 1650, when Fairbairn was certainly Deacon. John Frazer was maker of a cup of 1638, formerly at Monifieth.

dated 1642 and 1643, that it is almost certain he was acting as deacon for James Dennistoun in those years. He was then the youngest master. This same form of his mark occurs at Dalmellington in 1650, when he was deacon for the first time himself. It is different in a later period of office.

5. *George Cleghorn* was deacon of the craft in the year 1648-9, and again 1655-6; we have his punch as G·C three times on church-plate, from 1646 to 1650. He made a cup for New-battle Church in 1646, and some Old Grey Friars Church plate in 1649 bears his mark as deacon. [He was admitted in 1641.]

The deacon's monogram we have five times between 1629 and 1646, name Adam Lamb; it occurs on the Dunfermline plate in 1629, on the Haddington Church plate in 1645, and in connection with the mark of George Robertson on an alms-dish now at St. Patrick's Church, Brighton, but formerly the pro-perty of the church of Duffus, co. Elgin. This is probably of the year 1629.

6. *Dunbar* parish Communion-plate, maker's punch [John Wardlaw, adm. 1642] occurs from 1644 to 1657. It is found with London marks at Canongate Church, Edinburgh.

Deacon's punch, James Fairbairn, as above, No. 4. It occurs in 1659 at Dalgety, and it is heart-shaped in this second period of office.

7. *Alexander Reed* [admitted 1660] was deacon of the craft in 1677-8 and other years, and made some of the Pittenweem parish church-plate, dated 1677. His mark is found 1670 to 1677—in 1670 as both maker and deacon, and again as deacon in 1674.

The deacon's mark is for W. Law; we have his punch, usually as a maker, five times between the years 1667 and 1681. It occurs in 1673 at Mid Calder, and in 1667 at Glencross. [He was admitted 1662.]

8. *From Dunblane* parish church Communion-plate. Maker's name James Penman. He appears as a maker five times between the years 1685 and 1695, and as assay-master sixteen times from 1695 to 1707. The date-letter is a defective one for 1686.

The deacon's, or rather in this case and henceforwards, the assay-master's, mark is *ℬ* in a shaped border; we have his punch twenty times between the years 1681 and 1696. [His

name was John Borthwick] assay-master 1681-96.   From 1681
a date-letter appears.

9. *Robert Ingles* [Inglis, adm. 1686] was deacon of the craft
in 1691, and again 1701; we have his punch seven times, as a
maker, between the years 1692 and 1719.   It is on Communion-
plate at Cromdale, in Morayshire, given in 1708.   Assay-master
as in No. 8.

10. *Patrick Turnbull* [adm. 1689] as found on the Legerwood
parish church communion-plate.   He must have acted as assay-
master for a time in 1717, in an interregnum, owing perhaps
to an illness or absence of the proper assay-master, Edward
Penman; but it seems rather an inexplicable circumstance, as
no other indication of such an interruption occurs, except once
later between 1741 and 1744.

11. *William Ayton* [adm. 1718] who was deacon of the craft
in the years 1730-1.   We have his punch four times between
the years 1729 and 1733.   The assay-master EP [Edward
Penman] held that office from 1708 to 1729.   During that
period we have his punch six times as a maker, and twenty-
four times as assay-master.

12. *James Kerr* [adm. 1723] was deacon of the craft three
times, and for two years at each time, in the years 1734-5,
1746-7, and in 1750-51.   He was also a Member of Parliament;
we have his punch six times between the years 1721 and 1745.

The mark AU [Archibald Ure] appears as that of the assay-
master from 1729 to 1740.   During that period we have his
punch twelve times as such.   From 1741 to 1744 it is uncertain
who was assay-master, but Dougal Ged seems to have acted as
such in 1741, and Edward Lothian in 1742 and 1743.*

13. *Edward Lothian* [adm. 1731] was deacon of the craft
in the years 1742-3, and from the Hammermen's Arms (a
hammer with Imperial Crown) which the device over his initials
is intended to represent, he had been a member of that corporation; we have his punch both as maker and deacon, in all
five times, from 1742 to 1759, and then with the standard mark

---

* It seems to the author that in that
interval the Deacon for the year, Dougal
Ged and E. Lothian successively, acted
as assay-master, but Mr. A. J. S. Brook,
no doubt on better authority, says that
from 1740-44, pending a dispute, plate
was stamped by the oldest and youngest
masters.   See list of examples on p. 178.
1741 to 1743.

(the thistle) introduced in 1759, instead of the deacon's or assay-master's mark, as in the next example.

The assay-master, *Hugh Gordon* [adm. 1727] was deacon of the craft in 1732-3, and seems to have been in office as assay-master 1744 to 1759. During that period we have his punch sixteen times.

14. *Robert Gordon* [adm. 1741] was deacon of the craft in 1748-9; we have his punch three times between the years 1744 and 1760. The Castle and Thistle, in square punches, differ a little at this date from the same marks as used a few years later.

15. *Patrick Robertson* [adm. 1751] was deacon of the craft in the years 1754-5; and again in 1764-5; being two years in office each time; we find his punch fourteen times as maker between the years 1766 and 1790.

EXAMPLES OF EDINBURGH PLATE, prior to 1681.

With Maker's and Deacon's Marks.

1561		Maker, Alex. Auchinleck. Deacon, Thos. Ewing. Mazer, dated 1567.—St. Mary's Coll., St. Andrew's.*
1586?		Maker and Deacon, probably John Mosman. Com. cup, undated.—Rosneath.
1596-9?		[Maker, Hugh Lyndsay, adm. 1587. Deacon, David Heriot, adm. 1592.]—Com. cup, undated. Currie.
c. 1610		Maker, Robt. Dennistoun [adm. 1597]. Deacon, illegible. The George Heriot Loving Cup, formed of a Nautilus shell.—The Heriot Trust, Edinburgh.*
1617-8	GK^T I·L	Maker, G. Kirkwoode, as in 1623-4. Deacon, John Lyndsay. Com. cups, undated.—Carstairs and Glencairn.
1619-20	GK†	Maker as last. Deacon, James Dennistoun [adm. 1598]. Com. cup, undated.—Blantyre.
1623-4		Maker and Deacon, Gilbert Kirkwoode. Com. cups, undated.—Marnock and Beith.
1633		Maker, probably Thos. Cleghorn [adm. 1604]. Deacon, George Crawfurd. Com. cups, dated 1633.—Old Grey Friars Ch., Edinburgh.
1638	I·F IS	[Maker, John Frazer, adm. 1624]. Deacon, John Scott. Com. cup, tazza form on baluster stem, given 1638 to Monifuth.—Messrs. G. Lambert, 1888.

* From *Scottish National Memorials.* Glasgow, 1890.

† Mr. Brook gives both these makers as Gilbert Kirkwoode (see 1623).

1642-3			Maker, Nicol Trotter [adm. 1635]. Deacon, James Fairbairn (see p. 164). Com. cups, dated 1643.—Tolbooth Ch., Edinburgh.
Do.		Do.	Maker, John Scott. Deacon as last. Com. cup, dated 1644.—Canongate Parish Ch., Edinburgh.
Do.?		Do.	Maker [Robert Gibson, adm. 1628]. Deacon as last. Com. cup, undated.—Dalkeith.
1645			Maker as in 1633. Deacon, Adam Lamb. Com. cup, dated 1646.—Newbattle.
1645		Do.	Maker [Andro Dennistoun, adm. 1636]. Deacon as last. Com. cup, dated 1646.—Newbattle.
1649			Maker, John Scott. Deacon, George Cleghorn. Com. cup on baluster stem, dated 1650.—Dalmellington.
Do.		Do.	Maker, Andrew Burnett [Burrell]. Deacon, George Cleghorn. Basin, dated 1649. — Old Grey Friars Ch., Edinburgh.
1650			Maker, George Crawfurd. Deacon, James Fairbairn, as above in 1642-3. Com. cup, dated 1650.—Dalmellington.
1653-4			Maker and Deacon, Andrew Burnett [Burrell]. Com. cup, undated.—Paisley.
1655-6			Maker, Peter Neilsone [adm. 1647]. Deacon, George Cleghorn. Spoons.—Heirs of Thomas Maxwell.*
1663-4?			Maker, Alex. Scott [adm. 1649]. Deacon, Edward Cleghorn [adm. 1649]. Com. cups, undated.—Linlithgow.
1667			Maker, W. Law. Deacon, James Symontone. Com. cup, dated 1667.—Glencross. Also Com. cup, dated 1673.—Mid-Calder.
1670			Maker and Deacon, Alex. Reid. Com. cups, dated 1670.—North Berwick.
1680			Maker and Deacon, Edward Cleghorn. Com. cup, dated 1681.—Newbattle.

EXAMPLES OF EDINBURGH PLATE, from 1681.

With Maker's Marks and the Assay-master's Mark till its discontinuance in 1759:

1682			[Probably James Cockburn, adm. 1669.] Jug.— The late Lord Murray. Assay - master, John Borthwick, 1681-96.
Do.		Do.	Duddingston Church plate, dated 1682. [Rev. T. Burns reverses this mark and attributes it to E. Cleghorn.]

* From *Scottish National Memorials*, Glasgow, 1890.

1682		Do.	[Andrew Law.] Baptismal basin.—Tron Church, Edinburgh.
Do.		Do.	Com. cups.—Culross. [Rev. T. Burns attributes these to W. Law.]
Do.		Do.	Com. cup.—Pittenweem.
1683		Do.	(Thos. Yourston.) Com. cup.—Peebles.
1685	· ·	Do.	Jas. Cockburn, as in 1632. Communion cups, dated 1686.—Auchtermuchtie.
1689	· ·	Do.	(Do.) Benholm Church plate, dated 1690.
1690		Do.	[Walter Scott, adm. 1686.] Church-plate, dated 1689.—Temple Ch., Edinburgh.
1691		Do.	[John Lawe, adm. 1662.] Com. cup, gift of Hay. —Falkland.
1692		Do.	[James Sympsone, adm. 1687.] Church-plate, dated 1693.—Benholm.
1694		Do.	(Robert Ingles.) Church-plate, dated 1694.—Prestonkirk.
1695		Do.	(Thos. Cleghorn, adm. 1689.) Com. cups.—Prestonpans.*
1698			[Thos. Ker, adm. 1694.] Trinity College Church plate, dated 1698. Also 1704 Com. cups, given 1705.—St. Michael's, Dumfries. Assay-master, James Penman, 1696—1708.
1701		Do.	[Geo. Scott, adm. 1697.] Communion cup, dated 1702.—New North Kirk, Edinburgh.
Do.		Do.	[J. Penman.] Com. plate, dated 1702.—Dunning, Perthshire.
Do.		Do.	(Thos. Cleghorn, as in 1695.) Dalmeny Church plate, presented by Lord Rosebery, 1702. Also 1703 Com. cups, dated 1703.—Mertoun Kirk, St. Boswell's.
1702		Do.	Com. cup, given 1702.—Pittenweem.
1703		Do.	Com. cup, given 1704.—New North Kirk, Edinburgh.
Do.	G	Do.	(Maker as in 1701.) New North Kirk Communion cup, dated 1704.
1704	AK	Do.	[Alex. Kincaid, adm. 1692.] Carmichael Church plate, dated 1705.
1705		Do.	[James Taitt, adm. 1704.] Rattray Church plate. Also 1731 Com. cups.—Crichton.
1707	R.I	Do.	(Robert Ingles, as in 1694.) Communion cup, Cromdale, Morayshire, given by Jean Houston, Lady Grant, 1708.
Do.	WS		(Maker as in 1690.) Communion cups, dated 1708.—Lady Yester's Ch., Edinburgh. Assaymaster, Edward Penman, 1708-29.

* T. Cleghorn's bill for these, dated and receipted July, 1695, is still preserved.

1707	(MY)	Do.	[Mungo Yourstone, adm. 1702.] Baptismal laver, dated 1708.—New North Kirk, Edinburgh.
1708	Do.	Do.	Eddleston Communion cups, dated 1709. Also 1714 Com. cups, dated 1714.—Maryton.
Do.	(RK)	Do.	[Robt. Ker, adm. 1705.] Com. cups.—Irongray.
1712	[AF]	Do.	[Alex. Forbes, adm. 1692.] Candlesticks.—Cluny.
1716	**RI**	Do.	(Robert Ingles, as in 1694.) Abbotshall (near Kirkaldy) Church plate, dated 1717.
1717	See No. 10, p. 169.		(Patrick Turnbull.) Legerwood Com. cups, dated 1717.
Do.	**RI**	(EP)	(Robert Ingles, as in 1694.) Errol Church plate, dated 1718.
Do.	[IS]	Do.	[John Seatoune, adm. 1688.] Com. cups, dated 1719.—Corstorphine.
1718	**RI**	Do.	(Robert Ingles, as in 1694.) Galashiels Church plate, dated 1719.
1719	[WG]	Do.	[Wm. Ged. adm. 1706.] Punch bowl of the Royal Company of Archers, dated 1720.
1720	[AS]	Do.	[Alex. Simpson, adm. 1710.] Pencaitland Church plate, dated 1721.
1721	(HB)	Do.	[Harry Beatone, adm. 1704.] Kelso Church plate, presented by Christiana Kerr, " daur. of the Master of Chatto and widow of Frogden, 1722."
1722	(CC)	Do.	[Colin Campbell, adm. 1714.] Spoons.—Alexander Drysdale, Esq. Also 1723 Com. cups, dated 1723.—Dalziel.
Do.	{CD}	Do.	[Chas. Dickson, adm. 1719.] Com. cup, dated 1722.—Ayr.
1726	[HB]	Do.	[Qy. Harry Beatone.] Forteviot (Perth) Church plate, given 1727.
1727	(PG)	Do.	[Patrick Gream, adm. 1725.] Table-spoons.—Marquis of Breadalbane.
1728	(AE)	Do.	[Alexr. Edmonstoune, adm. 1721.] Com. cups, dated 1729.—Anstruther Easter.
1729	(I·K)	[AU]	(James Kerr.) St. Ninian's Church plate. Also 1733 Com. cups, given 1734. — Auchinleck. Assay-master Archibald Ure, 1729-40.
1732	(IM)	Do.	[John Main, adm. 1729.] Kincardine Church plate, given 1733. Also 1733 Com. cup, dated 1734.—Panbride.
1733	[WA]	Do.	(Wm. Ayton.) Com. cup.—Kilrinney.
1735	I·K	Do.	(James Kerr, as in 1729.) Bowl on feet.—Castle Grant.
1736	Do.	Do.	(Do.) Set of salvers. Do.
Do.	[HP]	Do.	[Hugh Penman, adm. 1734.] Com. cups, dated 1737.—Kinross.
1741	**WA**	**GED**	(Maker as in 1733, Dougal Ged, Deacon 1740-1, acting as Assay-master.) Com. cup, dated 1742.—Newburgh.
Do.	[LO]	Do.	[Maker, Laurence Oliphant, adm. 1737.] Deacon as last. Com. cup, dated 1742.—Alloa.

Date	Maker's mark	Assay mark	Description
1742	*RG*	EL	[Maker, Robt. Gordon, adm. 1741, as on p. 169,] Edw. Lothian, Deacon 1742-3, acting as Assay-master. Beakers, dated 1744.—Auldearn.
1743	EL	EL	[Maker, Edw. Lothian, and again as Deacon for Assay-master as above.] Com. cups, dated 1744.—Kembach.
Do.	Do.	Do.	Do. Do. Com. cups, dated 1744.—Kirkcudbright.
Do.	Do.	Do.	Do. Do. Silver club, dated 1744.—Edinburgh Golf Club.
1747	CL	HG	Guthrie Church plate, dated 1748. Assay-master, Hugh Gordon, 1744-59.
1749	K&D	Do.	[Ker and Dempster.] Old Church, Edinburgh, Communion cups, dated 1750.
1751	CLARK	Do.	[John Clark, adm. 1751. Forks. Noted by author.
Do.	EO	Do.	[Ebenezer Oliphant, adm. 1737.] Kettle and stand. Noted by author.
1752	GED	Do.	(Dougal Ged, adm. 1734.) Spoons.
1753	IG	Do.	[James Gillsland, adm. 1748.] Pepper-box.—Sir George Home, Bart. Also 1762 Com. cups, dated 1763.—Gordon.
1754	LvR	Do.	[Lothian and Robertson.] Lochgoilhead Church plate, given by Sir James Livingstone, of Glenterran, Bart., 1754.
1755	K&D	Do.	[Ker and Dempster.] Double-handled porringer.—Castle Grant.
1760	ALT		[Alexr. Aitcheson, adm. 1746.] Com. cup, dated 1761.—Langton.
1762	WD		[William Drummond, adm. 1760.] St. Cuthbert's Parish Chapel of Ease, Edinburgh, Communion plate, dated 1763.
1763	Do.		(Do.) Do., baptismal laver, dated 1763.
1765	K & D		(Maker as in 1755.) Auchinleck Church plate, from Lady Auchinleck, "given by Lord Auchinleck, 1766."
1766	PR		(Patrick Robertson, adm. 1751.) Cake-basket.—Messrs. Mackay and Chisholm.
1770	Do.		(Do.) Spoons.—Capt. Gordon, of Cluny.
1771	IxW		[James Welsh, adm. 1746.] Plain bowl.—Castle Grant.
1776	WD		[William Davie, adm. 1740.] Oxnam Church plate, dated 1776.
1777	PR		(Patrick Robertson, as in 1766.] Mauchline Church plate, dated 1777.
1783	WD		(William Davie, as in 1776.) Cramond Church plate.
1784	JH		[James Hewitt, adm. 1760.] St. Andrew's (Edinburgh) Church plate.
1785	FH		(Francis Howden.) Leecroft (Bridge of Allan) Church plate.
1788	PR		(Patrick Robertson, as in 1766.) Mauchline baptismal basin.
1789	Do.		(Do.) Pencaitland Church plate, given 1789.
1790	Do.		(Do.) Kippen Church plate, given 1790.
Do.	AG		[Alex. Gairdner, ent. 1754.] Carmylie Church plate, given 1791.

1791	WC PC	[William and Patrick Cunning- } Tolbooth Church baptis- ham, adm. 1776.] } mai basin, renewed 1792.
1795	WR	(William Robertson, adm. 1789.) Westerkirk Church plate.
1799	FH	(Francis Howden, as in 1785.) Kincardine Church plate, dated 1799.

SCOTTISH PROVINCIAL MARKS.

Before coming to the establishment of the modern assay office of Glasgow, we must pause to notice some provincial towns in Scotland, where plate was marked in olden times.

These, and possibly other towns, availed themselves of the privileges conferred by the Act of 1457, the provisions of which in this behalf will be remembered. It is certain that these provisions were not very strictly attended to, for in many cases the mark of the assay-master's tool is the only proof that the metal had been examined and tested by any authorised person; the maker's and the town mark being found unaccompanied by a deacon's. The following marks have been selected as illustrations of the mode of marking plate in the Scotch provincial towns; and an explanatory note of each is added to conclude this section of the subject.

In *Glasgow* the old town mark was the arms, with the bell on one side of the tree, a letter G on the other, the fish's head is sometimes to the dexter, and sometimes to the sinister side, and has a ring in its mouth : of this mark we have above twenty examples between the years 1694 and 1766.

On early plate the town mark is on a small round punch, so small that it is often difficult to recognise the bearings at all. In most examples we have a date-letter, but it is impossible to place them in regular order, except for a very short period. It seems probable, that the letters used at the end of the seventeenth, and beginning of the following century, were of the same character as those of the first two Edinburgh alphabets, and that the same letters stood for nearly the same years at both places.

The Glasgow letters seem to occur about three years later than the corresponding letter at Edinburgh, thus the small Gothic O for 1694 at Edinburgh would be for 1697 at Glasgow.

But the letter S in various escutcheons which appears on several of the following examples in 1734, and later, and the letter O at c. 1770, seem not to have been date-letters. Mr. A. J. S. Brook suggests that S denotes "standard" quality.

Glasgow, 1697. [Robert Brook, 1673.] Church plate, dated 1697.—Hamilton.

Glasgow, 1701. Com. cups, formerly at Cardross.*— Sudeley Castle.

Glasgow, 1703. Renfrew Church plate.

Glasgow, 1708. Greenock, West Church plate.

Glasgow, 1710. Com. cups, dated 1709.—Barony Church, Glasgow. Also at Kilmarnock, 1709.

Glasgow, 1727. [Johan Biltzing, adm. 1717.] Com. cups, dated 1727.—Dumbarton.

Glasgow, 1734. Com. cups, dated 1734. — Barony Church, Glasgow.

Glasgow, 1752. Com. cup, dated 1752.—Dalmellington. Also cups dated 1752.—Bothwell.

Glasgow, 1765. [Probably Bayne and Napier.] St. Quivox Church plate.—Ayr.

Glasgow, c. 1770. [Milne and Campbell.] Com. cups, undated.—Inverary.

In *Dundee* also the town mark was the arms, a pot of three growing lilies, of which we have only a few examples. The shape of the flowers is not always quite the same. One of those given is of the year 1652; the other is on a large circular alms-dish of 1665, with the coat of arms of the donor, Johannes Fethens. The RG of 1652 is also found on the cover of a cup belonging to the Church of Perth, said to have been given by Mary, Queen of Scots, and repaired in Dundee in 1637. The original part of the cup is of beautiful Nuremberg work.

---

* The initials **I.L** and **R.L** are attributed to members of the Luke family, goldsmiths in Glasgow from about 1660 to 1750.—**IG** to James Glen, who succeeded to Robert Luke in 1753.—*Scottish National Memorials*, Glasgow, 1890. The author has also seen a spoon of about 1685 with the initials of George Luke [adm. 1680].

AL in a square, repeated twice, appears on the Communion cups at Kettins, Coupar Angus, which are dated 1636. [Alex. Lindsay, 1628.]

Dundee, 1652. Forgan Church plate, Fife.
    [Qy. Robert Gairdyne.]

Dundee, 1665. Dundee parish church, alms-dish.
    Also St. Vigean's, Arbroath, dated, 1667.
    [Thos. Lyndsay, 1662.]

In *Aberdeen*, the town mark was a contraction BD or ABD. The first Aberdeen mark lower on this page gives it as it appears on the Mace of the King's College, which is marked with the maker's name, *Waltervs Melvil Fecit* 1650, whose mark occurs at Ellon as early as 1642; the XX may be the quality of the silver. The same marks but ABD instead of BD are on a cup dated 1653, belonging to Aberdeen University. In most cases the town mark is as in this last mentioned, and the next example of 1666, though the contraction mark is not always found. $\mathcal{ABD}$ script letters were used about 1770-80.

Aberdeen, 1650. King's College mace. (Walter
    Melvil, Deacon, 1662.)

Aberdeen, 1666. Com. cup dated 1666; Ellon,
    Aberdeenshire. (George Walker, adm. 1685.)

Aberdeen, 1680. Three medals. — Grammar
    School, Aberdeen. [Wm. Scott. adm. 1666.]
Aberdeen, 1685. Com. cup, Ellon, Aberdeen-
    shire. (George Walker.)

Early in the eighteenth century some makers at Aberdeen used a shield with three small castles, not unlike the better known Newcastle mark, instead of the letters ABD. Examples of this are the following :—

1715. [John Walker, adm. 1713.] Com. cups,
    dated 1715.—Marykirk.
1731. [Alex. Forbes, adm. 1728.] Com. cup,
    dated 1731.—St. Fergus.

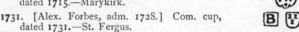

The mark of AF is also known with the three castles' mark

and date-letter A on com. cups dated 1728 at Logie-Pert; and with date-letter B on com. cups dated 1731 at Maryculter.

Later in the century the town mark in script letters is found, as for example, at Dyce, in 1770 (A.B.D) [IW] the mark of James Wildgoose, adm. 1763; and at Birnie, in 1778, with [J.L] the mark of James Law, adm. 1777.

Montrose. A mark formerly given in these pages as belonging either to Aberdeen or Montrose, seems now to be fairly identified by Mr. Brook as that of William Lindsay of Montrose from 1671 to 1708. It is found as follows, and the hammer shows that he belonged to the Hammermen's Society.

Montrose, 1682. Fordown Church plate, Kincardineshire.

Montrose, 1683. Com. cup, Aberlemno.   Do.   Do.

The *Inverness* town mark was, like that of Aberdeen, a contraction INS, but has no mark over these initials. It is found on a communion cup given in 1708 by a Lady Grant to Inverallan (Grantown) Church, Morayshire. It has a maker's mark [M.L] on each side of it, and the remains of a Roman letter C in a plain shield. This, it may be noted, is also the Edinburgh letter for 1707-8, so perhaps at that time Inverness used the same letters as the capital. This suggestion is rather confirmed by the marks on a com. cup at Forres, mentioned by Rev. T. Burns, showing a letter T in a plain shield on a repair dated 1724. This would be the Edinburgh letter for 1723-4. A more modern maker's mark met with is that of *Charles Jamison*, who was in business there about the year 1810. Besides his initials there is an animal (very small) something like a dromedary, which happens to be the dexter supporter to the Inverness arms. The animal is found usually turned to the left, but sometimes to the right.

Inverness, 1810.—(Charles Jamison.)

Inverness. Soup ladle, late 18th cent.—Late Dr. Diamond, F.S.A.

Inverness. Tea-spoons.—Marquess of Breadalbane

The *Perth* town mark was a spread eagle, sometimes single and sometimes double-headed, part of the town arms, and was used along with the Edinburgh marks, as shown on the West Church communion plate. The double eagle with RK (Robert Kay) is found on spoons of modern date; and this maker's mark is also found with a single-headed eagle on a plain rectangular stamp on spoons, the property of the Marquess of Breadalbane. It should be mentioned that the mark of a lamb and flag for Perth, with RG for maker's mark, occurs on the communion cups of Coupar Angus, which are dated 1687, and on an undated cup at Meigle, Perthshire. [Robert Gardiner, deacon 1669, 1673, and 1674,] and as below.

Perth. Com. plate.—Yorks.

Perth, 1771.   The West Church, Perth.

The *St. Andrew's* town mark was a St. Andrew's cross, as shown on the parish church Communion plate; the same marks occur on a silver dish, thought to be a salt-cellar, belonging to St. Mary's College there.

St. Andrew's, 1671.   The parish church-plate,
    St. Andrew's.   [Patrick Gairden.]

Canongate, Edinburgh.   A jug bearing these marks is mentioned in a History of the Burgh of Canongate published in 1879.   The mark, borne as is usual on Scottish provincial plate between the reduplicated maker's mark, is the Canongate crest.

Canongate Burgh, Edinburgh.

Mr. Brook gives some other examples, but always with a stag's head not having a cross above it.

Banff.   A small quantity of table plate seems to have been made here, of which the spoon cited is a good example. [Patrick Scott, c. 1710-31.]

Banff. Spoon, Hanoverian pattern. (Late Dr. Diamond,
    F.S.A.)

Elgin.   A soup-ladle has been noted by the author bearing the mark ELGIN with four other marks, viz., a castle with two towers (twice repeated); a standing figure with a staff, and the maker's initials CF. Mr. A. J. S. Brook reads these marks as the figure of St. Giles, the west front of Elgin Cathedral, and the maker's mark of Charles Fowler, 1790-1820.

Greenock. Mr. Brook attributes the small mark of an anchor often found on Scottish plate to Greenock.

UNCERTAIN SCOTTISH MARKS.

Racing bell described as the "Bell of Lanark, presented to the Burgh of Lanark by William the Lion in the year 1160." (Exhibited at the Grosvenor Gallery, London, in the Arts and Sports Loan Collection, 1890.)—A. H. Laidley, Esq.

R XID H.

This curious bell resembles the bell of 1655 engraved in Chapter X. It has a closed mouth with a number of small shields hanging round it, in the Dutch manner, one of which bears date 1628, whilst the rest are modern. It is of the early part of the seventeenth century, not much earlier than the date of its oldest shield, and the maker is probably Hugh Lindsay and the deacon Robert Dennistoun, which would give the bell to 1608-9, a not improbable date. The centre mark denotes the "elleven pennie fine" of the Act of 1555.

Pair of beaker cups, given 1750.—Drainie by Elgin.

FB ✿ FB

Com. cup, dated 1633.—Fintray, Aberdeenshire.

AH ✿ AH

MODERN GLASGOW.

Lastly, we come to the establishment of a new assay office in Glasgow, by an Act of 1819 (59 Geo. III. c. 28), which formed a Company in that city whose powers should extend for forty miles round, and appoints the marks to be used by it. These marks have been used ever since, notwithstanding any references to Glasgow in the more general Act 6 & 7 Will. IV. The distinguishing mark was to be the arms of the city of Glasgow,—a tree, fish, and bell; and its date-letters, complete alphabets of twenty-six letters each, have been regularly changed. They are given in Appendix B. A new alphabet of Italic capitals commenced in 1897. The standard mark is the lion rampant: these three, together with the maker's mark and Sovereign's head, make up the set of marks used there.

For silver of the higher standard, the "Britannia" mark is, however, added, and gold of eighteen carats is marked with the figures 18. The special remark must be made, that as the marks for gold of twenty-two carats have been, until quite lately, the same as those used for sterling silver, an article made of sterling silver stamped as such and afterwards gilt, often cannot, by the marks alone, be distinguished from gold. The figures 22 seem to be now used on gold of this quality. The parliamentary inquiry of 1773 did not extend to Scotland; but in 1848, both Edinburgh and Glasgow were in fair work, the former doing somewhat more than the latter. Edinburgh in 1847 had stamped nearly 29,000 ounces, and paid to the government a sum of £2152.

A tabular summary of the marks used in Edinburgh and Glasgow concludes the present chapter; whilst the tables of date-letters used will be found amongst other such Tables in Appendix B. at the end of the volume.

Those readers who require still further information on the question of Scottish hall-marks cannot do better than refer to the large work of Rev. T. Burns on *Old Scottish Communion Plate*, Edinburgh, 1892.

TABLE OF MARKS USED IN EDINBURGH AND GLASGOW.

OFFICE.	QUALITY.	STANDARD.		DATE.	DUTY.	MAKER.	TOWN MARK.
EDIN-BURGH.	Silver, O S.	Deacon's mark 1457 to 1759, then the thistle.	...	Annual letter from 1681.	Sove-reign's head from 1784 to 1890.	Initials, some-times in mono-gram, from 1457.	Castle from 1483.
	Ditto, N.S.	Ditto.	Britannia.				
GLAS-GOW from 1819.	Silver, O.S.	Lion rampant.	...	Do. from 1819.	Do. from 1819 to 1890.	Do. from 1819.	Tree, fish, and bell.
	Ditto, N.S.	Ditto.	Britannia.				

For gold of 18 carats since 6 & 7 Will. IV., and quite recently of 22 carats, add those figures respectively to the marks for silver, O.S.
For gold of the three lower standards, the quality is marked for 15, 12, or 9 carats, with those figures, in addition to the marks for silver, O.S.

CHAPTER VII.

IRELAND.

THE Goldsmiths' Company of Dublin, incorporated by a charter from Charles I., dated 1638 (22 Dec., 13 Car. I.), has the entire regulation of the goldsmiths' trade in Ireland. Their Charter is given at full length by Mr. Ryland in the little book before alluded to,* from which some of the following details relating to it have been taken.

The company was to have the correction of all abuses within the kingdom of Ireland, and to exercise the same powers as the Goldsmiths' Company of London had in England. The incorporated members were William Cooke, John Woodcocke, William Hampton, James Vanderbegg, William Gallant, John Banister, Nathaniel Stoughton, James Acheson, Clement Evans, George Gallant, Sylvanus Glegg, William St. Cleere, Gilbert Tongues, Edward Shadesy, Peter Van Eijndkoven,† Matthew Thomas, William Crawley, Thomas Duffield, John Cooke and John Burke, all styled of the city of Dublin, goldsmiths; and the above-named William Cooke, John Woodcocke, William Hampton, and John Banister were appointed the first wardens. Their successors and future wardens were to take office on All Saints' Day. No gold or silver of less fineness than the standard in England was to be wrought, and the " King's Majesty's stamp called the Harp crowned now appointed by his said Majesty" was not to be put on any silver below his Majesty's standard. These privileges have been exercised to the present time, subject to the various subsequent Acts of Parliament which are presently to be noticed; and the books of the Company have been kept with regularity even through troublous times. The early entries occasionally give the annual date-letters, as in 1644 and some succeeding years, but this is not

---

* *Assay of Gold and Silver Wares*, London, 1852.   † Per Mr. Westropp.

often the case. In that year, too, it is recorded that Thos. Parnell, Daniell Bellingham, Gilbert Tongues, Robert Coffee,* Nathaniell Stoughton and Peter Van Eijndkoven * had plate assayed. Two of these, therein called Gilbert Tongues and Peter Vandenhoven, with Sir John Veale, Knt., had been named in the previous year 1643 as goldsmiths, in a Proclamation relating to melting plate for the King.

Notices of civic importance are not wanting, such as the riding of the franchises of the city of Dublin, in which the Company of Goldsmiths took a prominent part in 1649, and other years. In that year, we have a detailed account of the attendance of the Company with horse and armour, and after the names of those who bore their part in the cavalcade, including Gilbert Tongues as captain, and also a Captain Waterhouse, comes a note which serves to indicate that the goldsmiths were of no mean importance socially speaking, for it adds, "certain above-named were not of our corporation, but of their own goodness forsook more ancient corporations and rode as loving brothers in our company, viz., Captain Water-house; some were invited by Mr. Sheriff Vandyndhown to his tent, the rest with us at Mr. Sumpnour, having no tent in the field." The minute of this event ends with the words " Sic transit gloria hodiei."

The list of the goldsmiths contributing to the expenses of the day contains the following names :—

Nathaniell Stoughton, Mʳ Warden.	Edward Bentley.
Danyell Burfeldt, Warden.	Ambrose Fewtrell.
Danyell Bellingham, Warden.	Joseph Stoker.
Gilbert Tongues.	Christopher Wright, and
Thomas Sumpnour.	Thomas Taylor.
Edward Shadsey.	

Another such festivity is recorded in 1656, Joseph Stoker being Master of the Company, but later on the times seem changed, for we come upon a motion in 1776 resolving that the Company was incapable of riding the franchises that year. It was not unmindful of its duty of prosecuting the fraudulent, for in 1777 it is entered that one Michael Keating, whose mark was MK, was convicted of counterfeiting marks, and sentenced to a fine of £50 and six months' imprisonment "at the last commission of Oyer and Terminer." As some of their initials

* Per Mr. Westropp.

occur on pieces of plate, a list of Dublin masters for a certain
number of years may be added as follows.   Most of these had
served as wardens in various years before being master, and
the dates of their becoming apprentices is added where known.

1671.	Thos. Rutter.	1696.	Vincent Kidder, Assay
1672.	John Dickson.		Master, 1697—1726.
1673.	Richard Lord, Assay Master	1697.	John Clifton.
	before 1692.	1698.	John Humphry.
1674.	Paul Lovelace.	1699.	David King, A. 1681.
1675.	Do.	1700.	W. Bingham, A. 1673.
1676.	Abm. Voisin.	1701.	Joseph Walker, A. 1683.
1677.	James Cottingham.	1702.	Robt. Rigmaiden.
1678.	James Kelly, A. 1654.	1703.	John Harris.
1679.	John Cope, d. bef. 1787.	1704.	James Welding, died.
1680.	Gerrard Grace.	1705.	Robt. Smith.†
1681.	Samuel Marsden.	1706.	Edward Slicer.
1682.	Abel Ram, Aldm. Sir.	1707.	Do.
1683.	Edward Harris.	1708.	Thos. Browne.
1684.	Capt. James Cottingham.	1709.	Mortagh Dowling.
1685.	Do.	1710.	Benj. Racine.
1686.	Adam Soret.	1711.	Thos. Billing.
1687.	John Shelly, A. 1674.	1712.	Edw. Workman, A. 1693.
1688.	John Cuthbert.*	1713.	W. Archdale, A. 1695, Assay
1689.	John Dickson.		Master, 1736—51.
1690.	Wm. Drayton, A. 1676.	1714.	John Hamilton.
1691.	Adam Soret.	1715.	Erasmus Cope.
1692.	Th. Bolton, Assay Master,	1716.	John Pallet, A. 1695.
	1692—97.	1717.	John Sterne.
1693.	John Phillips, A. 1666.	1718.	Wm. Barry.
1694.	Capt. Benj. Burton, A. 1678.	1719.	Do.
1695.	Do.		

A Company of Goldsmiths existed also at Cork from 1656
and regularly elected its master and wardens each year for a
long time onwards.   Other trades are included in the guild.
The Cork goldsmiths marked their plate with a galleon and a
castle with a flagstaff on separate stamps, but they did not use
a date-letter.   Plate thus marked is found towards the end of the
seventeenth century in and near the city of Cork.   One Robert
Goble was a very prominent member of the Company at that
period.   He was master in 1694 and 1695, and his mark RG
appears on a mace dated 1696 in the South Kensington Museum
(No. '69.31), and on communion cups, one dated 1692 at
Inishannon, and the other 1694 at Midleton, both in co. Cork.
The mark WB of one Walter Burnett, warden in 1694 and
master in 1700, occurs on more than one example.   Later the
word STERLING seems to have been used with a maker's

---

* He went to England February 14th, 1688, and appointed John Dickson to act.
† Elected June 27th for remainder of year, and re-elected 1705—6.

mark. It occurs thus on a flagon at Carrigaline, near Cork, and at other places in the South of Ireland.

It may be useful to add a list, for which readers are mainly indebted to Mr. Cecil C. Woods, of Cork, of the chief working goldsmiths of Cork from the incorporation of the guild in 1656. His list is much longer, containing some eighty names from 1601-1835. Not all were working goldsmiths.

1656. JOHN SHARPE.	1719. JOHN BISS.
1667. NICHOLAS GAMBLE.	Do. ROBERT GOBLE, Jr.
1673. JAMES RIDGE.	1721. WM. NEWENHAM.
1674. RICHARD SMART.	1723. REUBEN MILLERD.
1678. SAMUEL PANTAINE.	GEORGE HODDER, living 1745.
1680. JOHN HAWKINS.	MICHAEL MCDERMOTT, living 1757.
1690. GEORGE ROBINSON.	WM. REYNOLDS, living 1758.
1691. JOHN JAMES.	STEPHEN WALSH, living 1761.
1692. KALEB WEBB.	JOHN HILLERY, living 1762.
Do. CHARLES MORGAN.	CARDEN TERRY, living 1766.
1693. CHAS. BEHEGLE.	RICHARD WALSH, living 1768.
1694. ROBERT GOBLE.	JOHN NICHOLSON, living 1770.
Do. WALTER BURNETT.	CARDEN TERRY, jr., adm. 1785.
1702. CALEB RATHRUM.	JOHN WILLIAMS, living 1795.
Do. GEORGE BRUMLY.	(These last two were partners,
1706. JOHN HARDINGE.	(1795-1810.)
1710. WILLIAM CLARKE.	JOSEPH GIBSON, 1795.
1711. JOHN MAWMAN.	JOHN TOLEKIN, 1795.
1712. JAMES FOULKS.	WM. TEULON, 1795.
1716. WM. MARTIN.	

The dates down to 1723 are the years in which the goldsmith first served as either master or warden of the guild.

EXAMPLES OF CORK PLATE.

Chalice, dated 1663.—Lismore Cathedral.

Do.

Communion-plate given 1670 and 1671.—Carrigaline, Cork.

(John James, Master, 1692.) Plain tumbler cups. —Earl of Ilchester. Mr. Westropp ascribes this to Limerick.

STERLING

Chalice, dated 1694.—Inoshannon, Cork. Also paten, dated 1694.—Ballymodan, Bandon.

Sterling

(William Clarke, Master in 1714.) Flagon.— Carrigaline, Cork.

STERLING WM

(William Martin, Master, 1720 and 1727.) Maces repaired 1738 by Martin.—Corporation of Cork.

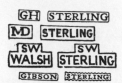

(George Hodder, living 1745.)　Cup.
(Michael McDermott, living 1757.)　Plain double-
　　handled loving cup.—Capt. M. Longfield.
(Stephen Walsh, living 1761.　Another smaller.
—Do.
(J. Gibson, 1795.)　Spoon.

It is possible that a little plate was made at Youghal, Limerick, and other places; but examples bearing what seem to be local Irish marks are very rare, and most of the church plate at Limerick is either of London or Dublin make.　Youghal received power by charter in 1608 to subdivide its corporation into guilds and to appoint a clerk of assay; and in 1631 Cork was granted "the same privileges as those enjoyed by Youghal," without specific mention of what they consisted.　There is no evidence of either place having exercised its privileges as far as establishing an assay office is concerned.

Nothing in the way of legislation need be noted till 1729 (3 Geo. II. c. 3, Ireland), when the Irish Parliament enacted that all articles of gold and silver should be assayed at Dublin by the assay-master appointed by the Company of Goldsmiths, fixed the standard of gold at 22 carats, and silver at 11 oz. 2 dwts., and ordered that the articles should be marked with the marks then used, which, we may add, would be the harp crowned, a date-letter, and the maker's initials.　The English enactments as to silver of the higher standard were not imitated in Ireland, and no plate of that standard has ever been made there.　To these marks, however, another was added in the following year 1730, by order of the Commissioners of Excise, who introduced the figure of Hibernia, to denote the payment of the duty first charged upon plate in that year.　The subsequent Act of 1807, requiring the king's head to be stamped on plate for the same purpose, took no notice of the Hibernia mark, and the two marks have since that year been used together till 1890.

In 1783 a second statute (23 & 24 Geo. III. (Irish) c. 23), repealed that of 1729, as far as gold was concerned, and fixed three standards for gold, viz., of 22, 20 and 18 carats.　All articles of gold were to be marked with the maker's mark, consisting of the first letters of his Christian and surname, and the various qualities were to be distinguished as follows:—
22-carat gold was to be marked at the assay office in Dublin with the harp crowned, and at the assay office at New Geneva

then established with the harp crowned having a bar across its
strings; 20-carat gold at Dublin with a plume of three feathers,
and at New Geneva with a plume of two feathers; and 18-carat
gold at Dublin with a unicorn's head, and at New Geneva with
a unicorn's head with a collar round its neck.   It further ordered
that the punches were to be so constructed that the impression
should be indented, instead of being in relief, so as to prevent
its being defaced.   It will be remembered that in England the
duty mark of the King's head introduced at about this same
time, is at first found "indented" in the fashion here described.
Certain specified gold wares, and all that should weigh less than
6 dwts., were exempted from the operation of the Act.

New Geneva is a village near Waterford where in 1783 a
colony of foreign Protestants was established after some persecution on the Continent.   Many Swiss were among them, prin-
cipally Genevese, whence the name.   They exercised various
trades, especially working in silver and jewellery, and hence
the establishment of an assay office and particular marks.
After a few years and the expenditure of £30,000, the settlement
was abandoned; the Genevese became discontented at not
having obtained as much as they wanted, and quitted the
country, and the place has dwindled to a small obscure village
without any trade.   It is therefore probable that very few if
any articles were assayed or marked there.

It remains to be said that date-letters have been used in Ireland from the time of the Charter of 1638, and as elsewhere
have formed more or less regular alphabets, the course of which
is, however, not always quite certain.   Plate of about the
middle of the eighteenth century is sometimes found bearing
the other proper marks, but no date-letter at all.

The lists at the end of the volume have been most carefully
compiled from the books of the company, and from a number
of specimens of plate, several of the latter kindly noted by Mr.
W. D. Waterhouse, who has paid much attention to the subject.
As might be expected, some few difficulties have been met with.

The old English ℭ for 1680-1 for example, and the 𝕂 for
1693-4, leave us an interval of thirteen years, but only six
letters to distribute over it.   If these six letters succeeded each
other in regular order, from 1680 to 1686, historical events
might be left to account for the next few years.   The charters

of all Irish Corporations were annulled for a time in 1687, and little trade in silver or gold work could have been carried on in Ireland, between the landing of King James at Kinsale in 1689, and the Treaty of Limerick which was concluded in October, 1691.

It must be confessed that it is less easy to account for a second gap between the years 1695 and 1709, and if the Dublin records are to be trusted, work seems to have been regularly carried on through the most troublous times. It is understood that the matter has attracted the attention of the Royal Irish Academy, and there is therefore reason to hope that some day an authoritative explanation of it will be furnished. The tables given may be depended on as nearly, if not quite, accurate; and all recent research, by fixing that the R of the alphabet which begins in 1678-9 must be certainly put at 1705-6, and the S which is the first letter which occurs in a shield with an escalloped top, at 1707-8, has gone to show that each letter probably stood for two consecutive years from 1695 to 1715. It may also have been so from 1680 to 1693, but hardly any hall-marked examples of plate are known for that stormy period.

Mr. Ryland states that the small Roman letter alphabet commencing in 1821-2 was changed at the letter e (for 1825), to one of Roman capitals, by order of the Commissioners of Stamps, to denote the transfer of the duties then made to them from the Commissioners of Excise by 6 Geo. IV. c. 118, and to mark the reduction of the allowance of $2\frac{1}{2}$ dwts. per lb., which had up to this time been made from the standard, to the allowance of $1\frac{1}{2}$ dwt. in accordance with the better practice of the London assay office. A careful investigation into the matter by Mr. Waterhouse, gives the letters for that cycle as they are found in the appended lists. They are all of them Roman capital letters, but a small Roman letter e in a shaped escutcheon is found in addition to the usual large letter in 1825.

From the alphabetical tables a good deal of additional information may be obtained, if one or two leading facts be borne in mind. The harp crowned will be found of larger size, and on a punch adapted to the outline of the mark, until 1787; after which, and until 1794,* it was smaller, and placed in a plain oval escutcheon, like the Hibernia which is to be looked for from the year 1730. The letters of the alphabet which

---

* Per Mr. Westropp.

commences in 1746, are to be distinguished from those of the next by their being somewhat bolder, and their shields larger and more angular at the bottom than those of the later alphabet, which last have the harp in an oval from the letter P of 1787* as remarked above, a second distinction. Both these hints are due to the observation of Mr. Waterhouse. From about 1794 to 1808,* both the harp crowned and Hibernia were in square stamps with the corners slightly cut off, and from 1808 to the end of that alphabet they are in shaped shields like the date-letter.

The letter L of 1807-8 is found both with and without the sovereign's head. During the last century the shapes of the other stamps seem to have pretty much corresponded with the shape of the shield used for the date-letter of the year; when that is plain or merely has the corners cut off, the same sort of shields are used for the harp, Hibernia, and King's head; but when shaped the escutcheons of these others correspond with it.

In 1848, Dublin was stamping from 20,000 to 40,000 ounces of silver per annum, besides a small quantity of gold, the annual totals varying very much, being about as much as the Edinburgh office, though a great deal less than Birmingham, Exeter, or Sheffield. At the time of a Parliamentary enquiry held in 1856, it was doing a somewhat smaller business, nearly all the country work having fallen off, especially that coming from Cork. The business originating in Dublin itself appeared to be somewhat on the increase.

EXAMPLES OF DUBLIN PLATE.

1638	. . .	Communion flagon—Trinity College, Dublin.
1639		(Probably John Thornton.) Communion cup, dated 1639. —Fethard, Wexford.
1640	Do.	Paten, dated 1640.—Do.
Do.		(Probably William Cooke, master 1637.) Communion cup and paten, dated 1639-40.—St. John Evangelist, Dublin.
1641	Do.	(Do.)—Communion cup, given 1637.—Derry Cathedral.
1659		Communion cup, given 1659.—St. John's-in-the-Vale, Cros-thwaite, Cumb. (Probably Joseph Stoker, master 1656.)
1663	Do.	Communion cup, dated 1665.—Corporation of Drogheda.
Do.	Do.	Communion cup and flagon, both dated 1667.—St. Peter's, Drogheda.
		Note.—A Communion plate, date 1669, *ex dono* Belling-ham, at Trinity College, Dublin, is by this maker.
1676		(Samuel Marsden, master 1681.) Communion cup and paten, given 1676.—St. Michan, Dublin.

* Per Mr. Westropp.

Date	Mark	Description
1679	E·S	Cups, dated 1674 (probably E. Swan) Sir J. K. James, Bart. Also flagon, dated 1677.—St. Werburgh, Dublin.
Do.	:M	(The other initial indistinct, probably SM as in 1676.)—Casket of St. George's Guild, dated 1678.
1680	AG	(Andrew Gregory, sworn 1673.) Tankards (see woodcut, Chap. x.).—Merchant Taylors' Co., London.
Do.	Do.	(Do.) Small Communion cup, originally the property of a Dean of Cork.—Late Rev. H. H. Westmore.
Do.	IP	(Probably John Phillips, master 1693.) Tankard-flagon, —St. John's, Limerick.
Do.	GG	(Gerrard Grace.) Ch. flagon, H. E. Taylor, Esq., Whickham.
1684	IH	(Probably John Humphry, master 1698.) Communion cup, called the new challess in 1686.—St. John's, Dublin.
Do.	Do.	(Do.) Communion cup, given 1685.—St. Werburgh, Dublin.
Do.	WL	Alms-dish, dated 1683 (Walter Lewis, A. 1666.)—Do.
Do.	I↑C	"Doggett" paten, given 1693.—Do. (Probably John Cope, master 1679, or John Cuthbert, master 1688).
1693	B	(Thos. Bolton, Alderman of Dublin and Assay-Master 1692-97.) Cup, given 1696.—Mansion House, Dublin.
Do.	Do.	(Do.) Cup, *ex dono* Duncombe.—Trinity College, Dublin.
Do.	AS as in 1686	(A. Gregory.) A pair of candle cups and cover.—Noted by West and Son. Dublin.
Do.	JW	(Joseph Walker, master 1701.) Paten, dated 1693.—Ch. Ch. Cathedral, Dublin. Also paten, given 1693.—St. Michan, Dublin.
Do.	Do.	(Do.) Communion cup, dated 1696.—St. Nicholas', Dublin.
Do.	AS	(Probably Alex Sinclare, warden 1699.) Piece of plate, dated Jan. 169⅔.—Abbey Leix. Also alms-dish, given 1694.—Ch. Ch. Cathedral, Dublin.
1694	DK	(David King, master 1699.) Flagon, dated 1698.—St. Michan's, Dublin.
1695	. . .	(Thos. Bolton, as in 1693.) Cup given 1696.—Mansion House, Dublin.
Do.	. . .	Flagon, dated 1700.—Trinity College, Dublin.
1697	S	Large monteith with arms and inscription.—Noted by Messrs. West and Co. (Rt. Smith, master 1705, or E. Slicer, master 1707.)
Do.	DK	(David King, master 1699.) Gadrooned salver from the same collection.—Do. The foot of this is by A.S.
1699 } 1700 }	Do.	(Do.) Mace, dated 1701, formerly belonging to the borough of Lifford.—Earl of Erne.
Do.	. . .	Paten, dated 1703.—St. Mary's, Dublin.
Do.	JW	(Joseph Walker, as in 1693.) Flagon and paten, dated 1720.—Ch. Ch. Cathedral, Dublin.
1701 } 1702 }	AS	(Alex Sinclare, as in 1693.) Tankard.—Noted by Author.
1705 } 1706 }	JW	(Joseph Walker, as in 1693.) Communion cup and paten, dated 1706.—St. Nicholas', Dublin.
Do.	DK	(David King, as in 1694.) Paten, undated. — Ch. Ch. Cathedral, Dublin.
Do.	Do.	(Do.) Small salver on foot.—Noted by Messrs West. and Co.

1706	H·M	(Hy. Mathews, warden 1711.) Paten, dated 1705.—St. Mary's, Dublin.
1707, 1708	. . .	(Thos. Bolton, as in 1693.) Paten, dated 1707.—Staplestown, Carlow.
Do.	J·W	(Joseph Walker, as in 1693.) Cup, dated 1709, *ex dono* Palliser.—Trinity College, Dublin.
Do.	DK	(David King, as in 1694.) Mace.—Corporation of Enniskillen.
Do.	. . .	Communion cup, dated Feb. 1703-4.—Cloyne Cathedral.
1709 1710	J·W	(Joseph Walker, as in 1693.) Alms-dish.—St. Mary's, Dublin.
Do.	Do.	(Do.) Communion cup and paten, dated 1706.—St. Nicholas', Dublin.
Do.	. . .	(Thomas Bolton, as in 1693.) Flagon; legacy, dated 1712.—Cloyne Cathedral.
Do.	. . .	(Communion cup dated 1709.) St. Margaret's, Dromiskin.
Do.	PT Crown and Shaped Shield	(Probably Philip Tough, warden 1711.) Com. plate at St. Dogmaels, Pembroke.
Do.	DK	(David King, as in 1694.) Flagon, dated 1711.—St. Audoen's, Dublin.
1711 1712	Do.	(Do.) Communion cup, given 1713.—Killeshranda, Cavan.
Do.	. . .	Paten, dated 1712.—St. Mary's, Dublin.
1713 1714	. . .	(Thos. Bolton, as in 1693.) Fine fluted monteith.—Capt. M. Longfield.
1715	. . .	Communion plate, dated 1715.—Cashel Cathedral.
Do.	J·W	(Joseph Walker, as in 1693.) Paten, dated 1716.—St. Luke's, Dublin.
Do.	I·C	Paten.—Daglingworth, Glouc. (Perhaps John Clifton, master 1697.)
1716	. . .	(Thos. Bolton, as in 1693.) Candlesticks with square bases, the corners cut off, winged busts on the stems.— Earl of Ilchester. Also two-handled cup. Col. Tremayne, Carclew.
Do.	E·W	(Edward Workman, warden 1712.)—Flagon dated 1717.— St. John Evangelist, Dublin.
Do.	DK	(Probably another mark of David King.) Flagon, dated 1716.—Templeport, Cavan.
Do.	Do.	Flagon, dated 1716.—Killeshrandra, Cavan.
1718	. . .	(Thos. Bolton, as in 1693.) Mace.—Corporation of Dublin.
Do.	AS	(Probably Alex. Sinclare, as in 1693.) Plain salver on foot. Noted by West and Co.
Do.	PK	(Philip Kinnersley, master 1720.) Alms-dish, dated 1720. —Noted by Lambert and Co.
1719	TW	Thos. Walker, as in 1726. Paten, Rhoscrowther, Pembrokeshire.
1720	R·H	(Robert Harrison.)* Fluted salver.—late Col. Meadows Taylor, C.S.I.
Do.	. . .	Salver on feet, bearing Gore arms.—Lord Harlech.
Do.	H·D	(Henry Daniell.)* Plain two-handled cup.—Capt. M. Longfield.
1724	R.H	(As in 1720.) Coffee-pot.—Rev. F. Sutton,
1725	H·C	Two-handled cup and cover—late J. R. Daniel-Tyssen,Esq.
Do.	I·H	(John Hamilton, master 1714.) Alms-dish, dated 1724.— St. Michan's, Dublin.

* Per Mr. Westropp.

1726	(mark)	(Perhaps Matthew Walker, master 1724.) Communion cup.—St. Nicholas', Dublin.
Do.	T·W	Plain salver on foot.—Noted by Messrs. West and Co. (Probably Thomas Walker.)
1728	WW	Mace, dated 1728.—Goldsmiths' Co., London.
1729	(mark)	Plain bowl—Blair O. Cochrane, Esq.
1730	I·H	(I·H, as in 1725.) Plain bowl.—Noted by Messrs. West and Co.
1731	DK	(Crowned, as in 1716.) Small salver.—Marquis of Breadalbane.
1732	T·W	(As in 1726.) Flagon, dated 1731.—St. Nicholas', Dublin.
Do.	I·T	Rat-tail spoon (probably John Taylor, warden 1725–27–28).
Do.	A·L	Mark noted by Author. (Ant. Lefebure.)
1733	T·W	(As in 1726.) Two-handled cup.—late Lord Holmpatrick.
1734	. . .	Flagon, dated 1733.—St. Patrick's, Waterford.
Do.	I·W	Jug, won by " Smileing Bald," at Waterford Races.—Lord Harlech. (Probably John Wilme, master 1739.)
1735	E·C	Racing cup, dated 1734.—Earl of Enniskillen. (Eras. Cope, master 1722.)
1736	I·H	(As in 1725.) Large shaped salver and pair of small two-handled cups. — Sold at Christie & Manson's in 1875. Also cake-basket in imitation of wicker-work.—Capt. M. Longfield.
Do.	AB	Mark noted by Author.—(A. Brown.)
Do.	R·H	Mark noted by Author.—(Robt. Hopkins, master 1760.)
Do.	W W	(As in 1728.) Gold snuff-box, presented with the freedom of Naas, 1737.—Earl of Shannon.
1738	DK	(Crowned, as in 1716.) Paten. — Llanelian-yn-Rhos, Denbighshire.
1739	FW	Communion cup, dated 1741.—Kildare Cathedral. (Fras. Williamson.)
1740	AG	Mark noted by Author. (Andrew Goodwin,* master 1746.)
1743	I·H	(As in 1725.) Table-spoons.—Lord Amherst of Hackney.
1744	T·W	(As in 1726.) Do.—Noted by Messrs. Waterhouse.
1745	AR	Mark noted by Author.—Alex. Richards.*
1747	W·W	Flagon.—St. Nicholas', Dublin. (Probably W. Wilson.)
1753	ID	Table-spoons, Hanoverian pattern. — Col. Tremayne, Carclew. (Probably Isaac D'Olier, master 1752.)
c. 1755	R+C	Salvers and tankard.—Lord O'Neill. (Robt. Calderwood, master 1736.)
1755	D·P	(David Petre.) Fluted soup-ladle. — Col. Tremayne, Carclew.
1756	I P	Spoons.—Noted by Messrs. Waterhouse.
Do.	J·S	Table-spoons, feather-edged.—Late J. J. Lonsdale, Esq. (Probably John Sherwin, master 1769.)
1759	I·L	Mark noted by Author.
1765	A·N	Mark noted by Author.—Arthur O'Neill.*

* Per Mr. Westropp.

1767	IC	Dessert-spoons.—Noted by Messrs. Waterhouse.
1769	WJB	Large circular salver.—Late Col. Meadows Taylor, C.S.I.
Do.	JK	John Karr.—Noted by Author. (A. 1751.)
1770	CT	Two-handled cup.—J. Y. Burges, Esq. (Chas. Townshend.)
1776*	I·K	Snuff-box, presented with an address, 1778. — Earl of Shannon. (Perhaps John Keane, warden 1799.)
1778	MK	In plain oblong (Michael Keating). Plain table-spoons with pointed handles.—Capt. M. Longfield.
Do.	J·B	In oval. Salad spoon and fork, feather-edged.—Do.
1782	IK	As in 1776. Table-spoons with pointed handles, feather-edged.—Do.
1783	GS	Spoon.
1785	MW	Sugar-basin, on three feet.—From the Staniforth Collection.
1789	TJ	Mark noted by Author. (Thos. Jones, master 1791.)
1794	L&B	Mark noted by Author.
1796	RW	Mark noted by Author. (Richd. Williams, master 1785.)
1805	I·S	Cake-basket, repoussé and chased.—Late Rev. C. Daniel. (John Stoyte, master 1799.)
1807	J·P	Large gravy-spoon.—Messrs. Waterhouse. (John Pittar, master 1796.)
1811	I·L·B	(Le-Bas.) Teapot (also stamped with dealer's name WEST).—Late Rev. C. Daniel.
1815	Do.	(Do.) shaped salver, on feet.—Do.

TABLE OF DUBLIN MARKS SINCE 1638.

QUALITY.	STANDARD.	DATE.	DUTY. 1730—1890.	MAKER.
Silver, O.S.	Harp crowned. 17th cent. 18th cent. till 1787. 1787-94. 1794 to 1808. (See pp. 193-4.)	Annual letter.	Hibernia from 1730, and King's Head in addition from 1807. 1730 to 1792. 1792 to 1808. (See p. 194.)	Initials.
Gold, 22 c., till 1784.†	Ditto.	Ditto.	Ditto.	Ditto.

N.B.—The provisions as to gold of 15, 12, and 9 carats, of 17 & 18 Vict. c. 96, extend to Ireland, and these qualities are denoted by the same decimal numbers as in England, by way of standard marks.

* The date letters F, H and M of this alphabet, and others, have a small dot or pellet beneath them within the shield (see p. 520).

† Since 1784, for standard marks on gold of 22, 20, and 18 carats, and for the New Geneva marks, see the notice of the Act of that year (23 & 24 Geo. III. c. 23), p. 191.

CHAPTER VIII.

FRAUDS AND OFFENCES.

THE lessons that may be derived by the plate-buyer from a
little practical experience, as well as from a record of some of
the offences that have from time to time been attempted in contravention of the legislation of which we have now considered
the course, are so important, that a short chapter may be fairly
devoted entirely to them.

Frauds are no new thing, and a description of the deceits of
the goldsmiths in Queen Elizabeth's days might almost word
for word have been written in those of His present gracious
Majesty. They are amusingly set out in Stubbes' *Anatomy of
Abuses,** thus :—

"*Theodorus.* Be there Goldsmithes there any store also, as in
some other countries there be ?

"*Amphilogus.* There are inow, and more than a good meanie.
They are (for the most part) very rich and wealthye, or else
they turne the fairest side outwards, as many doe in *Dnalgne.*†
They have their shops and stalles fraught and bedecked with
chaines, rings, gold, silver, and what not woonderfull richly.
They will make you any monster or antike whatsoever of golde,
silver, or what you will. They have store of all kinde of plate
whatsoever. But what ? Is there no deceit in all these goodlye
shewes ? Yes, too many. If you will buy a chaine of golde, a
ring, or any kinde of plate, besides that you shall paye almost
halfe more than it is woorth (for they will persuade you the
workmanship of it comes to so much, the fashion to so much,
and I cannot tell what) ; you shall also perhaps have that golde
which is naught, or else at least mixt with drossie rubbage, and
refuse mettall, which in comparison is good for nothing. And
sometimes, or for the most part, you shal have tinne, lead, and
the like, mixt with silver. And againe, in some things some will
not sticke to sell you silver gilt for gold, and well if no worse too
now and then. But this happeneth very seldome, by reason of

---

* Phillip Stubbes' *Anatomy of Abuses
in England*, Part II. 1. Tricks of
Goldsmiths and Vintners.—New Shake-
speare Society, Series VI., No. 12.
† England.

good orders, and constitutions made for the punishment of them
that offend in this kind of deceit, and therefore they seldome
dare offend therein, though now and then they chance to stumble
in the darke."

There is little here that would differ from an account of
practices that are, unhappily, too prevalent at the present time.

The earliest provisions against fraud concern themselves with
the use of metal worse than standard, the setting of false stones
in gold, and of real stones in base metal, the price at which
goldsmiths' work shall be sold, and the prevention of working
in secret; later on penalties were instituted, not only for selling
silver of inferior quality, but for selling even fine silver before
it was marked with the proper touches and the maker's own
mark, whilst in 1597 we come as a third stage to proceedings
instituted against those who counterfeited marks, which resulted,
as we have seen, in the offenders being put in the pillory and
losing an ear. Some of these offences owe their very existence
to a state of things, socially speaking, which has long passed
away. The very notion of legislating against working in a
back street, or at night, or fixing the price at which articles
should be sold, is enough to raise a smile at the simplicity of
mediæval economy. Neither need we notice here the statutes
directed against exporting silver and melting down the coin of
the realm to make plate.

It may, however, be of interest to recall that from 1635 for
some time onwards the Pewterers gave much umbrage to the
Goldsmiths' Company by placing on their wares marks counterfeiting those on the Goldsmiths'. This practice seems to have
prevailed more or less for a century, say till 1739, for the Act
of that year made it for the future practically impossible.

Coming to modern days, a short review of the reported cases
will answer the useful purpose of suggesting to the reader the
sort of frauds against which he should be on his guard, even
though changes in the law, and the abolition of the intricacies
of special pleading, have deprived them to a certain extent of
their legal interest.

Several such cases were appended to the report presented to
the House of Commons in 1773, this appendix being in point
of fact an account of the prosecutions carried on by the Goldsmiths' Company against persons for frauds and abuses in

matters relating to gold and silver plate during the seven years then last past.

They were four in number, and omitting technicalities they were as follows :—

(1.) In 1767, for soldering bits of standard silver to tea-tongs and shoe-buckles, which were worse than standard, and sending them to the Company's assay office in order fraudulently to obtain their marks to the same.

(2.) In 1768, for making salt-cellars worse than the standard, and selling them for standard.

(3.) In 1770, for making and also for selling gold watch-chains worse than standard.

(4.) In the same year for selling two silver watch-cases without being marked.

To this report of 1773 was appended the remark that the heavy penalty (no less than death as a felon) imposed by 31 Geo. II. c. 32, for counterfeiting hall-marks, had greatly put a stop to frauds in wrought plate.

It is more than doubtful whether as much could be said at the present day, though the goldsmiths' trade is now regulated by an Act which does all that can be effected by careful provisions in the direction of rendering abuses difficult or impossible ; but such is the temptation to the forger of these days, in consequence of the demand for " antique " plate, that a single walk through the streets of London will be enough to show that present legislation is powerless against his cunning arts. The Quarterly Reviewer has not overstated the case in saying that a buyer may return home, after traversing our great thoroughfares for a day, with " a cab-load of real old English plate," if he be not too fastidious, and has money in his purse.* By the time the reader has got to the end of this chapter, if he ever does, and if he did not know it before, he will have found where all this stuff comes from, and how little genuine antique plate is to be had at a moment's notice, or indeed at all, however much one may be willing to pay for it.

First, let us recount the main provisions of the Acts which now regulate the craft ; then note a case or two that have

---

* *Quarterly Review*, April, 1876.

been dealt with under them; and conclude the chapter with some personal experiences of the modes in which they are evaded.

We may ignore, as this is not a legal treatise, the various minor provisions of the last and present centuries, altering penalties from time to time, and also certain details found only in the Sheffield and Birmingham Acts. Everything of general interest is practically summed up in the most recent Act,* which, with the Act of the reign of Geo. II.,† are those to which we now turn : the latter still providing for the maintenance of the standards, whilst the Act of 7 & 8 Vict., c. 22, deals with abuses in the marking of wares.

As to the standards, then, the Act of 1739 provided that all gold wares should be not less in fineness than 22 carats of fine gold, and all silver wares not less than 11 oz. 2 dwts. of fine silver in every pound weight Troy, and inflicted by s. 1 a penalty of £10 for every offence.

It is, however, not quite certain but that these offences are still indictable as misdemeanours under older legislation; for the ancient Acts of 28 Edw. I., 2 Henry VI., 18 Eliz., and 12 Will. III. are recited but not repealed by the Act we are now considering : and since the passing of it, prisoners have been sentenced to fine and imprisonment on indictment under 28 Edw. I. for making silver plate worse than standard. Instances of this occurred in 1758, 1759, and 1774, the last case being tried by Lord Mansfield.‡

The Act of 1739 also inflicts a penalty of £10, or in default imprisonment, for selling, exchanging, or exposing to sale any gold or silver ware before it is duly marked; it directs the entry of makers' marks at the Goldsmiths' Hall; and it details under penalties the particulars which must accompany every parcel of wares sent to the assay office for stamping. These last are repeated in the duty Act of 1784.

Turning now to the other branch of the subject, we find that everything relating to the prevention of frauds and abuses in the marking of gold and silver wares in England is summed up

---

* 7 & 8 Vict. c. 22 (1844).   † 12 Geo. II. c. 26 (1739).
‡ R. v. Jackson. Cowper, 297.

in the Act of 1844,* which enumerates the following offences all punishable as felonies :—

Sec. 2. Forging or counterfeiting any Die for marking Gold or Silver Wares or knowingly uttering the same ;

Marking Wares with forged Dies, or uttering them ;

Forging any Mark of any Die, or uttering the same ;

Transposing or removing Marks, or uttering them ;

Having in possession knowingly any such Die, or Ware marked with the same ;

Cutting or severing Marks with Intent to affix them upon other Wares ;

Affixing any Mark cut or severed from any other Wares ;

Fraudulently using genuine Dies.

Later sections deal with other offences, as follows :—

Sec. 3. Selling or having possession of any Wares with forged or transposed Marks without lawful excuse (even unknowingly that the Marks were so forged or transposed) ; penalty £10 each offence.

Sec. 4. Dealers to be exempt from the above penalties on giving up the names of the actual manufacturer of such wares of gold or silver or base metal, or of the person from whom they received them, but not from the consequence of uttering them with guilty knowledge.

Sec. 5. Adding to, or altering by addition or otherwise, the character of wares already marked and so as to increase the weight by more than one-third of the original weight, without having them re-assayed as new ; or in certain cases, with the assent of the Company, the added part only assayed ; or selling such ware without the same being marked ; penalty £10 for each offence and forfeiture of the ware.

Sec. 6. Exceptions to the preceding section corresponding to those of section 4.

Sec. 7. If any officer of any of the Halls shall mark any base metal with any die, etc., such Company to be liable to a penalty of £20, the officer to be dismissed and the ware seized.

Sec. 8. Dealers to register every place where they work or carry on business or deposit wares, under a penalty of £5.

Sec. 9. Dealers not to fraudulently erase, obliterate, or deface any mark under a penalty of £5.

Sec. 11. Upon information given upon oath against persons suspected of having in possession illegal wares, etc., Justices may grant search-warrants, but not for wares not required to be marked.

Sec. 13. Actions to be commenced within three months after the fact committed.

This being the state of the law, at the risk of repeating what has been said by other writers, some notice must be taken of the most instructive case that had occurred under it down to the year 1876, condensing our account from that given by Mr. Ryland.†

Two silversmiths were tried before Lord Denman at Taunton

---

* 7 & 8 Viet. c. 22.   † *Assay of Gold and Silver Wares*, London, 1852.

Spring Assizes, 1849, for having in their possession, without lawful excuse, a silver spoon and soup-ladle having thereon marks of dies used by the Goldsmiths' Company, which had been transferred from silver skewers. The spoon and ladle were of modern make, but bore the mark of the year 1774. An officer from the Goldsmiths' Company proved that, on clearing off the gilding and using a blow-pipe he found that the spoon and ladle were not made in one piece, which would be the ordinary mode of manufacture, but that the parts bearing the marks were "inserted" or "brought on." A working silversmith proved that by direction of the prisoners he had made and sent to them two silver bowls for spoons; that they afterwards were returned to him with handles attached to be gilt, and when he burnished them he perceived the old hall-marks; he proved also that the bowls and stems, or handles, were generally made together.

The defence set up was that this did not amount to a *transposition*, but was only an *addition*, a minor offence under the Act and entailing a lesser penalty; and it was suggested that the spoon and ladle were made by using old silver skewers with the old hall-mark for the stems, and adding to them bowls and figures at the top called "apostles" in order to give them the appearance of old plate, and that *this* was an addition, which, though a fraud in contravention of the Act, would not be a felony. This ingenious transposal of the process commended itself to the jury, and they acquitted the prisoners, though evidently against the summing-up of the learned judge, who thought that the description of *transposition* in one section, and of *addition* in another, came to much the same thing, and avowed that he was at a loss to see any difference between taking out just merely the mark and putting it into a new article, which would clearly be a transposition, and doing the same thing with some more dexterity and more disguise in a considerable length. A more recent case is not less suggestive.

D. L. G., a dealer, carrying on business in London, was convicted at the Central Criminal Court in August, 1876, of feloniously altering and transferring a certain mark of a die used by the Goldsmiths' Company under the following circumstances. A customer found displayed in the prisoner's shop, and purchased for £10, a coffee-pot, hall-marked and bearing

the letter m of the year 1747, there being appended to it a
label with the words "120 years old." He also purchased of
the prisoner a small silver ewer, bearing the goldsmiths' letter
for 1744.

It being found that the articles were of recent manufacture,
the Goldsmiths' Company issued a writ against the prisoner
to recover penalties under s. 3 of the Act we are considering,
in regard to which, under another section, a dealer could, however, be protected if within twenty-one days he gave up the
name of the person from whom he bought the article. At first
stating that he had bought the article in the way of trade and
did not know from whom, he afterwards gave the name of a
working electro-plater, who was thereupon arrested and, on the
prisoner's evidence, being committed for trial, pleaded guilty.
Judgment was postponed, and his evidence taken against the
principal offender, from which it appeared that he had transferred to the coffee-pot and ewer certain old marks from pieces
of silver brought to him by the prisoner for that purpose, the
prisoner agreeing to purchase those articles if the witness would
put the old marks on. The offenders were thereupon sentenced,
the dealer to six months and the electro-plater to two months'
imprisonment, in both cases with hard labour. A number of
penalties were sued for in the course of the year 1878, by the
Goldsmiths' Company; and in one case no less a sum than £240
was paid on account of the sale of 24 forks bearing forged
hall-marks of a good period. It would be very desirable to
give fullest publicity to all such convictions; without this they
have but little effect.

A few words may conveniently be said here about the importation of plate bearing forged English marks. Legislation upon
this abuse seems to commence with a Customs Act of 1842
(5 & 6 Vict. c. 47), which enacts that foreign plate shall not be
sold unless duly assayed and marked, but does not oblige the
importer to send such plate to be marked *at the time of its
importation*, nor indeed at any time. Another Act of the same
year (5 & 6 Vict. c. 56), provides that ornamental plate made
prior to 1800 may be sold without being marked. Shiploads of
modern forgeries avail themselves of this convenient provision.

A third such Act, passed in 1867 (30 & 31 Vict. c. 82), directs
that any imported plate sent to an assay office to be marked,

shall be marked with all the usual marks, and with the letter F in an oval escutcheon in addition. This act has been repealed; but the provision in question was re-enacted (39 & 40 Vict. c. 35) in the same words. We then find in the *London Gazette* of Dec. 9, 1887, an Order in Council under the Merchandise Marks Acts of the same year, prescribing special marks for foreign watch-cases admitted to assay, after a declaration as to place of manufacture. For gold, the word "Foreign" on a cross. For silver, the same on a regular octagon. These to be used together with the year-letter, and other usual marks.

The following further Acts of Parliament, mostly passed since the above has been written, may be of interest :

1883.—46 & 47 Vict. c. 25 (The Revenue Act, 1883) sect. 10 is an important provision which requires the Customs to secure that all gold and silver plate imported into the United Kingdom for sale shall be bonded, and removed from the warehouse in charge of an Officer of Customs, and be delivered into the hands of the officers of the Assay Office nearest to the port of importation. This section also provides that if such plate shall be found upon assay to be of standard quality it may be " cleared " for home use, but that if such plate shall be found not to be of standard quality it shall not be broken (as was formerly necessary), but shall be removed from the Assay Office and returned to the warehouse for export.

Plate imported for private use, and not for sale, is exempted upon proof by Statutory Declaration that such plate is not intended for sale or exchange.

1884.—47 & 48 Vict. c. 62 (the Revenue Act, 1884) sect. 4 provides that articles of foreign plate which, in the opinion of the Commissioners of Customs, may be properly described as hand-chased, inlaid, bronzed, or filigree work of oriental pattern shall, subject to the payment of the proper duties of Customs, be exempted from assay in the United Kingdom.

1887.—50 & 51 Vict. c. 28 (the Merchandise Marks Act, 1887) sect. 8 provides for a declaration of origin of all watch-cases sent to any Assay Office in the United Kingdom for the purpose of being assayed and marked, and for the marking of foreign watch-cases with a special mark to be prescribed by Order in Council.

This mark was prescribed by Order in Council of Nov. 28, 1887, and changed by Order in Council of May 7, 1907.

1890.—53 & 54 Vict. c. 8, part II. provides that on and after May 1, 1890, the Stamp duties and duties of Customs on gold and silver plate shall cease to be payable, and the drawback upon the exportation of plate shall cease to be allowed.

1904.—4 Edw. VII. c. 6 (the Hall-marking of Foreign Plate Act, 1904) repeals the Customs Tariff Act, 1876 (39 & 40 Vict. c. 35) sect. 2, and provides that where any plate or other article imported from a foreign part is brought to an Assay Office in the United Kingdom to be assayed and marked the plate or article shall be marked in such manner as His Majesty may determine by Order in Council, so as to readily distinguish whether the plate or other article was made in England, Scotland or Ireland, or was imported from foreign parts. The Act also provides that any person who brings or causes to be brought any plate or other article to be assayed and marked at an Assay Office shall make a written declaration of origin (unless the plate or other article is brought in charge of an Officer of Customs as having been imported from foreign parts), and that if such person does not know the place of origin he shall make a written declaration to that effect, and the plate or article shall be marked as foreign.

A person knowingly making a false declaration is made liable to a penalty of £5 for every article.

The special mark was provided by Order in Council of October 24, 1904, and changed by Order in Council of May 11, 1906.

1907.—7 Edw. VII. c. 8 (Assay of Imported Watch-cases (existing stocks exemption), Act 1907), provides that foreign watch-cases imported before June 1, 1907, shall be exempted from assay and marking, but throws the burden of proof upon the person claiming exemption. There are also provisions for securing identification of such watch-cases as may be exported and subsequently reimported.

7 Edw. VII. c. 13 (the Finance Act, 1907) sect. 5 amends sect. 10 of the Revenue Act, 1883, by providing that imported plate may be sent to any Assay Office selected by the importer (not only the nearest office) and may be so sent without being in charge of an Officer of Customs upon certain security being given.

An Order in Council of May 11, 1906, enacted the following, as to the marking of foreign plate introduced into Great Britain :

For gold, the hall mark particular to each Assay Office ;

and the carat value of the gold, together with the decimal
equivalent of the carat value. For silver the hall mark
particular to each Assay Office, together with the decimal
equivalent of the standard value of silver.

The mark for the London Assay Office is the sign, Leo ;
for Birmingham, an equilateral triangle ; Sheffield, the sign of
Libra ; Chester, acorn and two leaves ; Edinburgh, St.
Andrew's Cross ; Glasgow, double block letter F inverted ;
Dublin, Boujet. The annual date letter of each office has to be
added. These marks are the same for gold and silver.

It will easily be seen that none of these enactments offer
any real hindrance to the importation of plate bearing forged
English marks, and some stringent legislation is sorely needed
to put a stop to fraudulent practices and to protect the honest
dealer and the public alike.

There is nothing, however, so telling as personal experience :
let us see what can be picked up in this way by the amateur of
old plate as he walks along the London streets.

He will soon see that in consequence of the first series of
imitations having been usually of seventeenth century plate,
and the better credit that silver work of the reigns of Queen
Anne and the earlier Georges therefore maintained, the latter
period became in time the more profitable one to attack, and
that the market is now flooded with the plain and fluted plate
of those reigns, which is made to all appearance, both at home
and abroad for importation hither, by the waggon-load.

Next he will find that the modern forger scorns to be at
the trouble of transposing or adding, call it which you will,
genuine old hall-marks to modern plate. He boldly fashions
antique plate, marks and all ; and here we may say that so far
from giving him information to turn to base advantage, as one
writer has feared would be the case, the published lists of date-
letters and other marks have, by their very inaccuracies, proved
pit-falls for those who have used them for purposes of fraud.

How shall we distinguish the real from the spurious ? Well,
one chance is, that our enquirer finds in nine cases out of ten
that the forger has not learned his lesson thoroughly. A living
amateur has seen, for instance, at a public exhibition in London,
a large jug conspicuously labelled as by the famous George
Heriot, but bearing marks which could only belong to the end

of the seventeenth century, if they were genuine at all; and they were not if the said amateur knew anything about the matter. He has also seen, as conspicuously labelled in a shop-window, a pair of Queen Anne pattern candlesticks, bearing what purported to be a well-known maker's mark, and beside it the date-letter of a year that had elapsed long before the adoption and registration by that maker of the particular mark in question.

What would the unsophisticated collector say to finding that two specimens of Queen Anne plate in his cabinet, with their gadrooned edges, court-hand date-letters and all, of some five or ten years apart, and by quite different makers, proved on a careful examination of the ornamentation, to have come from one and the same modern *atelier*, a small defect in one of the tools used having left its fatal sign on both articles alike?

What, again, if he should see an Elizabethan treasure, say of 1576, put into a sale by its disgusted owner, who had arrived at a knowledge of its real age all too late, and knocked down by the auctioneer for a small sum as what is called in the trade a "duffer," amid the pleasantries of an appreciative audience of dealers who will possibly welcome it again before long under much the same circumstances?

Another surprise may await him if he should be fortunate enough to secure for his collection some relic of thrilling historical interest, such as a cup proved by the inscription upon it to have been the gift of Mary Queen of Scots to Darnley; for it is not beyond the bounds of possibility that he may meet ere long with a second cup, of precisely similar pattern, and proved as conclusively to have been the one given in exchange by Darnley to that unfortunate lady.

As he will hardly expect to pick up a third treasure of this description, he may perhaps turn his attention to real old "family plate," of which he may think that there is likely to be more in the market. It would be very odd if he did not soon come across plenty to be sold, "in strict confidence," and "under peculiar circumstances," with a condition that the ancient coats of arms with which it is decorated are to be carefully erased.

Much of this precious stuff has been bought by those who have afterwards found that, like some other people who preceded them—*sero sapiunt Phryges*,—they have come by their wisdom too late.

A most flagrant case came to light long after the publication
of the first edition of this volume in 1878, and it is full of
warning, illustrating almost every point that has been mentioned
in the last few pages. Were it not an actual fact, it would be
hard to believe that dealer dared sell, or buyer could be found
to buy, a set of many hundreds of spoons, forks, and other table
plate marked as of the first ten or fifteen years of the eighteenth
century. More astonishing still is it that, though he marked
his wares as of Britannia standard, the manufacturer should
not have taken the trouble to make up his metal to that quality,
for the chance of avoiding detection by the assay ; and most
astonishing of all that he should have included in his set, dessert-
knives, fish-slices, and other articles unheard of in bygone days.
The handles of the forks appear to have been cast, marks and all,
in a mould made from a spoon-handle, and then fastened on to
prongs, for which cast metal would not have been sufficiently
hard and unbending. Great numbers of these had the letter
for 1703-4, with the Britannia standard marks, and for maker's
mark the letters *PE* with a crown above, and a pellet below
them, all within a circle. Others had the letter for 1712-3, with
II for maker's mark on a stamp with indented edge; others,
again, had *HB* as it appears in Appendix A at the year 1782,
together with the London hall-marks for 1683-4. And many
other blunders of the same sort came to light as soon as the
objects were submitted to careful examination.

On the institution of proceedings the dealer who sold all this
rubbish gave up, under the provisions of section 4 of the Act of
1844, the name of a person from whom he said he had received
it in the ordinary way of business; and in the end judgment
was signed by the Goldsmiths' Company against this person
for the full amount of £10 for each of the articles, of which
there were 647, bearing forged marks. It seems very much
open to question whether the Act works at all well, or for
the interests of the public. Penalties are nominally recovered,
it is true, by the Goldsmiths' Company; but the forger goes to
work again as before at his profitable trade, escaping in most
cases, by judicious and timely surrender, the exposure which
would be the only effectual hindrance to his operations. If

full advertisement in the newspapers of all penalties recovered
by the Company were part of the punishment inflicted upon
such offenders, it would probably be much more dreaded and
more effectual.

Quite recently there have occurred one or two cases in which
the culprits seem to have more adequately received their deserts.
In March, 1898, a silversmith was convicted at the Central
Criminal Court of having forged several hall-marks of the Goldsmiths' Company, and of having had in his possession articles
bearing forged hall-marks. He was sentenced by the Recorder
of London, who dwelt upon the gravity of the offence, to twelve
months' imprisonment with hard labour. Still more recently,
an offender has paid fines amounting to more than £3,000,
besides forfeiting the plate bearing the forged marks, making
a very heavy loss to him in addition to the amount of the
penalties incurred.

It is sometimes possible to guess correctly the very shop from
which articles purporting to be of the Queen Anne period have
come, from the marks used upon them. A much-abused mark
has been that of William Gamble; being the letters **GA** under
a crown with a pellet on each side, all in a circle.

There is no need to condemn all plate found bearing these
various marks; but much that is spurious having been put into
circulation so marked, it will be well to be cautious about such
and the like specimens. The date-letters for 1683, 1739 and
1746 have been seen by the author so well executed as almost
to defy detection, did they stand alone.

Should the collector fail in finding ready to his hand anything
of sufficient historical or family interest to tempt him, let him
further beware of giving orders for articles not to be found of
the date he covets,—a coffee-pot, of the reign of Queen Elizabeth
for example,—or he will run the risk of finding his newly
acquired possession, when at last some fortunate agent has
picked up one for him, to be formed of the sloping body of an
ordinary chalice of a well-known type in those days turned
bottom upwards to get the slope the right way and fitted with
a foot, lid, handle and spout of suitable fashion, the position
of the hall-marks upside down in a row round the lower
part of the pot revealing to the initiated alone the ingenious
adaptation.

Here we may remark that the observant amateur will soon find a good guide in the situation of the hall-marks; those marks were always placed by rule, and will be found in unusual positions on pieces of plate that have been altered from their original shape.

An early tankard ought to be marked on the side near the handle, and straight across the flat lid in a parallel line with the purchase or perhaps upon the flange of the lid, but a more modern one will be stamped on the bottom and inside the lid ; a standing cup of Queen Anne or earlier bears the marks round the margin, one of thirty years later on the bottom of the bowl up inside the hollow stem, and so on in other cases.

Time was when ornamentation of one date coupled with hall-marks of another would have passed muster, and for the detection of such anomalies as these the illustrations given in later chapters will be of some use; but blunders of this kind are not so frequent now, and the buyer is left to the careful examination first of the metal itself, then of the execution rather than the fashion of the ornamentation, and lastly of the hall-marks. The silver in spurious specimens will be rolled perhaps, instead of hammered, and betray to the practised eye and hand what has been called "a fatal air of newness;" the same fatal air may condemn the fashion and decoration, especially the gilding if any be present; and the hall-marks are still so little understood that forgeries almost court detection by trained eyes, but trained they must be. Failing this, the buyer can scarcely do better than resort for what he wants to one or other of the great houses of goldsmiths whose names are household words, and leave himself in their hands, or to some one whom he knows to be a respectable and well-skilled trades-man. Good plate and genuine after all can be got, and it is into such hands that what is really valuable generally passes. Patience and money the collector will require, and plenty of both ; for such houses as these do not make old plate to order, and they are as much as other people under the laws of supply and demand which regulate the price of it when it comes into the market.

But if the buyer prefer foraging for himself, whether in highway, bye-way, or sale-room, to be forewarned is to some extent to be forearmed; and surely he is better off with the means of forming a good judgment placed at his disposal than if ignorant of facts the greater part of which are already well known to the fraudulent, and daily used by them against their victims.

We cannot end this part of the subject better than with the words—*caveat emptor.*

But equally useful lessons of another kind may be learned from the eventful history of a piece of old family plate mentioned later as having been lost and recovered again by its owner (see p. 376). This cup was missed from its home in Gloucestershire in the summer of 1892, and all trace of it lost till early in 1901, when it was recognised by the present writer in a Loan Collection of old plate exhibited in London that year. It proved to have passed through the hands of several dealers in quite different parts of London so swiftly and unquestioned, although known by all to be a piece of plate the subject of an illustration in this work, that it was already in the possession of its eventual purchaser and exhibitor even before its loss was known to the owner. Information was at that time given to the various police authorities, and an engraving of the cup inserted in the London *Police Gazette;* but neither the Metropolitan nor the City of London police succeeded in learning anything of the transactions, amounting to a series, which had then so recently taken place within their jurisdiction. More unfortunately still, neither authority was able to show, when its attention was again called to the matter in 1901, that any enquiry had been made in 1892 amongst pawnbrokers and dealers, or any steps taken to bring the loss to the knowledge of such persons. This rendered any proceedings in 1901 almost impossible, and the moral is not only that owners must take all care of their valuables for themselves, but that they need not place much reliance on official help in time of need. It will perhaps occur to readers that there would be no thieves if there were no receivers, and if purchasers were less apt to shut their eyes to circumstances which ought to arouse suspicion, and to avoid asking inconvenient questions in their eagerness to acquire objects of interest for their collections.

CHAPTER IX.

ECCLESIASTICAL PLATE.

EPISCOPAL CONSTITUTIONS RELATING TO CHURCH PLATE—CHURCH GOODS, HOW
AFFECTED BY THE EVENTS OF THE REIGNS OF EDWARD VI. AND QUEEN
ELIZABETH — CHALICES EXCHANGED FOR COMMUNION CUPS — PRE-REFOR-
MATION CHALICES AND PATENS—ELIZABETHAN COMMUNION CUPS—MODERN
CHALICES, COMMUNION CUPS AND PATENS — FLAGONS — ALMS-DISHES —
CANDLESTICKS.

THE preceding chapters have dealt with the marks by which
the age and authenticity of ancient plate may be verified, and
it is time to turn to what remains of the possessions of our
ancestors, and to see what additional information may be
gathered from its fashion and other circumstances.

It will be convenient to divide the subject into two portions,
devoting the present chapter to ecclesiastical plate, and reserving
decorative and domestic plate for separate consideration.

The misfortunes that befell the goods of the Church in
England during the sixteenth century, and the simplicity of
later ritual, have shortened the history of our church-plate a
good deal. The examples of pre-Reformation art now left in
England are comparatively few; those of any importance are
very few indeed; for the rest, cathedral and church alike
possess certain simple articles of communion and altar plate of
dates ranging from the reign of Edward VI. to the present day,
and varying in their design from time to time, as we shall see,
but hardly ever rising to any high level of art excellence.

It is difficult to realise the splendour of the display that
would have met the eye of him who entered one of our great
cathedrals or wealthy parish churches on any high festival day
in the three or four centuries that preceded the Reformation.
The church was the nursing-mother of the arts, which lent
themselves in their turn to the adornment of her services; the
monks were the goldsmiths of the middle ages; St. Dunstan
himself was the patron of their craft in England; what
wonder, then, that the wealth of gold and silver in its shrines

and treasuries was immense, so immense as to be almost incredible.

It would be foreign to our present purpose to reprint long lists of treasures of which not so much as an article remains ; but some few historical remarks are necessary to enable us to understand the earlier specimens of English church-plate that still exist.

Let us take for a starting point the episcopal constitutions which ordained what ornaments and furniture were necessary for the ordinary service of the church. One of the best of these is that of Robert Winchelsey, Archbishop of Canterbury, 1293—1313, who directs, in 1305, that parishes should provide, and keep in proper repair, the following articles :—*

" Legendam, antiphonarium, gradale, psalterium, troperium, ordinale, missale, manuale, calicem, vestamentum principale, cum casula dalmatica tunica et cum capa in choro, cum omnibus suis appendiciis, frontale ad magnum altare cum tribus tuellis, tria superpellicia, unum rochetum, crucem processionalem, crucem pro mortuis, thuribulum, lucernam, tintinabulum ad deferendum coram corpore Christi in visitatione infirmorum, pixidem pro corpore Christi honestam, velum quadragesimale, vexilla pro rogationibus, campanas cum chordis, feretrum pro defunctis, vas pro aqua benedicta, osculatorium, candelabrum pro cereo Paschali, fontem cum serura, imagines in ecclesia, imaginem principalem in cancello."

In another edition of these same constitutions a chrismatory is added to the above requirements.

We have given the complete list, as it is a very full and interesting one, and more of it has some relation to the art of the goldsmith than might seem likely at first sight ; for besides the sacramental vessels the pyx, censor (thuribulum), chrismatory, and pax (osculatorium), the images also and the covers of the service books were often of silver and of great weight. The image of its patron saint, taken from the chapel of St. Stephen at Westminster in the time of Henry VIII., weighed no less than thirteen score and thirteen ounces, and the inventory of St. Olave's, Southwark, in 1552, includes a " gospeller booke garnyshed with sylver and parcell gylte with Mary and John, weynge cxx. ounces," and a " pisteler booke

---

* Lyndewode, *Provincialis*, Lib. iii. tit. De ecclesiis edificandis. fo. 137.

with Peter and Palle garnyshed with sylver and parcell gylte
weynge C. ounces." Such covers as these served as pax-bredes
or osculatories.

The requirements of Winchelsey are almost identical with
those of Archbishop Simon in 1368; and if certain other
articles, such as phials for wine and water and also candlesticks,
are mentioned by an earlier prelate, Gilbert de Bridport, Bishop
of Sarum in 1256, the pyx, the vessel for holy-water, and the
pax—all included by Archbishop Winchelsey—are omitted from
the more ancient list. The constitutions of William de Bleys
in 1229 add but a single item of interest, an unconsecrated
chalice, which might be of tin, for burial with the priest.*

Further, it is clear that even in early days country churches
were properly supplied with all these vessels, vestments, books,
and other necessaries. The inventories taken by William de
Swyneflete, Archdeacon of Norwich in or about 1368, the year
of Archbishop Simon's Constitutions, may be quoted to show
that the Norwich churches were all amply supplied at that
time, and later visitations give the same testimony.†

A very beautiful Thurible or Censer of the end of the reign of
Edward III. was sold at Messrs. Christie, Manson & Woods'
Auction Rooms in the Grenville Wells Collection, in the
summer of 1890. It was found, together with a Ship or
Incense Boat, in Whittlesea Mere; and is figured in Shaw's
Decorative Arts, and described in *Archæological Journal*,
Vol. VIII. The Incense Boat bore rams' heads on its two
extremities, part of the arms of Ramsey Abbey, to which no
doubt both pieces belonged. They were purchased by Lord
Carysfort at the sum of £1155 for the Censer, and £900 for the
Boat. The Incense Boat is of early Tudor work.‡

In the days of Edward VI. there is good evidence of the great
value of parish church plate years after the events of his father's
reign had bestowed the still greater treasures of cathedrals and
monasteries upon the king under the general name of "Church-
stuff." St. Olave's, Southwark, in 1552 still possessed no less
than 1062 ounces of silver in chalices, crosses, basins, mounted
covers for the books, pyxes, a pax, a chrismatory, censers,

---

* For these two last-mentioned Constitutions, see Wilkins's *Concilia*, Vol. I.,
pp. 714 and 623.

† *Norfolk and Norwich Archæology*,
Vol. V. 93.

‡ Both were acquired by the Victoria
and Albert Museum in 1923.

cruets, and the like; a church in Norwich returned a list of 857 ounces to the commissioners about the same time; and it was the same everywhere, the amounts varying with the importance of the parishes.

It is hardly fair, therefore, to charge King Henry VIII. and his advisers with the whole course of spoliation which the Church suffered in the years which followed 1536. On the contrary, it was reserved for succeeding reigns to carry on and complete the work of destruction which was then only commenced. The seizure of parish church plate was not decided upon until the last year of King Edward VI., and some was left untouched till the days of the Protestant reaction which marked the accession of Elizabeth and resulted in some places in a repetition of the excesses in which the puritanism of her brother's reign had vented itself.

Whilst all this was going on it is not wonderful that parochial authorities, alarmed at the misfortunes befalling their more powerful neighbours, the monasteries, guilds, and fraternities, took advantage of the excuse afforded by the necessity of altering their churches, and adapting them to the new and more simple ritual, and of repairing the damage done by the destruction of painted glass, images, and all that could come under the denomination of "monuments of superstition," to dispose of a portion of their more valuable property by way of meeting these extraordinary expenses. This practice, commencing about 1536, soon became so general, that the commissioners sent through the land more than once in the reign of Edward VI. professed to take their inventories for the purpose of stopping it, and insuring the preservation of all that was left. In fact, their proceedings go far to show that up to that time, whilst much that was valuable had been alienated by churchwardens themselves for repairs and other like expenses, real or pretended, neither plunder nor embezzlement from other quarters had done much harm. This, however, compels us to note in passing the extraordinary number of losses by thieves that are mentioned in the returns of these churchwardens. If they are to be believed, almost every church in many counties was broken into and robbed at some time or other in the interval between 1547 and 1553. It may have been so, but when we remember that the commissioners of the year last mentioned were ordered to

make strict comparison of the returns now made to them, with
the best of the inventories compiled in answer to the earlier
inquisitions of the reign, and that under these circumstances it
became very doubtful how much of the proceeds of any sales
of church furniture that had been effected, the parishes would
be allowed to retain, even under the pretence of their having
been spent upon repairs, it is hardly possible to get rid of a
suspicion that such an allegation as a loss by robbery was found
the simplest mode of accounting for missing articles.   Many of
the returns honestly represented that by "the consent and
agreement of all the parishioners," the churchwardens had sold
some of their plate, and spent the proceeds on improvements
and necessary expenses.   Large quantities of church stuff came
in this way into private hands ; and this would seem to dispose,
to some extent, of the charges so broadly made by Heylin, and
repeated also in Fuller's *Church History*, of general plunder and
spoliation.   Both these authorities comment upon the parlours
to be found hung with altar-cloths, tables and beds covered with
copes, carousing cups made of chalices, and the like ; Fuller
saying that "as if first laying hands upon them were sufficient
title unto them ; seizing on them was generally the price they
had paid for them ; " and Heylin that, "It was a sorry house
and not worth the naming, which had not somewhat of this
furniture in it."   But how, we may remark, could it be otherwise if churchwardens provided themselves as best they could
with the funds they required for such purposes as the following,
which may be taken as a fair sample,* viz. :—" altering of oure
churche, and fynisshing of the same according to our myndes
and the parisshioners.   Itm., for the new glassing of xvii.
wyndows wherein were conteyned the lyves of certen prophane
histories and other olde wyndows in church.   Itm., for and
towards the paving of the kinge's highe way in stoans aboughte
our Churche and in our Parisshe which was foule and needfull
to be doon.   Item, for a cheste and a box sette in our Churche
according to the Kinge's Maties Injunctions."
    Such were the objects upon which some Norwich church-
wardens had spent the money ; and after all, these and the like
alterations and repairs were ordered by the Injunctions issued

---

* *Norfolk Archæology*, Vol. VI. p. 364.

on the accession of Edward VI. in 1547 "to all his loving subjects, clergy and laity," though it was not perhaps intended that they should be paid for by the sale of valuables which might eventually be seized by the Crown when decent pretext offered.   Much of these injunctions reappeared in the following year in the Visitation Articles of the province of Canterbury, which at the same time straitly enquired of the clergy " whether they have not monished their parishioners openly that they should not sell, give, nor otherwise alienate any of their Church goods."*   But royal injunctions were more imperative than episcopal monitions, and the expenses were no doubt met in the most obvious way; indeed, these injunctions actually authorised the churchwardens to bestow part of their property upon the reparation of the church, " if great need requires, and whereas the parish is very poor, and not able otherwise to repair the same."   So things went on until the last year of Edward VI., when the final step was taken of seizing all that was then left, or nearly all, for the Commissioners were directed even then to leave " one, two, or more chalices or cuppes according to the multitude of people."

For this the Crown may have said in excuse that by this time all the repairs and alterations rendered necessary by the Reformation had been effected, and that what was still over after making all due provisions for the future use of the Church according to the simplified ritual was superfluous if not super- stitious, and in either case proper for conversion to His Majesty's use.

It may be asked where then are these " one, two, or more chalices," even if all the rest have perished ?   Will they not form an ample remnant by which to judge the ecclesiastical goldsmith of earlier times ?

Alas! it must be said that they too have perished with the rest, for whilst the instructions of the Commissioners directed their return, the King's injunctions ensured their destruction ; by the latter, after more minute provisions, it being directed in one sweeping general clause that "all monuments of feigned miracles, pilgrimages, idolatry and superstition " were to be taken away, utterly extinguished, and destroyed, " so that there

---

* Cardwell's *Documentary Annals*, Vol. I. 42.

remains no memory of the same in walls, glass windows, or elsewhere within churches or houses." The holy vessels that had been used at the Mass were from this point of view no less " monuments of superstition " than the representations of saints in windows of painted glass, or sculptured in stone to occupy the canopied niches of the reredos, and all fell under the same ban.

Let us illustrate its practical working by the case of the parish of Dartford in Kent, where the Commissioners are found expressly ordering, in 1553 (6 Edward VI.), that the chalices and patens, and a pax to add to the quantity of silver retained by the inhabitants, should " be exchanged by the said church-wardens for ij cuppes to receyve the Communyon in to amount to the like weyght and value." Some parishes, in compliance with the feeling of the time and the injunctions, had already altered their chalices into communion cups. Quite as many of the parishes in the county of Surrey in the year last-mentioned certify to the possession of communion cups as of chalices; some return in their list of plate one of each marking the distinction, and some mention the exchange of one for the other. The churchwardens of St. Andrew's, Norwich, mention such a transaction, also in 6 Edward VI. :—

" There do nowe remayne in the seide Churche at this day one Communyon Cuppe weing xl. unces parcell gilt at v° the unce S^m x li. whiche was made of twoo peir of challeis w^t the patens parcell gilte."

St. Saviour's, Southwark, sometime between the inventory taken in 1548 and that of 1552, had parted with four chalices weighing fifty-four ounces to one Calton at the sign of the Purse in Cheap, of which the said Calton made two communion cups weighing but fifty-two ounces. The parish was constrained to charge the difference, being 17s. 8d. against itself, on the occasion of the later of the above inventories being taken.*

The parochial authorities of Wimbledon, co. Surrey, record among the receipts for 1552 the following :—

" Receivede for thre chalisses waying xxx^li and v ounces at v^s the ownce whereof went to the communyon cuppe xx^j ounces and a quartern which commeth to v^li vi^s iij^d. And so

---

* *Surrey Church Notes*, by J. R. Daniel-Tyssen.

remayneth xiij ownces and thre quartours which commythe to iii^{li} vii^{s} ix^{d} whereof paide to Robert Wygge goldsmythe of London for the making and gilding of the communyon cupp after xx^{d} an ounce which commyth to xxxv^{s} v^{d}." *

A few such communion cups provided under Edward VI. may still be seen. Two are the property of St. Margaret's, Westminster, to this day; but most of them were only made to be almost directly destroyed again, as unfit for the purposes of the restored ritual of the reign of Queen Mary. True it is that the respite consequent upon her accession following so quickly upon the heels of the Commissioners, for the King died that same year, saved for a time some of the few ancient chalices left by them in accordance with their instructions in the hands of their owners: for such of these as had not been immediately destroyed, like those at Dartford, were brought again into use, and of course carefully preserved until the end of Queen Mary's short reign. In some cases, too, the Commissioners had not had time to carry out their work at all. Chelmsford, for example, is found dealing with plate in 1558, which would not then have been in existence at all if the Commissioners of Edward VI. had ever got there. But at last these relics, which had weathered all previous storms, fell victims to the stringent orders of Queen Elizabeth and her prelates at the head of the outburst of Protestant zeal which ensued on her accession.

Once again were the injunctions of King Edward VI. reenforced and repeated almost word for word in those issued by Elizabeth. The proscribed church goods were again followed even into private hands, for the Visitation Articles of 1558 enquire, as did those of 2 Edw. VI., "whether you know any that keep in their houses any undefaced images, tables, pictures, paintings, or other monuments of feigned and false miracles, pilgrimages, idolatry and superstition, and do adore them, and especially such as have been set up in churches, chapels, and oratories."

Inclination and injunction seemed now to work in harmony, and each parish vied with its neighbour in the haste with which it proceeded to melt up what remained of its plate, especially all that had been profaned by use at the Mass, and to get rid of its other church furniture. The books were sold to pedlars "to

---

* *Surrey Church Notes*, by J. R. Daniel-Tyssen.

lap spices in ; " the sacring bell was " hung about a calf's neck " or " at a horse's ear," and the holy water vat was turned into a swine's trough.* But still it seemed to the bishops of the reformed church necessary to maintain the stringency of former orders, and even as late as 1569 we find amongst articles to be enquired of within the diocese of Canterbury at the ordinary Visitation of Matthew Parker, the following :†—

" Whether they do minister in any prophane cuppes, bowles, dishes, or chalices heretofore used at masse or els in a decent Communion cuppe provided and kept for the same purpose only."

Lastly, we may quote the Visitation Articles of Archbishop Grindal, in 1576, enquiring " Whether you have in your Parish Churches and Chapels, a fair and comely Communion Cup of Silver, and a Cover of Silver for the same, which may serve also for the ministration of the Communion Bread."

The churchwardens' accounts of every year from 1558 teem with notes of changes made in obedience to these orders ; a few examples may be taken from town and country.

Amongst the parochial payments of St. Andrew-Hubbard in London for 1558 is the following :—

" Paide for the Eschaunge of two chalices with the covers weyghing xxxii oz. halfe for a communion cup waying xxx. oz. and halfe thexchaunge with the odde oz. at xiiij^s viij^d."

At Chelmsford these items occur in 1560 :—

" Received of Mr. Mustchampe goldsmyth at the syne of the ring with the rube in Lumbarde St. for a gylt challys with a paten gylt waying xxiii oz. and a quarter at v^s iiij^d the ounce, som is vi^{li} iiij^s."

" Paid to Mr. Muschamp in Lombard St. at the sygne of the ring with the rube for a coupe of gilt weighing 19 oz. 3 qr., 6^s 8^d the oz., som is £6. 11. 7."

Bungay St. Mary in 1568 pays " For a Co'mmunyon cuppe made of one payer of chalice havyng a cover, for workmanship and some silv', xxi.^{s}"

The Leverton churchwardens in 1570 pay "Thomas Turpyn the goldsmith for facyonenge of the Communyon Cuppe weynge xii. oz., x^s.

---

* Peacock's *Church Furniture.*
† Cardwell's *Documentary Annals,* I. 321.

" It^{m} he putt to the same cupp a q^{ter} and a half of an ounce of his own silver ij^{s}."

At Eltham they exchange a chalice and paten weighing 13¾ oz. for a cup and cover only 10 oz. in weight.

At Lyminge in Kent there is a curious little cup of the year 1561-2, bought with a bequest to the church of vli. by one Daniel Spycer in 1558 for the purchase of a *chalice*. Four years later, at the Archbishop's visitation in 1562, it is recorded as decreed " that a *Communion Cuppe* shall be bought with the money." The cover of this cup is of different make, and engraved with the date 1578; this was added no doubt in compliance with the enquiry in that behalf made by the Visitation Articles of Archbishop Grindal in 1576. The cup itself had always been supposed to be of the date engraved on the cover, but the present rector's discovery of the visitation of 1562 has proved the hall-mark to be a safe guide. It may be added that the cup is by the same maker as the oldest Protestant Communion cup known, being one of those at St. Lawrence, Jewry.

In some parts of the country, perhaps owing to the energy of the diocesan, these changes were effected more promptly than in others. In the diocese of Norwich so many of the cups that remain are either of the year 1567 or 1568 that it suggested an enquiry whether the Bishop of Norwich of that day, John Parkhurst, was not an exceptionally zealous reformer. He had been one of the exiles at Zurich, and Strype says of him, " and so delighted was he with the discipline and doctrine of that Church, that he often wished that our Church were modelled exactly according to that."* The annalist goes on to say, " this bishop was supposed to be inclinable to the puritans, and to wink at them."

To these notes may be added an extract from his injunctions of 1561, the year of his first visitation, in which he directs his clergy to " see the places filled up in walles or ellswhere where imagies stode, so as if ther hadde been none there."

Again, in later injunctions of 1569, he asks,

" Item, whether you have in your Church a decent pulpit and Communion table, furnished and placed as becometh, with a comely Communion cup with a cover." . . .

---

* *Annals*, I. ii. pp. 508-9.

In Worcestershire so many cups of the year 1571 occur, that the late Archdeacon Lea, when enquiring into the subject was led to suppose that this was the case all over England, and to search for some reason for the coincidence, just as the present writer had done some years before for Norfolk. In the neighbouring county of Gloucester, cups of 1576 or 1577 are much more common than those of any other years. In Dorsetshire, Mr. Nightingale found nearly all were of the years 1570 to 1574 inclusive; whilst the experience of the Rev. A. Trollope in his Leicestershire researches puts the greater number of the *dated* Elizabethan pieces in that county as from 1567 to 1571.

In the West of England, Devon, and Cornwall, most of these cups were obtained quite as late as in Gloucestershire, but every village far and near was properly provided by 1580; and not only were they so provided, but in many a church the very same "fair and comely Communion Cup" is in existence and in use at the present day.

Some have urged that these exchanges were made merely because the chalices were too small for congregational use; but it will be observed that in many of the above-mentioned instances the communion cup is no larger, and in more than one case is of even less weight, than the chalice it replaces. The tone of the episcopal visitation articles is, however, conclusive as to the real reason for it, and some of the earlier ones speak in plainer terms than the later versions we have already quoted.* For instance, Grindal, when Archbishop of York, had in 1571 required his clergy "to minister the Holy Communion in no chalice nor any profane cup or glasse, but in a Communion Cup of Silver, and with a cover of Silver appointed also for the ministration of the Communion bread."

Since this chapter was originally printed, the late Rev. J. Fuller Russell, B.C.L., gave in the *Archæological Journal* (vol. xxxv. p. 48), the reply of George Gardiner, one of the Prebendaries of Canterbury, to Archbishop Parker's "articles to be enquired of," in Canterbury Cathedral in 1567. "This respondent saith that their divine service is duely songe in maner and forme, according to the Queen's Injunctions: saving that the Communion, as he saith, is ministered in a chalice, contrary,

---

* Appendix to Second Report of the Ritual Commission, p. 411.

as he saith, to the Advertisements . . . . He wold have service songe more deliberately with Psalms at the beginning and ending of service, as is appointed by the Injunctions; and their chalice turned into a decent communion cup."

Mr. Russell observed that neither chalices nor cups are even mentioned in Archbishop Parker's Advertisements of 1566; but that in 1562 he had, according to Strype, intended to order "chalices to be altered to decent cups." His proposed articles of 1562, were "exhibited to be admitted by authority, but not so allowed," and therefore never issued; but as Mr. Russell proceeds, "Master Gardiner may have had some inkling of the Archbishop's inclination in favour of the alteration of chalices to decent cups and sagaciously opined that his recommendation of it might advance him in the good graces of his Metropolitan, who notwithstanding his failure to obtain the allowance of authority for such a change in 1562, did not scruple to enjoin it in 1575, if not before." It may be noted as a curious fact that a great number of the Elizabethan communion cups still preserved in the arch-diocese of Canterbury are of the very year 1562.

We are now in a position to say what the antiquary may expect to find around him in church or cabinet.

It may be summed up very shortly : he will find a few chalices of Norman or late Romanesque type, chiefly coffin chalices, and succeeding to them a few—a very few—Gothic and Tudor chalices and their patens, remains of Pre-Reformation art. Of the latter hardly a dozen were known when these pages were first printed, little more than forty-eight years ago; and to this small number the addition of about thirty examples at the outside has been the result of the more general interest taken in the subject of old church-plate and the very extensive, and in many counties and dioceses exhaustive, search that has since been made for what remains of it.

He will find here and there a communion cup with its cover of the reign of Edward VI., made no doubt of the materials afforded by some more ancient chalice. Of these there are still fewer than of the chalices which preceded them; and next in order he will find broadcast over the whole country a multitude of examples of the communion cups provided in the first years of Queen Elizabeth under the circumstances that have been

A TABULAR CLASSIFICATION OF PF

A. NORMAN TYPE. *CHALICES WITH CIRCULAR FEET* . .
circa 1170—1350.

(1) 12 & 13 cent. . .
Bowls wide and shallow.

Chichester I., slight lip.
Canterbury, 1205. Abp. H. Walter, slight lip.
Berwick St. James, slight lip (*illustration*).
Chichester II., slight lip.
Lincoln, 1253. Bp. Grostête, slight lip.

Lincoln, 1279. Bp. Gravesend, slight lip,
Salisbury, 1297. Bp. Longespée.
Lincoln, 1299. Bp. Sutton.
Exeter, 1307. Bp. Bitton.
Hereford, 1316. Bp. Swinfield.

(2) Early 14 cent. , . *York, 1340. Abp. Melton (*illustration*)
Bowl conical.

B. GOTHIC TYPE. *CHALICES WITH HEXAGONAL FEET* . .
circa 1350—1510.

(1) 1350—1510 . . .
*Bowls conical at first,
then less so.
Feet without toes.*

Hamstall Ridware. Goathland.
Nettlecombe, 1479 (*illustration*). Manning
Abbas. Victoria and Albert Mus.
B. N. C. Oxford, 1498. Hinderwell. Amplef
Abbey. R. C. C. West Grinstead.

(2) 1490—1510 . . .
*Bowls as before.
Feet with toes.*

Clifford Chambers, 1494. Very Rev. Dr. Da
1496. West Drayton, 1507. Claughton.
*Leominster, c. 1510 (stem buttressed as in P
ton Hall chalice of following class and t
hemispherical), and twelve others ; inclu
Coombe Keynes (*illustration*) and Llanel

C. TUDOR TYPE. *CHALICES WITH SIX-LOBED AND FLOWING FE*
circa 1510—1536.

(1) 1510—1536 . . .
*Bowls often less conical.
Feet six-lobed.*

C. C. C. Oxford, 1507 (*illustration*). Pillaton I
Leyland, 1518. C. M. W. 1518. Jurby,
(*illustration*).
Ebbesbourne. St. Sampson, Guernsey. Victori
Albert Mus., 1527. R. C. Cathedral, Wes
ster, 1529. Sturminster Marshall,
Highworth, 1534. Exhib. Soc. of Ant.,

(2) 1525—1536 . . .
*Bowls nearly hemi-
spherical.
Feet flowing outline.*

Wylye, 1525 (*illustration*).
Trin. Coll. Oxford, 1527 (*illustration*).

---

* The bowls of the York and Leominster chalices serve to mark transitions.

EFORMATION CHALICES AND PATENS (see p. 224).

THEIR PATENS.		Depression.	Device.
ichester I.		4-foil.	Agnus) with inscription
nterbury, 1205.		Plain plate.	Agnus } in uncial
yke (*illustration*).		8-foil.	Agnus) letters.
ichester II.		8-foil.	Manus.
ncoln, 1253.		4-foil.	Bp. blessing.
orcester, 1266.	Bp. Cantelupe	4-foil.	Manus.
(*illustration*).			
ncoln, 1279.		4-foil and square.	Manus.
lisbury, 1297.		8-foil.	Manus.
ncoln, 1299.		Plain plate.	Manus.
eter, 1307.		Plain plate.	Manus.
reford, 1316.		Plain plate.	Manus, inscription.
rk, 1340.		6-foil (as in earliest ol next class at Hamstall Ridware).	Manus.

THEIR PATENS.

mstall Ridware.	6-foil.	Manus (as in preceding class).
pleforth Abbey.	do.	do.

With these exceptions, almost all the patens now have a rude "vernicle" for ice.† The six-foil depression (quite at last) occasionally gives way to plain ular depression, as at Hinderwell, with "agnus" or "ihc"; and some of the st have legend round rim, like those in following class. These are at Happis- igh, 1504, and Claughton.

tlecombe, 1479 (*illustration*).	6-foil.	Vernicle.

THEIR PATENS.

The Patens are as in preceding class, till *circa* 1520.† From c. 1520, "vernicle" laborated with rays, &c., the six-foil depression giving way more often than re to the plain plate, as at C. C. C. Oxford, 1507, Great Waltham, 1521, and Edmund's, Salisbury, 1533; and a legend round rim is the rule.

. Coll. Oxford, 1527 (*illustration*).	6-foil.	Vernicle elaborated.
		Legend round rim.

† All the hall-marked patens down to c. 1520, of which about twenty-five are known, are six-foil with vernicle; except C. C. C. Oxford, 1507, which is a plain plate; and Happisbrough, 1504, which has legend in addition.

narrated, each with its paten-cover ; and he will find flagons of shapes varying with their date, and other special considerations to be mentioned later.

Coming to more modern times there is less and less to be said; the needs of an increased population, and the pious liberality of donors, have added from time to time to the quantity of our church plate, but not to its interest or artistic value. Art in these matters appears to have steadily declined from the middle of the sixteenth to the middle of the present century, when a salutary reaction has directed attention to the examples that Gothic art has left for our study and guidance. Modern reproductions of these, in some cases admirable, in others still leave much to be desired ; a slavish adherence to ancient models that cannot be surpassed would be better than the bastard results of coupling pure Gothic form with inappropriate ornamentation, or of adapting beautiful Gothic adornment to articles of tasteless modern shape.

CHALICES.

In the early days of the Church, chalices were no doubt formed of various materials, some of them simple and quite the reverse of costly. But in process of time objections were found to these ; wood was porous, and liable to absorb a portion of the sacred element placed within ; horn was an animal substance and so formed by blood; glass, crystal and precious stones were all brittle and liable to fracture; and at length the precious metals alone were allowed to be employed. It was decreed by the Council of Rheims in 847 that if not of gold, chalices should be wholly of silver ; tin being allowed only in cases where means to provide anything better were wanting. Other materials were forbidden altogether. Silver is prescribed by a constitution of Stephen Langton (1206),* the commentator in Lyndewode adding " *vel aureum.*"

Something may be gathered as to the fashion of the chalices of the thirteenth and next centuries from wills and mortuaries. Nicholas de Farnham in 1257 bequeaths to the monks of Durham "j calix cum lapidibus pretiosis in pede ; " and John, Earl of Warrenne, in 1347, another such to Durham Cathedral. It is

---

* Lyndewode, lib. iii. fol. 136.

described in his will as "unum calicem magni valoris de auro purissimo cum multis lapidibus pretiosis insertis."

In the inventory of the goods of a bishop of Durham who died in 1381, his chalices are mentioned as follows : "j calicem magnum argenteum et deauratum in cujus pede est ymago Domini crucifixi et super nodum ejusdem Scuta armorum ejusdem Episcopi cum iij leunculis argenteis. It^m j cuppam infra deauratam et extra anemelatam pro Eukaristiâ."

Proof could be adduced that chalices were cups of a somewhat fixed and well-known form, from the fact that drinking-vessels were sometimes described as "chalyswyse," or "ad modum calicis factum." Stephen Lescrop, Archdeacon of Richmond, makes a bequest in 1418, of "unum chalescuppe cum longo pede de argento deauratum et coopertum cum j knop in sumitate." Sir R. de Roos mentions in his will, dated 1392, "unum ciphum qui vocatur chaliscopp"; an almost identical entry is to be found in the will of John Stoke, a burgess of Bristol, proved in 1393;* whilst among a number of articles of table-plate bought by Edward III. in 1366 of Thomas Hessey his goldsmith, and presented to the Constable of Flanders and other personages as gifts from the King, was "un coup de chalice endorr' et esm'."

But it is hardly necessary for the purposes of such a handbook as this to discuss at any length the form of ancient chalices which no longer exist. We may pass by the chalices with handles which were often found and perhaps necessary till the denial of the cup to the laity, and come to the known if rare examples of the twelfth century.

Most of the earliest chalices known to exist, are those which have been discovered in the tombs of ecclesiastics of about this epoch, but one or two massing chalices of the twelfth and thirteenth centuries also remain.

Mr. Octavius Morgan says as to the form of the Pre-Reformation English chalice, "A chalice consists of three parts—the cup or bowl; the stem, which in its middle swelled into a bulb called the knop; and the foot. The bowl itself was usually quite plain, in order that it might be more easily kept pure and clean. The stem, knop and foot were frequently

---

* The Bristol *Great Orphan Book.*

ornamented with enamels, or chased work representing the
emblems of the Passion or other sacred subjects; and on the
foot, which was usually made hexagonal,* to prevent the chalice
rolling when laid upon its side to drain, there was also a cross
which the priest kept towards himself at the time of celebration.
In the thirteenth century the chalices seem to have been short
and low, and the bowl wide and shallow, as exemplified by the
celebrated chalice of St. Remy, once at Rheims, but removed
to the Bibliothèque Nationale, which is considered to be of the
time of St. Louis, as also by the chalices of silver and pewter
which have been found in the tombs of the priests of that
century. In the fourteenth century they were made taller, the
bowls assumed a decidedly conical form, being narrow at the
bottom, and having the sides sloping straight outwards. In
the fifteenth century they were usually broader at the bottom,
with the sides still forming part of a cone, like that at Nettlecombe, co. Somerset, till a form altogether hemispherical was
assumed, of which a fine chalice at Leominster, figured in
Archæologia, vol. xxxv. p. 489, is a noble specimen. Of this
type also is one at Comb Pyne in Devonshire."

A great many recent discoveries have only confirmed the
value of this original description by the accurate observer, to
whom the author owes so much; and if we follow his account
by its steps, and distinguish old English chalices into classes,
we shall find the most ancient group with "wide and shallow"
bowl and circular foot, which we have called late Romanesque,
or Norman, includes, as Mr. Morgan notes, the coffin chalices,
together with the Berwick St. James example to be mentioned
again presently.

The "decidedly conical" and narrower bowl of the fourteenth
century is well exemplified by the latest known of such coffin
chalices, that found in the tomb of Archbishop Melton of York,
who died in 1340. This bowl we shall also find in the earlier
examples of the succeeding group or class, which consists of
the Gothic or hexagonal-footed chalices, the earliest known of

---

* The author is indebted to Mr. T. M.
Fallow for a reference in the will of Sir
John Foxley, dated 1378, which seems to
indicate that this hexagonal form of foot
may then have been something new. The
testator, after speaking of a chalice with
circular foot (*cum pede rotundo*), describes
another as having a foot of the shape of
a mullet of six points (*cum pede de forma
moletta sex punctorum*).

which are at Hamstall Ridware in Staffordshire, and at Goathland, Yorkshire.

This Gothic class includes amongst its later examples the
well-known Nettlecombe chalice, used by Mr. O. Morgan to
illustrate the characteristic features of its period, one of which
is the bowl "broader at the bottom, but with the side still
forming part of a cone," a form which carries us on, as the
Archbishop Melton chalice did earlier, to the first of the next
or Tudor class, the chalices with six-lobed and flowing or wavy-
sided feet but less conical bowls, which are found during a
period almost exactly coinciding with the reign of Henry VIII.
These form our third and equally well-marked group, and
bring us gradually through such bowls as that at Jurby to the
"hemispherical" bowl noticed by Mr. Morgan as a feature of
the latest chalices of Pre-Reformation form.

The first type is found till about 1350; the second from then
for a full century and a half, say till 1510; and the third carries
us onward to 1536, the date of the latest example.

These main and typical forms cover so many and varied
details of ornament, that in a recent admirable paper on the
subject,* the authors have found it possible to divide Pre-
Reformation chalices into eight or perhaps nine types, some of
them referring to the form, and others to the ornamentation
of the vessels; and the corresponding patens into two forms
and seven types, the latter relating to their decoration. A
number of divisions, taking note of almost every distinguishing
feature in turn, are very useful for classifying new finds; and
apart from considerations of chronology the arrangement could
not be improved upon. But, for historical purposes, divisions
are not very convenient, the dating of which is obviously subject
to much uncertainty in consequence of the types sometimes
being contemporaneous, sometimes overlapping one another in
point of time, and sometimes reappearing after an interval.
It is in fact almost, and in the earlier epochs quite, impossible
to date a series of groups formed upon this principle.

A very early chalice like that discovered in the tomb of
Archbishop Hubert Walter at Canterbury, who died in 1205,

---

* *English Mediæval Chalices and* | and T. M. Fallow, M.A., *Archæological*
Patens, by W. H. St. John Hope, M.A., | *Journal*, vol. xliii.

would fall, owing to its decoration, into a class by no means the most ancient ; whilst the much later example from the tomb of Bishop Swinfield of Hereford, who died in 1316, would be placed amongst those of the rudest and therefore the supposed earliest type. It is very far from certain that excellence in workmanship and decoration is any sure proof of lateness of date, or rudeness in those respects good evidence of greater antiquity.

It seems preferable, therefore, in the present chapter, to divide chalices, according to their form, into types or classes that are chronologically, as well as in point of fashion, more

No. 1.—PEWTER COFFIN CHALICE AND PATEN. 13 CENT.

certainly distinct ; and without treating details of workmanship as if they indicated differences of period. These can be easily sub-divided if necessary, for minor considerations, but a single subdivision for each group seems all that is required. Such an arrangement will be found on page 226 in a tabular form, the three main groups of which correspond in a general way with the late Romanesque or Norman, the Gothic and the Tudor styles in architecture, at all events nearly enough to be called by those names for the sake of distinction, and includes the patens, as well as the chalices, under the same headings and indications.

If the first group extends through more than one architectural epoch, the second covers almost exactly the Perpendicular period, and the third coincides, as we have said, with the reign of Henry VIII.

Turning now to each of our three groups successively we find that the earliest (A) consists almost entirely of the chalices which have from time to time been discovered in the coffins of bishops and priests of the eleventh and following centuries.

They are the oldest pieces of plate known to exist in England, and they have been found usually of silver, but sometimes of pewter, in coffins at Canterbury, York, Lincoln, St. David's, Hereford, Salisbury, Exeter, and Chichester Cathedrals, and also at other places.   Amongst the very oldest of silver are chalices from the coffins, which are supposed to be those of Bishops Seffride and Hilary, successively occupants of the See of Chichester in the twelfth century.   These are of silver-gilt and have their patens.   But there is a still earlier one of pewter at Chichester, probably buried with Bishop Godefridus, who

No. 2.—CHALICE IN THE BRITISH MUSEUM.   13 CENT.

died in 1088; and this also has its paten.   Similar chalices of silver have been found at York Minster of the later part of the twelfth or the first half of the thirteenth century.

So many coffin chalices are of pewter that it may be permissible to give an illustration of a very early specimen made of that metal.   It was found in the coffin of a priest at Cheam in Surrey (No. 1), and gives a good idea of such a vessel in the thirteenth century.

No better illustration of the general character of the early silver chalices can be found than a massing chalice (No. 2)

formerly at Berwick St. James, Wiltshire, but now in the
British Museum.   It has all the points to be observed in those
of earliest date, including the slight lip to the bowl which only
occurs upon the most ancient of these vessels, quite disappearing
before the end of the thirteenth century.

The wood-cut would do almost equally well for one of the
coffin chalices found at York or Chichester.   But the finest

No. 3.—COFFIN CHALICE OF ABP. MELTON (D. 1340) AT YORK MINSTER.

chalice of this earliest class is without doubt one which is said
to have been found in 1890 with its paten near Dolgelly.   It
is of unusual size and character, showing the early lip but
coupled with an elaborate knop and ornamentation on the
stem and foot of decidedly Early English design.   The paten
has six lobes with ornamental spandrils, and in the central space
the Saviour sitting, with the right hand raised as in blessing,
an inscription in plain capitals running round the device,

features which, with the characteristics of the chalice itself, place both vessels in the early or middle part of our first class or group; but which it would be difficult to include under any one head in the more detailed system of classification, mentioned at an earlier page. The Dolgelly vessels are little, if at all less ancient than those lately found in Archbishop Hubert's tomb at Canterbury.*

A later example, found in the tomb of Bishop Longespée of Salisbury, who died 1297, is of good execution, the bowl wide and shallow without a lip, the stem and foot, like all the rest, circular but decorated with a little chasing, and having an ornamental knop. It is slightly more Gothic in feeling and finish. Plainer vessels resembling the early ones at York and Chichester, are from the tombs of Bishop Sutton of Lincoln, who died in 1299, and of Bishop Swinfield of Hereford, who died in 1316. Almost the latest of its class is a chalice with similar foot and

No. 4.—CHALICE (1479) AT NETTLECOMBE, SOMERSET.

stem to the other examples, but with the deeper and more conical bowl proper to the fourteenth century, preserved at York, and found in the coffin of Archbishop Melton, who died in 1340; and this (No. 3), with its transitional features, brings us to the middle of the fourteenth century and to examples of a more definitely Gothic type (A 2 in our table).

Of the second and third groups or types (B and C in the table) to which we now come, the chalice mentioned by Mr. O. Morgan as at Nettlecombe, together with examples at Coombe Keynes in Dorsetshire, at Corpus Christi College,

* Doubts as to the Dolgelly vessels being English have recently been raised.

Oxford, at Jurby in the Isle of Man, at Trinity College, Oxford, and at Wylye, Wilts, have been selected as illustrations. The first two represent the Gothic, and the rest the Tudor class. They are all of great beauty and merit, and whilst five out of

No. 5.—CHALICE (C. 1495) AT COOMBE KEYNES, DORSET.

the six are hall-marked, and their dates therefore accurately known, the date of the sixth is not less well ascertained.*

The Nettlecombe Chalice and its Paten were brought to light by Mr. Octavius Morgan some years ago, and are of the greatest interest, not only from their beauty and perfect

---

* Bishop Fox's chalice at Corpus Christi College, Oxford, possesses the rare interest of being the only known chalice made of gold, and there is a gold communion cup at Welshpool, given 1662.

condition, but from their antiquity, for they are older than any other hall-marked example of English goldsmith's work. The chalice is described by Mr. Morgan as follows:—*

"The chalice stands very nearly six inches high. The bowl is in form between a cone and a hemisphere, that is, the bottom is broad and round, whilst the sides continue straight and conical, a form which is rather indicative of its date. This bowl is supported on a hexagonal stem divided into two portions by the knop, which is a beautiful piece of goldsmith's work formed by the projection from the angles of the stem of six short square arms, each terminating in a lion's mask, or in proper heraldic language 'a leopard's head,' and having the intermediate spaces filled up with elegant flowing Gothic tracery of pierced open work. The lower part of the stem rests on a curved hexagonal foot, being united to it by Gothic mouldings, and the foot terminates in an upright basement moulding, which is enriched with a small vertically reeded band. One of the six compartments of the foot was ornamented, as is usual in ancient chalices, by a representation of the Crucifixion. The metal of this compartment has been cut out, and a silver plate engraved with the Crucifixion has been rudely riveted in. This silver plate is, I think, the original work, and it was formerly enamelled— for it would probably have been found easier and more convenient to prepare the enamel on a small separate plate and then fix it in its place, than to have subjected the whole chalice to the heat of the enameller's furnace, which must have been the case had the enamel been done on the foot itself. The silver plate is deeply engraved, or rather the metal is tooled out to receive transparent enamel in the style of the work of the fourteenth or the beginning of the fifteenth century, and small traces of the enamel with which it has been filled may still be discovered. It will be seen at once that the design was made for the place from the peculiar attitude of the figure, the arms being drawn up over the head to adapt it to the form of the compartment."

This last feature is a typical one, appearing in most of the chalices of this type and period, sometimes with the addition of

* This description originally appeared in *Archæologia*, vol. xlii. 405, and was accompanied by coloured lithographs of the chalice and paten of the actual size of the originals, from which the engravings prepared for this volume have been carefully reduced.

figures standing beside the Cross, and other modifications of the like kind according to the fancy or the skill of the artist.

The date of this chalice is 1479, though from the want of examples it was difficult in former days to positively assign the date-letter which it plainly bears to that year. This letter was supposed to stand for the year 1459, but the date-letters are now well understood and the many points of resemblance between this and chalices more recently discovered, the dates of which are well ascertained, are conclusive as to its age, though to judge from the enamelling alone, it might have been of a somewhat earlier date than 1479.

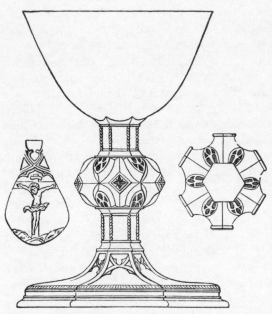

No. 6.—BISHOP FOX'S GOLD CHALICE (1507) AT CORPUS CHRISTI COLLEGE, OXFORD.

The only special feature to notice about the next illustration (Class B 2 in the table), the Coombe Keynes chalice, is that it has a small projecting ornament or toe at each angle of the foot. Mr. Hope and Mr. Fallow called these "knops" on the authority of an early mention of them, and record a notice in 1525, in which they are described as "half mones, otherwise called Knappes." But as "knop" was the word exclusively applied to the projection on the stem of the chalice by Mr. Octavius Morgan, it would not be appropriate to follow a newer and less established use here. The usual design of these projecting toes is that of an ornamental letter M, and this is often so decidedly the case that it may be intended to indicate the name of the Virgin. Chalices with this ornamental addition are the latest of the Gothic group. Two of them are hall-marked as of 1494 and 1496 respectively, dates which happily coincide with the period at which these chalices

NO. 7.—CHALICE (1521) AT JURBY, ISLE OF MAN.

had been placed already by their fashion in the absence of any known dated or hall-marked example.

Of the eighteen specimens at present known, several have lost some or all of their toes. They were somewhat easily broken off: and when a chalice had lost one or more of them, the easiest way of restoring the symmetry of its appearance was no doubt to lop off the rest. Mr. Hope suggests that their liability to catch in the altar linen or the vestments of the priest caused the change in the form of foot which we soon have to notice.

It is with some hesitation that they have been classed as a sub-division of the Gothic group to which they belong; for it

No. 8.—CHALICE (1527) AT TRINITY COLLEGE, OXFORD.

is not at all impossible that some of the earlier chalices, now without toes, may originally have been so ornamented.

It will be seen from the engravings of Bishop Fox's chalice (No. 6) and the chalices at Trinity College (No. 8), and Wylye (No. 9), that they form a regular series, the cable-like edges to the stem and the engraving on the foot of the chalice of 1507 giving an intermediate point between the very beautiful simplicity of the earlier Nettlecombe and Coombe Keynes chalices and the later

pair.   Much of Mr. Octavius Morgan's description of the Nettlecombe chalice is equally applicable to the other examples.

NO. 9.—CHALICE (1525) AT WYLYE, WILTS.

But these bring us to the third type (Class C in the table),
which we have called the Tudor; and as the chalice of 1340
was treated as a transitional example between the two earlier

groups, so Bishop Fox's, with the chalice at Leominster, the
former dating back and the latter looking forwards, may illustrate the passage from the better Gothic of the second to the
debased of the third and latest class.   In the Corpus College
chalice we still have the conical bowl of the middle type
coupled with the lobed foot which now replaces .the more
Gothic and angular form; whilst in the Leominster example
we have the features reversed, the foot being of the earlier
fashion, but the bowl of the coming hemispherical form.   At
Jurby we come to the debased form of bowl as well as the
lobed foot.   Traces of this form of bowl may have been seen
before, but at the time of the Jurby chalice the change from
the Gothic to the Tudor hemispherical bowl is well in progress,
and it is not a change for the better.

With the Trinity College and Wylye cups we have arrived
at the full development of the Tudor type.   (Class C 2 in the
table.)   To all the ornamentation of the older vessels they add
a complicated flowing foot, a highly elaborated stem, in the
details of which almost all Gothic feeling is lost, and with
these features a nearly hemispherical bowl which abandons
the extreme simplicity of the Gothic period, by showing an
engraved inscription on a belt running round the centre of it,
to match in the case of the Trinity chalice an inscription
similarly engraved upon its paten.   This inscription is not
unusual.   "A chalice with a patent gilt graven with *Calicem
Salutaris* weing xxi. onz.," is mentioned amongst the gilt plate
belonging to Henry Fitzroy, Duke of Richmond, at his death in
almost the very year in which the Wylye chalice was made.

The beautiful example at Wylye is one of those discovered
by the late Mr. J. E. Nightingale, F.S.A., who described it as
follows:—" It is of silver gilt and in excellent preservation;
6¾ inches in height, stem and base hexagonal.   Some of the
ornamentation corresponds with the Trinity College chalice at
Oxford.   It has the same cable ornament at the angles of the
stem, and the same Gothic open embattled work at the foot of
it, but not the open tracery work between the cables.   The
knop is similar to that of the Nettlecombe chalice, except that
it has human heads instead of lions' heads; the moulding of
the base, too, is like the Nettlecombe cup, and likewise the
form of the bowl, which is not so globular as that of the Trinity

College example. It has an inscription both on bowl and foot, and the usual crucifix on the base; the lettering on the cup is small Gothic, and that on the base in capitals of the early sixteenth **h** century type." The hall-mark is a Lombardic capital **h** and will give us the year 1525 as the date of this interesting cup. It is as close to the Trinity College, Oxford, chalice in point of date, as it is in the style of its ornamentation. The six engravings given of the chalices of the Gothic and Tudor period, give for each of these groups one example in outline, followed by another in full perspective. It may be not undesirable in conclusion to give a complete list of the known Pre-Reformation chalices, as nearly as may be in chronological order, omitting the coffin chalices. They are as follows:—

TYPE A.

1. British Museum (from Berwick St. James, Wilts.) . early 13th cent.
2. Dolgelly, chalice found near (Do.) Cardiff Museum.

TYPE B.

3. Hamstall Ridware, Staffs. . late 14th century.
4. Goathland, Yorkshire . early 15th century.
5. Nettlecombe, Somerset . . 1479
6. Brasenose Coll., Oxford, a pair 1498
7. Manningford Abbas, Wilts. .
8. Hinderwell, Yorks. .
9. Ampleforth Abbey, Yorks. .
10. R. C. C., West Grinstead .
11. Victoria and Albert Museum .
12. Clifford Chambers, Glouc. . 1494
13. Very Rev. Dr. Darby . . 1496
14. Codford St. Mary, Wilts. .
15. Beswick, Yorks. . . .
16. Hornby R. C. Church, Lancs.
17. Old Hutton, Westmorland .
18. Bacton, Herefordshire . .
19. Blaston St. Giles, Leicesters.

20. Little Faringdon, Oxfordshire
21. Coombe Keynes, Dorset .
22. Llandudwen,* N. Wales .
23. Chavenage, Glouc. . .
24. Llanelian yn Rhôs, Denbighshire . . .
25. Comb Pyne, Devon .
26. West Drayton, Middlesex .
27. Claughton, Lancs. . .
28. Leominster, Herefordshire c. 1510

TYPE C.

29. Pillaton Hall, Staffs. . .
30. Corpus Christi College, Oxford 1507
31. St. Sampson, Guernsey. .
32. Ebbesbourne, Wilts. . .
33. Leyland, R. C. Church, Lancs.
34. Chalice, sold at C.M.&W. 1905 1518
35. Chalice, exhib. at Soc. of Ant.
36. Jurby, Isle of Man . . 1521
37. Sturminster Marshall, Dorset . 1536
38. Victoria and Albert Museum † 1527
39. Wylye, Wilts. . . . 1525
40. Trinity College, Oxford . 1527
41. R. C. Cathedral, Westminster 1529
42. Highworth, Wilts. . . 1534

Would that many more such remained, but the chalices mentioned in the foregoing list are all that have come to the author's knowledge, after years of inquiry, and with the advantage of the researches of many friends and a constantly increasing band of fellow-labourers in this interesting archæological field; amongst whom must be specially mentioned the late Mr. J. E. Nightingale, F.S.A., who brought to light no less than eight chalices in Wilts and Dorset, and

---

* Jones, Bangor Church-plate   † The bowl of this seems restored.

Mr. T. M. Fallow, F.S.A., who has been as successful in the Yorkshire and Lancashire district.

The examples from No. 9 to No. 24 inclusive, form a beautiful group, having much good work and interesting features, including the projecting toes which have been described as peculiar to them. One of the first discovered of these was the chalice at Old Hutton, found by Miss Ellen K. Goodwin (now Mrs. Ware) in the course of examining the church-plate

NO. 10.—PATEN (C. 1200) AT WYKE, HANTS.

of the Deanery of Kendal for publication in the Cumberland and Westmorland Antiquarian and Archæological Society's Transactions. This was the only piece of Pre-Reformation plate remaining in the diocese of Carlisle. It is to the great interest excited by the successful volume upon the church-plate of the Carlisle Diocese, edited by the late Chancellor Ferguson, which was the first complete Diocesan or County account to see the light, that we owe the admirable works on the same subject which have succeeded it, and a number more which are in hand, some of them rapidly approaching completion.

We now come to Patens, which are more numerous, and a good many of which are still in use. Above ninety are now known, by far the greater part of them of the very end of the fifteenth or the early part of the sixteenth century. One of the most beautiful and the oldest at the same time is at Wyke in Hampshire (No. 10). With an octofoil depression, it exhibits both the characteristic features of the most ancient examples, viz.:—the Agnus for central device, and an inscription running round the rim of the plate in uncial lettering. The inscription is **CUN [C] TA CREO VIRTUTE REGO PIE TATE REFORMO.** Very similar lettering is to be seen on the paten found at Canterbury in the tomb of Archbishop Walter who died in 1205. A third very early example is at Chichester bearing, like the Canterbury example, the inscription **AGNVS DEI QVI TOLLIS PECCATA MVNDI MISERERE NOBIS,** both of them having the "Agnus" for

No. 11.—COFFIN PATEN OF BP. CANTELUPE (D. 1266) AT WORCESTER CATHEDRAL.

central device. The spelling in all these examples is more or less abbreviated or incorrect, and in the case of the Canterbury paten the letters **NN** are engraved, as we should say, upside down. The Canterbury paten has around the rim a second band with a curious inscription which does not occur elsewhere in England. In the thirteenth century, the "Manus Dei" became the usual device for the centre, and the depression seems more often than not of quatrefoil shape. An engraving (No. 11) is given of a very typical example of c. 1266 found in the tomb of Bishop Cantelupe of Worcester.

By the time we come to the Gothic period, we have a more settled form and fashion of Paten. Instead of the plain plate or the tenfoil or octofoil or quatrefoil depression, we have now almost invariably a six-lobed depression corresponding to the hexagonal form of the foot of the chalice, and the "agnus" and "manus" give way to the "vernicle" or face of the Saviour. rudely engraved in the middle of the depression.

This is illustrated by the Nettlecombe paten, which Mr. O.

No. 12.—PATEN (1479) AT NETTLECOMBE, SOMERSET.

Morgan described as follows:—"The paten is $4\frac{7}{8}$ inches in diameter, with a narrow moulded edge and a brim like an ordinary plate, within which is sunk a six-lobed depression. The centre points from which the workman formed the lobes are still visible, and the spandrels between the lobes are filled with a small radiating ornament as is usual in similar patens which are not unfrequently met with. In the centre is a still further depression, in which has been inserted from the back a small silver plate having in transparent enamel sunk in the metal a representation of the vernicle or face of our Saviour surrounded by a cruciform nimbus. It fortunately remains perfect. This central depression with an inserted plate of enamel is very unusual, the surface of patens being usually made as smooth as possible. The back of this small plate is gilt and engraved with the sacred monogram (see No. 12) in black letter of the fifteenth century." Such patens were commonly made to match the chalices with which they were used.

and the two were called "a chalice with his paten" in the old inventories of church goods. The depression of the paten often fitted exactly into the top of its chalice if placed upon it.

As we get later into the Gothic period the form of the paten becomes a little more uncertain, the six-lobed depression giving way to the single depression of a plain plate; and in the late Gothic times too, we find the sacred monogram instead of the vernicle. In the Tudor time the paten is elaborated to match

NO. 13.—PATEN (1527) AT TRINITY COLLEGE, OXFORD.

the chalices of which we have already spoken, and as an inscription around the bowls of the chalice became usual, so did the same addition become a common feature around the rim of the paten, and they were engraved to match one another. Of this final development the fine paten (No. 13) at Trinity College, Oxford, supplies us with an illustration.

The lettering of the Tudor period will be noticed, and the elaboration of rays with which the vernicle is surrounded as with a halo, spreading over the whole surface within the six-

lobed space left round the central portion of the paten. The
paten at St. Edmund's, Salisbury, of the year 1533, much
resembles the Trinity paten.

Of the whole number of known patens, some twenty-five
are hall-marked. They are as follows :—

Nettlecombe, Somerset . 1479 . Vernicle.	Late Rev. Thos. Staniforth	
Stow Longa, Hunts . 1491 . do.	1517 . Vernicle	
Shirley, Derbyshire . 1493 . do.	Paten sold at C. M. W.,	
Clifford Chambers, Glouc.	1905. . . . . 1518 .	do.
1494 . do.	Durham Cathl. Library . 1519 .	do.
Childrey, Berks . . 1496 . do.	(from Hamsterley, Durh.)	
Cossey, Norf. . . . 1496 . do.	Hartshorne, Derb. . c. 1520 .	do.
Happisbrough, Norf. . 1504 . do.	Great Waltham, Essex . 1521 .	do.
C. C. C., Oxford . . 1507 . do.	Beachamwell, Norf. . 1523 .	do.
West Drayton, Midx. . 1507 . do.	Trin. Coll. Oxford . . 1527 .	do.
Hockham, Norf. . . 1509 . do.	Vict. & Albert Mus. . 1527 .	do.
Orcheston St.Mary,Wilts 1510 . do.	Gissing, Norf. . . . 1530 .	do.
Scremby, Lincs. . . 1512 . do.	St. Edmund, Salisbury . 1533 .	do.
Heworth, Durh. . . 1514 . do.	Llanmaes, Glamor. . 1535 .	do.
	Cofton Hackett, Worc. 1535 .	do.*

It will be noticed that no less than five of these hall-marked
patens come from Norfolk, a county which can boast of
possessing more than thirty out of the whole number of Pre-
Reformation patens remaining at the present time.

Besides the paten, a spoon sometimes appertained to the
ancient massing chalice. A chalice is mentioned in a will of
1422, as "calicem sanctificatam cum patena et cocliari eidem
calici pertinente." The use of this chalice spoon is told us by
an entry in the York Minster fabric rolls, 23 Dec., 1370, which
adds to the mention of a silver gilt spoon that it was "ad pro-
porcionandum vinum sive aquam pro calice magni altaris."

This brings us to Protestant times and the new form of
communion cup introduced in the reign of Elizabeth, or rather
of Edward VI.

Cups of the earlier reign are seldom to be found. Those known
to the author were, until lately, only ten in number ; but to this
short list Mr. Edwin Freshfield, junr., F.S.A., has added no less
than five, all found in the City of London, and three have come to
light since. The nineteen now known are as follows :—St. Lawrence, Jewry, 1548 ; St. Peter, Cornhill, St. James, Garlickhithe,
St. Mildred, Bread Street, St. Michael, Wood Street, 1549 ; Cup,
Derbyshire ; Bridekirk, Cumberland, St. Michael, Cornhill, 1550 ;
St. Margaret, Westminster (2), Hunstanton, Norfolk ; Totnes,

---

* Per Th. Barnett, Esq.

Devon ; Beddington, Surrey ; St. Michael, Southampton, Mrs. Milligan, sold at Christie's since 1914, 1551 ; Owlysbury, Hants ; St. James, Garlickhithe ; Cup, Sussex, 1552 ; Great Houghton, Northants, 1552. Most of these so much resemble the engraving we have given (No. 14) of the communion cups of 1570 still preserved at Cirencester, that more need not be said about them. Their peculiarity is the plain bowl with at most a little dotted ornament and the conical stem with gadrooned flange close up under the bowl. The Cirencester pair no doubt owe their early fashion to the fact that though they are themselves of Elizabethan date, they were made by a silversmith who had been much employed upon such work in the time of King Edward VI., and who continued, as it seems, to use his original shop pattern long afterwards. They are plain standing cups, with conical stem, as shown, and without knops. Their large size adapted them for the use of the whole congregation, now that in 1547 the administration

NO. 14.—COMMUNION CUP (1570) AT CIRENCESTER.

of the Communion in both kinds was restored according to the practice of the early Church, and in this respect they are a great contrast to the chalices they replaced.

There is fortunately no lack of examples of the Elizabethan communion cup. They are found everywhere, and of the same

IS76
CRIST CHRCH

No. 15.—COMMUNION CUP AND PATEN COVER
(1576) AT CHRISTCHURCH, CO. MONMOUTH.

form, and bearing the same style of ornamentation, from one end of England to the other. (No. 15.) There are sixteen within a walk of Cirencester, and as many in one county as another. Mr. Morgan has given the following account of them :—

"The chalice still consisted of the same parts — bowl, stem, and foot — though I have known two instances in small parishes where the chalices consist of the cup only, without stem or foot. The stem, although altered in form and character, still swells out in the middle into a small knob, or the rudiments of one, and is occasionally ornamented with small bands of a lozenge-shaped ornament, or some other such simple pattern, and the foot is invariably round instead of indented or angular.* The form of the cup, however, is altogether changed, and instead of being a shallow wide bowl, it is elongated into the form of an inverted truncated cone slightly bell-shaped. The form of the paten is also much changed, the sunk part of the platter is often considerably deepened, the brim narrowed, and thereon is fixed a rim

* Several examples of the conical stem of Edw. VI., varied so as to be almost pear shaped, occur in several London churches, dated 1559.

or edge by which it is made, when inverted, to fit on the cup as a cover, whilst a foot is added to it which serves also as a handle to the cover, as though it were intended to place the wine in the chalice and cover it with the paten-cover until the administration of the Sacrament, when the cover would be removed and used as a paten for holding the bread. On the bottom of the foot of the paten was a silver plate which almost always bears the date when it was made, and the name of the parish to which it belongs. The ornamentation on all these chalices and paten-covers, as they may be called, is invariably the same; it consists simply of an engraved band round the body of the cup and on the top of the cover formed by two narrow fillets which interlace or cross each other with a particular curvature in every instance the same, the space between them being occupied by a scroll of foliage, sometimes replaced by plain lines of short strokes like hyphens, as at Cirencester, and as shown also on the Christ Church paten (No. 15), and this ornament is marked by a total absence of letters, monograms, emblem, or figures of any kind.* It is curious how this exact uniformity of shape and ornament was so universally adopted, unless there had been some regulation or standard pattern to go by, but I have not been able to find any such, to guide the makers."

To this it may be added, that some years ago, before much attention was paid to hall-marks, a silversmith assured the present writer that these cups were all made by order, and issued one to every parish by Government under an Act of Parliament; it is, however, hardly necessary to say now that no such Act can be found. They were made by provincial as well as London goldsmiths; plenty were made at York, Exeter, and Norwich, and there are almost as many different makers' marks upon them as there are cups themselves. In Yorkshire and in Worcestershire they are of 1570 or 1571; in Norfolk five years earlier, and in Gloucestershire and the west of England about as much later.

---

* Sometimes the band is close round the lip. A number of examples of this variation occur between 1564 and 1570. Sometimes there are two separate bands; many are known from 1568 to 1573. Sometimes a wider compound band is found at about the same period; but the design is of the same general character in all these cases.

No two again are exactly alike in size or finish, there is everything from the tiny cup of some village church weighing no more than five or six ounces, and destitute of all ornament, up to a tall vessel a foot high, holding nearly a quart of wine and fully ornamented as in the engraving, some few having a second belt around the cup.   Local deviations in detail from the cup described by Mr. Morgan prevail, however, here and there.   The cups made at Norwich have wider, shallower bowls, and no knob in the stem. The name of the parish is engraved round the bowl instead of the usual band of ornament, as for example, FOR THE TOWNE OF RANYNGHAM.   In Suffolk the bowl is generally bell-shaped, and the knob is either missing or placed immediately below the bowl.   In South Wales the cups occasionally follow the Norwich shape, but usually have deep bowls with the name of the parish in Latin round them in addition to the ornamental band.   The York made

No. 16.—COMMUNION CUP (1568), NORWICH PATTERN.

cups are fine vessels often with square-shaped bowls, and the band of ornament is found as late as 1690. The Exeter cups, too, are also very handsome vessels, tall and deep, like the London pattern, the bowls vase-shaped, larger at the top than at the bottom, the sides just at the rim turning up for about a quarter of an inch rather than forming a lip.   In Worcestershire a number of the cups noted by Archdeacon Lea have stems of the Edward VI. pattern or a modification of it.   These have usually a single mark only,

probably that of a local man; but several of them are dated
1571. Except for such small differences and local peculiarities,
they are all so alike in shape and style, that it is indeed somewhat wonderful, as Mr. Morgan remarks, that no authority
or direction for their formation has ever been found. Burnet
and Strype, the Constitutions and Canons of the Church,
the Acts and Proceedings in Convocation, the Documentary
Annals of the Reformation, the Injunctions, Declarations and

No. 17.—TWO COMMUNION CUPS (1600, 1622).

Orders, were all searched by Mr. Morgan without finding any
specific direction that would account for the extraordinary
uniformity of shape and pattern which could hardly have
been the result of the taste or caprice of churchwardens
or silversmiths. To this long list may be added the
Statute Book, the Registers of the Privy Council, and every
other likely record, which have all since been searched in
vain.

There is one suggestion left, that some regulation on the
subject, though unrecorded, may have emanated from the

Convocation held in London in 1562, at which many important matters concerning the doctrine, articles, rites and discipline of the Church of England were settled. The earliest cup of this fashion is of the year 1558, at S. Michael's le Belfry, York.

The same pattern found favour from this time to about the middle of the next century, but in examples of a later date than 1600 the engraved belt is usually wanting, and the bowls are perhaps rather straighter sided. There are good specimens of these at the Temple Church made in 1609 by one Terry, a goldsmith of note,* and a pair of rather plainer finish at Hackney Church of the year 1637. All these are about nine inches high.

Plain upright beakers are found doing duty as communion cups in various places. An example of 1608 is preserved at Stickney, Lincs., and another of the following year at Armathwaite, also one at Castle Bythe of 1630. Later ones of London make in 1676, and dated 1678, are at Maiden Newton, Dorset, and at Ashby, Lincs., dated 1737.† They are very common all through the seventeenth century as communion cups in Scotland. The Dutch Church community at Norwich had a set of four such cups of Elizabethan date, made by one of the local goldsmiths.

Between 1600 and 1630 the cup is often found shaped something like the letter V, and supported by a baluster stem. An engraving (No. 17) is given of an example of this kind and date, together with a cup of 1622, which also shows the baluster stem, and much resembles the chalice in which King Charles I. received his last communion on the morning of his execution. This sad historical relic was made in 1629, and is preserved at Welbeck. The wine-glass shaped vessels, and tazza-form cups like that engraved later, No. 92, were the popular shape for communion cups in Scotland. It is not too much to say that most Scottish communion cups of the seventeenth century are of one or other of these two patterns, or else of beaker fashion. Of the tazza form of communion cup, only three are known in England. These are at Peatling Magna, Leicestershire, of 1603 ; at Shenton, in the same county, of 1641 ; and a third, in Somersetshire, of 1602.

The last two illustrations with the pair which follow next (No. 18) give us four of the most usual forms of communion

---

* *Calendar of the Records of the Inner Temple.* F. A. Inderwick, K.C.

† Five have been noted in Yorks between 1593 and 1772, one at Llanfillen of 1598 (see p. 375).

cups in the seventeenth century. They all have been reproduced for the sake of convenience from some of the very
accurate outlines given by Mr. A. Trollope in his Leicestershire
church plate, as follows:—

(1.) Com. cup, 1600.　Pickwell,　Leicestershire　.　.　.　½ scale.
(2.) Com. cup, 1622.　Ashfordby　　do.　.　.　.　.　do.
(3.) Com. cup, 1630.　Melton Mowbray do.　.　.　.　do.
(4.) Com. cup, 1686.　Carlton Curlieu　do.　.　.　.　.　⅓ scale.

The first gives an illustration of the V-shaped cup in vogue
for a few years from 1600; and the second, of the wine-glass

No. 18.—TWO COMMUNION CUPS (1630, 1686).

shaped cup which succeeds the last and is found till about 1650.
Of the earlier type are cups at Scaleby, Cumberland; at
Pickwell, Leicestershire; and Newbold Pacey, Warwickshire,
all of them of the year 1600; at Glooston, Leicestershire, of
1601; and at Gilmorton in the same county of 1605. Of the
latter, there are a host of examples from 1622 to 1642. The
fourth represents the rude vessels of the later part of the century.
But the third is for many reasons of unusual interest, and

deserves more detailed notice. It is a form of cup constantly found from 1630 to 1640, and many of them are by the same maker, who used an escallop for his mark. No less than twenty-nine cups of this make are known to the author. Of these cups the peculiarity is the stem and foot. Instead of the baluster stem more usual at this period, or the evenly divided and knopped stem of the Elizabethan type which was not yet out of date,

No. 19.—PEWTER COMMUNION VESSELS, CIRCA 1640.

we have a collar or flange around the upper part of a trumpet-shaped stem which plainly recalls the form of foot which has been already described as first found in the reign of Edward VI., and then again later in the case of some cups of the early years of Elizabeth.

It will be remembered that the re-appearance of this shape of foot at the later of these dates, when the general fashion of foot was somewhat different, was accounted for by the fact that it must have been a shop pattern of the smith, whose mark of a stag's head proved that the same hand had fashioned both groups of cups. And now again in the seventeenth century there is a coincidence which seems to account as happily for its

No. 20.—COMMUNION CUP (1676) AT ASHBY-DE-LA-ZOUCHE.

second re-appearance. The author has always been of opinion that the resemblance of the new foot of c. 1630 and that of the communion cups of the time of Edward VI. was too marked to be accidental, and that the smith of the escallop shell must have been acquainted with the work of him who so many years before

had used the stag's-head mark.   The very earliest in date known
of the later group is this of 1630 at Melton Mowbray, and
curiously enough an older cup belonging to the same parish is
one of the very rare examples of the early Elizabethan group
marked with the stag's head.   That this last formed the model
for the newer cup which was probably ordered to match it, is
almost certain ; and it is an interesting conjecture that the rest

No. 21.—COMMUNION CUP (C. 1510) AT SANDWICH, KENT.

of this large and well-marked group of communion cups by the
smith of the escallop shell, owe their fashion directly to the
pattern originally supplied him by his customer at Melton
Mowbray.   It may be added that in 1628, only two years before
the old pattern thus came to his notice, he is found producing
a cup for Witley in Surrey of the usual Elizabethan type.
     It will be seen from the pewter vessels (No. 19) formerly at a
village church in Gloucestershire, that the pewter communion

cups and flagons of this period are very much like those made of more precious metal.

Of the Commonwealth period and some ten years on either side of it, are found a few communion cups, such as those at Rochester Cathedral, which seem to have been fashioned after Pre-Reformation models. They have the six-sided or else eight-sided foot with cherub-heads at the points, but the bowls are deeper and straighter than those of the Gothic period. The fine set at Rochester is of 1653; and equally fine vessels by the same maker are at Staunton Harold, Leicestershire, of the following year.

A fine example of this class is at Ashby-de-la-Zouche, an engraving (No. 20) of which is given from an original drawing furnished by the kindness of the late Rev. J. Denton. It was given in 1676, and resembles, in general form, an undated and not so highly ornamented cup used in Lambeth Palace chapel. This last is by a maker the whole of whose dated work is of c. 1636. Somewhat similar ones dated 1637 are at St. Mary's, Lambeth, and one at Lichfield Cathedral, dated 1670. These dates fairly mark the period during which such cups are met with.

From about the time of the Restoration a ruder fashion prevailed; many cups are then found of great size, with straight sides having somewhat of a lip, and mounted on a plain circular stem and foot, wholly unrelieved by any ornament, save that the stem perhaps swells out at its centre into a simple boss or ring as plain as the rest of it. (See the cup of 1686, No. 18.) The paten-cover fitting on is still found as on those at Westminster Abbey, dated 1660, and many other places.

Another pattern in vogue then and later had an even ruder stem and foot all in one, it being merely a truncated cone somewhat of the shape of the bowl of an Elizabethan communion cup turned upside down, and attached to the bottom of the cup. There are examples of them dated 1661 at St. Margaret's, Westminster, and they are not at all uncommon; from this time the paten-cover is often wanting.

Before we leave the sixteenth and seventeenth centuries, note must not be omitted of other cups of quite exceptional form which are occasionally found, some of great excellence; these have, no doubt, been originally secular drinking cups, but since devoted by the piety and liberality of their owners to more sacred purposes. They are found of all dates and shapes. The earliest known to the author is a beautiful Gothic cup with conical bowl at Marston, near Oxford. Its stem is as a truncated cone, and has beautiful pierced mouldings at its outer edge which rests upon three talbot dogs, themselves upon small oblong stands or pedestals.

No. 22.—CUP (1535) WITH COVER SURMOUNTED BY THE BOLEYN BADGE,* USED AS A CHALICE AT CIRENCESTER.

Three most singular cups are those at Wymeswold, Leicestershire, Sandwich, Kent, and Deane, Hants (1551). They are exactly alike, simple, shallow, circular, tazza-shaped, flat-bottomed, straight-sided bowls, on truncated cone feet; and they each have an inscription running round the bowl in Tudor lettering: SOLI DEO HONOR ET GLORIA being on the Wymeswold cup, and the words THIS IS THE COMMVNION COVP on the cup at Sandwich which has a cover (No. 21)†; and on the Deane cup. GYVE GOD THAKES FOR ALL THYNGS. The inscription at Wymeswold is the same as that which appears on a very similar cup in the possession of Lord Swaythling of the year 1500; but the inscription on the Sandwich cup can hardly have been placed upon it before c. 1550.

The Leicestershire example is hall-marked 1512, a circumstance which may be taken to date its fellow at Sandwich at all events approximately.

* The Boleyn badge was a crowned falcon bearing a sceptre in the dexter claw and having a mount of lilies growing in front of its breast. The above engraving gives the lilies rather too much in profile to be intelligible without explanation, and makes the sceptre, the upper portion of which is now broken off in the case of the cup at Cirencester, too like a dagger.

† The inscription on the Dunn Gardner bowl of 1521 in similar Henry VIII. lettering is :—" BENE · DICTUS · DEUS · IM · DONA · SUIS · AME."

Perhaps the most beautiful of all these secular cups is one at Cirencester, made in 1535, and in all probability for the unfortunate Queen Anne Boleyn. An engraving of this is given (No. 22). It is not known at what time it came into the possession of the churchwardens at Cirencester, but it is not improbable that it was one of the royal New Year's Day presents, made by Anne Boleyn's daughter, Queen Elizabeth, after the fashion of those days, to her physician, Dr. Richard Master (to whom the lands of the Abbey of Cirencester were granted in 1565), and by him given to the parish with which his descendants have ever since been connected. Another very ancient cup at Gatcombe, Isle of Wight, bears the hall-mark of the year 1540. (No. 23.)

No. 23.—CUP (1540) USED AS A CHALICE AT GATCOMBE, ISLE OF WIGHT. (Half scale.)

A fine hanap at Watford in Hertfordshire, is of the year 1561. Sir John Maclean notes a very good one, dated 1576, at St. Mabyn, Cornwall. It is some 13 inches high, and has a cover surmounted by a boy nude holding a shield, both bowl and cover engraved in arabesque style with birds and foliage. Kensington parish church has a tall standing cup of 1599, the bowl ornamented with escallop shells in bold repoussé-work ; and at Hucknall Torkard is a very similar hanap, of about 1610, in character much like the Edmonds' Cup of the Carpenters' Company, of which an engraving is given in the next chapter (No. 81) ; but the steeple is in this case wanting, or more probably has been broken off. A magnificent cup of 1611 at Yarlington, Som., another of 1614 at Odcombe, Som., a third of 1617 at Bodmin, with a fourth of 1619 at Linton, Kent, are as fine as that at Carpenters' Hall ; others of the same fashion are at Welland, Worc., and at Braunstone, whilst there are no fewer than four in the Diocese of Carlisle. Simple beaker cups are in use at Llanfyllin, N. Wales, Welcombe, Devon, Stickney, Lincs., and at Armathwaite, in Cumberland. These are of the years 1598, 1601, 1608, and 1609 respectively. Such cups were popular also for secular use at this period. (See No. 94.)

Last of all comes an ordinary two-handled fluted porringer, like No. 98, Chap. X. Made in 1708, it has done duty as a chalice at a village church in Gloucestershire ever since. A similar vessel of 1709 is to be seen at the Independents' Chapel in Oswestry.

It is interesting to find examples, and fine examples too, of each successive fashion of secular drinking-cup among the ancient possessions of our parish churches. It may, perhaps, be thought by some at the present day inappropriate to use such vessels for the sacred purposes to which their former owners have dedicated them, but surely they should be carefully treasured and preserved instead of exchanged, as they too often are, for articles of modern design that cannot be thought of without a shudder of horror. Less suitable they may seem to a few for their present use than such models of mediæval art as the chalices at Nettlecombe or at Oxford, but they have an interest and value of their own that can never attach to the brand-new vessels decorated with sham jewels and nineteenth century filigree-work, that are too often obtained in exchange for them.

To return to ordinary cups. At the commencement of the eighteenth century, cups were made very upright, much like those of 1660 at Westminster Abbey, but narrower and straighter, and always perfectly plain. It is said that Queen Anne presented most of the American churches of that day with silver altar vessels ; some of these are preserved still, and it is much to be hoped that many more examples will be found sooner or later.

There is even now in use, or was in 1861, the hundredth anniversary of the foundation of the church, at Christ Church, Cambridge, Mass., a silver paten, cup and flagon bearing the date 1694, originally part of a service presented by King William and Queen Mary "for the use of their Majesties' Chappell in New England," that is, the King's Chapel, Boston. This set seems to have been given by the Church to Governor Hutchinson in exchange for a more valuable set in 1772, and by

him divided equally between Christ Church, Cambridge, and
St. Paul's Church, Newburyport.*

The silver service sent to Grace Church, Jamaica, in Long
Island, by the Society for the Propagation of the Gospel,* in
the year 1704, is still in existence there, engraved "Ex dono
Societatis pro promovendo Evangelis in partibus transmarinis,
1704," and the record of the grant of money with which it was

NO. 24.—COMMUNION VESSELS (1707), AT HYATTSVILLE, MARYLAND, U.S.A.

bought is to be traced in the Journal of the Society on Nov. 17
in that year. It was made by John Wisdome of London.
Plate of the year 1708, given by Queen Anne, remains at St.
George's Church, Hempstead, Long Island, and at St. Peter's
Church, Westchester, N.Y., both cups being made by John
Eastt. The service with royal arms and **AR** at Trinity Church,
N.Y., is of the following year and by Francis Garthorne. A
set of communion plate given in 1711 by Queen Anne "to her
Indian Chapel of Onondawgas," is now in use at St. Peter's

---

* Note kindly communicated by Rev. H. W. Tucker, M.A., Secretary S.P.G.

Church, Albany, N.Y.   Other plate of this same year, and like
the last bearing the royal arms and **AR**, is at Brantford and
also at Desoronto, both in Canada.   The plate at Christ
Church, Boston, Mass., was given by King George II. in 1733,
and was made in that year by Joseph Allen and Mordecai Fox,
of St. Swithin's Lane.

Again, Trinity Church, Boston, and St. John's, Portsmouth,

No. 25.—PATEN (1673) AT ST. CUTHBERT'S, YORK.

New Hampshire, were given plate by the same sovereign in
1742, made in 1741 by the same silversmiths as the last.

The latest royal gift yet traced in the United States is an
alms-basin at Trinity Church, New York, by the well-known
Thom. Heming, in 1766.   It is engraved with the royal arms,
and bears the initials **GR**.   Of the same year is some of the
plate at Ch. Ch. Bruton, Virginia, which is marked **GIIIR**.

But little attention was now paid to art in ecclesiastical
matters, and it can only be said that the church plate of the
eighteenth and much of the last century was well suited to the

churches of the period. No better general illustration of the taste of the reign of Queen Anne and later, in such matters, could possibly be found than the Cup and Flagon (No. 24) at Hyatts-ville, Maryland, made by the well-known London smith, M. E. Lofthouse.   These were originally at Patuxent or Upper Marl-boro, but eventually came to the church at which they are now preserved.   Many an English town and village can show just such vessels. Fortunately, older churches in most cases treasured the better plate acquired at an earlier period, and well would it be if this were still so, and fewer Elizabethan communion cups were seen in the shop-windows of the modern silversmith. Many of them are made of the very same silver as the more ancient chalices which they replaced, vessels that had, per-chance, belonged to their parishes from time immemorial.   It is to be feared that they are constantly parted with for the mere price of the silver of which they are made, by those who are in ignorance, or are regardless, of the curious historical associa-tions which surround these ancient and interesting relics of the Reformation period.

Modern chalices may be seen in use at St. Paul's Cathedral, and at Kensington parish church, to mention places that are easily accessible, and these may be usefully compared with the illustrations of older chalices given in this chapter by those who are interested in such matters.

So much for chalices, but a few more words must be added to carry down the history of patens.

The paten usual in the seventeenth century was not fitted to the cup, but was a plain circular salver on a central circular and conical foot like the stem of the rudest of the communion cups, and that of the eighteenth century was a plain plate.   In fact, everything may be found from a plain but solid plate, about the size and shape of a dinner-plate, down to a small domestic waiter, standing on the three usual small feet, and made, if not of silver, of Sheffield plate.

As an illustration of the patens of the seventeenth century, a woodcut (No. 25) is given of an unusually fine one of St. Cuthbert's, York, by the kindness of the Yorkshire Archæological Society.   It affords also a good example of the stiff feather mantling that so often surrounds the coats of arms engraved on plate of the Charles II. period.

FLAGONS.

The earliest of these are of the reign of Elizabeth, and succeeding as they·did the phials or cruets of earlier days, one of which was for wine and the other for water, they are usually found in pairs, although a single vessel of the kind would have been all that was actually necessary, even to bring to the church the larger quantity of wine that was now used. Tankard-flagons of an Elizabethan pattern with tapering sides that will be found described under the title Tankards later on, are in use as communion flagons, one at Fugglestone St. Peter, Wilts, and another at Corpus Christi

T.HOBBS

No. 26.—COMMUNION FLAGON (1576) AT CIRENCESTER.

College, Cambridge, with a third at Heddington, Wilts, this last being of 1602, but there is nothing to identify their fashion especially with ecclesiastical uses. We may, therefore, pass on to the very early pair of "round-bellied" or jug-shaped flagons at

Cirencester church (No. 26), which were made in 1576, and
supply us with a distinctive form of flagon which was used till
about 1615. Several examples of them have been found at intermediate dates ; a pair at St. Margaret's, Westminster, and also
one at St. George's Chapel, Windsor, are of 1583 ; and at Rend-
combe in Gloucestershire, there are flagons of the same shape
ornamented round the bowls with engraved belts of the usual
Elizabethan communion-cup pattern. They are of the year
1592. Then come a fine pair of 1598 at Wadham College,
Oxford. These are gilt and covered with engraved strapwork
all over the necks and bowls. They were a legacy of the
foundress. A plainer flagon of 1604 is at Salisbury Cathedral.
A second at St. George's Chapel, Windsor, is as late as 1613 ;
but it was no doubt made to match the one of 1583. It is
curious to note that there are no less than seven or eight large
flagons of this exact shape and of English make, amongst the
treasures of the Czar and of the Patriarch of Moscow in the
Kremlin. The Russian examples are ornamented all over in
flat repoussé work, and are of various dates from 1596 to 1612.

Flagons were probably not so invariably made of silver as
were chalices. The churchwardens of Wing, co. Bucks, are
found in 1576, paying " for a tynne wyne bottell for the churche,
xviij*d*.," and in 1605 the authorities of Leverton ij*s*. vi*d*. " for a
puter communion pott."

The word " pott " will remind us of the Canons of 1603, by
which (Canon 20) the wine was required to be brought to the
communion table in " a clean and sweet standing pot or stoup
of pewter if not of purer metal."

Every now and then a later flagon is found to recall the
earlier pattern. For instance, a pair of very large gilt vessels,
chased all over with decoration as feather-work, and of the year
1660, at the Chapel Royal, St. James's Palace, are almost
exactly of the " round-bellied " shape ; but from this time the
" round-bellied " flagons, as they are called in a MS. inventory of
the plate of St. George's Chapel, disappear from common use,
and the usual tankard pattern comes in which has ever since
been used and is so familiar. A rare example of an upright-
sided plain tankard-flagon is at Teffont Ewyas, Wilts. This is
of 1572. Early examples like this are of small size compared
with the more common tall and large vessels which came in

with the seventeenth century. The earliest of these tall
tankard-flagons known to the writer is an example at C. C. C.,
Oxford, of 1598; the next is at New Coll., Oxford, and of 1602,
to which succeed a pair quite plain, save for one or two small

No. 27.—COMMUNION FLAGON (1664) AT CANTERBURY CATHEDRAL.

bands of moulding, at Brasenose College, Oxford. These are of
1608. Then come a pair at Salisbury Cathedral of 1610, given by
John Barnston, Canon of Salisbury, and of Brasenose College,
Oxford. Possibly as both pairs are by the same maker, both
were presented by Barnston. Following these are two of the

same year, 1618, a plain one belonging to Gray's Inn Chapel, and a beautiful specimen ornamented with belts and scrolls of strapwork, the property of the parish of Bodmin: a very similar one to the last at Kensington Church, London, was made in 1619. The illustrations later under the article on Tankards, of tall tankards at Norwich and Bristol, give a good idea of the church flagon-tankards of this period. Later than this, and to the present day, they are all of the general shape and character of the pewter example shown on page 256, which is of 1640 or thereabouts. Usually plain, and often of great size, and with a spreading base or foot, in the reign of Charles II. they are found covered with heavy Louis XIV. scrolls and flower ornamentation in repoussé work all over the drum. Very occasionally exceptions occur, as in the case of those at Canterbury Cathedral, which are of a jug shape with swelling bowls on short stems or feet, and have spouts, their lids being surmounted by crosses. (No. 27.) They are ornamented with flat appliqué silver ornamentation of the kind sometimes called by amateurs "cut card work," for want of a better name, and are of the year 1664. The jug-shaped flagon is occasionally found in the eighteenth century. A pair at Durham Cathedral, which are of the year 1766, are ornamented with flower-sprays in repoussé work, and are not very unlike the coffee-pot of the same period in shape and general style, except that a short lip at the rim replaces the long spout inserted lower down in the bowl, which would be proper to a coffee-pot. The ordinary flagon of the eighteenth century is shown by the woodcut (No. 24) on p. 263.

The word "flagon" seems to have been always appropriated to a vessel intended to hold wine, and has therefore been continued to these communion vessels, which would otherwise be more appropriately called "tankards," or "pots," as in the language of the Canons of 1603.

The very derivation of the word connects it with "flask," and with the travelling bottles, or costrels, suspended by a cord or chain, similar to what are now called "pilgrims' bottles." A large and handsome bottle of this description bearing the arms of General Charles Churchill, younger brother of the great Duke of Marlborough, and said to have been used by him as a campaigning wine-flask, was sold in 1892 in London. This was by P. Platel, and its date was between 1702 and 1714, probably nearer to the earlier than the later year. In England the wine was brought to the communion table in the sort of vessels described above; but it is a curious fact that at this very day, at All Souls' College, Oxford, the flagons used to contain the wine for consecration at the Sacrament, are two very ancient large silver-gilt flasks, or pilgrims' bottles, having chains to which the stoppers are attached. It is said that they were spared at the Reformation, as having nothing popish about them. They are of foreign, and, from the goldsmiths' marks, almost certainly of French, workmanship; their precise date is unknown. Possibly they are the very vessels described in the will of Richard Andrew, Dean of York (1477), as bequeathed to the College; but from their general character, and particularly that of their stoppers, they are probably of the beginning of the sixteenth century. Similar vessels must have been the "two bottles, parcel gilte with cheynes and stoppelles white, weing clxx. oz., cli." in the list of Katherine of Aragon's Plate of the year 1533.*

ALMS-DISHES OR BASINS.

These in early days may have been of various forms, such as ships, but were more often basins. The wardrobe accounts of 1296 (24 Edward I.) mention "j navis argenti cum pede p' elemos'," and in the time of Edward III. occurs an entry, "una magna olla p' elemosinar'," but these were probably articles of table plate intended for the reception of broken meat to be given to the poor. Another such alms-dish of gold, called the "Tygre," and standing upon a golden bear ornamented with rubies and pearls, is mentioned in Palgrave's State Inventories at the year 1431 (9 Henry VI.). This appears from other entries to have been a ship, like the dish of 1296, and was pledged over and over again for loans of money.

Basins in great number, whatever they may have been used for, are mentioned in the church inventories of 1552 and other years, but those which are now found in our cathedrals and churches are not ancient ones. A large plain gilt alms-dish, with Tudor rose on the central boss, of the year 1556, at St. George's Chapel, Windsor, is the oldest known to the writer.†
Next to that comes another gilt dish at Lambeth Palace

---

* P. R. O. State Papers [Anno 1533], Vol. VI., 340.
† A secular dish of 1524, at St. Magnus, London Bridge, seems to have been altered a good deal at the time of its presentation in 1564 to the Church of St. Michael, Crooked Lane, now linked with St. Magnus.

Chapel, of 1635, and this is followed by a curious fluted dish decorated with punched work in spirals, dated 1639, and belonging to the parish of Bermondsey. Small shallow trays with punched ornamentation, of this period, are used as alms-basins at several village churches, amongst which are Chalton, Hants, 1630, and Bredgar, Kent, 1632, also Alderton, Wilts, 1639. They are almost all included between the years 1630 and 1640. One or two similar basins are, however, of 1660-70.

A plain dish, that might serve for either alms-dish or paten, part of the Gray's Inn Chapel plate, is of the year 1639. Later ones are always plain plates or dishes of silver or silver gilt, differing from one another only in size, some few having a coat of arms engraved on the centre or rim. Hardly any of them are of earlier date than 1660, and few are as old as that. A magnificent altar dish of that year is at the Chapel Royal, St. James' Palace. The centre is filled with a representation of the Last Supper in very high relief, and on the wide rim are other subjects, the chased and repoussé panels being surrounded by Louis XIV. decoration.

There is a fine large dish of 1684 ornamented with repoussé work at Westminster Abbey, and a pair of plainer ones, of about the same date, engraved with the well-known heraldic bearing of a cross between five martlets, the coat assigned to Edward the Confessor.

CANDLESTICKS.

Those used before the Reformation were usually in pairs, and made of latten, or of copper gilt; often they were of silver. Such a pair are found amongst the plate of Henry Fitzroy, Duke of Richmond, natural son of Henry VIII., in 1527, described as follows:—

" Pair of candelstikkes chaced wrethen for an aulter, weing lxxviij. oz. iii. qts. Another pair, lxiij. oz. iij. qts."

They have all entirely disappeared, those which were of intrinsic value in the time of Edward VI., and those made of commoner materials were destroyed as "monuments of superstition" in the early years of Elizabeth.

Pricket candlesticks, or candlesticks with an upright spike upon which to place a large candle, are found among the plate of our cathedrals, but are seldom older than 1660, and still seldomer of any artistic interest. Candlesticks such as these are at Rochester, Canterbury, Gloucester, and other places. The Rochester examples are the earliest known to be still in use, being of 1653. Those preserved in Salisbury Cathedral are of 1662. A very fine pair of chased candlesticks of great size on tripod stands and of good workmanship belong to Westminster Abbey, but these are somewhat later, being of the year 1684. Others at Exeter Cathedral are fluted columns on pedestals, and were made in 1681.

Good candlesticks of more modern design, ornamented with fluted work, chased flowers, and the like, may be seen at Durham. These were made in 1767.

The dates of all these specimens suggest the concluding remark that comparatively little communion plate of any kind is found in our cathedrals older than the Commonwealth and Restoration periods.

Rochester has a pair of tazze with one cover to them, temp. Henry VIII., besides a full set of Commonwealth plate.

Peterborough Cathedral has a single Elizabethan communion cup with its paten-cover of 1569 ; and Wells has a large flagon of 1572, as well as two communion cups of the same year with paten-covers. The following extract from the Wells Cathedral records gives this interesting history of these cups :—" The plate that beforetime were used to superstition shalbe defaced, and of the greatest challaice shalbe made a fayer Communion cuppe with as much convenient speede as maye be before the ffeaste of Easter and of the lesser challaice another by the tyme before limited 19 Nov. 1572."

Probably cathedrals were more exposed to spoliation during the Civil War than parish churches, which could better deny the possession of any treasure worth taking; at all events but little of their Elizabethan plate now remains, and not very much to represent the earlier half of the seventeenth century.

CHAPTER X.

DECORATIVE AND DOMESTIC PLATE.

INTRODUCTION—EFFECT OF THE WARS OF THE ROSES—PROSPERITY OF THE SIX
TEENTH CENTURY—GREAT DESTRUCTION OF OLD PLATE AT VARIOUS TIMES
—GOLD PLATE—OBSOLETE VESSELS—SPOONS—MAZERS—SALTS—STONEWARE
JUGS—EWERS, BASINS, AND SALVERS—STANDING CUPS AND HANAPS—
TANKARDS—SMALLER CUPS OF VARIOUS KINDS—PLATES—FORKS—MON-
TEITHS—CANDLESTICKS, SCONCES, ETC.—TOILET SERVICES—CASTERS AND
CRUET-STANDS—TEA AND COFFEE SERVICES, KETTLES, ETC.—CAKE BASKETS
AND EPERGNES—MACES AND OARS—RACING BELLS, ETC.

PASSING from ecclesiastical to secular plate, it needs no
apology to commence a chapter which is intended to form part
of a practical guide to the plate-collector, with the period to
which the oldest extant specimens belong.

It may be said at once that the Wars of the Roses were to
secular plate what the events of the next century were to the
treasures of the Church. Domestic plate of an earlier date
than the reign of Henry VII. is as scarce as Pre-Reformation
church-plate. The known examples may be almost reckoned
on the fingers, and none of them are hall-marked except the
Nettlecombe Chalice and Paten, and the Anathema Cup at
Pembroke College, Cambridge. They comprise the few chalices
and patens of which particulars have been given in the preceding chapter ; several mazers which will be mentioned later ;
about half-a-dozen drinking vessels of note ; and a salt or two.
The cups are the Lynn Cup, the Horn at Queen's College,
Oxford, the Foundress' Cup at Christ College, Cambridge, and
a Cocoa-nut Cup at New College, Oxford. Almost the only salt
is the Huntsman or Giant Salt at All Souls' College, Oxford.

But in prosperous Tudor times the goldsmith had once more
become a dependent of no mean consideration in the households
of the great. The will of Katherine of Arragon mentions her
goldsmith, to whom she gives a year's wages, and one Robert
Amadal held a similar office in the domestic establishment of
Cardinal Wolsey.

Very early in the sixteenth century an English gentleman's
house of the better sort would have been found well supplied

with silver plate. Sir John Heron, Knt., Treasurer of the Chamber to King Henry VIII., bequeaths to his wife in 1525, "my daily usual plate being in my buttery, that is to say, three saltes silv' with a cover, xxii^t of silver spones, two standing cuppes with ij covers gilt, three Gobletes with a cover and ij white bolles of silver oon pounced and another playn."

The same testator had more covered cups, covered salts, ewers and basins, and other things besides to leave to his children; but the terms of the bequest to his wife give a good idea of what was thought necessary for ordinary domestic use in such a house as his at that period.

By the middle of the reign of Queen Elizabeth the wealth and luxury of the country had been on the increase for almost a century, and an extract from the *Description of England*, by William Harrison, Chaplain to Lord Cobham, which is prefixed to Holingshed's Chronicles, will supply us with a convenient preface. Writing in 1586 he quaintly comments as follows on the times in which he was living :*—

" Certes in noble men's houses it is not rare to see abundance of Arras, rich hangings of tapestrie, silver vessell, and so much other plate as may furnish sundrie cupbords to the summe often-times of a thousand or two thousand pounds at the least, whereby the value of this and the rest of their stuffe dooth grow to be almost inestimable. Likewise in the houses of knights, gentlemen, merchantmen, and some other wealthie citizens, it is not geson to behold generallie their great provision of tapestrie, Turkie work, pewter, brasse, fine linen, and thereto costlie cupbords of plate worth five or six hundred or a thousand pounds to be deemed by estimation. But as herein all these sorts do far exceed their elders and predecessors, and in neatnesse and curiositie the merchant all other; so in time past the costlie furniture stayed there, whereas now it is descended yet lower, even unto the inferior artificers, and manie farmers who by vertue of their old and not of their new leases have for the most part learned also to garnish their cupboards with plate, their joined beds with tapestrie and hangings, and their tables with carpets and fine naperie, whereby the wealthe of our countrie (God be praised therefore and give us grace to employ it well) dooth infinitelie appeare."

---

* Book II. cap. 12.

Plenty of evidence here, of the wealth of plate possessed by men of every degree late in the sixteenth century, and a little farther on he gives in more detail the amount of it that might be found amongst what may be called the lower middle classes. He speaks of the exchange of "treene platters into pewter, and wooden spoones into silver or tin"; and after stating that in old times all sorts of "treene" stuff were so common that a man would hardly find four pieces of pewter, of which one was usually a salt, in a good farmer's house, whereas there was now a fair garnish* of pewter in his cupboard, he concludes with a list of such a farmer's plate, consisting of "a silver salte, a bowle for wine (if not a whole neast), and a dozen of spoons to finish up the sute."

And as it was three hundred years ago, so it is now. Emerson says of the Englishman of to-day that "he is very fond of his plate, and though he have no gallery of portraits of his ancestors, he has of their punch-bowls and porringers. Incredible amounts of plate are found in good houses, and the poorest have some spoon or saucepan, gift of a godmother, saved out of better times."†

Smaller curiosities too have ever had a charm, for the fairer sex especially. And if our sisters carry their treasures about with them hung round their waists, their grandmothers did not value theirs the less because they kept them at home in a Chippendale cabinet.

"With what admiration of the ingenuity of the fair artist," says Sir Walter Scott, "have I sometimes pried into those miscellaneous groups of *pseudo-bijouterie*."‡

"Blessings," adds the great novelist, "upon a fashion which has rescued from the claws of abigails and the melting-pot of the silversmith those neglected *cimelia* for the benefit of antiquaries and the decoration of side-tables."

It is the plate of the century or more beginning with the reign of Henry VII., and ending with that of Queen Elizabeth, which furnishes the modern sideboard with its choicest specimens; and rare as they are, the only wonder is that so many have been preserved, when we consider the events of subsequent times.

---

* A garnish = a full set of an established number of pieces, such as a dozen of each sort. "A garnish" and "half a garnish" are both often spoken of.

† Emerson's *English Traits*.

‡ *St. Ronan's Well*, Chap. X.

It is needless to say that the requirements of King or Parliament in the following century swept much away; but two
less obvious causes have wrought the destruction of even more
than can be laid to the charge of Cavalier and Roundhead put
together.   One of them has already been alluded to in detailing
the measures adopted by William III. to remedy the scarcity of
bullion so grievously felt at the end of the seventeenth century.
The premium then offered for hall-marked silver brought to the
Mint was only too tempting, and a vast quantity of ancient
plate was sacrificed to the cupidity or the necessity of its
owners in 1697.   But scarcely less must have been melted
down a century afterwards to furnish the mere metal required
for the immense dinner equipages which the altered fashions of
the day then rendered indispensable.   No new supply of silver
was available, such as that which had once poured in from
Spanish America; whence then came the tons of silver which
were fashioned into dinner services with their various appen-
dages by the industry of London silversmiths, from Lamerie to
Rundell and Bridge?   It is clear that at that time another and
perhaps the largest consignment of old-fashioned and disused
plate must have gone to the melting-pot, to be returned to its
owners in the shape of the plates, dishes, forks, and spoons
with which our houses are even now to a great extent supplied.
The grand service of plate which graced the royal table at the
great banquet given by Sir Samuel Fludyer at the Mansion
House on Lord Mayor's Day, 1761, which the King and Queen
honoured with their presence, was made new for the occasion
by Mr. Gilpin, the goldsmith, with whom the City exchanged
a quantity of old plate for the new; and many royal and other
services still in use were thus provided between that time and
the end of the century.   Table-services of plate were provided
at the public expense for certain great personages of state, on
taking office, such as Ambassadors, Viceroys of Ireland, and
the Speakers of the House of Commons.   It may be gathered
from account-books preserved by the Messrs. Garrards for the
interval between 1712 and 1720 that a set of the first class was
about 7,000 ounces, and of the second rank about 4,000 ounces.
The largest sets never included more than two or three dozen
forks, one set silver, and another gilt; nor do we find mention
of butter-boats, sauce-ladles, fish-knives, or butter-knives.   A
large cistern and fountain were usually provided, and these

were probably used for washing the forks on the sideboard.
These last articles often weighed 2,000 ounces or more; but
they seem to have gone out of fashion by about the year 1720.
The grandest services were sometimes, but very rarely, of silver
gilt, and such are popularly called "gold services," a mistake
which suggests a remark as to the very small quantity of real
gold plate that is now to be seen.

Only five examples were exhibited amongst the art treasures
collected at South Kensington in the Loan Collection of 1862
—a gold cup and cover of seventeenth century work, given
by Bishop Hall to Exeter College, Oxford; a cup on baluster
stem, given to the Corporation of York in 1672; a covered cup
of the following year, the property of Hon. L. Walrond; a
chocolate cup and cover with one handle, found in the lake
at Knowsley, belonging to the Earl of Derby; and last in
date, but not least, a pair of massive ice-pails from Blenheim,
weighing together no less than 365 ounces, the gift of Queen
Anne to the great Duke of Marlborough. There are two
gold salvers in the collection of plate of His Majesty the
King at Windsor Castle, and a small salver of pure gold
was noted by Mr. Morgan amongst the plate of King
William IV., which was said to have been made of the presentation rings of Serjeants-at-Law. This is no doubt still
preserved. Besides these there is a double-handled gold cup
at Berkeley Castle made by P. Lamerie in 1717, a legacy
from the then Countess of Berkeley to her celebrated daughter,
Lady Betty Germain. It is of the usual plain Queen Anne
pattern. Another was noticed lately in London.

A small racing cup of the same period and shape by Benjamin Pyne, a well-known goldsmith, is in existence, engraved
with a horse ridden by a jockey, and underneath the words
"Saltby Stakes." This was sold in London in December 1923.
It bore the hall-mark of the year 1710-11. The late Sir F. A.
Milbank had a very similar one of 1705-6 by Harracke. It
weighed 23 ounces, and realised in 1898 the sum of £450 at the
sale of the Milbank Collection. Resold in 1911 for £1,800. Lord
Yarborough possesses two such gold cups, both of small size.

The Corporation of Oxford has a solid gold porringer with
two handles and cover, of the year 1680; and at Tredegar
there is a gold cup presented to Sir Charles Gould, Bart., by
the Equitable Assurance Society, about 1780.

It is very possible that a good many other specimens of gold plate may exist, but enough has been said to prove its extreme rarity at the present day; indeed so little has been the demand for gold plate for a long time past that the Goldsmiths' Company in 1664 replied to an enquiry on the subject by the Secretary of State that "it is so seldom that any is made that it hath never been the usage and custom of the Company, as we can find, to make any entry thereof in any of their books."

No. 28.—SIDEBOARD OF 16TH CENTURY.

It was in fact included in the returns relating to silver plate. Formerly it was by no means uncommon. Gold plate is frequently mentioned in the Wardrobe Accounts; and in the Introduction to the State Papers of the reign of Henry VIII., printed by order of the Master of the Rolls, a banquet given by that monarch is mentioned, at which two cupboards (by which we must understand a sort of sideboard of many stages), reaching from the floor to the roof, were covered with a large and varied assortment of vases all of massive gold, silver-gilt dishes of another sort being used for the service of the meats.

An engraving of such a sideboard of five stages, taken from a volume published at Dilingen in 1587, descriptive of the

ceremonies at Prague when the Grand Duke Ferdinand of
Austria invested the Emperor and the Grand Dukes Carl and
Ernest with the order of the Golden Fleece, was given by
the late Mr. W. Fairholt in his description of the celebrated
Londesborough Collection, and is reproduced here (No. 28).
That eminent antiquary reminds us that the series of receding
steps not only served for the due display of the plate, but to
indicate the rank of the person who used it ; persons of royal
blood alone being allowed to use dressers of five " degrés " or
stages, whilst those of four were appropriated to nobles of the
highest rank, and so on down to stages of two or but a single
step, which were proper for knights-bannerets, and unennobled
persons of gentle descent respectively.

The engraving is also valuable for the examples it presents
of many quaint forms of plate then in use, and fitly introduces
a few words about such obsolete articles before we go on to
those that are still found and can be classed under definite heads.

The tall tankard at the servitor's feet would in those days be
called a " can "—a German as much as an English word.

The large double cups made to shut upon the rims of each
other are also noticeable. These, too, are mentioned occasionally in English inventories, and are called "double" or
" trussing " cups. The will of a north-country ecclesiastic
proved at York in 1395, describes his " ciphum duplicem
argenti deaurati vocatum le trussyng coppe," and other early
examples of them occur.

A conspicuous object is the " nef," or ship, which was used
in England as well as abroad ; it seems to have originally been
used to contain the articles used by the noble at his banquet.*
The writer knows of no example of English workmanship or
bearing an English hall-mark, but there were a number of
specimens in the Londesborough Collection of foreign make.

Like the "nef," the "just," the "goddard" and the "voider"
have all disappeared, but they deserve a passing word.

Of the "justa," de Laborde says that it was a vase or flagon
for the table of an invariable size as to capacity, but that its
form varied. This agrees in general terms with the definition
of the word as given by Du Cange.

The " goddard " seems to be derived from the French *godet*,

---

* See p. 339, note.

a sort of goblet or cup, often with a cover. Under the head of "mazers" a little later, we shall find some cups of that description called "goddards," in an account of the year 1444.

The "voyder" was a large dish in which were collected the broken victuals which were removed from the table with a large knife with a broad flat blade called the *voyder-knife*, from *vider*, to empty, clear, or make void.

The *Boke of Nurture*, by Hugh Rhodes, the date of which is 1577, one of the curious set of handbooks of manners and etiquette reproduced by the Early English Text Society, speaks of these vessels as follows :—

" See ye have Voyders ready for to avoid the Morsels that they doe leave on their Trenchours. Then with your Trenchour knyfe take of such fragments and put them in your Voyder and sette them downe cleane agayne."

A "new voyder or charger " of silver is included in a list of plate made in the course of a lawsuit in 1616 ;* and a " great silver voyder with a lardge ewer belonging to it," occurs in a Tredegar inventory of 1676. Few silver ones remain, but some large brass voiders or dishes which have probably been so used, may still be seen, of the history of which nothing is known by their present owners.

The student of mediæval wills and inventories will find many other vessels mentioned here and there which it is difficult or impossible to identify with any existing forms. A "skinking pot " occasionally occurs, deriving its name from the obsolete Saxon word *scencan*—to serve drink at table.   What is the cup called a " costard " in one Bristol will of 1491 ; or the article styled a " custerd coffyn " in another of 1580 ? A " chaffar " of silver for " partrich mynced " is included in a list of plate of the year 1443 (*Test. Ebor.*). A " little silver pot with two ears called a little conscience," is another curious entry in the list of articles of plate in dispute upon the death of Sir H. Lee in 1616 of which mention has already been made.†   But as we are not primarily concerned with this kind of enquiry, it is now time to turn to articles that may be met with by the amateur and collector of the present day, not without a caution to him not to look for more in his subject than there is.   The beginner is very apt to jump at theories which have nothing in them, too

---

* *Masters' Reports*, 1616, F. to N.   *The Ordinary*, a play by Cartwright,
† A " conscience "=a bellarmine, see   1651.

apt to think he has discovered as stages of progress in art workmanship what are really nothing but differences of detail attributable to the better or worse taste and skill of individual and perhaps contemporary workmen. He almost invariably, too, goes through a period when the authenticity of a piece of plate seems to depend upon nice points of detail in regard to its hall-marks. It is wonderful how long it is before the collector finds out how little such niceties signify, or can be depended upon, and how different the very same mark can look upon different pieces of old plate bearing it, entirely owing to the effect of time and wear. It is through these experiences that the collector eventually becomes a connoisseur.

SPOONS.

Our notices of domestic plate must begin with spoons by right of seniority, for, says the learned de Laborde,* " Les cuillers sont vieilles, je ne dirai pas comme le monde, mais certainement autant que la soupe "; after this we shall not be surprised to find that amongst the most ancient pieces of English hall-marked plate in existence are simple spoons.

In early days, when forks were as yet unknown, spoons played an even more important part at meals than they do at the present day, and persons of every rank seem to have striven to possess a spoon, if only a single one, of silver. Our ancestors evidently anticipated, in their way, the view of Professor Wilson—

" A plated spoon is a pitifu' imposition,"

though, be it said, their alternative would have been honest pewter or wood; and no bad substitute either, according to the same modern authority, who adds :—

" A wudden ladle; indeed, gents, I'm no sure, but it's no sae apt to be stown; in the second, maist things taste weel out o' wud; thirdly, there's nae expense in keepin 't clean."†

It would be difficult any time for the last six hundred years to find a man, of however humble station, without a spoon or two to bequeath to his widow or his son. The wills and inventories of the rich mention them in great numbers; and

---

* *Notices des Emaux, etc.*, par M. de | † *Noctes Ambrosianæ*, XXXI. Laborde, IIᵉ Parte, 238.

the quaint treatises, to which reference has been made on a
preceding page, contain many directions as to the service and
management of the spoon at board.

The *Boke of Kervyng*, which was printed in 1513 by Wynkyn
de Worde, perhaps from a MS. of much earlier date, instructs
the panter as to setting on the salt and trenchoures, and
proceeds :—"then laye your knyves and set your brede one
lofe by an other, your spones and your napkyns fayre folden
besyde your brede, then cover your brede and trenchoures
spones and knyves." The *Babees Book* of 1475 deals with the
polite use of the spoons so laid :—

> "And whenne your potage to yow shall be brouhte,
> Take yow sponys and soupe by no way,
> And in youre dysshe leve nat your spone, I pray."

The *Young Children's Book* adds (1500) the further advice,

> " Ne pleye with spone trenchere ne knyffe."

The spoons of the thirteenth and two following centuries
seem to have had stems terminating in a spear point, diamond
point, pine cone, a plain knop, or sometimes an acorn. An
entry of 1410 (*Test. Ebor.*) *de uno cocliari plexibili*, seems to
point to a folding-spoon, as also do "my foulden sylver spoone"
in another will of the same century, and *unum coclear argenti
falden* in 1432 (*Test. Ebor.*). The first mention known to the
author of spoons with the image of the Virgin—*cum ymaginibus
Beatæ Mariæ in fine eorundem*—occurs in a will of 1446. These
were known later as " maidenhead " spoons; they are so
called in a Bristol Orphan Book will of 1493, and are common
enough in the sixteenth century, but not before.

The same may be said of Apostles' spoons, which are seldom
found before 1500, but were very popular for a century and a
half afterwards. It was an old English custom for sponsors at
christenings to present these spoons to the children for whom
they answered ; the wealthy giving a complete set, others a
smaller number, a poor person a single spoon with the figure of
the saint in honour of whom the child was named, or perhaps
the patron saint of the donor.

Hone's *Every Day Book** gives some amusing notices of this

---

* Hone's *Every Day Book*, vol. i., 176.

laudable custom collected from various writers, Ben Jonson, Middleton, and Beaumont and Fletcher, amongst the number. A character in Ben Jonson's *Bartholomew Fair* says, " and all this for the hope of a couple of apostle-spoons, and a cup to eat caudle in." Beaumont and Fletcher likewise in the *Noble Gentleman*, say :—

> " I'll be a Gossip. Bewford,
> I have an odd apostle-spoon."

Hone notes, too, that in 1666, the usage was on the decline, quoting from Shipman's *Gossips :*—

> " Formerly, when they us'd to troul,
>   Gilt bowls of sack, they gave the bowl ;
>   Two spoons at least ; an use ill kept ;
>   'Tis well if now our own be left."

A certain number of these spoons, which were called apostles' spoons from the figures of the apostles they bore on their handles, are still to be seen, and they are of considerable value from their antiquity and comparative rarity. Good specimens have fetched high prices, varying from £5 to £10 each, and even much more of late years;*whilst a complete set of thirteen is

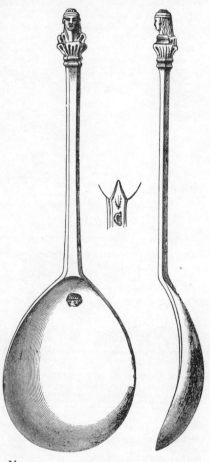

No. 29.—MAIDENHEAD SPOON, CIRCA 1540.

so seldom to be met with, that a fine early set of matched spoons would doubtless realise a very large sum, perhaps not less than a thousand guineas, if put up to auction to-morrow. This opinion is borne out by the mention in the *Quarterly Review* of April, 1876, of the sale in 1858 of a set of twelve spoons dated 1592, but not all apostles, once the property of

* In Feb., 1905, at Christie's, single spoons sold from £50 to £115; at the D. Gardner sale one went for £690.

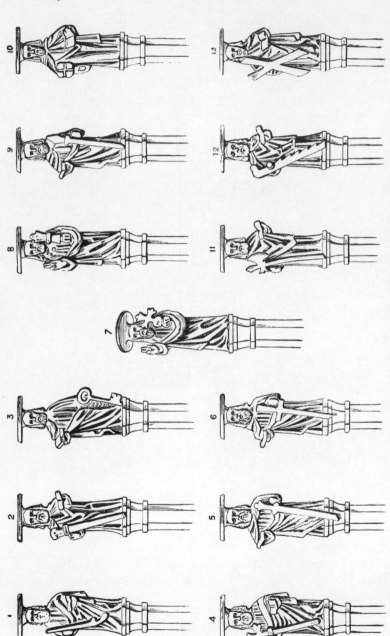

No. 20.—SET OF THIRTEEN APOSTLES' SPOONS (1626)

1 St. James the Less, with a fuller's bat. 2. St. Bartholomew, with a butcher's knife. 3. St. Peter, with a key, sometimes a fish. 4. St. Jude, with a cross, a club, or a carpenter's square. 5. St. James the Greater, with a pilgrim's staff and a gourd, bottle or scrip, and sometimes a hat with escallop shell. 6. St. Philip, with a long staff, sometimes with a cross in the T: in other cases a double cross, or a small cross in his hand, or a basket of fish. 7. The Saviour, or "Master," with an orb and cross. 8. St. John, with a cup (the cup of sorrow). 9. St. Thomas, with a spear; sometimes he bears a builder's rule. 10. St. Matthew, with a wallet, sometimes an axe and spear. 11. St. Matthias, with an axe or halberd. 12. St. Simon Zelotes, with a long saw. 13. St. Andrew, with a saltire cross.

Sir Robt. Tichborne, Lord Mayor in 1656, for £430. A set of eight apostles' spoons of 1527, the property of Bp. Whyte of Winchester, temp. Q. Eliz., realised £252 at Christie, Manson & Woods' Rooms in 1890; and a very interesting set of twelve spoons, in two sets of six spoons each, the earlier being of the year 1524 and the later of 1553, but these last evidently made in that year to complete the set, which had always been in the same hands, were sold at the same Rooms in March, 1892, for £400.* St. Paul replaces St. Jude in this set.

Only four sets of thirteen are known to the writer: one of them is in the possession of Corpus Christi College, Cambridge, and consists of thirteen spoons, one of which is supposed to represent St. Paul. They are of the year 1566-7, with the exception of the St. Paul spoon, which is of the year 1515-6. In the second set, presented to the Goldsmiths' Company by Mr. George Lambert, F.S.A., Matthias takes the place of Judas Iscariot. These spoons are all of one year, 1626, and by the same maker. The third was sold at Christie's Sale Rooms in 1901 for £1060, although rather worn, realising at last what has been said above as to the probable value of a complete set. Since then the fourth set of thirteen was sold at Christie's in 1903 for £4,900.

A set of twelve spoons, forming a series of the Master with eleven apostles, was secured by the late Rev. T. Staniforth at the Bernal sale, and is of great value from its antiquity, having been made in 1519. Only eleven of these seem traceable at the present time. That gentleman also possessed the most ancient hall-marked apostle spoon known, it being of the year 1493.

The set of 1626 has been selected for our engraving (No. 30), owing to the presence of the rare "Master" spoon, and the fact of the whole being made by one maker at the same time. A reference to the various emblems by which the apostles are here distinguished will facilitate the identification of individual figures found in private or public collections.

The figure of St. Paul distinguished by a sword, or sometimes two swords, is frequently found, St. Jude being omitted from the set of twelve to make room for him, and St. Luke and St. Mark occasionally replace St. Simon and St. Matthias.

In the Byzantine Manual, James the Less, Jude and Matthias are all omitted, their places being taken by St. Paul, St. Luke and St. Mark.

---

* Sold in the Swaythling sale, May 1924, for £700.

As to the emblems attributed to each, there is not much
variation to be noted, but the saw is sometimes given to Jude
as well as to Simon.   This is the case in the representations of
the apostolic college, by Agostino Caracci.*   As it appeared
advisable to give the whole of these emblems on a single page,
that they might be seen at one view, an illustration is given
of a group of three other apostle-spoons from a set which
belonged to the late Rev. S. Lysons (No. 31), in order that the
general shape and character of such spoons, their bowls as well
as handles, may be clearly understood.   The figures represent
St. Simon Zelotes, St. Andrew and St. James the Less.

The most modern specimen that has come to the knowledge
of the present writer is one of 1660, and belonged to Mr.
Staniforth.   Mr. Octavius Morgan had seen one of as late a
date as 1665, bearing the figure of St. James.   This bears out
what was said by Shipman in 1666, as to the custom of
presenting them at christenings being then on the wane.

Besides " maidenhead " and " apostles," spoons are found
some with sejant lions for knops.   Other devices than these
three are more uncommon, though balls and spear-points for
handle ends still occur.   The lion sejant spoon is found both in
the sixteenth and early in the seventeenth century.   A good
specimen in the author's possession is of 1547.   This is a very
early example, and came from the Ashford Collection.   The
spoons with the ends of the handles simply cut off at an angle,
as if they might once have been apostles' spoons but had
had the figures roughly lopped off, are very commonly called
" Puritan " spoons ; but spoons seem to have been often so
made, and were not unpopular for a long period.   Our subjoined
list speaks of them in heraldic terminology as " slipped in the
stalks " in 1500, and again as " sleppe-ended " in 1580.   It may
be remarked that when made in this fashion, the date-letter is
often stamped at the end of the handle close to the slip end,
perhaps to show that it had not been shortened or tampered with.

The ordinary spoon of domestic use down to the Restoration
period had probably a seal-headed and baluster top to its
handle more often than any of the devices we have mentioned,
but before turning to the ordinary domestic spoon, two special
spoons must be mentioned, and first the coronation spoon

---

* Mrs. Jameson's *Legendary Art.*

preserved among the regalia at the Tower of London. Some
think that the date of this is early in the thirteenth century,

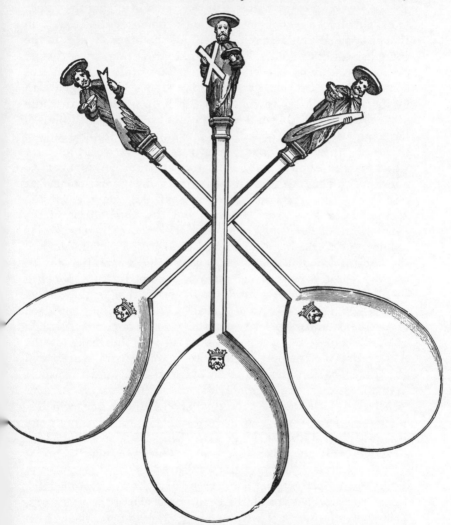

Nc. 31.—APOSTLES' SPOONS, 16TH CENTURY.

and that it may be the original spoon, notwithstanding the
goldsmith's account for the fabrication of a new one, at the
coronation of King Charles II., which has been given at

page 43. But many consider that the fashion of its bowl points conclusively to the later period, and this opinion is shared by the present writer. It may be added that its weight (3 oz. 8 dwts.) corresponds closely with the account of 1684, and that it is of silver as therein stated, all the other articles in the same list being of gold. The original Anointing Spoon would almost certainly have been of gold. The other is the ancient spoon said to have been given by King Henry VI. together with his boots and gloves to the loyal Sir Ralph Pudsey, at whose seat, Bolton Hall, that unfortunate monarch concealed himself for some weeks after the battle of Hexham. Of the antiquity of this spoon there is no doubt, even if its identity with the spoon which is the subject of the historical tradition is open to question. The head of its handle is octagonal, somewhat resembling the capital of a Gothic shaft, and on the flat top is engraved a single rose, the badge of the king. It is of the usual form of ancient spoons, and the marks thereon are as follows : inside the bowl is stamped the leopard's head,—and all the ancient London spoons previous to the Restoration are so marked ; on the back of the stem is stamped with a punch a small heart for maker's mark; and above that is the annual letter, also stamped with a punch. This was long supposed to be the Lombardic letter for the year 1445-6, which would certainly agree both with the history and the make of the spoon; but there is now much more known about marks, and strong reason to assign it to the year 1525-6, and to suspect that the story has by some chance in the course of ages transferred itself from the original spoon to this one, which is ancient enough to have an interest of its own, but is not quite old enough to have belonged to King Henry VI. These accidents will sometimes happen. The "Godwin" cup at Berkeley Castle, " the property of Earl Godwin in 1066, and regilt by the Earl of Berkeley 1766 " as the inscription tells, seems to be formed out of the head of a mace of the year 1610. The silver furniture at Knole, long thought to have been provided in honour of a visit of King James I., was the boudoir suite of a Countess of Dorset probably presented in 1680, by her second husband Henry Poole, Master of the Rolls, and certainly made in that year. The form of spoons used in England seems to have continued the same from the middle

of the fifteenth century to the time of the Restoration, when a
new fashion was introduced which completely superseded the
more ancient pattern.

The more ancient model, with its common baluster and seal-
headed end, is shown by No. 1 (engraving No. 32).* The
bowl was pear-shaped and its stem a regular shaft made in one

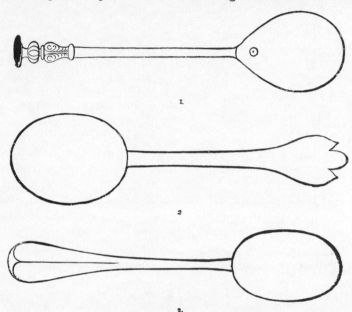

No. 32.—SPOONS OF 16TH, 17TH, AND 18TH CENTURIES.

piece with the bowl, the head being affixed by a plain spliced
joint or else by a deep V-shaped socket or notch.　Spoons
of this type were in common use as late as 1660.　The date of
a very late one known to the author is 1659, and the earliest
specimen of the next form (No. 2) being of 1652, a decade seems
to cover the whole change.　The shape was then altogether
altered.　The stem and handle became flat and broad at the
extremity, which was divided by two clefts into three points,
slightly turned up, whilst the bowl was elongated into a regular
ellipse, and strengthened in its construction by a tongue which

---

* An unusually slight and tapering
shaft or stem—" stele " as it is called in
old inventories—indicates an early spoon
of the fourteenth or fifteenth century.

ran down the back.   This form of spoon, the handle of which is termed by French antiquaries *pied de biche* or the hind's foot, obtained till the reign of George I., when a third fashion was becoming known, but in the latest part of its period, temp. Q. Anne, the outer points of the *pied de biche* handle were just lopped off, so that the splay narrowed to the blunt point, which was bent backwards rather than upwards.   In the third form (No. 3), the bowl was more elongated and elliptical, and the handle was round at the end and turned up, the front of it showing a high sharp ridge down the middle.   Mr. Morgan noticed that one of these changes occurred at the Restoration, and the second nearly at the accession of the House of Hanover, and the approximate correspondence of dates supplied him with the convenient names for these spoons by which they are now generally known, viz., the Restoration and the Hanoverian.

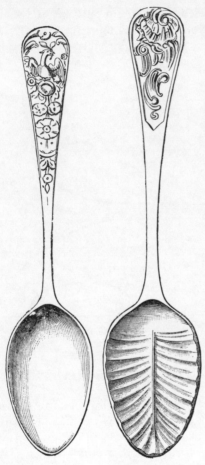

No. 33.—TEA-SPOONS, CIRCA 1760, AT BARBER-SURGEONS' HALL, LONDON.

The Hanoverian spoon, hardly known temp. Q. Anne, became the spoon of the period in the next reign, and continued to be made certainly till 1760 and later, but not to the exclusion of other patterns, for towards the end of the reign of George II. another new fashion came into use, which has continued to the present time.   The bowl became more pointed, or egg-shaped, the end of the handle was turned down instead of up, whilst the tongue, which extended down the back of the bowl, and is so well known by the name of " the rat's tail," was shortened into a drop. This is the well-known plain spoon of common use from 1760 or 1765 till 1800, and is called by the trade the "Old English" pattern. Transition spoons with the Hanoverian handle, but the strengthening drop and not the rat-tail at the back of the bowls, appear in 1754 and 1762. The fiddle-headed pattern, in which a sharp angular shoulder was introduced on either side the stem, just above the bowl and also near the end of the handle, came into vogue in the early part of the late century, and still seems popular. The bowl is now always pointed and quite ceases to be elliptical. Tea-spoons follow the fashion of larger spoons. Other patterns not popular enough to establish themselves as representative of a period need not be mentioned specially. They indicate the fancy of an individual smith or of a particular customer. As regards ornament, scroll-chasing is sometimes found on the back of bowls and at the insertion of the handle of all periods from Charles II. onwards. Tea-spoons of the Louis XV. period especially have been decorated with ornaments of the time, both in bowl and on handle, and their handles were sometimes of fancy shapes, formed as vine tendrils, flower rose-sprays, and other such devices. From about 1775 to 1785 feather-edging and beaded edging not unfrequently adorn the handles of the plain " Old English " spoons then in use. Straining spoons for tea are mentioned later in this chapter. It is entirely unnecessary to go into detail about the many fashions of ornamentation used in workshops since 1800. They may, any of them, be applied to spoons of the " Old English " or the " fiddle pattern " type as the case may be.

NOTES OF ANCIENT SPOONS, ARRANGED IN CHRONOLOGICAL ORDER.

1259. xii coclearia argenti. (Will of Martin de St. Cross.)—Surtees Society Trans. Wills and Inv.*

---

* Many references are made in this chapter to the invaluable collection of Mortuaries, Wills, and Inventories published by the Surtees Society, under the following titles :—
Testamenta Eboracensia. Wills registered at York. (*Test. Ebor.*)
Wills and Inventories from the Registry of the Archdeaconry of Richmond. (*Rich. Wills.*)
Wills and Inventories from the Registry of the Diocese of Durham. (*Wills and Inv.*)
These volumes have also supplied some of the materials for Chapter IV.

1296. ix coclear' auri, j coclear' argenti magnū p coqūa pond. xxis. iijd.—Wardrobe
       Accounts, 24 Edw. I.

1300. 7 coclear' auri, 8 coclear argenti signata in collo signo Parisius scilt de quodam
       flore glegelli.—Wardrobe Accounts, 28 Edw. I.

1366. coclearia nova ultimo facta in Ebor.—Surtees Society Trans. Test. Ebor.

1385. xxx cocliaria argenti.—Will of Ric. de Ravenser, Archdeacon of Lincoln.

1392. sex coclearia argentea cum acrinsse de auro.—Test. Ebor.

1421. xij cocliaria arg. de opere London.—Idem.

1432. calicem sanctificatam cum patena et cocliari eidem calici pertinente.—Idem.

1440. sex cocliaria argenti de fradelett.—Idem.

do.   unum cocliar' argenti cum longo brachio pro viridi zinzebro.—Idem.

1441. vj cocliaria argenti cum quodam signo viz hawthornleves.—Idem.

1444. xxiiij coclear' argenti de opt. (Will of Thos. Brygge de Salle.)—Norwich
       Registry.

1446. ij coclearia argentea et deaurata unius sectæ cum ymaginibus Beatæ Mariæ in
       fine eorundem. xii coclearia argentea cum glandibus in nodis. vii coclearia
       argentea cum nodis deauratis.

do.   x^{xx}xi coclearia argenti diversorum operum et ponderis.   (Inv. of Duiham
       Priory.)—Surtees Society Trans. Vol. II. 91.

1452. sex cocliaria argenti de Parysh.—Test. Ebor.

do.   vj cocliaria arg. de una sorte signata cum flore vocato flour de lice.—Idem.

1459. dim. dos coclearium arg. cum akehorns.—Test. Ebor.

1463. xii coclearia argenti operis Paris' de unâ sectâ signata cum litera 跭.—Idem.

1474. ij sylver sponnes marked wt lybbard hedys and square knoppis.—Idem.

1477. half doz. spones wt lepardes hedes prynted in the sponself.—(Will of Robert
       Bagworth, C.P.C. 30 Wattys.)

1487. ij dozen and vi sponys with dyamond poyntes pond xli unc. i qua. at 3s. 2d.
       vi. li. xs. viid ob. (Inv. of Robert Morton, gent.)—Brit. Mus. Add. MS.
       30,064.

1490. vj cocliaria arg. cum fretlettez. vi coclearea arg. cum lez acornez deaur'. —
       Test. Ebor.

1497. sex coclearia cum capitibus puellarum.—Idem.

1498. a spone and a forke for grene ginger. (Will of Anne, Lady Scrope.)—Idem.

1500. xii coclearia argenti slipped in lez stalkes pond. inter se xiiij unc. (Will of
       Thos. Rotherham, Abp. of York.)—Idem.

do.   12 great spones with knobs wrought and gilt 24 oz. at 4s. 4l. 16s. ; a dozen
       of spones not gilt 14 oz. at 3s. 2d. ; a little spone of gold.—Inv. of Thos.
       Kebeel S.L.

1505. xl doz. sponis, ij dos. gylt sponys.—Lord Mayor's Feast. (E. E. Text. Soc.)

1506. 6 spoons with owls at the end of the handles. See Appendix A.—C. C. C.
       Oxford.

1515. ij silv' sponys being in a purse, 1 whrof being a gemewe spone and the other
       a spone with a forke.—Norf. Arch. Soc. Trans.

1516. 6 spoons with balls on the ends of the stems gilt. See Appendix A.—C. C. C.
       Oxford.

1525. spone knopped with the image of our lady.—Bury Wills.

1527. a spone of golde with a rose and pomegranat 11 oz. qt. di. (Inv. of Henry
       Fitzroy, Duke of Richmond.)—Camden Society Trans.

1533. xii spones white wt gilte knoppes writhen at th' endes weing xv. oz. di. Inv.
       of Katherine of Aragon's plate.—P. R. O. See p. 270.

1542. a longe silver spone (and a longe forke) for sokett, a spone with an acorne
       doble gilt. (Will of Countess of Northumberland.)—Coll. Top' et Gen.

1546. ij sylver sponys withe angells on the knoppys gyltyd.—Wills and Inv.

1546.　3 silver spones with mayden heids.—Rich. Wills.

1558.　xii silvr spones wt skallap shells on their heads, one silv' spone kilt wt ar
accorne on the head.—Idem.

1560.　syxe silver spones of ye mayden heddes.—Idem.

do.　4 silver spones with lyons off thends gilt.—Idem.

1565.　spoons with diamond knops.　See Appendix A.—Mercers' Company.

1567.　½ dosune lyons and ½ doss. madine hedes xvi oz., ij doss flat ended spones,
xxviii oz.—Rich. Wills.

do.　thre spones wt knoppes of our ladie, and v wt lyons p'cell gilt.—Idem.

1570.　i doss silver spones with maden heades.—Idem.

1577.　vi silver spoones with lyons on the ends of them.—Idem.

1580.　dosen spones, theis spones being sleppe endyd.—Wills and Inv.

1582.　3 silver spoones, with acornes.—Idem.

1583.　xi sylver spones with lyone knopes gilte at the ends.—Wills and Inv.

do.　xij spones called slippes weying xxiiij ownces and a halfe, and preised at Vs
the ounce.—C. P. C. Inv. of William Dallison, Esq.

1588.　xi sponnes with maden heads weing xiiij ounces and ½ at 4s. per ounce, 2l. 18s.
—Idem.

1596.　six lesser sylver spones with the knobs at th' endes.—Rich. Wills.

1618.　spoons with slipped ends.　See Appendix A.—Mercers' Company.

1620.　a sugar box spoon.　(The Unton Inventories.)—Berkshire Ashmolean Soc.
Trans.

1660.　a dosson of sillver spouns wᵗʰ flat handels.—Will of Eliz. Gresham of Titsey.

APOSTLES' SPOONS.

1493.　Apostle spoon.　See Appendix A.—From the Staniforth Collection.

1494.　xij cocliaria arg. cum apostolis super eorum fines.—Test. Ebor.

1517.　xiij spones with xii appostells.　(Will of Sʳ Ralph Shirley.)—Stem. Shir.

1519.　eleven apostles' spoons.　See Appendix A.—From the Staniforth Collection.

1536.　xiij spones of Chryst and the xii apostells, whereof j gylt and the rest sylver
with mages gylt.—Inv. of Minster Priory in Shepey.

1555.　xii silver spones with xii apostles on heads.—Rich. Wills.

do.　Apostle spoon.—W. R. M. Wynne, Esq., Peniarth.

1566.　12 Apostles' spoons.　See Appendix A.—C. C. C. Cambridge.

1567.　xiiij postle spones, xxv oz.—Rich. Wills.

1570.　vi silver spones with postle heads.—Idem.

1580.　one dozen of postell spoones of silver weyng 24 ounces at 4s.—Idem.

1582.　a dozen spones with apostles' heads xxxv oz. 5l. 16s. 8d.—Idem.

1587.　my xii silver spones called the xii apostells.—Wills and Inv.

1588.　xii appostell spons, the ends being gilted weing xx ounces at 4s. 8d. per ounce.
—Idem.

1626.　13 Apostles' spoons.　See Appendix A.—Presented to Goldsmiths' Company
by G. Lambert, Esq., F.S.A.

For further notes of apostles' and other spoons now in
existence, see chronological list in Appendix A.

MAZERS.

If spoons are as old as soup, drinking vessels have been in use as long as spoons, and from spoons it is therefore convenient to pass to the ancient and interesting bowls that are known as mazers.

It is easier to say that these were for centuries amongst the commonest articles in domestic use, than to give a satisfactory reason for their being usually called "murræ" in mediæval inventories, or to define the material of which they were made. On the former of these points a great deal of learning has been expended by the antiquaries of past generations, so much indeed that it ought to have gone farther than it has towards settling the latter.

Du Cange only ventures to say that mazers were "pretiosiora pocula," adding that opinions differed as to what they were made of. First he quotes Somner, a well-known writer of the early part of the seventeenth century, who supposed that they were wooden vessels and made of maple; but he proceeds himself to say that the better opinion is that they were the vessels called "myrrhine" in classical ages. Other authorities are then cited who in turn suggest gum, porcelain, shell, metal and lastly onyx as the materials of which they were probably fashioned. Somner was guided by the fact that the word "maeser" signified in the Flemish language an excrescence of the maple-tree; and notwithstanding the opinion of Du Cange, which was no doubt influenced by the inventories of the twelfth and following centuries, in which he found these vessels actually described as "de murrâ," "de murro," or by the adjective "murreus," there can be no doubt that nothing but wood was in ordinary use in mediæval days for utensils such as these.

The menders of broken cups in Paris are said by John de Garlandia in the eleventh century to have worked upon cups made of many different kinds of wood, "de murris, planis, brucis, de acere, et tremulo," and he gives it as the opinion of some that the "murra" was a tree mentioned by Lucan—*in auro murrave bibunt.*

In England too, "treen" vessels preceded pewter, as pewter did silver plate :—

"Beech made their chests, their beds, their join'd stools ;
Beech made the board, the platters and the bowls."

COWLEY.

A reference to the older English poets, or to early wills and the inventories which are often appended to them, will go far to convince us that mazers were merely the best sort of wooden bowls, and that these favourite drinking vessels were made of the speckled portions of the maple-tree, from which they derived their name.

The word "maser" is explained by Skinner, an antiquary of the same century and as trustworthy as Somner, to mean a wooden cup, "poculum ligneum, a Belg. *maeser*, tuber ligni aceris ex quâ materiâ præcipue hæc pocula confici solebant" : and to this may be added Planta's definition of it, "un neud ou bosse à un arbre nommé erable." *

The same vessel was called in French *madre*, which, says Cotgrave, is used "of wood whose grain is full of crooked and speckled streaks or veins."

The German *Maser* is a spot, speck, or the grain of wood; *Maserholz* is veined wood in the same language, and *Maserle*, maple-wood or the maple-tree. From this source our word mazer is clearly derived. In old inventories the word is often turned into an adjective; *mazereus* and *mazerinus* are Latin, and *meslyn* or *messilling* English forms in which it is found. The latter recalls the lines of Chaucer :—

> " They fet him first the swete win,
> And mede eke in a maselin,
> And real spicerie."
> *Rhime of Sire Thopas*, V. 13, 780.

Such a meslyn or mazer is described more in detail by Spenser :—

> " A mazer ywrought of the maple wood
> Whereon is enchased many a fair sight
> Of bears and tigers that make fierce war."
> *Shepherd's Calendar, August.*

That "masere" was a wood of price may be gathered from the old romances, French and English. Several of the French are quoted by Du Cange and de Laborde, and with these extracts may be read the lines from *Syre Gawene and the Carle* : †—

> " The harpe was of masere fyne,
> The pynnys were of gold I wene."—V. 433.

---

* Planta.   *Thresor du Lang. Bas. Alman.*

† These are taken from a valuable notice of mazers, and especially of the Scrope bowl at York, to be found in the Transactions of the Archæological Institute for 1846.

The Scottish ballad of Gil Morrice * places the silver cup and the mazer dish together on the baron's table:—

> " Then up and spake the bauld baron,
>   An angry man was hee ;
>   He's tain the table wi' his foot,
>   Sae has he wi' his knee ;
>   Till siller cup and mazer dish
>   In flinders he gard flee."

It may be noted that, in the reign of Edward III., the manor of Bilsington Inferior was held by the service of presenting three "maple" cups at the king's coronation. Hone records that this service was performed by Thomas Rider at the coronation of George III., when the king, on receiving the maple cups, turned to the Mayor of Oxford who stood on his right hand, and, having received from him for his tenure of that city a gold cup and cover, gave him these three cups in return.†

Whilst the best and most highly prized bowls were always of maple, it is quite possible that the term " mazer," originally proper to those of maple-wood only, was afterwards extended to all bowls of similar form, regardless of the materials of which they were made : " dudgeon " wood, whatever that may be, occurs in more than one English will;‡ beech has already been mentioned, and some have supposed that even if the word " mazer " sometimes signified maple, it was more properly applied to walnut-wood.§

If gourds, eggs, nuts, and other rare substances were used when obtainable, wood and the turner's art more often provided drinking-vessels for our forefathers; and whilst the simple " beechen goblets " so dear to the poets have perished, a few of the more valuable sort have been preserved to our own time. Those which have come down to us are of maple-wood, almost without exception.

So much for the name and materials of these bowls, which

---

* Percy's *Reliques*, 4th Ed. Vol. III. p. 94.

† Hone's *Table Book*, p. 616.

‡ *Unum ciphum de Degun* in 1387. Bristol Orphan Book.

§ Parker's *Domestic Architecture*, I. 144, which quotes from Nicholas Bollarde's Version of Godefridus super Palladium, MS. Harl. 116, fo. 158, that from ripe walnuts soaked in water in a moist pit, " ther shalle growe thereof a grett stok that we call ' masere.' "

seem to have been valued in proportion to the beauty of the wood of which they were made, the knots and roots of the maple being especially prized for their veined and mottled grain. As knots would not be very thick, and therefore the bowls made of them shallow, their depth was increased by mounting them with the high metal rim which is one of the characteristic features of mazers. This rim answered the further purpose of ornamenting and adding to the value of choice specimens of wood, and it was frequently of silver or silver-gilt, and bore an inscription running round it.

Their second characteristic feature, the boss, which is almost invariably found in the bottom of these vessels, is also simply accounted for. When the half of a calabash or gourd having a hard rind was employed as a drinking-cup the necessity would arise of covering with a plate of metal the point where the fibres of such gourds were clustered in a knot. Badly turned wooden bowls would present a similar imperfection, and Mr. Octavius Morgan considered that the " prints " or bosses of mazers had their origin in the desire to conceal the blemish with an ornament. This may well be so, but similar bosses are commonly found in very ancient cups of silver, as well as of wood or gourd; so much so that an ornament in the bottom of a drinking-cup may be considered a general fashion.

The elaborate enamelling found upon some of these bosses has sometimes suggested a doubt whether the vessels containing them were really intended for use as drinking-cups; but their enumeration in all cases amongst other domestic utensils for the service of the table, would be conclusive evidence on this point, even if their use were not often expressly mentioned.

Such a cup was, " le hanap du Roy S. Louis dan lequel il beuvote, fait de Madre avec son couvercle de mesme matiere garny d'un pied d'argent doré et dedans icelui hanap au milieu du fond en email de demy rond taillé de fleurs-de-lys d'or à champs d'azur."*

The accounts of Stephen de la Fontaine, silversmith to the king of France in 1350, include " un hanap de madre fin, a tout le couvercle, duquel l'en sert le Roy a table ; " also "madres et caillers pour boire vins nouveaux," and other similar entries.

---

* Doublet, p. 344, quoted by Du Cange.

A will proved at York in 1446 disposes of no less than thirty-three "murræ usuales," besides twelve "murræ magnæ et largæ," and two of such importance as to have had names assigned to them. These must almost necessarily, judging by their description and number, have been ordinary household requisites. Others bore inscriptions which of themselves prove, if proof were needed, that they were intended for wine-cups. The well-known specimen (No. 34) in the collection of

No. 34.—MAZER (15TH CENTURY).

the late Mr. Evelyn Philip Shirley, of Eatington, bears the legend:

In the name of the Tirnite
Fille the kup and drinke to me.

This cup is of polished maple, and is figured in Parker's *Domestic Architecture of the Middle Ages*. The annexed engraving of it was taken by permission of Mr. Parker from the same wood-block.

In more than one country church a mazer now serves as an alms-dish; but perhaps even these were originally acquired for festive purposes. To the description of one that was amongst the church goods at St. Saviour's, Southwark, in 1552, it is added "whiche maser was geven to the wardeyns when they mete to drynk in."*

---

* Mr. J. R. Daniel-Tyssen's *Surrey Church Goods, temp. Edw. VI.*

In one of the smaller mazers, belonging to the Harbledown Hospital, near Canterbury, as well as in the print or boss of a small mazer at Fairford Church, Gloucestershire, a white crystal is fixed, much resembling that found in the cover of the so-called "Poison Tankard" at Clare College, Cambridge. It may be that in all these cases such a crystal was selected for its supposed virtue in detecting poison.

No. 35.—THE SCROPE MAZER (CIRCA 1400) AT YORK MINSTER, AND INSCRIPTION ON THE BAND.

The list, long as it is, which is appended to this section, has been carefully selected from notes of a much larger number of English mazers, with the view of indicating their antiquity, variety, value, the domestic purpose they served, and the period at which they fell out of use.*

Turning meanwhile to extant specimens that we may see for ourselves what manner of vessels these ancient bowls were, it is found that within certain limits they are all very much alike.

---

* An interesting catalogue of foreign instances, extending from the year 1080 down to about 1600, and taken from romances, royal accounts and other sources, is given by de Laborde, under the title "madre" in his glossary, which has been before referred to (page 281).

They are of two kinds, large bowls holding half-a-gallon or more, usually standing on a foot, and smaller bowls about six or seven inches across, which are with or without a foot as the case may be.

The earliest known example belongs, like the crystal mounted mazer mentioned above, to the hospital at Harbledown, and is of the time of Edward II. It has a plain gilt foot or stem, and a plain rim or mount, whilst within it is a large silver-gilt medallion, bearing the figure of Guy, Earl of Warwick, with a curious inscription running round the edge of it in good Lombardic lettering.

Next to this venerable relic, precedence must be given to the so-called "Scrope" mazer at York, which is a fine specimen of the larger sort, and, more than this, has supplied us with important evidence as to the course of the date-letters used in that city. It is 12 inches across by 3½ inches deep.

By the kindness of the Royal Archl. Institute, in whose Transactions for the year 1846 an account of it by Mr. Robert Davies appears, we are enabled to give an engraving (No. 35) of the cup and its curious inscription. In an inventory of 1465 it is thus described :—

"Unus ciphus magnus de murro cum ligatura plana ex argento deaurato, qui vero ciphus indulgentialis digno nomine censetur et hac de causâ :—Beatæ quidem memoriæ dominus Richardus Scrop, quondam archiepiscopus Ebor., vere pœnitentibus et confessis qui si de hoc cipho sobrie tamen cum moderamine et non excessive, nec ad voluntatem, mente pura potaverint, quadraginta dies indulgentiæ contulit gratiose. Eadem enim murra appret. xls.   Quam quidem murram seu ciphum Agnes Wyman, olim uxor Henrici Wyman, quondam majoris civitatis Ebor'. fraternitati Corporis Christi obtulit quam devote, cujus anima pace requiescat perpetua.   Amen."—(From a list of jewels belonging to the Guild of Corpus Christi. Lansd. MSS. cccciii. fo. 1.)

Its somewhat interesting history seems to be shortly this, that presented originally to the Corpus Christi guild at York by one Agnes Wyman, who died in 1413, and consecrated by Abp. Scrope as suggested by the inscription it bears, which fixes its date as from 1398 to 1405, it passed from that guild on its dissolution in 1546, or later, to the Company of Cordwainers, with whom it remained till, on their dissolution in turn in the last century, it passed into the hands of the then master of the company, and by him was placed in the custody of the dean and chapter of York, its present owners.

It is suggested that possibly the plate on the foot, recording the names of the searchers and beadle of the company in 1622, denotes the date at which it came into the possession of the Cordwainers.   However this may be, the tradition that it was presented to the Cordwainers by Abp. Scrope himself can hardly stand in the face of so much identification of the cup as the one originally belonging to the C. C. Guild.

The successive repairs to the silver mounts of this ancient

No. 36.—MAZER (C. 1440) AT ALL SOULS' COLLEGE, OXFORD.

cup bear not only the goldsmiths' date-letters but the dates themselves, and so afford important aid in putting together the alphabets anciently used in York.

Another large mazer, with silver-gilt rim and foot less elaborately ornamented but far older than the mount of the last, is at All Souls' College, Oxford : on the boss of this is the coat of arms in enamel, and initials (T B) of Thomas Ballard. He died in 1465, but gave the mazer some years before, as it is mentioned in a College inventory of 1448 (Nos. 36, 37).   This mazer is of the fifteenth century, as also are a pair of smaller and plainer bowls at the same College. These are about six inches in diameter, and the plain gilt mounts which extend down, inside as well as outside, 1¼ inch from the brim, seem to have been added to give them greater depth.

This College is the fortunate owner of a set of mazers, of which the above form a portion, probably part of the plate given to it by Archbishop Chichele in 1442, or other early benefactors, and of unique interest. Besides the mazers already

No. 37.—BOSS OR PRINT IN THE BOTTOM OF THE LAST MAZER.

mentioned, there is a small but beautiful bowl of light yellowish maple-wood with a cover, the knop or handle of which is a projecting ornament of gold, having a pale ruby polished but uncut set in the top. Four pearls have originally been fixed on wires projecting from the centre of the ruby; but of these only two remain, and it is curious to note that there were no more than two left at the date of an inventory made in the time of Warden Hoveden, circa 1583.

A large mazer was exhibited by Rev. G. W. Braikenridge in 1862.* This is known as "the Tokerys bowl," and is 9⅝ inches in diameter, and 7¾ inches high. It is inscribed in Tudor

---

* Sold for £2,500 Feb. 27, 1908.

lettering of the period, much resembling that of a small mazer
(No. 41) in the Franks Collection—" ✠ *Be yow more and glade
and soo the Masters Tokérys do byde*,"—an invitation to drink
which has no doubt often been accepted. The words are
divided by an ape, a dog, a pig, a stag, a huntsman, fruit or
flower. The mount of the bowl is of the year 1534, but as
usual the bowl itself seems older, whilst the foot which it had
in 1862 bore the hall-marks proper for 1560-1. The foot was
simply a fine tazza inverted and fastened beneath the mazer,
from which it differs much in style, being quite Renaissance
whilst the mazer is Gothic. This hybrid composition has since

NO. 38.—MAZER (CIRCA 1450) AT IRONMONGERS' HALL, LONDON.

been divided and two fine pieces of 16th century plate have
been restored to their proper condition without injury to either.
   A fine specimen of the larger bowls is at Armourers' Hall
London. It is nearly a foot in diameter, and of considerable
depth ; the rim and foot are of silver-gilt, and are united to each
other by vertical bands, all the metal-work being covered with
inscriptions, from which it appears that it was repaired in 1579,
the year of its hall-mark (1578-9), though the original bowl was
older, having been presented by Everard Frere, the first master
of the Armourers' Company after its incorporation in 1453.
Within the bowl are the arms of the Company, St. George and
the Dragon, and a cross within a wreath.
   Coming to the smaller mazers, some of which have already
been spoken of, we find the same style of ornament on nearly
all of the extant bowls of the fifteenth century; but some
of them bear inscriptions on the band, which is left plain
in others. One of a pair amongst the ancient plate of the

Ironmongers' Company (No. 38), bears a Latin inscription from
Luke i. verses 28 and 42, in old Gothic letters :—

𝔄𝔟𝔢 . 𝔐𝔞𝔯𝔦𝔞 . 𝔤𝔯𝔞 . 𝔭𝔩𝔢𝔫𝔞 . 𝔡𝔲𝔰 . 𝔱𝔢𝔠𝔲𝔪 . 𝔟𝔢𝔫𝔢𝔡𝔦𝔠𝔱𝔞 . 𝔱𝔲 𝔦𝔫 𝔪𝔲𝔩𝔦𝔢𝔯𝔦𝔟' . 𝔢
𝔟𝔢𝔫𝔢𝔡𝔦𝔠𝔱𝔲𝔰 . 𝔣𝔯𝔲𝔠𝔱𝔲𝔰.

Its fellow has no inscription. They are of about the same
size and date.

A somewhat similar specimen is at Oriel College, Oxford.
The Oriel mazer, said to have been given to the College by
Bishop Carpenter, circa 1470, is described minutely in Shaw's

No. 39.—MAZER (CIRCA 1470) AT ORIEL COLLEGE, OXFORD.

Ancient Furniture, and Skelton's *Oxonia Antiqua Restaurata*, to
which the reader is referred. For the beautiful wood-cut
(No. 39) of it, prepared by the late Sir A. W. Franks to
illustrate a proposed paper by Mr. Albert Way, but unhappily
never put into use owing to Mr. Way's lamented death, the
author is indebted to the Council of the Royal Archæological
Institute. The bowl is of about the date of its gift to the
College, and is somewhat larger than the smaller pair at All
Souls', being as much as 8 inches across, and 2½ inches in
depth. The inscription upon it is in Gothic characters :—

"𝔙𝔦𝔯 𝔯𝔞𝔠𝔦𝔬𝔫𝔢 𝔟𝔦𝔟𝔞𝔰 𝔫𝔬𝔫 𝔮𝔲𝔬𝔡 𝔭𝔢𝔱𝔦𝔱 𝔞𝔱𝔯𝔞 𝔟𝔬𝔩𝔲𝔭𝔱𝔞𝔰
𝔖𝔦𝔠 𝔯𝔞𝔯𝔬 𝔠𝔞𝔰𝔱𝔞 𝔡𝔞𝔱𝔲𝔯 𝔩𝔦𝔰 𝔩𝔦𝔫𝔤𝔲𝔢 𝔰𝔲𝔭𝔭𝔢𝔡𝔦𝔱𝔞𝔱𝔲𝔯."

It should be remarked that with the end of the fifteenth century we come also to the end of Gothic lettering of this description, which gives place to the sort of Tudor capitals that

No. 40.—MAZER (1532) FORMERLY AT NARFORD HALL, CO. NORFOLK, PART OF ENGRAVED BAND, FULL SIZE.

are found on the Tokerys bowl and on the mazer long preserved at Narford Hall, Norfolk.

The Narford mazer was engraved many years since in *Archæologia.** It is of the early part of the sixteenth century, and has a silver-gilt rim with inscription, as follows: CIPHUS REFECTORII ROFENSIS PER FRATREM ROBERTUM PECHAM. Of

No. 41.—MAZER-BOWL (CIRCA 1530-40), IN THE FRANKS COLLECTION.

part of this rim and inscription an engraving (No. 40) is given of the full size, which may be of use in identifying lettering of the period upon other specimens, for the hall-mark fixes the date of this interesting bowl as of the year 1532. It has an enamelled boss bearing the figure of St. Benedict with staff and book, with flowers in green and red, and S. BENIT inscribed

---

* Vol. xxiii. p. 392.

round the border. At the Fountaine sale, in 1884, it passed into the hands of the late Sir A. W. Franks. Another mazer in the Franks Collection is very like the last.

The inscription on this is taken from Job xix. 21, Vulgate version: MISEREMINI · MEI · MISEREMINI · MEI · SALTEM · VOS · AMICI · MEI, and the similarity of some of the letters to those on the Narford mazer will be seen by the annexed engraving (No. 41).

It has been already remarked that some of these small mazers were mounted on feet; and it will be convenient to close this section with an illustration of one of the latest now preserved having this addition (No. 42). It is one of the All Souls' College series and of the year 1529. It is of interest to note that it bears the name of " R. Hoveden* Custos, 1571," scratched on the inside of the foot with a pointed instrument, apparently by the

NO. 42.—STANDING MAZER (1529) AT ALL SOULS COLLEGE, OXFORD.

warden's own hand, for it corresponds with his signature as appended to the College inventory of 1583, which has already been mentioned.

There seems to be but a single mazer known of more modern date than the three last-mentioned specimens, which are all temp. Henry VIII., and which like the chalices of that reign show, it will be noticed, almost hemispherical bowls instead of the more conical or " splayed " bowls of earlier times.

This, therefore, brings us to the end of English mazers, but

---

* Robert Hoveden, of the well-known yeoman family of Hovenden (as the name is usually found). of Harrietsham, Cran-   brook and other places in Kent, became Warden in that year. He died in 1614

a notice of mazer-bowls would be incomplete without some
reference to another form of wooden cup which, though of
considerable rarity, is represented in several English collections.

No less than five of these
have come under the
notice of the Society of
Antiquaries at different
times, to whom, as well
as to Mr. Octavius
Morgan, we are indebted
for the accompanying
engravings. They all
appear to be of the
fifteenth century, or
earlier, and from their
occurrence in German
heraldry, it has been
thought probable that
they are chiefly of
German and Swiss
origin. Cups of this
kind appear as the arms
and crest of the family of
Liebenberg, of the Can-
ton Zurich, in a curious
Roll of Arms published
by the Society of Anti-
quaries at Zurich, *Die
Wappenrolle von Zürich*,
which is of the middle of
the fourteenth century ;
and in some remarkable

No. 43.—SILVER-GILT CUP, WITH ARMS OF THE
RODNEY FAMILY.*

German illuminations of the early part of the fifteenth century,
now preserved in the British Museum (Add. MS. 24,189), being
illustrations to Mandeville's Travels, a covered cup of the kind in
question occurs. It stands on a table set out for a feast, and is
apparently all of one material ; a similar cup is held by one of the
attendants.†

* Sold in Swaythling sale for £7,600, May 1924.

† There are some other early German and French notices of them given in the *Proceedings of the Society of Antiquaries* for June 20, 1861, from which the above have been taken.

The suggestion, then, that they were the German representatives of mazer-bowls, like them used for drinking, and the
smaller ones—for some of them are very small—employed in
testing or taking assay of the drink, seems a very good one, but
it is by no means safe to conclude that they were not also
fashionable in England at the same time, and to be included

No. 44.—SILVER-GILT CUP OF MAZER FASHION, FORMERLY THE PROPERTY OF
THE DUKE OF HAMILTON.

equally amongst the English drinking vessels of the period.
One such cup was in the possession of the Rodney family
till lately, and bears their arms; another formerly belonged
to the Hamilton Palace Collection. Like mazers, too, they
lent their peculiar form to vessels made of other materials than
wood, and whilst some of them are of maple, others, including
the Rodney and Hamilton Cups, are of silver gilt.
    The former is shown in the wood-cut given here (No. 43).

It is 6½ inches high, and 4½ inches in dia meter at the widest part. It probably, says Mr. Morgan, was made for, and belonged to, Sir John Rodney, Knt., of Rodney Stoke, who was living in 1512, as the arms of the Rodney family— three eagles dis played — are en graved on the top of the handle of the cover in a style very ancient, and not im probably coeval with the make of the cup.

The Hamilton cup is of about the same size as the last, or a little smaller, but in the wood-cut (No. 44) is drawn on a somewhat larger scale. It has no cover, and no orna ment save the nar row Gothic bands shown.* Neither

* At the sale of the Hamilton Collection at Messrs. Christie and Man son's in 1882, this piece was sold for no less a sum than 405 guineas. It is now, with so many other choice pieces, in the Franks Collection at the British Museum.

No. 45.—CUP OF WOOD MOUNTED IN SILVER GILT, DATED 1492.
(From the Soltykoff Collection.)

No. 46.—CUP OF WOOD MOUNTED IN SILVER GILT.
(In the Franks Collection.)

of these cups is hall-marked. Other specimens, of which engravings are here given (Nos. 45 and 46), were exhibited by John Webb, Esq., and Octavius Morgan, Esq., but both of these are probably of foreign make. The Webb cup was from the Soltykoff Collection, and is now in the South Kensington Museum.

On Mr. Morgan's death the choice cup in his collection (No. 46) was presented by his nephew, the late Mr. H. S. Milman, Director of the Society of Antiquaries, to Sir A. W. Franks, by whom it was bequeathed, together with the other mazers above mentioned, to the British Museum, where they are all now preserved.

NOTES OF ANCIENT MAZERS, ARRANGED IN CHRONOLOGICAL ORDER.

1253. cupam meam magnam de Mazera.—Will of Will : de la Wych, Bishop of Chichester.
1296. j maser cū coop'clo cum pede et pomelle arg.—Wardrobe Accts. 24 Edw. I.
1302. plates "argenti" to fix in a mazer-bowl.—Rogers' *History of Prices*, ii. 568.
1311. unum magnum mazerum.—Will of Sir Wm. de Vavasour.
1337. a mazer cup valued at 6s. in an inventory of a felon's goods.—Riley's *London Life*, etc.
1338. a hanap of mazer with impression of St. Thomas of Lancaster.—Sale Indenture of Jocalia, 12 Edw. III.
1345. ciphum meum de murrâ unum ciphum parvum meum de murro cum pede argenti, unum ciphum de murro cum ymagine Sci. Mich. in fundo.—Test. Ebor.
1348. unum mazerum cum pede argenti. —Idem.
1351. unum ciphum de murro meliore quem habeo.—Idem.
1359. unum ciphum murreum cum quadam ymagine de Trinitates depictâ in fundo. —Idem.
1365. meliorem ciphum de murro vocatum knopmazer unum ciphum de murro cum uno founce. *—Idem.
1366. unum parvum mazereum cum cooperculo de mazar.—Idem.
1369. parvum mazerinum meum cum circulo deaurato.—Idem.
1381. les mazers.—Idem.
1382. one mazer cup bound with silver gilt value 10s., another smaller value 5s., stolen from John Frensshe, goldsmith.—Riley's *London Life*, etc.
1391. viij mazeris argenti ligatis et deauratis (from an indictment for house-breaking). —P. R. O. per late W. D. Selby, Esq.
1391. unum mazerum vocat *Godezere.*—Bristol Orphan Book.
1392. j ciphum de mazero et j cocliar argenti ad facturam unius calicis.—Test. Ebor.
1395. unum ciphum de mazer cum cooperturâ et pede argenti deaurati signatum cum diversis literis de bees (BB).—Idem.

---

* *Frownce* of a cup, frontinella, in modern goldsmiths' art the ornament called "gadrooned" from Fr. gode-

ronné—knurling. Cotg., it implies a "wrinkle"—*Prompt. Parvul.*—Camden Society.

1395. unus godet de murro cum cooperculo murrio.—Idem.

1396. unum mazerum quem nuper emi de executoribus Domini Johannis de Bysshop eston cum uno cooperculo argenteo deaurato ligato in summitate ejusdem scriptum.

> ho so ys lengyst a lybe
> tak this cope with owtyn stryfe.—Idem.

1399. It^m j aut'e petit hanap de mazer ove le cov'cle a guyse dun pot steant s iij peez t̄ garnis darg' d' enorrez pris vi^s viijdi. It^m j large mazer cont' iij galons liez environ' d'arg endorrez enbossez en le founce,* itm j g'nt pee endorrez pr la dc̄e maser, pois xiiij lb iiij unc.
It^m j maser tour de nutte garnisez d'argent enorrez t̄ cov'ez.—Treasury Inv. 1 Hen. IV.

1400. cum uno cypho de mazer nomine mortuarii mei.—Test. Ebor.

do. unum mazer vocatum Spang ; meliorem ciphum meum de murreo scilicet mazer. These were bequeathed by Sir R. le Scrop (Lord Bolton) to his son the Archbishop of York.—Idem.

1404. unam murram in cui fundo infra scribit. hoc nomen Jhc in asura p'cii xs.— Bristol Orphan Book.

1406. unus ciphus masar stans super pedem argenti deauratam mobilem portatum super tres leones cum bordurâ argenti deaurata et ymagine Sancti Johannis Baptistæ in fundo cooperculum borduratum de aquilis argenti deauratis et pomellum aimellatum de azuro cum j chapelletto viridi et iiij rosis albis. Will of a Bp. of Durham.—Test. Ebor.

1415. unu' ciphum vocāt grete maser qui quondam fuit ciphus p'ris mei ad te'minu' vitæ suæ.—Coll. Top. et Gen.

1433. unum mazer flat cum singula liga argenti deauratum ; unum mazer cum ymagine Sanctæ Katherinæ vocat Frounce in fundo.*—Test. Ebor.

1434. majorem patellam de meslyn.—Idem.

1436. unam murram quæ vocatur cossyn.—Idem.

1442. unum standyng maser ligatum cum argento.—Idem.

1444. a standing maser of silver and gilt, uncov'ed, wt þ'armes of England and F'aunce, and wt a poyse write *Good Edward,* weyng xxi ounces p's þeunce iij^s iij^d Smā., lxx^s, also ij litil masers called *Godardes,* cov'ed and anoþer litil maser uncov'ed, weyng togydre ij lb. i unc t. dī. p. unc ij^s vi^d Sma. lxij^s ix^d.—Inv. of Treasury of Exch. 22 Hen. VI.

1446. j murra cum pede deaurato vocata HERDEWYKE cum cooperculo ; alia murra larga et magna vocata ABELL sine cooperculo : xii murræ magnæ et largæ, cum uno cooperculo quorum iij cum pedibus ; xxxiii murræ usuales. —Test. Ebor.

1452. murræ altæ ; murræ bassæ.—Idem.

1453. unum ciphum murreum coopertum vocatum j nott.—Idem.

1454. unum maser harnasiatum cum argento et deaur' cum uno rose prynte.—Idem.

1455. unam murram cum uno browne shell.—Idem.

1459. unam murram vocatam Crumpuldud.—Idem.

1463. aliam murram coopertam habentem in summitate castellum deauratum.—Idem

1464. unam murram sine Frounce.*—Idem.

1471. matri meo unam parvam murram.—Idem.

---

* See note on preceding page.

1485.   my litle mazer.—Idem.
1486.   a mazer the printe of an emying of Seynt George.—Idem.
1487.   vii. lytell masers with duble bonds pond xli unc di at 2s. 4d. ııiiꬷ xviˢ xᵈ v
        masers with sengyll bonds, and an olde blak nutte with a cover, with iij
        knoppys for coverynges of mazers pond xliiij un at 2s. 2d. iiiiꬷ xvˢ iiijᵈ.
        Inv. of Robert Morton.—Brit. Mus. Add. MS., 30,064.
1490.   j mazer shell.—Test. Ebor.
  do.   a little mazer bounden with silver and gilt, which that I bought upon Palme-
        sondaie in the furst yere of the reign of King Edward the iiijᵗʰ.—Idem.
  do.   unam murram cum j frounce* et Jhesus insculpt in eodem ; unam murram
        cum fronce fracto.—Idem.
1496.   unum ciphum vocatum nut de mazer coop.—Idem.
  do.   a mazer with a playne band sylver and gilt ; a standing nutte of mazer with a
        foot of silver and over-gilt wt. a coveryng to the same, wt. three ostrich
        fedders of silver and over-gilt.—Idem.
1497.   ij mazer bandes inde factur' unam murram.—Idem.
1498.   a masser wt. the prynt in the bottom.—Idem.
1499.   a standynge maser wt. cover of wode.—Idem.
1502.   j pelvim de meslyn.—Idem.
1506.   a pardon maser (having round the brim an indulgence of 40 days to the
        drinker).—Idem.
1534.   a standynge maser wt. a cov' and shell wtall weyng xxvi unces di. ; Itm one
        great maser wt a sengle band wt a prynt in the bottom gilt wt an ymage of
        Allmyghti god sittynge at the iugement in the myddes of iiij evangelistes
        weynge xlix unces di. ; Itm a masar wt a sengle band wt a prynt in the
        bothom of the passion of saynt Thomas the martir and a plate of sylv' and
        gilte wt an Ape lokynge in an vrynall written wt these woordes " this wat'
        is p'olows" weynge xv unc. di. These and many other mazers are
        described in an Invent. of the Guild of the B. V. M. at Boston, co. Linc.—
        Peacock's *Church Furniture.*
1535.   v grete masers with small bonds of sylver and gylt ; iiij masers whrof iij of
        them be with gylt bonds and the fourth with a sylver bonde dailye occupied
        waying xxiiij uncs. ; ij masers with brode bands sylver and gilt and a littel
        mazer with a fote and a small bande sylver and gylt waying xviij uncs. ;
        ij small masers with brode bands of sylver and gilt. Inv. of Maison
        Dieu at Dover, 26 Hen. VIII.
1536.   a standynge maser with a cover, the fote gilt ; ij greate, and ij less mazors
        with brymmys and rosys in the botome save j lacketh a roose.—Inv. of
        Minster Priory in Shepey.
1542.   a silver masser.—Rich. Wills.
1543.   a masour cuppe and three silver spones, to each of testator's two daughters.—
        Idem.
1555.   ij messilling bassens.—Idem.
1557.   j masser egged about with silver.—Idem.
1577.   one mazer with one edgle of sylver.—Idem.
1578.   ij massers.
1585.   j silvar mazar.—Wills and Inv.
1592.   A maser cuppe 2s. 6d.—Idem.

---

* See note on page 310.

THE SALT.

We now come to what was the principal article of domestic plate in English houses of whatever degree. The massive salt-cellar, which adorned the centre of the table, served to indicate the importance of its owner, and to divide the lord and his nobler guests from the inferior guests and menials, who were entitled to places " below the salt " and at the lower ends of the tables only. It seems rather to have served this purpose than to hold salt for the meal, a supply of which was usually placed near each person's trencher in a smaller salt-cellar, called a " trencher " salt. There are many allusions in the poets to the distinction marked by the position of the salt amongst the guests, and to the social inferiority of " humble cousins who sit beneath the salt." The great salt was, therefore, an object of considerable interest, and it was often of great magnificence and of curious device. Edmund Mortimer, Earl of March, in 1380, had such a salt-cellar, " in the shape of a dog "; John Earl of Warenne's was in the form of an " olifaunt " (1347); salt-cellars, enamelled or gilt, nearly all with covers, are found on every table. Fifteenth century wills mention salts

No. 47.—THE HUNTSMAN SALT (15TH CENTURY) AT ALL SOULS' COLL., OXFORD.

of every shape and size and kind. Salts square, round, plain, wreathed, high, low, with covers and without, are all found; the words "*pro sale*" being often added to the description of the vessel. Salts formed as dragons occur, and also those shaped as lions. Silver, silver-gilt, and " berall"* are the

---

* *Test. Ebor.* 1471

materials of which most are made.   Whoever could afford an
article of plate, besides his spoon, had it, in those days, in
his salt, even in preference to a silver cup for his own particular
use.   A very fine and early salt is the Huntsman Salt
(**No. 47**) at All Souls' College, Oxford, and of the fifteenth

century.   It is so called from the
standing figure bearing upon his head
the receptacle for salt, which, be it
noted, is a box made of rock-crystal
with a hinged lid of the same.   A description of the principal salt of Henry
Fitzroy,   Duke   of   Richmond,   the
natural son of Henry VIII., taken from
the inventory made on his death in
1527, gives a good idea of those which
graced the board of royalty.   It was
" a salte of golde with a blak dragon
and v perles on the bak, and upon the
fote iij course saphirs, iij course balaces
xxiij course garnisshing perles, and
upon the cover of the same salt vij
saphirs or glasses, and iiij course
balaces, and xxxij garnishing perles,
upon the knoppe a white rose with
rubyes and a pyn of silver to bere the
salt going through the dragon and the
bace made fast to a plate of silver and
gilt under the said bace weing xxv onz.
di."   To this may be added that one
of his small salts was " a little salt of
birrall, the cover and fote well gar-
nisshed with golde stones and perles,
sent from my Ld. Cardinelle for a New
Yere's gift, anno xixmo, with a ruby

No. 48.—SALT (1493) AT NEW
COLLEGE, OXFORD.

upon the cover, weing vi. onz."
     Another, of even less weight but of no less value, was " a
salte of gold, supposed to be of an unycorn horn, welle wrought
and sett with perles, and the cover with turkasses sent from the
king by Mr. Magnus, v onz. di."
     A Lincolnshire will of 1558 mentions " my silver salte with

a cover doble gilte, having in the middle of it a pece of Birrall."

Let the little treatise of 1500 entitled *Ffor to Serve a Lord*, say how the chief salt-cellar should be placed :—

"Thenne here-uppon the boteler or panter shall bring forthe his pryncipall salte . . . he shall sette the saler in the myddys of the tabull accord-yng to the place where the principall soverain shall sette . . . thenne the seconde salte att the lower ende . . . then salte selers shall be sette uppon the syde-tablys."

The *Boke of Kervyng* too directs that the salt shall be set on the right side "where your soverayne shall sytte." Furthermore, it was not graceful to take the salt except with "the clene knyfe," so says the *Young Children's Book*, in 1500, far less to dip your meat into the salt-cellar. The

No. 49.—SALT (1518) AT IRONMONGERS' HALL, LONDON.

Babees Book is strong upon this point, even a generation before (1475) :

> "The salte also touche not in his salere
> With nokyns mete, but lay it honestly
> On youre Trenchoure, for that is curtesy."

Omitting for the present the smaller trencher salts, there are four patterns of Old English salt-cellars, of which examples have come down to our time, and of each of them an illustration must be given. First come the hour-glass salts of the reigns of Henry VII. and Henry VIII., of which some five or six hall-marked specimens are known to the writer, besides one or two undated.   The undated ones are the older, and they comprise some of the finest workmanship and great beauty.   Two are at Oxford, Corpus Christi College and New College each boasting of one.   The Corpus salt was given by the founder, Bishop Fox; and bearing the letters R and E amongst the ornamentation, it seems safe to refer it to the period during which he held the see of Exeter, 1487 to 1492.   The New College specimen, given by Walter Hill, is dated 1493, and serves well as an illustration of these beautiful salts (No. 48).   Both these are figured in Shaw's *Specimens of Ancient Furniture.* A pair at Christ's College, Cambridge, part of the plate of the foundress, Margaret, Countess of Richmond, are of about the same period. They are ornamented with a double rose in repoussé work on the alternate lobes and Gothic work with pinnacles at the angles round the waist.

NO. 50.—CYLINDRICAL SALT (1569) IN THE POSSESSION OF THE CORPORATION OF NORWICH. A SIMILAR SALT FETCHED £1550 AT C. M. & W

Amongst the later and hall-marked examples is a third given to Christ's College, Cambridge, by its foundress. This is engraved with Tudor rose, fleur-de-lys and portcullis on alternate lobes, and was made in 1507. The next is at Cotehele and of 1516; whilst the pair from which our second illustration (No. 49) of this class of salt is taken, are of 1518 and 1522, and in the possession of the Ironmongers' Company in London. All alike are six-sided in plan, with raised lobes alternately ornamented and plain, only differing in the details of the decoration. The salt at Cotehele has beautiful Gothic pinnacles around the knop or waist, like the earlier pair at Christ's College, Cambridge.

By the middle of the sixteenth century we come to the second type, and the earliest of this class again is at Corpus College, Oxford. It is a cylindrical standing salt, of the year 1554, and with its cover, is ornamented with repoussé and engraved work in a pattern formed of three principal cartouches with central bosses, the intervals filled with foliated scrolls. The cover is surmounted by a statuette of a boy with a staff and shield. It was exhibited in the South Kensington Loan Collection of 1862, and has been erroneously catalogued at different times as of 1613 and of 1594.

Later specimens of this fashion of salt are in the

No. 51.—SALT (1569) AT VINTNERS' HALL, LONDON.

possession of the Goldsmiths' and the Armourers' Company. These cylindrical salts occur oftener than the square ones. The example selected to represent them (No. 50) is one in the possession of the Corporation of Norwich, given by Peter Reade, who died in 1568. It was made in Norwich in the following year. The drawing is after one published some years ago in a volume relating to Norwich antiquities, but for want of shading hardly gives it a sufficiently rounded form. It

affords a good example of Norwich work, and of this style
of salt.

Of the same type, but square instead of cylindrical, is the
beautiful salt of the year 1569, belonging to the Vintners' Company. From this the illustration No. 51 is taken, and it is a
possession of which its owners are justly proud. It is thus
described in the catalogue of the works of art exhibited at the
Hall of the Ironmongers' Company some years ago :—

" A square salt silver gilt with cover. It is 12 inches high,
and 4½ inches square; on
the panels at the sides, in
bold relief, are four female
figures, representing Virtues,
viz. : 1. Justice, with sword
and scales ; 2. Fortitude,
holding in her left hand a
blazing heart, and in her
right a dart ; 3. Temper-
ance, pouring from a vessel
into a cup; 4. Chastity,
with a lamb at her feet; all
within landscapes, and at
the angles are therm figures.
The cornice and foot are
boldly moulded and richly
embossed. The whole rests
on four sphinxes, crowned ;
above the arch of each panel
is an escallop. The cover is
surmounted by a female

No. 52.—SALT (1595) AT HABERDASHERS'
HALL, LONDON.

figure, standing on a richly embossed vase; a serpent is coiled
round her, and she holds a shield, whereon are the arms of
the Vintners' Company."

The Hammersley salt (No. 52), at Haberdashers' Hall, is of
1595. The drum is repoussé with pastoral subjects in bold
relief, which have a very pleasant effect, and contrast with the
conventional decoration which was more usually affected at
that period.

At the very end of the sixteenth century we find a circular
bell-shaped salt, or spice-box, in three tiers or compartments,

No. 53.—SALT (1607) AT CHRIST'S HOSPITAL, LONDON.

No. 54.—SALT (1661) AT CLOTHWORKERS' HALL, LONDON.

much in fashion, but only for a few years.   They are no doubt
the " Bell " salts of contemporary inventories.   " The bell salt
of silver with his cover " was an item in the will of Sir Thomas
Scott, of Scot's Hall, which is dated 1594; and a Durham will

No. 55.—OCTAGONAL SALT (1685) AT MERCERS' HALL, LONDON.

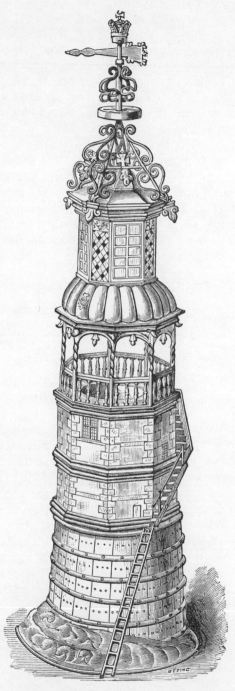

No. 56.—THE EDDYSTONE LIGHTHOUSE SALT (1698).

of 1593 refers to "a white bell salt" as well as "a trencher salt." The specimen from which our illustration (No. 53) is taken belongs to Christ's Hospital, London, and is fourteen inches high. Its style of ornamentation speaks for itself, and is very representative of its period. The two lower compartments form salt-cellars, and the upper one serves as a pepper-castor. A similar salt of 1594, found at Stoke Prior, is now in the S. Kensington Museum; and a third specimen was in the collection of Mr. Octavius Morgan. A pair, one of 1599 and the other of the following year, were in the possession of the late Sir G. Dasent. As to their value, it may be mentioned that a piece in the Hailstone Collection, almost exactly like the Christ's Hospital salt, was sold for 330 guineas in 1891 It had been bought at Exeter in the year 1858 for five pounds.*

About the middle of the seventeenth century we find a rare

1629.   No. 57.—TRENCHER SALTS.   1667.

example of a style of decoration more affected in Holland than in our own country, in the Waldo salt of 1661 at Clothworkers' Hall (No. 54). The Dutch repoussé work of the Utrecht School was marked by the skill with which silver was hammered into volutes, which shape themselves at every point into grotesque faces or masks, testifying to a mastery of the art of metal-working which has never been surpassed.

Next comes a simple and well-known form of salt, which carries us all through the seventeenth century, from 1638, the date of one of the earliest known, to 1685, when some in the possession of the Worshipful Company of Mercers were made, from one of which our engraving (No. 55) is taken. These salts of the Mercers' Company show the stiff feather decoration under the shield of arms, which is so characteristic of the period from 1670 to 1685. It is most common of all about the year 1675. Similar salts of intermediate date are amongst the splendid plate of the Clothworkers' Company. Some of them are circular, others are square or octagonal.

* In 1903 one was sold (1613) for £1,150.

It will have been observed how carefully the earlier salts were covered to preserve the cleanliness of the salt, and perhaps to prevent the introduction of poison; in these later ones the small projecting arms were for supporting a napkin with which it now became usual to cover the salt-cellar with the same object.

Last of all must be described the curious and unique salt-cellar of which mention, so far as its marks are concerned, has already been made (see p. 135). Built in storeys, not unlike the "bell" salts of an earlier generation, the lighthouse formerly at Tredegar is a most interesting piece of plate. On the top will be observed (No. 56) a lantern surmounted by a scroll work, and terminating in a vane, and beneath the lantern a dome or cupola above an open arcade with a gallery, within which is a depression for salt; the lantern itself being perforated for pounded sugar. Beneath this gallery are three storeys—the upper one empty, the next has a lid perforated for pepper, and the lowest storey forms a larger box, empty like the uppermost. There is a winding outside staircase, leading from the basement storey of masonry to the upper storey and gallery, and a little ladder hangs on to the foot of the staircase, to reach down to the rock on which the lighthouse is based, or the sea. It is 17 inches in height. For generations it was supposed to represent the lighthouse on an island called the Flat Holme in the Bristol Channel, but, on closer examination by Mr. Octavius Morgan, it proved to be an exact model of the first and original Eddystone lighthouse, erected by Winstanley, and first lighted in November, 1698. This was much altered and strengthened in 1699, but in November, 1703, was swept entirely away by a fearful storm, Winstanley himself and all hands perishing with it. In Smeaton's account of the Eddystone, the drawing of the original lighthouse, which did not exist more than a year without alteration, corresponds in every detail with the silver copy, which we may therefore safely conjecture was made in the year 1698.

"Trencher" salts are at first triangular or circular, with a depression in their upper surface; of the former shape and of simple fashion was a little salt of 1629, bearing for inscription "John Lane, Vintner, at ye Mermaide, near Charing Crosse."

which was sold in 1869 in the Hopkinson collection for £20 10s., and re-sold for no less a sum than £30 in the Dasent sale, only six years afterwards. Small circular salts of 1667 are in use at Cotehele, and a set of the year 1683 are in the possession of the Innholders' Company.

These, and such as these, obtained till the reign of George II., when a small cir-
cular salt standing upon three feet came in, which gave way in its turn to the boat-shaped pattern, with pointed end sometimes termi-nating in handles, so common at the end of the eigh-teenth century, when everything was made oval, that could by any pos-sibility at all be got into that shape.

No. 58.—STONEWARE JUG, MOUNTED IN SILVER GILT (1562) AT VINTNERS' HALL.

STONEWARE JUGS.

There are few collectors who have not tried to secure for their cabinets one or more of the mottled stoneware jugs, with silver cover and neck-mounts, and sometimes also silver foot-band, which were in vogue for the greater part of the sixteenth century. The jugs themselves were imported from Germany, probably from Cologne, and were mounted by the English silversmiths. The earliest notices of them occur about 1530 to 1540, and from that time to the end of the century they were common enough; but they seem then to have gone out of fashion, for it would be difficult to find a single specimen with a seventeenth century hall-mark. As regards ornamentation they are all very much alike; the well-known Elizabethan interlaced fillets, with running foliage, are often engraved around the neck-bands of the earlier ones, whilst the later specimens are more often decorated with repoussé work.

An engraving (No. 58) is given of one of 1562, which shows Elizabethan engraving on the mount, and also some repoussé work on the lid. A description of one of those exhibited at Kensington in 1862 will give a good idea of all of them.

"A stoneware jug of mottled brown glaze, mounted in silver gilt as a tankard, engraved neck-band of interlaced straps; the cover repoussé with lions' heads and fruit, surmounted by a flat-rayed button and small baluster, purchase formed of two acorns; round the foot is a border of upright strawberry leaves and a gadrooned edge." This

No. 59.—STONEWARE JUG (1581) BELONGED UNTIL LATELY TO WEST MALLING, KENT.

would describe a specimen of about 1565; and later ones would differ from it only in the engraving of the neck-band being replaced by cartouches of lions' heads, masks, fruit, and flowers or the like, in repoussé work.

Some mounts, bearing ancient Exeter goldsmiths' marks, have been already mentioned in an earlier chapter. (See page 114.)

Jugs or "covered pots" of the same shape are found in silver sometimes, just as we shall see the cocoa-nut or the ostrich egg suggested shapes to the goldsmiths. Such a vessel is the jug of 1567 at Armourers' Hall, and a similar one of 1571, and of English make, in the Treasury of the Patriarch at Moscow.

Three stone jugs from the Staniforth collection were sold in 1889 at Messrs. Christie, Manson and Woods, for £215, £54, and £105 respectively. A good specimen of 1549 passed into Sir A. W. Franks' possession. A small but good jug of 1560 was sold at the same rooms in 1890 for £71 8s., a price which seemed below its real value.

A stoneware jug of 1581 belonged until lately to West Malling, Kent—and an engraving of it is added to further illustrate this section (No. 59). It was sold under a faculty, Feb., 1903, for 1,450 guineas.

The following notes sufficiently indicate the period during which they were found :—

1535. a stone pot garnished with silver and gilte with a cover of silver and gylte.—Inv. of the Maison-Dieu, Dover.

1546. Lid and mount of jug, button enamelled with Parr arms ; bought at Strawberry Hill sale.—Sudeley Castle. (This is of glass.)

1551. Stoneware jug with cover engraved with musical instruments.—Messrs. Garrards.

1557. iij stone drinking potts covered with silver ij oz. ix s iiij d.

1562. Stoneware jug, cover engraved in Elizabethan fashion ; see engraving No. 58. —Vintners' Company.

1567. Silver jug with handle and cover engraved with Elizabethan strapwork.— Armourers' Company.

1570. 2 ston pottes, wth covers and bands doble gilt and one pot covered with silv', vi li xiij s iiij d.—Rich. Wills.

1571. Silver jug with handle and cover ornamented with Elizabethan engraving like that of 1567 at Armourers' Hall.—Treasure of the Patriarch, Moscow.

1572. a stone cupp garnished with sylver and gylte.—Inv. of Thomas Lee, of Marton, co. Bucks.

1573. stoneware jug with repoussé and engraved mount used as flagon.—Lowthorpe, Yorks.

1574. 1 stone pott garnished with silver pcell gilt.—Rich. Wills.

1577. twoo stone pottes layde with silver gylte.—Wills. and Inv.

1578. ij stone potts bounden with silver doble gilt.—Rich. Wills.

1580. my stone pot with a cover of sylver.—Wills. and Inv.

do. one stone pott garnished with sylver, wth a cover and gilt.—Rich. Wills.

1583. a stone cruse with cover brim and foote of silver doble gilt.—Bristol Orphan Book.

1585. ij stone pottes with silver covers gilte and imboste.

1588. one stone jugge double gilted 1 li 10 s ; one stone jugge covered with silver, 1 li 10 s.—Wills and Inv.

1596. ij stone jugges garnished with silver and double gylted.—Wills. and Inv.

EWERS, BASINS, AND SALVERS.

These occur in every old will and inventory of any importance, and being articles in daily use at every table, must have been very common indeed, making up as they did for the want of any such utensil as the modern fork.

We must remember that sometimes more than one person ate off the same dish, and that with the fingers, aided only

No. 60.—SALVER (1545), AT CORPUS CHRISTI COLLEGE, CAMB.

with the knife or spoon, as the case required; and even if a rule prescribed in the *Boke of Nurture* were never transgressed,—

> "Sett never on fysche nor flesche beest nor fowle trewly
> More than ij fyngurs and a thombe for that is curtesie,"

still we shall agree with de Laborde in his remark on ancient basins, "que l'absence de fourchette et l'habitude de manger à deux dans la même écuelle et à plusieurs dans le même plat, rendaient nécessaire la propreté des mains, pour les autres avant le diner, pour soi-même après."

Ewers and basins were accordingly handed before and after every meal, and after every course, the hands being held over the basin whilst water, hot, cold, or scented, was poured over them from the ewer by the server. In the houses of the great they were of costly material, and fine naperie for use with them is found in abundance amongst the household goods of the middle ages.

The *Boke of Kervyng* and the *Babees Boke* do not omit to regulate the serving of the ewer and basin.

The *Boke of Kervyng* directs the attendant to see before meat that " thyn ewery be arayed with basyns and ewers and water hote and colde, and se ye have nap-kyns . . ." and the manner in which they should be used at the end of the meal is laid down in the *Babees Boke* :—

No. 61.—EWER (1545), AT CORPUS CHRISTI COLLEGE, CAMB.

" Thanne somme of yow
for water owe to goo
Somme holde the
clothe, somme poure
uppon his hande."

The little manual entitled *Ffor to serve a Lord* directs this service before and after meat in 1500, and even in 1577 the *Boke of Nurture* mentions " a basen ewer and towell to aray your cupbord."

With the appearance of forks the use of the basin was to a great extent discontinued, and most of the basins themselves have disappeared, perhaps to be converted into forks. It may well be that some of the forks now in use were made out of the ewers and basins which their invention rendered superfluous.

The few now remaining are used for sideboard decoration, or for handing rose-water after dinner, and the most ancient of them are only of the middle of the sixteenth century.

Amongst the earliest specimens are the silver-gilt ewer and

salver engraved with foliated arabesques, which were the gift of Archbishop Parker to Corpus Christi College, Cambridge, in 1570. They bear the hall-mark of 1545. Of these the engravings (Nos. 60 and 61) give a good idea, showing the arabesques which were the usual decoration of the Henry VIII. period. Next to these rank a silver-gilt ewer and salver of 1579 and

No. 62.—ROSE-WATER SALVER (1597), AT MERCHANT TAYLORS' HALL, LONDON.

1581 respectively, the property of the Duke of Rutland, the former formed of agate rings with silver-gilt bands between them, ornamented, as well as the top and bottom of the vase in repoussé, with dolphins and tritons in cartouches, snails, shells, fruit, flowers, birds, lobsters, tortoises and many other objects, "the mounts connected by four projecting female terminal figures, with figures on their heads ending in scrolls; the handle is formed by the head and body of a warrior, and terminates in twisted serpents' tails.   On the back of the warrior is a large snail, with a smaller snail on the top of its shell, under the lip a female mask.   The circular foot is

No. 63.—EWER (1617), THE PROPERTY OF THE CORPORATION OF NORWICH

repoussé with lions' claws, masks, and fruit between, with a boss of four projecting eagles' heads."   The salver is 18 inches in diameter, and has eight oval pieces of agate inserted on the border, and a circular piece in the raised boss, the whole field being filled with repoussé scrolls and arabesques of birds, etc., and the centre ornaments being a shrimp, lobster, dolphin and tortoise.

In the early part of the seventeenth century they were orna-mented with beautiful repoussé strap-work, interlaced and enclosing boldly treated flowers or marine monsters, and have

No. 64.—SALVER (1617), THE PROPERTY OF THE CORPORATION OF NORWICH

raised bosses, or "prints" in the centre of the basin, some-times enamelled, but oftener engraved, with coats of arms or other devices.

The engraving (No. 62) is of a rose-water dish belonging to the Merchant Taylors' Company, one of two such dishes exhibited by them in the loan collection of 1862 at South Kensington. It is described in the catalogue as "a circular rose-water dish, silver, parcel gilt. On a boss in the centre, much raised up, is a coat of arms, viz., a fess between eight

billets. Round the boss are six panels, containing dolphins
and flowers, all in repoussé. Dolphins and flowers in panels
are also repeated in the rim. The other part of the dish is
engraved with flowers in scrolls." It may be added that the

No 65.—EWER (1741), BY PAUL LAMERIE, AT GOLDSMITHS' HALL, LONDON.

arms are those of Maye; one Richard Maye was Warden of
the Company in 1575, and Master some few years later.
Marine monsters are frequently found from 1595 to 1635.

Of this fashion is the salver of 1595, with a ewer to match of
1617, which are the oldest specimens of English silver work in
the Royal Collection at Windsor Castle. By the gracious

permission of Her late Majesty Queen Victoria, these were given as the frontispiece to this volume.*

The Corporations of Bristol and Norwich possess fine sets,—that at Bristol bearing the date-letter for 1595, and the other the marks for 1617. These are admirable examples of the goldsmiths' art of this period. The Norwich ewer and salver are given as illustrations (Nos. 63 and 64).

Such examples are found down to the end of the reign of Charles I., after which a plainer fashion prevails, the salver being quite unornamented, and the ewers somewhat rude cup-shaped jugs, with or without stems, and with a plain handle. With the accession of James II. come in the well-known helmet-shaped patterns which afterwards became very usual, and lasted till about 1720. The later ones were sometimes of elaborate design and finish; and, by permission of the Gold-smiths' Company, an engraving is given of the finest known specimen by that celebrated smith, Paul Lamerie (No. 65).

"On the lower part of the vase is a winged mermaid with two tails, accompanied by two boy-tritons blowing conches. The foot consists of marine flowers, shells, and reptiles. On the upper part of the vase are festoons of flowers and the Company's badges, the leopards' heads. The handle has a very bold half-length figure of a sea-god, terminating in foliage." It is of the year 1741.

This is perhaps the appropriate place to comment upon the remarkable absence in English work of examples of the more extravagant *rococo* fashion found in French collections from 1735 to 1755. English specimens of this character may be counted upon the fingers, and are chiefly by Paul Lamerie. The Goldsmiths' ewer may be taken as a good example of the class. A curious soup-tureen with its cover piled with grapes and pears, and the bowl resting upon two goats, whose heads belong to the bowl and bodies to the stand, of a very French type, was sold in 1888. It was made by Paul Crespin in 1740, and was probably designed to match a pair of *soupières* (sold for £1,600 the pair) in the same collection by J. Roettiers. These were of 1739, and were made, of course, in Paris. The English piece seems to have owed its inspiration to its foreign companions.

The great cistern mentioned later (No. 107), by Kandler, of

---

* Omitted from this edition.

1734, is a third of these rare examples; but this is more distinctly English in its design and workmanship than the other pieces described above.

The salver of 1741, at Goldsmiths' Hall, is of workmanship to correspond with the ewer, the border being designed boldly in Louis Quatorze scrolls, and panels enclosing figures of boys representing heathen gods. It is not, however, very effective.

The salvers of the seventeenth and the beginning of the eighteenth centuries were plain circular dishes, and repoussé work gave way to plain engraving towards the middle of the former century. Those which accompany the helmet-shaped ewers are usually quite plain.

In the reign of Queen Anne, chasing is found, the edges of the salvers being both chased and shaped, the salvers themselves standing on three, or sometimes four, small feet. Some are both engraved and chased; the talents of Hogarth were for some six years employed in engraving plate for Mr. Ellis Gamble, the silversmith, to whom he was apprenticed in 1712; and salvers or waiters, decorated by him, are said still to be seen. Strangely enough, the mark of his master is not to be found amongst those registered at Goldsmiths' Hall at that period. The plainer salvers of this date have often a gadrooned edge. Some simple but effective ornamentation is given to some salvers, circa 1735, by small semi-circular notches, eight or ten in number, in the moulded rim.

This style of ornament was succeeded by the beaded edges of the time of George III., and circular or shaped salvers were replaced by the plain oval trays, having handles at the ends, which are then found almost to the exclusion of any other patterns.

The following list gives a selection of examples, of all dates from the earliest :—

1284. par pelvium arg' emp Lond.—Account of "jocalia" purchased for the king's use and presents, 12 & 13 Edw. I.

1296. 1 par pelvium; 1 lavator' arg' p aula, 1 bacinus arg' p eodem.—Wardrobe Accounts, 24 Edw. I.

1324. un ewer a triper dorre aymall t̃ taille d'une vyne.—Indenture of royal plate, 17 Edw. II.

1339. un eawer endorre od doubles ymages (aymals) en* founce t̃ en pomel chisellez d'une vigne.—Indenture of "jocalia" found in the Treasury, 12 Edw. III.

---

* These images were slipped trefoils, the alternate ones being turned upside down.

1347.   ij bacyns, ma hure d'argent dore, un petit ewer d'argent dorre (will of John, Earl of Warren).—Test. Ebor.

1349.   duos baciones enaymaillatos in fundo quorum in uno est judicium Salamonis et in alio est rota fortunæ, duo magna lavatoria (will of Henry, Lord de Percy).—Idem.

1369.   un peire des bacyns ove swages endorres et enammaylles ; ewers ove spoutes.— Vessels bought of the executors of John Hiltoft, goldsmith, 42 Edw. III.

1392.   Richard, Earl of Arundel, leaves to his wife Philippa a pair of basons, "in which I was accustomed to wash before dinner and supper."—Nichols' Test. Vet.

1400.   unum perepelvm de argento cum coopert' cum armis meis et Domini de Nevylle in fundo ; cum ij pelvis et ij aquariis argenti cum armis meis in fundo (will of Richard de Scrop).—Test. Ebor.

1419.   duos pelves argenteos cum rosis in medio deauratis, duos aquarios cum ij idriis argenteis (will of Will. Gascoigne, L. C. J.).—Idem.

1433.   unum ewer argenti cum le spowte in certis partibus deauratum.—Idem.

1444.   j laver cum ij spowtes deaurat'.—Idem.

1463.   iij pelves cum pryntis et boses argenti et enameld in medio eorundum.—Idem.

1500.   two basons and two ewers part gilt weighing 117 oz. at 3s. 4d. per oz. ; two great basons with two ewers partly gilt 183 oz. at 3s. 4d.—Will of Thomas Kebeel, S.L.

1503.   an ewer and basin ot silver the swages gilt.

1505.   a payyer of gilt basons, xviij basins with ewers.—Inv. of Lord Mayor's Feast. (E. E. Text Society.)

1519.   duos pelves argenti cū lavat's in medio unius est una Rosa in alio scutū armor' meor' (will of Rawf Lathom citizen and goldsmith).—C.P.C. 32 Ayloffe.

For existing specimens see Appendix A. :—

1545, 1590, 1595, 1616, 1617, 1640, 1651, 1668, 1670, 1675, 1676, 1677, 1679, 1680, 1685, 1705, 1706, 1715, 1720, 1721.

STANDING CUPS AND HANAPS.

An article of hardly less importance in mediæval times than the great salt-cellar, was the standing cup in which lord, abbot, or gentleman received his wine from the butler's hand after it had been duly "essayed."

Whilst simple "treen" cups were used by the lower classes, those which graced the table of the high-born and wealthy were always of great magnificence and of costly material. The splendour of the cup marked the consequence of him who used it, as the standing salt did the position of the lord of the feast; and if not of gold, silver, or silver-gilt, it was formed of some then rare material, such as the egg of the ostrich, the shell of the cocoanut, or, at least, of curiously mottled wood mounted on a foot and surrounded with bands of precious metal. Such cups were of great value, and some were prized no less for the historical or other associations which surrounded them than for their intrinsic worth.   They were often known, not only in the household of the owner, but even in the district in which he lived, by special names, and the custody of the cup has signified the ownership of an estate.

The "Constable Cup" of Sir Richard de Scrop in 1400, and the great silver cup with a cover called "Le Chartre of Morpeth," mentioned in the will of John, Lord of Greystock, in 1436, must have been of some such importance as this.* Richard, Earl of Arundel, in 1392 bequeaths to his wife Philippa "her own cup called Bealchier."†

This was no doubt a family possession of much interest; and in many other less notable cases, drinking-cups are found to bear particular names, sometimes being called after saints. Mazers named "Spang," "Cossyn," and "Crumpuldud" have already been mentioned, all of the fifteenth century; and a still earlier one called "Godezere" was bequeathed by a burgess of Bristol to the chapel of St. Thomas there in 1391.‡   These few instances will be enough to show that favourite drinking-cups were often given pet or special names; but the list might be prolonged indefinitely.   The same Bishop of Durham whose Indian nut will be presently mentioned, calls one of his cups "Chanteplure" in 1259; § whilst Edmund de Mortimer, Earl of March, has a cup of gold with an acorn called "Benesonne" and another of silver called "Wassail," at his death in 1380.‖ John Halle, rector of Buscot, leaves to his friend and neighbour the vicar of Lechlade, a cup called "Cobbard" in 1400.   The prior of Durham called one of the cups of his house "Beda" in 1446,¶ whilst two others there were named "Herdewyke" and "Abell" respectively.

A few words must be said both as to the term "hanap," so often applied to cups of this description, and as to the mode of using them, before going into further detail as to their varying fashion.   The Norman-French word "hanap," then, which has at last come to mean a basket for package, in fact a hamper, is derived from the Saxon *hnæp*, a cup or goblet, and was applied

---

* Surtees Society.—*Test. Ebor.*
† Nichols.—*Test. Vet.*
‡ *Bristol Orphan Book*, Will. No. 45.

§ *Test. Ebor.*
‖ *Test. Vet.*
¶ Surtees Society, Vol. II.

in mediæval days to standing cups with covers, but only as it would seem to cups of some size and importance. As drinking vessels grew up, with the increasing luxury of the times, from wooden bowls into the tall "standing cups and covers" which is the proper description of the cups called hanaps, the use of the latter term became confined to such cups alone, and the place where such hanaps were kept was termed the *hanaperium*.

This was necessarily a place of safe keeping and therefore a sort of Treasury. The hanaper accordingly was the safe place in the Chancery where the fees due for the sealing of patents and charters were deposited, and being received by the Clerk of the Hanaper (or Clerk of the Chancery Treasury), the term hanaper office has continued to the present time. The hanaperium may originally have been a strong chest, and so the terms "hanaper" or "hamper" may have been applied and continued, at last exclusively, to a chest-like basket with a lid, used for various purposes.*

A very few notes will show the importance of the hanap. A statute of 1285,† speaking of the security for good conduct to be given by tavern-keepers, prescribes that an offender should be bound over by " *soen hanap de la taverne ou par altre bon gage.*" This was evidently his principal drinking vessel. Again, William Lord Latimer specially mentions " *la grant hanaper d'argent endoere appelle Seint George* " in his will dated 1381, and John of Gaunt in 1394 bequeaths " *moun plus grant hanap d'or.*" In both these cases the cup is one of price. Far later on, in 1670, it is found that " he which is mayor of London for the time shall have an hanap d'or or golden tanker at the coronation of every king."‡

Sometimes these grand cups were placed upon the table and at others were handed to the lord when he chose to drink. The *Boke of Nurture*, by Hugh Rhodes, written in 1577, directs the server as follows :—" When he (the master) listeth to drinke and taketh of the cover, take the cover in thy hand and set it on agayne "; and the *Boke of Curtasye*, circa 1430, another of

---

* 13 Hen. VII., hanaperium de twiggys, *Kal. and Inv. of the Exchequer*, Vol. III.

† 13 Edw. I., stat. 5, Statuta Civitatis London'.

‡ Calthrop's Reports, 1670, cited in Wright's *Dict. of Obsolete and Provincial English*.

these treatises, shall describe in its own words the mode of
serving wine at that still earlier period :

> " The kerver anon withouten thought
> Unkovers the cup that he hase brought
> Into the couvertoure wyn he powres out
> Or into a spare pece* withouten doute
> Assayes an gefes tho lorde to drynke
> Or settes hit doun as hym goode thynke . . ,"

It further proceeds to say :

> " Bothe wyne and ale he tase indede
> Tho botler says withouten drede
> No mete for mon schalle sayed be
> Bot for kynge or prynce or duke so fre . . ."

This obliges us to note the constant fear of poison in which
our ancestors lived, and their curious belief in the power of
certain substances to detect its presence.   It has already been
remarked that cups and salt-cellars in many cases had covers
to prevent the introduction of poison; but besides this, all
meats and drinks were tasted or assayed by him who served
them before they were partaken of by the lord, the books of
etiquette prescribing the extent to which these precautions
should be carried in serving at the tables of personages of
various ranks.   The most exalted had both meat and drink
tested, those of lower station only their beverages.

"Cups of Assay" are not unfrequently found in the inventories of the great; they are usually of small size.   Henry
Fitzroy, Duke of Richmond, in 1527 had no less than four,
graven with various devices in the bottom, such as a rose, a
ring, or an eagle, and weighing from six to nine ounces each.
Katherine Countess of Northumberland, in 1542, has "a cope
of assay gilt with cresande sett on the bodome," and half a
century later, in 1614, Henry Howard, Earl of Northampton,
has such a cup nine ounces in weight.

The cover, or a " spare pece " according to our rhyming
authority, was used instead of a special cup by people of less
consequence.   A further precaution was sometimes adopted in
making the cup itself of one or other of the substances alluded

---

* *Pece,* cuppe ; *Pecia, crater.* " A pece   *—Prompt. Parv.*   It is of constant
of silver or of metalle, a pyece of wyne   occurrence in old inventories.
cuppe " = crater.   A cuppe, tasse, hanap.

to above.　Salts, as we have seen, and cups, as we shall also find, were formed of the horn of the narwhal, which did duty for that of the fabulous beast known as the unicorn, and was firmly believed to have the power of detecting poison.*　Turquoises were supposed to turn of a paler blue, and certain crystals to become clouded, in the presence of poisons, and both were used in this faith for the decoration of cups.　The well-known "Poison cup" at Clare Coll., Cambridge, has such a crystal mounted in the centre of the lid.

Turning now to standing cups as we find them, precedence must be given to those made of ostrich eggs and cocoa-nuts, mounted in silver, and having feet of the same metal.　These were very popular in early times, and they were classed together because they are of similar size and shape, and their mounting is of the same character.　Sometimes the cup itself was formed of silver or silver-gilt, shaped as an egg or nut, and in these cases it is difficult to say which of the two it is intended to represent.　It has been suggested that the silver examples only occur when the earlier nut or egg has been broken, and the owner not being able to procure another has refilled the mount with a silver bowl or lining of similar shape ; but to set against this, it may be said that some of the silver linings are found of the same date and fashion as the feet and other mountings with which they are fitted.　A notice of some of these cups will serve to show for how many centuries they held their ground.　As early as 1259, a bishop of Durham bequeaths his "cyphum de nuce Indye cum pede et apparatu argenti"; and at the opposite end of the social scale, the inventory of a felon's goods in 1337 comprises amongst other things "one cup called a note with foot and cover of silver value 30s."†　An indenture of the

---

* Mr. F. W. Fairholt, in his *Descriptive Catalogue of the Londesborough Collection*, speaking of a *nef* mentioned in the inventory of Charles V. of France, which is said to hold "his essay, his spoon, knife, and fork," alludes to essaying by the narwhal horn as follows:— "The essay was a piece of horn believed to be that of the unicorn, but really obtained from the narwhal ; and which was supposed to be an antidote to poison, and to detect its presence by becoming agitated when plunged in liquor containing it ; for which reason it was attached to a chain of gold for the greater convenience of dipping it in the cup, and it was the butler's duty to make trial or essay of the wine when presenting it to his lord."

† Riley's *Memorials of London and London Life*, pp. 199, 203.

following year mentions "a nut on a foot and silver covercle" amongst jewels sold. In 1399 occur *un oef de griffon* as well as *un pot d'une noite noyre* and *un corn de griffon.**

In 1349 Henry Lord Percy dies possessed of "unam copam de uno gripe";† and a Treasury Inventory of 1399 (1 Henry IV.) contains the following item : "j maser tour de nutte garnisez d'argent enorrez t̃ cov'erc." Perhaps a cup of silver "called the rocke," in the will of a Bristol merchant of 1569, was one formed of what was supposed by its owner to be a roc's egg.

In the next two centuries they are often mentioned, as the following list, compiled from the volumes of the Surtees Society and other sources, may serve to show :

1419.   alius ciphus vocatus a grypey ligatus cum argento et deaurato.—Will of Judge Gascoigne.—Test. Ebor.

1420.   unum note argenti herneisiatum et deauratum optimum cum coopertorio unum ciphum vocatum Note cum cooperculo deaurato.—Will of John Fromond, Archl. Jour. XVI., 166.

1428.   j hanape dargent dorrez fait a la m de j notte poissant de troye iij lb. iiij unz q at le lb. xlviijs. viij li.—Treasury of the Exchequer, Inv. 6 Henry VI.

1429.   a coupe made of gripes eye garnysshed wt siluer and ouer gilt with a fote and a couercle.—Will of Sir Gerald de Braybroke of Danbury, Knt.

1431.   unum nigrum nott coopertum et deauratum cum unâ aquilâ in summitate cooperculi ; unum chalescopp argenti et deaurati ad modum unius gripe egg cum scriptura in cooperculo.—Test. Ebor.

1433.   unum ciphum vocatum le nutt coopertum cum pede argenti stantem.—Idem.

1444.   iij Gripes eyes cov'ed garnysshed wt silver and gilt weyng vi lb. vunc p's the unce ijs. vid. Sma. ixli. xiis. vid. ; also ij notes cov'ed garnysshed wt silver t̃ gilt weyng xxiii unces ijs. vid. Sma. lviis. vid.—Treasury of the Exchequer Inv. 22 Henry VI.

1454.   unam peciam vocatam Grypeg deaur'.—Test. Ebor.

1459.   meum optimum nutt, meum less nutt.—Idem.

1476.   j standyng blake nutte quæ fuit matris meæ.—Idem.

1481.   a standyng gilt nutt.—Will of Sir Thos. Lyttelton. Nichols' Test. Vet.

1490.   a cup of silver called the grype's egg.—Test. Ebor.

1492.   unum ciphum vocatum le nutte stantem argen' in toto cum coopertorio.—Idem.

1508.   a notte paynted the coveryng silver and gilt.—Idem.

1535.   a littell olde nut with a bonde of sylver and gylt and a littell bonde of sylver and gylt; ij nutts with ij covers of sylver and gylt, and the seid nuts garnysshod with sylver and gylt, xxxiii uncs.—Inv. of Maison-Dieu, Dover ; 26 Henry VIII.

1536.   a gylt nut with fote bryme and rybbes of sylver and gylt ; a small nut with the fote brimme and cover of sylver.—Inv. of Minster Priory in Shepey.

1558.   a nutt gilt with a cover.—Surtees Society. Wills and Inv.

1570.   one nutt double gilt weinge xxxv. ounces xili. xiiis. iiijd.—Idem.

---

* *Kal and Inv. of the Exch.*, Vol. III. | *Gripe* or *Grypey* = egg of the grype or
† Surtees Society Trans.—Test. Ebor. | griffin.

1572. a nutt enclosed with silver and gilte of accorne woorcke and a cover gilte for
       the same.—Bristol Orphan Book.
1577. my black nut with the cover.—Wills and Inv.
1596. one nutte of silver to drink in dwoble gilte with a cover.—Wills and Inv.

These notes plainly indicate that just as a silver-gilt bowl shaped as a mazer would sometimes be called by that name, silver cups were called nuts or eggs if they were so formed. Cups of all three materials are extant. Cocoa-nut cups of the fifteenth century are to be seen at Oriel and New Colleges, Oxford, the latter society owning two specimens. The great City Companies possess several; the Vintners, the Armourers, and the Ironmongers each have one, from the latter of which our engraving (No. 66) is taken. It gives a very good idea of the way in which they were generally mounted at the beginning of the sixteenth century. The example at Vintners' Hall is very like this, and bears the hall-mark of 1518. Ostrich-egg cups are not so common, perhaps because they were rather more easily broken. Exeter College, Oxford, possesses an egg-cup of the first years of the seventeenth century (No. 67), and the Earl Howe another of earlier

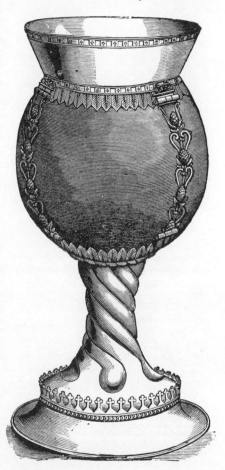

No. 66.—COCOA-NUT CUP (CIRCA 1500) AT
IRONMONGERS' HALL, LONDON.

date; all these were exhibited in the Loan Collection at South Kensington in 1862.

There is a very ancient ostrich egg at Corpus Christi College, Cambridge, the history of which can be traced to the fourteenth century. It was originally used for carrying about the Host, and being broken in the mastership of one Moptyd, or between 1553 and 1557, it is said to have been renewed at the expense of Richard Fletcher, when Bishop of Bristol (1589-92). This account of it, given by Masters in his history of the college, written late in the 18th century, is borne out by the hall-mark which is still legible on the mount, and fixes its date as of the year 1592. The cup, now much broken, is held together by its very plain silver tripod mounting, the only ornament of which is a little Elizabethan engraving.

The Exeter College cup is of 1610, and has a characteristic foot of that period with a stem formed as ostriches' legs; the cover is surmounted by an ostrich standing on a plume of ostrich-feathers (No. 67).

A third, somewhat more modern but an excellent and typical specimen nevertheless, is the beautiful cup in the collection of Lord Swaythling (No. 68).

Its history is told by an inscription running round the top of the cup and on the flag borne by the figure surmounting the cover. The date of its presentation as engraved on the cup accords with the hall-mark, which gives the year 1623.

No. 67.—OSTRICH-EGG CUP (1610), AT EXETER COLLEGE, OXFORD.

The Earl of Ducie has a silver-gilt cup of ostrich-egg or cocoa-nut shape, mounted with vertical hinged bands to hold the bowl, which rests in a socket or frame supported by four dolphins placed

on the top of a circular foot.
This specimen, which is
almost unique, is of the year
1584.

Other drinking hanaps, no
less ancient than the eggs,
are formed of horns mounted
in silver, as shown in the accompanying engraving (No.
69), of the Queen's College
horn, now used as a loving-
cup. It is traditionally called
poculum caritatis, or loving-
cup, and is said to have been
presented to the college by
Philippa, queen of Edward
III., its founder in 1340 being
her chaplain, Robert de Egles-
field. According to the
statutes the members of the
college were to be summoned
together by the sound of a
horn; possibly this was the
horn originally used for the
purpose. It is formed of a
buffalo-horn, and is 19½ inches
high, the horn itself being no
less than 25 inches long.
The cover with its eagle is of
later work than the bands of
the horn.

A similar horn (No. 70) is
in the possession of Christ's
Hospital, London. Either
because horns as well as the
other substances previously
mentioned were supposed to
have the property of revealing
the presence of poison in any
liquor poured into them, or

No. 68.—OSTRICH-EGG CUP (1623), SOLD
1925 FOR £5,700.

for some better reason, they have been used as drinking vessels
from early times. A drinking-horn originally represented estates
held by Cornage or by the horn ; one of the most ancient being
the Pusey horn,* by which the family of the same name hold
the village of Pusey in Berkshire. The gift of King Canute, it

No. 69.—WASSAIL HORN (14TH CENT.), AT QUEEN'S COLLEGE, OXFORD.

has gone with the estate from time out of mind, and has been
the subject of a Chancery suit in which it was held that the heirs
were entitled to it if the land was held by cornage. (Pusey *v.*
Pusey, 1 Vernon, 272.) The same great ecclesiastic who died
possessed of a nut in 1259, also had a drinking-horn, which he
left to his sister Agatha, describing it as "cornu meum magnum

* *Archæologia*, iii. 3. *Archæologia*, xii. 377.

ad bibendum cum apparatu argenti." Sir Brian de Stapleton in
1394 had " j corne esteaunt sur deux pees," which must have
been very like our engraving; whilst Chief Justice Gascoigne
leaves a cup called "Unicorn" to his son in 1419. Three quarters
of a century later Sir Brian Rowcliffe mentions in his will " unum
cornu ad bibendum garnesiatum cum argento et deaur'. '* A
fifth example may be given from the inventory of the Guild of
the Blessed Virgin Mary at Boston taken in 1534. "Itm a

NO. 70.—MOUNTED DRINKING-HORN AT CHRIST'S HOSPITAL, LONDON.

drynkynge horne ornate with silv' and gilte in three p'tes of it
wt ij feit of silv' and gilte wt a stone sett in silv' and gilte
weyng in the whole xiiij unc. di."

This is of the same date or thereabouts as the horn engraved
above.

Of a little earlier period was a celebrated horn long preserved
at Golden Grove. An engraving of this (No. 71) was kindly
placed at the author's disposal by His Grace the late Duke of

---

* All these are from the often-quoted
Testamenta Eboracensia; the wills cited

were proved 1259, 1394, 1419, and 1494
respectively.

Beaufort.   It had a foot of silver, ornamented with the royal
supporters, the date of which is somewhere about 1485, and it
is said to have been the first drinking vessel used by Henry,
Earl of Richmond, after landing in England in that year, and
presented by him to David ap Evan, son of Roderick the Great,
who lived in Llwyndafydd in Llandisiliogogo, and there enter-
tained the Earl and his men in his expedition against
Richard III.   This cup seems to have disappeared, and another
horn with similar supporters, but of seventeenth-century work,
at some time or other replacing the original relic, is now preserved at Golden Grove
by the Earl of Cawdor,
and is shown in its
stead. An elephant's
tusk, carved with
figures and mounted
with silver of sixteenth-
century work, is to be
seen at the British
Museum.

No. 71.—THE CAWDOR HORN (TEMP. HENRY VII.).

Lastly, we come to
standing cups made
entirely of the precious
metals themselves.
These are not confined
to any one century, and
there are extant speci-
mens to illustrate the work of successive generations of goldsmiths for three hundred years.   In speaking of the word hanap
it appeared that such cups as these were in fashion as far back
as records go.   The earliest specimen, however, bearing a recognised English hall-mark, and therefore of an ascertained date, is
no older than 1481 ; not but that there are a few still more ancient
cups in existence.   The enamelled cup at Lynn, for instance, is
of the fourteenth century, a covered cup of beaker shape at Oriel
College, Oxford, and one or two others at Cambridge are of the
fourteenth and fifteenth centuries, but of none of them can it
positively be said that they are of English make.   Some notice
must nevertheless be taken of them in passing.   The Lynn cup
is one of the most interesting cups in existence ; it has been

known as "King John's cup" for centuries, and is said to have been given to the town by that king. This can hardly be the case, as the costumes of the enamelled figures with which the bowl is covered are of the fourteenth century; but it is of no less interest for this, being still the most remarkable specimen of the goldsmiths' work of the period, ancient enough, to which it really belongs. It has been suggested that the King John was John of France, who may have visited King's Lynn with Edward III. and Queen Philippa on one of their progresses, and this is a suggestion which accords well with the workmanship of the cup. It is of silver gilt, 15 inches high, with a cover, and enriched, as we have said, with enamels, the bowl being divided into compartments by vertical ribs, in which figures appear, male and female. The stem is very slender, and rises from a circular foot. It was exhibited at South Kensington in 1862, and

No. 72.—THE FOUNDRESS' CUP (CIRCA 1440), AT CHRIST'S COLLEGE, CAMBRIDGE.

had before that been engraved in *Examples of Art Workmanship*. The curious cup at Christ's College, called the Foundress' cup, is of fifteenth-century work (No. 72). Its diagonal bands, ornamented with running foliage in repoussé, and the Gothic cresting which surrounds the cover and the

No. 73.—CUP (15TH CENT.) AT ORIEL COLLEGE, OXFORD.

base, might be of the second half of that century, or even a
little later, but the arms enamelled on the boss within the cup

are those of Humphrey, Duke of Gloucester, impaled with Cobham of Sterborough, and this impalement, being the distinctive coat of Duke Humphrey's second wife Eleanor Cobham according to the heraldry of that day, would point to 1440, or a year or two earlier, as the true date of the cup. The arms long passed for those of Countess Margaret; and the cup itself is supposed to have come into the possession of the College at her death in 1509, along with a beaker or stoup and her salt-cellars. The beaker, or stoup at Oriel Coll., Oxford, of which an engraving* (No. 73) is given, is another very ancient cup, but, like the Lynn cup, not of the date that tradition would assign to it. The letters and Lancastrian badges seem to refer to Prince Edward, son of Henry VI.; but at any rate the cup is nearly a century and a half later than the reign of Edward II., whose gift to the College it was formerly supposed to be.

No. 74.—BEAKER (1507) AT CHRIST'S COLLEGE, CAMBRIDGE.

It much resembles the stoup given to Christ's College, Cambridge, by its foundress Margaret, Countess of Richmond. This at Oriel College is probably of Paris make and of the year 1462,

---

* For this engraving, as for that of the Oriel College mazer and others, the author | is indebted to the Council of the Royal Archæological Institute.

No. 75.—THE LEIGH CUP (1499) AT MERCERS' HALL, LONDON.

whilst the Cambridge
one is certainly Eng-
lish and only a little
later in date — 1507
(No. 74). The daisy,
the Tudor rose, and
the portcullis forming
the letter M, are all
emblematic of the
Countess' name and
family, just as the
ornamentation of the
Oriel beaker indicates
the Lancastrian
prince, who no doubt
once owned it.

The "Leigh" cup
of the Mercers' Com-
pany (No. 75) is the
second earliest of the
hanaps known to be
hall-marked, the Ana-
thema cup being the
first. It is of the year
1499, and notwith-
standing some small
alteration and repair,
is a beautiful speci-
men of goldsmiths'
work. It is silver
gilt, sixteen inches
high and six and a
half inches in dia-
meter. The pierced
band of Gothic tracery
with a cresting of
Tudor flowers is re-
peated around the
cover, and in the

No. 76.—THE RICHMOND CUP (CIRCA 1500–1520),
AT ARMOURERS' HALL, LONDON.

lozenge-shaped panels, into which the bowl of the cup is

No. 77.—STANDING CUP (1569),
AT CORPUS CHRISTI COLLEGE,
CAMBRIDGE.

divided by the intersection of corded bands, are maidens' busts and flagons alternately, the former much like the busts on the sides of the Mercers' Company beakers, an engraving of which will be given later. A demi-virgin gules within an orle of clouds, forms the coat of arms borne by this Worshipful Company; and this is further alluded to by the figure of a pure virgin with a unicorn reposing in her lap, which surmounts the cover of the cup. The coat-of-arms around the knop, and the lettered bands, are in enamel.

The cup next to be noticed is of the same or possibly even of a little earlier date than the last. It is the beautiful " Richmond " cup of the Armourers' Company, so called because presented in 1557 by one John Richmond (No. 76). It is thirteen inches high, and weighs fifty-one ounces. Its style speaks for itself, and recalls the simple but elegant make of the hour-glass salts of about the same date. The bowl is not unlike that of the Leigh cup in shape, though the real outline of the latter is somewhat hidden by the ornaments; they both resemble in this respect a cup of 1511, used as a chalice at Chewton Mendip, and the Anathema cup, at Pembroke College, Cambridge, which is of the year 1481.

We now come to a typical specimen of Elizabethan art in the tall cup (No. 77), given by Archbishop Parker to Corpus College, Cambridge. Not the less English because it reminds

us of the fine Dutch and
German hanaps of the same
period, it is one of the finest
of its class.   Dutch and
English ornaments were
wonderfully alike at this
time.   As characteristic is
the "Chapman" cup of
the Armourers' Company
(No. 78).   The gift of one
Edmond Chapman in 1581,
its hall-mark corresponds
with its history, whilst the
egg-and-tongue moulding
and the bands of engraven
foliage identify the cup at
a glance as of the reign
of Queen Elizabeth.   The
present cover is of 1610,
but there is good reason
to think it an exact copy
of an older one.   The belt
of foliage around the upper
part of the cup is just
what is found upon the
communion cups of this
period.

Before passing to the
seventeenth century a few
words must be said of cups
of exceptional form or
material.   Ivory standing
cups are sometimes found,
and of these the best known
example is the celebrated
cup called Thomas à
Becket's,* formerly at

No. 78.—THE CHAPMAN CUP (1580) AT
ARMOURERS' HALL, LONDON.

* It now belongs to His Grace the
Duke of Norfolk.

No. 79.—PEA-HEN CUP (CIRCA 1643), AT SKINNERS' HALL, LONDON.

Corby Castle. This is a very ancient ivory cup bearing the initials
TB and a mitre, from which it has been supposed that it once

belonged to the saint and archbishop himself; but it was over-

looked that the initial letter of his family name would be replaced by that of the See in the case of a prelate, and although very old, the cup can hardly be referred to as early a period as the twelfth century whilst the mounting is of the reign of Henry VIII. The date-letter which suits the fashion of the mount, is the Lombardic H of 1525, the date properly assigned to it many years ago by Mr. Octavius Morgan. The interesting history of the cup, which was given by Sir Edward Howard, Lord High Admiral, to Queen Katharine of Arragon, and afterwards reverted to the Earl of Arundel, points to the time at which it was mounted in its

No. 80.—DOUBLE CUP (17TH CENTURY), AT VINTNERS' HALL, LONDON.

present fashion, and coincides happily with the hall-mark. The style of the belt, which bears in Tudor characters the

inscription VINUM . TVVM .
BIBE . CVM . GAVDIO, and the
groundwork of the letters, which
also carries the hall-mark, closely
corresponds with the inscribed
bands on the chalice at Trinity
College, Oxford, and the Narford
mazer, which are of the years
1527 and 1532 respectively.

Early in the reign of Elizabeth, cups are found fashioned
as gourds or melons, with feet
formed as their twisted stems
and tendrils. The Armourers'
Company and the Honourable
Society of the Inner Temple
each have one, the former of
the year 1585, the latter dated
1563. Cups, too, shaped as
birds and other animals, their
heads taking off to form them
into drinking vessels, sometimes
occur. The set of fine large
cups formed as cocks, and called
the "Cockayne" cups of the
Skinners' Company, are the best
known examples of these. They
were made in 1605. The pea-
hen cup of the same Guild is
as characteristic as the Cockayne cups; the engraving of
it (No. 79) conveys a good idea
of this class of cup generally.
It was presented by the widow
of one Peacock. In both these
cases the name of the donor has
of course suggested the design
for the cup.

In Germany drinking-cups
often took these and other

NO. 81.—THE EDMONDS CUP (1613), AT
CARPENTERS' HALL, LONDON.

No. 82.—THE BLACKSMITHS' CUP (1655).

quaint shapes, such as windmills, at about this time, and until
the middle of the seventeenth century. The windmills seem

OEP—N

always of foreign origin, but another favourite cup is found of English make as well as German. These are the well-known ones, sometimes called "wager cups," in the form of a woman, holding a small cup over her head with up-stretched arms. A very beautiful seventeenth century cup of this kind is amongst the plate of the Vintners' Company, an engraving of which is given (No. 80). It is not quite certain whether it is of English or foreign workmanship. They are all very much alike.

A little later another very distinctive fashion prevailed. The "Edmonds" cup of the Carpenters' Company is an admirable illustration of it (No. 81). This is one of a set of four such cups, in the possession of the Company, given by the wardens whose names they bear. The foot resembles those of earlier cups, but the stem is different, being formed as acanthus or other leaves, the upper part of it baluster-shaped. It forms a link between the Elizabethan and the plain baluster stems which are so often found in the seventeenth century.

The bowl is as characteristic of its period as the stem, the pointed shape being general for a time; and the covers of all these cups are surmounted by three brackets bearing a triangular spire of pierced work ending in a spearhead as shown in the engraving. This "Edmonds" cup was given in 1613, and was made that same year: the others are of 1609, 1611 and 1628. Magnificent cups of this period and fashion are in use as chalices at Odcombe, co. Somerset, at Bodmin in Cornwall, and several other places. In a few instances the pyramid is surmounted by a statuette, man with long spear and shield or other such figure, instead of ending in a point.

The Armourers' Company have two very similar cups, called the "Leycroft" and the "Foster" cup, the former of 1608, and the latter of 1631; and the Trinity House other two of the years 1611 and 1627 respectively. These dates serve to plainly mark the interval within which these cups remained in full vogue. The covers in each of these instances are surmounted by open-work pyramidal spires, those at the Trinity House being supported by mermaids. The pyramidal finials occur occasionally as early as 1599 or 1600. Such a cup of gold was given to the King by the Inner and Middle Temple

No. 83.—THE ROYAL OAK CUP (1676), AT BARBER-SURGEONS' HALL, LONDON.

No. 84.—THE PEPYS CUP (1677), AT CLOTHWORKERS' HALL. LONDON.

in 1609. It is described* as "in the upper part thereof adorned with a fabric fashioned like a pyramid, whereon standeth the statue of a military person leaning with the left hand upon a Roman fashioned shield or target."

A cup of this fashion, gilt, and weighing 46 oz., was sold at Christie and Manson's Rooms in June, 1875, for £200, or about four and a half guineas an ounce. †

A specimen of 1639, now bereft of its spire, is to be seen in the Treasury of the Czar at Moscow; and a stray example of as late a date as 1646, called the " Rawlinson " cup, is at Vintners' Hall. This is the very last known to the writer.

To these succeeded a much less artistic form of cup, which held its own, however, much longer, being found from about 1631 to 1694, the dates of the earliest and latest of them that have been noted. The example of 1631 is at Haberdashers' Hall. Queens' College, Cambridge, has one of 1636.

The engraving (No. 82) is taken from one of the year 1655, which was once the property of the Blacksmiths' Company, but found its way into the Bernal Collection and thence to Mr. Dexter. At the Dexter sale it passed to Messrs. Hancocks for no less a sum than £378, and from them into the fine collection of the late Sir F. A. Milbank.

It is about twelve inches high, and stands on a large circular foot. Its stem is of somewhat exceptional form, being a figure of Vulcan. In the general run of the examples known of this pattern of cup the stems are plain balusters. The bowls of a great many of them are covered with granulated ornament, as shown in the engraving, or sometimes show a matted surface, and are of the same shape, whilst a few are chased with a band of upright acanthus foliage round the lower part.

Most of the City Companies, the Trinity House, and the Inns of Court are supplied with one or more of these favourite loving cups, which were made in great numbers for more than half a century.

It is not to be supposed, however, that there was no demand for a more decorated style of cup, especially in the festive reign of Charles II. Cups of the greatest magnificence are found of that period, of which two examples may be given to show what the Caroline goldsmith could accomplish.

---

* *Calendar of the Inner Temple Records.*—F. A. Inderwick, K.C.

† A tall cup, pyramid lost, 19 in. high, at the Dunn Gardner sale, sold for £4,000.

The " Royal Oak " grace cup (No. 83) was presented by the merry monarch to the Barber-Surgeons' Company in 1676. It is 16¾ inches high, including the cover, and is formed as an oak-tree, the bowl being supported by the trunk and branches. It is profusely ornamented with chased leaves and garlands, and has an arched royal crown as a cover.

The other example is the cup (No. 84) given by Samuel Pepys to the Clothworkers' Company. It is of about the same date as the last, 1677, but of greater size, being 23 inches high, and 166 ounces in weight.

Its general shape is much like that of the plainer loving cups on baluster-stems which have already been described; but in this case the plain bowl is surrounded by a removable silver casing of pierced flowers and scrolls of very elaborate and beautiful work, and the foot and baluster-stem are ornamented in a similar manner.

This may bring us to the eighteenth century, and the simple but massive two-handled cups with covers that mark the reigns of Queen Anne and the earlier part of the Georgian period.

These seem to have been the only cups made for a long time, and they are of every size and degree of finish, from those of simplest workmanship up to the beautiful specimen by the master hand of Paul Lamerie, from which our illustration (No. 85) of the class is taken, by permission of the Goldsmiths' Company.

It is one of the best possible examples of a well-known form of cup, of the decoration of the period, and of the work of this celebrated artist, who flourished from 1712, when he entered into business, till his death in the summer of 1751. It may be remarked that his fame was fairly and honourably earned by the personal attention he seems to have devoted to his art throughout his whole career. Much of the beautiful work which bears his mark must have been executed by his own hand, for it appears from his will, which, dated in May and proved in August, 1751, gives us the period of his death within a few weeks, that he kept only two journeymen, to one of whom, Samuel Collins, he entrusted the duty of preparing his unfinished plate for sale by auction for the benefit of his widow and three daughters. That he had no son accounts for the disappearance of the name from the books of the Goldsmiths'

Company. He was of French extraction, as his name and
the names of the personal friends who were his executors,
sufficiently denote. He worked under the name of Lamerie,
but used the prefix " de " in signing his last will.

No special forms or fashions can be identified with any

No. 85.—TWO-HANDLED CUP AND COVER (1739), BY PAUL LAMERIE, AT
GOLDSMITHS' HALL, LONDON.

particular period from the middle of the eighteenth century
onwards, if we except the oval-pointed cups, sometimes fluted,
but more often ornamented with hanging festoons sometimes
carried over medallions, which are also found on Wedgwood
ware of the time of Flaxman. The potters and the goldsmiths
have often copied each others' designs, or else have resorted to
the same designers; and as in the reign of William III. Staffordshire ware made by the well-known John Philip Elers, from
1690 onwards, reproduced the Chinese ornament patronised by

the goldsmiths a decade earlier, so now Flaxman and his school influenced the goldsmiths' work of the day almost as much as the ornamentation of ceramic ware, with which his name is more popularly associated.   The Wedgwood ware, for which

No. 86.—CUP (1795), AT MERCHANT TAYLORS' HALL, LONDON.

Flaxman for many years furnished models, won extraordinary fame.   It is not so generally known that the same great artist was employed also by Rundell and Bridge, the crown goldsmiths, notwithstanding the fine examples executed by them after his designs that are at Windsor Castle and other places.

No better illustration of the style could be found than the vase-like cup which has been selected for our engraving (No. 86). It is one of a pair made in the year 1795, and is the property

of the Merchant Taylors' Company, by whose permission it has
been engraved.

It is generally admitted that the English goldsmiths of the
present century are not behind those of days gone by, and
have of late years even outstripped their continental brethren
in an art which is capable of so much.

TANKARDS.

The use of the word "tankard," in its now familiar sense of
a large silver drinking vessel with a cover and handle, is of comparatively modern introduction.   No article of plate is called
by this name in any of the volumes of wills and inventories published by the Surtees Society, which carry us down to the year
1600.   The word seems to first occur in this sense about 1575,
and from that time is constantly applied to the vessels that
have ever since been known as tankards.   In earlier days it
was used for the wooden tubs bound with iron, and containing
some three gallons, in which water was carried.   The men
who fetched water from the conduits in London were called
"tankard-bearers," and in a Coroner's Roll of 1276, for the
ward of Castle Baynard, tankards are mentioned as the vessels
they bore.   This roll sets forth that one Grene, a water-carrier,
who had come to St. Paul's Wharf, "cū quodam tancardo,"
intending to take up water with it, entered a boat there, and
after filling the tankard attempted to place it on the wharf,
but the weight of the water in the tankard making the boat
move away as he was standing on its board, he fell into the
water between the boat and the wharf, and was drowned, as
the coroner found, by misadventure.*

Again in 1337, the keepers of the conduits received a sum
of money for rents for "tynes and tankards," thereat; and in
1350 a house is hired for one year at 10s. to put the tankards—
les tanqers—in, and two irons costing 2s. 6d. were bought for
stamping them.†

Similar utensils are found in farming accounts of the same
period.   In 1294 at Framlingham, co. Suffolk, the binding with
iron of thirteen tankards costs 3s., and six years later, a

---

* Coroner's Roll, **17** June, 4 Edw. I. | *London Life*, p. 6.
—Riley's *Memorials of London and* | † Riley's *Memorials*, etc., pp. 201, 265

three-gallon iron-bound tankard is priced in Cambridge at 1s.
At Leatherhead a two-gallon tankard is valued at 2d. in 1338,
and two such vessels at Elham together cost 4d. in 1364.*

All this time tankards are mentioned in no other connection;

No. 87.—TANKARD (1574), AT THE ASHMOLEAN MUSEUM, OXFORD.

but when we come to the sixteenth century, a notice of "lether"
tankards occurs. This is in a church account of 1567, and they
were no doubt used as fire-buckets. A churchwardens' inventory of the same period (1566) speaks of a "penny tanckerd
of wood used as a holy-water stock." Even later than this,
tankards appear in household accounts classed with other

---

* Prof. Rogers' *History of Agriculture and Prices in England*, Vol. II., pp. 577,
568, 571, 573.

kitchen goods, for an inventory of the chattels of one Edward
Waring, Esq., of Lea, taken in 1625, includes "two tankerds
and one payle," certainly not amongst his plate. Some time
before this, however, the term was occasionally applied to silver
vessels. The will of Sir George Heron of Harbottell, proved

No. 88.—THE POISON TANKARD (CIRCA 1565), AT CLARE COLLEGE, CAMBRIDGE.

at Durham in 1576 or thereabouts, mentions his "three silver
tanckards" valued at VI*li*.; and in a Norwich will of 1583,
there is an entry of " one Canne or Tanckerd of sylver." In the
inventory of the plate of Dr. Perne, Master of Peterhouse, Cambridge, which is of the year 1589, occur the following articles :*—

Item a tankerd barred lipt and covered v ounces xxiiij*s*. ij*d*.

Item a white horne tankerd with a cover barres and lipt double gilt vi ounces xxi*s*.

* Camb. Univ. Registry. Drawer 13. Kindly communicated by A. P.
Humphry, Esq.

These are some of the earliest instances of a then new application of the word, which soon became common, and eventually superseded the old.

It was, after all, not very unnatural to transfer a word originally used for a capacious water-tub to a drinking vessel that was also large of its kind, and it is difficult to understand why etymologists should have taken so much trouble, as they have, to find fanciful derivations for it. Duchat and Thomson would both derive "tankard" from *tin-quart*, and Dr. Thomas Henshaw from the twang or sound the lid makes on shutting it down; but, after all, if tank is derived, as it surely is, from the French *estang*, a pond or pool, it is not necessary to go further for a derivation of the name of a vessel which was originally intended to hold water than to connect it with tank, and derive it from the same source. Johnson's Dictionary describes it as "a large vessel for strong drink," and cites Ben Jonson: "Hath his tankard touched your brain?"

No. 89.—TANKARD (1618), IN THE POSSESSION OF THE CORPORATION OF NORWICH.*

One of the earliest extant specimens of what we should now call a tankard is preserved at Corpus Christi College, Cambridge

---

* A tall gilt tankard of 1607 like this, 12¼ in. high and weighing 39 oz., was sold in 1898 at Messrs. Christie's Rooms for £458 5*s*.

(see page 266). It is of the year 1571, and is elaborately ornamented with arabesque bands of repoussé and engraved work.
Caius College, Cambridge, has one of 1570. Both this and
the tankard at
Corpus Christi
College, were
given by Arch-
bishop Parker,
who also gave one
to Trinity Hall,
which is of 1571.
The Ashmolean
Museum at Oxford
has a beautiful
example of 1574
(No. 87). A little
later comes a good
example of 1602
now used as a
communion flagon
at Heddington,
Wilts. It is very
like the Ashmo-
lean Tankard.
These are all of
moderate size, not
more than six or
seven inches high,
and the Oxford
example tapers a
good deal from
the bottom up-
wards.

The "Poison
Cup" at Clare
College, Cam-
bridge (No. 88), which has already been mentioned in another
connection, is a glass tankard enclosed in silver filigree casing
of about the same date as the last.

No. 90.—TANKARD (1634), THE PROPERTY OF THE
CORPORATION OF BRISTOL.

The earliest straight-sided upright tankard flagon is one of

1572, at Teffont Eywas, Wilts. It is of smaller size than later flagons of this pattern, and has the rayed-button knop on the cover, instead of the rounded dome.

To these succeed the taller, upright, and straight-sided tankards, often beautifully ornamented, that are found in the reigns of James I. and Charles I. One of these, belonging to

Thes Tankers were made John Hart. Wardens in the and eightie. being the plate

No. 91.—IRISH TANKARDS (1680), AT MERCHANT TAYLORS' HALL, LONDON.

the Corporation of Norwich, and made in the year 1618, is given on p. 368 (No. 89). The drum is repoussé, ornamented with strapwork, forming diamond divisions, which are filled with flowers and fruit, and with medallions bearing the usual marine monsters of the period. This is strikingly like a flagon of the year 1619, which has been referred to before, at Kensington parish church. A pair of similar fashion and of the same date are at Bodmin Church, and another pair, perhaps more elaborate, are amongst the valuable possessions of the Corporation of Bristol. These last are of 1634 (No. 90).

Later tankards are plainer, and are of constant occurrence. Seventeenth-century inventories frequently mention them, and plenty of specimens are still in existence.

A splendid pair, from one of which our engraving (No. 91) is taken, came into the possession of the Merchant Taylors' Company in London, on the dissolution of a Dublin Guild some years ago, and they show round the lower part of the drum the acanthus-leaf ornament which is so characteristic of the time at which they were made. They bear the Dublin hall-marks for 1680. A note as to prices may not be inappropriate. From an early account-book of the Clockmakers' Company it may be quoted that a pair of tankards, ordered to be bought at about this time, and weighing together 100 oz., cost £31 19s. 5d.

These domestic tankards of the second half of this century are very plain, sometimes of great diameter in proportion to their depth, and have flat lids and very massive handles, the lower part of the latter often being notched to form them into whistles, which might be used for summoning the servitor, when the vessel required replenishing. They came in at the Restoration, and are found till about 1710 or 1720, when a pot with swelling drum and dome-shaped lid, with or without a knob, was introduced, of a fashion so well known at the present day, both in silver and pewter, that it is unnecessary to describe it more fully. The tankards of the last two centuries are perhaps as often without lids as with them, and examples of the more usual shapes in pewter may be seen in every tavern.

It has already been remarked that the so-called flagons used ordinarily in English churches are, properly speaking, tankards, and the origin of the application of the word flagon to them has been explained in the previous chapter.

Tankards of the tall, highly ornamented kind will be found in the chronological list at the years 1618, 1619, 1634, a plain one of the same shape at 1634; and the ordinary flat-lidded tankard at 1664, 1666, 1669, and onwards.

SMALLER CUPS.

INCLUDING TAZZE, SAUCERS, BEAKERS, TASTERS, CAUDLE-CUPS, PORRINGERS,
TUMBLERS, ETC.

Side by side with the standing cups, which were often more fitted for decorating the "cup-board" than for use except on state occasions and bearing the same relation to them that the trencher-salt did to the standing salt-cellar, are found a number of smaller cups and basins adapted for every-day requirements. A short chronological notice of their forms will perhaps be of more practical use to the collector than the preceding section ; for whilst standing cups are seldom for sale, and when they are, command prices that are beyond the reach of any but the very wealthy, good specimens of smaller drinking-cups are more easy of acquisition.

TAZZE.—Very elegant cups, usually on baluster-stems and with bowls shaped like the low open champagne glasses of nineteenth-century use, are found from about 1570 till the outbreak of the Civil War in the reign of Charles I. Specimens of these are much prized by the collector, and they are by no means common, though the Armourers' Company are fortunate enough to possess a number of them. Their bowls are often punched all over with small bosses in rings or other patterns from the outside, decreasing in size towards the centre and somewhat resembling

No. 92.—TAZZA (1633), FROM THE OCTAVIUS MORGAN COLLECTION.

the designs now produced by engine-turning. This was possibly in imitation of the Venetian glasses which were much used for drink at this period by those who could afford them. One of 1599, the property of Mr. Octavius Morgan, is so ornamented ; and several of the Armourers' Company cups are similarly treated.

Others have plain bowls, or have a simple band of ornament round the rims, such as may be observed in the case of the beautiful example of which a woodcut is given (No. 92). This is of the year 1633. Very many Scottish communion cups are of this, and the V-shaped or wine-glass pattern cups shortly to be mentioned. A large number of these are found all over Scotland from about 1615 to 1650.

SAUCERS.—Ornamented usually with punched patterns are found several shallow trays or saucers, like the bowls of the tazze of which we have been speaking, deprived of their stems and feet. These generally occur from 1630 to 1655, but there are one or two of a later period, say 1660 to 1670. Sometimes

No. 93.—SAUCER (CIRCA 1632), USED AS AN ALMS-DISH AT BREDGAR, KENT.

they have small flat handles formed as escallop shells, or else scroll handles of wire. Several in use as alms-plates at village churches have been already mentioned. These small trays were all no doubt originally intended to hold sweetmeats or trinkets. The illustration is of one used as a paten at Bredgar in Kent (No. 93).

TASTERS are the small shallow circular bowls with a flat handle that are sometimes called bleeding-basins, but incorrectly, the latter being a different class of vessel, sometimes found in nests. They are constantly mentioned in the plate-

lists of Elizabethan days, but rarely earlier than 1570, nor more
than a single one in each list.

> Item a white taster xiij ouncs, iij quarters, iij li., vi s., vi d.
> Item a white taster with a cover xiiij ouncs and one quarter, iij li., viii. s.
>
> Inv. of Dr. Perne, Master of Peterhouse, Cambridge, 1589.

A silver bowl called *le Taster* is mentioned in a Bristol will
of 1403, and in another of 1545 a "taster of silver waing by
estymacion vi. ounces" occurs.   Half-way between these dates
"a taster with a cover" is included in an inventory of 1487,* but
this was in all probability a cup of assay.   The ordinary tasters
weighed about three ounces, and were valued at about ten
or twelve shillings.   The extant specimens are mostly of the
middle or end of the seventeenth century.   Bleeding-basins
of the first years of the eighteenth century about 4½ inches
in diameter, and having a single flat pierced handle, are not
uncommon.   They are found of pewter as well as of silver.

BEAKERS.—These come next in order, occurring first at the
very beginning of the seventeenth century; a few may be found
of earlier but not much earlier date, though their names occur
long before in inventories.   In England, at all events, they are
more often seen in the cabinet of the collector than amongst
the ancient treasures of great people or great corporations, a
fact which must be left to explain itself as best it can.   Early
foreign examples are more common.   They are usually Dutch,
or from the north of Europe.

Dr. Johnson derived the word from *beak*, and defined the
beaker as a cup with a spout in form of a bird's beak, an
opinion shared also by Skinner.   Other authorities content
themselves with saying that it was a kind of vessel probably
derived from Flanders or Germany, without fixing its shape ;
and Forby would trace it to the Saxon *bece*, ordinary drinking-
vessels being made of beech-wood.

The learned de Laborde connects the English word *byker* with
the German *becher* and the French *buket*; giving for authority the
cases in which the latter is used for a holy-water bucket, and for
a large cup of silver with cover, enamelled in the bottom.   The
vessels commonly called beakers are plain upright drinking-cups,
widening at the mouth and without spout or handle, somewhat

---

* **Inv.** of Robert Morton, gent., 3 Henry VII., Brit. Mus. Add. MS. 30,064.
Arch Jour. XXXIII. 321.

resembling the tall glass tumblers used in modern times for sodawater and the like. The engraving is taken from those of the Mercers' Company, dated 1604 (No. 94). A beaker of 1609, with belts and flower-scrolls engraved round the top, is used as a communion cup at Armathwaite, in Cumberland; and another of 1598 is at Llanfyllin, N. Wales. In Scotland they seem quite a favourite form of communion cup in the seventeenth century.

1346. ciphum meum biker argenti. Will of a canon of York.—Test. Ebor.

1348. Bikers, cups intended for ladies, see Beltz, *Memorials of the Order of the Garter*, p. 385.

1379. un hanap tour de beker.

1399. two bikers of silver gilt, 29½ oz., one other biker gilt, 16 oz. (amongst the stock of a jeweller's shop in Cheapside). *

1446. vi bikkez diversarum sectarum, It^m xiij bikkes cum ij cooperculis, It^m xij bik'kez antiqua.—Inv. of Durham Priory.

1582. a sylver becker.—Rich. Wills.

1604, 1605. Plain gilt beakers, each ornamented with three maidens' heads on the sides (see engraving No. 94).—Mercers' Company.

1625. One white beaker.—Inv. of Edward Waring of Lea, Esq.

V-SHAPED CUPS on baluster-stems were very common from about 1600 to 1630, and cups on baluster-stems but with more conical bowls for about thirty years more. These last are very like the ordinary wine-glasses of the present day, but are somewhat larger. Communion cups, especially in Scotland, as well as secular drinking-cups, are often found of this shape. Examples in silver and pewter have been given in the chapter upon ecclesiastical plate, pp. 253, 255.

With these may be classed the very small hexagonal or octagonal grace-cups on high stems that are found in the reign of James I. These are quite peculiar to that period. Specimens are preserved at Christ's Hospital, and by the Armourers' Company. They seem to occur in sets of three.

CAUDLE-CUPS AND PORRINGERS.—These two classes of vessels, the former of which were often called " posset " cups or " posnets," include all the two-handled cups with covers and sometimes also trays or stands, that were so commonly used in the seventeenth and the earlier part of the following century.

The former are somewhat pear-shaped, swelling into larger bowls at the base, and were used for drinking posset, which

---

* It may be noted that his whole stock in trade consisted of 132 oz., valued at 2s. 4d. an ounce. Riley's *Memorials of London and London Life*, p. 550.

was milk curdled with wine and other additions, like our own white-wine-whey and treacle-possets. The curd floated above the liquor, and, rising into the narrow part of the cup, could be easily removed, leaving the clear fluid at the bottom. Their fashion differs with their date. A well-known pattern in the

middle years of the seventeenth century, is shown in the engraving (No. 95). This is one of three such cups at Clothworkers' Hall. It affords a rather late example of a fashion of wreath, formed of leaves and berries like myrtle or bay, which was very common about 1635. It is found from 1630 to 1654, but is very seldom seen either earlier or later. Lincoln's Inn also possesses some, and there are many at Oxford, where they are used in college halls as beer-cups. A very fine and extremely early caudle-cup of 1616 is at Mercers' Hall. In the gayer times of the merry monarch, they are of more elaborate design; many are ornamented very boldly with flowers and monsters in repoussé work. A beautiful example, of the year 1670,

No. 94.—BEAKER (1604), AT MERCERS' HALL, LONDON.

is engraved (No. 96), by the kind permission of Earl Bathurst. This cup was stolen some years ago, but has fortunately been recovered recently.

Porringers, on the other hand, were wider-mouthed bowls, but with covers and handles like the last. Their less flowing shape necessitated a somewhat different style of treatment in the way of decoration; and they are sometimes found, in the middle of the century, octagonal or even twelve-sided, without any ornament.

From about 1665 to 1685, they are often decorated with flat appliqué leaves round the bottom of the bowl and the knop of the cover. These thin plates of metal, cut into various shapes and applied to the surface, have been called by Mr. Octavius Morgan "cut-card" work, for want of a better name, and it has been somewhat generally adopted. The engraving is of a very good specimen exhibited in the Loan Collection of 1862 by the late Paul Butler, Esq. (No. 97). The cover is furnished with three small projecting handles that form feet if the cover is used as a tray or saucer for the cup, for which, as well as for a cover, it is adapted. A fine cup of this fashion made in 1671 is at Wadham College, Oxford.

Some bowls are decorated with the upright acanthus leaf as found on the great tankards of the Merchant Taylors' Company in 1680, of which an engraving has been given, No. 91. This acanthus ornament was much in vogue for a short time, say from 1675 to 1685.

Another well-known but a short-lived style of decoration covered everything with Chinese figures in engraved work (for which see woodcut, No. 104). The mania for Chinese porcelain which pre-vailed for a few years

No. 95.—CAUDLE-CUP (1657), AT CLOTHWORKERS' HALL, LONDON. *

in the reign of William III., and affected even the queen her-self, has been immortalised by the satirists of the day. It did not die out before the goldsmiths first and the potters following them had covered their wares with Chinese designs. Upon Elers ware of about 1690 is found a whole series of representa-tions illustrating the cultivation and use of the tea-plant, an old and a young viceroy of Canton, and the like. A vast quantity of plate was decorated in this way in the years 1682, 1683, and 1684, and a few pieces are found up to about 1690, but not much later. Amongst other specimens is the small gold cup found in the lake at Knowsley, and already mentioned as one of the few articles of gold exhibited at South Kensington in 1862. It was then catalogued as of "circa 1650." This is surely too early, especially as the

* A pair of such cups (1690) sold at the Dunn Gardner sale at 430s. per oz.

maker's mark, RL, is well known, and agrees with the usual date of Chinese decoration, having been noted on plate from 1680 to 1693.

A small tankard, with the same sort of engraving, is in the South Kensington Museum; but the barrel is of one year, the cover of the next, and the decoration ten or fifteen years later than either.*

Last of all come the fluted porringers of the reign of Queen

No. 96.—CAUDLE-CUP (1670), THE PROPERTY OF EARL BATHURST.

Anne, of which it is necessary to say that, as they have much attracted the attention of collectors, imitations of them have been manufactured by the cart-load. These modern copies would very often be detected by an assay, for they are all marked as made of the Britannia standard of silver, and many of them if tested would no doubt prove to be of silver of lower quality. Their period almost exactly coincides with the first quarter

---

* As of the Chinese period, but rather earlier than the kind of engraving mentioned above, being of the year 1674, may be mentioned a set of three large silver vases, and two tall beakers, given to Horace Walpole by the Lady Betty Germain, and sold at the Strawberry Hill Sale. They are of the form of the blue and white Chinese porcelain sets, which are sometimes arranged on the top of library book-cases. They are of great size; the jars twenty inches high, and twelve inches in diameter, and the beakers fourteen inches high. They passed through the hands of Messrs. Lambert, to the last Marquis of Breadalbane in 1857. There are others at Knole of about the same date.

of the eighteenth century. An engraving is given of a good example selected from a large number of these porringers in the collection of the late R. Temple Frere, Esq. (No. 98).

No. 97.—PORRINGER (1674) *

TUMBLERS.—These useful articles have been rather pushed out of their place in the chapter by the necessity of classing

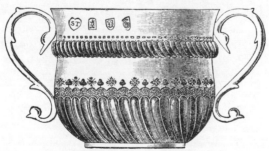

No. 98.—FLUTED PORRINGER (1699).

together porringers and caudle-cups; for they are decidedly more ancient than the last-mentioned class of porringers. They are so called because they will not lie on their side but will only rest on the bottom, tumbling or rolling from side to side

* A similar porringer (1681) sold for £582, in Feb., 1903.

like a tumbler, till they steady themselves in an upright position. The name has somewhat improperly been transferred to our flat-bottomed drinking glasses. Such round-bottomed cups are frequently met with from about 1670 onwards, and are used in some of the colleges at Oxford for drinking beer. They were sometimes called bowls, and, being of different sizes, the larger ones were called beer-bowls, and the smaller wine-bowls, in old inventories. "Bolles" are mentioned from very early times. "vi Ciphos vocat. bolles de argento" were left by Robert Cheddre of Bristol, to his son Richard, in 1382, and they constantly occur afterwards.

PLATES.

Plates of silver or silver-gilt were used both at dinner and at what is now called dessert. The dessert-plates are the more common, though silver "trenchers" are sometimes mentioned, as for instance in the will of Christopher Urswyke, Rector of Hackney, co. Midx., who died in 1521. The "conceites after dinner," such as "appels, nuts, or creame,"* were no doubt placed upon them.

Silver "spice-plates" occur in the inventories of the fourteenth and fifteenth centuries: one of the earliest is of a "plate argenti pro speciebus imponendis," in a list dated 1358.† Two or three known sets of small silver plates, parcel gilt and elaborately engraved, are of the middle of the sixteenth century. One of these sets, consisting of twelve plates, the borders engraved with medallions, heads, flowers, and other ornaments of the Elizabethan period, and the centres with the labours of Hercules after Aldegrever, was sold by auction at Messrs. Christie and Manson's Rooms in the summer of 1876 for £480, a price far below their real value. They are of the year 1567, and once belonged to the Cottons of Connington, one of whom was that great antiquary, Sir Robert Cotton, Bart., the collector of the Cottonian Library. They were oddly enough catalogued for sale and sold as of 1667, and as engraved by Magdalene de Passe, one of the celebrated family of engravers of that name. The well-known signature of M P in monogram, which some of the set bear, almost certainly signifies Martin Poeham, who is known to have

---

* Hugh Rhodes, *Boke of Nurture*, 1577.   † *Test. Ebor.*, 1358.

worked after Aldegrever's designs, although it is described as
that of "un graveur inconnu" in some of the best dictionaries.
Other engravings by the same hand and bearing the same
mark are dated 1577. These very plates had supplied Mr.
Octavius Morgan many years ago with the shape of the small
old English ƙ proper to the year 1567.

Similar plates of the years 1568 and 1569 have also been
noted by Mr. Morgan, as in the possession some years since of
Messrs. Thomas of New Bond Street. This class of plate will
not fail to remind the antiquary of those curious sets of little
painted sycamore-wood trenchers, which he knows by the name
of "roundels." Much has been said of these interesting objects,
and the learning on the subject has been collected in a contri-
bution to the *Portfolio* (Sept. 1885), by Prof. A. H. Church.
Their use and the meaning of the posies upon them has been
alike discussed, but possibly the simplest explanation is the
best, that they were for serving fruit or cheese. More than one
reference of Elizabethan date quoted by Prof. Church points
to this, and no doubt the silver plates were used for the same
purposes.

Dinner-plates of silver with shaped and gadrooned edge, are
found commonly in the eighteenth, and sometimes of the preceding, century, replacing the simple pewter of a still earlier
period. For the reason of this we must appeal for a second
time to Prof. Wilson.

> NORTH. Deep must be the foundation and strong the superstructure, of that
> friendship which can sustain the shock of seeing its object eating mock-turtle
> soup from a plate of imitation silver.
> SHEPHERD. Meaner than pewter !*

There was no "imitation silver" to fall back upon in the
seventeenth century, and pewter becoming in the reign of
Charles II. too mean for the times, the only substitute was
silver itself. Dishes and dinner-plates of this more costly
material accordingly began to make their appearance. Prince
Rupert buys five dozen plates, amongst other things, of
Alderman E. Backwell in 1670, and Prince George of Denmark
24 plates and 24 trenchers of Child and Rogers in 1686. These
plates weighed 17¾ ounces each, and were paid for at the rate

---

* *Noctes Ambrosianæ*, No. XXXI.

of 5s. 8d. per ounce.   The trenchers were 21 ounces each, and
cost the same per ounce as the plates.   Very early examples
are the plates of the year 1686, still to be found amongst the
family plate of the Earls Bathurst.

Lord St. Oswald has a set of as early a year as 1697, part of
it made by one Chadwick, and the rest by a smith named
Gibson.   A very similar set of 1732, bearing a maker's mark
known as Paul Crespin's, belongs to Lord Hotham.   After that
they are of common occurrence.   An enormous number, with
dishes to match, were made by Paul Lamerie for the Mansion
House in 1737, and are in regular use there.

FORKS.

These are a modern invention compared with spoons ; so
much so that, to avoid doing our ancestors grave injustice, we
shall be glad to agree with the learned de Laborde, who speaking of forks, and remembering that the exquisites of Greece
and Rome all ate with their fingers, concluded that the use of
forks at meals is rather a conventional matter than a test by
which to measure the advance of civilization.

Certain it is that no mention of forks is to be found in our
fifteenth century treatises on etiquette and manners; whilst in
early wills and inventories no forks ever occur, except now and
then one or two mounted in crystal or other ornamental
handles, and used for eating pears or green ginger.   These had
usually two prongs only.

The *Boke of Kervyng*, directing the servitor to "laye your
knyves and set your brede one lofe by an other your spones
and your napkyns fayre folden besyde your brede," would have
told him where to dispose his forks, had there been any ; and
the *Boke of Nurture* in 1577 would have included them in its
caution against the improper use of the knife which runs as
follows :—

> Pick not thy teeth with thy knyfe,
>   nor with thy fyngers end,
> But take a stick, or some cleane thyng
>   then doe you not offende.

Again, the *Young Children's Book* only warns its readers not
to play with "spone trencher ne knyffe," not adding fork.

Even later than this, the long and detailed inventory of the goods of Dr. Perne, Master of Peterhouse, Cambridge, which is dated May 10, 1589, only mentions one fork, but spoons and every other sort of table-plate in abundance. The entry mentioning this single fork is rather a curious one.

Item, a peece of plate having in it a chafinge dyshe vj spones one forke ij gobletts ij cuppes ij saltes vi trenchers and a pepper box, all waying vii^{xx}xj ounces—xxxviiⁱⁱ.

The common use of the fork was introduced from Italy about the beginning of the seventeenth century ; and a well-known passage from Coryat's *Crudities* has been often cited as the first mention of forks in England. That gentleman, describing in 1611 his travels in Europe, notes the "little fork" used by the Italians instead of their fingers, when they cut meat out of the dish, and records how he was called *furcifer* by a friend when he continued the use of his fork on his return home. Their Italian origin is also referred to by Ben Jonson, who speaking of the manners of Venice, puts into the mouth of Sir Politick Would-be—

> . . . Then you must learn the use
> And handling of your silver fork at meals.
> *Volpone or the Fox*, Act IV. Sc. 1.

This was written in 1607, but a few years later (1616) the same writer speaks of them as known in England :—

> SLEDGE. Forks ! what be they?
> MEER.   The laudable use of forks,
>   Brought into custom here, as they are in Italy,
>   To the sparing of napkins.
> *The Devil is an Ass*, Act V. Sc. 3.

Massinger too, about the same time, recognises the use of the fork in polite society :—

> I have all that's requisite
> To the making up of a signior . . .
> . . . and my silver fork
> To convey an olive neatly to my mouth.
> *The Great Duke of Florence*, Act III.

This fork for eating olives might be one of the more ancient kind, but at all events the employment of dinner-forks was now becoming more general, and a fork was added to the knife and spoon which most persons seem to have carried about with them for their own use wherever they went. The same knife, fork

and spoon no doubt served for the whole meal, perhaps wiped
and sometimes washed, for few families had any great number,
especially of forks.   The large dinner-forks which we now cali
" table " forks are said to have been first used in France by the
Duke de Montausier, circa 1645.   Prince Rupert purchased
24 forks with his plates in 1670, and Prince George of Denmark
a dozen in 1686, besides his plates and trenchers.   These cost,
the spoons, two shillings apiece for the making, and the forks
two shillings and sixpence, besides the silver at 5s. 2d. per
ounce.   A set of twelve forks amongst the domestic plate at
Cotehele was made in 1667, and it is believed that these are
the oldest now in use.   They were probably all that the Sir
Richard Edgcumbe of that day possessed, and were no doubt
considered an unusually handsome equipage.   They have plain
flat handles like the spoons of the period, of which the spoon
No. 2 in the engraving given at page 283 is an example; but
the tops are not so much cleft, the two side projections being
rounded off like the central one.   One of the handles is
lengthened out to form a marrow-spoon.   Another such set is
mentioned by Viscount Gort in *Notes and Queries*, as bought by
one of his ancestors, in 1698, of a Dublin silversmith named
Bolton, whose account for them was as follows:—" For 12
forks, wt. 30 oz. 14 dwt. at 6s. 10d. per oz., £10 10s."   There
are only seven forks in a long Tredegar inventory of 1676.   All
these would resemble our wood-cut, No. 99.

A split-ended, flat-handled fork of the year 1683 with four
prongs has been dug up in the grounds of Eden Hall.   It bears
the Musgrave crest engraved in the fashion of that day, and if
genuine it must take rank as the most ancient English four-
pronged table-fork known.   Most probably, however, this fork
has been fashioned out of a spoon.

When the custom arose, most likely in the early part of the
eighteenth century, of the host supplying his own table with
the plate requisite for the use of his guests, a much larger quantity was needed, and more and more as time went on.   Mr.
Octavius Morgan suggests that a great deal of old-fashioned, un-
used plate—ewers and basins and the like—was, in the middle
years of the eighteenth century, melted down to supply this new
want; and that the magnificent services of gilt and silver plate
which were then made for royal and other tables were provided

in this way.   An enormous quantity of metal must have been
required to provide silver for the number of plates, dishes, sauce-
boats* (never found much before the reign of
George II.), spoons and forks, which were made
by Rundell and Bridge, the Garrards, and other
firms their immediate predecessors, and the spoon
and fork makers of a hundred or more years ago;
and, as at that period old plate was not valued,
every one was glad to change antiquated silver
articles for those of a newer and more useful fashion.
This will partly account for the comparatively
small quantity of ancient plate to be found in the
plate-rooms and treasuries of the present day.

The older dinner or table forks (see No. 99)
are three-pronged, but about the middle of the
eighteenth century four-pronged forks came into
fashion; the earliest four-pronged forks known to
the writer, except the Eden Hall fork above mentioned, are of the years 1726 and 1727, and are at
Narford Hall, Norfolk, but they were not common
before the reign of George the Third. The handles
of modern forks follow the fashions of spoons.

NOTES OF FORKS, ARRANGED IN CHRONOLOGICAL ORDER.

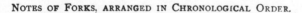

No. 99.—FORK
(TEMP. CHARLES II.)
DUG UP IN COVENT
GARDEN.

1300.   unum par cultellorum cum manicis argenti aymellat' cum
        uno furchetto de Cristallo.—Wardrobe Accounts,
        28 Edw. I.

1304.   duo furchetti arg' deaur' et duo manubriæ de cristallo.—
        Wardrobe Accounts, 32 Edw. I.

1349.   Henrico filio meo . . . dimidiam duodenam furcarum argenti deauratarum
        Margaretæ filiæ meæ . . . duas furcas argenti deauratas. (Will of Henry
        Lord Percy.)—Test. Ebor.

1395.   unum instrumentum argenteum pro zinzibo.—Idem.

1399.   j furche darg' poisant xv unc' di'.
        Itm ij furches p' zinzibr' v't darg' ennorrez.
        Im j fourche de beryle garnis darg' enorrez debrusez.
        Im j large furche d'arg' endorrez p' gingr vert pois vi unc t di.
        Itm j large fourche en p'tie endorrez meindre pois j unc'.—Treasury
        Accounts, 1 Hen. IV.

* The earliest sauce-boats are double-
spouted, so that the sauce could be poured
from either end, and have two handles
at the middle of the boat-shaped body,
one on each side, which facilitated the
passing of the vessel from hand to hand.

1443.   ij forkes for grene gynger.   (Will of Sir Hugh Willoughby.)—Test. Ebor.
1463.   my silver forke for grene ginger.—Bury Wills.
1487.   ij gynger forkes.   (Inv. of Robert Morton, gent.)—Brit. Mus. Add. MS.
        30,064.
1498.   a forke for grene gynger.   (Will of Anne Lady Scrope.)—Test. Ebor.
1500.   a prange of silver for grene gynger.—Will of Sir John Treffry, Knt.
1515.   a silver spone wt a forke.—Norf. Archæology.
1523   Itm too forkes with ther spones doble gylte to eete grene gynger with all.
        Itm one fork with hys spone parcell gylte to eete green gynger with all.
        Itm a forke of sylver doble gylte graved with lybertes on the end.—Inv. of
        Lady Hungerford, attainted 14 Hen. VIII.
1542.   A longe forke of silver for sokett.   (Will of Kateryne Ctess. of Northumber-
        land.)—Coll. Top. et Gen.
1554.   spone wt a forke in the end.
1567.   one long silver spone with a forke in the end double gilt.
1615.   a knife a spoone and forke of a greene and white stone garnished with gold.
        (Inv. of Duke of Somerset.)—Loseley MSS.

For more modern specimens see Chronological List, Appendix
A, 1667, 1715, 1727, 1737, 1738.

MONTEITHS.

The Monteith was a punch-bowl so called after a gentleman
of fashion, of the name of Monteith, who was remarkable for
wearing a scalloped coat.

> New things produce new words, and so Monteith
> Has by one vessel saved himself from Death.
> King's *Art of Cookery.*

Ant. à-Wood under 1683 mentions this vessel as follows:—
" This yeare in the summer time came up a vessel or bason
notched at the brim to let drinking-glasses hang there by the
foot, so that the body or drinking place might hang in the water
to cool them.   Such a bason was called a ' Monteigh,' from a
fantastical Scott called ' Monsieur Monteigh,' who at that time,
or a little before, wore the bottome of his cloake or coate so
notched."   It had a moveable rim, ornamented around the top
with escallops or else battlements to form indentations, in
which the glasses were placed with the feet outwards for the
purpose of bringing them into the room without breaking.
The bowl was of course brought in empty, the punch being
made in the room, each gentleman fancying he had an especial

talent for concocting the beverage, and a silver ladle and lemon-
strainer were brought in with it.   When the glasses were taken
out, the bowl was placed on the table, the rim was removed,
and the process of punch-making commenced.   The pierced
bowl of the old-fashioned wine-strainers (in general use when
gentlemen decanted their own port wine in the parlour) served
as a lemon-strainer, there being generally a small flat hook

NO. 100.—MONTEITH (1702), AT VINTNERS' HALL, LONDON.

at the side of it, by which it was appended to the side of the
bowl. *

Besides the characteristic rim, their fluted bowls should be
noted, their gadrooned bases or feet, and the large rings hanging from lions' mouths which are almost invariable,—amongst
the few exceptions known to the writer being one of the earliest
and one of the very latest specimens he has ever seen.   The
former has no handles, but all of the other characteristics
of the true Monteith ; it is of 1696, and is the property of the
Fishmongers' Company.   And the latter, which was given to

---

* The lemon-strainers with two long flat handles were no doubt also used with
these bowls.

the Clothworkers in 1718, by Sir John Bull, has bull's-head handles instead of lions' heads, the variation being, no doubt, adopted in allusion to the donor's name. The engraving (No. 100) is of a Monteith in the possession of the Vintners' Company.

The following references clearly mark the period of their introduction, and comprise the best Monteiths that the writer has had the opportunity of examining; but to these must be added a good and very early specimen noted by Mr. Morgan, the property of the Corporation of Newark. Its moveable rim is shaped like the top of a chess-castle, and it bears an inscription as follows:—" This Monteith and thirteen cups were given by the honourable Nicholas Saunderson of the Corporation of Newark upon Trent, A.D. 1689." A Monteith appears in 1690 as a " Mountbeth," in a list of the plate at Tredegar. In a later inventory of 1698 it is spelled " Monteth." For others see Appendix A, 1696, 1698, 1699 (three specimens), 1700 (two specimens), 1702, 1707, 1713, 1716, and 1718.

CANDELABRA, CANDLESTICKS, AND SCONCES.

These are occasionally, but not very frequently, mentioned in wills, accounts, and other documents of every period. There is, however, but little to be said about them that could not equally well be gathered from the subjoined lists. No really ancient specimens are known to exist in the precious metals, the earliest now to be found being the candlesticks shaped as fluted columns which are found in the reign of Charles II. (No. 101). They have square bases, which are sometimes cut off at the corners so as to become octagonal, and have also a projection to match the base, but smaller, and a convenient distance above it, to serve as a knop by which to hold or carry them. In the time of William and Mary, and of Queen Anne, the fashionable candlestick was equally simple, but with a baluster-stem, terminating in a square base, which has the corners cut off or else set back and rounded. Additional ornament was gradually added to the plain baluster. A candlestick of 1735 illustrates a transition period, after which, at about the middle of the last century, the baluster-stem already a little modified as will be seen by

the cut (No. 102) became much ornamented with the oblique
gadrooning of Louis XV. taste.   Towards 1765 this last finally
gave way to the Corinthian column pattern (No. 103), which
was the first, it may be observed in passing, that is always found
with removable socket-pans or nozzles.*   These Corinthian

No. 101.—CANDLESTICK (CIRCA 1670), AT PENIARTH.

columns in turn were replaced by candlesticks ornamented
with festoons of flowers, or drapery hanging between bosses
or medallions which bear masks or other devices of the
fashion introduced by those who designed for silversmiths
and potters of the time of Josiah Wedgwood.   Removable
nozzles are sometimes found on candlesticks of the reign
of Geo. II., but not often.   The sockets of the candlesticks
of the later part of the century are in many cases shaped as
vases ornamented with hanging wreaths.

---

* Their bases were sometimes formed as three or four square steps.

Silver sconces are very seldom seen ; there are good examples at Sudeley Castle, the back plate being repoussé and having a single branch for the light ending in a tulip-shaped cup.   They are of 1668.   Prince Rupert buys six sconces of Alderman E. Backwell in 1670.   At Knole a number of sconces are preserved, the back plates showing the Dorset arms and coronet in beaten-work.   Some of them bear the London marks for 1685.   The

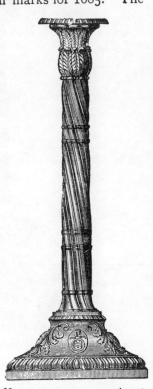

No. 102.—CANDLESTICK (1735).

No. 103.—CANDLESTICK (1773), AT NEW COLLEGE, OXFORD.

author has also seen a tiny toy-sconce by Anthony Nelme of the Queen Anne period bearing the arms of Russell on the back plate in a lozenge.   There is hardly a single entry of sconces in old-English wills ; but it may be as well to say that " un chandelier d'argent blanc, en manière d'esconce," occurs in the inventory of Charles V., which is ascribed by de Laborde to the year 1380.

1324.   Chaundelabres.—Indenture of plate, 17 Edw. III.
—   vi candelabr' arg. alb. et deaur. in pede.—Wardrobe Accounts temp. Edw. III.
1346.   duos candelabras argenti.   (Will of a Canon of York.)—Test. Ebor.
1400.   candelabra.   (Inv. of an Archdeacon of Richmond.)—Idem.
1438.   an hond candilstikke. —Treasury Inv. 16 Hen. VI.
1443.   chaundeliers of silver.   (Will of Sir Hugh Willoughby.)—Test. Ebor.
1453.   ij candilsticks of silver for qwerios parcell gilt.   (Will of John Lord Scrope.)—
        Idem.
1458.   ij rounde chaundelers of silver, w^t pykes.   (Will of Sir Thos. Cheworth.)—
        Idem.
1527.   four chaundelers, gilt prykettes for a table, ciij oz. (Inv. of Henry Fitzroy,
        Duke of Richmond.)—Camden Society.
1572.   vi candlesticks.—Inv. of Thos. Lee of Marton, co. Bucks.
1625.   one small silver candlesticke.—Inv. of Edward Waring of Lee.

For more modern examples, see Appendix A, 1668, 1685, 1690, 1699, 1715, 1716, 1721, 1734, 1735, 1759, 1775.

TOILET SERVICES AND BOUDOIR FURNITURE.

The luxury of the later years of the Stuarts is suitably illustrated by the rich toilet services which are one of its creations. They came into fashion at about the Chinese period of which mention has been made, and more than one set is found decorated in that style. They usually consist of a number of pieces of silver or silver-gilt, a mirror with silver frame, candlesticks, snuffers and trays, pin-cushion, tazze, boxes for trinkets and soap, sometimes a basin and ewer, and a variety of other articles. The set at Knole is perhaps the best known of all. It is composed of a number of toilet-boxes and a table-mirror, the boxes plain oblong and octagonal with frosted panels, and their covers bearing coronets and pierced cyphers fastened on with pins and nuts. The date of this service is 1673. There is also preserved at Knole a table entirely covered over with plaques of silver, beaten and chased with acanthus foliage, scrolls, amorini, etc. Like the toilet-boxes, it has coronets and pierced monograms attached in the same way ; in this case the initials are those of Frances Countess Dowager of Dorset and her second husband Henry Poole, Master of the Rolls, and M.P. for Cirencester. It was made in 1680. On each side of this table stand tall silver tripods (gueridons) for candlesticks, and above it hangs a mirror in silver framing to match the table. The tripods are of 1676, and the mirror was

probably made at the same time as the table, being evidently
of the same workmanship. The whole forms a suite of great
magnificence, and it was long supposed to have been provided
in anticipation of a visit of King James I. to Knole ; but there
is now no doubt that it was acquired by gift or purchase upon
occasion of the second marriage of the Countess Frances, whose
first husband Richard, 5th Earl of Dorset, had died in 1677. A
toilet-box from a service of the year 1682 is given as a good

NO. 104.--TOILET-BOX (1682).

specimen of engraving in the Chinese style (No. 104). Two
somewhat similar boxes of 1695 from the Marquis of Exeter's
Collection sold for 275 and 291 guineas respectively in 1888,
which was at the rate of about 60s. per oz. A pair of scent-
bottles at 82s. per oz., and a pair of small cups engraved with
birds at 130s. per oz. These were all by P. Harrache. Other
toilet-table sets are known of the years 1681, 1682, and 1683 ;
the Berners set, and the beautiful service formerly belonging
to the late Sir C. Trevelyan, Bart., and now in the South
Kensington Museum, being both of them of the latter year.
Sir F. A. Milbank, Bart., had a set of 1686. Somewhat later

ones were exhibited at South Kensington in 1862. One of the finest possible of eighteenth century sets is the property of Sir W. Williams-Wynn, Bart. It is gilt in the very best Louis XV.

No. 105.—FIRE-DOG (CIRCA 1685), AT KNOLE.

taste, and of the year 1768. One of the above earlier sets had lain for generations forgotten in the cellars of the Bank of England, where it had once upon a time been deposited for safe custody, and only came to light on the falling to pieces from age of the case containing it long after all record of its ownership had been lost. Heraldic or other internal evidence was, however, forthcoming, which enabled the authorities to restore it to the descendants of the original owners. It is very possible that other treasures remain unknown in the same repository.

There are several boudoir-tables, either made of or mounted with silver plaques like those at Knole. Amongst them are two at Windsor Castle. One of these is of the time of Charles II., the other a little later. Silver fire-dogs or andirons also occur of the same period and fashion. Examples of these are preserved both at Windsor and Knole; and reproductions in facsimile of the fire-dogs and the tables in these collections may be seen in the South Kensington Museum.

Of the andirons there are no better examples than those at Knole, from one of which No. 105 is taken. A pair of fire-dogs of the first year of George I. is known to the author.

With these the large jars mentioned at a previous page naturally class themselves. They mark both the luxurious fashions of this part of the seventeenth century and the Chinese taste which prevailed, as we have seen, in the reigns of James II. and of William and Mary. No. 106 is also from Knole,

WINE CISTERNS AND FOUNTAINS.

Not less magnificent than the boudoir furniture that has just been mentioned are the great wine-cisterns that are found of the same period. These cisterns range from 1665 to 1735, but the earlier ones are not accompanied by fountains. The oldest are of gigantic size, and their use may be indicated by the fact that one of the finest of them, now at Welbeck, bearing Harley arms, was made in the year in which the great statesman Robert Harley, who became in turn Speaker, Lord High Treasurer, and Earl of Oxford and Mortimer, came of age. This was in 1682. The great cistern at Belvoir Castle was bought of Child and Rogers in 1681. Its weight was 1,979½ oz., and its cost £616 10s. A still earlier one, of 1667, was amongst the plate of the Cootes, Earls of Mountrath. The later ones are somewhat smaller, and have fountains or great covered urns or vases with taps. It has been conjectured that those which have already been mentioned in the preface to this chapter, in speaking of ambassadors' and other official services of plate, were really not used for wine but for washing-up the forks as required on the sideboard. The finest and largest of such pieces is a cistern at the Winter Palace, St. Petersburg, made in 1734 by one Charles Kandler, a silversmith in London, from a design by Henry Jernegan (No. 107). It weighs nearly 8,000 ounces, and holds 60 gallons. Perhaps the most immense and one of the most elaborate pieces of decorative plate in the world, it is no doubt the very cistern referred to in the Journals of the House of Commons for 1735 in a somewhat curious connection. In that year a lottery was authorised by Parliament for raising the funds necessary for building a new bridge over the Thames at Westminster; and this same Jernegan is found petitioning the House to take as a lottery prize a very magnificent cistern upon which he had expended a vast sum of money and years of work, and which had been pronounced by all to excel anything of the kind that had ever been attempted.

No. 106.—JAR (CIRCA 1685), AT KNOLE.

He represented, that although he had offered it to various foreign sovereigns through their ambassadors, it remained upon his hands unsold, and in the end Parliament ordered its disposal in the lottery. How it got eventually to the Winter Palace, the author, who himself discovered it there, has not yet been able to ascertain, though an old engraving describes it as " the property of the Empress of Russia."

The first design or sketch for this great cistern seems to have been made by G. Vertue, who presented his drawing to the Society of Antiquaries in 1740. This differs in many particulars from the finished piece, but in a note on the drawing in Vertue's own writing, it is described as his own design, and as " exhibited

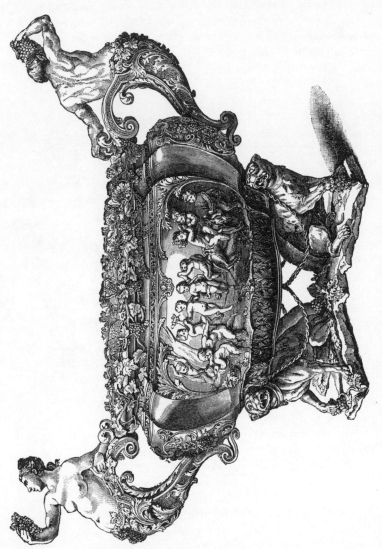

No. 107.—WINE CISTERN (1734), AT THE WINTER PALACE, ST. PETERSBURG.

to the publick when finished " by Mr. Henry Jerningham.   The
same note records that in the lottery it was won by . . .
Batten, Esq., of Sussex; that the modeller in wax was M.
Rysbrake for the figures and basso-relievos ; and that whilst
several chasers were employed to finish it, the work took at
least three years to complete.*

CASTERS AND CRUET-STANDS.

Of these the former first occur at the commencement of the
eighteenth century, or a few years earlier, and are occasionally
found of great size.   The larger ones must have been intended
as standing-pieces for the decoration of sideboards ; but it would
be difficult to produce legal proof of the genuineness of some
of the specimens that have changed hands of late years.   The
natural tendency of a demand to create a corresponding supply
should never be forgotten by the plate-collector any more than
by the economist.   A gigantic sugar-caster is often doubtful,
about in proportion to its size.

One of the earliest cruet-stands known is of plain massive
silver with five rings and central handle, the rings containing
two glass cruets with plain silver caps to slip over the necks by
way of stoppers, and three shaped casters of silver with pierced
tops for sugar, pepper, etc.—one large, and two to match of
smaller size.   These are of much the same fashion as the sets
of three casters so often seen, of dates ranging from 1720 to
1770, but they are of plainer fashion than more modern
examples.   This cruet-stand is by Pyne, made in 1706, and
is the property of Lord Tredegar.   The separate casters above
mentioned seemed to have formerly formed part of the fittings
of cruet-stands.   See Appendix A, 1706, 1733, 1734, 1758, 1775.
Count A. B. Bobrinsky of Moscow possesses beautiful sets of
casters fitting into a great cruet-frame or centre-piece, the work
of Paul Lamerie in 1735.

TEA AND COFFEE SERVICES, KETTLES, ETC.

Tea and coffee must have been well known in England many
years before we find silver tea-pots or coffee-pots in common
use.   Ant. à Wood mentions the first introduction of coffee and

---

* Soc. Antiq. Lond.   Drawings presented by G. Vertue.   Vol. I., f. 83.

coffee-houses into Oxford in the year 1650. Tea follows in
1664. A toy tea-pot with tea-cup and tea-spoon of the year
1690 is known. This is also about the date of the first earthenware tea-pots. The earliest tea-pot known to the author in
actual domestic use is of 1682. It is of hexagonal form, each
side forming a panel chased with Chinese scenes, very minute
in detail, and deeply cut. It must have been copied exactly

No. 108.—OCTAGONAL COFFEE-POT (1715), THE PROPERTY OF AUTHOR.

from a Chinese original. The second is of 1709. This has a
raised conical lid and a small flap shutter to the spout; and is
closely followed by specimens in the possession of the Earl
of Ilchester and Earl Amherst. A few small melon-shaped
tea-pots are found about 1685; but a great number of tea
and coffee pots, tea-caddies, and kettles were made in the
reigns of George I. and George II., at first of very plain
design, but afterwards more freely ornamented with chasing
and repoussé work.

The coffee-pot of the reign of George I. was a plain one, tall and tapering, often octagonal, and with a conical octagonal lid to match (No. 108). Tea-pots are found of very similar fashion as far as regards the lids, but with the round or octagonal body swelling out at the lower part into a bowl instead of having

No. 109.—COFFEE-POT (1764), AT SALTERS' HALL, LONDON.

straight upright sides. Chocolate-pots of the Queen Anne period and later are of plain tapering cylindrical form, with lid to match, sometimes having a small hole at the apex, with a flap cover to admit the pestle or stirring rod.

In the time of George II. and the early days of George III. (No 109) gadroons and flower-wreaths in the Louis Quinze taste will be looked for; and later on, oval tea-pots engraved with festoons, knots of riband and medallions, are usually found.

Tea-kettles are found from the first years of the century. The earliest are globular, either quite plain, or with a little

engraving; sometimes they are fluted so as to resemble melons
or gourds. They are always on openwork stands, with feet;
and to these, spirit-lamps, often of a later date, are fitted.

There is no better example of the melon-shaped tea-kettle
than one in the royal collection at Windsor Castle; it has been

No. 110.—TEA-URN (1771), AT BARBER-SURGEONS' HALL, LONDON.

copied for the South Kensington Museum. This stands in a
triangular tray, and is of the year 1732.

Later in the century urns succeeded to kettles; many of them
are of the pointed oval shape then so popular, and are chased or
engraved with festoons and medallions to match the tea-pots of
the period. (See No. 110.)

Tea-caddies are not commonly found till the time of George II.;
but all through that reign sets of two tea-caddies and a basin
fitted into shagreen cases were very fashionable. Some of them
afford good examples of chased flowers and foliage, which are

very sharply executed in high relief. Such caddies were often also supplied with a small spoon with pierced bowl and long pointed handle used for straining the tea and clearing the spout of the tea-pot before the introduction of the fixed strainer at the inner end or insertion of the spout. These are often but erroneously called straw-berry-spoons.

Of the minor accessories to the tea-table, a few words may be said. A wire basket or strainer was sometimes hung in the spout of the tea-pot, answering the same purpose as the pierced spoon.

Of another kind was " the silver strainer, on which, in more economical times than ours, the lady of the house placed the tea-leaves, after the very last drop had been ex-hausted, that they might after-wards be hospitably divided amongst the company to be eaten with sugar, and with bread and butter."* About tea-spoons there is nothing to be said that cannot be gathered from the general article on spoons. A very small toy tea-spoon, only two inches long,

No. 111.—CHOCOLATE-POT (1777), IN THE SOUTH KENSINGTON MUSEUM.

of the year 1689, and having the usual flat handle of those days, is the oldest tea-spoon of any kind known to the author. Cream-jugs simply follow the fashion of larger vessels ; the earliest being plain, solid, and slightly bellied like miniature blackjacks, with the same short spouts and no stem nor foot. Others are like tiny helmet ewers, whilst later ones are of rococo or of Louis XV. design, and the latest not unlike the

---

* St. Ronan's Well, chap. x.

chocolate-pot 1777 given on the preceding page (No. 111), but
with a small square foot and without the lid.

CAKE-BASKETS AND EPERGNES.

These are classed together because the former often formed
the central or uppermost portion of the latter, and they are of
precisely similar style of workmanship. They are objects of considerable importance in the plate-collections of the eighteenth
century, and great taste and skill were expended upon their

No. 112.—CAKE-BASKET (1731), BY PAUL LAMERIE.

production. Most of them were made between 1730 and 1780.
An early basket of a design peculiar to Paul Lamerie (No. 112),
was acquired by the late Mr. J. C. Dent of Sudeley Castle, at the
Strawberry Hill sale. The bottom is engraved with the arms of
Sir Robert Walpole, encircled with the Garter, but without a
coronet. It will be remembered that Sir Robert enjoyed the rare
distinction of the Garter whilst still a commoner. This cake-
basket is of imitation wicker-work, with handles of the same.

A more elaborate example by the same good hand is the
property of the Count Bobrinsky at Moscow. It consists of
a basin on feet as the centre, with baskets round it which

may be removed, and has candlestick branches, double sets of casters, and cruets, which may be substituted for the baskets or for each other at will. It is of the year 1735. The body of the central bowl is chased as wicker-work.

To this, which seems to have been a favourite pattern, succeeded the pierced baskets ornamented also with chasing and repoussé work, which were very common in the middle of the century. Many of them are of excellent design and

No. 113.—CAKE-BASKET (1749), BY PAUL LAMERIE.

finish. One of the finest, in the possession of Lady Amherst of Hackney, is amongst the latest and most remarkable specimens of the work of Paul Lamerie, being of the year 1749. An engraving of this is given (No. 113); the chasing of the insects is of the very highest excellence.

The piercing of the later baskets is sometimes rather rude; the holes being merely punched out of the sheet of silver without much additional ornament except some intervening rows of small punched bosses.

During the last quarter of the century baskets were not

pierced, but are solid and either fluted or lobed like escallops, or ornamented with chased bands of foliage.

Where these pierced baskets form the crowning ornament of epergnes, or centre-pieces for table decoration, they are accompanied by a number of smaller baskets of the same design as the large one, all of which could be detached from the branched stand which supported them, and handed with the fruits or sweetmeats they were made to contain. A very massive epergne of open scroll work chased with fruit and flowers, a basket in the centre and branches with leaf-shaped dishes on a stand with fruits and animals' heads in high relief, was sold in 1888 for £360. It was of 1755 and by Edward Wakelin.

Many examples are noted in Appendix A.

MACES AND OARS.

A notice of English plate would be incomplete without a few words about corporation maces and oars. Originally, no doubt, weapons of offence, in modern times maces have become mere symbols of authority or emblems of State. Imagination easily carries us back to the days when the escort of some great personage bore simple clubs upon their shoulders with which to clear the way. We may watch the growth of the simple club into an elaborate weapon, and of the elaborate weapon into a work of art, useless for any purpose but adding to the state of legal, civic or academic dignitary. Somehow or other maces seem to have got turned upside-down in the course of these changes; for the handles of some of the more ancient, as they are now borne, look very like the heads, as they would have been used in case of being required for real work.

The city of London with its various wards can show as many as thirty maces, but none of them are as ancient as some of those in the possession of provincial corporations : two of the very oldest being at Hedon in Yorkshire. These are of the fifteenth century. Not much more modern are the small pair (No. 114), which belong to the little town of Winchcombe in Gloucestershire. They are 15½ inches long. The handles of these are an admirable illustration of what has been said above as to the changing of ends. Very uncomfortable to grasp, they are well fitted to form the striking heads of weapons of offence. A degree more modern, especially as regards the head and plain handle, is the Great Mace of Morpeth (No. 115), for an illustration of which the author was indebted to the late Mr. R. S. Ferguson.*

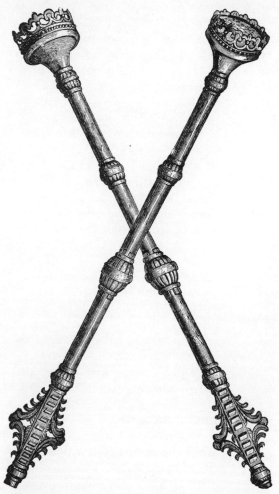

No. 114.—MACES AT WINCHCOMBE. CO. GLOUCESTER.

It is of silver, with bowl and knops gilt, has a cresting of thirty fleur-de-lis, and on the top the royal arms as borne by the Stuarts.   Below the cresting appears the inscription in italic

* *Archæological Journal*, XLII., p. 90.

No. 115.—MORPETH
GREAT MACE (1604).

characters, describing it in Latin as the gift of
William Howard, Lord of Morpeth, and the
lady Elizabeth, his wife, in 1604. Then
under a cable moulding come eight shields
with the Howard arms and quarterings; and
below the foot another coat, in Mr. Ferguson's opinion once undoubtedly enamelled,
but from which the coloured matter has completely disappeared. It is 26½ inches in
length.

The period of small maces with uncrowned
heads about ends with the reign of James I.
The arched crown occasionally found in the
time of Charles I., and rather oftener, if of
different fashion, under the Commonwealth,
becomes usual at the Restoration ; and from
the middle of the century, State maces increased immensely in size also.   Smaller
maces too from this period, as made for persons and places of less than the first importance, are mostly reproductions of the large
examples on a reduced scale.   Sometimes
crowns have been added to earlier maces,
and the crowns are all much alike.   The
mace of the ward of Cheap (No. 116) is the
earliest of the London maces, and is a good
example of a mace of the time of Charles I.,
with a more modern crown. This addition was
made in 1678, at the request of the Ward, as
one of the inscriptions upon it tells.

It will be noticed that the arches spring
from a narrow band, which is evidently itself
an addition also.   The remainder of the bowl
with its cresting, which has been mutilated
to make room for the upper band, together
with the shaft, give a good idea of the earlier
maces. When the city maces were exhibited
at the Society of Antiquaries in 1860, this
one was selected for engraving by Mr. Octavius
Morgan, because it so admirably illustrated

the changes which maces underwent at various times.

The bowls are usually ornamented with royal badges that fix their date; but most of the maces then in existence underwent alteration in this respect in pursuance of an order of Parliament made in 1649, the arms of the Commonwealth being substituted for royal bearings. Mr. A. P. Humphry notes that the cost of this change in the case of the four maces of the University of Cambridge was £9 17s. 3d. The expense of restoring the royal arms on the Yeoman-Bedell's mace in 1663 is also recorded. The considerable difference between maces as agreeable to Commonwealth notions and those of Royal pattern, may be gathered from Mr. W. H. St. John Hope's general description of the Commonwealth maces still preserved at Congleton, Buckingham, and several other places.* He notices that "the coronet consisted, not of regal fleur-de-lis and crosses, but of an intertwined cable enclosing small cartouches with a St. George's cross for England and a harp for Ireland, and instead of a jewelled circlet there was a band inscribed 'THE FREEDOME OF ENGLAND BY GOD'S BLESSING RESTORED' with the date of the making of the mace. The jewelled or beaded arches of the crown were replaced by four gracefully curved members like ostrich feathers, but adorned

* *Reliquary*, N.S., Vol. V., No. 1.

No. 116.—MACE OF WARD OF CHEAP, LONDON (1625).

with oak foliage, which nearly met in the centre, and supported
not the time-honoured orb and cross but a handsome cushion
wrought with cartouches of the arms of England and Ireland and
surmounted by an acorn. The staff was chased throughout with
longitudinal branches of oak or other foliage encircled by a
narrow spiral riband and the knots were wrought with spirally
laid gadroons." Some public attention has on more than one
occasion been devoted to the history of the mace borne before
the Speaker of the House of Commons, and various opinions
given as to whether the present mace is or is not one of these
Commonwealth maces remodelled at the Restoration. Nothing
is now known of any mace which may have been used before
1649; but it is clear that a new one was provided in pursuance
of an Order of the House in that year, and that it was made by
one Thomas Maundy or Mandye of Fetter Lane, London, who
was to have a monopoly of the making of " all other great maces
to be used in this Commonwealth " according to the same form
and pattern as that which was ordered for use in the House of
Commons. The mark of this worthy is to be found on maces
at Gloucester, dated 1660. In 1650 he made a new mace for
Wallingford, allowing a sum of £10 2s. 6d. for older maces
made in 1615 by Anthony Bennett of the Sunne in Foster
Lane. The stem of the mace now at Wallingford is that of
Maundy's mace of 1650, though the mace is now royalist in
other respects. This is also the case at Gloucester. Here
economy seems to have been a consideration; and the changes
necessary in 1660 were carried out with strict regard to it;
for we find that the sword and maces were to be altered only,
and that the mayor was charged to "cause the same to be
done to the best advantage of the chamber." The present
maces at Gloucester are these very altered ones, the heads of
which were then re-made with royal emblems and arched
crowns, whilst the old shafts with their diaper of oak foliage
and acorns, appropriate to Commonwealth times, were retained.
All four appear to be of the same make, though two of them
are dated as of 1652 and the other two as of 1660, only the
latter having Maundy's mark. According to the Corporation
accounts, the whole set with the sword were bought of Aldn.
Vyner of London in 1651 for £85 5s. 0d., and were altered in
1660 by Mr. Cuthbertes of London, goldsmith, at the further

cost of £74 1s. 0d. The date of 1660 was no doubt placed
upon two of the maces, together with the name of the mayor
for that year, Toby Jordan, in course of the alteration: and
Aldn. Vyner must have employed Maundy to make them, as
one who devoted his attention specially to the manufacture
of such articles. Returning to the House of Commons mace
and the question whether it is in reality " the fool's bauble "
of Cromwell's high-handed proceedings in 1653, under a newer
royalist guise given it at the Restoration, or is an entirely new
one made in pursuance of a further Order of the House—which
resolved on May 21, 1660, " That two new maces be forthwith
provided, one for this House, and the other for the Counsell of
State with the Crowne and the King's Majesties Armes and
such other ornaments as have bin usuall, and it is referred to
the Counsell of State to take care that the same be provided
accordingly "—the weight and the make of the present mace
both indicate that it is an entirely new one, made in 1660.

In the first place it is probable* that Maundy's mace was
considerably lighter than the present one. The goldsmith
himself states in a letter preserved amongst the records of the
borough of Leicester that he was paid at the rate of 13s. 4d.
per ounce for it; and from the orders of Parliament it may be
gathered that its cost was £146 11s. 8d. This gives its weight
as 219 oz. 14 dwt.; whereas that of the present mace is
engraved on the head as 251. 2. 2, which rather understates its
present weight than otherwise. This is not perhaps in itself a
discrepancy of much importance; but when we come to the
fashion of the mace as it is, it seems to the author that the fact
of the royal badges—rose, thistle, harp, and fleur-de-lys—being
hammered out of the solid material of which the head of the
present mace is formed, is as conclusive that it is practically
a new head of 1660, even if the old metal was used again, as
the fact that the diaper on the stem reproduces the rose and
thistle found on the head—royal emblems which were certainly
not on the head of the Commonwealth mace—is indicative of
the stem being of the same date as the head itself. It would

---

* These extracts from the House of
Commons Journals and the Leicester
Records are taken from a paper by Mr.
W. H. St. John Hope, in the *Reliquary*,
New Series, Vol. V., p. 26.

have been even more difficult to re-engrave the stem than to alter the head. If this is so, there is very little left of the "fool's bauble" now. In reality the mace now appertaining to the Serjeant-at-Arms attending upon the Speaker of the House of Commons, and the two maces similarly used by the House of Lords (two being required in this case, as the Lord Chancellor is sometimes sitting in Court, and by deputy in the House of Lords at the same time) are three out of the eleven maces in all possessed by the Lord Chamberlain's Department, and borne by His Majesty's ten Serjeants-at-arms. The House of Commons mace is returned to that Department when the House is not in session; whilst the Upper House provides for the safe custody of the maces of the Serjeant-at-Arms in attendance upon the Lord Chancellor. The other eight Serjeants-at-Arms are seldom required to bear their symbols of office; and as these maces are kept at the Tower they are familiar objects to sightseers.

The author has had opportunities of carefully examining most of the eleven maces, including those at the Houses of Lords and Commons. All these are of the second half of the seventeenth century, and four of them bear the marks of well-known goldsmiths; two being by Francis Garthorne, who enjoyed much royal favour, and other two by a maker, like him, of the last quarter of the century. It is just worth adding that the maces are most of them so much alike in size, their general length being about 4 feet 10 inches, as well as in weight and appearance, that in days when no great attention was paid to such matters, almost any one of them might have been issued for use after a Parliamentary recess in mistake for its fellow, though there is no ground for saying that this has ever actually happened. At any rate the mace now used at the House of Commons is wholly of the Charles II. period, and too closely resembles several of the others to make it in the least degree probable that any part of it is of more ancient date than the year 1660. No more typical example of the usual mace of the later half of the seventeenth century could be found than the mace given to the Corporation of Norwich in 1671 by Lord Henry Howard.

It shows every characteristic of the maces at either House of Parliament, and, indeed, is so very like them, as well as the other maces at the Tower, in general appearance, that the engraving of it (No. 117) would serve almost equally well for any of them.

Reference was once made by Mr. Speaker Peel* to the tradition held in Jamaica that a mace at Kingston, in that island, is the veritable "fool's bauble," which is supposed by some to have found a home there when turned out of the House by Cromwell. It is true that an older mace than either of the two now preserved in the island was once in existence. This was taken out by Lord Windsor, temp. Charles II., as a present to the House of Assembly, and was long supposed to have been lost at the time of the great earthquake of 1692, when Port Royal was overwhelmed, its houses engulfed forty fathoms deep by the sea. Though this is doubtful, as at a Council held at St. Jago July 11, 1692, the mending of the mace was ordered, which looks as if it had been damaged, not lost, it has since disappeared.† It seems to have been a little overlooked that the "fool's bauble" of 1649 would have required very great alteration before it was fit to send out as a royal present to a colony in 1664. The present maces in Jamaica, which have not been in use of late years owing to the changed form of government in the colony, and are now deposited in the Institute for safe custody, are comparatively modern. The older one is of the year 1753, and was made by Mordecai Fox, of London; and the newer mace by the hand of Henry Green, also of London,

No. 117.—THE "HOWARD" MACE (1671), AT NORWICH.

* In a speech at Leamington, August, 1890.
† Journal of the Institute of Jamaica, Vol. I., No. 7, p. 287, communicated by Mr. F. Cundall, F.S.A.

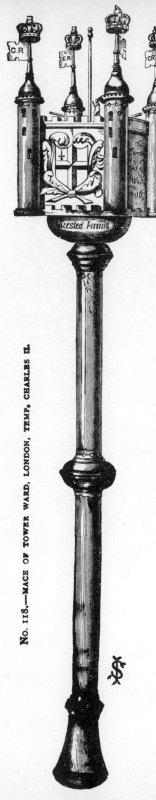

dates from 1787. They are both of great size, being about 5 feet 4 inches in length, and the mace of 1753 weighs no less than 297¼ oz. There are other good specimens in the West Indies. The Speaker's mace at Barbadoes is a fine one supplied by Rundell and Bridge in 1812; and the Grenada mace made, like the later mace at Kingston, Jamaica, by Henry Green in 1781, is 276 oz. in weight, being almost as massive as the Jamaica mace of 1753.*

It may be of interest to add to these notes that a mace now used by the Speaker of the House of Representatives at Charleston, South Carolina, U.S.A., is of 1756, the work of Magdalen Feline, of London. All kinds of traditions quite inconsistent with its real date have attached themselves to this mace, as to others. Sometimes the heads of maces are made to unscrew from the shaft and to fasten on to short stems with feet so as to form standing cups, the arched crowns also being removable and serving as covers. This is the case with the mace-heads of the towns of Cambridge and Gravesend. A standing cup called the "Godwin cup," preserved at Berkeley Castle, is formed of a mace-head of the time of James I.

---

* Most of these interesting notes of maces in the West Indies were made for the author by the late Mr. Stanley Leighton, M.P., who visited those islands in the autumn recess of 1890.

mounted as a drinking-cup in the same way. The stems of maces are quite plain in older examples; but in Commonwealth times it was the fashion to chase them with a diaper of oak foliage, and afterwards of rose, or rose and thistle.

As an example of a mace of exceptional form, is given an engraving (No. 118) of the mace of the Tower Ward, London. The tower head is of the reign of Charles II. Eighteenth century maces are very common —Paul Lamerie made a small pair at Hythe in 1744. The grand maces at Rye and Winchelsea are by T. Heming in 1767. They follow the fashion of maces of the Charles II. period; and differ from one another, and from our typical engraving (No. 117) of such maces, only in matters of details.

Certain sea-port towns have maces formed as silver oars. There are large and small oars of this description. The larger ones were used as maces and symbolized the Admiralty jurisdiction of the town. Specimens are preserved at Southampton, Rochester, Dover, and Yarmouth, whilst a fine one, formerly at Boston, is now the property of Earl Brownlow. The smaller ones were borne by the water-bailiffs. They are made to contain the oar inside the barrel when not in use, the blade being pulled out, reversed, and screwed into one end of the handle when required to be shown by the water-bailiff as an emblem of authority on occasion of arresting anyone on board ship. Such as these were to be found at Rochester, Colchester, Dover, and Deal, but the last mentioned is now in private hands. As illustrations are given the large and small oar-maces (Nos. 119 and 120) at Dover. The larger oar is the mace of the Cinque Ports Admiralty Court held

1

NO. 119.—OAR-MACE (C. 1690) OF CINQUE PORTS ADMIRALTY COURT.

from time immemorial in St. James's Church there, and is of the end of the seventeenth century. Of very much the same fashion is the oar-mace of the High Court of Admiralty; but of this no part is older than 1798, except the royal arms and supporters on the blade, which have been transferred from some older mace, and are temp. Henry VII. It was re-made by Pitts and Preedy in 1798.

The case of the small oar is of brass. Oars are of all periods, from the Elizabethan example at Boston (which must, however, have been modernized, or, in fact, re-made in 1725; for it bears the hall-marks of that year with the maker's mark of Benj. Pyne on every part of it), to the small oar of Deal, which is of the year 1819. The silver oar of the Governor of Bermuda is dated 1701, but was made in 1697. That of Great Yarmouth is of 1744; whilst the large Rochester oar is of 1748. The small Rochester oar was made in 1723, though it has the year 1721 inscribed upon it.

This is perhaps all that can be said about the oar-maces considered as articles of plate; but those who feel interested in their use and history may be referred to the *Archæological Journal*, Vol. XXX., page 91, and Vol. XXXI., page 82, for some additional particulars relating to them.

No. 120.—DOVER
WATER-BAILIFF'S MACE.

RACING AND COCKING BELLS.

Two curious cuts of racing and cocking bells were placed at the author's disposal by Mr. R. S. Ferguson, to complete the concluding section of this sketch of Old English Plate.

There are probably not many examples of either to be found.

The racing-bells (No. 121) are the property of the Corporation of Carlisle, and it would appear that such a prize was not an uncommon one there. Bells were also given, says Mr.

Ferguson, at York, and at Chester. The York bell in 1607 was of gold; the Chester one, about 1600, of silver only. A reference to these Chester bells will be found amongst the notes about the old goldsmiths of Chester (p. 110) in an earlier chapter: and a Scottish racing bell is mentioned in the chapter

No. 121.—RACING-BELLS (TEMP. ELIZ.), THE PROPERTY OF THE CORPORATION OF CARLISLE.

on Scottish Plate. This last, which is not unlike the cocking-bell engraved below, with the same closed mouth, has the addition of small hanging shields, the oldest dated 1628, which

No. 122.—COCKING BELL (1655).

is no doubt the date of the piece. Its traditional history, which has been given earlier, need not be repeated here.

The donor of the larger Carlisle bell was probably Elizabeth, daughter of George Talbot, fourth Earl of Shrewsbury, and wife of William Lord Dacre of Gillesland, who was Governor of Carlisle in the reign of Queen Elizabeth. It is of silver-gilt,

2¼ inches in diameter, and bears as shown in the woodcut the rhyming couplet for inscription—

✠ THE ✠ SWEFTES ✠ HORSE ✠ THES ✠ BEL ✠ TO ✠ TAK ✠
FOR ✠ MI ✠ LADE ✠ DAKER ✠ SAKE

The smaller bell bears the initials of Henry Baines, Mayor of Carlisle, in 1599. The Cocking-bell of 1655 (No. 122) is a curious relic of the Commonwealth, and may indicate that there was a lighter side to the severity which we are prone to identify with that period in the history of our arts, as well as of our manners.

CONCLUSION.

The history of plate-working in England has now been surveyed in as much detail as is possible within the compass of a general hand-book. Many of the subjects only touched upon here would require a volume if they were dealt with exhaustively, but enough has been said about each to give the plate-collector an idea of the varying fashions of each successive art period. The antiquary would wish to expand the notices of mazers or salts into chapters; the artist, to dwell upon the history of shapes and ornament at more suitable length; the working goldsmith, on the technicalities of the art-workmanship which distinguish many of the most remarkable pieces we have considered. But all will agree that there is a singular interest in English goldsmiths' work, and it is this: that whilst it has preserved to us in comparatively imperishable materials specimens of the art-workmanship of every decade, from the Gothic period to our own, it has given us at the same time the means of dating these specimens with far greater certainty and accuracy than is the case with any other series of art-objects that have come down to our time. In this way it becomes possible to use old English silver work as a key for the dating of very many and very different objects, which could only be assigned in a general way to their period in art-history, but for the indirect aid that our ancient English system of hall-marking has thus incidentally supplied. In no other way can the gradual melting of Gothic into Renaissance style be so delicately measured, or the sequence of the art-epochs which we are in the habit of calling by the names of the French monarchs of the eighteenth century. The accuracy with which both French and English silver work can be dated enables us to trace the style known generally as 'style de Louis XV.' through three separate developments, in a way that would otherwise be almost impossible; and the same may be said in a greater or less degree of almost every other well-known period from early days to the end of the eighteenth century. This is the point at which it has seemed convenient to break off the various notices which make up the foregoing sketch. The art of the goldsmith in the early days of the nineteenth century made less than no progress. Like other seasons of rest, this interval has in our times been followed by a revival which promises much, and especially in our own country; but it need hardly be said that a consideration of contemporary work, however interesting in itself, would be inconsistent with the design of a handbook on " Old English Plate."

APPENDIX A.

CHRONOLOGICAL LIST, PART I.,

OF

THE ARTICLES OF PLATE

WHICH HAVE SERVED AS AUTHORITY FOR

THE CONSTRUCTION OF THE TABLES OF DATE-LETTERS
USED AT GOLDSMITHS' HALL, LONDON,

AND FOR THE MAKERS' MARKS.

To be used with Part II. following it, as a single List.

In the following list, the years must be understood to begin in the month of May of the year given as the date, and to end in the same month of the year following :—

DATE	MAKER'S MARK.		ARTICLE AND OWNER.
			ALPHABET I. 1478—1497.
1479		Dimidiated fleur-de-lys.	Chalice and paten. Nettlecombe, Som.
1481	. .	. . . .	The Anathema Cup, given 1497. Pemb.Coll.Camb.
1491		. . . . .	Paten. Stow Longa, Hunts.
1493		. . .	Apostle-spoon. (Staniforth Coll.)*
1496		A pod with peas in it (?)	Paten. Costessey, Norf.
			ALPHABET II. 1498—1517.
1498	. .	. . . .	Pair of chalices. B.N.C. Oxford.
1499		. . . . .	The Leigh Cup. Mercers' Company.
Do.	. .	. . . .	Spoon. Alnwick Castle.
1500		. . . . . .	Spoon. (Staniforth Coll.)
1504		A barrel or ton	Paten. Happisbrough, Norf.
1506		. . . . .	Bp. Fox's spoons, with owls at the ends. C.C.C. Oxford.
1507		. . . .	Bp. Fox's gold chalice and paten. C.C.C.Oxford.

* Sold in London, May 1925, for £100.

DATE	MAKER'S MARK.		ARTICLE AND OWNER.
1507	(image)	A maidenhead, no shield.	Chalice and paten. West Drayton, Midx.
Do.	Do.	Do.	Mazer. Saffron-Walden Almshouse, Essex.
Do.	. .	A fish as in 1491 .	Foundress' beaker and hour-glass salt. Christ's Coll. Cambridge.
1508	(image)	No shield . . .	Mazer. Whitgift Charity, Croydon, Surrey.
1509	(image)	Two links of chain .	Paten. Hockham Parva, Norf.
1510	(image)	No shield . . .	Mazer. (Franks Coll.)
1511	. .	. . . . .	Cup used as chalice. Chewton Mendip, Som.
1512	. .	A barrel or ton as in 1504.	Low bowl used as chalice. Wymeswold, Leic.
1514	(image)	Man with staff . .	Paten. Heworth, Durham.
1515	. .	. . . . .	Low bowl with cover. C.C.C. Oxford.
Do.		. . . . .	Apostle-spoon (St. Paul), gift of Abp. Parker. C.C.C. Camb.
1516	Do.	As in 1515 .	Bp. Fox's spoons, with balls on the ends. C.C.C. Oxford.
Do.	(image)	. . . . .	Hour-glass salt. Cotehele House, Cornw.
1517	(image)	Some small animal .	Paten. (Staniforth Coll.)

ALPHABET III. 1518—1537.

1518	. .	Two links as in 1509	Chalice. St. Mary's R. C. Church, Leyland, Lanc.
Do.	. .	. . . . .	Cocoa-nut cup, with hinged straps. Vintners' Company.
Do.		. . . . .	Hour-glass salt. Ironmongers' Company.
Do.		. . . . .	Do. Saddlers' Company.
1519	(image)	. . . .	Set of eleven apostles' spoons from the Bernal Collection. (Staniforth Coll.)
Do.		. . . . .	Paten. From Hamsterley, Durh. (Durham Cathl. Library.)
1520	. .	Crescent and star as in 1516.	Standing cup * with imbricated pattern on bowl. Christ's Coll. Camb.
1521	. .	. . . . .	Low bowl with imbricated pattern, and inscription round in Tudor capitals. (Dunn Gardner Coll.) Sold 1902 for £4,100.
Do.	. .	Two links as in 1509	Chalice. Jurby, Isle of Man.
Do.	.	Do.	Paten. Great Waltham, Essex.
Do.		. . . . .	Mazer, with rose enamelled on boss. C.C.C. Camb.
1522	. .	. . . . .	Hour-glass salt. Ironmongers' Company.
1523	. .	. . . . .	Cup, given 1540 by Henry VIII. Barber-Surgeons' Company.
1525	(image)	. . . . .	Mount of ivory cup, called Thomas à Becket's cup. Duke of Norfolk.

* The arms on the knop of the cover of this cup have never been identified. They are thus described by the late Mr. Albert Way :—Arg. on a chevr. sa. 3 estoiles of the field betw. 3 adders' heads of the second, a crescent for difference.

DATE	MAKER'S MARK.		ARTICLE AND OWNER.
1525	(mark)	. . . .	Chalice. Wylye, Wilts.
Do.	. .	A heart as in 1515 .	Seal-headed spoon, called the Pudsey spoon. Mayer Museum, Liverpool.
1527	(mark)	A saint's head . .	Chalice, gift of Sir Thos. Pope. Trin. Coll. Oxford.
Do.	. .	. . . . .	Spoon. The late Sir G. Walker, Bart.
1528	(mark)	Manasses Stockton was of the " Keye " in 1569.	Spoon, with spirally fluted knob. (Staniforth Coll.)
Do.	(mark)	. . . . .	The St. Nicholas spoon. (Dunn Gardner Coll.)
1529	Do.	As in 1528 . .	Small standing mazer. All Souls' Coll. Oxford.
Do.	. .	Fringed S as in 1519	Apostle-spoon (St. Philip). Dug up at Moreton, near Thornbury, Glouc. Late J. H. Cooke, Esq.
1530	. .	. . . . .	Apostle-spoon. (Staniforth Coll.)
1531	. .	Orb and cross between I C as in 1528	Cover to a cup. C.C.C. Camb.
1532	(mark)	No shield . . .	The "Narford" mazer. (Franks Coll.)
Do.	. .	Fringed S as in 1519	Apostle-spoon (St. Andrew). Dug up at Moreton. Late J. H. Cooke, Esq.
Do.	(mark)	John Mabbe was of the " Cuppe " in 1569.	Tazza, used as almsplate. Arlington, Devon.
Do.	Do.	Do. . . .	Cover to pair of similar tazze (the tazze are of 1530 and 1531). Rochester Cathdl.
1533	TW	. . . .	Paten. St. Edmund, Salisbury.
Do.	. .	. . . . .	Two-handled cup with cover, engraved scrolls. C.C.C. Oxford.
1534	(mark)	John Harysson was of the "Broad Arrow" in 1569.	Mazer, known as the "Tokerys" bowl. (Braikenridge Coll.) Sold for £2,300.
1535	(mark)	. . . . .	The "Boleyn" cup, used as a chalice. Cirencester, Glouc.
1536	TW	As in 1533 .	Chalice. Sturminster Marshall, Dorset.
1537	. .	Fringed S as in 1519	Apostle-spoon. (Staniforth Coll.)
		ALPHABET IV. 1538—1557.	
1539	. .	Fringed S as in 1519	Apostle-spoon (St. Julian). Innholders' Company.
1543	. .	. . . . .	Standing cup, with cover surmounted by statuette. St. Peter Mancroft, Norwich.
1545	(mark)	Maidenhead . .	Ewer and salver, engraved with foliated arabesques, given by Abp. Parker. C.C.C. Camb.
1546	(mark)	. . . . .	Mount of glass jug, cover enamelled with arms of Parr. (From Strawberry Hill Coll.) Sudeley Castle.
1548	(mark)	Covered cup . .	Plain communion cup. St. Lawrence Jewry, London.
Do.	(mark)	See 1557 . . .	Mount of glass jug. (Franks Coll.)

DATE	MAKER'S MARK.		ARTICLE AND OWNER.
1549		AC linked letters .	Mount of jug. (Staniforth and Franks Coll.)
Do.		BN linked letters, probably for Nichs. Bartlemewe.	Seal-headed baluster-top spoon. (R. Temple Frere Coll.)
1550		Leg in armour. One Beereblocke was of the "Legge" in 1569.	Communion cup, engraved with arabesques, Bridekirk, Cumb.
1551		. . . . .	Pair of communion cups. St. Margaret, Westminster.
Do.		A dexter hand open under a crown.	Plain communion cup. Hunstanton, Norf.
Do.		AK linked letters .	Plain communion cup. Totnes, Devon.
1552		Robert Danbe . .	Plain communion cup. Messrs. Thomas, 1883.
Do. 1553	. . . .	RD linked as in 1552	Seal-headed baluster-top spoon. Armourers' Co. Standing cup with cover, surmounted by statuette. Armourers' Company.
1554		TL monogram . .	Cylindrical standing salt, with cover surmounted by statuette. C.C.C. Oxford.
Do. 1555	. . . .		Sir Martin Bowes' cup. Goldsmiths' Company. Two-handled cup. C.C.C. Camb.
Do.		A bird . . .	Nautilus cup, with hinged figure straps, foot repoussé with masks and flowers. Messrs. Christie, Manson, & Woods. 1885.
1556		. . . . .	Alms-dish, with Tudor rose boss. St. George's Chapel, Windsor.
1557		See 1548 . . .	Covered cup on stem, with Eliz. engraved belt. Waterbeach, Cambs.
Do.	IF	. . . . .	Seal-headed spoon. Messrs. West, Dublin, 1882.

ALPHABET V. 1558—1577.

DATE	MAKER'S MARK.		ARTICLE AND OWNER.
1558	. . . . .		Communion cup and cover. St. Michael-le-Belfry, York.
1559		Mark very indistinct	Plain communion cup, gilt, no engraved belt; egg and dart moulding round foot. St. Peter ad Vincula, Tower of London.
1560		Probably bird's claw.	Spoon, with lion sejant on stem. (Date-letter not in a shield.) Sudeley Castle.
Do.		. . .	Very small communion cup with engraved belt. (Date letter in a regular shield.) Ugglebarnby, Yorks.
1561	. . . .		Standing cup used as a chalice. Watford, Herts.
Do.		Sun in splendour, with W in centre, on plain shield.	Apostle-spoon. Innholders' Company.
Do.	. .	A covered cup as in 1548.	Bell-shaped communion cup, paten cover dated 1578, no engraved belt. Lyminge, Kent.

DATE	MAKER'S MARK.		ARTICLE AND OWNER.
1561	(✳)	. . . .	Wide Norfolk-shaped com. cup, engraved **belt.** St. Lawrence Jewry, Lond.
1562	P·C	. . . . .	Com. plate. Beeford.
Do.		Stag's head, as in 1551	Mount of stoneware jug. Vintners' Company. Also com. cup. Swingfield, Kent.
Do.	N	NS interlaced, probably Nichs. Sutton	Cup and cover surmounted by statuette. Armourers' Company.
Do.	D	. . . . .	Seal-headed spoon. Armourers' Company.
Do.	⚜	No shield . . .	Communion cup, gilt and handsomely engraved in usual style. St. Olave, Old Jewry, Lond. Also Com. plate, 1569, 1571.
Do.		. . . .	Plain com. cup, no belt. High Halden, Kent.
Do.	W C	A cricket or grasshopper below.	Com. cup, double belt. Headcorn, Kent.
Do.	P	. . . . .	Communion cup, usual Elizabethan belt. Avening, Glouc.
Do.	. .	RD in monogram as in 1552.	Circular standing salt and cover repoussé in relief with strap work, cartouches, masks, foliage, &c.; given 1570, by Abp. Parker. C.C.C. Camb.
1563	HW	. . . .	Standing cup formed as a melon, with melon stalk and tendrils for foot. Hon. Soc. of Inner Temple.
Do.	. .	. . . . .	Com. cup, usual pattern. Old Alresford, Hants.
1564	. .	Fleur-de-lys as in 1562.	Com. cup, usual pattern. New Alresford, Hants.
Do.	. .	. . . .	Communion cup, usual pattern, but with two belts. All Souls' Coll. Oxford.
Do.	🤚	A hand grasping a cross-croslet fitché	Communion cup. Sherburn Hospital, Durh.
1565	HW	As in 1563 . .	Communion cup and cover. Little Ness, Salop.
Do.	IF	As in 1557 . . .	Seal-headed spoon. Armourers' Company.
Do.	M	. . . .	Com. cup and **cover,** usual Elizabethan belt. Daglingworth, Glouc. Ch.-plate, Pembrokes.
Do.	RK	. . . . .	Seven spoons with pear-shaped bowls and angular kn⌒ps. Mercers' Company.
Do.	I C	An animal's head .	Small com. cup, usual belt. Hawkinge, Kent. Another. Temple Ewell, Kent.
1566	. .	. . . . .	Mount of stoneware jug. Messrs. Garrards.
Do.	. .	Bird's claw, as in 1560	Set of twelve apostles' spoons, given by Abp. Parker, probably in 1570, as their weight is recorded on the salt of 1562-3, which he gave in that year. C. C. C. Camb.
Do.	IP	. . . . .	Plain gilt com. cup, no belt. Westerham, Kent. Much church-plate made by him, 1565—76.
1567	. .	Crescent and three stars as in 1560.	Small com. cup, usual belt, with paten-cover; formerly at Beding. British Museum.
Do.	A	. . . . .	Small communion cup, usual pattern. Oxburgh, Norf. Also paten-cover. E. Horndon, Essex.

DATE	MAKER'S MARK.		ARTICLE AND OWNER.
1567	🛡	A hooded falcon. Thos. Bampton was of "The Falcon" at this period.	Twelve parcel-gilt plates, engraved after Alde-graver with the Labours of Hercules, formerly the property of the Cotton family. Formerly at Messrs. Garrard.
Do.	🛡	Hand with hammer, shaped shield.	Fine parcel-gilt ewer with Bishop Parkhurst's arms on button of lid. Corpn. of Guildford.
Do.	. .	RD in monogram, as in 1553.	Jug or pot, with cover and handle. Armourers' Company.
Do.	🛡	. . . .	Plain communion cup and cover, no belt. Christ's Coll. Camb.
1568	🛡	A bunch of grapes .	Gilt cup and cover, ornamented with chasing. Armourers' Company. Tazza, Southampton, 1567.
Do.	. .	. . . . .	Six engraved plates. Messrs. Thomas.
Do.	Ⓡ	. . . . .	Communion cup. Sutterton, Linc.
1569	🕊	A falcon . . .	Standing Salt. Vintners' Company.
Do.	W.H	. . . . .	Communion cup and cover, usual engraved belt. Poulton, Glouc.
Do.	. .	A bull's head erased on shaped stamp.	Communion cup and cover, usual engraved belt. Avening, Glouc.
Do.	. .	A bunch of grapes, as in 1568.	Tall standing cup and cover, surmounted by a statuette; given in 1569 by Abp. Parker. C.C.C. Camb.
Do.	✚	. . . .	Communion cup. Horncastle, Linc.
Do.	IP	As in 1566 . . .	Com. cup and cover, usual belt. Barlings, Linc. Also a very fine one. Eton Coll. Chapel. Also a small one with good belt, dated 1569. Titsey, Surrey.
Do.	NS	Interlaced, as in 1562	Broken lid, probably from stoneware jug, centre repoussé with portrait of Henry VIII. British Museum.
1570	AK	Linked letters, as in 1551.	Communion cups. Sneaton, Yorks., and St. Bees', Cumb.
Do.	. .	Stag's head, as in 1551	Large plain communion cups and covers. Ciren-cester, Glouc.
Do.	🛡	HS interlaced, proba-bly Henry Sutton.	Communion cup, usual belt. Formerly at Alder-maston, Berks.
Do.	Do.	Do.	Do., do., dated 1571. Ingleby Arncliffe, Yorks.
Do.	🛡	SE interlaced . .	Tazza cup or bowl on stem, used as chalice. Bas-church, Salop.
Do.	IP	As in 1566 .	Two-handled cup to match one of 1555, q. v. C.C.C. Camb.
Do.	🛡	. . . .	Communion cup. Stow Longa, Hunts.
Do.	HW	As in 1563 . .	Communion cups. Lanchester, Durh., and Pilton, Som.
1571	. .	. . . . .	Apostle-spoon. Innholders' Company.
Do.	. .	A dove on shaped shield.	Small gilt tankard, ornamented with arabesques, medallions and masks. Given by Abp. Parker in 1571. C.C.C. Camb.
Do.	BT	Linked letters, as in 1567.	Jug or pot with Elizn. engraving like that of 1567 at Armourers' Hall. Treasure of the Patriarch, Moscow.

DATE	MAKER'S MARK.		ARTICLE AND OWNER.
1571	IF	. . . .	Communion cups, usual pattern. Bothal, Northmb. and Sutton Ashfield, Notts.
Do.		Pair of bellows . .	Communion cup. Greatham, Durh.
Do.	RF	Linked letters, as in 1568.	Com. cup, usual belt. The Chapel, St. Michael's Mount, Cornw.
Do.	I·H	. . . .	Communion cup, usual pattern. Great Smeaton, Yorks.
Do.	RD	Linked letters, as in 1553.	Communion cup. Adlingfleet, Yorks.
1572		. . . .	Gilt tazza in form of a Venetian glass. Christ's Coll. Camb.
Do.	. .	An eagle displayed in circular escutcheon	Seal-headed spoon. Armourers' Company.
Do.	HB	. . . .	Paten cover, engraved 1572. Northleach, Glouc.
1573	. .	. . .	Communion cup, parcel gilt, two engraved belts. St. Martin, Exeter.
Do.	IP	As in 1566 . .	Communion cups and covers, usual pattern. Rodney Stoke and Mark, Som.
Do.		This mark occurs on a similar spoon of 1575.	Seal-headed spoon. Armourers' Company.
Do.	A	As in 1567 . .	Blue and gray stoneware jug. Alnwick Castle.
1574	C·P	A halberd between the letters.	Tankard. Ashmolean Museum, Oxford.
Do.	M	As in 1565 .	Communion cup and cover, usual belt. Kemble, Glouc.
1575	M	. . . .	Communion cup and cover, usual belt, parcel gilt. Preston, Glouc.
Do.	WC	Grasshopper below, as in 1562.	Stoneware jug, with usual repoussé mount and lid. Sudeley Castle.
Do.	AK	Linked letters, as in 1551, but larger.	Communion cup with paten cover, usual belts, etc. St. Kew, Cornw.
Do.	. .	Crescents and star, as in 1570.	Gilt com. cup and cover, dated 1575. Oswestry, Salop.
1576		Three trefoils . .	Simon Gibbon's salt. Goldsmiths' Company.
Do.	M	As in 1575 . .	Communion cup and cover, dated 1576, two belts. Somerford Keynes, Wilts.
Do.	RH	. . . .	Pair of large bowl flagons, dated 1577. Cirencester, Glouc.
Do.		? what . . .	Communion cup and cover, dated 1577, usual pattern, but very handsomely engraved. Fairford, Glouc.
Do.		Sun in splendour .	Communion cup and cover, dated 1577, usual belt. Baunton, Glouc.
Do.		. . . .	Communion cup, usual pattern. Christ Ch. Monm.
Do.	IH	As in 1571 .	Communion cup, dated 1576. Caerleon, Monm.
Do.		Compasses with points downwards, a mullet between them.	Standing cup with cover surmounted by statuette, now used as a chalice. St. Mabyn, Cornw.
Do.		. . . .	Chalice of tazza form. Wishford, Wilts.
1577	. .	. . . .	Communion cup. Magor, Monm.
Do.	RH	. . . .	Seal-headed spoon. Armourers' Company.

DATE	MAKER'S MARK.		ARTICLE AND OWNER.
			ALPHABET VI. 1578—1597.
1578		PG, as shown . .	Mount of large mazer-bowl. Armourers' Company.
Do.		A windmill. Robt. Wright was of the "Wyndmylle" in 1569.	Small cup, lower part fluted, upper part engraved with festoons and animals. St. Mary the Virgin, Romney Marsh.
Do.	IC	Animal's head between, see 1565.	Mount of stoneware flagon. Menheniot, Cornw.
Do.		. . . .	Gilt cup, dated 1578. Drapers' Company.
Do.		An escallop . .	Apostle-spoon. (Staniforth Coll.)
1579		. . . .	Communion cup and paten-cover, dated 1579. Crawley, Suss.
1580		. . . .	Standing cup, gift of Chapman. Armourers' Company.
1581		Three trefoils slipped in trefoil shield.	Gilt salver, partly formed of agate. Ewer to match, is of 1579. Duke of Rutland.
Do.		No shield . . .	Mount of stoneware flagon. Formerly at Malling, Kent.
Do.		Double-seeded rose in pentagon.	Communion cup. Exton, co. Rutland.
Do.	RW	. . . .	Com. cup, Eliz. belt, conical stem, knop under bowl. Grimston, Leic.
1583		. . . .	Large gilt communion cup. Gray's Inn Chapel, Lond.
Do.		A flag with staff bendwise.	Pair of large flagons. St. Margaret, Westminster.
1584		. . . .	Mount of stoneware jug. (Franks Coll.)
Do.		. . . .	Gilt cup, shaped as an ostrich egg, hinged straps, foot surmounted by four dolphins. Earl of Ducie.
1585	Do.	. . . .	Gourd-shaped standing cup and cover, stem as double twisted tree-trunk. Armourers' Comp.
Do.		. . . .	Very massive seal-headed spoon. Earl of Mount-Edgcumbe.
Do.	Do.	This mark occurs on similar spoons of 1590, 1596, 1602, 1603, 1609, 1611, 1612.	Seal-headed spoon. Armourers' Company.
Do.		Three leaves with 3 pellets as in 1576.	Mazer. Rev. H. F. St. John.
1586		This mark occurs on similar spoons of 1596, 1599, 1600, 1601.	Seal-headed spoon. Armourers' Company.
Do.	Ð	. . .	Small gilt paten. St. Margaret, Westminster.
Do.		A newt on a ton (rebus for NEWTON).	Communion cup with paten cover, usual belts. Stanford, Kent.
Do.		. . . .	Very large standing salt, finely repoussé with flower-swaggs and masks, cover with scroll supports to a vase, over all three more supports and an acorn knop. South Kensington Mus.

DATE	MAKER'S MARK.		ARTICLE AND OWNER.
1588	RF	. . . . .	Cocoa-nut mounts. Cooks' Company.
Do.		. . . .	Plain cylindrical salt, statuette on cover, ball and bird's-claw feet. Armourers' Company.
1589		. . . .	Gilt cup on baluster stem, with knop, engraved with flowers. (Staniforth Coll.)
Do.	IM	. . . .	Flagon, tapering barrel, repoussé decorations. Fugglestone St. Peter, Wilts.
1590	RM	. . . . .	Rose-water salver with raised boss, engraved with arms, etc. Merchant Taylors' Company.
Do.		This mark occurs on a similar spoon of 1597.	Seal-headed spoon. Armourers' Company.
Do.	. .	IS interlaced, as in 1588.	Ostrich-egg cup. Noted by the late Mr. Albert Way in 1864, as then in the possession of a family in Kent.
1591		. . . . .	Cup on baluster stem, oviform bowl, engr. with foliage. Messrs. Garrards, 1882.
1592		An anchor. This mark occurs on a similar spoon of 1597.	Seal-headed spoon. Armourers' Company.
Do.	RW	As in 1581 . .	Ostrich-egg cup. C.C.C. Camb.
Do.	WH	A rose below . .	Pair of flagons. Rendcombe, Glouc.
Do.	HL	. . . .	Tall cup made of the great seal of Ireland, anno 1593. Marquis of Ely.
1593	D	As in 1586 . . .	Small paten. St. Olave, Old Jewry, Lond.
1594		. . . . .	Seal-headed spoon. Armourers' Company.
Do.	IM	. . . . .	Jug-shaped flagon. Westwell, Kent.
1595	I·B	Small rose or a mullet below.	Ewer and salver. Corporation of Bristol.
Do.	TN	. . . .	Salver, repoussé strapwork, marine monsters in cartouches, etc. H.M. the King.
Do.	Do.	. . . . .	The Hammersley salt. Haberdashers' Company.
1596		. . . .	Seal-headed spoon. (Staniforth Coll.)
Do.	. .	Newt on ton, as in 1586.	Jug-shaped flagon, bowl repoussé with strap-work. Treasure of the Patriarch, Moscow.
Do.	IG	Linked letters, as in 1591.	Communion cup. Rokeby, Yorks.
1597	IH	A bear passant below	Small communion tankard, or flagon, chased and engraved. Christ's Coll. Camb.
Do.		Double-headed eagle displayed.	Jug-shaped flagon. Westwell, Kent. (The eagle's heads are between letters T S.) Also 1587. Tankard-flagons, St. Mary Woolnoth, London.

DATE	MAKER'S MARK.		ARTICLE AND OWNER.
			ALPHABET VII. 1598—1617.
1598	☾	. . . .	Circular bell-shaped salt with compartments. (Octavius Morgan Coll.)
Do.	TF	. . . . .	Cup with cover, gift of Adam Dixon. Armourers' Company.
Do.	WI	. . . .	Communion cup. East Gilling, Yorks.
Do.	RP	. . . . .	Beaker-shaped communion cup. Llanfyllin, N. Wales.
1599		A squirrel .	Tall gilt cup, bowl ornamented with large escallops. Kensington, Midx.
Do.	M	. . . . .	Tazza-cup, bowl having ornament punched from the outside. (Octavius Morgan Coll.)
Do.		No shield . .	Small gilt cup on baluster stem. Armourers' Company.
Do.	RC	. . . . .	The Gwalter cup, dated 1599. Innholders' Co. Also paten-cover. Throwley, Kent.
Do.	IB	. . . .	Large plain gilt bowl. Whitgift Charity, Croydon.
1600	JS	Interlaced .	Bell-shaped salt or spice-box. From the Dasent collection.
Do.	. .	W within crescent, as in 1585.	Seal-headed spoon. Innholders' Company.
Do.		. . . . .	Pair of great sejant leopards supporting shields. Imperial Treasury, Moscow.
1601		Hart lodged as in 1598.	Standing cylindrical salt, *ex dono* Rogers. Goldsmiths' Company.
Do.		. . . . .	Seal-headed spoon. Armourers' Company.
Do.	. .	A squirrel, as in 1599	Silver gilt cup engr. with flowers; found in one of the lakes at Knowsley. Earl of Derby.
Do.	IG	Linked letters, as in 1591.	Gourd-shaped cup, stem as twisted tree-trunk. Treasure of the Patriarch, Moscow.
1602	. .	See 1585 . . .	Seal-headed spoon. Armourers' Company.
Do.	AB	. . . .	Cup on stem, straight-sided bowl, like the Elizabethan communion cups, cover with statuette, *ex dono* Champernowne. C.C.C. Camb.
Do.		Animal's head erased	Communion cup. Ellel, Lanc.
Do.		Harp betw. initials, probably L M, shaped shield.	Plain gilt tankard, straight sides, dome lid with rayed button. Corpn. of Guildford.
1603	IB	. . . .	Cup, dated 1640. Corporation of Hedon, Yorks.
1604	AB	Linked letters, as in 1602.	Beaker. Mercers' Company.

DATE	MAKER'S MARK.		ARTICLE AND OWNER.
1604	[D]	This mark occurs on similar spoons of 1606, 1608, 1610, 1611, 1612, 1613, 1615, 1617, 1619, 1620.	Seal-headed spoon. Armourers' Company.
Do.	IA	. . . . .	Cup, presented 1588, but must have been re-made this year. The Burgesses of Westminster.
Do.	. .	Animal's head, as in 1602.	Fine jug, snake-handle. Imperial Treasury, Moscow.
Do.	IH	Bear passant below, as in 1597.	Jug-shaped flagons. Romanoff House, Moscow.
1605	AB	Monogram, as in 1602	Beakers to match that of 1604. Mercers' Com.
Do.	[RW]	. . . .	Rose-water dish, repoussé with marine monsters, Elizabethan belts and foliage. Clothworkers' Company.
Do.	[G]	, ...	The Cockayne cups. Skinners' Company.
Do.	[ɔ]	As in 1585 . .	Spoon with lion sejant handle. British Museum.
Do.	Do.	Do.	Apostle spoon. Melbury House, Dorset.
1606	[CB]	. . . .	Shallow cup on baluster stem, bowl ornamented with punched pattern from the outside. Armourers' Company.
Do.	Do.	. . . . .	Cup of similar shape, on bell-shaped stem, with three arms to support bowl, which is ornamented with engraving. C.C.C. Camb.
Do.	. .	. . . . .	Communion cups and patens. Halifax, Yorks.
Do.	. .	. . . . .	Gilt salt in form of a temple. R. Neville Grenville, Esq.
1607	NR	Negro's head below	Circular bell-shaped salt or spice-box. Christ's Hospital, Lond.
Do.	[CW]	. . . . .	Spoons *ex dono* Ferris. Trinity House, Hull.
Do.	[IV]	. . . .	Communion cup. North Meols, Lanc.
Do.	[C]	This mark occurs on similar spoons of 1609, 1611, 1612.	Seal-headed spoon. Armourers' Company.
Do.	[ɔ]	. . . .	Apostle-spoon. (Staniforth Coll.)
Do.	Do.	. . . . .	Seal-headed spoon. Armourers' Company.
Do.	. .	. . . . .	Gilt foot of glass cup. Founders' Company.
Do.	[TW]	T rising from middle of W.	Cup, repoussé with marine monsters in medallions. C.C.C. Camb.
Do.	[SF]	SF interlaced . .	Cup, with pyramid on cover. Cutlers' Company.
Do.	[MB]	. . . . .	Paten. Chelmorton, Derby. Also Com. plate 1593.
1608	WC	W within C, as in 1607.	Apostle spoon. British Museum.
Do.	[SO]	. . . . .	Straight-sided tankard-flagons. Brasenose Coll. Chapel, Oxford.

DATE	MAKER'S MARK.		ARTICLE AND OWNER.
1608	W.R	. . . .	Cup and cover, engraved all over bowl with flowers. Armourers' Company. Ch. plate, Jersey.
Do.	IK	. . , . .	Tall shaped repoussé cup, surmounted by open-work triangular steeple and statuette. Armourers' Company.
Do.	(casque)	A casque; found on a similar spoon of 1610.	Seal-headed spoon. Armourers' Company.
Do.	IS	. . . . .	Cup on stem, bowl ornamented with leaves, cover with steeple. C.C.C. Camb.
Do.	IA	As in 1604 . . .	Plain communion cup. Bermondsey, Surrey.
1609	TI *	Do.	Box in form of escallop. Lord Hotham. Also 1621.
Do.	. .	A cross within a crescent, as in 1607.	Apostle spoon. Innholders' Company.
Do.	F	Mr. Terry . . .	Handsome gilt communion cups and covers. Temple Church, Lond.
Do.	Do.	Do.	Ansell's cup. Carpenters' Company.
Do.	. .	. . . .	Gilt tazza-cup to match one of 1572, q. v. Christ's Coll. Camb.
Do.	A	. . . .	Communion cup. Halsall, Lanc. Also plain deep dish. G. E. L. Baker, Esq.
1610	G	As in 1605 . . .	Communion cup, V-shaped, on baluster stem, formerly at Stanley Pontlarge Church, co. Glouc. Sudeley Castle.
Do.	TF	Monogram as in 1609	Gilt cup and cover. Armourers' Company.
Do.	IB	. . . .	Cup called "Earl Godwin's Cup." Berkeley Castle.
Do.	SO	As in 1608 . . .	Ewer and salver, repoussé with marine monsters in oval cartouches, etc., given 1613. Eton College.
Do.	T·A	. . . .	Communion cups. Prior's Marston, Warw.
1611	TF	Monogram as in 1609	Reeves's Cup. Carpenters' Company.
Do.	F W	. . . . .	Tall cup, richly repoussé, pyramid cover. Barford St. Martin, Wilts.
1612	Do.	. . . . .	Communion cup, *ex dono* Ferris. Holy Trinity, Hull.
Do.	TF	Monogram as in 1609	Tall standing cup, cover with finial supported by three mermaids. Trinity House, Lond.
Do.	IV	As in 1607 .	Communion cup, cover with knob. St. George's Chapel, Windsor.
Do.	CB	Monogram as in 1606	Tall cup with cover surmounted by open-work steeple. Bongate Church, Appleby, Westmrld.
1613	IV	As in 1607 . .	Plain bowl-shaped flagon (like Cirencester, 1576). St. George's Chapel, Windsor.
Do.	W	. . . .	Seal-headed spoon. Armourers' Company.
Do.	RS	. . . . .	Thomas Edmonds' Cup. Carpenters' Company.
Do.	T·C	. . . .	Jug-shaped flagon, repoussé ornament. Imperial Treasury, Moscow.

DATE	MAKER'S MARK.			ARTICLE AND OWNER.
1613	Do.	• • •		Tall cup with pyramid on cover. Holm Cultram, Cumb.
Do.	WR	As in 1608	• •	Tankard-flagon, repoussé ornament. Treasury of the Patriarch, Moscow.
Do.	RB	• • •		Cylindrical salt with cover, ball and claw feet. Imperial Treasury, Moscow.
Do.	Do.	• • • •		Another, with triangular pierced pyramid on cover. Romanoff House, Moscow.
1614	IV	As in 1607	•	Flagons, dated 1695. St. Michael's, Coventry.
Do.	RB	• • • •		Cylindrical standing salt with steeple cover, dated 1635. Innholders' Company.
Do.	IM FB	• • •		Tall cup with steeple on cover. Odcombe, Som. Also cup. Kirkburton, Yorks.
Do.	RC	• • • •		Seal-headed spoon. Armourers' Company.
1615	WC	• • •		Three small grace cups on high stems. Christ's Hospital, London.
Do.	S	This mark occurs on similar spoons of 1617, 1621.		Seal-headed spoon. Armourers' Company.
Do.	HS	• • •		One of three small octagonal cups on high stems. Armourers' Company.
Do.	IR	Do. • • •		Communion cup and paten-cover, usual Elizabethan pattern. Cricklade St. Sampson, Wilts.
Do.	G M	A key between	•	Communion cup on baluster stem. Cumrew, Cumb.
1616	RB	• • •		Rose-water dish, repoussé with marine monsters on medallions, etc. Clothworkers' Company.
Do.	IV	As in 1607 •	•	Communion cup with paten cover, dated 1616. St. Andrew, Plymouth.
Do.	Do.	Do. • • •		Com. cup to match that of 1612. St. George's Chapel, Windsor.
Do.	EL	• • • •		Flagon with marine monsters for decoration. Queen's Coll., Oxford.
Do.	RW	• • •		Oviform cup on baluster stem, ex dono Johnson, dated 1616. C.C.C. Camb.
1617	Do.	• • • •		Gilt cup, repoussé with flowers, etc. on high stem. Armourers' Company.
Do.	IS	• • •		Tall hanap with steeple and figure on cover. Bodmin, Cornw.
Do.	IP A	A bell below	•	Oviform cup on stem, with scroll bracket supports to bowl. Treasure of the Patriarch, Moscow.
Do.	SF	Interlaced as in 1607		Oviform cup on baluster stem. Chignal, Essex.
Do.	TF	Monogram, as in 1609		Communion cup, usual engraving, given 1618. Sevenoaks, Kent.
Do.	IF	• • •		Spoons with lion sejant handles. British Museum.
Do.	IV	As in 1607 •	•	Ewer and salver. Corporation of Norwich.
Do.	WC	A dart between		Ewer, flat strap-work decoration. H.M. the King.

DATE	MAKER'S MARK.		ARTICLE AND OWNER.
			ALPHABET VIII. 1618—1637.
1618	WR	As in 1608 . . .	Tall repoussé tankard. Corporation of Norwich.
Do.	RC	In plain shield .	Tall upright gilt communion flagon. Hon. Soc. of Gray's Inn.
1619	AB	. . . .	Tall upright gilt communion flagon, repoussé in panels with straps, etc. Kensington, Midx.
Do.	RS	A heart below . .	A pair of flagons, very like the last, given 1620. Bodmin, Cornw.
Do.	CB	Monogram, as in 1606.	Tall cup, with steeple and figure with shield and spear on cover. Linton, Kent.
Do.	. .	A bird alighting with wings erect, shaped shield.	Communion plates. All Souls' Coll., Oxford.
Do.	CM	As in 1615 . .	Communion cup. St. Mary's, Hull.
Do.	I I	. . . . .	Communion cup. Ansley, Warw.
Do.	IS	As in 1617 . .	Pilgrim-bottle vase with chains to stopper. Imperial Treasury, Moscow.
Do.	TF	Monogram, as in 1609	Tall cup with pyramid on cover. Northleach, Glouc.
1620	Do.	Do.	Plain communion cup, dated 1621. Chelmsford, Essex.
Do.	. .	See 1604 . . .	Seal-headed spoon. Armourers' Company.
1621	. .	See 1615 . . .	Seal-headed spoon. Armourers' Company.
Do.	IF	As in 1617 . .	Spoon, with lion sejant on stem. (R. T. Frere Coll.)
Do.	FW	Linked letters, as in 1611.	Pair of patens. St. Andrew's, Plymouth.
1622	. .	. . . . .	Apostle spoon. Innholders' Company.
Do.	FT	. . . .	Small cup, given 1648. Corporation of Hull.
1623	. .	A trefoil slipped, on shaped shield.	Mount of an ostrich-egg cup decorated with masks in repoussé, cover bearing figure of Minerva with spear and flag, dated 1623. (H. Willett Coll.)
Do.	HS	Blazing star below, as in 1615.	Plain cup, no engraved belt. Sir T. Thornhill, Bart.
Do.	WC	As in 1617 . . .	Communion plate, beautifully repoussé, gift of Duchess Dudley in 1627. Ladbroke, Warw.
1624	RC	. . . .	Communion plate. St. Margaret, Westminster.
Do.	DV	Crowned, shaped shield.	Mace, dated 1625. Ward of Cheap, Lond.
Do.	P.B	. . . .	Paten or plate. Mark, Som.
Do.	TF	Monogram, as in 1609	Tall plain communion cup with two ribs round bowl. Eton Coll. Chapel.
Do.	RL	. . . . .	Plain ewer. Eton College.
Do.	RB	. . . . .	Communion cup, *ex dono* Lady Cutts, 1625. Shipborne, Kent.
1625	HT	Monogram, as in 1622	Plain communion cup and cover. Coln St. Aldwyns, Glouc.

DATE	MAKER'S MARK.		ARTICLE AND OWNER.
1626	(I T)	. . . .	Plain communion flagon. Avening, Glouc.
Do.	HS	As in 1615 . . .	Pair of salts like short columns, dated 1626. Innholders' Company.
Do.	. .	. . . . .	Gilt basin, like a deep soup-plate. Fishmongers' Company.
Do.	(PH)	Linked letters PH .	Very large plain communion flagons. Christ's Coll., Camb.
Do.	(BY)	Probably Benjamin Yates.	Set of thirteen Apostles' spoons. Goldsmiths' Company.
1627	(T.8)	. . . .	Seal-headed spoon. Armourers' Company.
Do.	CB	Monogram, as in 1606.	Tall standing cup given 1626. Trinity House.
Do.	TF	Monogram, as in 1609.	Pair of large plain gilt patens. Temple Church, London.
Do.	(J)	. . . . .	Communion cup. Berners Rooding, Essex.
Do.	(R.I ★)	. . . .	Apostle-spoon. Innholders' Company.
1628	Do.	Do.	Seal-headed spoon. (R. Temple Frere Coll.)
Do.	RS	As in 1619 . .	Communion cup, given 1628. St. Andrew, Plymouth.
Do.	TF	Monogram, as in 1609.	Tall cup, like Edmonds cup, cover surmounted by modern statuette of Britannia. Christ's Coll., Camb.
Do.	(RM)	. . . .	Cup and paten, given 1628. Spaldwick, Cambs.
Do.	HS	As in 1615 .	Small plates with flat rims, dug up in the Castle grounds. Mereworth Castle.
Do.	(B.P)	. . . . .	Tall cup, gift of Jarman. Carpenters' Company.
1629	RA	A cinquefoil below .	Triangular salt. (Dasent Collection.)
Do.	RC	As in 1624 . .	V-shaped cup, on baluster stem, in which K. Charles I. received the communion on the morning of his death. Welbeck Abbey.
Do.	(W^S)	Walter Shute.	Flagon, dated 1628. Totnes, Devon.
Do.	(C↑C)	A column or tree between the letters.	Small gilt paten. St. Peter ad Vincula, Tower of London.
Do.	HS	As in 1615 .	Bowl with handle (see 1628). Mereworth Castle.
Do.	RS	As in 1619 . . .	Flagon. St. Stephen, Bristol.
Do.	(R C)	As in 1624, but heart dotted.	Four gilt communion flagons. Exeter Cathedral.
1630	(D↑G)	Anchor between .	Small paten. St. Mary's, Beverley, Yorks. Com. plate, 1624, 1633, 1652. Lincs.
Do.	PB	As in 1624 .	Communion cups, dated 1631. Queen's College, Oxford.
Do.	(D W)	. . . . .	Plain cups on baluster stems. Charterhouse, London.

DATE	MAKER'S MARK.		ARTICLE AND OWNER.
1630	RS	Heart below, as in 1619.	Pair of communion cups. Charterhouse, Lond.
Do.	(W M)	W. Maunday . .	Small alms-saucer with two handles. Chalton, Hants.
1631	CB	. . . .	Small tazza cup, baluster stem, bowl punched with bosses. Armourers' Company.
Do.	WM	One above another, as in 1630.	Alms-plate. St. Stephen's, Bristol.
Do.	(shield)	Mullet above escallop between pellets.	Small frosted cup, gift of Stone. Haberdashers' Company.
1632	(shield)	. . . .	Communion cup and paten cover. St. James, Dover.
Do.	CB	Monogram, as in 1606	Tazza cup, baluster stem, punched bosses, etc. Armourers' Company.
1633	(WS)	Another mark of Walter Shute.	Tazza cup, baluster stem, punched bosses, etc. Armourers' Company.
Do.	(IG)	. . . .	Tazza cup, baluster stem, punched bosses, etc. Vintners' Company.
Do.	.	C within D, as in 1604	Apostle spoon. Innholders' Company.
Do.	RC	. . . . .	Tall gilt communion flagon, dated 1633. Hon. Soc. of Gray's Inn.
Do.	(W C)	. . . .	Paten. Sandal, Yorks. Also com. cup given 1634. Sevenoaks, Kent.
Do.	(RS)	. . . . .	Deep plate engr. with arms, dug up in the grounds. Mereworth Castle.
Do.	WS	Walter Shute, as in 1629.	Plain communion cup, gift of B. Hyde. Chiddingstone, Kent.
1634	. . . . . .		Tankards. Corporation of Bristol.
Do.	(RM)	. . . .	Plain communion flagons. Trinity Coll., Oxford. Also flagon. Prior's Marston, Warw.
Do.	(RH)	. . . . .	Seal-headed spoon. (Octavius Morgan Coll.)
1635	(shell)	An escallop shell .	Large communion paten and pair of plain flagons, given 1635. St. Olave, Old Jewry, Lond.
Do.	(CO)	Probably Cardinall Orme.	Large plain gilt alms-dish. Lambeth Palace Chapel.
Do.	(BF)	Probably Benjamin Francis.	Plain patens. Christ's Coll., Camb.
Do.	(owl)	Owl standing upon small animal.	Small communion cup. Llangadwaldr, N. Wales.
Do.	(F)	. . . .	Plain alms-dish, *ex dono* Bainbrigge. Christ's Coll., Camb.
1636	Do.	. . . . .	Communion cup, without belt. Ampney Crucis, Glouc.
Do.	(F)	. . . .	Spoon. (Staniforth Coll.)

DATE	MAKER'S MARK.		ARTICLE AND OWNER.
1636	[S/W]	. . . .	Small trencher-salt, engr. 1636. Erddig, N. Wales.
1637	RB	A mullet below, shaped shield.	Plain gilt communion cups with paten covers. Hackney, Midx.
Do.	[mark]	Mullet above escallop as in 1631.	Plain gilt flagon, dated 1637. St. Mary at Hill, Lond.
Do.	[RS]	. . . . .	Paten. Glaston, Rutland.
Do.	[PB]	. . .	Communion cup. All Saints', Maidstone.
Do.	RM	As in 1634 . . .	Tall gilt communion flagons. Temple Ch., Lond.
Do.	[G·D]	Probably George Day	Plain communion cup. Holy Trin., Minories, Lond.
Do.	CC	As in 1629 . . .	Plain communion cup. St. Peter ad Vincula, Tower of London.
		ALPHABET IX. 1638—1657.	
1638	[BF]	See 1635 . . .	Frosted cup and cover on baluster-stem, given 1638. Trinity House.
Do.	[RB]	. . . . .	Tall tankard, given 1638. Trinity House.
Do.	[F]	Monogram, CF .	Large gilt salt. Mercers' Company.
Do.	[OM]	. . . . .	Gilt communion cups and a paten, dated 1637. St. Mary, Lambeth.
Do.	[I·B]	A buckle beneath, probably for name BUCKLE.	V-shaped cup on baluster-stem. Vintners' Co.
Do.	[W]	. . . .	Paten. St. Giles, Durham. Also paten, 1675.
1639	TF	Monogram, as in 1609	Frosted cup on baluster-stem. Trinity House.
Do.	RM	As in 1634 . . .	Plain communion flagon to match one of 1637. Temple Church, Lond.
Do.	[M]	T. Maunday .	Fluted dish, punched pattern in spirals. Bermondsey, Surrey.
Do.	[IM]	A pig passant below.	Butter-dish. S. E. Shirley, Esq.
Do.	[TH]	. . . .	Seal-headed spoon. (R. T. Frere Coll.)
Do.	[RC]	. . . . .	Apostle-spoon. British Museum.
1640	[WS]	. . . .	Rose-water dish. Trinity House.
Do.	Do.	Do. . . .	Another. Charterhouse, Lond.

DATE	MAKER'S MARK.	ARTICLE AND OWNER.
1640	IM	Pig below as in 1639	Pair of flagons. St. Ives, Cornw.
Do.	DW	. . . .	Flagon, dated 1639. St. Stephen's, Bristol.
Do.	IT	. . . . .	Apostles' spoons. Corporation of Hedon.
Do.	RK	. . . .	Sets of communion plate, gift of Lady Frances Kniveton. Bradley, Kniveton, Ormaston, etc. Derbys.
Do.	I·I	Probably Jeremy Johnson . .	Apostle spoon. Late W. R. M. Wynne, Esq.
1641	ᵀᴄ	Linked letters CT .	Communion paten. Halsall, Lanc.
Do.	IT	. . . .	Ewer and basin, *ex dono* Lister, 1640. Trinity House, Hull.
1642	I·I	As in 1640 . .	Communion paten. (Staniforth Coll.)
1643	WJ	John Wardlaw (see p. 174).	Communion cups dated 1644. Canongate Ch., Edinburgh.
1645	TG	. . . .	Communion cup, given by Capt. Poyer, the royalist, 1645. St. Mary's, Pembroke.
1646	AF	Probably Ant. Fickettes.	Standing cup with open-work steeple cover, and statuette of man on horseback. Vintners' Co.
Do.	NW	Probably Nichs. Wollaston.	Wineglass-shaped communion cup on baluster-stem. Rendcombe, Glouc.
Do.	RV	Probably Richard Vaghan.	Shallow lobed bowl, standing on foot, used as a paten. Marshfield, Monm.
Do.	SA	SA linked letters, probably Abr. Smith.	Communion cup and paten, *ex dono* Bedford. Charles Ch., Plymouth.
1648	IH	IH linked letters .	Plain rude communion cup, gift of Robert Jenner, 1648. Marston Meysey, Glouc.
Do.	WM	. . .	Plain communion flagons, frosted sides. St. Stephen, Exeter.
1650	HG	Probably Henry Greenway.	Frosted cup, on baluster stem. Mercers' Co.
Do.	IW	. . . .	Communion cup with baluster stem. St. Tudy, Cornw.
1651	R·S	. . . . .	Ewer and salver, *ex dono* Wandesford, 1652. Hon. Soc. of Lincoln's Inn.
Do.	HG	As in 1650 . .	Pint tankard, chased masks, etc. Sir Hedworth Williamson, Bart.
Do.	HB	. . . .	Loving cup, gift of Dashwood, 1654. Saddlers' Company.
1652	ES	. . . .	12-sided gilt porringer and cover with handles, said to have been given by Oliver Cromwell to Lady Falconberg. In the collection of the late Paul Butler, Esq.

DATE	MAKER'S MARK.		ARTICLE AND OWNER.
1652	(KF)	. . . . .	Salt, gift of Wrightington, 1653. Trin. House, Hull.
1653	(IV)	. . . .	Frosted cup on baluster stem, *ex dono* Bloodworth. Vintners' Company.
Do.	(ET)	. . . . .	Small cup with punched ornament. Earl Amherst.
Do.	WM	As in 1648 .	Dish deep like soup-plate. Lord Harlech.
Do.	(⚜)	Hound sejant . .	Set of communion and altar plate. Rochester Cathedral.
1654	(SV)	Probably Stephen Venables.	Seal-headed spoon. (Staniforth Coll.)
Do.	. .	. . . .	Frosted loving cup on baluster-stem. Innholders' Company.
Do.	. .	. . . .	Very small cup like that of 1659 at Marshfield. Late Sir T. Thornhill, Bart.
1655	(FW)	Probably Field Whorwood.	Plain communion cups and patens. St. Paul, Covent Garden, Lond.
Do.	(W·H)	. . . .	Pair of alms-dishes. St. Olave, Old Jewry, Lond.
Do.	(WC)	. . . .	Apostle-spoon (St. Andrew). (Octavius Morgan Coll.)
Do.	(IW)	An oval object below	The Blacksmiths' Cup. (F. A. Milbank Coll.)
Do.	(IG)	. . . .	Plain communion cup on baluster-stem. Wythburn, Cumb.
Do.	(DR)	Probably Daniel Rutty.	Communion cup. Navenby, Linc.
1656	(HG)	. . . .	Tall plain communion flagon. St. Mary, Sudeley Manor, Glouc. Another. Escrick, Yorks.
Do.	WC	As in 1655 .	Spoon. (Staniforth Coll.)
Do.	(HN)	Bird with olive branch below.	Communion cup, given 1656. Thornbury, Devon.
1657	I·I	As in 1640 . .	Seal-headed spoon. Kensington, Midx.
Do.	Do.	Do.	Seal-headed spoon. Hackney, Midx.
Do.	HG	As in 1656 . .	Plain rude communion cup, *ex dono* Scotson, 1657. Bermondsey, Surrey.
Do.	(H)	. . . .	Plain caudle-cups, ring handles. Clothworkers' Company.
			ALPHABET X. 1658—1677.
1658	(R·I)	. . . . .	Pint tankard. Messrs. Lambert.
Do.	(G/S)	Probably George Sull . . .	Small caudle-cup. Trin. House, Hull.

DATE	MAKER'S MARK.		ARTICLE AND OWNER.
1658	WM★	. . . . .	Bowl with cover, repoussé with flowers, etc. Viscount Midleton.
Do.	J	. . . .	Apostle-spoon, dated 1658. Innholders' Co.
Do.	PB	. . . . .	Frosted loving cup on baluster-stem, *ex dono* Osborne, 1658. Innholders' Company.
			NOTE.—This cup and the above spoon both have for date-letter the black-letter capital 𝔞 in the damaged state.
1659	HN	Bird with olive branch in beak below, as in 1656.	Part of mount to Elizabethan stoneware jug. (Staniforth Coll.)
Do.	M	. . . .	Communion cup, bowl ornamented with flat repoussé work. Marshfield, Monm.
1660	SV	As in 1654 . . .	Spoon, plain cut-off end to handle. (R. T. Frere Coll.)
Do.	RA	. . . .	Plain communion cups and flagons. Westminster Abbey. (See also p. 132.)
Do.	. .	Animal sejant, as in 1653.	Communion plate. Gloucester Cathedral.
Do.	. .	Do. . . . ,	Standing cup, repoussé, on baluster-stem. Clothworkers' Company.
Do.	TA	. , . . .	Plain communion flagon. Lambeth Palace Chapel.
Do.	TG	. . . .	Altar candlesticks and alms-dish. Ch. Ch., Oxford.
Do.	NW	As in 1646 . . .	Paten. Skelton, Yorks.
Do.	RN	Probably Richard Neale.	Flagon. Charles Ch., Plymouth.
Do.	DR	As in 1655 . .	Communion cup. St. Teath, Cornw.
Do.	SV	As in 1654 . .	Apostle-spoon. Innholders' Company.
1661	Do.	Do. . . .	Another. Innholders' Company.
Do.	PB	As in 1658 . .	Flat tankard. Innholders' Company.
Do.	TD	. . . . .	Communion cups and paten covers. St. Margaret, Westminster.
Do.	IG	. . . , .	Plain alms-dish. Gloucester Cathedral.
Do.	. .	Animal sejant, as in 1653.	Gilt pricket candlesticks. Gloucester Cathedral.
Do.	HN	As in 1656 . .	Two-handled caudle-cup. Messrs. Lambert.
Do.	WC	. . . , .	Small caudle-cup, ring handles. Hon. Soc. of Lincoln's Inn.
Do.	RN	. . . .	Flagons, given 1662. Charles Ch., Plymouth.
Do.	CS	Probably Christopher Shaw.	Loving cup, given 1662. Saddlers' Company.
Do.	ET	As in 1653 . .	Plain communion cup, baluster-stem. Brigham, Cumb.
1662	WM	. . . , . .	Frosted cup on baluster-stem. Mansion House, Lond.
Do.	IW	As in 1655 .	Plain communion flagons. Bermondsey, Surrey.
Do.	Do.	Do. . . , .	Quart tankard, flat lid. In the collection of the late Paul Butler, Esq.

DATE	MAKER'S MARK.		ARTICLE AND OWNER.
1662	R.N	As in 1661 . . .	Patens. Chester Cathedral.
Do.	(TP)	. . . . .	Caudle-cup, with cover and handles. Queen's Coll., Oxford.
Do.	(IR)	. . . .	Communion cup. Linton, Yorks.
Do.	(IN)	. . . . .	Jug-shaped flagons. Chester Cathedral.
Do.	(TD)	. . . .	Small gilt paten. Chester Cathedral.
Do.	TA	As in 1660 . . .	Two-handled porringer. Emmanuel Coll., Camb.
1663	(WN)	. . . .	Frosted cup on baluster-stem, *ex dono* Henley, 1664. Hon. Soc. of Middle Temple.
Do.	AF	Probably Ant. Fic- kettes.	Another smaller, *ex dono* Barker. Hon. Soc. of Middle Temple.
Do.	HN	As in 1656 . .	Small plain paten. Hackney, Midx.
Do.	GS	As in 1658 . . .	Large paten. Hunstanton, Norf.
Do.	CS	As in 1661 . .	Paten, dated 1663. Leamington Hastings, Warw.
Do.	HG	As in 1656 . . .	Tall tankards, strap foliage. Imperial Treasury, Moscow.
Do.		A mullet above an escallop between pellets & annulets.	Pair of repoussé candlesticks. Imperial Treasury, Moscow.
1664	FW	. . . .	Plain communion flagon, purchased 1664. Also pair of smaller flagons. St. Mary, Lambeth.
Do.	R·S	. . . . .	Plain two-handled drinking-bowl. Armourers' Company.
Do.	Do.	. . . . .	Flat quart tankard. Lord Tredegar.
Do.	. .	Escallop under mul- let, as in 1663.	Jug-shaped communion flagons. Canterbury Cathedral.
Do.	S	. . . .	Large paten on central foot. St. Stephen, Exeter.
1665	M	. . . . .	Hanbury's cup. Goldsmiths' Company.
Do.	HR	. . . .	Large paten or alms-dish. St. Margaret, West- minster. Also 1683 Com. plate. Shrewsbury.
Do.	C	. . . . .	Communion cup, given 1666. Otford, Kent.
Do.	TH	. . . .	Gilt dish, repoussé flowers. Erddig, N.Wales.
1666	M	. . . . .	Plain tankard. Fishmongers' Company.
1667	TK	. . .	Four plain small trencher salts. Cotehele House, Cornw.
Do.	IK	. . . .	Set of three-pronged forks. Cotehele House, Cornw.
Do.	FW	As in 1664. . . .	Plain communion cup and paten. Messrs. Garrards.

DATE	MAKER'S MARK.		ARTICLE AND OWNER.
1667	TH	Anchor between, as in 1665.	Flat-lidded tankard, dated 1666. Cordwainers' Company.
1668	IC	. . . . .	Gilt salver, dated 1668. St. Paul, Covent Garden, Lond.
Do.	RD	. . . .	Rose-water dish. Trinity House.
Do.	WM	Crowned, mullet below, shaped shield	Plain communion flagons. Holy Trinity, Minories, Lond.
Do.	IN	As in 1662 . . .	Wall brackets or sconces, repoussé. Sudeley Castle.
Do.	I*G	. . . .	Plain plate, *ex dono* Raikes, 1668. Trin. House, Hull.
1669	IC	As in 1668 . . .	Great communion flagon. St. Paul, Covent Garden, Lond.
Do.	T*A	. . . .	Small cup on low foot, cable pattern round lower edge. Armourers' Company.
Do.	I·B	See 1670 . . .	Communion cup, dated 1670. The Dutch Church, Austin Friars, Lond.
Do.	TM	. . . .	Porringer and cover, cut-card work. Lord Tredegar.
Do.	WH	Cherub's face below.	Cup on high stem, cut-card work. Hon. Soc. of Gray's Inn.
Do.	TH	Anchor between, as in 1665.	Loving cup, given 1669. Oriel Coll., Oxford.
Do.	RL	. . . .	Paten. Elland, Yorks.
Do.	WW	. . . . .	Large mace, given 1669. Corporation of Hedon.
1670	PP	. . . .	Flat tankard. Trinity House.
Do.	WH	. . . . .	Porringer and cover repoussé with animals and flowers. Earl Bathurst, C.M.G.
Do.	TM	As in 1669 . .	Rose-water ewer and salver, plain. Hon. Soc. of Inner Temple.
Do.	TK	. . . .	Flat tankard. Armourers' Company.
Do.	I*B	See 1669 . . .	Mace. Ward of Billingsgate, Lond.
Do.	Do.	. . . .	Porringer with cover, cut-card work ornament, dated 1670. Queen's Coll., Oxford.
Do.	RL	As in 1669 . . .	Plain alms-plate. Hatherop, Glouc.
Do.	RH	. . . .	Small tankard, engraved Chinese figures. South Kensington Museum.
1671	Do.	. . . . .	Lid of the above. South Kensington Museum.
Do.	Do.	. . . . .	Plain alms-dish, gift of Katherine Cheney, 1671. Hackney, Midx.
Do.	Do.	. . . . .	Plain tumbler cup. All Souls' Coll., Oxford.

DATE	MAKER'S MARK.		ARTICLE AND OWNER.
1671	E G	. . . . .	Flat tankard. Armourers' Company.
Do.	I:D	. . . .	Loving cup. Fishmongers' Company.
Do.	W W	As in 1669 . . .	Tankard set with Greek coins and bearing scenes from life of Penn. H.M. the King.
Do.	O S	. . . .	Communion cup. Nunnington, Yorks.
1672	S	Crowned, as in 1664.	Loving-cup and cover, repoussé scrolls, etc. Grocers' Company.
Do.	L C	See 1686‾ . . .	Flat-handled forks. Charterhouse, Lond.
Do.	M	. . . . .	Plain communion flagon. Ashridge House Chapel.
Do.	W H	Cherub's face below, as in 1669.	Grace cup on high stem, ornamented with cut-card work. Hon. Soc. of Gray's Inn.
Do.	M	. . . . .	Tankard, cut-card work. Queen's Coll., Oxford.
1673	H E	. . . .	Plain alms-dish. Cirencester, Glouc.
Do.		BG in cypher, star above.	The Knole toilet service. Lord Sackville.
Do.	W·W	. . . .	Alms-plate, dated 1673. Crediton, Devon.
1674	I N	As in 1662 . . .	Two-handled porringer and ewer, called the "Cutler" cup. In the collection of the late Paul Butler, Esq.
Do.	A K	. . . .	Flat-stemmed spoon dug up at Brogyntyn. Lord Harlech.
Do.	D R	. . . . .	Tankard. Christ's Hospital, London.
Do.	I C	As in 1668 .	Plain paten or alms-plate. North Cerney, Glouc.
Do.	I B	As in 1669 . . .	Set of vases and beakers like Chinese porcelain jars. In the collection of the late Marquess of Breadalbane.
Do.	I A	. . . .	Flagon, given 1678. Titsey, Surrey.
Do.	G G	. . . . .	Alms-plate, given 1673. Chiddingstone, Kent.
1675	T L	. . . .	Ewer and plain salver, the gift of the Earl of Anglesey, 1675. Hon. Soc. of Lincoln's Inn.
Do.	O S	. . . . .	Large paten. Ansley, Warw.
Do.	$	. . . .	Plain paten. Rendcombe, Glouc. (This maker's mark is found on much plate.)
Do.	C M	. . . . .	Paten, dated 1675. Offham, Kent.
1676	Do.	. . . .	Plain rude communion cup. Steyning, Sussex.

DATE	MAKER'S MARK.		ARTICLE AND OWNER.
1676	(RM)	. . . .	Ewer and salver, the gift of Sir Joseph Williamson, 1676. Clothworkers' Company.
Do.	A M	Monogram, as in 1672	Tankard on lion feet. Lord Harlech.
Do.	FS	. . . .	Small flat tankard. Corporation of Oxford.
Do.	OS	As in 1675 .	Flat-lidded tankard. All Souls' Coll., Oxford.
Do.	(TF)	. . . .	Cup given by Countess of Burlington, 1677. Keighley, Yorks.
Do.	(ASI)	Thos. Ash . .	Octagonal flat hour-glass salt. Saddlers' Com.
1677	(TM)	. . . .	Two-handled caudle-cup. Hon. Soc. of Lincoln's Inn.
Do.	(I·R)	. . . . .	Frosted cup on baluster-stem. Fishmongers' Company.
Do.	(TC)	Found 1677–88 on Kent church plate.	Plain communion cup, given 1677. Winchcombe, Glouc.
Do.	IS	Monogram, as in 1675.	Ewer and basin, gift of Samuel Pepys, 1677. Clothworkers' Company.
Do.	RM	Monogram, as in 1676.	Square salt, with four projecting arms. Clothworkers' Company.
Do.	(JG)	JG Monogram, reversed . .	The "Pepys" cup, open-work silver casing over gilt standing-cup. Clothworkers' Company.
Do.	(W·S)	. . . . .	Plain silver flagons. Welbeck Abbey.
Do.	(IH)	. . . .	Loving cup with acanthus ornament. Stationers' Company.

ALPHABET XI. 1678—1696, Part 1.

1678	IS	Monogram, as in 1675	Pair of flagons. St. Nicholas, Bristol.
Do.	(A·R)	. . . .	Tall flagon, given 1679. Skinners' Company.
1679	(BP)	Probably Benj. Pyne	Rose-water salver. Hon. Soc. of Middle Temple.
Do.	I.R	As in 1677 .	Flat tankard, acanthus pattern round lower part of barrel. Trinity House.
Do.	(IS)	. . . .	Flat-handled spoons, dated 1679. Cutlers' Company.
Do.	(IK)	. . . . .	Flat-handled spoons. Cotehele House, Cornw.
Do.	(IB)	. . . .	Straight-sided porringer, acanthus decoration. G. E. L. Baker, Esq.
1680	(RL)	Probably Ralph Leeke.	Rose-water ewer and salver. Hon Soc. of Middle Temple.
			NOTE.—There is plate at Westminster Abbey and other places by this maker, but without date-letter.

DATE	MAKER'S MARK.		ARTICLE AND OWNER.
1680	FS	As in 1676 . .	Large plain gilt alms-dish. All Souls' Coll., Oxford.
Do.	I·B	. . . .	Tall loving cup on baluster-stem, given by the Spanish Ambassador who was in England at the time of the plague. New Coll., Oxford.
Do.	·T·L·	. . . .	The Knole silver table. Lord Sackville.
Do.	. .	. . , .	Porringer, 6¾ inches high, with two handles and cover, made of solid gold. Corporation of Oxford.
Do.	IS	Monogram, etc., as in 1675.	Frosted cup, on baluster-stem. Fishmongers' Company.
Do.	RH	. . , .	Pair of ditto, given by John Brett, senr. and junr., 1680. Merchant Taylors' Company.
Do.	EG	As in 1671 .	Alms-dishes. St. Martin, Exeter.
Do.	M	. . . .	Tall flagons, *ex dono* Beckford. Clothworkers' Company.
Do.	·TA·	. . .	Large paten. Guisbro', Yorks.
1681	R.L	As in 1680 . .	Immense ice-cistern, exhibited in Loan Collection of 1862. Duke of Rutland.
Do.	IC	, , ,	Flat tankard, barrel with acanthus ornament. Fishmongers' Company.
Do.	F·W	. , ,	Large paten or alms-plate, given 1682. St. Peter ad Vincula, Tower of London.
Do.		. . .	Pair of small plain communion cups, dated 1681. Minchinhampton, Glouc.
Do.	W·S	. , , .	Shallow basin ornamented with cut-card work on cover. Earl Bathurst, C.M.G.
Do.	MK	. . .	Communion flagon, given 1681. Cricklade St. Sampson, Wilts.
Do.	II	. . . .	Large tankard with acanthus ornament round bottom. Christ's Coll., Camb.
Do.	.	. . ,	Tall pricket candlesticks, like columns. Exeter Cathedral.
Do.	AH	. . . .	Two-handled cup, gift of Rich, 1681. Saddlers' Company.
Do.	RH	. . . .	Large paten, given 1681. Whiston, Yorks.
Do.	L·S	. . . .	Plain paten. Leeds, Kent.
1682		A water-bird; found 1678—93.	Frosted cup on baluster-stem. Hon. Soc. of Middle Temple.
Do.	EG	. . .	Alms-dish, plain. Cirencester, Glouc.
Do.	GG	Probably George Garthorne.	Plain communion cup, given 1684. Stow-on-the Wold, Glouc.

DATE	MAKER'S MARK.		ARTICLE AND OWNER.
1682	I·W ✿	. . . . .	Communion flagon, given 1683. Ampney Crucis, Glouc.
Do.	✱ P·M ✚	. . . .	Small tankard, repoussé strap-work. **Trin. Coll.,** Oxford.
Do.	D	. . . .	Toilet service, engraved with Chinese subjects. Messrs. Lambert.
1683	BG	Cypher with star above, as in 1673.	Cup and cover, acanthus ornament and fluted, given 1683. Hon. Soc. of the Middle Temple.
Do.	FS	As in 1676 . .	Communion paten, given by President Bathurst. Trin. Coll., Oxford.
Do.	PK ✱	. . . . .	The "Berners" toilet set.
Do.	TC	As in 1677 .	Very small plain communion cup. Kensington, Midx.
Do.	I·V	(EV Damaged letters)	Cup with handle and spout. Holy Trinity, Minories, Lond.
Do.	SR	. . . . .	Plain tankard. Clothworkers' Company.
Do.	WF	. . . .	Toilet service. (Late Sir Charles **Trevelyan,** Bart.) South Kensington Museum.
Do.	RS	In heart, mullet below.	Small spoon, with two-pronged fork handle. (O. Morgan Coll.)
Do.	RP	. . . .	Flagon, dated 1683. St. Mary-le-Port, Bristol.
Do.	WF	WF linked letters .	Gilt tankards repoussé with battle-scenes. H.M. the King.
1684	R	Found 1677—93 .	Communion flagons, ornamented all over with repoussé work; also tall pricket candlesticks. Westminster Abbey.
Do.	T	. . . .	Gilt punch-ladle. Fishmongers' Company.
Do.	RC	. . . . .	Porringer and cover, engraved with Chinese subjects. T. W. C. Master, Esq.
Do.	Do.	. . . .	Porringer and cover, *ex dono* Mansell. Jesus Coll., Oxford.
Do.	TA	. . . . .	Square salts, with four projecting arms. Clothworkers' Company.
Do.	P	Benj. Pyne; see 1723	Communion cup. Chedworth, Glouc.
Do.	H	SH linked letters .	Large flagon, bought 1685. Kensington, Midx.
1685	J	. . . . .	Octagonal salt. Mercers' Company.
Do.	Do.	. . . .	Doric-column candlesticks. Merchant Taylors' Company.

DATE	MAKER'S MARK.		ARTICLE AND OWNER.
1685	IS	. . . . .	Table-spoons. Mercers' Company.
Do.	PK	As in 1683 . .	Helmet cup, ornamented with cut-card work, given 1684. Merchant Taylors' Company.
Do.	DB	Probably Buteux .	Pair of salvers on circular central feet, given 1684. Merchant Taylors' Company. Also 1696.
Do.	*D*	As in 1682 . .	Punch-bowl. Lord Harlech.
Do.	TI	Probably T. Issod .	Communion cup and paten. Dumbleton, Glouc.
Do.	TI	Another mark for T. Issod . .	Also pair of maces, dated 1590. Bodmin. Cup. Goldsmiths' Hall.
Do.	ST	In monogram crowned, as in 1681	Set of sconces, repoussé with arms. Lord Sackville.
Do.	P·R	. . . .	Plain flat tankard. Clothworkers' Company.
Do.	IₘY	. . . . .	Bowl repoussé and engraved in alternate divisions, handles formed of plain flat coiled silver riband. (Staniforth Coll.)
Do.	(3 storks)	3 Storks . . .	Pair of jugs, cut-card ornament. Wynnstay.
Do.	GG	As in 1682 . . .	Plain punch-bowl, given 1686. Skinners' Co.
Do.	IC	As in 1681 .	Plain tankard, *ex dono* Sebright. Jesus Coll., Oxford.
1686	Y·T	Two pellets above fleur-de-lys below.	Two com. cups gilt. St. Mary Abchurch, London.
Do.	S	As in 1664 .	Two-handled cup, cover and stand. Christ's Hospital, London.
Do.	S⊙D	Probably Samuel Dell.	Plain alms-plate. Winchcombe, Glouc.
Do.	RL	As in 1680 . .	Set of dinner-plates, with shaped and gadrooned edge. Earl Bathurst.
Do.	L·C	Probably Lawrence Coles ; see 1672	Flat-stemmed, split-ended spoon. (Octavius Morgan Coll.)
Do.	DB	Buteux, as in 1685 .	Pair of candlesticks with baluster-stems. Leeds Castle, Kent.
Do.	WE	. . . .	A similar pair. Welbeck.
1687	NG	Probably Nat. Greene	Alms-dish, given 1688. Avening, Glouc.
Do.	EG	As in 1682 . .	Plain half-pint tumbler. All Souls' Coll., Oxf.
1688	IC	. . . .	Flat-stemmed, rat-tailed table-spoons. Hon. Soc. of Middle Temple.
Do.	*GJ*	Linked as in 1684 .	Plain paten on central foot. St. Mary Arches, Exeter.
Do.	FG	Probably Fras. Garthorne.	Plates, dated 1689. St. Mary-le-Bow, Durham.
Do.	I·I	Probably John Jackson.	Two handled-cup, Chinese engraving. Coachmakers' Company.
1689	P	As in 1684 . .	Large repoussé paten, given 1690. Uffington, Linc.

DATE	MAKER'S MARK.		ARTICLE AND OWNER.
1689	FG	As in 1688 . . .	Plain-gilt casters. H. M. the King.
Do.	P♣H	Probably Peeter Harache. See p. 63	Circular stand with gadrooned foot. Sir F. Milbank, Bart.
Do.	⟨C	Probably Ant. Nelme	Toilet-mirror frame, Chinese style. Leeds Castle, Kent.
1690	*A*	As in 1682 . . .	Caudle-cup, called a "plate" at Queen's Coll., Oxford.
Do.	WB	. . . .	Large Doric-column candlesticks. Hon. Soc. of Middle Temple.
Do.	K	. . . . .	Communion flagons, dated 1690. Preston, Glouc.
Do.	P	As in 1684 . .	Alms-dish, dated 1690. Kensington, Midlx.
Do.	R	R. Timbrell . .	Plain flat tankard, dated 1690. Clothworkers' Company.
1691	FG	See 1688 and 1728 .	Salver, gadrooned edge, centre chased with "The Last Supper." St. Margaret, Westminster.
Do.	FS	As in 1676 . .	Plain half-pint tumbler. All Souls' Coll., Oxford.
Do.	IY	As in 1685 .	Another. All Souls' Coll., Oxford.
Do.	R·T	Probably R. Timbrell	Frosted cup, baluster-stem. Fishmongers' Company.
Do.	IC	Probably James Chadwick.	Large flagon, dated 1691. St. Mary Arches, Exeter.
Do.	MH	. . . . .	Loving cups, acanthus decoration, dated 1692. Stationers' Company.
1692	IY	As in 1685 .	Flagons, dated 1692. St. Petrock, Exeter.
Do.	Do.	Do.	Flagons, dated 1692. St. Martin, Exeter.
Do.	P	As in 1684 .	Plain gilt toilet service, gadrooned edges. Marquis of Breadalbane.
Do.	GG	As in 1682 . .	Jug-flagon with scroll-handle and cut-card ornament. Kensington Palace Chapel.
1693	RL	As in 1680 , .	Communion plate given by " Sarah, late dutchess of Somerset," 1694. St. Margaret, Westminster.
Do.	·R·T·	As in 1691 . .	Plain jug-shaped communion flagon. Foulden, Norf.
Do.	ME	. . .	Small rudely shaped communion cup, dated 1694. Poole Keynes, Wilts.
Do.	RC	As in 1684 . .	Small communion cups with covers, given 1694. St. James', Westminster.
Do.	T·K	Fish above .	Cup with paten-cover. Old Romney, Kent.
Do.	. .	Water bird, as in 1682.	Tall flagon, dated 1694. Weston Subedge, Glouc.
Do.	WK	Probably Wm. Keatt.	Flagons. Holy Trinity, Hull.
1694	IR	Probably John Ruslen.	Frosted cups, baluster stems, gift of the Bank of England. Mercers' Company.

DATE	MAKER'S MARK.		ARTICLE AND OWNER.
1694	I·I	As in 1688 . .	Communion cup, dated 1694. Llangedwyn, N. Wales.
Do.		Probably Robert Cooper.	Communion cup and paten cover, very plain and rude. Didlington, Norf.
Do.		Probably Thomas Allen.	Alms-plates, dated 1695. Halifax, Yorks.
Do.	TI	Escallops, as in 1685.	Ewer, gadrooned. Lord Sackville.
Do.		. . . . .	Tankard, flat lid. Magd. Coll., Oxford.
Do.		. . . .	Oblong box inkstand, acanthus ornament. Col. Warde, Squerries, Kent.
Do.	FG	As in 1688 . . .	Credence paten with royal arms. Trin. Ch., New York, U. S. A.
1695	I·I	As in 1688 .	Pair of communion flagons, given 1695. St. Margaret, Westminster.
Do.	I·C	As in 1691 . . .	Large paten or alms-plate on central foot, gadrooned edge. St. Winnoe, Cornw.
1696 (1st pt.)		As in 1682 .	Monteith, ex dono Abney. Fishmongers' Com.
Do.		. . . . .	Paten on central foot, gadrooned edge, given 1698. Byfield, Northants.
Do.		Thos. Brydon .	Jug-shaped flagon, dated 1696. St. Mary, Beverley, Yorks.
Do.		. . . . .	Spoon. St. Nicholas, Bristol.
Do.		. . . .	Plain communion cup, dated 1696. Boughton Monchelsey, Kent.
Do.		Probably Andrew Moore.	Pair of fire-dogs. H. M. the King.
1696 (2nd pt.)	. . . . . .		ALPHABET XII. 1696, Part 2—1715. Communion flagon. St. Bride, Chester.
1697		Wm. Denny and John Bathe.	Tall communion cup on baluster-stem, with paten-cover. Kensington, Midx.
Do.		. . . . .	Straining-spoon. Westminster Abbey.
Do.		Hugh Roberts in Newgate Street.	Communion cup with gadrooned knop and foot; also a paten. Byfield, Northants.
Do.	. .	. . . .	Pair of large communion flagons, dated 1697. Chelmsford, Essex.
Do.		Joseph Bird . .	Candlesticks, baluster-stems. Welbeck.
Do.		James Chadwick .	Dinner-plates. Lord St. Oswald.

DATE	MAKER'S MARK.	ARTICLE AND OWNER.
1697	William Gibson .	Dinner-plates. Lord St. Oswald.
Do.	Richard Hutchinson of Colchester.	Large flagons, dated 1697. Chelmsford, Essex.
1698	John Ruslen at yᵉ Golden Cup in Swithin Lane.	Monteith, punch-ladle and salver. Fishmongers' Company.
Do.	Benj. Watts, ent. 1698.	Rat-tailed spoon. Late W. R. M. Wynne, Esq., Peniarth. Also flagon, dated 1699. Haxey, Lincs.
Do.	Denny and Bathe, as in 1697.	Plain gilt alms-plate engraved with Mann arms, Linton, Kent.
Do.	Robert Peake, ent. 1697.	Large paten on foot. Melbury, Dorset.
Do.	William Fawdery .	Tall flagons, given 1698. New Romney, Kent. Another. Leamington Hastings, Warw.
1699	Robert Timbrell . .	Pair of fine Monteiths. Mercers' Company.
Do.	Benj. Traherne .	Four small patens. St. Margaret, Westminster.
Do.	Simon Pantin, ent. 1701.	Flat taper candlestick. Earl Bathurst, C.M.G.
Do.	Joseph Stokes, ent. 1697.	Fluted porringer. (R. T. Frere Coll.)
Do.	Francis Singleton .	Large plain salver, gift of Lord Chancellor Somers, as Recorder of the City. Corporation of Gloucester.
Do.	Samuell Hood . .	Monteith. (Staniforth Coll.)
Do.	Samuel Thorne, ent. 1697.	Monteith, gilt, noted by the author.
Do.	John Chartier, ent. 1698.	Communion plate. Ch. Ch., Oxford.
Do.	William Lukin, ent. 1699.	Preserving saucepan. G. E. L. Baker, Esq.
Do.	Samuel Dell, ent. 1697.	Large alms-dish. Holy Trinity, Coventry.
Do.	William Gamble, ent. 1697.	Paten. Great Ouseburn, Yorks.
1700	Peeter Harracke, jun., ent. 1698.	Very large salver. Earl Bathurst, C.M.G. NOTE.—Some of the splendid plate made for the great Duke of Marlborough, and exhibited in the Loan Collection of 1862 by Earl Spencer, was by this maker.
Do.	Anthony Nelme . .	Fine large Monteith, dated 1700. Merchant Taylors' Company.

DATE	MAKER'S MARK.		ARTICLE AND OWNER.
1700	(Co)	John Cory . . .	Paten. Auborn, Linc.
1701	(BO)	George Boothby, at the sign of the Parrot.	Helmet ewer. Eton College.
Do.	(BO)	John Bodington .	Plain communion flagon. North Cerney, Glouc.
Do.	(LE)	George Lewis, ent. 1699.	Plain communion cup, goblet shape, and cover. Cricklade St. Sampson, Wilts.
Do.	(PY)	Benjamin Pyne, see 1684 and 1723.	Circular salvers, on round central feet. Hon. Soc. of Gray's Inn.
1702	(WA)	Joseph Ward, ent. 1697.	Plain communion cup and cover. Sapperton, Glouc.
Do.	Do.	Do.	Plain communion cup and cover. Duntisbourne Rous, Glouc.
Do.	(FA)	John Fawdery (A smaller than the F).	Monteith. Vintners' Company.
Do.	(PL)	Pierre Platel, ent. 1699.	Helmet-cup with strap-work ornament, and two-handled cups. Messrs. Garrards, 1878.
Do.	(CO)	Robert Cooper, ent. 1697.	Large paten, dated 1703. Weston Subedge, Glouc.
1703	(SV)	John Sutton . .	Paten. Long Marston, Yorks.
Do.	(AN)	William Andrewes .	Tankard. South Kensington Museum. Also much Kent church plate 1697–1707.
1704	(LA)	John Ladyman . .	Table-spoon. W. Cripps, Esq., C.B.
Do.	Do.	Do.	Spoon, flat stem, cut end. (Staniforth Coll.)
Do.	(Ro)	Philip Rolles . .	Fire-dogs. Welbeck.
Do.	(SM)	John Smith . . .	Communion cup. Driffield, Glouc.
1705	(Lo)	Seth Lofthouse, ent. 1697.	Plain half-pint tumbler. All Souls' Coll., Oxford.
Do.	HA	Peeter Harracke, as in 1700.	Helmet-shaped ewer. Vintners' Company.
Do.	Do.	Do.	Large two-handled cup and cover. Berkeley Castle.
Do.	Do.	Do.	A small racing cup of gold. Thorp-Perrow.
Do.	(EA)	John Eastt, ent. 1697.	Communion plate. Newton, Norfolk.
Do.	(St PE)	John Martin Stocker and Edwd. Peacock, ent. 1705.	Large paten, *ex dono* Pendarves. St. Ives. Cornwall.

DATE	MAKER'S MARK.		ARTICLE AND OWNER.
1706	**Ti**	R. Timbrell, as in 1699.	Large flat-lidded tankard. Vintners' Company.
Do.	[mark]	David Willaume in the Pell Mell.	Helmet-cup with mermaid-handle and a salver. Fishmongers' Company.
Do.	[mark]	Edward York, ent. 1705.	Pair of patens on circular central feet. Gray's Inn Chapel.
Do.	**PY**	B. Pyne, as in 1701.	Cruet-stand. Lord Tredegar.
Do.	[mark]	J. Barbut, ent. 1703	Rat-tailed spoons. Hon. Soc. of Inner Temple.
Do.	[mark]	John Gibbons, ent. 1700.	Paten. Springthorpe, Linc.
Do.	[mark]	John Downes, ent. 1697.	Paten. Paull, Yorks.
Do.	[mark]	Andrew Raven.	Paten, dated 1706. St. Mary Bishophill, senior, York.
1707	**PA**	Simon Pantin, as in 1699.	Very large two-handled cup and cover. Earl Bathurst.
Do.	[mark]	Alice Sheene, ent. 1700.	Plain paten or alms-plate. Chedworth, Glouc.
1708	**FA**	Wm. Fawdery, as in 1698.	Punch-ladle. Hon. Soc. of Middle Temple.
Do.	[mark]	John Wisdome, ent. 1704.	Small plain chocolate pot. Lord Hotham.
Do.	. .	Edward York, as in 1706.	Paten on foot. Kemble, Wilts.
Do.	**WI**	David Willaume, as in 1706.	Large round salver on foot. Earl Bathurst, C.M.G.
Do.	**CO**	Robert Cooper, as in 1702.	Communion cup and patens, given 1708. Lincoln's Inn Chapel.
Do.	[mark]	"Goyce Issod widdow."	Two-handled fluted porringer, used as a chalice. Uley, Glouc.
1709	[mark]	Thomas Allen in Gutter Lane.	Rat-tailed table-spoons. Hon. Soc. of Middle Temple.
Do.	[mark]	Samuel Hood, as in 1699.	Pair of salvers, gadrooned edge. Mercers' Co.
Do.	**PA**	Simon Pantin, as in 1699.	Globular box, perhaps for soap. Lord Hotham.
Do.	[mark]	Gabriel Sleath, ent. 1706.	Another. Lord Hotham. NOTE.—These boxes are like the object above the initials in Sleath's mark.
Do.	[mark]	Humphrey Payne, ent. 1701.	Large plain communion flagon, dated 1709. Winchcombe, Glouc.
Do.	[mark]	Francis Garthorne, ent. 1697.	Communion plate, gift of Q. Anne. Trinity Ch., New York, U.S.A.
Do.	[mark]	John Read, ent. 1704.	Communion cup. Wrexham, N. Wales.
1710	**PY**	B. Pyne, as in 1701.	Gilt two-handled drinking cup and cover. St. Margaret, Westminster.

DATE	MAKER'S MARK.		ARTICLE AND OWNER.
1710	**PY**	B. Pyne, as in 1701 .	Gold two-handled cup and cover. Noted by the author.
Do.	(Ⓖ🅡)	Richard Greene, ent. 1703.	Paten or alms-plate on foot. Oxburgh, Norf.
Do.	𝕃o	Seth Lofthouse, as in 1705.	Paten. Bradford, Yorks.
Do.	(🅡⚓)	Philip Rolles, junior, ent. 1705.	Small chocolate pot. Lord Sackville.
Do.	(SL)	Another mark of Gabriel Sleath.	Large monteith, lion handles, &c. The Winter Palace, St. Petersburg.
1711	Do.	Do.	Paten and flagon. Sapperton, Glouc.
Do.	**GA**	A within the G. as in 1709. Francis Garthorne.	Communion plate, gift of Q. Anne. St. Peter's, Albany, N. Y.
Do.	(Lo)	Nath. Lock, ent. 1698.	Plain alms-plate. Bermondsey Church, Surrey.
Do.	**EA**	John Eastt, as in 1705.	Paten. Buxton, Norf.
Do.	(PE)	Edmund Pearce, ent. 1704.	Two-handled cup and cover. Lord Harlech.
1712	(Ⓛ)	Matth. E. Lofthouse, ent. 1705.	Fine half-gallon tankard. All Souls' Coll., Oxford.
Do.	(TW)	William Twell, ent. 1709.	Candlesticks with octagonal bases. Noted by the author.
1713	(V★I)	Probably Edward Vincent.	Helmet-ewer. Trin. Coll., Oxford.
Do.	𝕃u	William Lukin, as in 1699.	A fine monteith. Mansion House, Lond.
Do.	**PA**	S. Pantin, as in 1699	Shaped salvers. Hatfield House.
1714	. .	Matth. E. Lofthouse, as in 1712.	Plain communion cup. Coates, Glouc.
Do.	. .	Do.	Large repoussé and chased salad bowl. W. Cripps, Esq., C.B.
Do.	(BA)	John Bathe, ent. 1700.	Plain dinner plates. Viscount Falmouth. Also 1720, church-plate.
1715	**PY**	B. Pyne, as in 1701.	Hand candlestick. Ravensworth Castle.
Do.	**BO**	John Bodington, as in 1701.	Plain octagonal chocolate pot. W. Cripps, Esq., C.B.
Do.	**PY**	B. Pyne, as in 1701.	Helmet-ewer and salver. Berkeley Castle.
Do.	(LI)	Isaac Liger in Heming's Row, ent. 1704.	Three-pronged table forks. Lord Amherst of Hackney.
Do.	**Pa**	H, Payne, as in 1709	Paten. Llangedwyn, N. Wales.
Do.	(FL)	Wm. Fleming, ent. 1697.	Small oval tray, edge lobed outwards. Lord Amherst of Hackney.
Do.	**EA**	John Eastt, as in 1705.	Plain communion cup and cover. Foulden, Norfolk.
Do.	(T𝔅)	Robert Timbrell	Communion flagon. Belton, Linc.

DATE	MAKER'S MARK.		ARTICLE AND OWNER.
1715		William Spackman, ent. 1714.	Paten. Dent, Yorks.
Do.		Petley Ley, ent. 1715	Paten. Borden, Kent.
Do.		Samuel Hitchcock, ent. 1712.	Rat-tailed table-spoons. Lord St. Oswald.
			ALPHABET XIII. 1716—1735.
1716	SL	Gabriel Sleath, as in 1710.	Flagon dated 1716, given by the widow of Sir Robert Atkyns. Coates, Glouc.
Do.	Pa	H. Payne, as in 1709	Loving cups on baluster stems, monteiths, salvers, etc. Salters' Company.
Do.		Henry Jay . . .	Alms-plates, dated 1718. Hunton, Kent.
Do.		Niccolaus Clausen, ent. 1709.	Massive ink-tray. Welbeck.
Do.		Samuell Lea, ent. 1711.	Tankard. G. E. L. Baker, Esq.
1717	WI	John Wisdome, as in 1708.	Communion flagon. Kemble, Wilts.
Do.		Paul Lamerie, ent. 1712.	Gold two-handled cup and cover. Berkeley Castle.
Do.	• •	M. E. Lofthouse, as in 1712.	Plain paten or alms-plate on central foot. Foulden, Norf.
Do.	TA	David Tanqueray, ent. 1713.	Circular salver on central foot. Narford Hall, Norf.
Do.	BA	Richard Bayley, ent. 1708.	Taper candlestick. Late Rt. Hon. Sir J. R. Mowbray, Bart.
1718	Ho	Edward Holaday in Grafton St., ent. 1709.	Immense upright flagons given by the Corporation of Mines Royal, etc., 1718. Mercers' Co.
Do.	FA	W.Fawdery as in 1698	Monteith, given 1718. Hon. Soc. of Lincoln's Inn.
Do.	TA	Tanqueray, as in 1717	Coffee-cup saucers, with frames to hold the cups. Narford Hall, Norf.
Do.	SL	G. Sleath, as in 1709.	Monteith, bull's-head handles. Clothworkers' Co.
Do.		Jonah Clifton, ent. 1703.	Patens. Whixley, Yorks.
1719	• •	Anthony Nelme, as in 1700.	Dinner plates, shaped and gadrooned edge. Lord Hotham.
Do.	Wi	John White, ent. 1719	Low open dishes, fluted. T. W. C. Master, Esq.
Do.	CL	Nicolas Clausen, as in 1716.	Shaped dinner plates. Viscount Midleton.
Do.	Ma	Thomas Mason, ent. 1716.	Plates, given 1720. Westerham, Kent.
Do.		Louys Cuny, ent. 1703.	Salver. Late Col. Warde, Squerries, Kent.

DATE	MAKER'S MARK.		ARTICLE AND OWNER.
1719	(MA)	Samuel Margas, ent. 1714.	Candlesticks. Late Col. Warde, Squerries, Kent.
1720	LA	P. Lamerie, as in 1717	Large two-handled cup and cover, chased. Lord Hotham.
Do.	PY	B. Pyne, as in 1701 .	Very large shaped ewer with lid and handle. Mansion House, Lond.
Do.	(EC)	John Eckfourd, in Red Lion Court, Drury Lane, ent. 1698.	Large two-handled cup and cover. Narford Hall, Norfolk. Also cup dated 1719. Doncaster, Yorks.
Do.	(JE)	John Edwards .	Flagons, dated 1720. Scarboro', Yorks.
1721	PY	B. Pyne, as in 1701 .	Three pairs of ewers and salvers, Brit. st. Mansion House, Lond.
Do.	(I·B)	John Bignell, o. s., ent. 1720.	Plain communion cup and cover. Holy Trinity, Minories, Lond.
Do.	· ·	R. Greene, as in 1710	Tankard, Brit. st. Hamon le Strange, Esq.
Do.	(IC)	Joseph Clare, old sterling mark, ent. 1720.	Pint mug. Messrs. Lambert.
Do.	(CO)	Aug. Courtauld, ent. 1708.	Square salver, Brit. st. Messrs. Lambert.
Do.	(EV)	Probably Edw. Vincent.	Communion cups, dated 1722. Orton, Westmor.
1722	(BN)	Bowles Nash, ent. 1721.	Alms-dish, given 1723. St. Margaret, Westminster.
Do.	(GU)	Nathaniell Gulliver, ent. 1722.	Paten, dated 1722. Howden, Yorks. Also 1724, Com. plate. Lincs.
1723	(AB)	Abraham Buteux, ent. 1721.	Oblong salver given by Lady Trollope, 1724. Uffington, Linc.
Do.	(PIa)	Wm. Paradise, ent. 1718.	Small paten, Brit. st. Poole Keynes, Wilts.
Do.	(T·F)	Thos. Ffarrer in Swithing Lane, ent. 1720.	Punch-bowl. Lord Harlech.
Do.	(I·E)	John East, ent. 1721	Large tankard. Armourers' Company.
1724	LI	Isaac Liger, as in 1715.	Low bowl, lobed edge, Brit. st. Narford Hall, Norf.
Do.	Wh	John White, as in 1719.	Communion plate. St. German's, Cornw.
Do.	(MG)	Meshach Godwin, ent. 1722.	Small communion cup, dated 1724. St. Thomas Cliffe, Lewes.
Do.	(MEP)	M. Arnett and E. Pococke, ent. 1720.	Communion cup. Barmston, Yorks.
Do.	(IS)	Jas. Smith, ent. 1720	Communion plate. Owston, Yorks. Also church-plate, 1730. Shrewsbury.

DATE	MAKER'S MARK.	ARTICLE AND OWNER.
1725	Humphrey Payne, old sterling mark, ent. 1720.	Plain beer-jug. Sudeley Castle.
Do.	. . . . . .	Small plain paten, cover to an older cup, both given 1725. Folkestone, Kent.
Do.	George Wickes, ent. 1721.	Paten. Holy Trin., Coventry.
Do.	Paul Hanet, ent. 1721	Dessert forks. Lord Sackville.
Do.	John Edwards, ent. 1724.	Square Salver. Viscount St. Aldwyn.
Do.	David Willaume, ent. 1720.	Dinner plates. Viscount Falmouth.
1726	Edward Wood, ent. 1722.	Repoussé sugar-basin. Lord Amherst of Hackney.
Do.	RC	Paten. Portslade, Sussex.
Do.	LA	P. Lamerie, as in 1717.	Square salver on feet. Messrs. Hunt & Roskell.
Do.	William Atkinson, ent. 1725.	Alms-dish. Burstwick, Yorks.
1727	John Tuite . . .	Shaped snuffer-tray on feet. Lord Amherst of Hackney.
Do.	Paul Crespin, old standard mark, ent. 1720.	Four-pronged table-forks. Narford Hall, Norf.
1728	E·W	Edward Wood, as in 1726.	Small oblong salts. All Souls' Coll., Oxford.
Do.	Do.	Do.	Small oblong salts. (Staniforth Coll.)
Do.	James Gould, ent. 1722.	Table-candlesticks. Lord Amherst of Hackney.
Do.	Edw. Cornock, ent. 1723.	Salver, given 1729. Chart Sutton, Kent.
1729	CR	Paul Crespin, NS1720 (scallop and mullet as in 1727).	Epergne, chased, etc., bearing the royal arms, Brit. st. Lord Hotham.
Do.	Aug. Courtauld, ent. 1729.	Two-handled cup, cover and salver to match. Trinity House, Lond.
Do.	LA	P. Lamerie, as in 1717.	Four small square waiters, Brit. st. Lord Amherst of Hackney.
Do.	Francis Nelme, old standard mark, ent. 1722.	Dinner plates, shaped and gadrooned edge. Earl Bathurst.
Do.	Humphrey Payne, as in 1725.	Plain communion cup. Middle, Salop.
Do.	Lion rampant above. Edward Pocock, ent. 1728.	Small teapot. (Staniforth Coll.)
1730	Probably Jona Kirk, ent. before 1697.	Pair of two-handled cups with covers. Hon. Soc. of Middle Temple.

DATE	MAKER'S MARK.		ARTICLE AND OWNER.
1730	**LA**	P. Lamerie, as in 1717.	Chocolate pot, Brit. st. Lord Amherst of Hackney.
Do.	**T·F**	Thos. Ffarrer, as in 1723.	Pair of alms-plates. Holy Trin., Minories, Lond.
Do.	**AB**	Abraham Buteux, as in 1723.	Two-handled cup and cover, ornamented with raised belts. Sir W. Williams Wynn, Bart.
Do.	(W)	George Wickes, as in 1725.	Set of four gilt maces, arched crown heads. Corporation of Exeter.
Do.	**R·B**	Richard Bayley, NS 1720. Plain oblong	Flagon and alms-dish. Halsall, Lanc.
Do.	(GS)	Gabriel Sleath, ent. 1720.	Covers to pair of older cups. Merchant Taylors' Company.
Do.	[DW]	David Willaume, ent. 1728.	Set of table candlesticks, square bases with corners cut off. Lord Sackville.
Do.	(WL)	William Lukin, ent. 1725.	Small salver. Late Rt. Hon. Sir J. R. Mowbray, Bart.
1731	**LA**	Paul Lamerie, as in 1717.	Set of four small circular salts, with masks above the feet, and wreaths between, Brit. st. Lord Hotham.
Do.	Do.	Do.	Open-work cake-basket, imitation of wicker-work, Brit. st. Sudeley Castle.
Do.	*JJ*	John Tuite, as in 1727.	Set of tea-caddies in shagreen case. Late W. R. M. Wynne, Esq.
Do.	(WD)	Wm. Darker, ent. 1731.	Communion flagon. Sandal, Yorks.
Do.	Do.	Do.	Sauce-pan. Lord Harlech.
Do.	**I·K**	As in 1730 . . .	Tankards (one made of British silver). Mansion House, Lond.
Do.	(I·S)	Joseph Smith, ent. 1728.	Tankard on lion-feet. Ironmongers' Company.
1732	**PC**	Paul Crespin, as in 1727.	Dinner plates, shaped and gadrooned edges. Lord Hotham.
Do.	**EP**	Edward Pocock, as in 1729.	Small square waiters, corners shaped. All Souls' Coll., Oxford.
Do.	(GH)	George Hindmarsh, ent. 1731.	Salvers. Viscount St. Aldwyn.
Do.	(CH)	Caleb Hill, ent. 1728	Table forks. G. E. L. Baker, Esq.
1733	(PL)	Paul Lamerie, 2nd mark, ent. 1732, "old sterling mark"	Large two-handled cup and cover, chased with strap-work ornaments. Lord Amherst of Hackney.
Do.	Do.	Do.	Large oblong salver. Late Sir T. Thornhill, Bart.
Do.	(IG)	John Gamon, ent. 1726-7.	Small pepper-caster. Clothworkers' Company.
1734	(S·W)	Samuel Wood . .	Sugar-casters, plain shape. Clothworkers' Company.
Do.	**AC**	Aug. Courtauld, as in 1729.	Melon-shaped kettle, with lamp and stand. Lord Amherst of Hackney.
Do.	(W·G)	William Gould, ent. 1732.	Taper candlesticks. Clothworkers' Company.
Do.	(KA)	Charles Kandler, ent. 1727.	Immense wine cistern. The Winter Palace, St. Petersburg.

DATE	MAKER'S MARK.	ARTICLE AND OWNER.
1735	R·A	Robert Abercromby, ent. 1731.	Waiter on feet, shaped edge. Late Sir A. H. Church.
Do.	*H P*	Humphrey Payne, as in 1725.	Waiter. J. Vaughan, Esq., Nannau.
Do.	T R·G C	Richard Gurney & Co., old sterling mark, ent. 1734.	Pair of candlesticks. Lord Amherst of Hackney. NOTE.—This mark was first entered in 1727 by Thomas Cooke and Richard Gurney, living at yᵉ Golden Cup in Foster Lane.
Do.	G·S	Gabriel Sleath, as in 1730.	Plain two-handled cups. Clothworkers' Company.
Do.	PA	Peter Archambo . .	Pierced cake-basket. W. C. Master, Esq.
Do.	Do.	Do.	Pierced cake-basket. Lord Harlech.
Do.	GH	Geo. Hindmarsh, ent. 1735.	Fine-shaped salver, given 1735. Clothworkers' Company.
Do.	P·L	Paul Lamerie, as in 1733.	Centre-piece with branches for small baskets, candlesticks, casters, cruets, &c., all interchangeable, with beautifully chased upper basket. Count Bobrinsky, Moscow.
Do.	IE	John Eckford, junior, ent. 1725.	Plain flagon. Minchinhampton, Glouc.
Do.	GW	George Wickes, ent. 1735.	The first mark entered as of the house now occupied by the Messrs. Garrard.

ALPHABET XIV. 1736—1755.

DATE	MAKER'S MARK.	ARTICLE AND OWNER.
1736	R·B	Robert Brown, ent. 1736.	Plain tankard. Vintners' Company.
Do.	RA	Robert Abercromby, as in 1735.	Chased salver on feet. W. C. Master, Esq.
Do.	IA Mᶜ	Joseph Allen and Mordecai Fox, ent. 1729.	Alms-plate. Kensington Palace Chapel.
Do.	IS	John Le Sage, ent. 1722.	Tall sugar-casters. Viscount Falmouth.
1737	P·L	Paul Lamerie, as in 1733.	Dinner plates and dishes to match. Mansion House, Lond.
Do.	L·D	Louis Dupont, ent. 1736.	Two-handled cup and cover. Lord Tredegar.
Do.	IC	Isaac Callard, old sterling, ent. 1726.	Three-pronged table forks. Lord Amherst of Hackney.
Do.	I·S	Joseph Smith, as in 1731.	Pint tankard. Lord Amherst of Hackney.
Do.	*J J*	John Tuite, as in 1727.	Waiter. Lord Harlech.
1738	BS	Benj. Sanders, ent. 1737.	Kettle and stand to form epergne, with candle-branches and sweetmeat trays to fit on. (Octavius Morgan Coll.)
Do.	IS	Joseph Sanders, ent. 1730.	Mark found on portions of the above.
Do.	TT	Thos. Tearle, old sterling, ent. 1720.	Tea-pot repoussé with flowers. (Octavius Morgan Coll.) Also much Kent church-plate, 1725—37.

DATE	MAKER'S MARK.		ARTICLE AND OWNER.
1738	IC	Isaac Callard, as in 1737.	Three-pronged table forks. Lord Tredegar.
Do.	F·S	Fras. Spilsbury, ent. 1729.	Flagon, dated 1738. Tideswell, Derbyshire.
Do.	BG	Benj. Godfrey, ent. 1732.	Broth-basin, with cover, tray, and spoon. Viscount Midleton.
Do.	TR	Thos. Rush, ent. 1724	Flagon, given 1738. St. Mary's, Sandwich, Kent.
1739	PL	P. Lamerie, 3rd mark, ent. 1739.	Two-handled cup and cover, handsomely chased. Lord Tredegar.
Do.	Do.	Do.	Another. Goldsmiths' Company.
Do.	JKing	Jeremiah King, ent. 1739.	Rat-tailed dessert-spoon. Lord Tredegar.
Do.	GW	George Wickes, King's Arms, Panton St., ent. 1739.	
Do.	WG	William Garrard, ent. 1739.	First entry of the name of Garrard, which at length in 1792 becomes associated with that of Wakelin, the successor of Wickes in Panton St.
Do.	TT	Thos. Tearle, ent. 1739.	Flagon. Holy Trin. Micklegate, York.
Do.	AC	Augustin Courtauld, ent. 1739.	Paten, *ex dono* Bathurst. Siddington, Glouc.
1740	RG	Gurney & Co., ent. 1739.	Communion flagon, given 1741. Steyning, Sussex.
Do.	PL	P. Lamerie, as in 1739.	Two-handled cup and cover, chased strap ornaments. Clothworkers' Company.
Do.	WH	William Hunter, ent. 1739.	Pierced and chased cake-basket. All Souls' Coll., Oxford.
Do.	GS	Gabriel Sleath, ent. 1739.	Two-handled cup with cover, and salver to match. Mansion House, Lond.
Do.	TF	Thos. Farren, ent. 1739.	Tankards. Charterhouse, Lond.
Do.	FS	Fras. Spilsbury, ent. 1739.	Small tea-pot. Sir W. Williams Wynn, Bart.
Do.	LP	Lewis Pantin, ent. 1739.	Kettle with lamp and stand. Noted by the author.
1741	PL	P. Lamerie, as in 1739.	Plain saucepan. Messrs. Lambert.
Do.	Do.	Do.	Ewer. Goldsmiths' Company.
Do.	DW	D. Willaume, ent. 1739.	Dinner plates. Viscount Falmouth.
Do.	JA MF	J. Allen and Mordecai Fox, ent. 1739.	Communion plate, gift of K. Geo. II. Trin. Ch. Boston, New England.
1742	EF	Edward Feline, ent. 1739.	Coffee-pot. Sir W. Williams Wynn, Bart.

DATE	MAKER'S MARK.		ARTICLE AND OWNER.
1742	𝕴𝕭	Jeconiah Ashley, ent. 1740.	Large inkstand. Sir W. Williams Wynn, Bart.
Do.	EG	Elizabeth Godfrey .	A paten or alms-plate. St. Minver, Cornw.
Do.	CH	Chas. Hatfield, ent. 1739.	Globe-shaped kettle, lamp and stand. W. C. Master, Esq.
Do.	SW	Samuel Wells, ent. 1740.	Small salver or alms-plate. St. Margaret, Westminster.
Do.	A C I N	John Neville and Ann Craig, ent. 1740.	Spoons and three-pronged forks. E. R. Wingfield, Esq.
Do.	WG	Wm. Gould, ent.1739	Table candlesticks. W. C. Master, Esq.
1743	J.King	As in 1739 . .	Dessert-spoon. W. Cripps, Esq., C.R.
Do.	BW	Benj. West, ent.1739	Baptismal bowl. St. Clement's, Sandwich, Kent.
1744	PL	P. Lamerie, as in 1739.	Plain mug with handle. Lord Amherst of Hackney.
Do.	Do.	Do.	Oblong tea-caddies, masks at corners, panels chased with Chinese subjects. Quentin Hogg, Esq.
Do.	EF	Edward Feline, as in 1742.	Pierced and chased cake-basket. (Octavius Morgan Coll.)
Do.	IR	John Robinson, ent. 1739.	Large salvers on feet, shaped edges. Lord Amherst of Hackney.
Do.	PA	Peter Archambo, ent. 1739.	Candlesticks. Late Rt. Hon. Sir J. R. Mowbray, Bart.
1745	J R·G C	Gurney & Co., as in 1740.	Two-handled cup and cover. Lord Harlech.
Do.	PP	Pézé Pilleau, ent. 1739.	Coffee-pot. Late W. R. M. Wynne, Esq.
1746	Do.	Do.	Kettle, lamp, and stand. Late W. R. M. Wynne, Esq.
Do	PL	Paul Lamerie, as in 1739.	Three plain mugs with handles. Lord Amherst of Hackney.
Do.	HM	Hugh Mills, ent. 1745.	Small salver, shaped edge. Hon. Soc. of Middle Temple.
Do.	J R·G C	Gurney & Co., as in 1740.	Large tankards and also butter-boats. Hon. Soc. of Gray's Inn.
Do.	EG	Eben. Coker, ent. 1739.	Three-pronged forks. Hon. Soc. of Gray's Inn.
Do.	EG	Elizabeth Godfrey, as in 1742.	Pierced and chased cake-basket. Lord Tredegar.

DATE	MAKER'S MARK.		ARTICLE AND OWNER.
1746	WP	William Peaston, ent. 1745-6.	Salver. Late W. R. M. Wynne, Esq.
Do.	J*G	Thos. Gilpin, ent. 1739.	Salver. Late Rev. G. F. E. Shaw.
1747	WG	William Grundy, ent. 1743.	Two-handled cup and cover, chased, given 1747. Fishmongers' Company.
Do.	HM	Hugh Mills, as in 1746.	Salver. Late W. R. M. Wynne, Esq.
Do.	E·W	Edw. Wakelin, ent. 1747.	(See 1739).
Do.	W·C	William Cripps, ent. 1743.	Pierced cake-basket. Late Col. Warde, Squerries, Kent.
Do.	TH	Thos. Heming, ent. 1745.	Jug with cover. Melbury House, Dorset.
1748	GS	Gabriel Sleath, as in 1740.	Plain communion cup, given 1748. Dursley, Glouc.
Do.	ST	Samuel Taylor, ent. 1744.	Tea-caddies in shagreen case. (Edkins Coll.)
Do.	AV	Ayme Vedeau, ent. 1739.	Oval salver, shaped and chased edge. Fishmongers' Company.
1749	PL	P. Lamerie, as in 1739.	Cake-basket, circular salver, also coffee-pot. Lord Amherst of Hackney.
Do.	FW	Fuller White, ent. 1744.	Communion flagon, given 1749. Chapel-Allerton, Yorks.
Do.	JP	John Pollock, ent. 1739.	Sauce-boat. Late W. R. M. Wynne, Esq.
Do.	FK	Fredk. Kandler, ent. 1739.	Kettle, with lamp and stand. E. R. Wingfield, Esq.
1750	WP	William Peaston, as in 1746.	Large lobed rose-water bowl. Trin. Coll., Oxford.
Do.	I·R	John Rowe, ent. 1749.	Two-handled cup. Clothworkers' Company.
Do.	H·P	Humphrey Payne, ent. 1739.	Flagon, dated 1750. Navenby, Linc.
Do.	B·G	Benj. Gignac, ent. 1744.	Small trays, formerly part of epergne. G. E. L. Baker, Esq.
1751	EC	Elias Cachart, ent. 1748.	Table spoons. Lord Amherst of Hackney.
1752	S·C	Sam. Courtauld, ent. 1746.	Set of table candlesticks. Narford Hall, Norf.
Do.	R·G C T	Gurney & Co., ent. 1750.	Plain two-handled cup. Late Rev. G. F. E. Shaw.
1753	JB	John Bayley, ent. 1751.	Communion flagon, dated 1754. Llangedwyn, N. Wales.
Do.	F·W	Fuller White, as in 1749.	Communion flagon. Hunmanby, Yorks.

DATE	MAKER'S MARK.		ARTICLE AND OWNER.
1753	𝕵𝖜𝕾	James Shruder, ent. 1739.	Oblong box and other pieces of various dates. Melbury House, Dorset.
Do.	I·Q	John Quantock . .	Candlesticks. Do.
1754	DP	Dan. Piers, ent. 1746.	Large butter-boats with handles and feet, gadrooned edges. Hon. Soc. of Gray's Inn.
Do.	J:C	John Cafe, ent. 1742	Table candlesticks. Late W. R. M. Wynne, Esq.
Do.	P·G	Phillips Garden, ent. 1751.	Pair of large jugs. Viscount St. Aldwyn.
1755	J·P	John **Payne,** ent. 1751.	Plain coffee-pot. Lord Amherst of Hackney.
			ALPHABET XV. 1756—1775.
1756	S𝕿	Samuel Taylor, as in 1748.	Pair of tea-caddies in shagreen case, chased and repoussé with flowers, spiral flutes, etc. In the collection of the late Paul Butler, Esq.
Do.	P·C	Paul Crespin, ent. 1739.	Massive circular salts. Welbeck.
Do.	JS	John Swift, ent. 1739.	Half-pint tumbler cups. All Souls' Coll., Oxford.
Do.	FW	Fuller White, as in 1749.	Quart tankard. Lord Tredegar.
Do.	WG	Wm. Grundy, as in 1747.	Gilt patens, gadrooned edge, on central feet. Canterbury Cathedral.
Do.	Do.	Do.	Cheese-toaster, *ex dono* Charles Morgan. Queen's Coll., Oxford.
1757	DP	Dan. Piers, as in 1754.	Set of candlesticks, also meat-dishes. Lord Hotham.
Do.	I E A S	Edw. Aldridge and John Stamper, ent. 1753.	Pierced basket. Late Rt. Hon. Sir J. R. Mowbray, Bart.
Do.	W·I P·G T	Pierre Gillois, ent. 1754.	Tea-caddies. Idsworth, Hants.
1758	MP	. . . . .	Set of three casters, one larger and a pair smaller. Lord Hotham.
Do.	WC	. . . .	Parish mace. St. Margaret, Westminster.
Do.	Do.	. . . . .	Pierced cake-basket. Lord Tredegar.
Do.	W·P	Wm. Plummer, ent. 1755.	Cake-basket pierced and having spiral flutes. Lord Amherst of Hackney.
Do.	C T·W W	Thos. Whipham, and Chas. Wright, ent. 1757.	Communion flagons and alms-basin. St. Paul, Exeter.
Do.	J·P	John Payne, as in 1755.	Small tumbler cups. (Octavius Morgan Coll.)
1759	W I·P E·W	Parker and Wakelin, goldsmiths to the Prince of Wales.	Inkstand. Soane Museum, London.
Do.	RR	Robert Rew, ent. 1754.	Large salver. Noted by the author.

DATE	MAKER'S MARK.	ARTICLE AND OWNER.
1759	C T·W W	Whipham & Wright, as in 1758.	Helmet-cup, merman handle ornamented with strapwork. Fishmongers' Company.
Do.	WC	Wm. Cafe, ent. 1757.	Candlesticks. Earl of Durham.
Do.	I·L I·S·L	John Langford and John Sebille.	Inkstand. Noted by the author.
Do.	J·S	John Swift, as in 1756.	Large tankard. All Souls' Coll., Oxford.
Do.	W· W·S P	Wm. Shaw and Wm. Priest, ent. 1749.	Quart tankard. Lord Amherst of Hackney.
Do.	SWW	· · · ·	Tripod pricket altar candlesticks, ornamented with wreaths, cherubs, etc. Trin. Coll., Oxford.
1760	AP	Abraham Portal, ent. 1749.	Two-handled cup and cover. Sir W. N. Throck-morton, Bart.
Do.	R·R	Richard Rugg, ent. 1754, smaller size letters than Robert Rew of same year.	Hand candlesticks. Late W. R. M. Wynne, Esq.
1761	CM	· · · ·	Small wired basket with entwined wreaths. Earl of Ducie.
Do.	C T·W W	Whipham & Wright, as in 1758.	Spiral fluted tea-urn on square open-work foot. Salters' Company.
1762	I*M	Jacob Marshe, ent. 1744.	Pint tankard. W. Cripps, Esq., C.B.
Do.	FW	Fuller White, ent. 1758.	Communion flagon. Dursley, Glouc.
1763	E·A	· · · ·	Pierced cake-basket. Trin. Coll., Oxford.
Do.	T W·C C	· · · ·	Gravy spoons. Hon. Soc. of Gray's Inn.
Do.	IP EW	Parker and Wakelin, as in 1759.	Two-handled racing cups and covers, vase-shaped and chased. Duke of Cleveland.
Do.	W·S	William Shaw, ent. 1749.	Communion flagon, usual pattern, given 1763. Byfield, Northants.
Do.	J·S	John Swift, as in 1756.	Inkstand, gilt, Louis XV. style. Sir W. Williams Wynn, Bart.
Do.	F L*H B	Lewis Herne and François Butty, ent. 1757.	Shaped dishes in sets. Earl Amherst.
Do.	T·P	Probably Thos. Powell, ent. 1756.	Epergne with pierced baskets, etc. The Schloss, Berlin.
Do.	W·P R·P	Probably W. and R. Peaston.	Tankards. Gift of K. George III. and Q. Charlotte. Eton College.
1764	S·C * I·C	Septimus and James Crespell.	Large oblong inkstand with lids. Viscount Midleton.
Do.	H S·H B	Samuel Herbert and Co., ent. 1750.	Cake-basket. Sir H. Pelly, Bart.
Do.	R· D·H H	David and Robert Hennell, ent. 1763.	Large salt-cellar. Sir W. Williams Wynn, Bart.

DATE	MAKER'S MARK.		ARTICLE AND OWNER.
1764	E·C	Probably Ebenezer Coker.	Small waiter used as paten. Ickburgh, Norf.
Do.	J W·B P	William Bond and John Phipps, ent. 1754.	Shaped coffee-pot, repoussé with scrolls and foliage. Salters' Company.
Do.	W G	Wm. Grundy, as in 1747.	Heads of parish beadles' staves, bought 1765. St. Paul, Covent Garden, London.
Do.	L·B	Louis Black, ent. 1761.	Table candlesticks. Corinthian caps. Late Sir Geo. Chetwode, Bart.
Do.	W P J P	William and James Priest.	Coffee-pot repoussé. G. E. L. Baker, Esq.
Do.	D·S R·S	Daniel Smith and Robert Sharp.	Salver. Welbeck.
1765	I W V L	. . . . .	Cake-basket. Sir H. Pelly, Bart.
Do.	J·S	John Swift, as in 1756.	Quart tankard. All Souls' Coll., Oxford.
1766	Do. I	Do.	Pint tankards. All Souls' Coll., Oxford.
Do.	W V L	As in 1765 . .	Tea-caddies. Sudeley Castle.
Do.	F·B N·D	François Butty and Nich. Dumee, ent. 1759.	Communion plate (flower sprays and gadroons). Durham Cathedral.
Do.	Do.	Do.	Alms-plate, dated 1766. St. German's, Cornw.
Do.	★ PW	Peter Werritzer, ent. 1750.	Candlesticks, Corinthian capitals. Sudeley Castle.
Do.	T·H I·C	Thos. Hannam and John Crouch.	Paten. Newchurch, Romney Marsh.
1767	U A·L ★	Aug. Lesage . . .	Plain kettle, lamp, and stand. Lord Amherst of Hackney.
Do.	Do.	Do.	Quart tankard. Lord Tredegar.
Do.	F·B N·D	Butty and Dumee, as in 1766.	Chased and fluted pricket altar-candlesticks. Durham Cathedral.
Do.		Thos. Heming . .	Large maces, dated 1767, engr. T. HEMING fecit. Corpn. of Rye.
1768	SC IC	S. and J. Crespell, as in 1764.	Butter-boats, gadrooned edge, handles at each end. Salters' Company.
Do.	C T·W W	Whipham & Wright, as in 1758.	Communion plate. Croft, Yorks.
Do.	I·C	Probably John Carter.	Salvers, gadrooned edges. W. C. Master, Esq.
Do.	R·R	Richard Rugg, as in 1760.	Salver. Sir W. Williams Wynn, Bart.
1769	Do.	Do.	Shaped and gadrooned salvers. Earl Amherst.
Do.	T. P.	As in 1763. . .	Epergne, with hanging baskets and larger basket. W. C. Master, Esq.
Do.	H I·S C	John Hyatt and Chas. Semore, ent. 1757.	Table candlesticks. W. C. Master, Esq.

DATE	MAKER'S MARK.		ARTICLE AND OWNER.
1769	**IH**	Joseph Heriot, ent. 1750.	Oblong box, chasing by Moser, presented with freedom of London to K. Christian VII. of Denmark. Rosenberg Museum, Copenhagen.
Do.	**F·C**	Fras. Crump, ent. 1756.	Communion cup, dated 1770. Sawley, Yorks.
1770	*J H*	Thos. Heming, as in 1767.	Soup tureen and cover. Hon. Soc. of Middle Temple.
Do.	**SC IC**	S. and J. Crespell, as in 1764.	Set of dinner plates. Earl Bathurst, C.M.G.
Do.	**I·C**	See 1768.	Waiters with shaped and gadrooned edges. Earl of Ducie.
1771	**W·P**	W. Plummer, as in 1758.	Pierced and repoussé cake-baskets. Earl of Ducie.
Do.	**T·P**	As in 1763.	Epergne, with pierced hanging baskets. Lord Amherst of Hackney.
Do.	**E·C**	See 1764.	Candlesticks like Corinthian columns. Merchant Taylors' Company.
Do.	**P·N**	Philip Norman .	Goblet-shaped communion cup and paten. Exeter Cathedral.
1772	**T I·D D**	Thos. and Jabez Daniel.	Muffineer. Sir A. Church, K.C.V.O.
Do.	**IP EW**	Parker and Wakelin, as in 1759.	Large circular salver, shaped and gadrooned edge. Earl Amherst.
Do.	**ER**	Probably Emick Romer.	Epergne with pierced work and flower-sprays. Late Rt. Hon. Sir J. R. Mowbray, Bart.
Do.	*J H*	Thos. Heming, as in 1767.	Chocolate pot. Hatfield House.
Do.	**CW**	C. Wright . .	Large two-handled cup and cover, with dragon handles, fluted stem, wreaths, cover surmounted by statuette. Mansion House, Lond.
Do.	**J·A**	Jonathan Alleine .	Set of candlesticks with gadrooned ornament on feet. Lord Amherst of Hackney.
Do.	**IB**	Probably John Barry, ent. 1758.	Snuffers. Lord Amherst of Hackney.
1773	**IP EW**	Parker and Wakelin, as in 1759.	Sauce-boats. Lord Hotham.
Do.	**W·P**	W. Plummer, as in 1758.	Pierced and repoussé cake-basket. (Edkins Coll.)
Do.	**I·K**	. . . . .	Plain tumbler, with belt round middle, fitted into a stand. Berkeley Castle.
Do.	**SC IC**	S. and J. Crespell, as in 1764.	Set of dinner plates. Lord Harlech.
1774	**WV**	William Vincent .	Open-work (vine pattern) sugar-basket. W. Cripps, Esq., C.B.
Do.	**I·C T·H**	Crouch and Hannam, see 1766.	Salver. Earl of Ducie.
Do.	**GS**	George Smith, ent. 1774.	Three-pronged forks. Hon. Soc. of Gray's Inn.
Do.	**WS RC**	Sumner and Crossley, ent. 1773.	Spoon-makers' mark.
Do.	**I·Y O·I**	James Young and Orlando Jackson, ent. 1774.	Two-handled oval vase with leaf straps. E. H. Luxmoore, Esq.

DATE	MAKER'S MARK.		ARTICLE AND OWNER.
1775	I·C	See 1768 . . .	Set of candlesticks ornamented with rams' heads, etc. From the Hopkinson collection. E. Waller, Esq.
Do.	TD	T. Daniell, ent. 1774.	Pierced and repoussé cake-basket. Sudeley Castle.
Do.	WS	. . . . .	Wine-strainer, beaded edge. Hon. Soc. of Gray's Inn.
Do.	R·P	Robert Piercy, ent. 1775.	Sugar-casters. Lady Amherst of Hackney.
Do.	I·Y	James Young, ent. 1775	Sugar vase, urn-shaped, with handles as ropes. Late Rt. Hon. Sir J. R. Mowbray, Bart.
			ALPHABET XVI. 1776—1795.
1776	R·I I·S	Robt. Jones and John Scofield, ent. 1776.	Set of salvers. Sir H. Pelly, Bart.
Do.	H C·A G	Chas. Aldridge and Henry Green, ent. 1775.	Claret jugs, festoons and medallions for ornament. Also a salver, with beaded edge. Clothworkers' Company.
Do.	BD	Burrage Davenport .	Open-work cake-basket. Lord Amherst.
Do.	A·F	Andrew Fogelberg .	Dinner plates. Viscount St. Aldwyn.
1777	WS	As in 1775 . . .	Alms-plate. Shrewsbury.
Do.	H C·A G	Chas. Aldridge and Henry Green, as in 1775.	Inkstand. Late Rev. C. Orlando Kenyon.
Do.	CW	As in 1772 . . .	Communion plate. Coln St. Aldwyns, Glouc.
Do.	R D·S S	Daniel Smith and Robert Sharp.	Toilet set, with medallions, wreaths, etc. National Museum, Stockholm.
1778	J H	T. Heming, as in 1767.	Salvers. Viscount St. Aldwyn. Also 1777, candlesticks. Melbury House.
1779	BD	B. Davenport, as in 1776.	Large bread-basket, shaped as a shell. Noted by the author.
Do.	T·N	Thos. Northcote, ent. 1776.	Feather-edged spoons. Late Earl of Glasgow.
1780	I·W W·T	John Wakelin and Wm. Tayler, 1776–92.	Plain kettle, lamp and stand. Sold at Christie and Manson's, 1876.
Do.	I·S	John Scofield, ent. 1778.	Candlesticks. Sudeley Castle. (This maker produced a great number of candlesticks and much other plate.)
1781	IB	Probably John Barry, as in 1772.	Snuffers. Lord Amherst of Hackney.
Do.	E·F	Edward Fennell, ent. 1780.	Flagon, dated 1786. Lympne, Kent.
Do.	D S R S	Daniel Smith and Robert Sharp, ent. 1780.	Pair of large tankards. Trin. Coll., Oxford.
1782	Do.	Do.	Chased salver. Trinity House.
Do.	Do.	Do.	Flat tankard. All Souls' College, Oxford.
Do.	HB	Hester Bateman, ent. 1774.	Small two-handled tray. Late W. R. M. Wynne, Esq.

DATE	MAKER'S MARK.		ARTICLE AND OWNER.
1783	EI	Edward Jay, ent. 1757.	Flat-candlestick. W. E. Oakley, Esq. Plas Tanybwlch.
1784	G S	George Smith, as in 1774.	Gravy spoons, feather-edged. (No King's head mark.) W. Cripps, Esq., C.B. (This maker made many spoons.)
Do.	SW	Samuel Wintle, ent. 1783.	Very small tea-spoons. (King's head mark in intaglio.) W. Cripps, Esq., C.B.
1785	TD	T. Daniell, as in 1775.	Oviform communion cup. Old Shoreham, Suss.
Do.	R·C	Richd. Crossley, ent. 1782.	Spoons. Lord Tredegar. (This maker made many spoons.)
Do.	HB	Hester Bateman, as in 1782.	Paten, dated 1785. Gateshead, Durh.
Do.	IL	John Lambe, ent. 1783.	Large tankard, ex dono Dilke. Trin. Coll., Oxford.
Do.	I·S	John Scofield, as in 1780.	Candlesticks. Earl Bathurst. C.M.G.
Do.	G S	George Smith, as in 1774.	Set of dessert-spoons, feather-edged. W. Cripps, Esq., C.B.
			NOTE.—All the above specimens of this year have the King's head in intaglio.
1786	G S W F	George Smith and William Fearn, ent. 1786.	This mark is found on a large number of spoons from this year till about 1792.
Do.	I·S	John Scofield, as in 1780.	Oval-pointed tea-urn, pointed handles. Late Miss Ker-Porter.
Do.	I·H	John Harris, ent. 1786.	Bread-basket. Late W. R. M. Wynne, Esq.
1787	H G	Henry Green, ent. 1786.	Barge-master's badge. Clothworkers' Company.
1788	H C	Hen. Chawner, 1786–96.	Oval-pointed, boat-shaped salts, with handles at each end. Late E. Waller, Esq.
Do.	I·C T·H	Crouch and Hannam, as in 1774.	Salver. Sudeley Castle.
1789	Do.	Do.	Oval salver, with handles. Lord Amherst of Hackney.
Do.	HB	Hester Bateman, as in 1782.	Small plain communion cup. St. Paul, Covent Garden, Lond.
1790	W·P I·P	Wm. Pitts and Joseph Preedy, ent. 1791.	Small stand, with festoons and medallions. Earl Ducie.
Do.	W V	Wm. Vincent, as in 1774.	Oval waiter or teapot stand. Late Miss Ker-Porter.
1791	R·H	Robert Hennell, ent. 1773.	Plain circular sugar-basin, on square foot, two pointed handles of the period. Berkeley Castle.
Do.	W·A	Wm. Abdy, ent. 1784.	Oval-pointed, boat-shaped salt-cellars. W. Cripps, Esq., C.B.
Do.	H G	Henry Green, as in 1787.	Oval waiter or tea-pot stand. Ravensworth Castle.
Do.	P B A B	Peter and Ann Bateman, ent. 1791.	Oval-pointed, boat-shaped sugar-basin. W. Cripps, Esq., C.B.
Do.	H C	Henry Chawner, as in 1788.	Ewer. Sir H. Pelly, Bart.

DATE	MAKER'S MARK.		ARTICLE AND OWNER.
1792	**H C**	Henry Chawner, as in 1788.	Fluted baptismal basin. St. Margaret, Westm.
Do.	I·K	John King, ent. 1785.	Plain communion cup. Bagendon, Glouc.
Do.	**I·S**	John Scofield, as in 1780.	Fluted oval tea-pot (Rundell and Bridge). Lord Tredegar.
Do.	P·S	Paul Storr, ent. 1792-3.	Oval-pointed cup with cover and handles. Lord Sackville.
Do.	R S	Robert Sharp, ent. 1789.	Large and also smaller candlesticks on square bases. Salters' Company.
Do.	G S T H	George Smith and Thos. Hayter, ent. 1792.	This mark is found on many spoons.
1793	I M	John Moore, ent. 1778.	Small plain paten, given 1793. Marston Meysey, Wilts.
1794	**W P** **I·P**	Pitts and Preedy, as in 1790.	Epergne and plateau. Mercers' Company.
1795	Do.	Do.	Inkstand. Trinity House.
Do.	**I·S**	John Scofield, as in 1780.	Very fine Wedgwood-shaped, two-handled vases and covers. Merchant Taylors' Company.
Do.	I T	John Thompson of Sunderland, ent. 1785.	Coffee-pot. Lord Harlech.

ALPHABET XVII. 1796—1815.

DATE	MAKER'S MARK.		ARTICLE AND OWNER.
1796	**I·S**	John Scofield, as in 1780.	Oval tea-pot and stand (bought of Rundell and Bridge). W. Cripps, Esq., C.B.
1797	Do.	Do.	Tea-pot stand. Late W. R. M. Wynne, Esq.
Do.	**W A**	Wm. Abdy, as in 1791.	Oval solid cake-basket. Late H. Bertie Williams Wynn, Esq.
Do.	R H D H	Robert and David Henell, ent. 1795.	Large shaped and gadrooned dish for fish. (Staniforth Coll.)
1798	G S	. . . . .	Table-spoons. Royal North Gloucester Militia.
Do.	**R·C**	Richard Crossley, as in 1785.	Table-spoons. Royal North Gloucester Militia.
Do.	J·E	John Emes, 1796-1808.	Fish-slice. Royal North Gloucester Militia.
Do.	I·W R·G	J. Wakelin and Robt. Garrard, 1792-1802	Oval-pointed soup-tureen with handles. Lord Tredegar.
1799	I·R	John Robins, ent. 1774.	Communion plate. South Cerney, Glouc.
Do.	W E W F	Wm. Ealey and Wm. Fearn, ent. 1797.	Soup-ladle. Royal North Gloucester Militia.
1800	I·B	. . . . .	Table-forks. W. Cripps, Esq., C.B.
Do.	P B A B W B	Peter, Ann, and Wm. Bateman, ent. 1800.	Pair of small beaker-cups. Sudeley Castle.
1802	R H D H S H	Messrs. Henell . .	Tea-pot, raised rim, and coffee jug or pot to match. Noted by the author.
1804	H N	Henry Nutting, ent. 1796.	Tea-pot, raised rim. Welbeck.

CHRONOLOGICAL LIST, Part II.,

TO BE USED

IN CONJUNCTION WITH THE PRECEDING PORTION.

DATE	MAKER'S MARK.		ARTICLE AND OWNER.
			ALPHABET I. 1478—1497.
1494	🐦	Bird's head . .	Chalice and paten. Clifford Chambers, Glouc.
1496	• •	Dim. fleur-de-lys, as in 1479.	Chalice. Very Rev. Dr. Darby, Dean of Chester.
Do.	🍃	Indented leaf, no shield.	Plain paten, with vernicle. Childrey, Berks.
			ALPHABET II. 1498—1517.
1503	✚	Cross-bow . .	Cup. Goldsmiths' Co. Formerly Col. Tufnell.
1510	• • • • •		Paten, sexfoil depression, usual vernicle. Orcheston St. Mary, Wilts.
1512	• •	Fish, as in 1507 .	Do. do. Scremby, Lincs.
1518	• •	Do. . . .	Chalice. C. M. and W., 1905.
			ALPHABET III. 1518—1537.
1523	• •	Fleur-de-lys, &c., as in 1525.	Paten. Beachamwell, Norf.
1524	✚ shield	• • • •	Alms-basin, indented Gothic moulding round rim, engraved with Elizabethan medallions. —St. Michael's, Crooked Lane (now with St. Magnus, London Bridge).
1525	🛡	• • •	Low bowl on foot, same size. Dunn Gardner Coll.
1527	🛡	• • •	Chalice and paten. Victoria and Albert Museum.
1528	• •	Fringed S, as in 1519.	Apostle spoon. British Museum.
1529	• •	Fleur-de-lys, &c., as in 1525.	Chalice. R. C. Cathedral, Westminster.
1535	• •	Broad arrow, as in 1534.	Plain sexfoil paten, with rude vernicle. Llanmaes, Glamor.
Do.	• •	Illegible . .	Sexfoil paten, with vernicle.
1536	🏹	Sheaf of arrows .	Thirteen Apostle spoons. C. M. & W., May 1903.
			ALPHABET IV. 1538—1557.
1541	• •	Fringed S, as in 1519.	Spoon, noted by Sir Hercules Read.
1543	• •	Sheaf of arrows .	Maidenhead spoon. Late Sir A. W. Franks.
1547	**BN**	Linked letters, as in 1549.	Spoon with lion sejant end. W. Cripps, Esq., C.B.
1549	**RD**	Linked letters, as in 1552.	Com. cup, bell-shaped bowl, conical stem. St. Peter, Cornhill, London.
Do.	🛡 FB	• • • •	Com. cup and paten without foot. St. James, Garlickhithe, London. Also another, St. Mildred, Bread Street, London.
1551	🛡	Swan erased .	Church-plate. Hants.
1552	• •	Bird, as in 1555 .	Com. cup. Owlysbury, Hants.

DATE	MAKER'S MARK.	ARTICLE AND OWNER.
1553	*[mark: RM]* Perhaps R. May-narde.	Com. cup on short stem. Gt. Houghton, North-ants.
		ALPHABET V. 1558—1577.
1559	. . Stag's head, as in 1551.	Com. cup. Melton Mowbray, Leics.
Do.	*[mark: lamp]* Lamp . . .	Com. cup and cover gilt, with unusual stem. St. Mary-le-Bow, London.
Do.	*[mark: star]*	Com. cup with pear-shaped stem. St. George-the-Martyr, London.
1562	*[mark]* Letter S, surroun-ded by rays, alter-nately straight and waving.	Com. cup. Ruckhorn-Weston, Dorset.
Do.	*[mark]*	Com. cup, lower part of bowl fluted. St. Stephen's, St. Albans, Herts.
1563	. . Three mullets and crescent, as in 1560	Standing salt, in two storeys. South Kensing-ton Museum.
Do.	*[mark]* Ths. Metcalfe was above bell.	Crystal cup. Leeds sale, C. M. & W., July 1920.
1564	*[mark: A]* See 1567 . .	Large shallow tazzo gilt, head repoussé in centre. Christie's Rooms, May 1895.
1567	*[mark]* Bull's head erased, as in 1569.	Com. cups with paten covers. Kinecote, Goadby Marwood, &c., Leics.
Do.	*[mark]* Fleur-de-lys .	Cup and paten. Halton, Holgate.
1568	*[mark: MG]*	Com. cup with two belts. Rotherwick, Hants.
Do.	*[mark: globe]* Globe . . .	Church-plate. Hants.
1569	. . Bull's head as above in 1567.	Netherhampton, Dorset.
Do.	*[mark: IC]*	Com. cup, usual belt. Northleach, Glouc.
Do.	*[mark: IH]*	Elizabethan com. cup. P. R. Meldrum, Esq.
1570	*[mark: HE]*	Cups with paten covers. Walditch and Tarrant, Keystone, Dorset.
Do.	*[mark: IJ]*	Com. cup, usual belt, dated 1571. Doncaster. Another, dated 1571. Caundle Purse, Dorset. Another, dated 1571. St. Mary-le-Bow, Durham.
Do.	*[mark: IH]*	Com. cup. St. Stephen, Bristol.
Do.	*[mark: horse head]* Horse's head couped to sinister.	Com. cup, usual belt. Fugglestone St. Peter, Wilts.
Do.	*[mark: covered cup]* Covered cup .	Com. cup. Shapwick, Dorset.
Do.	. . Orb and cross, as in 1569.	Com. cups. Saddington, Leics.; Long Bridy and Charminster, Dorset, &c.
Do.	*[mark]* No shield . .	Com. cup. St. Bees, Cumb.
Do.	. . Elephant . .	Church-plate. Denbighs.
Do.	*[mark]*	Church-plate. Hants.
1571	HW As in 1563 . .	Com. cups, usual belt. Cropthorne, &c., Worc. Also small cup, usual belt, dated 1571. Holm Cultram, Cumb.

DATE	MAKER'S MARK.		ARTICLE AND OWNER.
1571	(mark)	. . . .	Com. cup and paten. St. Mildred, Bread Street, London.
Do.	(mark)	Animal's head erased.	Com. cups. Isel, Cumb., and Thorncomb, Dorset.
Do.	(mark)	. . . .	Com. cup and cover. Yetminster, Dorset, also 1584.
Do.	IF	As in 1571 . .	Com. cup, dated 1571. St. John, Dinsdale, and Roos, Yorks. Also paten cover. Loweswater, Cumb.
Do.	(mark)	. . . .	Paten cover, dated 1571. North Perrott, Som.
1573	. .	Bird, as in 1567 .	Cup made of the Great Seal. Late Rt. Hon. E. R. Wodehouse.
Do.	(mark)	Helmet . .	Com. cups with covers. Maperton and Yarlington, Som.
1575	(mark)	. . . .	Cup and cover. Ash, Surrey.
1576	(mark)	. . . .	Com. cups. South Newton and W. Grimstead, Wilts. ; and at Hever, Kent.
Do.	(mark)	. . . .	Com. cup. Ashmore, Dorset.
Do.	(mark)	Small animal, ? snail.	Com. cup Chilmark, Dorset.
Do.	(mark)	. . . .	Com. cup, dated 1577. Dunn Gardner Coll.
1577	AH	. . . .	Com. cup and cover. Lympley Stoke, Wilts.
1578	(mark)	. . . .	Shallow cup with wide pointed bowl and baluster stem (found at Stoke Prior). South Kensington Museum, also 1580.
			ALPHABET VI. 1578—1587.
1579	(mark)	As in 1578 . .	Tapering tankard. Ashford Coll.
Do.	HW	As in 1563 . .	Pair of vase-shaped jars, with screw-stoppers and chains passing to lions'-head rings on the bowl. The Schloss, Berlin.
Do.	(mark)	. . . .	Tazza, helmeted head engraved in bowl. Loan Cat. 1862, No. 5744. H.R.H. the late Duke of Cambridge.
1580	SB	As in 1580 . .	Com. cup. St. Mary, Monmouth.
1581	(mark)	. . . .	Com. cup and cover. West Dean, Wilts.
Do.	(mark)	Trefoil in shaped shield.	Dishes. Formerly Mrs. Cator.
1583	FR	Linked, as in 1568	Round-bellied flagon. St. George's Chapel, Windsor.
1584	(mark)	Bird . . .	Cup. Bassingthorpe.
1585	SB	As in 1580 . .	Gourd-shaped cup. Troitsa Mon, Russia.
1592	(mark)	. . . .	Church-plate. Hants.
1593	(mark)	MB over ton .	Elizabethan church-plate.
1594	(mark)	. . . .	A bell salt with strapwork of the period (found at Stoke Prior). South Kensington Museum.

DATE	MAKER'S MARK.		ARTICLE AND OWNER.
1594		. . . .	V-shaped cup on baluster stem. St. Botolph, Aldgate, Lond.
1595	IA	As in 1604 . .	Plain com. cup, conical stem. Woodchurch, Kent.
1596	T	. . . . . .	Oviform cup on baluster stem. Leigh, Wilts.
1597	RB	Mullet below shaped shield, as in 1624. See p. 432.	Maye rosewater dish. Merchant Taylors' Co.
Do.	B	. . . . .	V-shaped com. cup. St. Giles, Camberwell, Surrey.
Do.	T	. . . . .	Com. cup. Whitminster, Glouc.
			ALPHABET VII. 1508 – 1617.
1598	. .	Eagle displayed, as in 1597.	Flagons, tankard-shaped. C. C. C., Oxford.
Do.	HB	. . . . .	Mounts of cup, with glass egg-shaped bowl. St. Kew, Corn.
Do.		Hart lodged . .	Pair of fine gilt round-bellied flagons, chased with usual strap-work. Wadham Coll. Chapel, Oxford.
1599	ER	. . . . .	Bell salt in three tiers. (Dasent and Ashford Colls.)
Do.	IE	. . . . .	Tall gilt cup with escallops on bowl and pyramid on cover. Charing, Kent.
Do.	IB	. . . . .	Dishes. Formerly Mrs. Cator.
Do.	L	. . . . . .	Do.
Do.	E	. . . . .	Do.
1600	HD	. . . . . .	Cup with baluster stem. Whitgift Charity, Croydon.
1602	IR	. . . . . .	Tankard-flagon. Headington, Wilts.
1603	AT	Tun below . .	Small saucer, punched ornament. Lacock, Wilts.
1605	TH	. . . . .	Church-plate. Som.
Do.	LA	. . . . .	Do. do.
1606	LB	. . . .	Tazza cup with punched ornament. Late Sir A. W. Franks.
Do.	W	. . . . . .	Com. cup, usual belt; paten cover dated 1607. Crowmarsh, Oxon.
Do.		Open right hand .	Com. cup and cover. Newland, Glouc.
1608	FS	. . . . .	Beaker communion cup. Stickney, Lincs.

DATE	MAKER'S MARK.		ARTICLE AND OWNER.
1609		. . . . .	Ostrich egg, mounted as a jug, with lid and handle and engraved band round mouth. Late Sir A. W. Franks.
Do.		Perhaps R. Peacocke.	Church-plate. Hants.
1610	WR	As in 1608 . .	Com. cup, dated 1610. Woodhouse, Leics.
Do.	.	W within Crescent	Apostle spoon, St. Matthias. (Ashford Coll.) W. Cripps, Esq., C.B.
1611		. . . . .	Tall gilt cup with chased bands and engraved hunting scenes. South Kensington Museum.
1612		. . . . .	Church-plate. Hants.
1613		. . . . .	Tall narrow tankard-flagon, lid with arms enamelled on small boss. Allhallows, Lombard Street, London.
1614		. . . . .	Seal-head spoon. (O. Morgan Coll.).
Do.	RG	As in 1619 . .	Apostle spoon. Church-plate. Som.
1617		. . . . .	Paten on foot, dated 1618. Ch. Ch., Newgate Street, London.
Do.		. . . . .	Small hexagonal cup on high stem. St. Giles', London.
Do.		. . . . .	Thirteen apostles' spoons. Formerly at Swettenham Hall, Cheshire.
Do.		. . . . .	Paten. Church Oakley, Hants.
		ALPHABET VIII. 1618—1637.	
1618		. . . . .	Slip-ended spoons. Mercers' Co.
Do.		. . . . .	Plain drum standing salt. Mercers' Co.
1619		. . . . .	Small cup on high stem, upper part of bowl octagonal. Formerly Rev. J. E. Kempe.
Do.		. . . . .	Church-plate. Som.
1622		. . . . .	Com. cup. Chillingham, Northumb.
1623		. . . . .	Com. cup dated 1624. East Ham, Essex.
1624		. . . . .	Church-plate. Hants.
Do.	DG	As in 1630 . .	Com. cup. Lyme Regis, Dorset.
1625		And see 1633 . .	Pair of tall tankard-flagons, given 1625. St. Peter's, Cornhill, London.
1626		. . . . .	Church-plate. Hants.

DATE	MAKER'S MARK.		ARTICLE AND OWNER.
1629	[mark]	Lombardic A	Church-plate. Lincs.
1630	[mark]	. . . . .	Com. cup, dated 1630. Bilsington, Kent. Others, dated 1630 and 1633. Burmarsh and Stodmarsh, Kent.
Do.	[mark: RA]	. . . . .	Beaker cup. Castle Bythe, Pembrokeshire.
1631	[mark: B]	And see 1660 . .	Paten. Wootton Basset, Wilts.
Do.	WS	As in 1629 . .	Paten. Lancs.
1632	IM	Pig below, as in 1639.	Com. cup, dated 1633. Doddington, Kent.
Do	. .	Escallop shell as in 1635.	Com. cup. Ashford, Kent. Twenty-nine com. cups by this maker, all between 1628 and 1636, have been noted by the author.
Do.	[mark: IM]	. . . . .	Plain com. cup, usual stem. Shorncott, Wilts.
Do.	[mark: RW]	. . . . .	Flagon, dated 1626. St. Nicholas, Gloucester.
1634	. .	Italic F as in 1635	Com. cup, dated 1635. Lythe, Ugthorpe, Yorks. Twelve pieces of ch.-plate by this maker, 1634 to 1641, have been noted by author.
Do.	[mark: PG]	. . . . .	Com. cup, with paten cover, given 1634. St. Dunstan-in-the-West, London. Four pieces of ch.-plate by this maker, all 1634 to 1638.
Do.	[mark: RW]	RW, rose below .	Paten. Radnorsh.
1635	[mark: ES]	. . . . .	Com. plate. Chester.
1636	[mark: IW]	. . . . .	Frosted-sided cup. Queen's Coll., Camb.
Do.	[mark: GM]	. . . . .	Com. cup and cover. Fetcham, Surrey.
		ALPHABET IX. 1638—1657.	
1638	[mark]	Probably Fras. Snow's widow.	Com. cup, wine-glass shape, on baluster stem. St. Nicholas, Gloucester.
1639	. .	W with I above, as in 1636.	Paten. Sturminster Newton, Dorset.
Do.	IB	Buckle beneath as in 1638.	Com. cup. Chelsfield, Kent.
Do.	[mark: IM]	. . . . .	Small saucer. Alderton, Wilts.
Do.	[mark: W]	. . . . .	Church-plate. Som.
1640	[mark: RP]	. . . . .	Com. cup. Winterborne Came, Dorset.
Do.	[mark: WC]	. . . . .	Com. cup. Tirley, Glouc.
1641	[mark: WM]	. . . . .	Plain tankard-flagon with splayed foot. St. Margaret, N. Fish Street, London.
Do.	[mark: WM]	. . . . .	Broad tankard-flagon. Freefolk, Hants.
Do.	[mark: RW]	. . . . .	Com. cup, dated 1641. Lechlade, Glos.
Do.	[mark: CP]	. . . . .	Church-plate. Som.

DATE	MAKER'S MARK.		ARTICLE AND OWNER.
1641	(RW)	. . . .	Church-plate. Hants.
Do.	(A)	. . . .	Com. cup, dated 1641. Radnors.
1644	. .	Illegible . .	Church-plate. Jersey.
1646	WT	. . . .	Church-plate. Hants.
1647	. .	Bird in plain shield	Com. cup. Guiseloy, Yorks.
1649	. .	Do. Do.	Com. cup. Stapleton Iwerne, Dorset.
Do.	KF	As in 1652 . .	Three cups in original case, given 1649. Co.´of Merchant Adventurers, Newcastle-on-Tyne.
1650	(IG)	. . . .	Flagon. Lydiard Tregoze, Wilts.
1651	(C)	. . . .	Com. Cup. Brokenborough, Wilts.
Do.	(RW)	. . . .	Large com. cup. Sherfield-on-Loddon, Hants.
Do.	(RW)	. . . .	Church-plate. Hants.
Do.	(IB)	. . . .	Do. Do.
1652	(AF)	. . . .	Tall flagon and deep dish. Ossington, Notts.
Do.	Do. .	. . . .	Spoon, of foreign shape. R. Day, Esq., junr.
1655	NW	As in 1646 . .	Shallow tray for sweetmeats, punched ornt. Lord Biddulph.
1656	(E·D)	. . . .	Wide tankard, given 1656. Innholders' Company.
Do.	WM	As in 1648 . .	Church-plate. Lincs.
1657	IC	As in 1668 . .	Do. Do.
Do.	WG	As in 1670 . .	Do. Do.
		ALPHABET X. 1658—1677.	
1658	. .	Hound sejant as in 1653.	Pair of cups and paten. Hinckley, Leics.
1660	(F·L)	. . . .	Flat tankard, with arms and mantling in repoussé. Noted by author.
Do.	(M)	No doubt Thos. Maundy. See p. 406.	Arched-crown maces, dated 1660. Corpn. of Gloucester.
Do.	(B)	And see 1631 .	Jug - shaped flagons, feather - work bodies. Chapel Royal, St. James's Palace. (Others are at St. George's Chapel, Windsor Castle.)
Do.	MA	Linked as in 1665 .	Tall tankard-flagons. Chapel Royal, St. James's Palace.
Do.	HG	As in 1656 . .	Large salver, repoussé flowers and animals. Do.
Do.	(I)	. . . .	Tall tankard-flagon. Kensington Palace Chapel.
1661	Do. .	. . . .	Large gilt alms-dish. Eton Coll. Chapel.
Do.	(A)	Italic A. C. linked.	Plain plate engraved with arms. St. George's Chapel, Windsor Castle.
Do.	WM	As in 1658 . .	Com. cup, flagons and patens. Do.
Do.	(H)	T. H. linked .	Church-plate. Som.

DATE	MAKER'S MARK.		ARTICLE AND OWNER.
1662		. . . .	Church-plate. Hants.
Do.	MM	As in 1665 . .	Church-plate. Lincs.
Do.		. . . .	Paten. Hants.
1663		. . . .	Plain com. cup on conical stem. Steventon, Hants. Also com. cup, 1670. N. Wales.
1664	AF	As in 1663 . .	Com. cup. Broxholme, Lincs. (Eight pieces by this maker, 1660 to 1675, noted by author.)
Do.		Italic A. C. linked, as in 1661.	Plain com. cup on short baluster stem. Ken. Pal. Chap. Church-plate. Addington, Kent.
Do.		. . . .	Church-plate. Hants.
Do.	'S	Crowned, as in 1664	Com. plate. Chapel Royal, Whitehall.
Do.		. . . .	Large tankard with flat lid. Batcombe, Som.
1665		. . . .	Church-plate. Som.
1668	GV	. . . .	Com. cup, dated 1669. Kirkby Cane, Norf.
1669		. . . .	Caudle cup. Noted by author. This mark also occurs on an undated cup at Chapel Royal, St. James's Palace.
Do.	SR	. . . .	Plain com. cup. Harley, Salop. Church-plate, 1674 and 1682. N. Wales. Com. cup. N. Wales.
1670	WG	. . . .	Com. cup, given 1670. Barnard Castle, Durh.
1671	WG	. . . .	Alms-dish. Southampton.
1674	SR	As in 1662 . .	Church-plate. Lincs.
1675	W.S	. . . .	Alms-dish and paten. Manch.
Do.	B	. . . .	Church-plate. Hants.
1676	SN	. . . .	Plain com. cup, conical stem. Overton, Hants.
Do.		I.C. monogram .	Caudle cup used as com. cup. Lincs.
Do.	WB	. . . .	Civic plate. Denbigh.
Do.	. .	IB and running stag, as in 1684.	Church-plate. Lincs.
1677	IR	. . . .	Civic plate. Chester.
			ALPHABET XI. 1678—1696, Part I.
1678	TC	Fish above, as in 1677.	Com. cup, dated 1678. Birchington, Kent. (This maker's mark occurs on much Kent church-plate, 1677 to 1688.)
Do.		. . . .	Church-plate. Sansthorpe.
1679	CK	. . . .	Tankard. Eton College.
Do.	FM	. . . .	Civic plate. Chester.

DATE	MAKER'S MARK.		ARTICLE AND OWNER.
1679	SR	As in 1662 . .	Church-plate. Lincs.
1681		. . . .	Flat-handled spoon. Colt-Williams Collection.
Do.		. . . .	Flagon, dated 1678. Gillingham, Dorset.
Do.	TS	As in 1689 . .	Church-plate. Lincs.
Do.		. . . .	Com. cup. Sedgefield, Durh.
Do.		. . . .	Com. cup and cover, dated 1682. Up. Nately, Hants.
1682		Italic A . .	Frosted loving-cup. Innholders' Company.
Do.		. . . .	Tall gilt tankard-flagons with splayed feet. Merton Coll. Chapel, Oxford.
1683		. . . .	Gilt alms-dish, arms engraved in centre. All-hallows, Lombard Street, London.
Do.		. . . .	Flat-handled spoon. P. R. Meldrum, Esq.
1684		. . . .	Oval gilt tobacco-box. Late S. Leighton, Esq.
Do.	IN	As in 1662 . .	Com. plate, dated 1685. Hatfield, Herts.
Do.		. . . .	Paten. Hants.
1685	TI	Escallop above and below, as in 1685, p. 443.	Large mace, dated 1685. Wilton, Wilts.
1686		. . . .	Com. cup. Thrybergh, Yorks.
Do.	TS	As in 1689 . .	Church-plate. Lincs.
Do.		. . . .	Paten. Kirkland, Cumb.
Do.		Italic F. C. . .	Church-plate. Lancs.
1687		. . . .	Paten. Collingbourne Kingston, Wilts.
Do.		. . . .	Paten, dated 1688. Crudwell, Wilts.
1688		. . . .	Plain com. cup, with conical stem. Fulletby, Lincs.
Do.		. . . .	Large flagon, dated 1689. Wootton, St. Lawrence, Hants.
Do.		T. B. R. in monogram.	Church-plate, Hants.
1689		. . . .	Com. cup, dated 1689. Thornford, Dorset.
Do.	TN	As in 1683 . .	Church-plate. Lincs.
Do.		. . . .	Alms-dish. Durnford, Wilts.

DATE	MAKER'S MARK.		ARTICLE AND OWNER.
1690		. . . .	Flat-handled spoon, found under floor of hall. Oriel Coll., Oxford.
Do.		. . . .	Flagon. Pangbourne, Berks.
Do.		Probably Timothy Ley. See 1699 and 1727.	Flagon. St. Nichs., Whitehaven, Cumb.
Do.		. . . .	Plain porringer. C. M. & W., June 1900.
1692		Probably Wm. Gamble.	Paten. Tadcaster, Yorks.
Do.		Two italic B's addorsed.	Frame of toilet mirror. Earl Bathurst, C.M.G.
Do.		. . . .	Wall sconce, with arms and coronet. Hatfield House.
1693		. . . .	Beadle's arm badge. St. Giles', London.
Do.		. . . .	Church-plate. Som.
Do.		. . . .	Skellingthorpe, Lincs.
1694		. . . .	Tall flagon, given 1694. Deane, Hants.
Do.		. . . .	Church-plate. Cheshire.
1695	R G	As in 1684 . .	Church-plate. Lincs.
1696		. . . .	Bleeding-basin, usual handle. Norton Bavant, Wilts.
Do.		H. C. Linked .	Church-plate. Hants.
Do.	R G	As in 1684 . .	Church-plate. Lincs.
Part 1. c. 1696		Another mark for Fras. Garthorne.	Jug, with handle, cover, and spout, with " cut-card " ornt. Windsor Castle.

ALPHABET XII. 1696, Part 2—1715.

Do. Part 2.		Thos. Parr, ent. Apr. 1697.	Paten. Rilstone, Yorks.
1697		John Laughton, ent. 1697.	Snuffers. Col. Tremayne, Carclew.
Do.		Isaac Dighton .	Monteith. Late Lady Molesworth.
Do.		Stephen Edmonds	Snuffer and stand, noted by author.
Do.		Another mark for Jos. Bird.	
Do.		Thomas Brydon.	

DATE	MAKER'S MARK.		ARTICLE AND OWNER.
1697		Samuel Jefferys.	
Do.		Jona Kirke.	
Do.		Thomas Issod.	
1698		Philip Roker .	Also 1707. Tankard, dome lid. Merton Coll., Oxford.
Do.		Name unknown .	Caudle-cups, thumb-ring handles. Eton College.
Do.		William Keatt .	Plain tankard. Noted by author.
Do.		Another mark for Wm. ffawdery.	
1699		William Petley, ent. 1699.	
Do.		Timothy Ley, ent. 1697. See 1690.	Paten. Sherborne, Dorset.
Do.		Richare Syng, ent. 1697.	Com. cup. Puddletrenthide, Dorset.
Do.		John Leach, ent. 1697.	Mace. Corporation of Deal, Kent.
Do.		Alex. Roode .	Flagon. Ansley, Warw.
Do.		Charles Davaing, Carey Lane, ent. 1699.	
1700		Gabriell Player, ent. 1700.	
Do.		William Denny.	
Do.		Fras. Archbold, ent. 1697.	Hind's-foot spoons. Rev. W. H. Wayne.
Do.		. . . .	Paten. Hants.
1701		Samuell Wastell, ent. 1701.	
Do.		Willughby Masham, ent. 1701.	Salver. Corporation of Chester.
c. 1701		Lawrence Coles, ent. 1697.	Small flat-handled spoon. Colt Williams Collection.

DATE	MAKER'S MARK.		ARTICLE AND OWNER.
1702		Thos. Sadler, ent. 1701.	Flat-handled spoon. Noted by author.
Do.		Thos. Corbett, ent. 1699.	Tall standing cup and cover, gilt. Pewterer's Co.
Do.		Chas. Overing, ent. 1697.	Alms-plate, dated 1702. Chiddesden, Hants.
Do.		Geo. Garthorne, ent. 1697.	Large tankard. Noted by author.
Do.		Rich. Biggs, ent. 1700.	Large tankard flagon. Axbridge, Som.
Do.		Not ent. . .	Toilet set. Noted by author.
1704		John Read and Paul Sleamaker, ent. 1701.	Paten. St. Michael's, Glouc.
Do.		. . . .	Church-plate, 1701. Lincs.
Do.	PL	Pierre Plutel, as in 1702.	Small tea-pot, sold for £280—£60 per oz.—July 1919, C. M. & W.
1706		John Rand, ent. 1704.	Com. cup and cover. Hartley Wespall, Hants.
Do.		Probably Jacob Margas, ent. 1706.	
1707		John Abbott, ent. 1706.	Tankard. Noted by author.
Do.		Thos. Folkingham, ent. 1706.	Paten. Box, Wilts.
Do.		Thos. Burridge, ent. 1706.	Rat-tailed spoons. St. Margaret, Westminster, Lond.
Do.		Chas. Adam, ent. 1702.	Good sugar-castors. Noted by author. Also 1716 Chester Corp.
1708		. . . .	Small salver on foot. Earl Amherst.
Do.		Ambrose Steventon, ent. 1706.	Credence paten. Steynton, Pembrokeshire.
1709	PY	Benj. Pyne, as in 1701.	Great mace of Borough of Gravesend, Kent.
Do.		Thos. Ffarren, ent. 1707.	Plain gilt alms-dish, dated 1709. Allhallows, Lombard Street, London. Also flagon, 1714.
Do.		John Chartier, 2nd mark. See 1699, p. 448.	Plain cylindrical chocolate pot, flap on spout. Noted by author.
1710		Lewis Mettayer, ent. 1700.	Plain small table candlesticks, octagonal feet. Noted by author.
Do.		H. Clarke, ent. 1709.	Spoon.

DATE	MAKER'S MARK.		ARTICLE AND OWNER.
1711		. . . .	Church-plate. Hants.
1712		John Martin Stocker, ent. 1710.	Small salver on foot. Earl Amherst.
Do.	RU	As in 1698, John Ruston.	
Do.		Richard Raine, ent. 1712.	Also 1716. Paten dated 1716. Ockley, Surrey.
1713		Thos. Port, ent. 1713.	
Do.	PE	Mullet above and below. W. Penstone, ent. 1712.	Paten. Smarden, Kent. He made also other church-plate.
1714		Charles Jackson, ent. 1714.	Also 1715. Paten. Betchworth, Surrey.
Do.		W. England and John Vaen, ent. 1714.	Flagon. Nettleton, Wilts.
Do.		John Beesley .	Church-plate. Hants.
1715		Francis Plymley, ent. 1715.	
Do.		Nathl. Roe, ent. 1710. "Gone to live in Norwich."	Hanoverian-pattern spoon. Colt-Williams Collection.
Do.		Thos. Langford, ent. 1715.	Com. cup. Lillington, Dorset.
Do.		James Fraillon, ent. 1710.	Church-plate. St. Michael, Bosherston, Pembrokeshire.
		ALPHABET XIII. 1716—1735.	
1716		Joseph Clare, ent. 1713.	Paten. Steeple Grange, Dorset. Also flagon, 1718.
Do.		Michael Boult, ent. 1713.	Pair of candlesticks, octagonal feet. Noted by author.
Do.		Thos. Ewisden, ent. 1713.	Patens, given 1716. St. Nicholas, Gloucester.
Do.		Henry Miller, ent. 1714.	Hanoverian spoons. Rev. T. S. Cooper.
Do.		John Bell, ent. 1716.	Church-plate.
1717		See 1711 . .	Paten on foot, dated 1718. Halsall, Lancs.
Do.		Anne Tanqueray; probably widow of David Tanqueray.	This mark, and the same with AT instead of TA, are both entered at year 1717; the AT probably should be at 1720.

DATE	MAKER'S MARK.		ARTICLE AND OWNER.
1717		Réné Hudell, ent. 1717.	
Do.	Wa	. . . . .	Church-plate. St. Michael, Pembroke.
1718	DA	Wm. Darker at the Acorn, ent. 1718.	Plain shaped octagon sugar-castors. Merton Coll., Oxford.
1718	MO	Thos. Morse, ent. 1718.	New sterling mark.
1719	TE	Thos. Tearle, ent. 1719.	Paten. Corsham, Wilts.
Do.	Ba	Thos. Bamford, ent. 1719.	
Do.	BE	Wm. Bellanger, ent. 1716.	Cup and paten. S. Mary, Haverfordwest.
Do.	NE	Jonathan Newton, ent. 1718.	Paten given 1720. Beckford, Glouc.
Do.	EL	. . . . .	Flagon, dated 1720. S. Peter, Chester.
Do.	Hi	Rt. Hill, ent. 1716	Spoon. French Hospital.
1720	TB	Thomas Bamford, ent. 1720. Old sterling.	
Do.	SM	Samuel Margas, ent. 1720. Old sterling.	Same as in 1719, with SM for MA.
Do.	SA	John Sanders, ent. 1717.	Paten. West Chelborough, Dorset.
Do.	AR	Peter Archambo, ent. 1720.	New sterling mark.
Do.	I·S	John Sanders, ent. 1720. Old sterling.	Cup and cover. Street, Somerset.
Do.	DT	David Tanqueray .	Old sterling mark.
Do.	LM	Lewis Mettayer .	Do. Also 1721. Small square salver. Noted by author.
Do.	BW	Benj. Watts . .	Old sterling mark.
Do.	RB	Richard Bayley .	Do. Alms dishes, 1725. Paten, 1736.

DATE	MAKER'S MARK.		ARTICLE AND OWNER.
1720		William Fawdery .	Do. Alms dishes, 1725. Paten, 1736.
Do.		J. Barbut . .	Do.
Do.		Isaac Liger . . .	Do. **Also 1727.** Paten. Mildenhall, Wilts.
Do.		Charles Jackson .	Do. **Also 1727.** Fourteen " Puritan" spoons." Mercers' Company, London.
Do.		Samuel Hitchcock	Do.
Do.		. . . . .	Official inkstand, with bell, ink, and pounce-box. Viscount St. Aldwyn.
Do.		Paul Hanet, ent. 1715.	Tea-spoons, gilt. Narford Hall, Norfolk.
1721		Simon Pantin, ent. 1720.	Two-handled cup. Painter-Stainers' Company.
Do.		Edw. Turner, ent. 1720.	Candlesticks, baluster stems. (Staniforth Coll.)
Do.		Edw. Gibbon, ent. 1719.	Small octagonal pepper-box with handle. Noted by author.
Do.		John Wisdome, ent. 1720.	Com. cup. Pulham, Dorset.
Do.		S. Holaday, ent. 1719.	Double-handled and double-spouted sauce-boats. Noted by author.
Do.		Samuell Lea, ent. 1721.	Old sterling mark.
Do.		John Bathe, ent. 1721.	Do.
Do.		Matth. E. Loft-house, ent. 1721.	Do.
Do.	BE	As in 1719 . .	Church-plate. Norfolk.
Do.		As in 1696.	Gilt alms-dish. Witney, Oxon.
1722		Nic. Clausen, ent. 1722.	Old sterling mark.
Do.	IE	John Eckfourd .	Large mace. Henley-on-Thames.
Do.		W. Scarlet, ent. 1722.	Old sterling mark.

DATE	MAKER'S MARK.		ARTICLE AND OWNER.
1722		. . . .	Alms-dish.　Hants.
1723		Edw. Gibbon, ent. 1723.	Old sterling mark.
Do.		Thos. Morse, ent. 1720.　Old sterling.	Paten.　Dinder, Som.
Do.		Abraham Buteux. See 1723, p. 455.	New sterling mark.　Also 1727.　Candlesticks, George II. pattern.　Welbeck Abbey.
Do.		Benj. Pyne.　See 1684.	Beadles' maces.　Oxford University.
Do.		Thos. Ffarrer.　See 1723, p. 455.	New sterling mark, ent. 1707.
Do.		Arthur Dicken, ent. 1720.	Flagon, dated 1723.　Bradford-on-Avon, Wilts. Also church-plate, dated 1920.　Dowsby, Lincs.
Do.		Probably John Hill, ent. 1709.	Spoon.
1724		Arnett and Pococke.	New sterling mark, ent. 1719.　Also patens, Brit., 1726.　N. Wales.
Do.		John Wilkes, ent. 1722.	Great tankard-flagon, 98 oz., dated 1725.　St. Mary, Bridgwater, Som.
Do.		John Le Sage, ent. 1718.	Ewer and basin.　Montacute, Som.
Do.	TT	As in 1738 .　.	Church-plate.　Lincs.
Do.		John Gibbons, ent. 1724.	Patens.　Street, Somerset.
1725		George Wickes, ent. 1721.	New sterling mark.
Do.		Bernard Fletcher, ent. 1725.	Salver, shaped edge.　Late Lady Molesworth.
Do.		Isaac Ribouleau, ent. 1720.	Tea-pot, partly chased.　Noted by author.
Do.	. .	Benj. Payne, as in 1723.　See 1684.	The Boston Oar Mace.　Earl Brownlow.
Do.		Sarah Holaday, ent. 1725.	
Do.		Wm. Toone, ent. 1725.	Hanoverian-pattern table-spoons.　Park Hatch.
1726	P	Benj. Payne, as in 1723.	Great Mace of the Borough of Westminster.
Do.		Wm. Atkinson, ent. 1725.	New sterling mark.

DATE	MAKER'S MARK.		ARTICLE AND OWNER.
1727		Wm. Darker, ent. 1724.	Com. cup. Frome St. Quentin, Dorset.
Do.		Timothy Ley, as ent. before 1697.	Paten. Newchurch, Kent. T. Ley made much church-plate.
Do.		Jacob Margas, ent. 1720.	Oval lobed dishes. Welbeck. Also octagonal gilt dish. Hatfield House.
Do.		Chas. Hatfield, ent. 1727.	Also 1729. Sugar-castors, with good strap-work. Noted by author.
Do.		Wm. Shaw, ent. 1727.	
Do.		Edmund Bodington, ent. 1727.	
Do.		Hester Fawdery, ent. 1727.	
Do.		Th. Fawler (?) .	Com. cups. Lechlade, Glouc.
1728		James Gould, ent. 1722.	New sterling mark.
Do.		John Millington, ent. 1728.	
Do.	EV	Probably E. Vincent, as in 1721.	Church-plate. Lincs.
Do.		Thos. Mason, ent. 1720.	Alms-dish. Stour Provost, Dorset.
Do.		John ffawdery, ent. 1728-9.	Also 1736. Church-plate. N. Wales.
Do.		Jane Lambe, ent. 1719.	Three-pronged table-forks. Melbury.
Do.		Fras. Garthorne, as before 1697.	Flagon. Allerton Mauleverer, Yorks.
Do.		Ed. Jennings, "liveing in Little Britain," ent. 1720.	Spoon.
Do.		. . . .	Paten. Hants.
1729		Charles Kandler and James Murray, ent. 1729.	New sterling mark.
Do.		Do. . . .	Old sterling mark.
Do.		Richard Scarlet, ent. 1720.	Table-spoons, Hanoverian pattern. Corporation of Gloucester.

DATE	MAKER'S MARK.		ARTICLE AND OWNER.
1729	(R·L)	Robert Lucas, ent. 1726.	Flagon. Cannington, Som.
Do.	(IS)	Joseph Steward, ent. 1720.	Flagon. Crowcombe, Som.
Do.	SP	Sarah Parr, as in 1731.	Church-plate. Lincs.
1730	(WP)	William Petley, ent. 1720.	Straining spoon, Hanoverian pattern, half bowl pierced. St. Magnus, London Bridge.
1731	(T·E)	Thos. England, ent. 1725.	Cover to cup of 1709. Late Rt. Hon. Sir J. R. Mowbray, Bt.
Do.	IW	James Wilkes, ent. 1722.	Table-spoons, Hanoverian pattern. Corporation of Gloucester.
Do.	(EB)	Edward Bennett, ent. 1731.	
Do.	(PB)	Peter Bennett, ent. 1731.	
Do.	(EB)	Eliz. Buteux, ent. 1731.	
Do.	(SP)	Sarah Parr, ent. 1720.	Flagon, given 1732. Blandford Forum, Dorset.
Do.	(EY)	Edw. Yorke, ent. 1730.	Set of ch.-plate. St. John, Westmr., Lond.
Do.	(M·L)	Mary Lofthouse, ent. 1731.	Paten. Rattlesden, Suff.
Do.	R P	Richd. Pargiter .	Paten, given 1732. Abenhall, Glouc.
1732	(TP)	Thos. Parr, ent. 9 Feb., 1733.	Com. cup, given 1732. Blandford Forum, Dorset.
1733	(MP)	Mary Pantin, ent. 1733.	
Do.	LP	Lewis Pantin, ent. 1733.	
1734	GS	Gabriel Sleath, as in 1730.	Kettle with stand. Lord Walsingham.
Do.	JJ	John Jones . .	Com. cup. St. Benignus, Glastonbury, Som.
Do.	FP	. . . . .	Church-plate, Som.
1735	(G·E)	Griffith Edwards, ent. 1732.	Flagon. Upavon, Wilts.
Do.	(P·P)	Peze Pilleau . .	Plain globular soap-box on foot. Viscount Midleton.

DATE	MAKER'S MARK.		ARTICLE AND OWNER.
1735	IW	John White, ent. 1724. Old sterling.	Great gilt mace. City of London.
Do.	Sa	. . . .	Paten. Lancs.
			ALPHABET XIV. 1736—1755.
1736	DH	Daniel Hennell, ent. 1736.	
Do.	FM	The F and M are on 2 different punches.	Font bowl. Alford.
Do.	H·H	Henry Herbert, ent. 1734.	Plain paten or plate. Kensington Palace Chapel.
Do.	EB	Eliz. Buteux, as in 1731.	Finely-chased two-handled cup. Col. Tremayne, Carclew.
Do.	IN	John Newton, ent. 1726.	Chased tea-caddies in original case. W. Cripps, Esq., C.B.
Do.	F·S	Fras. Spilsbury, ent. 1729.	Com. cup. Desford, Leicester. Also com. cup and flagon. St. Nicholas, Leicester.
Do.	BC	Probably Benj. Cartwright.	Paten, given 1738. Pitney Lorty, Som.
Do.		. . . .	Com. cup. Boulston, Pembrokeshire.
1737	F·K	Fred. Kandler, ent. 1735.	Rococo sauce-boats, storks for handles. Noted by author.
1737	HS	. . . .	Plain round waiters. Lord Cromwell.
Do.	G·S	Gabriel Sleath, as in 1730.	Large plain two-handled cup. W. Cripps, Esq., C.B.
Do.	CA	Isaac Callard, ent. 1726.	New sterling mark.
Do.	T·M	. . . .	Com. cup and cover. Miserden, Glouc.
1738	RZ	Richard Zouch, ent. 1735.	Com. cup. Edington, Wilts.
Do.	P·B	Phil. Bruguier, ent. 1738.	
Do.	EC	Ebenezer Coker, ent. 1738.	
1739	DG	Dinah Gamon, ent. 1739.	
Do.	IH	John Harwood, ent. 1739.	Spoons, 1745 ; sauce-boats, 1760.
Do.	JH	John Harvey, ent. 1739.	
Do.	I·T	John Tuite, ent. 1739.	
Do.	R·P	Robt. Pilkington, ent. 1739.	
Do.	GH	Geo. Hindmarsh, ent. 1739.	

DATE	MAKER'S MARK.	ARTICLE AND OWNER.
1739	John Newton, ent. 1739. See 1736.	Mounts of fish-skin tea-caddy case. W. Cripps, Esq., C.B.
Do.	Edward Vincent, ent. 1739.	
Do.	Fras. Nelme, ent. 1739.	
Do.	Jas. Wilks, ent. 1739.	Table-spoons. Noted by author.
Do.	Lewis Pantin, as in 1740.	Chased castors. Col. Tremayne, Carclew.
1740	Probably D. Hennell; and see 1751.	Punch-ladle with double spout, given 1740. Corporation of Oswestry.
Do.	Jonathan Fossy, ent. 1739.	Short candlesticks. (Staniforth Coll.)
1740	T. Whipham and W. Williams, ent. 1740.	Chocolate-pot. Earl Amherst.
1741	Fras. Spilsbury, as 1740.	Fine kettle with stand. Sir F. Boileau, Bt.
Do.	Robt. Abercromby, ent. 1739.	
Do.	Paul Crespin, ent. 1739. (See p. 331.)	Tea-caddies in case. Rev. E. F. Wayne.
Do.	John Stewart.	Paten. Hants.
1742	Wm. Young, ent. 1739.	Spoon.
Do.	G. Edwards, ent. 1739.	
1743	Robt. Abercromby, as in 1741.	Alms-dish. Todber, Dorset.
Do.	Henry Brind, ent. 1742.	Pair of small salvers. Corpn. of Gloucester.
Do.	Edward Wood, ent. 1740.	Salts. Noted by author.
Do.	George Greenhill Jones, ent. 1739.	Church-plate, engr. George Greenhill Jones, fecit. Highworth, Wilts.
1744	Richard Gosling, ent. 1739.	Church-plate. Witney, Oxon.
Do.	. . . . .	Salver used as paten. Hants.
1745	John Neville, ent. 1745.	
Do.	. . .	Cruet frame. Warwick. Lord Cromwell.
Do	Isaac Callard, ent. 1739.	Table-spoons. W. Cripps, Esq., C.B.
1746	George Boothby, ent. 1739.	Coffee-pot. Noted by author.
1747	Wm. Williams, ent. 1742.	Gilt flagons, given 1747. St. John, Hampstead, Lond.
1749	Andrew Killik, ent. 1749.	

DATE	MAKER'S MARK.		ARTICLE AND OWNER.
1750	🔲	John Wirgman, ent. 1745.	Plain two-handled cup. Late E. A. Leatham, Esq.
Do.	ᵛ W	. . . .	Paten. Markby, Lincs.
1751	. .	Probably D. Hennell, as in 1740.	Salts on three feet, with satyr heads, grapes, and festoons, shell feet. Viscount St. Aldwyn.
Do.	F·K	Fredk. Knopfell, ent. 1752.	Com. cup, dated 1752. Bexley, Kent.
Do.	(IW)	. . . . .	Alms-plate. Hants.
1752	WA	Wm. Alexander, ent. 1742.	Enormous pendant chandelier, given 1752, 1330 oz. Fishmongers' Company.
Do.	🔲	Paul Callard, ent. 1751.	Spoons and forks. Col. H. M. Sholto Douglas.
Do.	R·C	Robt. Cox, ent. 1752.	Church salver. Stockland, Som.
Do.	🔲	James Morrison, ent. 1740.	Pair of salvers. North Perrott, Som.
1753	P·A	Peter Archambo and P. Meure, ent. 1749.	Pierced and chased (corn ears, &c.) cake basket. Noted by author.
Do.	🔲	William Gould, ent. 1753.	
1754	🔲	Simon Lesage, ent. 1754.	
Do.	DS	In plain oval. Dorothy Sarbit, ent. 1753.	Small George II. candlesticks. Elmore Court, Glouc.
Do.	JW	As in 1750 . .	Spoon. Noted by editor.
			ALPHABET XV. 1756—1775.
1756	W·P	W. and R. Peaston, ent. 1756.	
Do.	🔲	Thos. Whipham, ent. 1739.	Pair of com. flagons, dated 1757. Brit. stan. St. Mabyn, Cornwall.
1757	BC	Benj. Cartwright, ent. 1739.	Flagon. St. John's, Dinsdale.
Do.	JJ	John Jacobs, ent. 1739.	Large mace. Stratford-on-Avon.
Do.	IK TG	In plain square. John Kentenber and Thos. Groves, ent. 1757.	Soup-ladle. Noted by author.
Do.	E·J	Edward Jay, ent. 1757.	Paten. Silchester, Hants.
1758	CB	. . . . .	Flagon. Landford, Wilts.
Do.	TW	Thos. Wallis, ent. 1758.	
Do.	R·Cox	Robert Cox, ent. 1755.	Paten. Martock, Som.

DATE	MAKER'S MARK.		ARTICLE AND OWNER.
1759	I★T	James Tookey, ent. 1750.	Transition table-spoons. The author.
1760	M☆F	Mordecai Fox, ent. 1746.	Alms-basin. Trin. Ch., New York, U.S.A.
Do.	W·J	Italic W. T. . .	Church-plate. Som.
1761	E·A·A	. . . . .	Small sugar-basket. Noted by author.
Do.	. .	F. Kandler, as in 1749.	Set of ch.-plate, dated 1762. Mylor, Cornwall.
Do.	WC	As in 1759 . .	Church-plate. Lincs.
1762	M·W	Magdalen Feline, ent. 1753.	Shallow bowls or trays with lobed edges. Noted by the author.
1763	ER	Probably E. Romer.	Corinthian pillar candlesticks. Melbury Ho.
1764	T·H R·M	. . . .	Short candlesticks. Sudeley Castle.
1765	W·F	. . . . .	Alms-plate. St. Mabyn, Cornwall.
Do.	W·R	Wm. Robertson, ent. 1753.	Fretwork ink-tray. Late Rt. Hon. Sir J. R. Mowbray, Bt.
Do.	PG	P. Gardener . .	Church-plate. Cheshire. Also 1770 Church-plate. Lancs.
Do.	HL	. . . . .	Church-plate. Som.
1766	T·C W·C	. . . .	Plain table-spoons. Gran. Leveson-Gower, Esq.
Do.	T·O·B·I	Thos. Bumfriss and Orlando Jackson, ent. 1766.	Shaped tea-caddies in case. Park Hatch.
1766	LH	. . . . .	Two-handled vase-shaped cup with flower-sprays and oblique gadroons. Corpn. of Gloucester.
Do.	LC	In lozenge, Louisa Courtauld, widow	Tall two-handled cup and cover, oblique gadroons and flower-spray ornament. Elmore Ct., Glouc.
1767	. .	Fuller White, as in 1762.	Maces, dated 1767, and engraved Fuller White fecit. Rochester.
1768	C·W	. . . . .	Church-plate. Lancs.
1769	W·T	Probably Wm. Tuite, ent. 1756.	Small shaped salver on feet. Noted by author.
Do.	EV	. . . . .	Com. cup. Narberth, Pembrokes.
1770	AF	As in 1776 . .	Corinthian column candlesticks. Col. Tremayne, Carclew.
1771	O·J	Orlando Jackson, ent. 1759 and 1770.	Vase-shaped coffee-pot. Noted by author.
Do.	R D·S S	Dr. Smith and R. Sharp; see also 1764—1777.	Set of three sugar-vases. Earl of Ducie.
Do.	E·T	Eliz. Tookey . .	Table-spoons. Noted by author.
Do.	W·T	Wm. Turton, ent. 1733.	Church-plate. Som.

DATE	MAKER'S MARK.		ARTICLE AND OWNER
1772	I·D	John Deacon	Tankard-flagon. Wyke Kegis, Dorset.
1773	W·H N·D	Wm. Holmes and Nichs. Dumee, ent. 1773.	
Do.	BG	As in 1750 .	Ch.-plate. Lincs.
1774	T·T	Thos. Tookey, ent. 1773.	Table-spoons. Noted by author.
1775	AB	Abraham Barrier, ent. 1775.	
Do.	ELD	Louis Ducommien, ent. 1775.	
1776	N·D	Nichs. Dumee, ent. 1776.	ALPHABET XVI. 1776—1795.
Do.	RG	· · · ·	Flagon. Little Ponton, Lincs.
Do.	W·T	Walter Tweedie, ent. 1775.	Two-handled preserving pan. Viscount St. Aldwyn.
1777	RM RC	Robt. Makepeace and Richard Carter, ent. 1777.	Shaped and gadrooned salver. Noted by author.
Do.	JK	Fredk. Kandler .	Milkmaid cup. Earl of Ducie.
Do.	J★S	John Seede, ent. 1773.	Church-plate. Som.
1778	AB LD	Abraham Barrier and Louis Ducommien.	Table-spoons. Saltwood Castle, Kent.
Do.	RI	Richd. Jones, ent. 1778.	Church-plate. Lancs.
1779	TP RP	Thos. and Richard Payne.	Church-plate, given 1779. Whitton, Northants.
1780	JH	T. Heming, as in 1767.	Plain dinner-plates, beaded edge. Hatfield Ho.
Do.	IS	John Stamp, ent. 1780.	Cup, given 1779. Lincs.
1782	WS	Wm. S u m n e r, spoonmaker, ent. 1782.	
Do.	TC	Thos. Chawner, ent. 1773.	Com. cup. Nevern, Pembrokeshire.
Do.	RC	Richd. Carter.	
Do.	DS	Daniel Smith.	
Do.	RS	Robt. Sharp, ent. 1778.	
Do.	TW	· · · ·	Flagon, dated 1782. Radnors.
1783	GS	George Smith, bucklemaker, ent. 1775.	Church-plate. Som.
1784	EI	Edward Jay, ent. 1757.	Salver. Keble Coll., Oxford.
Do.	B·L	Benj. Laver, ent. 1781.	Oval dish-stand and lamp. Noted by author.
Do.	JH	· · · · ·	Urn. Mrs. Monk Gibbs.

DATE	MAKER'S MARK.		ARTICLE AND OWNER.
1786	ⓉⓁ	. . . .	Cover of com. cup, dated 1786. Mavis Enderby, Lincs.
Do.	BL	B. Laver, as in 1784	Church-plate. N. Elmham.
1787	⒤⒤	Joel Jacobsen, bucklemaker, ent. 1776.	Church-plate. Som.
1788	⒣Ⓒ	. . . .	Sauce tureens and covers. Lord Cromwell.
1790	TP	As in 1763 . .	Epergne, Louis XVI. style. Sudeley Castle.
Do.	ⓅⒷ ⒤Ⓑ	Peter and Jonathan Bateman, ent. 1790.	Small mugs, given 1791. Corporation of Oswestry.
Do.	ⓉⓅ ⒠Ⓡ	Phipps and Robinson.	Flagon, dated 1790. Wansted, Essex.
1791	Ⓓⓤ ⓃⒽ	Duncan Urquhart and Napthali Hart, ent. 1791.	
Do.	⒤·Ⓔ	John Edward, ent. 1788.	Small plain tea-pot. Welbeck Abbey.
Do.	AF SG	Andrew Fogelberg and Stephen Gilbert.	Alms-plate. Appledore, Kent.
Do.	DD	Daniel Denney, ent. 1786.	Heads of beadles' staves, dated 1792. St. Mary Abbotts, Kensington, Lond.
1793	⒤·Ⓕ ⒤·Ⓑ	John Fountain and John Beadnell, ent. 1793.	Oval salver, with handles. Lord Redesdale, C.B.
Do.	W·F I · F	Wm. and John Fisher, ent. 1793.	
Do.	IM	John Mewburn .	Initials, sometimes under coronet.
Do.	ⒼⒷ	Probably G. Bourne	Hatch Beauchamp, Som.
1794	ⓉⒽ	Thos. Howell, Bath, ent. 1791.	Flagon. St. Nicholas, Guildford, Surrey.
Do.	RM TM	Robert and Thomas Makepeace, ent. 1794.	In plain square.
Do.	TN GB	Thos. Northcote and Geo. Bourne, ent. 1794.	Do.
Do.	WF	Wm. Fountain, ent. 1794.	In two-lobed shield.
Do.	IB EB	James and Eliz. Bland, ent. 1794.	In plain square.
Do	ⓉⒼ	. . . . .	Church-plate. Som.
1795	RM	Robt. Makepeace, Serle St.	In plain oblong.
Do.	I·P I·P	Jonathan Perkins, sen. and jun.	In plain square.

ALPHABET XVII. 1796—1815.

1796	⒣·Ⓒ ⒤·Ⓔ	Henry Chawner and John Emes, 1796-98.	This firm is now represented by E. Barnard & Sons.
Do.	SG EW	Samuel Godbehere and Edward Wigan, ent. 1792.	In plain square. Com. cup. Oxenton, Glouc.
1797	⒥Ⓦ	. . . . .	Church-plate. Som.

DATE	MAKER'S MARK.		ARTICLE AND OWNER.
1798	HN	Hannah North-cote, ent. 1798.	Small letters in plain oblong.
1799	GS	George Smith, jr., ent. 1799.	
Do.	IL	John Lias, ent. 1799.	In plain oblong; sometimes a dot between the initials.
Do.	TS	Thos. Streetin, ent. 1799. Spoon-maker.	In plain oval.
Do.	DV	Ch. Duvaing, Carey Lane.	Church-plate. Jersey.
Do.	WP	Wm. Pitts, ent. 1799.	In plain oval.
Do.	RC	Richd. Cooke .	Alms-plate. Edington, Som.
Do.	WS	. . . .	Saltcellars. Lord Cromwell.
1800	I·P	Joseph Preedy, ent. 1800.	Do.
Do.	T·H L·C	Thos. Hannam and John Crouch, ent. 1799.	Speaker's set of plate. Lord Redesdale, C.B.
Do.	TW	Thos. Wallis, ent. 1792.	Spoons. Noted by author.
Do.	SG EW IB	Sam Godbehere, Edw. Wigan, and James Bult, ent. 1800.	In plain upright oblong.
Do.	CB TB	Christopher and T. W. Barker, ent. 1800.	In plain square.
1801	PS	Paul Storr, ent. 1799 (see also 1792). In plain two-lobed shield.	A Speaker's set of plate. Lord Redesdale, C.B.
Do.	A·B G·B	Alice and George Burrows, ent. 1801.	In plain square.
1802	SG W	Saml. and George Whitford, ent. 1802.	In plain square.
Do.	W·S	Wm. Sumner, ent. 1802. Spoon-maker.	In plain oval.
Do.	RG	Robert Garrard, ent. 1802.	In plain oblong, corners clipped.
Do.	R·H S·H	Robt. and Saml. Hennell, ent. 1802.	In plain square.
Do.	I·H	John Hawkins, ent. 1802. Spoon-maker.	In plain oblong.
1804	TP	Thos. Pitts, ent. 1804.	In plain oval.
Do.	GW	George Wintle, ent. 1804. Spoon-maker.	Do.
1805	D·U N·H	Duncan Urquhart and N. Hart, ent. 1805.	In plain square; and see 1791.
Do.	TD	Thos. Paine Dexter, ent. 1805.	In plain oblong.

DATE.	MAKER'S MARK.		ARTICLE AND OWNER.
1805	W B R·S	Wm. Burwash and Richd. Sibley, ent. 1805.	In plain square.
Do.	P B W B	Peter and Wm. Bateman, ent. 1805.	Do.
Do.	W.B	. . . .	Entrée dishes. Lord Cromwell.
1806	T G I G I C	Thos. and Joseph Guest and Joseph Cradock, ent. 1806.	In plain upright oblong.
1807	I·C	John Clarke, ent. 1807.	In plain oblong.
Do.	R C G S	Richard Crosley and George Smith, ent. 1807.	In plain square.
Do.	T·H	Thos. Halford, ent. 1807.	In plain oblong.
Do.	S W	Saml. Whitford, ent. 1807.	In plain oval.
1808	J C	John Crouch, ent. 1808.	In plain oblong, corners clipped.
Do.	W E W F W C	Wm. Eley, Wm. Fearn, Wm. Chawner, ent. 1808. In plain upright oblong.	Spoons. Noted by author.
Do.	R E E B	Rebecca Emes and Edw. Barnard, ent. 1808.	In four-lobed shield.
Do.	H N R H	Henry Nutting and Robt. Hennell, ent. 1808.	In plain square, corners clipped.
Do.	W.B	. . . .	Tea-tray. Lord Cromwell.
1809	M S E S	Mary and Eliz. Sumner, ent. 1809.	In plain oval.
Do.	H N	Henry Nutting, ent. 1809.	In plain oblong.
Do.	I W S W E	J. W. Story and W. Elliott, ent. 1809. In plain square.	Tea-pot, lion on lid; copied from the Chinese. Melbury House.
Do.	R H	Robt. Hennell, ent. 1809.	In plain oblong.
Do.	I C T H	John Cotton and Thos. Head, ent. 1809. Spoon-makers.	In plain square, corners clipped.
1810	T W J H	Thos. Wallis and Jonathan Hayne, ent. 1810.	In plain square.
1811	S·H	Saml. Hennell, ent. 1811.	In shaped oblong.
Do.	R R	Robt. Rutland, ent. 1811. Spoon-maker.	In plain oblong.
Do.	J B	James Beebe, ent. 1811. Spoon-maker.	In plain oblong, corners rounded.

DATE	MAKER'S MARK.		ARTICLE AND OWNER.
1812	GS	George Smith, ent. 1812. Spoon-maker.	In plain oblong.
Do.	IC WR	Joseph Cradock and W. Reid, ent. 1812.	In four-lobed shield.
1813	GW	Geo. Wintle, ent. 1813. Spoon-maker.	In plain oblong.
1815	WC	Wm. Chawner, ent. 1815. Spoon-maker.	Do.
Do.	W·B	Wm. Bateman, ent. 1815.	In two-lobed shield.
Do.	CR DR	Christian Ker Reid, Newcastle-on-Tyne, ent. 1815.	In plain square.
1816	TH GH	Thos. and Geo. Hayter, ent. 1816.	Do.
1819	PR	Philip Rundell, ent. 1819.	In plain square.
Do.	I·L H·L	John and Henry Lias, ent. 1819.	Do.
1820	(WB)	Wm. Burwash, ent. 1813.	Tea-pot, raised rim. R. N. Gloucester Militia.
1821	RG	Robert Garrard.	Under royal crown.
1822	CF	Charles Fox, ent. 1822.	In plain oval.
Do.	T·W	Wm. Traies, ent. 1822. Spoon-maker.	
1823	IL HL CL	John, Henry, and Chas. Lias, ent. 1823.	In plain upright oblong.
Do.	I·B	John Bridge, ent. 1823.	In plain square. Also the same initials under a royal crown.
1825	RC	Randall Chatter-ton, ent. 1825. Spoonmaker.	
1826	A·B·S	Adey Bellamy Savory, Cornhill, ent. 1826.	In plain oval and other shapes.
Do.	JW	Jacob Wintle, ent. 1826. Spoon-maker.	In plain oval.
1827	T·C·S	Thos. Cox Savory, Cornhill, ent. 1827.	In plain oblong.
1828	JCE	Jas. Chas. Eding-ton, ent. 1828.	Do.
1829	EE B JW	Edw. Barnard, Edw. Barnard, jr., John Barnard, and W. Barnard.	In plain four-lobed shield.

DATE	MAKER'S MARK.		ARTICLE AND OWNER.
1833	(PS)	Paul Storr . .	
Do.	AS JS AS	Adey Bellamy Savory, Joseph Savory, and Albert Savory, ent. 1833.	In plain upright oblong.
1837	RS	Richard Sibley, ent. 1837.	In plain oblong.
1838	WT RA	Wm. Theobalds and Robt. Metcalf Atkinson. Plate and spoonmakers, ent. 1838.	In plain square.
1839	FD	Fras. D. Dexter, ent. 1839.	In plain oblong.
Do.	IM & ISH	John Mortimer and John Saml. Hunt, ent. 1839.	The initials on shield under a royal crown.
Do.	WB DB	W. Bateman and Danl. Ball, Bunhill Row, ent. 1839.	In plain four-lobed shield.
1840	MC GA	Mary Chawner and Geo. W. Adams, ent. 1840.	In plain four-lobed shield.
Do.	GA	Geo. W. Adams, ent. 1840. Spoonmaker.	In plain two-lobed shield.
1841	JS AS	Jos. and Albert Savory, ent. 1841.	In plain square.
1844	ISH	John Saml. Hunt, ent. 1844.	The initials under a royal crown.

APPENDIX B.

―――◆―――

IMPROVED

TABLES OF THE DATE-LETTERS

USED BY ALL THE

ENGLISH, SCOTCH, AND IRISH ASSAY-HALLS,

FROM THE EARLIEST TIMES.

―――――――

NOTE.—It must be observed that the following tables of marks should be consulted by the light of the chapters that relate to them ; and it is thought better to refer the reader to those chapters, and especially to the tabular sheet appended to each, than to encumber the tables now to be given with a number of minute notes. For example, the tables give the marks as they are found on silver plate, and on gold plate until quite recently; but the marks now used to distinguish gold plate may be seen at a glance in the tabular sheets given at the end of Chap. II. for London plate, and at the end of Chaps. V., VI., and VII., for Provincial, Scotch, and Irish gold wares respectively.

CHARACTERS OF THE ALPHABETS OF DATE-LETTERS
USED BY GOLDSMITHS' COMPANY OF LONDON.

—◆—

I. 1478 to 1497.—Lombardic, double cusps.
II. 1498 to 1517.—Black letter, small.
III. 1518 to 1537.—Lombardic.
IV. 1538 to 1557.—Roman letter, and other capitals.
V. 1558 to 1577.—Black letter, small.
VI. 1578 to 1597.—Roman letter, capitals.
VII. 1598 to 1617.—Lombardic, external cusps.
VIII. 1618 to 1637.—Italic letter, small.
IX. 1638 to 1657.—Court hand.
X. 1658 to 1677.—Black letter, capitals.
XI. 1678 to 1696.— Ditto, small.
XII. 1696 to 1715.—Court hand.
XIII. 1716 to 1735.—Roman letter, capitals.
XIV. 1736 to 1755.— Ditto, small.
XV. 1756 to 1775.—Old English or black letter, capitals.
XVI. 1776 to 1795.—Roman letter, small.
XVII. 1796 to 1815.— Ditto, capitals.
XVIII. 1816 to 1835.— Ditto, small.
XIX. 1836 to 1855.—Old English or black letter, capitals.
XX. 1856 to 1875.— Ditto, small.
XXI. 1876 to 1895.—Roman letter, capitals.
XXII. 1896 to 1915.—Ditto, small.

The various forms of the leopard's head crowned, and of the lion passant, afford such material aid in determining the date of a piece of plate, and in enabling the letters of one alphabet to be readily distinguished from those of another, that engravings have been given of those marks at the foot of each alphabet. The Old English $ of 1695 may by their aid be instantly distinguished from the same letter in Alphabet V., the Roman capitals of Alphabet VI. from those of Alphabet XIII., and so on. It will be seen that in this way the addition of the leopard's head and lion's head erased renders any small and accidental inaccuracies in the letters and their shields of comparatively little importance.

I.		II.		III.		IV.	
	1478		1498		1518		1538
	1479		1499		1519		1539
	1480		1500		1520		1540
	1481		1501		1521		1541
	1482		1502		1522		1542
	RI. III. 1483		1503		1523		1543
	1484		1504		1524		1544
	HY. VII. 1485		1505		1525		1545
	1486		1506		1526		1546
	1487		1507		1527		ED. VI. 1547
	1488		1508		1528		1548
	1489		HY. VIII. 1509		1529		1549
	1490		1510		1530		1550
	1491		1511		1531		1551
	1492		1512		1532		1552
	1493		1513		1533		MARY. 1553
	1494		1514		1534		1554
	1495		1515		1535		1555
	1496		1516		1536		1556
	1497		1517		1537		1557

 1478—1547.    1548—1557.

 as occasionally found, *e.g.* 1515 and 1521, etc.

 1545—1549.   1550—1557.

V.		VI.		VII.		VIII.	
	ELIZAB. 1558		1578		1598		1618
	1559		1579		1599		1619
	1560		1580		1600		1620
	1561		1581		1601		1621
	1562		1582		1602		1622
	1563		1583		JAMES I. 1603		1623
	1564		1584		1604		1624
	1565		1585		1605		CHAS. I. 1625
	1566		1586		1606		1626
	1567		1587		1607		1627
	1568		1588		1608		1628
	1569		1589		1609		1629
	1570		1590		1610		1630
	1571		1591		1611		1631
	1572		1592		1612		1632
	1573		1593		1613		1633
	1574		1594		1614		1634
	1575		1595		1615		1635
	1576		1596		1616		1636
	1577		1597		1617		1637

		As before.					

MARKS.

1. Leopard's head crowned.   2. Maker's mark.   3. Date-letter.   4. Lion passant.

Letter	Year	Letter	Year	Letter	Year	Letter	Year
	1638		1658		1678		1696 Mar.toMa.
	1639 *		1659		1679		1697
	1640		CHAS. II. 1660		1680		1698
	1641		1661		1681		1699
	1642		1662		1682		1700
	1643		1663		1683		1701
	1644		1664		1684		ANNE. 1702
	1645 *		1665		JAS. II. 1685		1703
	1646 *		1666		1686		1704
	1647		1667		1687		1705
	1648		1668		W.MARY. 1688		1706
	CMWLTH. 1649		1669		1689		1707
	1650		1670		1690		1708
	1651		1671		1691		1709
	1652		1672		1692		1710
	1653		1673		1693		1711
	1654		1674		1694		1712
	1655		1675		WM. III. 1695		1713
	1656		1676		1696 MaytoMar.		GEO. I. 1714
	1657		1677		......		1715
As before.							

MARKS.
1. Leopard's head crowned.   2. Maker's mark.   3. Date-letter.   4. Lion passant.
NOTE.—From March, 1696-7, to June, 1720, Britannia and Lion's head erased substituted for the Leopard's head crowned and the Lion passant, on silver.

* These letters and their shields vary in some examples.

XIII.		XIV.		XV.		XVI.	
A	1716	a	1736	A	1756	a	1776
B	1717	b	1737	B	1757	b	1777
C	1718	c	1738	C	1758	c	1778
D	1719	d	1739	D	1759	d	1779
E	1720	e	1740	E	GEO. III. 1760	e	1780
F	1721	f	1741	F	1761	f	1781
G	1722	g	1742	G	1762	g	1782
H	1723	h	1743	H	1763	h	1783
I	1724	i	1744	I	1764	i	1784
K	1725	k	1745	K	1765	k	1785
L	1726	l	1746	L	1766	l	1786
M	GEO. II. 1727	m	1747	M	1767	m	1787
N	1728	n	1748	N	1768	n	1788
O	1729	o	1749	O	1769	o	1789
P	1730	p	1750	P	1770	p	1790
Q	1731	q	1751	Q	1771	q	1791
R	1732	r	1752	R	1772	r	1792
S	1733	s	1753	S	1773	s	1793
T	1734	t	1754	T	1774	t	1794
V	1735	u	1755	U	1775	u	1795
*		🦁 🦁		🦁 🦁		As before.	

MARKS.

1. Leopard's head crowned.   2. Maker's mark.   3. Date-letter.   4. Lion passant. And (from 1784) 5. Sovereign's head.

* From 1716—1720 as before. From 1720—1729 the punches are of uncertain shape; some look like old damaged punches of before 1697 brought again into use. From 1729—1739 the punches were a plain oblong rectangle for the lion passant, and a plain angular heraldic shield for the leopard's head crowned.

XVII.		XVIII.		XIX.	
A	1796	a	1816	A	1836
B	1797	b	1817	B	VICT. 1837
C	1798	c	1818	C	1838
D	1799	d	1819	D	1839
E	1800	e	GEO. IV. 1820	E	1840
F	1801	f	1821	F	1841
G	1802	g	1822	G	1842
H	1803	h	1823	H	1843
I	1804	i	1824	J	1844
K	1805	k	1825	K	1845
L	1806	l	1826	L	1846
M	1807	m	1827	M	1847
N	1808	n	1828	N	1848
O	1809	o	1829	O	1849
P	1810	p	WM. IV. 1830	P	1850
Q	1811	q	1831	Q	1851
R	1812	r	1832	R	1852
S	1813	s	1833	S	1853
T	1814	t	1834	T	1854
U	1815	u	1835	U	1855
As before.				As before.	

MARKS.

1. Leopard's head crowned. 2. Maker's mark. 3. Date-letter. 4. Lion passant. 5. Sovereign's head

NOTE.—The leopard's head is without a crown sometimes in, and always after, 1821.

XX.		XXI.		XXII.	
𝖆	1856	A	1876	𝖆	1896
𝖇	1857	B	1877	𝖇	1897
𝖈	1858	C	1878	𝖈	1898
𝖉	1859	D	1879		etc.
𝖊	1860	E	1880		
𝖋	1861	F	1881	**XXIII.**	
𝖌	1862	G	1882	𝖆	1916
𝖍	1863	H	1883	𝖇	1917
𝖎	1864	I	1884	𝖈	1918
𝖐	1865	K	1885	𝖉	1919
𝖑	1866	L	1886		etc.
𝖒	1867	M	1887		
𝖓	1868	N	1888	**NOTE.**	
𝖔	1869	O	1889	Since 1697, if not earlier, the London marks have been of several sizes so as to suit large and small articles, and whilst the largest size of punch bears the marks as they are here given, the smaller sizes often have the letter, lion passant, or other mark, on a plain square or oblong with the corners slightly cut off; sometimes, however, they are a small edition of the full-sized marks.	
𝖕	1870	P	1890		
𝖖	1871	Q	1891		
𝖗	1872	R	1892		
𝖘	1873	S	1893		
𝖙	1874	T	1894		
𝖚	1875	U	1895		
As before.		As before.			

MARKS.

1. Leopard's head.   2. Maker's mark.   3. Date-letter.   4. Lion passant.
5. Sovereign's head till 1890.

Old York Date-Letters, Prior to 1701.

	Year		Year		Year		Year
	1561	𝔄	1584	𝔍	1607	𝖆	1632
	1562	𝔟	1585	𝔅	1608	𝖇	1633
	1563		1586	ℭ	1609	𝖈	1634
	1564		1587	𝔇	1610	𝖉	1635
	1565		1588	𝔈	1611	𝖊	1636
	1566		1589	𝔍	1612	𝖋	1637
	1567		1590	𝔊	1613	𝖌	1638
	1568		1591	𝔥	1614	𝖍	1639
	1569		1592	𝔍	1615		1640
K	1570	𝔨	1593		1616	𝖐	1641
L	1571		1594	𝔎	1617	𝖑	1642
	1572		1595		1618	𝖒	1643
	1573		1596	𝔐	1619		1644
	1574		1597	𝔑	1620	𝖔	1645
	1575		1598		1621		1646
Q	1576		1599	𝔓	1622		1647
R	1577	𝔯	1600	𝔔	1623		1648
	1578		1601	𝔕	1624		1649
T	1579		1602	𝔖	1625	𝖙	1650
	1580		1603	𝔗	1626		1651
	1581		1604	𝔘	1627		1652
	1582		1605		1628		1653
Z	1583		1606	𝔚	1629	𝖝	1654
				𝔜	1630	𝖞	1655
				𝔷	1631		1656

MARKS.

1. Old York mark. 2. Maker's mark. 3. Date-letter.

𝔄	1657	𝔄	1683
	1658	𝔅	1684
	1659	ℭ	1685
𝔇	1660	𝔇	1686
ℰ	1661	𝔢	1687
𝔉	1662	𝔣	1688
𝔊	1663	𝔊	1689
ℌ	1664	𝔥	1690
	1665	𝔍	1691
𝔍	1666	𝔎	1692
𝔎	1667		1693
𝔏	1668	𝔏	1694
𝔐	1669	𝔐	1695
𝔑	1670	𝔑	1696
𝔒	1671	𝔒	1697
𝔓	1672	𝔓	1698
𝔔	1673	𝔔	
ℜ	1674		
𝔖	1675		
𝔗	1676		
	1677		
𝔙	1678		
𝔚	1679		
𝔛	1680		
𝔜	1681		
ℨ	1682		

MARKS.

1. Old York mark.　　**2.** Maker's mark.　　**3.** Date-letter.

(See p. 136.)

A	1565		1585		1605		1624
B	1566	b	1586		1606		1625
C	1567		1587		1607		1626
D	1568		1588		1608	D	1627
E	1569		1589		1609		1628
F	1570		1590		1610		1629
	1571		1591		1611		1630
	1572		1592		1612	H	1631
	1573		1593		1613	I	1632
	1574	Length of alphabet uncertain.	1594	Length of alphabet uncertain.	1614	K	1633
	1575		1595		1615	L	1634
	1576		1596		1616	M	1635
	1577		1597		1617	N	1636
	1578		1598		1618	O	1637
	1579		1599		1619	P	1638
	1580		1600		1620		1639
	1581		1601		1621	R	1640
	1582		1602		1622	S	1641
	1583		1603		1623		1642
	1584		1604				1643

MARKS.

1. Norwich mark.   2 Maker's mark.   3. Date-letter.
4. Double-seeded rose crowned.

NOTE.—This fourth mark is found in 1627-32-34-36-40, but not on the early Elizabethan specimens.

Probably no Date-letter used.	Probably no Date-letter used.	Marks		OLD CHESTER DATE-LETTERS, 1689—1697.	
1644	1664		1684		
1645	1665		1685		
1646	1666		1686		
1647	1667		1687		
1648	1668	&	1688		
1649	1669	B	1689	A	1689
1650	1670		1690	B	1690
1651	1671	d	1691	C	1691
1652	1672		1692	D	1692
1653	1673		1693	E	1693
1654	1674		1694	F	1694
1655	1675		1695	G	1695
1656	1676	I	1696	H	1696
1657	1677	K	1697	I	1697
1658	1678				
1659	1679				
1660	1680				
1661	1681				
1662	1682				
1663	1683				

MARKS.
1. City arms — Dagger betw. 3 garbs.
2. City crest—a sword erect, blade crossed by a ribbon.
3. Maker's mark.
4. Date-letter (character of alphabet see p. 112).

MARKS.
1. Norwich mark.   2. Maker's mark.   3. Date-letter.
NOTE.—Some specimens of 1660-85 bear a rose-sprig and a crown on separate stamps; others a seeded rose and a crown on separate stamps, in addition to the Norwich and maker's mark, but no date-letter.
Specimens of c. 1685-95 have a seeded rose crowned and an irregular date-letter.

						REMARKS.
Ⓐ	1787	𝖆	1812	A	1837	
	1788	b	1813	B	1838	
	1789	c	1814	C	1839	
ⓓ	1790	d	1815	D	1840	
ⓔ	1791	e	1816	E	1841	
ⓖ	1793	g	1818	G	1843	
	1792	f	1817	F	1842	
	1794	h	1819	H	1844	REMARKS.
ⓘ	1795	í	1820	I	1845	In consequence of the loss of the Assay-Office books, and the small amount of plate stamped at York, it is impossible to give alphabets for the interval between 1701 and 1787. Letters of varying character were used from 1701 to 1726, coupled with the marks for Britannia standard plate till 1720. The office did not work continuously, and seems to have ceased to record assays from about 1847, though plate was occasionally stamped until 1856.
ⓚ	1796	k	1821	K	1846	
	1797	l	1822	L	1847	
Ⓜ	1798	m	1823	M	1848	
Ⓝ	1799	n	1824	N	1849	
O	1800	o	1825	O	1850	
P	1801	p	1826	P	1851	
Ⓠ	1802	q	1827	Q	1852	
R	1803	r	1828	R	1853	(See p. 138.)
S	1804	s	1829	S	1854	
Ⓣ	1805	t	1830	T	1855	
U	1806	u	1831	U	1856	
V	1807	v	1832			
W	1808	w	1833			
X	1809	x	1834			
Ⓨ	1810	y	1835			
Z	1811	z	1836			

MARKS, 1787—1856.

1. Modern York mark.   2. Leopard's head crowned.   3. Maker's mark.
4. Date-letter.   5. Lion passant.   And (from 1784) 6. Sovereign's head.

🛡A	1701	*a*	1725	A	1749	A	1773
🛡B	1702	b	1726	B	1750	B	1774
C	1703	c	1727	C	1751	C	1775
🛡D	1704	d	1728	D	1752	D	1776
E	1705	e	1729	E	1753	E	1777
🛡F	1706	f	1730	F	1754	F	1778
G	1707	g	1731	G	1755	G	1779
H	1708	h	1732	H	1756	H	1780
🛡I	1709	i	1733	I	1757	I	1781
🛡K	1710	k	1734	K	1758	I	1782
🛡L	1711	L	1735	L	1759	K	1783
🛡M	1712	m	1736	M	1760	L	1784
N	1713	n	1737	N	1761	M	1785
🛡O	1714	o	1738	O	1762	N	1786
🛡P	1715	p	1739	P	1763	O	1787
Q	1716	q	1740	Q	1764	P	1788
🛡R	1717	r	1741	R	1765	q	1789
🛡S	1718	s	1742	S	1766	r	1790
🛡T	1719	t	1743	T	1767	ſ	1791
🛡V	1720	u	1744	U	1768	t	1792
🛡W	1721	w	1745	W	1769	u	1793
X	1722	x	1746	X	1770	w	1794
Y	1723	y	1747	Y	1771	x	1795
🛡Z	1724	z	1748	Z	1772	y	1796

MARKS.

1. Modern Exeter mark.   2. Leopard's head crowned.   3. Maker's mark.
4. Date-letter.   5. Lion passant.   And (from 1784) 6. Sovereign's head.
NOTE.—From 1701 till 1720, Britannia and Lion's head erased instead of the Leopard's head crowned and Lion passant, on silver.

Exeter Date-Letters.

Letter	Year	Letter	Year	Letter	Year	Letter	Year
A	1797	a	1817	A	1837	A	1857
B	1798	b	1818	B	1838	B	1858
C	1799	c	1819	C	1839	C	1859
D	1800	d	1820	D	1840	D	1860
E	1801	e	1821	E	1841	E	1861
F	1802	f	1822	F	1842	F	1862
G	1803	g	1823	G	1843	G	1863
H	1804	h	1824	H	1844	H	1864
I	1805	i	1825	J	1845	I	1865
K	1806	k	1826	K	1846	K	1866
L	1807	l	1827	L	1847	L	1867
M	1808	m	1828	M	1848	M	1868
N	1809	n	1829	N	1849	N	1869
O	1810	o	1830	O	1850	O	1870
P	1811	p	1831	P	1851	P	1871
Q	1812	q	1832	Q	1852	Q	1872
R	1813	r	1833	R	1853	R	1873
S	1814	s	1834	S	1854	S	1874
T	1815	t	1835	T	1855	T	1875
U	1816	u	1836	U	1856	U	1876

MARKS.

1 Modern Exeter mark. 2. Maker's mark. 3. Date-letter.
4. Lion passant. 5. Sovereign's head.

Letter	Year	Letter	Year	Letter	Year	Letter	Year
A	1701	A	1726	A	1752	a	1776
B	1702	B	1727	B	1753	b	1777
C	1703	C	1728	C	1754	c	1778
D	1704	D	1729	D	1755	d	1779
E	1705	E	1730	E	1756	e	1780
F	1706	F	1731	F	1757	f	1781
G	1707	G	1732	G	1758	g	1782
H	1708	H	1733	H	1759	h	1783
I	1709	I	1734	I	1760	i	1784
K	1710	J	1735	J	1761	k	1785
L	1711	K	1736	K	1762	l	1786
M	1712	L	1737	L	1763	m	1787
N	1713	M	1738	M	1764	n	1788
O	1714	N	1739	N	1765	o	1789
P	1715	O	1740	O	1766	p	1790
Q	1716	P	1741	P	1767	q	1791
R	1717	Q	1742	Q	1768	r	1792
S	1718	R	1743	R	1769	s	1793
T	1719	S	1744	S	1770	t	1794
U	1720	T	1745	T	1771	u	1795
V	1721	U	1746	U	1772	v	1796
W	1722	V	1747	V	1773		
X	1723	W	1748	W	1774		
Y	1724	X	1749	X	1775		
Z	1725	Y	1750				
		Z	1751				

MARKS.

1. Chester mark. 2. Leopard's head crowned. 3. Maker's mark.
4. Date-letter. 5. Lion passant. And (from 1784) 6. Sovereign's head.
NOTE.—From 1701 till 1720, Britannia and Lion's head erased instead of the Leopard's head crowned and Lion passant, on silver.

Chester Date-Letters.

A	1797	A	1818	A	1839	a	1864
B	1798	B	1819	B	1840	b	1865
C	1799	C	1820	C	1841	c	1866
D	1800	D	1821	D	1842	d	1867
E	1801	E	1822	E	1843	e	1868
F	1802	F	1823	F	1844	f	1869
G	1803	G	1824	G	1845	g	1870
H	1804	H	1825	H	1846	h	1871
I	1805	I	1826	J	1847	i	1872
K	1806	K	1827	K	1848	k	1873
L	1807	L	1828	L	1849	l	1874
M	1808	M	1829	M	1850	m	1875
N	1809	N	1830	N	1851	n	1876
O	1810	O	1831	O	1852	o	1877
P	1811	P	1832	P	1853	p	1878
Q	1812	Q	1833	Q	1854	q	1879
R	1813	R	1834	R	1855	r	1880
S	1814	S	1835	S	1856	s	1881
T	1815	T	1836	T	1857	t	1882
U	1816	U	1837	U	1858	u	1883
V	1817	V	1838	V	1859	A	1884
				W	1860	B	1885
				X	1861	C	1886
				Y	1862	D	1887
				Z	1863	E	1888

MARKS.

1. Chester mark. 2. Leopard's head crowned (till 1839).
3 Maker's mark. 4. Date-letter. 5. Lion passant. 6. Sovereign's head.

Mark	Year	Letter	Year	Letter	Year	Letter	Year
ℱ★	1702	A	*1721	A	1740	A	1759
B	1703	B	1722	B	1741	B	1760
	1704	C	1723	C	1742	C	1769
D	1705	D	1724	D	1743	D	1770
	1706	E	1725	E	1744	E	1771
F	1707	F	1726	F	1745	F	1772
	1708	G	1727	G	1746	G	1773
	1709	H	1728	H	1747	H	1774
	1710	I	1729	I	1748	I	1775
	1711	K	1730	K	1749	K	1776
M	1712	L	1731	L	1750	L	1777
	1713	M	1732	M	1751	M	1778
	1714	N	1733	N	1752	N	1779
	1715	O	1734	O	1753	O	1780
O	1716	P	1735	P	1754	P	1781
P	1717	Q	1736	Q	1755	Q	1782
Q	1718	R	1737	R	1756	R	1783
R	1719	S	1738	S	1757	S	1784
E	1720	T	1739	T	1758	T	1785
						U	1786
						W	1787
						X	1788
						Y	1789
						Z	1790

MARKS.

1. Newcastle mark. 2. Leopard's head crowned. 3. Maker's mark.
4. Date-letter. 5. Lion passant. And (from 1784) 6. Sovereign's head.

NOTE.—1702 till 1720, Britannia and Lion's head erased instead of the Leopard's head crowned and Lion passant, on silver.

* From 1721 to 1727 the Lion passant is found turned to the right, a most unusual circumstance. The letter for 1721 often resembles the Edinburgh letter for 1681.

Ⓐ	1791	Ⓐ	1815	Ⓐ	1839	ⓐ	1864
B	1792	B	1816	B	1840	b	1865
C	1793	C	1817	C	1841	c	1866
D	1794	D	1818	D	1842	d	1867
E	1795	E	1819	E	1843	e	1868
F	1796	F	1820	F	1844	f	1869
G	1797	G	1821	G	1845	g	1870
H	1798	H	1822	H	1846	h	1871
I	1799	I	1823	I	1847	i	1872
				J	1848		
K	1800	K	1824	K	1849	k	1873
L	1801	L	1825	L	1850	l	1874
M	1802	M	1826	M	1851	m	1875
N	1803	N	1827	N	1852	n	1876
O	1804	O	1828	O	1853	o	1877
P	1805	P	1829	P	1854	p	1878
Q	1806	Q	1830	Q	1855	q	1879
R	1807	R	1831	R	1856	r	1880
S	1808	S	1832	S	1857	s	1881
T	1809	T	1833	T	1858	t	1882
Ⓤ	1810	U	1834	U	1859	u	1883
W	1811	W	1835	W	1860		
X	1812	X	1836	X	1861		
Y	1813	Y	1837	Y	1862		
Z	1814	Z	1838	Z	1863		

MARKS.

1. Newcastle mark. 2. Leopard's head crowned. 3. Maker's mark.
4. Date-letter. 5. Lion passant. 6. Sovereign's head.

A	1773	a	1799	A	1825	A	1850	a	1875
B	1774	b	1800	B	1826	B	1851	b	1876
C	1775	c	1801	C	1827	C	1852	c	1877
D	1776	d	1802	D	1828	D	1853	d	1878
E	1777	e	1803	E	1829	E	1854	e	1879
F	1778	f	1804	F	1830	F	1855	f	1880
G	1779	g	1805	G	1831	G	1856	g	1881
H	1780	h	1806	H	1832	H	1857	h	1882
I	1781	i	1807	J	1833	I	1858	i	1883
J	1782	j	1808	K	1834	K	1859	k	1884
K	1783	k	1809	L	1835	L	1860	l	1885
L	1784	l	1810	M	1836	M	1861	m	1886
M	1785	m	1811	N	1837	N	1862	n	1887
N	1786	n	1812	O	1838	O	1863	o	1888
O	1787	o	1813	P	1839	P	1864	p	1889
P	1788	p	1814	Q	1840	Q	1865	q	1890
Q	1789	q	1815	R	1841	R	1866	r	1891
R	1790	r	1816	S	1842	S	1867	s	1892
S	1791	s	1817	T	1843	T	1868	t	1893
T	1792	t	1818	U	1844	U	1869	u	1894
U	1793	u	1819	V	1845	V	1870	v	1895
V	1794	v	1820	W	1846	W	1871	w	1896
W	1795	w	1821	X	1847	X	1872	x	1897
X	1796	x	1822	Y	1848	Y	1873	y	1898
Y	1797	y	1823	Z	1849	Z	1874	z	1899
Z	1798	z	1824						

MARKS.

1. Anchor.   2. Maker's mark.   3. Date-letter.   4. Lion passant.
And (1784 to 1890) 5. Sovereign's head.
NOTE.—For new standard silver the figure of Britannia is used instead of the Lion passant.

Letter	Year	Letter	Year	Letter	Year	Letter	Year	Letter	Year
E*	1773	E	1799	a	1824	A	1844	A	1868
F	1774	N	1800	b	1825	B	1845	B	1869
A	1775	H	1801	c	1826	C	1846	C	1870
R	1776	M	1802	d	1827	D	1847	D	1871
H	1777	F	1803	e	1828	E	1848	E	1872
S	1778	G	1804	f	1829	F	1849	F	1873
A	1779	B	1805	g	1830	G	1850	G	1874
C	1780	A	1806	h	1831	H	1851	H	1875
D	1781	S	1807	k	1832	I	1852	J	1876
G	1782	P	1808	l	1833	K	1853	K	1877
B	1783	K	1809	m	1834	L	1854		1878
I	1784	L	1810	p	1835	M	1855		1879
P	1785	C	1811	q	1836	N	1856		1880
K	1786	D	1812	r	1837	O	1857		1881
L	1787	R	1813	s	1838	P	1858		1882
W	1788	W	1814	t	1839	R	1859		1883
M	1789	O	1815	u	1840	S	1860		1884
L	1790	T	1816	v	1841	T	1861		1885
P	1791	X	1817	x	1842	U	1862		1886
U	1792	I	1818	z	1843	V	1863		1887
O	1793	V	1819			W	1864		1888
M	1794	Q	1820			X	1865		1889
O	1795	Y	1821			Y	1866		1890
Z	1796	Z	1822			Z	1867		1891
X	1797	U	1823						1892
U	1798							†	†

MARKS.

1. Crown. 2. Maker's mark. 3. Date-letter. 4. Lion passant.
And (1784 to 1890) 5. Sovereign's head.

NOTES.—For new standard silver the figure of Britannia is used instead of the Lion passant. The Crown and Date-letter are used on the same punch, or applied as separate marks, as best suits the article to be stamped.

* The letters of this alphabet cannot be accurately rendered in type. They closely resemble those of Alphabet XII. in the London tables.

† 1893 onwards small black letter alphabet in square shield, with corners clipped.

ALPHABET I.		ALPHABET II.		ALPHABET III.		ALPHABET IV.	
B	1681	A	1705	A	1730	A	1755
b *	1682	B	1706	B	1731	B	1756
c	1683	C	1707	C	1732	C	1757
d	1684	D	1708	D	1733	D	1758
e	1685	E	1709	E	1734	E	1759
f	1686	F	1710	F	1735	f	1760
g	1687	G	1711	G	1736	G	1761
h	1688	H	1712	H	1737	H	1762
i	1689	I	1713	I	1738	I	1763
k	1690	K	1714	K	1739	R	1764
l	1691	L	1715	L	1740	L	1765
m	1692	M †	1716	M	1741	M	1766
n	1693	N ‡	1717	N	1742	U	1767
o	1694	O	1718	O	1743	O	1768
p	1695	P	1719	P	1744	P	1769
q	1696	q	1720	2	1745	Q	1770
r	1697	R	1721	R	1746	R	1771
s	1698	S	1722	S	1747	S	1772
t	1699	T	1723	T	1748	T	1773
u	1700	U	1724	U	1749	a	1774
w	1701	V	1725	V	1750	D	1775
x	1702	W	1726	W	1751	X	1776
y	1703	X	1727	X	1752	Y	1777
z	1704	Y	1728	Y §	1753	Z	1778
		Z	1729	Z	1754	V	1779

MARKS.

1. The Castle. 2. Maker's mark. 3. Date-letter.
4. Assay-Master's initials till 1759, in which year the Thistle was substituted.

* 1682, also **b** and **b**. † 1716, also **M**. ‡ 1717, also **N** and **N**.

§ 1753, also **y**.

ALPHABET V.		ALPHABET VI.		ALPHABET VII.		ALPHABET VIII.	
A	1780	a	1806	A	1832	A	1857
B	1781	b	1807	B	1833	B	1858
C	1782	c	1808	C	1834	C	1859
D	1783	d	1809	D	1835	D	1860
E	1784	e	1810	G	1836	E	1861
F	1785	f	1811	F	1837	F	1862
G	1786	g	1812	G	1838	G	1863
G	1787	h	1813	H	1839	H	1864
H	1788	i	1814	I	1840	I	1865
I *	1789	j	1815	K	1841	K	1866
K	1790	k	1816	L	1842	L	1867
L	1791	l	1817	M	1843	M	1868
M	1792	m	1818	N	1844	N	1869
N	1793	n	1819	O	1845	O	1870
O	1794	o	1820	P	1846	P	1871
P	1795	p	1821	Q	1847	Q	1872
Q	1796	q	1822	R	1848	R	1873
R	1797	r	1823	S	1849	S	1874
S	1798	s	1824	T	1850	T	1875
T	1799	t	1825	U	1851	U	1876
U	1800	u	1826	V	1852	V	1877
V	1801	v	1827	W	1853	W	1878
W	1802	w	1828	X	1854	X	1879
X	1803	x	1829	Y	1855	Y	1880
Y	1804	y	1830	Z	1856	Z	1881
Z	1805	z	1831			†	

MARKS.

1. The Castle.   2. Maker's mark.   3. Date-letter.
4. Thistle. And (1784 to 1890) 5. Sovereign's head.

* 1789, also **J**.   † 1882 onwards, small black letter alphabet in oval shield.

A	1819	𝔄	1845	A	1871	𝒜	1897
B	1820	𝔅	1846	B	1872	𝓑	1898
C	1821	ℭ	1847	C	1873		
D	1822	𝔇	1848	D	1874	𝒞	1899
E	1823	𝔈	1849	E	1875		
F	1824	𝔉	1850	F	1876	etc.	
G	1825	𝔊	1851	G	1877	Letter in shield, as those in Glasgow table, p. 181.	
H	1826	𝔥	1852	H	1878		
I	1827	𝕴	1853	I	1879		
J	1828	𝔍	1854	J	1880		
K	1829	𝔎	1855	K	1881		
L	1830	𝔏	1856	L	1882		
M	1831	𝔐	1857	M	1883		
N	1832	𝔑	1858	N	1884		
O	1833	𝔒	1859	O	1885		
P	1834	𝔓	1860	P	1886		
Q	1835	𝔔	1861	Q	1887		
R	1836	𝔕	1862	R	1888		
S	1837	𝔖	1863	S	1889		
T	1838	𝔗	1864	T	1890		
U	1839	𝔘	1865	U	1891		
V	1840	𝔙	1866	V	1892		
W	1841	𝔚	1867	W	1893		
X	1842	𝔛	1868	X	1894		
Y	1843	𝔜	1869	Y	1895		
Z	1844	𝔷	1870	Z	1896		

MARKS.

1. Tree, fish, and bell.   2. Maker's mark.   3. Date-letter.
4. Lion rampant.   5. Sovereign's head to 1890.

A	1638	a	1658	A	1678		1698
B	1639	b	1659	B	1679		1699
C	1640	c	1660	C	1680		1700
D	1641	d	1661	D	1681		1701
E	1642	e	1662		1682	*D	1702
F	1643	f	1663		1683	*P	1703
G	1644	g	1664		1684		1704
H	1645	h	1665	G	1685	R	1705
I	1646	i	1666	Do.	1686	Do.	1706
K	1647	k	1667		1687	S	1707
L	1648	l	1668		1688		1708
M	1649	m	1669		1689	T	1709
N	1650	n	1670		1690		1710
O	1651	o	1671		1691	U	1711
P	1652	p	1672		1692	Do.	1712
Q	1653	q	1673	K	1693	m	1713
R	1654	r	1674	Do.	1694		1714
S	1655	s	1675		1695	Y	1715
T	1656	t	1676	M	1696	D	1716
U	1657	u	1677	N	1697		1717
				L	1698	A	1718
						B	1719
						C	1720

MARKS.

1. Harp crowned.   2. Maker's mark.   3. Date-letter.

NOTE.—The letters for 1644—48, 1656, 1659, and 1693, are from the Goldsmiths' books; the others, down to 1716, from dated specimens.

* Per Mr. Westropp.

A	1721	A	1746	A	1771	A	1796
B	1722	B	1747	B	1772	B	1797
C	1723	C	1748	C	1773	C	1798
D	1724	D	1749	D *	1774	D	1799
E	1725	E	1750	E *	1775	E	1800
F	1726	F	1751	F	1776	F	1801
G	1727	G	1752	G *	1777	G	1802
H	1728	H	1753	H	1778	H	1803
I	1729	I	1754	I *	1779	I	1804
K	1730	K	1755	K *	1780	K	1805
L	1731	L	1756	L *	1781	L	1806
M	1732	M	1757	M	1782	M	1807
N	1733	N	1758	N	1783	N N	1808
O	1734	O	1759	O	1784	O	1809
P	1735	P	1760	P	1785	P	1810
Q	1736	Q	1761	Q	1786	Q	1811
R	1737	R	1762	R	1787	R	1812
S	1738	S	1763	S	1788	S	1813
T	1739	T	1764	T	1789	T	1814
U	1740	U	1765	U	1790	U	1815
V	1741	V	1766	V	1791	V	1816
W	1742	W	1767	W	1792	W	1817
X	1743	X	1768	X	1793	X	1818
Y	1744	Y	1769	Y	1794	Y	1819
Z	1745	Z	1770	Z	1795	Z	1820

MARKS.

1. Harp crowned.   4 (From 1730). Hibernia.   2. Maker's mark.   And (from 1807) 5. Sovereign's head.   3. Date-letter.

NOTE.—The shape of the shield for each alphabet is given at the commencement; the then current alphabet was changed from a plain to an ornamental escutcheon in 1808, the N for that year being found in escutcheons of both shapes. * Same as F . G, dot inside, per Mr. Westropp.

Ⓐ	1821	a	1846	Ⓐ	1871	𝕬	1896
Ⓑ	1822	b	1847	B	1872	𝕭	1897
Ⓒ	1823	c	1848	C	1873	𝕮	
Ⓓ	1824	d	1849	D	1874		1898
ⓔ Ⓔ	1825	e	1850	E	1875	etc.	
F	1826	f	1851	F	1876	Letter in square shield with corners clipped.	
G	1827	g	1852	G	1877		
H	1828	h	1853	H	1878		
I	1829	j	1854	I	1879		
K	1830	k	1855	K	1880		
L	1831	l	1856	L	1881		
M	1832	m	1857	M	1882		
N	1833	n	1858	N	1883		
O	1834	o	1859	O	1884		
P	1835	P	1860	P	1885		
Q	1836	Q	1861	Q	1886		
R	1837	r	1862	R	1887		
S	1838	s	1863	S	1888		
T	1839	t	1864	T	1889		
U	1840	u	1865	U	1890		
V	1841	v	1866	V	1891		
W	1842	w	1867	W	1892		
X	1843	x	1868	X	1893		
Y	1844	Y	1869	Y	1894		
Z	1845	z	1870	Z	1895		

MARKS.
1. Harp crowned.   2. Maker's mark.   3. Date-letter.
4. Hibernia.   5. Sovereign's head to 1890.

NOTE.—From 1826 to 1870 the Date-letters are found in shields of many different shapes.

INDEX.

[Marks consisting of two or more letters should be looked for under the first letter of the pair or group.   Marks showing objects as well as initials are entered under the initials.]

Index.   539

THE END.